General Register Office Scotland

An Index, Drawn up About the Year 1629

Of Many Records of Charters, Granted by the Different Sovereigns of Scotland

General Register Office Scotland

An Index, Drawn up About the Year 1629
Of Many Records of Charters, Granted by the Different Sovereigns of Scotland

ISBN/EAN: 9783337143329

Printed in Europe, USA, Canada, Australia, Japan

Cover: Foto ©ninafisch / pixelio.de

More available books at **www.hansebooks.com**

AN

INDEX,

DRAWN UP ABOUT THE YEAR 1629,

OF MANY

RECORDS OF CHARTERS,

GRANTED BY THE DIFFERENT SOVEREIGNS OF SCOTLAND

BETWEEN THE YEARS 1309 AND 1413,

MOST OF WHICH RECORDS HAVE BEEN LONG MISSING.

WITH

AN INTRODUCTION,

GIVING A STATE, FOUNDED ON AUTHENTIC DOCUMENTS STILL PRESERVED, OF

THE ANCIENT RECORDS OF SCOTLAND,

WHICH WERE IN THAT KINGDOM IN THE YEAR 1292.

TO WHICH ARE SUBJOINED,

INDEXES OF THE PERSONS AND PLACES MENTIONED IN THOSE CHARTERS, ALPHABETICALLY ARRANGED.

PUBLISHED AT THE DESIRE OF

THE RIGHT HONOURABLE LORD FREDERICK CAMPBELL,
LORD CLERK-REGISTER OF SCOTLAND.

WITH A VIEW TO LEAD TO A DISCOVERY OF THOSE RECORDS WHICH ARE MISSING.

BY
WILLIAM ROBERTSON, Esq.
ONE OF THE DEPUTIES OF THE LORD CLERK-REGISTER FOR KEEPING THE RECORDS OF SCOTLAND.

EDINBURGH:
PRINTED BY MURRAY & COCHRANE.
AND SOLD BY THE BOOKSELLERS.
MDCCXCVIII.

1559029

PREFACE.

THE object of this Publication, is to recover some ancient Records of Scotland known to be missing; and the basis of it is an Index, compiled about the year 1629, and a very ancient Quarto Manuscript on vellum, lately discovered.

These materials came to the knowledge of the Editor by the following means.

The Lord Clerk-Register for Scotland, Lord Frederick Campbell, some years ago, in attending to the duties of his office, observed the perishing condition of the Parliamentary Records of Scotland, and formed the design of getting them printed for the public benefit, as the Journals of both Houses and the Parliamentary Rolls had been done in England.

Preparatory for this Work, the Editor transcribed, with his own hand, as much of the earliest and most decayed part of these Parliamentary Records as would make up two Folio Volumes; and was directed by the Lord Register, as soon as the business of his office would permit, to make an accurate research in the Tower of London, and in the Chapter-House at Westminster, to ascertain whether these ancient repositories contained any materials, from which the defects in the Parliamentary Records of Scotland might be supplied, it being well known, that King Edward I. had carried to England all the Records prior to the reign of King Robert I.

In the mean time, Mr Astle, one of the Trustees of the British Museum, whose knowledge in historical antiquity is not less known than his anxious endeavours to make it useful to the public, informed the Lord Register, that he had discovered some curious Manuscripts in the British Museum respecting Scotland, and in particular the Index now printed.

He likewise informed the Lord Register of a still more important discovery, which he had made as Keeper of his Majesty's State-Paper Office, which was a Quarto Manuscript on Vellum, written in a character of great antiquity, and which, besides Transcripts of many Deeds relative to Scotch affairs, contained Minutes of several Parliaments of Scotland antecedent to the earliest Parliaments mentioned in the printed Statute-Book.

In consequence of this very important information, the Lord Register directed copies to be

PREFACE.

immediately made, both of the Index in the Mufeum, and the Quarto Manufcript in the State-Paper office, preffing the Editor to repair to London as foon as he convenientlv could, for the purpofe of more effectually carrying on the intended refearch in all the above-mentioned repofitories.

The Editor accordingly, in Auguft 1793, repaired to London, where his firft care was to collate the two copies above mentioned with their originals.

The Index of Charters was found to be No. 4609. of the Harleian M nufcripts at the Britifh Mufeum; and on the firft page of that Index, at the top of it, there is written as follows.

" This Book contains Lifts or Inventories of feveral Rolls or Records of Charters, granted by
" King Robert I. King David II. King Robert II. and King Robert III. fucceffive Kings of Scot-
" land (*a*).
" This Lift is the more valuable, as feveral of thefe Rolls are loft."

On an attentive examination, this Index was found to comprehend Twelve Rolls and One Book of Charters which now exift, and have always been kept with the other Public Records of Scotland.

But befides thefe, it comprehends and relates to a much greater number of Rolls and Books of Charters which are not now to be found in the Public Records of Scotland. The number falling under this defcription is no lefs than Fifty-one Rolls of Royal Charters, and Three Books, confifting partly of Charters, partly of Decrees in Parliament.

Thefe Fifty-one Rolls and Three Books, together with Two Rolls of Decrees in Parliament, (mentioned in page 28. at the top), though proved by this Index to have been known and patent to infpection in the year 1629, have been miflaid or difappeared during fo long a period, that neither the Editor, nor any perfon known to him, had any knowledge of their having ever exifted, till he had accefs to and perufed the Index which makes the fubject of the prefent publication.

The Fifty-one Rolls and Three Books above mentioned as not now exifting in the Public Records of Scotland, feem to have contained about 1845 Charters and 30 Decrees in Parliament, exclufive of the contents of the two Rolls of Decrees in Parliament mentioned page 28. which do not appear to be particularly ftated in the Index.

The Manufcript difcovered by Mr Aftle in the State-Paper Office was, on examination, found to be the moft ancient Book of Scottifh Record now known to exift, and in everv refpect fo curious and important, that the Lord Regifter thought it incumbent on him to endeavour to recover it, for the purpofe of its being preferved in the Records of that part of the Kingdom to which it inconteftably appeared to have belong.d.

(*a*) It contains alfo Charters granted by Robert Duke of Albany as Regent of Scotland.

PREFACE.

For this purpose a petition was presented to his Majesty, who was graciously pleased to order the Manuscript Book to be removed from the State-Paper Office at London, with which it had no connection, and to be delivered to the Lord Register of Scotland, that it might be deposited in the General Register-Office kept at Edinburgh for the preservation of the Public Records belonging to that part of the Kingdom.

This Manuscript Book having been brought by the Lord Register to Scotland in November 1793, it was judged proper that it should be submitted to the examination of the Supreme Court of that country, in order to its receiving the sanction of that Court.

Accordingly, in the month of December 1793, a Committee of the Judges was, in consequence of a petition presented to the Court, appointed to inspect the Manuscript, and to report their opinion; who reported,

" That the Book is an authentic Record of Writings, Public and Private, relating to Scot-
" land."—Whereupon the Court made the following Resolution, to wit, " Approve of the Report;
" appoint the Manuscript Volume to be lodged among the other Public Records in the custody of
" the Lord Clerk-Register and his Deputies; and request the Lord President, in name of this
" Court, to return thanks to the Right Honourable Lord Frederick Campbell, Lord Clerk-
" Register of Scotland, for the trouble which his Lordship has taken in recovering to the public
" so valuable a Book of the ancient Records of this country. They further take this opportunity of
" expressing the high sense entertained by the Court of the benefit the public has derived from his
" Lordship's unremitting assiduity and eminent services in the execution of his office as Lord
" Clerk-Register, and particularly in the great attention which he has bestowed upon the con-
" struction, fitting up, and completing of the New Repository for the Public Records, as well as
" the internal arrangement of the business there; and last of all, in having solicited and obtained,
" by the favour of his Majesty, a permanent establishment for the preservation of the building,
" and for defraying the necessary expence attending the security and safe custody of the Re-
" cords (a); and appoint the Report, with this Commission, to be inserted in the Books of Sede-
" runt."

With regard to the Index before mentioned, discovered in the British Museum, it was judged proper that it should be printed for the information of the public; and accordingly the Lord Register gave orders for that purpose, as the most likely means of exciting the public attention to the Rolls and Books of Royal Charters which have been abstracted from the General Records of

---

(a) In November 1768, Lord Frederick Campbell was appointed Lord Clerk-Register of Scotland. On 27th June 1774 he laid the foundation-stone of the General Register-House. On 13th August 1787 his Lordship's Deputies for keeping the Records took possession of their apartments there, and began to remove the Records thither from the two vaults under the Court of Session, called the *Laigh Parliament House*, where they were formerly kept. On the 5th of October 1791 the Records were finally removed from those vaults, and arranged in the General Register-House. And in January 1792 his Lordship obtained, by the bounty of his Majesty, a permanent establishment of L. 500 a-year for the support of the fabric, and for defraying various contingent expences necessarily connected with it.

b

INTRODUCTION.

THE Index of Charters, which is the principal subject of the present publication, has been fully mentioned in the Preface. It exhibits a state of the Charters granted by the different Sovereigns of Scotland, from the accession of King Robert I. in the year 1306, till the 8th year of the regency of Robert Duke of Albany, in 1413, a period of about 108 years.

There are now in Scotland no Records of any kind anterior to the accession of King Robert I. (a)

The loss of our more ancient Records was one of the unhappy consequences of the fatal dispute about the succession to the Crown of Scotland in the years 1291 and 1292, which resulted from the failure of the direct line of the Royal Family of Scotland in the person of the infant grand-daughter of King Alexander III. commonly called the Maiden of Norway.

Fortunately, however, such monuments of those ancient Records are still preserved, in different Instruments drawn up on that occasion, as prove incontrovertibly, that Scotland, prior to the dispute about its Crown, had reached a pitch of internal polity not inferior to that of any kingdom in Europe at the same period.

King Edward I. of England having been chosen to decide on the claims of the different competitors for the Crown, issued a writ (b), directed to the Bishop of St Andrew's, to the Constable

---

(a) The ancient Book of Record discovered in the State-Paper Office, as mentioned in the Preface, appears to have been written in the reigns of King Robert I. King David II. and King Robert II. It contains indeed some Instruments that fall not within the period of those reigns, viz. the Discharge by King Richard I. to King William, p. 104. No. 13.; the Bull by Pope Boniface VIII. p. 100. No. 3.; the *Remissio seu abolitio criminis* by King Robert III. p. 104. No. 12.; and the renewal of the ancient league with France by the Regent Robert Duke of Albany, p. 111. No. 61. But the appearance of those entries in the Book, the Bull of Pope Boniface alone excepted, clearly evinces that they were not inserted there when the rest of the Book was written.

(b) " Rex et Superior Dominus Scotiæ, venerabili in Christo patri W. eadem gratia Episcopo Sancti Andreæ in
" Scotia, et dilecto et fideli suo Radulpho Basset de Drayton constabulario Castri sui de Edinburgh, et Willielmo de
" Dunfres Custodi Rotulorum regni Scotiæ, et omnibus ballivis et fidelibus suis ejusdem regni ad quos, &c. salutem :
" Sciatis, quod assignavimus dilectos nobis in Christo Abbatem de Dunfermelyn, et Adam Abbatem Sanctæ Crucis de
" Edinburgh, et dilectum et fidelem nostrum Johannem de Lithegreynes, Magistrum Willielmum de Lincoln, et Tho-
" mam de Ficheburn, ad investigandum, scrutandum, videndum, et examinandum Chartas, Instrumenta, Scripta, Literas
" Papales, Compositiones, Rotulos et Irrotulata, et omnia alia munimenta, jus petentium in regno Scotiæ et similiter
" nos et regnum quoquomodo tangentia, in Castro de Edinburgh, et alibi in eodem regno existentia, et ad ea recipienda,
" deferenda, et deponenda in locum per nos ad hoc assignatum ; et ideo vobis mandamus, quod eisdem Abbatibus,
" Johanni, Willielmo, et Thomæ, vel prædictis Johanni, Willielmo, et Thomæ tantum, cum prædictos Abbates ad
" hoc vacare non contigerit, intendentes sitis et auxiliantes quoticns ex parte nostra super hoc fueritis requisiti ; et vos,

c

of the Caſtle of Edinburgh, and to the Clerk Regiſter for Scotland, commanding them to deliver ſuch records as were within the Caſtle of Edinburgh, or any where elſe in Scotland, to certain perſons named in the writ, whom he had appointed to inſpect and to inveſtigate ſuch of them as had any relation to the claims of the competitors, or to himſelf and his kingdom ; and whom he had authoriſed to receive thoſe Records, and to convey the ſame to a place which he had pointed out.

In obedience to this order, many of the Records of Scotland appear to have been carried to Berwick-upon-Tweed, and to have been depoſited there the 23d of Auguſt, in the 20th year of the reign of King Edward I. viz. 1292.

Of the Records thus conveyed to Berwick, there is a Catalogue ſtill preſerved in the Chapter-houſe at Weſtminſter. In the Index of the Inſtruments in that Repoſitory made up by Mr Agarde between the years 1603 and 1625, the title of that Catalogue is entered in theſe words, viz. " In-" dentura de Evidentiis Jocalibus et aliis inventis in Caſtro de Edenburgh, 23. Auguſti, et illinc " deſertis uſque Berwick, 20 Edw. I."

That Catalogue was ſeen by the Editor in the Chapter-houſe at Weſtminſter in September 1793; and it is printed in Sir Joſeph Ayloffe's *Calendars of ancient Charters* (*a*), in the following words, ſome inaccuracies of the preſs being here corrected, and a few obſervations added in the form of notes. The corrections are incloſed in parentheſes, and printed in Italic characters.

" CATALOGUS

" MUNIMENTORUM quæ capta fuerunt in theſauria de Edenburg, in preſentia
" Abbatum de Dumfermelyn & de Sancta Cruce Edenburgi, & Johannis de Lythe-
" granes Ballivi de Lincoln, & Thomæ de Fiſſeburne, et Willielmi de Dumfreys
" cuſtodis rotulorum regni Scotiæ, et depoſita apud Berwick viceſimo tertio die
" Auguſti, anno 20 Edwardi Primi regis Angliæ, per præceptum ejuſdem regis,
" ſuperioris domini regni Scotiæ.

" CHARTA Richardi regis Angliæ facta Willielmo regi Scotiæ de feodo recipiendo, eundo
" & redeundo ad curiam Angliæ (*b*).

" Charta quod Alexander rex Scotiæ non inibit fœdus cum inimicis Henrici regis Angliæ, nec
" guerram procurabit.

" præfato Epiſcopo claves Theſaurariæ, necnon hoſtiorum, domorum, caſtri predicti, archarum, ciſtarum, et ſcriniorum
" quorumcunque in quibus predicta munimenta, literæ, rotuli, et cætera qualiacunque predicta inſtrumenta ſint recordata,
" predictis Abbatibus, Johanni, Willielmo, et Thomæ, cum eis ad hoc venire contigerit, liberetis ; in cujus, &c.
" Teſte Rege apud Berewyk ſuper Twed in Scotia, 12 die Auguſti."——Prynne's Collections, vol. 3. page 548. where
we ſee printed on the margin, " Rot. Scotiæ, an. 19 et 20 E. I. m. 11. De Chartis, Scriptis, et aliis inſtrumentis
" tangentibus Regem et petentes jus in regno Scotiæ ſcrutandis et examinandis," &c.

(*a*) Pages 327. 328. 329. and 330.   (*b*) Printed in the *Fædera*, vol. 1. p. 87.

INTRODUCTION.

"Charta quod adventus regis Scotiæ non trahatur in confequentiam de veniendo ad coronationem regis Angliæ.

"Obligatio domini Roberti de Brus junioris quod erit fidelis regi Scotiæ.

"Litera Richardi regis Angliæ de redditione caftrorum de Rokefburg & Berwick (*a*).

"Charta Ludovici filii regis Franciæ, facta regi Scotiæ.

"Charta regis Norwagiæ de homagio faciendo regi Scotiæ per infulanos.

"Obligatio hominum de Karryk quod erunt cum rege Scotiæ contra omnes.

"Litera majorum (*de*) Mann, miffa Alexandro regi Scotiæ.

"Charta baronum de Ergadia facta regi Scotiæ.

"Obligatio magnatum Scotiæ facta regi Alexandro, quod tenebunt domicellam Norwagiæ pro domina & regina Scotiæ (*b*).

"Charta baronum Angliæ miffa regi Scotiæ contra Johannem regem Angliæ.

"Charta baronum Angliæ & civium Londinenfium miffa regi Scotiæ contra Johannem regem Angliæ.

"Charta baronum Angliæ probis hominibus de Karleol' contra Johannem regem Angliæ de civitate Karl' reddenda regi Scotiæ.

"Charta baronum Angliæ miffa tenentibus Northumbriæ, Cumbriæ, (*a*) Weftmorlandiæ, contra Johannem regem Angliæ.

"Charta regis Angliæ quod rex Scotiæ & fui incolæ (*c*) poffint fe maritare, non obftante confederatione prius inter eos facta.

"Litera Henrici regis Angliæ miffa regi Scotiæ, de veniendo apud Norham die ftatuto.

"Charta Henrici regis Angliæ de advocationibus ecclefiarum Cumberlandiæ facta regi Scotiæ.

"Charta domini regis Angliæ facta Alexandro regi Scotiæ de terris de Penryth & aliis terris in Cumberlandia.

"Litera Majoris et civium Londinenfium miffa regi Scotiæ contra Johannem regem Angliæ.

"Litera regis Mann (*-iæ*) quod tenebit terram Mann de rege Scotiæ.

"Scriptum chirographatum inter Henricum regem Angliæ & Alexandrum regem Scotiæ, de comitatibus Northumbriæ, Cumberlandiæ, et Weftmorlandiæ, factum coram Otone legato (*d*).

"Litera regis Angliæ miffa regi Scotiæ & Davidi fratri fuo.

"Litera Edwardi regis Angliæ, quod adventus regis Scotiæ ad coronationem fuam, nec petita fervitia ibidem, ipfi regi Scotiæ fint prejudicialia.

"Scriptum obligatorium Anegi Dovenaldi quod exhæredetur fi forisfecerit contra regem Scotiæ.

"Finalis concordia inter reges Norwagiæ et Scotiæ facta apud (*de*) Man, et aliis infulis (*e*).

(*a*) This charter is more fully entered in Mr \gardc's Index of the "*Tractatus pacis,*" &c. p. 287. of Sir Jofeph's *Calendars*, &c. in thefe words, viz. " 1189. Litera regis Ricardi Primi, de redditione caftrorum de Rokfburgh et de Berwick, et de reftitutione omnium libertatum quas habuerunt reges Scotiæ ante captionem regis Willielmi ; et de literis reftitutis et reftituendis, fi quæ fuerint inventæ ; & quod literæ inventæ et non reftitutæ omnino non valeat. Dat. 5. Decembris, 1 Ric. I."——See Fœdera, vol. 1. p. 64. ; and p. 104. of this Index of Charters.

(*b*) See Sir Jofeph Ayloffe's Calendars, p. 288. ; and Fœdera, vol. 2. p. 266.

(*c*) The word *incolæ* is fufpicious, perhaps for "*fua foreret.*" See Fœdera, vol. 1. p. 240. et paffim.

(*d*) See this printed in the Fœdera, vol. 1. p. 375.   (*e*) See this Index of Charters, p. 101

INTRODUCTION.

" Litera Radolphi legati de prorogatione dierum.

" Litera Henrici regis Angliæ facta Alexandro regi Scotiæ de warda & maritagio Hugonis
" Bygot comitis Norfolciæ.

" Charta Johannis regis Angliæ, missa Willielmo regi Scotiæ de tractatu maritagii inter regem
" Franciæ & filiam Willielmi regis Scotiæ.

" Litera missa regi Scotiæ per magnates Angliæ post mortem regis Johannis, de veniendo usque
" Northampton.

" Quædam inquisitio facta apud Rokesburg per probos homines de regno Scotiæ super bondas
" marchiæ & etiam super discordias fluctus maris inter Berwick & Twedmuth.

" Scriptum chirographatum inter magnates Scotiæ sub pœna quatuor marcarum regi Scotiæ
" solvendarum.

" Bulla Honorii tertii de immediata subjectione ecclesiæ Scoticanæ ad ecclesiam Romanam.

" Alia bulla Clementis quarti, quod rex Angliæ possit recipere decimam de clero Scotiæ.

" Litera de conventione inter Edwardum regem Angliæ & custodes Scotiæ de maritagio domi-
" cellæ Norwegiæ (*a*).

" Scriptum regis Scotiæ Alexandri per quod concessit episcopo Sodorensi quod non iret super
" Mann usque ad tempus.

" Protectio Henrici regis Angliæ, facta domino Magno regi Mann, in partibus Walliæ.

" Quieta clamatio Johannis Cumyn patris, facta regi Scotiæ de libertate colpandi & communi-
" candi in boscis & dominicis ad manerium de Werk pertinentibus.

" Præter ista scripta, capta fuerunt ibidem transcripta irrotulata in capella domini regis.

" Una cedula que loquitur de warda castri de Rokesburg.

" Rotulus de bourgis & molendinis.

" Unus rotulus magnus de recognitionibus.

" Unus rotulus in cujus fine continetur charta demmera (*de mora*) de Aldenston.

" Alius rotulus de recognitionibus, in quo multa negotia utrumque Magnum tangentia continen-
" tur, & etiam negotium tangens com' de Mar' & Thomam ———.

" Alius minor rotulus de chartis & libertatibus de Berewyck, & ibi invenietur quod burgenses
" tenentur includere villam de Berewyck.

" Unus rotulus de titulis omnium chartarum quem W. de Dumfres facere fecit.

" Una cedula de chronicis de adventis regis Willielmi ad regem Angliæ.

" Una cedula tangens garderobam regis Scotiæ.

" Una cedula de armis regis Scotiæ traditis ingramo (*Ingeramo*) de Umframvell.

" *Unus rotulus de antiquis statutis regni Scotiæ* (*b*).

" Præterea tres ciphi de cristallo.

" Tres ciphi de nuce, & unus ciphus argenteus.

" Unum thuribulum argenteum deauratum.

" Duo godeta vitrea.

" Virgæ Aaronis.

" Tria cornua eburnea.

" Unus baculus unde Eustathius de Vesey saisivit regem Alexandrum in comitatu Northamp-
" toniæ cum esset apud Norham ad castellum obsidendum

(*a*) See Fœdera, vol. 2. p. 482. and 485.　　　(*b*) See the Note subjoined to this Introduction.

INTRODUCTION.

" Viginti duæ linguæ ferpentinæ pofitæ in argento.
" Una clavis Sancti Mahufei.
" Unus ciphus argenteus.
" Duo coftralli de criftallo.
" Quatuor cophini cum reliquiis diverfis.
" Unus cophinus cum cruce argentea in qua eft pars crucis dominicæ.
" Duo tamerella ligata argento.
" Duo antiqui rotuli de garderoba reginæ.

" *Omnia ifta inventa fuerunt in quadam cifta in dormitorio fanctæ crucis, & ibidem repofita per præ-*
" *dictos abbates, & alios fub eorum figillis.*

" Et in thefauria caftri de Edinburgh, inventa fuerunt ornamenta fubfcripta, fcilicet,
" Duæ cappæ brudatæ nobiles.
" Una cafula brudata nobilis.
" Alia non brudata.
" Tunicula, & dalmatica de rubeo famito.
" Duæ ftolæ & duæ fauenæ brudatæ cum uno amito, & una alba brudata,
" Unum manutergium cum frontali brudato.
" Duo filateria burellata in parte deaurata.
" Unum par fpatulariarum, & manetlorum cum cafula corporalium brudata.
" Una cappa de viridi famito.
" Duæ cappæ de famito purpureo, & duæ de famito rubeo.
" Una tunicula, & una dalmatica de baudekin.
" Unum amitum brudatum.
" Tres baudekins.
" Item plura minuta volutata panniculo lineo.
" Unum veftimentum integrum vetus, five cafula.
" Unum fcrinium argenteum deauratum in quo reponitur crux que vocatur *la blake rode* (*a*),
" unum pecten eburneum.
" Unum auriculare de baudekin, tria manutergia.
" Et una navis ad incenfum.

" In cujus rei teftimonium quilibet prædictorum abbatum & aliorum figilla fua fcriptis aliorum
" appofuerunt. Datum apud Edinburgh, die Jovis in vigilia Sancti Bartholomæi, anno Do-
" mini 1291" (*b*), (1292).

(*a*) See Fordoun's Scotichronicon, vol. 1. p. 307.

(*b*) Should probably be 1292; and yet as the *Vigil. S. Barth.* is 23d Auguft, if the year be 1292, the docquet, if not erroneous, has been fealed at Edinburgh the very day the deeds were depofited at Berwick. This is improbable: and there muft either be an error in the date of the depofitation, or in that of the docquet. But in every view 1291 feems wrong.

INTRODUCTION.

Again, after King Edward had pronounced his award in favour of Balliol, and after that unfortunate King had in the usual manner been crowned at Scone, and proclaimed King of Scotland, many of the Scottish Records appear to have been delivered by certain officers of King Edward to Alexander Balliol, the Chamberlain of Scotland, for the use of the King of Scots. A Catalogue of those Records is likewise inserted in Sir Joseph's *Calendars* (a); and among the " Rotuli Scotiæ" in the same book (b), the precept authorising that delivery occurs in these words : " De rotulis liberandis regi Scotiæ :" And in Mr Agarde's Repertory of the *Tractatus Pacis*, &c. the title of the Catalogue is entered in these words : " Indentura facta inter dictum Edwar-
" dum regem Angliæ superiorem dominum regni Scotiæ, et Dominum Johannem regem Scotiæ,
" de Bullis, Scriptis, Libris, Rotulis compotorum vicecomitum et aliorum ministrorum dicti
" regni Scotiæ, et de aliis memorandis inventis in castro de Edenburgh in regno Scotiæ, in manu
" Domini regis Angliæ existente, et liberatis per preceptum dicti regis Angliæ predicto regi
" Scotiæ. Dat. 30 Decembris, 21 Edw. I."

This Catalogue is singularly curious and interesting. It mentions, though in very general terms, a vast number of Records. It seems to be totally different from the *Catalogus Munimentorum* deposited at Berwick, which has been just laid before the reader ; and it evidently indicates a second removal of Records in the same year 1292, not to Berwick, but to the Castle of Roxburgh. It affords a presumption too, that the Instruments, Jewels, &c. contained in that first *Catalogus* were not returned. It is conceived in the following words, viz.

" MEMORANDUM. " Quod in isto chirographo continentur omnia & singula quæ dominus
" Radulphus Basset, custos castri puellarum constitutus per sereniſſimum principem dominum
" Edwardum regem Angliæ, dominum Hiberniæ, ducem Acquitaniæ, & superiorem dominum
" regni Scotiæ, ipso regno in manu dicti Domini regis existente per mortem Alexandri quondam
" regis Scotiæ defuncti, venire fecit, de dicto castro usque ad castrum de Rokesburgh, per man-
" datum R. Bathoniensis & Willielmi Dunelmensis, & W. Elyensis episcoporum, Gulielmi de
" Langetone custodis garderobæ dicti domini regis Angliæ, & W. de Karletone baronis de scac-
" cario dicti regis Westmonasterii, compota totius regni Scotiæ, ex parte prædicti regis Angliæ,
" videlicet, camerariorum, justiciariorum, firmariorum, dominicorum regni, thanorum, burgo-
" rum, et omnium ministrorum regni prædicti, apud dictum castrum de Rokesburgh, & castrum
" de Berewyck, audientium anno gratiæ 1292 ; et quæ omnia & singula adeo plene & integre,
" sicut recepta fuerunt, per auditores prædictos, sub sigillis suis liberata fuerunt domino Alexandro
" Balliolo, camerario dicti regni, per præceptum dicti domini regis Angliæ, &c. per manus
" dominorum W. de Langetone, W. de Karleton, prædictorum, & Johannis de Drokensford,
" clericorum domini regis Angliæ, ad opus Johannis de Balliolo, Dei gratia regis Scotiæ ; post-
" quam idem Johannes dictum regnum coram dicto domino rege Angliæ, plene fuit acceptus, &
" per gentes ipsius regis Angliæ, ac magnates Scotiæ, in sede sua regia de Scona aſſeſſus, & pro
" rege tentus, ac publice proclamatus : videlicet, duo coffri somerati in quorum uno fuerunt
" rotuli continentes compota totius regni, & in altero plura alia negotia, tam de compotis, quam
" aliis memorandis, & etiam plura scripta signata, & non signata, cum aliis diversis, prout inferius.
" continetur."

" Videlicet, In uno sacculo continebantur 23 rotuli magni & mediocres, de compotis vice-

---

(a) Pages 333. 334. 335. and 336.   (b) Page 109. Article 15.

INTRODUCTION.

" comitum, ballivorum, firmariorum, *thanorum* (*a*), burgorum, & aliorum, diverfis temporibus
" regum Scotiæ.

" In alio facculo 185 rotuli & memoranda de compotis omnimodis receptorum vel expen-
" forum aliquo modo tangentibus tam vicecomites, ballivos, & alios regni miniftros, quam
" aliorum compota aliqua de rebus quibufcunque reddentium, fcilicet, de redditibus & firmis
" quibufdam & exitibus eorundem, de inventoriis caftrorum, & aliorum locorum, de expenfis
" diverforum nunciorum regis & aliorum, de compotis monetariorum, & de initauris (*b*) *Wayting*
" regis & reginæ, & quibufdam expenfis eorundem, & liberorum, & aliis compotis diverfis de
" temporibus diverforum regum. Et in uno rotulo eorundem, continebantur quædam tangentia
" teftamentum Willielmi quondam regis Scotiæ.

" In tertio facculo 52 rotuli, cedulæ, & memoranda, videlicet, quidam rotuli de finibus
" factis per gentes Scotiæ regibus ejufdem regni, tam in vaccis quam denariis; et quidam de ....
" jufticiariorum & aliis perquifitis, de *auxiliis pofitis fuper barones regni*, & collectionibus eorun-
" dem, de catallis burgenfium diverforum appreciatis, & de aliis prædicta tangentibus, temporibus
" diverforum regum.

" Quarto facculo 93 rotuli parvi & cedulæ, & memoranda de diverfis inquifitionibus, per-
" ambulationibus, & exiftentis (*extentis*) terrarum, cuftodiis, & aliis hujufmodi prædia tangentibus.

" In quinto facculo 25 rotuli & memoranda de diverfis ordinationibus de hofpitio regis &
" reginæ diverfis temporibus, et aliis prædicta tangentibus.

" In fexto facculo 41 rotuli & cedulæ, & fcripta de obfidibus traditis in manibus diverforum
" regum Scotiæ, & de his qui fidelitatem fecerunt regibus prædictis temporibus præteritis, & de
" pluribus negotiis tangentibus terram Mann.

" In feptimo facculo 33 rotuli, cedulæ, & quædam fcripta figillata tangentia matrimonium
" Norwagiæ & Flandriæ, & negotia alia terrarum illarum hinc inde facta, & alia negotia de ma-
" ritagio filiæ comitis de Brus (*Drus*), ultimæ reginæ Scotiæ, nec non, & alia tangentia prælocu-
" tionem matrimonii inter filium regis Angliæ, & domicellam Norwagiæ hæredem Scotiæ (*c*).

" In octavo facculo 327 rotuli, cedulæ, fcripta figillata & memoranda de querelis & peti-
" tionibus diverfis factis regibus Scotiæ, & tranfcripta diverfarum literarum regibus prædictis mif-
" farum, & alia hujufmodi, & petitiones quædam regibus Angliæ per reges Scotiæ, & refponfiones
" ad quafdam.

" In nono facculo 40 rotuli, cedulæ, & memoranda, in quibus continentur tranfcripta qua-
" rundam literarum, bullarum & chartarum, una cum legibus marchiæ, & quadam inquifitione
" tangente marchiam, & tranfcriptum literæ epifcopi Dunelmenfis miffæ ad regem Scotiæ.

" In decimo facculo 21 rotuli, tangentes compota monetæ, & cambii, & alia monetam tan-
" gentia.

" Rotulus de confuetudine lanæ & correorum apud Berwick.

" In uno facculo 295 fcripta & munimenta figillata de diverfis obligationibus & receptis, ac
" liberationibus factis, nec non aliis diverfis mandatis, temporibus diverforum regum Scotiæ, una
" cum quodam fcripto per quod comes de Boghan tenetur ad Warantyam & equivalanteam
" faciendum fenefchallo Scotiæ de quibufdam terris.

(*a*) See Note fubjoined to this Introduction.   (*b*) There feems to be fome error here.
(*c*) See Fœdera, vol. 2. pages 482. and 485.

INTRODUCTION.

" Pedes finium levatorum in itinere justiciarii in Tyndale.

" In eodem facculo 13 bullæ Romanorum pontificum, & 30 literæ cardinalium.

" Unus rotulus magnus, qui continet 62 pecias ex utraque parte fcriptas, in quo *continentur*
" *diverfæ chartæ & confirmationes diverforum regum Scotiæ, ac etiam chartæ & recognitiones, &*
" *fcripta alia de regno illo,* tam de terris & tenementis regibus illis redditis, quam de aliis; nec
" non & placita in quibus omnia judicia fere refpectuantur vel amicabiliter terminantur, & etiam
" concordiæ & conventiones diverfæ fupra contraverfiis inter magnates & alios homines ejufdem
" regni habitis, & etiam inquifitiones, purprefturæ, & perambulationes, tam de hominibus infu-
" larum quam aliis ad pacem regum admiffis, & alia quædam dona & conceffiones per reges Sco-
" tiæ factæ, & alia diverfa muneranda inter reges prædictos & magnates ejufdem regni habita &
" tractata.

" Unus rotulus minor qui continet 11 membra, cum 16 cedulis eidem rotulo appenfis, *in*
" *quo continentur chartæ & confirmationes quædam, factæ per regem Alexandrum de diverfis annis,*
" *una cum diverfis chartis & fcriptis quorumdam magnatum Scotiæ,* & etiam una cum recogni-
" tionibus, & proceffibus querelarum, videlicet, querelæ tangentes Johannem de Balliolo fuper
" deliberatione Thomæ de Galwidiæ, & de aliis memorandis diverfis.

" Unus rotulus de novem peciis, fcriptus, in quo continentur chartæ & confirmationes factæ
" per A. regem Scotiæ ultimum, de diverfis annis regni fui, una cum quibufdam chartis fcriptis
" per quofdam magnates Scotiæ, & aliis confimilibus negotiis ut prædicitur.

" Unus rotulus de undecim membris de recognitionibus, & antiquis chartis, tempore regis
" Will. & Alex. regis filii fui, & de illis quibus dicti reges dederunt olim pacem fuam, & de illis
" qui fteterant cum Macvilla (*Mackwillam*) (*a*).

" In uno facculo continentur 46 rotuli, magni & parvi, quorum quidam funt de debitis, que de-
" bebantur domino regi, *& duo de legibus & affifis regni Scotiæ, & de legibus & confuetudinibus burgorum*
" *Scotiæ, & de quibufdam ftatutis editis per reges Scotiæ* (*b*); et duo rotuli de memorandis, videli-
" cet, unus magnus & alius parvus, quos fieri fecit magifter Thomas de Carnoco cancellarius, de
" fcriptis & aliis in depofito remanentibus infra caftrum puellarum poft mortem regis Scotiæ;
" et quidam parvus rotulus de purprefturis factis fuper regem Scotiæ, & unus rotulus de protef-
" tatione domini R. de Brus, & obligatio comitis de Monteth de navi domini regis, & aliis memo-
" randis, & alii rotuli dicti regis fuper comitatu de Monteth, et de arreragiis debitis de fermis, &c.;
" et de quibufdam provifionibus factis per cuftodes regni, & quoddam teftamentum regis Alex-
" andri ultimi confignatum; et duo rotuli tangentes garderobam regis liberati magiftro Welando
" per W. de Caremont apud Sconam, anno Domini 1282; et quidam rotulus de inquifitionibus
" faciendis fuper diverfis articulis; et quidam rotuli parvi & cedulæ, de diverfis recognitionibus
" & proceffibus habitis, & duobus placitis contentis in duabus cedulis de quibus judicia redduntur
" in præfentia regis; et quidam rotuli de negotiis tangentibus Johannem de Balliolo, & Thomam
" de Galwid.

" In uno hancpario ligneo novem fcripta patentia confignata, de centum marcis quolibet anno
" folutis regi Norwagiæ, in Orcadibus in quibus rex Scotiæ tenetur regi Norwagiæ, pro con-
" ventione infularum. Et funt dicta fcripta, videlicet, de annis gratiæ 1282, tertio, quarto,
" quinto, fexto, feptimo, octavo, nono, & 1291, fed de anno nonagefimo nulla.

(*a*) See Fordoun, vol. 1. p. 479. (*b*) See the Note fubjoined to this Introduction.

INTRODUCTION.

"Una litera comitis de Fiff, per quam attornavit Rogerum de Bathket ad reddendum compotum pro ipso.

"In una pyxide, una litera ad modum chirographi confecta, de inventoriis rerum & garneſturæ exiſtentium in caſtro de Dunbrittan, quando W. comes de Mar recepit cuſtodium.

"Litera Andoeni baronis regis Norwagiæ, & fratris Inari de ordine minorum, attornatorum domicellæ Scotiæ, de recognitione receptorum 350 marcarum ſterlingarum ad opus dominæ ſuæ, de fermis terrarum de Bathket & de Rathan (*Rathau*).

"Litera Malcolmi comitis de Levenax, per quam reſignavit & quietum clamavit Alexandro regi Scotiæ, totum jus quod habuit, vel habere potuit, in terris quæ quondam fuerunt Gil Patrick Mac Mol Bride.

"Litera Johannis de Balliolo, de reddendo regi Scotiæ Thomam de Galwidiâ & uxorem & filios.

"Duæ literæ Henrici regis Angliæ patentes, de viſta quadam inter ipſum & regem Scotiæ habenda.

"Litera R. Silward obligatoria, de reddendo regi Alexandro terram de Kelles, quam citius idem rex ſibi contulerit aliquod maritagium cum centum marcatis terræ.

"Litera Margaretæ de Ferrariis, comitiſſæ Derby, per quam reſignavit in manum Alexandri regis conſtabularium Scotiæ, una cum jure quod habuit in diverſis terris nominatis in eadem litera, ad feoſandum inde Alexandrum Comyn comitem de Boughan.

"Litera Dunkeldenſis & Dunblanenſis epiſcoporum, & Benumundi de vicic-canonici Aften. (*a*) collectorum decimæ, de executione mandati apoſtolici, facta ſuper negotio decimarum ſex annorum regi Scotiæ conceſſarum.

"Litera M. de Fiff, W. de Mar, & M. de Afceles (*Athcles*), comitum, & quorundam aliorum nominatorum, per quam obligant ſe ipſos eſſe plegios pro domino Eugenio de Argadia, ad ſolvendum Alexandro regi, quolibet anno 320 marcas pro quadam ſerma terrarum."

It is well known, that King Edward I. by reiterated perſonal inſults againſt Balliol individually, as well as by various national indignities againſt the people of Scotland in general, deliberately, as it ſhould ſeem, forced both the King and kingdom of Scotland to fly to arms.

This gave King Edward the opportunity he deſired, of attaining poſſeſſion of the country by conqueſt. He entered Scotland in the year 1296, at the head of a powerful army; and by the victorious progreſs of his troops, he quickly extorted from Balliol a formal ſurrender of his crown and kingdom, and obtained full and uncontrouled poſſeſſion of the country of Scotland.

It cannot be doubted that, along with the kingdom, King Edward got poſſeſſion likewiſe of its Records, with which his officers, who had ſo lately ſeen and examined them, were minutely acquainted. This ſeems to be proved by three ſchedules, entered in Mr Agarde's Index of the *Tractatus Pacis et Treugarum* in the Chapter houſe at Weſtminſter, in the following words, viz. "Tres ſchedulæ facientes mentionem de bullis, chartis, et aliis memorandis inventis in theſauro regis Scotiæ apud Edinburgh, 20 Edw. I.' (*b*)

(*a*) Some error probably in this name.

( ) *Calendars of Ancient Charters*, &c. p. 290. Inſtead of 20th it ſhould be 24 Edw. I. as is proved by the principal ſchedule itſelf, printed in the ſame book, p. 337. to be immediately laid before the reader.

c

xviii   INTRODUCTION.

Two of thofe *Schedulæ*, namely, a larger in the form of a roll, and a fmaller written on parchment and much decayed inclofed in the larger, were perufed in the Chapter-houfe by the Editor in September 1793, and again in April 1796. The larger contains all that is printed in the *Calendars* from p. 337. to the end of the firft nine lines on the top of p. 346. inclufive : and an inventory of inftruments infpected by the order of King Alexander III. in 1282 in the treafury at Edinburgh, is inferted in that larger fchedule, of which it forms the moft important part.

Omitting the paragraph in the middle of the 338th page of the *Calendars*, beginning with the words, " *The following fchedule*," which is not in the manufcript, and correcting a few errors of the prefs, the Roll or Schedule, as printed in the *Calendars*, runs thus, viz.

" MEMORANDUM, Quod omnia fubfcripta inventa fuerunt in caftro de Edinburgh,
" & liberata fuerunt domino Hugoni de Creflingham, thefaurario Scotiæ, apud
" Berewyck fuper Twedam, 16 Septembris, anno regni regis Edwardi vicefimo-
" quarto (1296).

" Unus rotulus continens 90 pecias, de compotis diverforum vicecomitum & aliorum miniftro-
" rum regni Scotiæ ab anno Domino 1218, ufque ad annum 1275, qui rotulus fic incipit, *Com-
" potum Job. de Makefwell*.
" Unus rotulus continens 7 pecias de eodem, de anno .... ufque ad annum 1215, qui fic in-
" cipit, *Vicefimum compotum Philippi* . . . . .
" Unus magnus rotulus continens 91 pecias de eodem, ab anno Domini 1218, qui fic incipit,
" *Compotum Alureti filii Elibern. &c.* ufque ad annum Domini 1248.
" Unus rotulus continens 19 pecias, de compotis auditis apud Rokefburgh, anno Domini 1292,
" de diverfis annis, qui fic incipit, *Compota audita apud Rokefburgh, &c.*
" Unus rotulus de compotis continens quatuor pecias de anno 1291, qui fic incipit, *Homines
" burgi de Dumfres, &c.*
" Unus alius rotulus continens fex pecias, de firmis molendinorum, unde compota redduntur
" (*reddita funt*) apud Rokefburgh, ut fupra.
" Rotulus continens duas pecias, de vifu compotorum anno 1292.
" Unus parvus rotulus unius peciæ, de compotis Reginaldi de Hen. vicecomitis de Invernaryn,
" de anno 1292.
" Unus rotulus unius peciæ, de .... arreragiis compoti Johannis de Kynres (*-ros*).
" Unus rotulus continens 20 pecias, de diverfis redditibus vaccarum, porcorum, & aliorum, &c.
" qui fic incipit, *Redditus vaccarum de Aberden*.
" Unus rotulus continens 3 pecias, qui vocatur, *Rotulus abbatis Archibaldi de antiquis redditibus
" in denariis & antiquis Waytingis*.
" Unus rotulus continens 3 pecias, de antiquis redditibus in bladis, & aliis, qui fic incipit,
" *Compotum Wilielmi Comyn, comitis de Buchan*.
" Unus rotulus continens 2 pecias, de compotis Willielmi Prat, vicecomitis de Invernaryn, anno
" Domini 1227.

INTRODUCTION.

" Unus rotulus de feodis militum, continens 3 pecias.
" Unus rotulus continens ..... pecias, de compoto Will. Frefekyn, vicecomitis de Inver-
" naryn, anno Domini 1204.
" Unus magnus rotulus antiquus de compotis burgorum Scotiæ.
" Unus rotulus de compotis epifcopatuum Scotiæ.
" Plures rotuli, fimul ligati, de particulis compotorum novæ confuetudinis burgi de Berewyck.
" Unus rotulus de collectione confuetudinis de lanis de Berewyck.
" Unus rotulus de reddita (*redditu*) comitatus de Strathern.
" Diverfi rotuli & parvi & memoranda de antiquis redditibus Strivelins & diverfarum fermarum.
" Una litera patens de .... ad firmam domino Galtero Moubray per Lufemiam de Kirk-
" patrick.
" Una litera patens obligatoria de decem doliis vini de Vafconia, folvendis domino Galfrido de
" Moubray, per Willielmum de Verfona, mercatorem de Cathurco."

" ANNO DOMINI millefimo ducentefimo octogefimo fecundo, die Sancti Michaelis,
" vifa funt munimenta & fcripta domini regis in thefauria apud Edinburg. ex
" præcepto regis, per magiftros Thomam de Carnoco, Radulphum de Bofco, &
" Willielmum de Dumfres (*a*).

" *Imprimis*, Bullæ papales, bulla Honorii papæ, quod ecclefiæ Scoticanæ immediate fint fubjectæ
" fummo pontifici, & confirmatio privilegiorum regis & regni.
" Similis bulla Celeftini.
" Similis In ocentii tertii.
" Bulla Innocentii quarti, de protectione & confirmatione jurium & libertatum regis & regni.
" Similis bulla Alexandri quarti.
" Bulla Innocentii quarti, ne prælati perturbent libertates & jura domini regis.
" Bulla Innocentii quarti confervatoria, ne feratur fententia excommunicationis in perfonam
" regis.
" Bulla Innocentii quarti duplicata, ne caufæ electionum vel aliæ examinentur extra regnum
" Scotiæ, & præcipue in diocefi Eboracenfi.
" Bulla Innocentii quarti, de participatione cum excommunicatis.
" Bulla Innocentii quarti duplicata, ne quis clericus vel laicus de regno Scotiæ trahatur extra
" regnum per literas apoftolicas.
" Bulla ejufdem Innocentii fuper ifto negotio confervatoria.
" Bulla Innocentii quarti de Alexandro filio regis, quod poffit audire divina in locis interdictis.
" Bulla Alexndri quarti, confirmatoria libertatum regis.
" Bulla Lucii papæ, confirmatoria libertatum ecclefiæ Scoticanæ.
" Bulla Celeftini papæ, ut regnum Scotiæ non poffit interdici, & quod ecclefiæ Scoticanæ im-

---

(*a*) This inventory is printed in the *Fædera*, vol. 1. p. 227.

INTRODUCTION.

" mediate fint fubjectæ ecclefiæ Romanæ, & quod nullus alienigena fit legatus in Scotia, nifi quem
" dominus papa ad hoc de corpore fuo fpecialiter deftinaverit.

" Bulla de fidelitate ab epifcopis domino regi præftanda, quæ dimiffa fuit in quadam parva
" pyxide, cum quibufdam aliis literis, ficut patet in fuperfcriptione ipfius pyxidis.

" MEMORANDUM. Quod dominus Willielmus de Dunfres dicit, quod eft quædam bulla con-
" fervatoria in depofito apud Melros, quam illuc portavit dominus Simon frater, ficut idem Simon
" confeffus fuit in vigilia Sancti Michaelis coram confilio domini regis, anno &c. octogefimo in
" fecunda pyxide.

" Dicit quod audivit a magiftro Ricardo de Lanerk procuratore regis in curia, quod eft quædam
" bulla in curia Romana, quod rex non tenetur reddere epifcopis regni fui bona aliqua de epifcopa-
" tibus, antequam ei fecerint fidelitatem.—Cat.

" Inventa eft quædam bulla contra clerum Scotiæ fuper decimis & aliis.

" Bulla Innocentii quarti de redemptionibus votorum in Scotia, non obftante conceffione facta
" regi Angliæ.

" Bulla Alexandri quarti de indulgentia conceffa capellæ regis.

"' Bullæ quatuor quod rex poffit fecum habere duos fratres prædicatores, ac duos minores,
" equitantes.

" Bulla quod papa voluit quod Johannes de Chicham, quondam epifcopus Glafguenfis, præftaret
" fidelitatis facramentum domino regi antequam ab eo reciperet temporalia.

" Bulla Innocentii quinti de conceffione decimæ papalis in regno Scotiæ domino regi, fi voluerit
" terram fanctam adire.

" Quædam bulla quæ innuit a contrario fenfu, quod rex poffit habere mobilia epifcopatuum
" poft mortem epifcoporum, fi hoc habeat a confuetudine.

" Sunt in quodam facculo per fe, præter iftas, quædam bullæ minus valentes."

" Negotia tangentia Angliam.

" Litera Richardi regis, promifforia regi Scotiæ, quod reftituet ei omnia jura fua; fed *vix*
" *apparet figillum.*

" Charta ejufdem Richardi regis de reftitutione jurium, & caftrorum, libertatum, & literarum
" regis Scotiæ (*a*).

" Litera regis Henrici de redditione honorum in Huntington.

" Litera regis Johannis, quod non poffit caftrum firmari fuper portum de Twedmuth.

" Litera Henrici regis Angliæ, de maritagiis fororum regis Angliæ, & fororum regis Scotiæ.

" Litera Henrici regis Angliæ, quod compofitio inita inter reges apud Novum Caftrum de
" Tyn, non præjudicat regi Scotiæ in maritagiis libere faciendis (*b*).

" Litera regis Johannis ad recipiendum 7500 marcas ad opus regis Angliæ, pro quodam fine, &
" de refiduo remittendo.

(*a*) See page 11. line 4. of this Introduction.   (*b*) See ditto, line 19.

INTRODUCTION.

" Litera monitoria epifcopi Elyenfis apoftolicæ fedis legati, ad folvendum quandam pecuniæ
" fummam regi Angliæ.
" Litera regis Angliæ de die ftatuto apud Norham.
" Litera quod non trahatur in confequentiam adventus regis Scotiæ ad coronationem regis
" Angliæ, nec per hoc præjudicium generetur.
" Ultima confederatio facta inter Henricum regem Angliæ, & Alexandrum regem Scotiæ,
" apud Novum Caftrum de Tyn ; et quod nullus eorum movebit guerram contra alium nifi ad
" ipfius defenfionem, ubi non funt figilla comitum Gloverniæ & Herfordiæ, nec videntur fuiffe
" appenfa.
" Litera conventionalis facta inter regem Angliæ & regem Scotiæ, fuper maritagio Margaretæ
" filiæ regis Angliæ.
" Litera regis Angliæ, de feodo præftando regi Scotiæ, vel de conductu, & eft duplicata.
" Litera arbitrii Ottonis legati inter reges Angliæ & Scotiæ, fuper arreragiis de ducentis libratis
" terræ.
" Litera regis Angliæ, quod non prejudicetur regi Scotiæ quod venit femel in Angliam fine
" conductu, ubi figillum vix apparet.
" Charta regis Angliæ, de advocationibus ecclefiarum de Penreth & de Cumberland.
" Charta de Lanwatby, &c. & de quadraginta libratis terræ in Penreth.
" Litera Edwardi, de fuccurfu petendo a rege Scotiæ, & eft duplicata.
" Litera regis Angliæ pro Rogero Bygot, de depofito pro maritagio fororis regis.
" Litera confederationis Richardi Marifcalli.
" Confederatio inter regem Scotiæ & Barones Angliæ olim facta.
" Adjudicatio terrarum Northumbriæ, & Cumberlandiæ, & Weftmorlandiæ, per barones An-
" gliæ, regi Scotiæ.
" Litera conventionalis inter regem Scotiæ & barones Angliæ, fuper quibufdam matrimoniis.
" Mandatum baronum Angliæ factum civitati Carlioli, fuper redditione & adjudicatione terra-
" rum Northumbriæ, Cumberlandiæ, & Weftmorlandiæ.
" Charta Regis Angliæ, de teftimonio offerendo inter regem Scotiæ & Hugonem Bygot, fuper
" debito 600 marcarum.
" Mandatum baronum Angliæ, directum baronibus Northumbriæ, Cumberlandiæ, & Weft-
" morlandiæ, per regem (*pro Rege*) Scotiæ.
" Litera conventionalis pro Rogero Bygot, de folvendis 600 marcis domino regi debitis ab
" eodem.
" Litera Majoris & burgenfium de London'.
" De fumma pecuniæ foluta (*pro*) maritagio fororis regis cum Marifcallo.
" Excufatio nunciorum regis Scotiæ, facta per quofdam magnates Angliæ, & de alia fecuritate
" facta per eofdem fuper quadam fumma pecuniæ deponenda ad Templum London'.
" Amicabilis compofitio inter regem Scotiæ & Walterum de Seburtham.
" Litera Roberti de Rofe & Euftachii de Vefey.
" Una litera cancellata quam non vidimus eo quod dominus Willielmus de Dumfres dixit fe
" velle prius oftendere regi tenorem ejufdem.
" Litera Ludovici filii regis Franciæ, de confirmatione chartæ baronum Angliæ.
" Alia confœderatio inter Scotos & Anglicos.

INTRODUCTION.

" Solutio 3750 mercarum regi Angliæ.

" Litera Lodovici filii regis Franciæ, de Northumbria, Cumberlandia, & Weſtmorlandia.

" Litera regis Angliæ de auxilio ſibi facto in denariis per dominum regem Scotiæ, quæ non
" trahatur in conſequentiam.

" Litera legati ſuper matrimonio contrahendo inter ſorores R. Angliæ & Scotiæ.

" Litera de tribus millibus librarum & amplius ſolutis regi Angliæ.

" Litera quietæ clamationis domini Gilberti, marſcalli regis Angliæ, de manerio de Jeddewod.

" Litera prioris Carliol', de amicabili compoſitione ſuper quibuſdam marchiis inter ipſum prio-
" rem & regem Scotiæ, de terra de Penreth, & de Soureby.

" Litera regis Angliæ quod non vertatur in præjudicium regi Scotiæ, quod homagii ſui receptio
" fuit prorogata de Tukyſbyri uſque London'.

" Litera inter regem & Adam de la Crokidayk de communia de Soureby.

" Litera inter regem Scotiæ & Galfridum filium Yvonis, de communia de Soureby.

" Litera Alexandri de Boultun, de communia de Soureby.

" Litera quod non cedat regi Scotiæ in prejudicium, quod ballivi ſui reddiderunt ei ballias ſuas
" apud Eboracum.

" Magna charta de Penreth facta apud Eboracum.

" Charta Regis Angliæ, de mille libris debitis regi Scotiæ, ratione dotis filiæ ſuæ.

" Litera regis Angliæ, quod adventus regis Scotiæ ad coronationem regis Angliæ Lundon' non
" cedat regno Scotiæ in præjudicium.

" Proceſſus de Quetly, habitus coram juſticiariis Angliæ.

" Nova charta regis Angliæ, de Aldemſtun."

" Negotium Flandriæ.

" Scilicet,
" Quatuor paria literarum.
" Litera Johannis de Weſey, cum litera abbatis de Melros.
" Litera epiſcopi Sancti Andreæ de quadam gratia regis ſibi facta.
" Litera baronum de Ergadia quod fideliter ſervient regi, ſub pœna exhæredationis, contra Ane-
" gum filium Dovenaldi, quod omnes inſurgent contra ipſum, ſi non fecerit voluntatem regis.

" Litera capitancorum & libere tenentium de Carrik obligatoria, quod ſervient domino regi
" contra omnes homines qui vivere poſſunt & mori.

" Obligatio abbatis de Melros de ſolutione facienda domino Johanni de Aconia.

" Litera Willielmi de Moravia, quod non alienabit terras, &c.

" Literæ quorundam magnatum conventionales quæ non multum tangunt regem.

" Litera vicecomitis Northumbriæ ſuper facto marchiæ.

" Obligatio Johanni de Swynburn, ſuper terram de Haultum.

" Septem pondera, & una balances, & octo conctæ veteres, in uno ſaculo veteri de corio."

INTRODUCTION. xxiii

"Negotia tangentia Norwagiam.

"Compofitio inter reges Scotiæ & Norwagiæ fuper infulis duplicata (*a*).
"Confeffio procuratorum mifforum a rege Norwagiæ pro dicta compofitione facienda.
"Mandatum regis Norwagiæ quod infulani faciant homagium regi Scotiæ, & ei intendant ut
"domino.
"Confeffio quorundam procuratorum regis Norwagiæ, de emendis (*amendis*) receptis pro qui-
"bufdam injuriis.
"Quædam litera regis Norwagiæ in lingua Norica.
"Charta regis Johannis Norwagiæ de naufragium paffis.
"Alia regis Sweni, regis Norwagiæ de codem.
"Confirmatio & donatio regis Norwagiæ, monafterio de Buffy in Mannia.
"Procuratorium regis Magni Norwagiæ.
"Charta regis Norwagiæ, fuper infula de Bot, & quibufdam aliis conceffis regi Manniæ.
"Litera regis Norwagiæ fuper terris de Inifter & Egyn.
"Quædam alia litera in lingua Norica, cum duobus figillis.
"Mandatum regis Norwagiæ de pacis reformatione.
"Litera regis Johannis Norwagiæ, & H. fratris ejus, de naufragium paffis.
"Litera regis Norwagiæ miffa Catanienfibus.
"Poteftas regis Norwagiæ ad recipiendum a rege Scotiæ 1100 marcas pro primo anno folu-
"tionis tantum poft compofitionem initam de infulis.
"Litera quietæ clamationis, de folutionibus factis in Orcadia de terminis præteritis, præter
"literas de mille & centum marcis de anno 1269, & de millæ & centum marcis de anno 127 ....
"inter alia fuit, præter alia de eadem fumma 1282, quæ creditur deberi portari ad prima com-
"pota."

"TRANSCRIPTUM CHIROGRAPHI primi tractatus de maritagio Norwagiæ, cancel-
"latum apud Berwyck.

"Ratificatio regis Norwagiæ fuper illo tranfcripto.
"Charta regis Norwagiæ, de affignatione donationis propter nuptias.
"Ratificatio magnatum & dominæ reginæ Norwagiæ & juramenta eorum quod procurabunt
"dictum matrimonium effe ratum.
"Promiffio eorundem bona fide fuper eodem.
"Sex paria procuratoriorum, & feptimum obfufcatum per mare, quorundam magnatum Nor-
"wagiæ, ad jurandum in animas eorum.
"Promiffio regis Norwagiæ, contrahendi cum domina Margareta filia regis Scotiæ, & ratificatio
"omnium prælocutorum in magno fcripto chirographato, quæ litera fuit portata per tales, fcilicet,
"dominum Robertum Lupelli & Godefridum.

(*a*) See page 101. No. 7. of this Book.

INTRODUCTION.

" Procuratorium regis Norwagiæ, ad perficiendum tractatum dicti maritagii.
" Ultimum scriptum chirographatum, apud Berwyc duplicatum, & alterum est obfuscatum in
" mari.
" Duo alia paria de eadem conventione, quæ sunt sigillata sigillo regis Norwagiæ, sed alterum
" obfuscatum est per mare ut prius.
" Litera quietæ clamationis regis Norwagiæ de 4500 marcis debitis de anno 1281, obfuscata
" per mare.
" Quieta clamatio sub sigillo dominæ reginæ Norwagiæ, & quorundam magnatum Norwagiæ
" de 4500 marcis debitis de anno 1282, obfuscata per mare.
" Quoddam transcriptum de rebus inventis post naufragium nunciorum.
" Duo procuratoria alia tangentia negotium Norwagiæ."

" RESIGNATIONES CHARTARUM redditarum domino regi, cum litera domini
" Roberti de Brus filii.

" Charta de Balernauch.
" Charta de Caldovyrcler.
" Charta Cofpatricii de Drem.
" Charta de Abirtarf.
" Charta de Dulb',
" Charta de Carcok.
" Charta de Tucok.
" Charta de Thorfopyn.
" Alia charta de Caldour.
" Donationes factæ abbati & conventui de
" Ruffy per Magnum dictum regem Manniæ.
" Charta Waranniæ de Caldovircler.
" Charta de Cambufnaythan.
" Charta de Torefta & de Kilrethnoc (Kil-
" reth ock) in Moravia.
" Charta de Suthirland.
" Charta quam Gilchrift Macnevyn de Le-
" venax reddidit domino regi.
" Alia charta Suthirlandiæ.
" Charta Walteri de Fontibus.
" Charta de Petyn.
" Charta Hofpitalis de Aberden.
" Charta de Forefta de Invirins.
" Charta regis Manniæ super receptione Man-
" niæ ad firmam.
" Charta de Burfchall.
" Charta de Abirkerdour.

" Charta Thomæ de Thirlefton.
" Charta M. Abel de hofpitio habendo in
" Strivelin.
" Charta de Fochober pro terra de Wynn
" (Boyne).
" Litera quietæ clamationis Ricardi Mauta-
" land de Terra de Abirtharf.
" Excambium factum per Priorem de Ur-
" chard de terra de Fochober pro terra de By-
" nin (Boyn.).
" Quieta clamatio Ottonis de Toniggo de qua-
" tuor marcatis terræ.
" Refignatio de Cambufnaythan & Caldovir-
" cler.
" Confirmatio de ecclefia de Ferindrauch.
" Charta de Neudofk.
" Charta de Polloc.
" Charta de Goger.
" Charta de terra empta de Willielmo de
" Valoniis, juxta Strivelyn, & obligatio ejufdem.
" Duæ chartæ de Balcolmo & una confirma-
" tio.
" Charta de nundinis de Strivelin.
" Charta Januæ de Treugar.
" Charta de Bredburg.
" Refignatio epifcopi Rofs de dimidia bovata
" terræ.

INTRODUCTION. xxv

" Quieta clamatio terrarum bondorum Ca-
" tannie, pro interfectione epifcopi.
" Refignatio Baroniæ de Menenvir.
" Charta de Gorgyn.
" Refignatio terræ de Pentland.
" Charta Walteri Biffet de Stratharkyk.
" Charta de Cultir.
" Charta de Glenkelk, quæ fuit regis Man-
" niæ.
" Charta de Cull.

" Charta de Kynmuk, quod teneatur in fo-
" refta.
" Charta de Neutun.
" Charta de Porthebrothec.
" Charta regis Willielmi de Neutun.
" Charta de Balernauch.
" Charta de Obeyn.
" Charta regis Alexandri de Kynmire, red-
" dita regi.
" Charta de Murtheby, reddita regi.
" Charta de Rethy."

" *Aliæ multæ literæ funt in thefauria domini regis, tam in pixidibus, cophinis, quam in facculis, de*
" *quibus nihil eft hic fpecificatum, quos tamen omnes vidimus & quæ fub figillis ponuntur, fcilicet,*
" *fub figillis magiftrorum Thomæ de Carnoco, Radulphi de Bofco, Willielmi de Dunfres, clerico-*
" *rum domini regis.*"

Befides the above fchedules, the Editor difcovered in the Chapter-houfe a fhort memorandum, in the following words, viz.

" MEMORANDUM, quod decimo die Maii, anno regni regis Edwardi tricefimo fecundo, Jo-
" hannes de Handekgleye clericus de garderoba domini regis liberavit domino de Dalileth recep-
" tori domini regis in partibus Scotie, decem & novem rotulos de extentis terrarum dominicorum
" domini regis, & compotis vicecomitum ex parte boreali maris Scotie de tempore regum Scotie,
" ad habendam evidentiam ad fuperindendum ftatum dictarum terrarum dominicorum in dictis
" partibus, per commiffionem factam magiftro Johanni de Weftoun & eidem domino Jacobo per
" figillum cancellarii Scotie ; in cuius rei teftimonium inter eofdem facta eft hec indentura apud
" Striuelyn, die & anno fupradictis."

No authentic inftrument has hitherto been difcovered that affords direct information how King Edward, after his conqueft of Scotland, difpofed of the other Records of that kingdom mentioned in the two firft fchedules or catalogues here printed. But is it not reafonable to fuppofe that the Records themfelves accompanied thofe catalogues? Is not the conclufion in fome meafure un- avoidable, that the other Records of Scotland continued to be kept along with King Richard's charters to King William, " *de redditione caftrorum de Rolfburgh,*" &c. and " *de fcolo præftando* " *regi Scotiæ de conductu fuo,*" &c. ; with the " *obligatio nobilium & magnatum Scotiæ,*" (*a*) &c. ; and with various other inftruments evidently belonging to Scotland, entered in different parts of Mr Agarde's Repertory of the *Tractatus Pacis*, and in the *Fœdera?*

It is certain that King Edward I. from the year 1296 till his lateft breath, regarded Scotland as part of his dominions. It cannot therefore be fuppofed that fo politic a Prince would inten-

---

(*a*) *Calendars*, pages 287. 288. 327. and 340. ; and *Fœdera*, vol. 1. p. 64. 8º. ; and vol. 2. p. 266.

g

INTRODUCTION.

tionally deftroy Records effentially neceffary to the government and to the general interefts of the country, as well as to the private interefts of many of the greateft landholders, who fupported his pretenfions to the laft (*a*). Indeed if the Records themfelves had been deftroyed, thofe catalogues of them muft have fhared the fame fate. But the prefervation of the charter by King Richard difcharging the conceffion of fuperiority extorted by his father from King William, than which a more decifive refutation of King Edward's claim of that fuperiority could not be devifed, affords, of itfelf alone, demonftration almoft that King Edward deftroyed none of the Records of Scotland.

Nor can the difappearing of thofe Records furprife us, when we confider the flovenly and carelefs manner in which the Records of England itfelf were kept (*b*) : And if many of the moft important Records of that country have been loft, we cannot wonder that the Scottifh Records, which may have been carried into England, attracted ftill lefs attention and care.

It is however a remarkable circumftance, that in the famous treaty of Northampton, (p. 101. &c. of this Index), concluded only about twenty-one years after the death of King Edward I. no notice is taken of the ancient Records which that King had ordered to be removed from the Caftle of Edinburgh, &c. Are we thence to conclude that they were then believed to be irrecoverably loft? or rather that the leading men at that time in Scotland having obtained grants of the large eftates of thofe who had been forfeited for their adherence to the Balliol and Englifh party, did not wifh to recover Records that might revive and perpetuate the pretenfions of the former proprietors or of their heirs (*c*) ?

Before concluding it may not be improper briefly to mention, that the problematical fate of thofe ancient Archives of Scotland did not efcape the attention of the prefent Lord Clerk-Regifter, Lord Frederick Campbell.

It has been ftated in the Preface, that preparatory to an intended publication of the exifting Parliamentary Records of Scotland, the Editor, at Lord Frederick's defire, and under his patronage, undertook a refearch in England, in the hope of finding there materials from which the defects in thofe Records might be fupplied.

(*a*) It is proved by King Edward's edict in 1305, "*pro ftabilitate regni Scotiæ*," printed in Prynne, vol. 3. p. 1053. and in the *Rotuli Parliamenti*, vol. 1. p. 267. and 268. that he intended to govern Scotland by its own laws.

(*b*) Many of them fell into the hands of private perfons; fome were depofited in the caftles of Pontefract, Tuttebury, and Tunbridge, and in monafteries, &c. See the Introduction to Sir Jofeph Ayloffe's *Calendars, paffim*. The following paffage is tranfcribed as a fample. " In the 3d year of King Edward VI. a great number of Records were " cafually difcovered in an old empty houfe within the Tower, which; by lying damp, and many of them being piled " up againft the walls, were much damaged and eaten with the lime," page 27.—Nay, it appears from notandums on different parts of Mr Agarde's Repertory, which was carefully perufed by the Editor, that many inftruments which exifted in his time have been miflaid fince.

(*c*) It feems clear by No. 13. page 179. vol. 1. of the *Rotuli Parliamenti*, that in the 1305, the 33d year of King Edward I. the Records of Scotland were exifting, and that they were in the cuftody of the Governor of Berwick, who was likewife Chamberlain of Scotland. The writ here referred to relates to the prior of Coldingham; and we read there as follows, viz. " Et quia Dominus Rex vult plenius certiorari in præmiffis, mandatum eft cuftodi partium de " Berwick & camerario Scotiæ, quod fcrutatis rotulis & aliis memorandis in cuftodia ejufdem camerarii exiftentibus, & " cifnou capta inquifitione diligenti per probos & legales, &c. inquirant de ftatu regum Scotiæ temporibus præteritis, " quatenus videlicet habere confueverunt in dicto prioratu," &c.

INTRODUCTION.

In the profecution of that refearch at London and Durham (*a*), in Auguſt, September, and October 1793, thofe more ancient archives which were in Scotland when King Alexander III. died, formed a principal and leading object. Every avenue that feemed likely to lead to a difcovery of their fate was traced with the utmoſt aſſiduity and care (*b*). But the enquiry proved in a great meafure fruitlefs. The *Catalogues* of them here prefented to the reader were indeed found, together with the difcharge by King Richard I. to King William of the extorted conceſſion of the fuperiority of the kingdom of Scotland; the obligation by the greater barons of Scotland to receive the Maiden of Norway for their Queen; and fome other detached original inſtruments; but no difcovery of the reſt could be attained.

Now although it be *poſſible* that thofe ancient Records, thrown afide in fome dark unexplored corner, may ſtill remain preferved, and that on a future occaſion fome fortunate accident may reſtore them to light; yet it feems, on the whole, but too *probable*, that they are now irrecoverably loſt.

(*a*) See page 152. of this book.

(*b*) Here it was intended to have given fome excerpts from the diary of the Editor's different proceedings relative to that inveſtigation. But as the prefent publication ſhould by thofe excerpts have been ſwelled much beyond the fize originally intended, they are omitted; efpecially as to many readers they might feem to favour too much of *egotiſm* and oſtentation.

xxviii   N O T E S.

NOTE on line 34. of page 12. and lines 24. and 25. of page 16. of the preceding INTRODUCTION.

" Unus rotulus *de antiquis statutis regni Scotiæ*;"—And again,

" In uno facculo continentur 46 rotuli magni & parvi, quorum quidam funt de debitis quæ debebantur
" domino regi, & duo de legibus & affifis regni Scotiæ, & de legibus & confuetudinibus burgorum Scotiæ, & de
" quibufdam statutis editis per reges Scotiæ."

THESE two entries prove indifputably, that in the year 1292, when the inventory in which they occur was drawn up, there exifted among the Archives of Scotland Rolls of Scottifh Statutes accounted ancient at the early period when thofe Rolls received their titles, which probably happened feveral, perhaps many years before 1292, the date of the inventory.

Suppofing the titles on thofe rolls to have been written no earlier than the reign of King Alexander III. it is not likely that the ftatutes contained in them were thofe of that King's father, or thofe of his grandfather King William, or even thofe of his granduncle King Malcolm, between whofe death and the acceffion of King Alexander III. about eighty-four years only had intervened. For ftatutes of a date not more remote than a century prior to the time when thofe rolls received their titles, could with no propriety be denominated ancient.

Under what King, then, or under what Kings were the ftatutes recorded in thofe rolls enacted ? And do any traces of thofe ftatutes now remain ?

Undoubtedly there is in Scotland a collection of ancient laws known during the fpace of more than 370 years by the name of *Regiam Majeftatem*, a name formed of the two firft words of the book,—that collection having been clearly and unequivocally recognifed as a book of Scots law by a public ftatute in the year 1425.

In the fequel, perhaps, we fhall be able to fhow, that that collection, though under a different name, was, many years before 1425, regarded as a genuine collection of the laws of Scotland. But it is certain, that from that year at leaft, it has been regarded by the lawyers of Scotland, with very few exceptions, as a fyftem of the more ancient law of that country.

This code of law, if it may be called fuch, is attributed to King David I. who filled the throne of Scotland twenty nine years, viz. from the year 1124 to the year 1153; a fuppofition which feems to derive fupport from the perfonal character of that King, from internal evidence in the book itfelf, and from a memorable edict of King Edward I. of England, of the moft unqueftionable authority.

But that collection muft not be confidered as containing only the laws enacted by King David himfelf. Its great bafis muft have confifted of the ftatutes and ufages of preceding times, collected under King David's authority, improved no doubt and enlarged by fome ftatutes of his own.

If we look into hiftory, we fhall perceive, that in point of perfonal character no King perhaps ever lived whofe difpofition was by nature better adopted to legiflation.

His unbounded liberality to the church and to churchmen has given occafion to much animadverfion. In our eyes, indeed, it fhould feem to border on profufion. But ignorant in a great meafure of the inductive circumftances that may have operated on King David's mind, we ought to view his conduct in that matter with candour, and to fpeak of it with diffidence and referve.

Now although much of King David's liberality to churchmen may be juftly afcribed to motives of innate piety, yet fome part of it may probably, with equal juftice, be imputed to a confiderable political motive, namely, to foften and to humanife his fubjects by religious fentiments. For a King fo zealous about the *fpiritual* concerns of his people, could not be regardlefs of their *moral* conduct, nor of their *civil* interefts.

This natural propenfity of King David to legiflation may reafonably be fuppofed to have derived additional energy from the example of his materna' anceftors. His mother's granduncle King Edward the Confeffor, and King Edgar, the grandfather of that Edward, were both diftinguifhed legiflators.

NOTES.

If then King David may be supposed to have had the inclination to civilize his subjects, and to regulate their conduct by laws, it cannot be denied that he possessed leisure and opportunity to carry his intentions into effect. For excepting the contest for the Crown of England between his niece Maud, the only child of his eldest sister, and Stephen, the husband of his other niece the daughter of his youngest sister, in which, during a few years, he was occasionally involved, his reign, upon the whole, was passed in uncommon tranquillity.

But on this point we are under no necessity to reason from conjecture founded on the general tenor of history.

King David's character has been drawn in striking colours by Baldredus abbot of Rieval in Yorkshire. That monkish historian was cotemporary with King David; and he seems to have been intimately acquainted with him, and to have been honoured with his patronage and friendship (a). We must therefore believe him to have been a man of integrity and veracity.

Baldred's account of King David appears to be a species of funeral oration, written immediately after the King's death, while the writer's mind was deeply impressed with that melancholy event, to the circumstances of which he had been an eye-witness. He addresses it to a distinguished personage who had seen and conversed with King David, and who must have been minutely informed of every particular advanced by the monk. This personage was King David's grandnephew, Henry Duke of Normandy and Aquitaine, and Earl of Anjou, who, eighteen months after David's death, succeeded to the Crown of England.

Baldred's narrative, therefore, seems on the whole to be superior to all suspicion.

The abbot speaks of King David as a man " qui non sibi vivebat sed omnibus, omnium curam agens, omnium " saluti prospiciens, rector morum, censor scelerum, virtutum incentor, justiciæ speculum."——" Unde tota illa gentis " illius barbaries mansuefacta, tanta se mox benevolentia et humilitate substravit, ut naturalis oblita sevitiæ legibus quas regia man- " suetudo dictabat colla submitteret." (b)

Baldred indeed did not enter into a particular description of King David's laws. As those laws were at the time universally known, a particular detail of them was unnecessary. But his words, though general, are clear and unambiguous.

That Baldred had no intention to enter into any detail of King David's laws, is evident from a subsequent passage in his narrative, where he is incidentally led to mention the *Leges Burgorum*. For when enumerating the bishopricks and the various religious houses founded by King David, he writes thus, " Et, ut quidam ferunt, monasterium sancti- " monialium Sancti Bartholomæi juxta Kaerleil, et canonicos Præmonstratenses Novi Castri, et ibi monasterium nigrorum " monachorum, et aliud monialium ibi, *ut patet in prologo ejus super statutis burgorum*, et etiam ad Dumfermelyn tresdecim " monachos, sciz. conventum, introduxit de Cantuaria, ac plura alia plena religiosis fratribus ordinata reliquit." (c)

Thus much in general on King David's title to the character of a legislator.

The book itself, too, without insisting on the words of its introductory chapter, contains direct evidence that King David was a legislator. For it presents us with several statutes expressly bearing to have been enacted by that King;—a circumstance which affords strong presumptive evidence, that the rest of the *original collection* was made under the *authority* of the same King David.

But the remarkable edict by the English Justinian King Edward I. to be afterwards noticed, seems to place this matter beyond all controversy.

In later times, however, in the course of the present century especially, the authenticity of *Regiam Majestatem* has been called in question by several writers, at the head of whom may be ranked the Lord Chief-Justice of England Sir

---

(*a*) " Ego autem, licet peccator et indignus, memor tamen beneficiorum tuorum, dulcissime Domine et Amice " (addressing himself to King David's spirit) quæ mihi, ab ineunte ætate mea, impendisti, memor gratiæ in qua me nunc " ultimo suscepisti (viz. when David was on his deathbed) memor benevolentiæ qua me in omnibus petitionibus meis " exaudisti, memor munificentiæ quam mihi exhibuisti, memor amplexuum et osculorum, in quibus me, non sine lacri- " mis, omnibus qui aderant admirantibus, dimisisti, libo pro te lacrimas meas, resolvo affectum meum, et totum refundo " spiritum meum." Fordoun, vol. 1. p. 310.

(*b*) " By these means the barbarity of the nation was softened into such gentleness, humanity, &c. that the people, " forgetting their natural fierceness, *bowed their necks to the laws which the royal clemency dictated*." Fordoun, vol. 1. p. 300.

(*c*) Fordoun, vol. 1. p. 301.

h

NOTES.

Matthew Hale. It has been by thofe writers held forth as little better than a fervile tranfcript of a reputed digeft of Englifh law, faid to have been written towards the end of the reign of King Henry II. when Ranulph de Glanville was Jufticiary of England, by whofe name that digeft is generally called.

The principal circumftance that feems to have induced thofe writers to form this general concluſion, is the fimilarity of the matter in the two books, which is ftated to be fo very ftrong, as could not have happened unlefs the one had been copied from the other, or both from fome common original; and no fuch common original having been pointed out, a variety of topics are adduced to prove that *Glanville* (by which name the Englifh work fhall be called on this occaſion) is the original, and *Regiam Majeſtatem* the copy.

The fimilarity fhall, for argument's fake, be admitted; for at prefent it is by no means intended to inveftigate all the minute particulars that have been advanced on this fubject. At fome other time, perhaps, fuch an inveftigation may be attempted; previoufly to which the two books muft be collated with care, as in a queftion of this nature difcrepancies that at a firft glance might appear immaterial, may, when more deliberately confidered, powerfully influence a final determination.

Nor will it be then lefs neceffary to inquire.—Whether the Englifh compilation was really digeſted when Glanville was jufticiary of England?—Whether it actually contains the laws of England as they ftood at that time (a)?—and, Whether its authenticity was ever fanctioned by any Englifh ftatute?

Thefe inquiries again will introduce feveral fubordinate queftions intimately connected with them,—What is the precife or the probable date of the moft ancient manufcript of Glanville now to be found?—What is the moft ancient book or manufcript in which Glanville is mentioned?—and, Does Glanville contain any reference to any law, or to any hiftorical fact, relative either to England or Scotland, of a date later than the year 1189, when King Henry II. died?

On the other hand, we know certainly, as obferved before, that more than 370 years ago *Regiam Majeſtatem* is under that very name mentioned in a public ftatute of Scotland as a book of Scots law. It is impoffible, therefore, to believe that it could have obtained that folemn parliamentary fanction, if it had not been deemed genuine and authentic for time immemorial antecedent to that period. This confideration feems effectually to overthrow the opinion of fome writers, who fix the introduction into Scotland of that fuppofed pilfered edition of Glanville to the reign of King David II. For that King having died only fifty-five years before the date of the act of parliament 1425, many perfons were probably then alive who had been men before the concluſion of King David II.'s reign, and knew exactly the character of authenticity which *Regiam Majeſtatem* then bore. Hence again it feems neceffarily to follow, that it bore the fame character for time immemorial prior to that King's reign; and that therefore its introduction into Scotland, and its adoption there as a fyftem of law, muft have happened at a period more early by many years than that King's reign.

But at whatever time that adoption took place, it muft appear a very extraordinary event; for one of two confequences feems unavoidable, viz.

Either that the Scots then laboured under a total privation of municipal law; an idea as abfurd in theory as it fhall be fhown to be falfe in fact:

Or that the Scots at once abandoned all their former ufages and laws, and fubftituted this Englifh code in their place.

In an abftract point of view, it is a violent fuppofition, that any nation, however uncivilized, would at once adopt in the grofs the juridical fyftem of a different country. Laws are the gradual refult of neceffity and focial experience. Even among a people but juft emerging from barbarity, eftablifhed cuftoms, however rude, bend flowly and reluctantly to the milder inftitutions of a more refined ftate of fociety.

Certainly at whatever time this adoption of Glanville's fyftem can be fuppofed to have taken place in Scotland, the

---

(a) " We have no authentic records of any acts of parliament before 9 Henry III.; and thofe we have of that King's reign are but few. Nor have we any reports of judicial deciſions in any conftant feries of time before the reign of Edward I. though we have the Plea-rolls of the times of Henry III. and of King John in remarkable order." Hiftory of the Common Law of England by Sir Matthew Hale, fecond edition, p. 58.——" The original or authentic tranfcripts of acts of parliament are not before the time of Henry III.; and many that were in his time are perifhed and loft."——And again, " And in the next age the ftatutes made in the time of Henry III. and Edward I. were loft." *Ibid.* p. 66.——" 'Tis true, we have no record of judicial proceedings fo ancient as that time," (viz. of " Henry II.), " except the Pipe-rolls in exchequer, which are only accounts of his revenue." *Ibid.* p. 138.

NOTES.

people of that country muſt have attained a ſtate of civilization altogether incompatible with ſuch an adoption. Between the acceſſion of King Edgar in 1098, and the death of King Alexander III. in 1286, a period of nearly two centuries, that nation appears to have enjoyed, both externally and internally, a ſtate of peace and quiet unprecedented in the hiſtory of any nation of Europe during the ſame period. On ſome few occaſions indeed their Kings were engaged in diſputes with thoſe of England. But thoſe diſputes were of very ſhort duration, and could not have diſturbed the general tranquillity in any material degree. In fact, the catalogue of Scottiſh records now before us, unaided by any other circumſtance, affords demonſtration, that the general polity of Scotland had, before the formation of that catalogue, reached a degree of perfection not inferior to that of any European ſtate in the ſame age.

Under ſuch circumſtances, it is incredible that the people of Scotland ſhould at once have aſſumed for their juridical ſyſtem the laws of a different kingdom; and thoſe too, not as detailed by Bracton, a later and more perfect work than Glanville (*a*); not as contained in the ſtill later and much more perfect ſyſtem of King Edward I. (*b*); nor as exhibited in the public ſubſiſting ſtatutes of that kingdom; but as preſented in the anonymous compilation of a private individual (*c*), which at the time of its ſuppoſed introduction into Scotland was in a great meaſure difuſed and antiquated in the kingdom from which it was borrowed (*d*).

But the learned Lord Chief-Juſtice carries the matter much farther. He maintains, that the laws of Scotland in general were imported from England. Nay, he argues, contrary to every degree of probability, and to the judgment of the foundeſt antiquaries, that the laws of Normandy, as exhibited in the *Grand Coutumier*, were likewiſe borrowed from the laws of England.

Here it may be obſerved, that if the feudal cuſtoms, inſtead of being *gradually* introduced into the different countries of Europe, as is moſt agreeable to the ordinary courſe of things, were at once adopted in the groſs by any nation, it is moſt likely that they would be copied from the ſyſtem eſteemed at the time the beſt and the moſt complete.

The learned Judge adduces various reaſons for the general importation of the Engliſh laws into Scotland,—the contiguity of the two countries, and the intercourſe between the inhabitants reſulting from that contiguity;—"the ſuperio-"rity and intereſt that the Kings of England obtained over the Crown and kingdom of Scotland;"—and finally and chiefly, the policy of King Edward I.; on which laſt point the words of the Chief-Juſtice himſelf ſhall be afterwards ſtated.

On the circumſtance of the contiguity of the two kingdoms, more ſtreſs perhaps is laid than on deliberate reflection it may appear to be entitled to, or than the fact will juſtify. For that contiguity, by furniſhing perpetual occaſion for mutual injuries and encroachments, was more likely to produce animoſity, diſcord, and hoſtility, than an adoption of each other's laws; a conſequence too clearly proved by the hiſtories of both countries.

It is unneceſſary here to enlarge on the trite ſubject of the Scottiſh dependence. Providentially it is now a ſubject totally inconſequential. It has become a point merely of curious inveſtigation among antiquaries; and every liberal and candid Engliſhman—and candour and liberality are now among the moſt prominent features of the character of an Engliſh gentleman—will liſten to any diſcuſſion on that ſubject with the cooleſt impartiality.

When, it may be aſked, did this dependence originate?—When the Romans poſſeſſed South Britain? No; their two celebrated pretenſions evince the contrary.—Was it obtained by the Britons after the Romans relinquiſhed the

---

(*a*) "If we do but compare Glanville's book with that of Bracton, we ſhall ſee a very great advance of the law "in the writings of the latter over what they are in Glanville." Hiſtory of the Common Law of England, ſecond edition, p. 156.

(*b*) "By all which, compared even with Bracton, there appears a growth and a perfecting of the law into a "greater regularity and order." *Ibidem*, p. 165.

(*c*) "The Tractate of Glanville, which though perhaps not written by that Ranulphus de Glanvilla who was "*juſticiarius Angliæ* under Henry II. yet ſeems to be wholly written at that time." *Ibidem*, p. 138.——"From theſe "words," (viz. the title to the printed edition of Glanville in 1604), "I infer," ſays Lord Lyttleton, "that this "treatiſe was not written by Ranulph de Glanville himſelf." Hiſtory of King Henry II. vol. 2. p. 267.

(*d*) See Sir Matthew Hale's Hiſtory of the Common Law of England, where quoted above, and in various other places.

NOTES.

ifland? By no means. On the contrary, the incurfions of the inhabitants of North Britain forced the Britons to the defperate refource of calling in the Saxons for their protection.

Was North Britain fubjected by the Saxons? No fuch event is mentioned in hiftory. A conqueft by fuch barbarians over a people ftill more barbarous than their conquerors, muft, like the conqueft of the Britons by the fame Saxons, have been marked, if not by an entire extirpation or expulfion of their opponents, at leaft by indelible traces of blood; and a heavy tribute, if not abfolute flavery, muft have been the lot of thofe who efcaped the fword. Feudal homage was the child of a later and fomewhat more civilized age.

It is probable, indeed, that the Saxons repulfed the northern barbarians from England, and, on the eaft fide of the ifland efpecially, drove them perhaps beyond the pretentures. But it is improbable that they paffed the Scottifh fea or Frith of Forth. The territory of South Britain prefented to them a lefs difficult as well as a more inviting prey, and immediately attracted their avidity. In conjunction with the very barbarians whom they had been hired to oppofe, they turned their arms againft thofe whom they had come to defend; and after a long and a fevere ftruggle, they deftroyed the greater part of the ancient Britons, and of the reft, forced fome to abandon the ifland entirely, and cooped up others in Wales, Cornwall, and Cumberland.

Hardly had the Saxons formed themfelves into feven feparate governments, called in hiftory the Heptarchy, than they began to quarrel with one another; and before thofe quarrels were concluded by the union of thofe feven governments under one head, the Danes had repeatedly committed depredations on the fea-coafts of England, and had commenced thofe invafions which they profecuted without intermiffion, and with inexpreffible lofs to the Saxons, till their leader Canute attained the throne of England.

Hence the Saxons do not appear to have had leifure either to fubdue North Britain, or to render it tributary.

It may be true that the Conqueror, by whom it is generally thought the feudal law was introduced into England, and his immediate fucceffors, obliged the cotemporary Kings of Scotland to hold the eftates they poffeffed in England by feudal tenure, and for thofe eftates to fubject themfelves to the feudal folemnity of homage and fealty (a). But that the Scottifh Monarchs became feudataries to thofe Kings of Norman extraction for the kingdom of Scotland, is as deftitute of probability as it is of proof.

Of the ancient independence of Scotland as a kingdom, an indirect, and negative indeed, but at the fame time a forcible argument arifes from the formal conceffion extorted (b) by King Henry II. from William King of Scots when King Henry's prifoner; by which King William became the liege-man of King Henry, and performed fealty to him as his liege-lord, for Scotland and all his, William's, other lands. For that declaration (c) contains not a fingle word

---

(a) Not to mention other acquifitions in England by the Scottifh Kings, it is certain, (if any faith at all can be given to the monkifh hiftorians of thofe early times), that as far back as the year 944, the province of Cumberland, which had formerly belonged to the Kings of Scotland, but had been wrefted from them by the Saxons, (Ford. vol. 1. p. 199.), was granted by King Edmond, the fon of Athelftan, to the apparent heirs of the Scottifh Crown. " Unde " Malcolmi regis auxilium, et animum placabilem firmiter fibi junctum contra Danos habere defiderans, totam ei Cum" briam in perpetuum, fub fide jurata, tradidit poffidendam."——" Provinciam, quæ vocatur Cumberland, regi Sco" torum Malcolmo, rex, fub fidelitate jurisjurandi, commendavit."——" Poftmodum vero ftatim inter eos concordatum " eft et amborum concilio decretum, ut in futurum pro bono continuandæ pacis utriufque regni, Malcolmi regis proximus " hæres Indulfus, cæterorumque regum Scotorum hæredes qui pro tempore fuerint, Eadmundo regi fuifque fucceffuribus " Angliæ regibus hominium pro Cumbria facerent ac fidelitatis facramentum." Fordun, vol. 1. p. 205.——" Mal" colmus autem rex cum Eadredo pacem habuit, facto fibi prius hominio pro Cumbria per Indulfum."——" Ad " Cumbriæ dominium, eo coronato, promotus eft Duffus, regis Malcolmi filius, Eadredo regi folita fidelitatis fide facta." Ibid. p. 206.——" Eo quoque ftatim coronato, Malcolmum filium Duffi fucceffioni proximum, fi vixiffet, in regulum " Cumbriæ libenter Eadgarus fufcepit, fub facramento fidelitatis confueto. Hujufmodi mutuæ pacis et amicitiæ pactum " inter reges et regna, feliciter a regibus Malcolmo Scotorum, et Anglorum Eadmundo primitus initum, abfque conten" tionis ftrepitu, jugiter et inconcuffe centum viginti perfeveravit annis et amplius 'etiam, ufque Willielmus Baftardus " invafit Angliam et obtinuit." Ibid. p. 209.

(b) " Præterea quietavimus mnes pactiones quas bonus pater nofter Henricus rex Angliæ, per novas cartas et per " captionem fuam" (viz. Willielmi regis Scotiæ) " extorfit." Fœdera, vol. 1. p. 64.

(c) Fœdera, vol. 1. p. 39. Prynne, vol. 3. p. 492.

NOTES.

that, in the most distant manner indicates any prior dependence of the kingdom of Scotland. But when it comes to mention the dependence of the church of Scotland, it is thus expressed, viz. " Quod ecclesia Scoticana talem subjec-
" tionem amodo faciet ecclesiæ Anglicanæ qualem illi facere debet *et solebat tempore regum singula prædecessorum suorum.*"
The prior alleged dependence of the church being thus pointedly stated, we may reasonably presume, that the prior dependence of the whole kingdom, had any evidence or even tradition of such prior dependence then existed, would have been likewise mentioned in terms equally explicit, especially as it would have afforded a colourable pretence for that new declaration of dependence.

It will be recollected, that this extorted concession was most solemnly discharged to the same King William by King Henry's son and successor King Richard I. in the year 1189, immediately after King Richard succeeded to the Crown of England.

This discharge is printed by Mr Rymer in the *Fœdera* (*a*). It was one of the Scottish deeds carried into England by King Edward I. and it still remains therein wonderful preservation, considering its antiquity, now more than 60° years (*b*).

No renewal of this feudal dependence having ever been obtained by any King of England anterior to the competition for the Crown of Scotland in the year 1292, the claim of superiority set up on that occasion by King Edward I. with King Richard's discharge in his pocket, is one of the grossest and most indefensible instances of usurpation that occurs in history. It is the more indefensible still, that in the marriage-articles between King Edward's eldest son and the infant Queen of Scots, only two years before, viz. in 1290, it is expressly declared, " Quod regnum Scotiæ remaneat
" separatum et divisum, et liberum in se, *sine subjectione* a regno Angliæ, per suas rectas divisas et marchias, *sicut a retro*
" *hactenus extitit observatum,* volentes et concedentes expresse quod deficientibus prædictis Edwardo et Margareta vel
" eorum altero absque liberis," &c. " regnum prædictum, integre, libere, absolute, et *absque vila subjectione,* revertatur et
" restituatur eisdem," (viz. proximioribus hæredibus) (*c*).

But viewing this question in the light the most unfavourable for Scotland, and supposing that country to have really been at some remote period a fief of England, certainly it was singularly glorious for the Scots, not only to have reconquered the territory between the two pretentures, but likewise to have decisively shaken off that dependence in a contest with the ablest and the most powerful of the English Monarchs.

But it is a wonderful circumstance, that the Scots, during this sanguinary contest, while prodigal of their blood for the independence of their own country, were in fact fighting against the English for the independence of England itself. For if the Scots, instead of combating the armies of England, had, as their auxiliaries and allies, displayed their banners in conjunction with them against the power of France, that kingdom, in all human probability, should have been subdued, the seat of government should have been transferred to Paris, and this noble island should have become a province dependent on France.

On the whole, if this supposed dependence of the kingdom and Crown of Scotland on the English Kings had been uniformly maintained by the English Monarchs, and enforced by the exaction of aids, scutages, and the other casualties resulting from feudal subjection, and if that dependence had been as uniformly acknowledged, and the exaction of all the feudal casualties voluntarily complied with by the Scots nation, it might have had a powerful influence in assimilating the laws of the dependent to those of the dominant kingdom. But as no vestiges remain of any of those feudal casualties having been ever demanded from the Scots, and as the alleged dependence appears to have been always strenuously denied and reprobated by that nation, except in the compulsitory declaration extorted by King Henry II. in consequence of the unfortunate captivity of their King, and that extorted by King Edward I. on occasion of the still more unfortunate competition for their Crown, the claim of dependence was more likely to have an effect directly opposite.

But the policy of King Edward I. furnishes the principal argument to the learned Chief-Justice for the introduction and establishment of the English jurisprudence in Scotland. On that head Sir Matthew expresses himself thus.

(*a*) Fœdera, vol. 1. p. 64.

(*b*) Page 105. and 106. of this Book. The preservation of this instrument, the most unfavourable to King Edward's pretensions of superiority that could be devised, will not allow us to suppose for a single moment that King Edward either meant to destroy, or did in fact destroy, any of the Scottish archives.

(*c*) Fœdera, vol. 2. p. 483.

NOTES

"King Ed....d I. having thus obtained the actual superiority of the Crown of Scotland (*a*), from the beginning of his reign until his 20th year, and then placing John de Balliol in that kingdom, and yet continuing his superiority thereof, and keeping his courts of justice, and exercising dominion and jurisdiction, by his officers and ministers, in the very bowels of that kingdom, and afterwards, upon the defection of this King John in the 24th of Edward I. taking the whole kingdom into his actual administration, and placing his own judges and great officers there, and commanding his courts of king's bench, &c. to issue their process thither, and continuing in the actual administration of the government of that kingdom during life ; it is no wonder that those laws which obtained and were in use in England *is and before the time of this King*, were in a great measure translated thither ; and possibly either by being enacted in that kingdom, or at least for so long time put in use and practice there, many of the laws *in use and practice* here in England, were in his time so rivetted and settled in that kingdom, that it is no wonder to find they were not shaken or altered by the liberal concessions made afterwards by King Edward III. upon the marriage of his sister ; but that they remain part of the municipal laws of that kingdom to this day.

"And that which renders it more evident that this was one of the greatest means of fixing and continuing the laws of England in Scotland is this, viz. This very King Edward I. was not only a martial and victorious, but also a very wise and prudent Prince, and one that knew very well how to use a victory, as well as to obtain it ; and therefore knew it was the best means of keeping those dominions he had powerfully obtained, *by substituting and translating his own laws* into the kingdom he had thus subdued. Thus he did upon his conquest of Wales, and doubtless thus he did upon his conquest of Scotland ; and those laws which we find there so nearly agreeing with the laws of England used in his time, especially the statutes of Westminster 1. and Westminster 2. are the monuments and footsteps of his wisdom and prudence," &c.

If, as Sir Matthew argues, the contiguity of the kingdoms, and the feudal dependence of Scotland on England, had naturally produced an introduction of the English laws into Scotland, what occasion was there for all this profound policy of King Edward ?

But overlooking this seeming defect in the deduction of Sir Matthew's argument, and supposing that King Edward, from those political motives, had really intended to establish the English jurisprudence in Scotland, why should he have preferred the antiquated system of Glanville,' as transcribed in *Regiam Majestatem*, to the more perfect and later system of Bracton ? or to his own system so much more improved than even that of Bracton ? (*b*)

(*a*) Common Law of England, p. 200. "King Edward I. having formerly received the homage and fealty of "Alexander King of Scots, was taken to be *superior Dominus Scotiæ Regni*." To this assertion the words of the instrument itself shall, without any commentary, be opposed ; "Et idem rex Angliæ homagium ejusdem regis Scotiæ recepit, salvo jure et clameo ejusdem regis Anglie et hæredum suorum de homagio prædicti regis Scotiæ et hæredum suorum de *Regno Scotiæ*, cum inde loqui voluerint :" And a little further, "Ego Alexander rex Scotiæ portabo bonam fidem Domino Edwardo regi Angliæ et hæredibus suis reibus Angliæ," &c. "debita *de terris et tenementis* quæ teneo de rege Angliæ supradicto." Fœdera, vol. 2. p. 126.—In the year 1237, by a solemn agreement between King Henry III. and King Alexander II. (Fœdera, vol. 1. p. 375.), the latter resigned in favour of King Henry the shires of Northumberland, Cumberland, and Westmorland, and had in lieu of them accepted *ducentas libratas terre* within the shires of Northumberland and Cumberland. These without question are the lands and tenements mentioned in the above act of homage and fealty.

(*f*) "Touching the former, viz. Bracton's Tractate, it yields us a great evidence of the growth of the laws between the times of Henry II. and Henry III. If we do but compare Glanville's book with that of Bracton, we shall see a very great advance of the law in the writings of the latter over what they are in Glanville." History of the Common Law of England, p. 156.——"We now come to the time of Edward I. who is well styled our English Justinian, for in his time the law, *quasi per saltum*, obtained a very great perfection."—And a little further—"The laws did never in any one age receive so great and sudden an advancement ; nay, I think I may safely say, all the ages since his time have not done so much in reference to the orderly settling and establishing of the distributive justice of this kingdom, as he did within a short compass of the thirty-five years of his reign, *especially about the first thirteen years thereof*." Ibidem, p. 157. and 158.——Here it may be observed, that King Edward had no opportunity of interfering in Scottish legislation till after the competition for the Crown, which began in the 20th year of his reign, about seven years, according to Sir Matthew Hale, after he had brought the English laws to their perfection. Glanville's compilation was more than an hundred years old when King Edward interfered in the affairs of Scotland.

NOTES.

The reasoning of the learned Lord Chief-Justice on this point furnishes an instructive lesson to every reader, "*not rashly to assent to arguments merely theoretical, however ingenious and plausible.*" For it shall here be shown, on the most unquestionable authority, viz. that of King Edward the English Justinian himself,

That when he intermeddled with the affairs of Scotland, the Scots nation had laws of their own; and

That King Edward never intended to establish any system whatever of English law in place of those Scots laws.

That the Scots had municipal laws of their own, and that they were particularly anxious that no innovation should be made in those laws by the interference of this same King Edward and his successors Kings of England, is evident from the remarkable instrument before alluded to, printed in the Fœdera, vol. 2. p. 482. and 483.

It will be recollected, that on the death of King Alexander III. without any other descendant of his body than an infant grand-daughter, the Maiden of Norway, King Edward employed all his influence to obtain her for wife to his eldest son, and by that means to effect an union of the two kingdoms. In this negotiation King Edward was successful. The marriage-articles were drawn up and ingrossed in the instrument here referred to, dated 18th July 1290, in the form of a declaration by King Edward's plenipotentiaries.

Of that instrument the very first article is expressed in the following words, viz.

"Cum, inter cætera, quæ contingunt negotium et tractatum, habitum inter excellentissimum principem, dominum
"nostrum suprædictum, ex parte una, et venerabiles patres custodes, et cæteros episcopos, abbates, et totum clerum,
"nobiles viros comites et barones, totamque communitatem regni Scotiæ, ex altera, super matrimonio contrahendo
"inter dominum Edwardum, filium et hæredem prædicti domini nostri regis, et dominam Margaretam, natam egregii
"principis domini Erici regis Norwagiæ, et ejusdem regni Scotiæ hæreditariam reginam, a nobis esset petitum ex parte
"eorundem custodum prælatorum, nobilium, et communitatis ipsius regni Scotiæ, quod pro domino nostro prædicto,"
(viz. Edwardo) "et hæredibus suis, eis concederemus et firmaremus *jura, leges, libertates, et consuetudines dicti regni*
"*Scotiæ*, tam ecclesiasticas quam seculares, hactenus usitatas et optentas, nos, habita consideratione diligenti ad pacem et
"tranquillitatem utriusque regni, et mutuam dilectionem habitantium in iisdem cunctis temporibus remansuram, con-
"cedimus nomine et vice domini nostri prædicti et hæredum suorum, quod *jura, leges, libertates, et consuetudines ejusdem*
"*regni Scotiæ*, in omnibus et per omnia per totum ipsum regnum, et ejus marchias integre et inviolabiliter perpetuis tem-
"poribus observentur."

In different parts of the same instrument the *leges et consuetudines Scotiæ* are repeated: and special provision is made in it for the safe custody of the reliefs, charters, privileges, and other monuments touching the royal dignity and the kingdom at large.

Can a more irrefragable proof be desired, that prior to the 1290 the Scots nation had a system of laws peculiar to themselves?

To prove again that King Edward, after having apparently conquered Scotland by his victories at Berwick and Dunbar in the year 1296, after having obliged King John Balliol to execute in his favour a solemn resignation of his crown and kingdom, and after quelling several formidable insurrections of the Scots, by which Scotland seemed to be completely subjected to his authority, was far from entertaining the design imputed to his wisdom by the Chief-Justice, but on the contrary was determined to govern the Scots by their own laws, the words of King Edward himself shall be here laid before the reader. The words shall be taken from an edict issued by King Edward for the government of Scotland, "*pro stabilitate regni Scotiæ,*" printed in Prynne, vol. 3. page 1053. and in the *Rotuli Parliamenti* of England, vol. 1. p. 267. and 268. It is dated in the year 1305, and contains this remarkable passage. "Endroit de leis et
"usages pur le governement de la terra d'Escoce, ordenee est, que l'usage de Scot et de Bret (*a*) desorendroit soit de-
"fendu, si que mes ne soit usez. Et ordene est aussit, que le Lieutenant le Roi, del houre qu'il serra venuz en la
"terre d'Escoce, face assembler les bones gentz de la terre, en aucun certyn liew le quel il verra que a ce soit covenable,
"et que illoeqes, en la presence de lui et de gentz quil y serront assemblez, soient rehercez les leis que le roi David
"fist, et aussint les amendementz et les addicions q'unt este puis faites par les Rois," (*b*) &c.

(*a*) The nature of this usage is now unknown; but it should seem to have been peculiar to Scotland.

(*b*) "In regard to laws and usages for the government of Scotland, it is ordained, that the usage of *Scot and
"Brit* be for the future prohibited, so that they may be no more used. And it is also ordained, that the King's Lieu-
"tenant, immediately on his arrival in Scotland, cause the good men of the country to assemble in any certain place

NOTES.

These words afford the most satisfactory evidence,

That King Edward had no intention of introducing into Scotland the laws of England; and That King David I. was a legislator, and that his laws were regarded as the basis of Scottish jurisprudence: and it is humbly conceived, that those laws of King David, with the *amendments and additions by succeeding Kings*, convey so exact a description of the book called by the general name of *Regiam Majestatem* as can scarcely be mistaken.

Thus, in a connected point of view, we see, that in the year 1292 there were among the archives of Scotland "rolls of the ancient statutes of the kingdom of Scotland, of the laws and assizes of that kingdom, and of the laws and usages of its burrows;"

That in the year 1305 King Edward directed " the laws of King David, with the improvements and additions made in those laws by succeeding Kings," to be publicly read in presence of the people of Scotland;

And that in the year 1425 a public statute was enacted, appointing a committee, consisting of eighteen of the states of Parliament, to " see and examine the bukis of law, yat is to say, *Regiam Majestatem* and *Quoniam Attachiamenta*, and mend the lawis that nedis mendment."

Little doubt, therefore, it is humbly thought, can be entertained, that the *Regiam Majestatem* and *Quoniam Attachiamenta* mentioned in this statute, are the *laws of King David, with the improvements and additions of succeeding Kings* mentioned in King Edward's edict just an hundred and twenty years before; and that the *Rotuli de Antiquis Statutis Scotiæ, &c.* put into King Edward's hands in 1292, thirteen years before his edict, contained those laws of King David, and the subsequent improvements and additions, &c.; in other words, that those three different references denote precisely the same thing, viz. the *Regiam Majestatem*.

No verbal or theoretical criticisms, however ingenious, can shake a weight of written evidence so firmly connected, and so direct.

The earliest manuscripts of *Regiam Majestatem* at present known, do not appear to be more ancient than the beginning of the fifteenth century, two hundred and fifty years at least after King David's code must have been compiled.

To assert that *Regiam Majestatem*, as contained in those manuscripts, is precisely the same with that drawn up by King David's directions, were very rash indeed. The *amendments* mentioned in King Edward's edict oppose such an idea. But without insisting on that expression, it is obvious, that before the invention of printing, interpollation and alteration could be practised with so little chance of detection, that the monkish transcribers had much latitude, both to alter the original text, and also to insert here and there passages suggested by their own fancies. Nay, in various instances a marginal observation or reference on a more ancient copy, might, by a later clerk, have been innocently mistaken for part of the text, and as such inserted in the body of the work, without any intention to deceive.

Under such circumstances, it were extraordinary indeed, if in the numberless transcripts of King David's code, which must have been made during the long period of two centuries and a half, the original manuscript had remained totally unaltered, without mentioning the intentional and deliberate alterations made by subsequent laws.

Certain passages from the Civil law, which appear suspicious to some; and other passages from the Canon law, and some references to Glanville, which prove a stumbling-block to others, have most probably found their way into the body of the work by such means.

At the same time, to suppose that before the discovery of the Pandects in one entire connected work, whether at Amalphi in 1137, before the middle of King David's reign, or at some earlier period; or that before particular promulgations of the Canon law, no fragments of the Civil or Canon law were any where preserved, is extremely improbable (*a*). Many unquestionable proofs of the contrary could, if necessary, be produced.

───────────────────────────────

" that he shall see convenient for the purpose, and that there, in presence of him and of those who shall be there assembled, be rehearsed the laws which King David made, and also the amendments and additions which have since been made by the Kings," &c.

(*a*) " These laws of King Henry I. are a kind of miscellany made up of those ancient laws called *the laws of the Confessor* and King William I. and of *certain parts of the Canon and Civil law.*" History of the Common Law of England, p. 135.——See also the authorities quoted by Lord Lyttleton, in support of the following passage, viz. " The law of England being a barrier against the whole system of Papal power, the prelates, who were become subservient to that power, and continually appealed to it in the affairs of the church, had recourse to the *Canon and Civil laws*, the authority of which they endeavoured to exalt above that of the former. *A professor of them, named Vacarius*,

NOTES.

If then such fragments were known in Europe before, or in the days of King David, some of the foreign ecclesiastics brought into Scotland to inhabit the various monasteries founded by the father and two elder brothers of that King, and by himself, must undoubtedly have imported such knowledge along with them. It cannot therefore appear in the least extraordinary, that traces of those laws might be discernible in any digest of laws formed by King David.

Nor was it at all necessary, as some writers seem to have supposed, that the people of Scotland should have derived their knowledge of the Civil and Canon law from England. The intercourse directly between Scotland and the continent of Europe in general, and Italy in particular, must, by means of the different churchmen, as well as by commerce (*a*), have been abundantly frequent; and it can hardly be doubted that the Scots would, on subjects of so high importance, prefer information flowing immediately from the source, to circuitous information transmitted through the channel of a hostile nation.

It has been urged as a suspicious circumstance, that in *Regiam Majestatem*, a code of laws supposed to have been altogether framed by King David, some particular statutes, not to be found in Glanville, occur, bearing expressly to have been enacted by that King.

But it is absurd to suppose, as has been already observed, that *Regiam Majestatem* contained nothing besides the acts of King David. It is much more reasonable to regard it as a general collection made by King David's authority of all the subsisting laws of preceding Kings, enlarged, no doubt, and improved by several acts of his own. Even in the former view, the objection has little force. In the latter, it has no force at all. On the contrary, in such a general collection it was proper to distinguish the particular enactments of David from the other laws in the book; and that circumstance, instead of throwing discredit on *Regiam Majestatem*, confers on it additional authenticity.

If, however, we may for a moment suppose the rolls of ancient Scottish statutes now under consideration to have fallen into the hands of some English monk, who observing in them a general resemblance to the ancient laws of England, and actuated by some illiberal motive, had formed the resolution to transcribe them, to alter the arrangement, and to exhibit them as an English compilation, such a man would be careful to omit every particular that might lead to a detection of his plagiarism, and of course would studiously omit those statutes of King David.

It has been urged too as a proof of *Regiam Majestatem* being a copy of *Glanville*, that the latter is not only the most methodical book of the two, but likewise in various respects the most perfect and complete.

Now, whether we shall suppose some private person in Scotland deliberately sitting down to copy Glanville, with a view to pass his copy on the world as an original digest of the ancient laws of his country, or several persons, by authority of the Parliament of Scotland, adopting Glanville in the lump as a body of Scots law, it is utterly incredible that in either case the copy should have been intentionally made more immethodical, or more imperfect than the original. No stronger argument, perhaps, can be adduced in support of the originality of *Regiam Majestatem*, than its being less methodical and less perfect than *Glanville*. (*b*)

" *was called over from Italy in the year* 1148 *by the Archbishop of Canterbury, and under his patronage they were taught in the Archiepiscopal Palace and in the university of Oxford. Some of the books brought and commented on by Vacarius* contained " notions and maxims," &c. " V. Johan. Salisb. Policraticon, sive de nugis curial. l. 8. c. 12.—Gerv. Actus Pont. " Cant. de Theobald.—Chron. Norm. p. 983.—D. Arth. Duck, de usu et auctoritate Jur. Civ. l. 1. c. 7. art. 10. " 11. 13."

(*a*) The Abbot Baldredus, the author of the eulogium on King David, referred to above, has the following remarkable passage. " Tu quondam (viz. terra Scotiæ) cæterarum inendica terrarum, cespite duro famem incolis inge- " rebas, nunc cæteris mollior atque fæcundior, ex tua abundantia vicinarum regionum inopiam allevias. Ipse (viz. rex " David) *portus tuos peregrinis mercibus fæcundavit, et aliorum regnorum divitias tuis deliciis aggregavit.*" Fordoun, vol. 1. p. 305. at the bottom.———The two following passages, though foreign to the present question, are so curious that we are induced to insert them in this place. " Ita enim populum illum" (viz. Scoticanum) ' rudem et agrestem ad " mores compositos et edomitos illicere satagebat, ut non solum de magnis re gni sui causis, verum et de minimis qui- " busque, utpote de *hortis, ædificiis, et pomariis* curam gereret, ut eos ad similia suo exemplo provocaret." Page 302.— And in another place, " Et ut nihil illi ad vitam honestam deesset, etiam hora conveniente honeste alicui operi, hoc est " aut *herbis plantandis, vel surculis a sua radice excisis*, alieno trunco inserendis operam dabat." Page 305.

(*b*) Lord Lyttleton, in his history of King Henry II. writes thus; " I will only add, that the *high encomiums* " on the then reigning King, in the prefaces to both these books," (viz. *Regiam Majestatem* and Glanville), " or

k

NOTES.

But in truth this whole matter is confined within limits so clear and so precise, as appear effectually to exclude all difficulty and misapprehension.

On the one hand, the statute 1425 must be admitted to carry back the character of authenticity attached to *Regiam Majestatem* fourscore years at least prior to that time.

On the other hand, the laws of King David, with the amendments and additions by succeeding Kings, ordered by King Edward's edict in 1305 to be publicly read in a general convention of the Scots nation, could be nothing else than those contained in the rolls of the ancient statutes of Scotland, of the laws and *assise* of the kingdom of Scotland, and *of the laws and usages of the burrows of Scotland*, put into King Edward's hands only thirteen years before, the contents of which must have been universally known.

That public rehearsal, again, in 1305, of those rolls, without mentioning the written documents of them, that, in consequence of so solemn a transaction, could not fail to have been spread through the country, must certainly have transmitted and preserved the perfect knowledge of them fourscore years at least after that rehearsal.

No time therefore seems to be left for the introduction into Scotland of this imperfect immethodical bungled transcript of Glanville, and for the adoption of it there, under the title of *Regiam Majestatem*, as a genuine system of the ancient laws of the Scots nation.

On the other hand, little doubt can be entertained that *Regiam Majestatem*, recognised by a public statute of Scotland in 1425 as a *book of law*, consisted of the " rotuli de antiquis statutis regni Scotiæ—de legibus et assisis regni " Scotiæ—et de legibus et consuetudinibus burgorum Scotiæ—et de quibusdam statutis editis per reges Scotiæ," mentioned in the inventory 1292; and that those *rotuli* again were " the laws which King David made, and also the amend- " ments and additions which have since been made by the Kings," ordered by King Edward's edict 1305 to be publicly rehearsed in a general convention of the people of Scotland.

It is proper too to keep in mind, that no more than an hundred and thirty-nine years had intervened between the death of King David in 1153 and the year 1292, the date of the inventory in which those rolls were mentioned; and an hundred and twenty years between the date of King Edward's edict and the 1425, when the statute was enacted; the longest period of the two being no more remote than from the Restoration to the present time, and, to use an expression of Sir Matthew Hale, perfectly *within time of memory*. Those indeed who lived in the reign of King Alexander III. cannot be supposed to have been ignorant of the laws of King David, enacted only about an hundred years before the commencement of that reign. Nor could those who lived in the time of King James I. have been ignorant of laws publicly rehearsed in a convention of their countrymen only an hundred years before King James's accession to the Crown.

Let it not then be deemed presumptuous to request, that before the severe sentence of final condemnation be pronounced against *Regiam Majestatem*, of being a spurious and bungled copy of Glanville, the question may be candidly and dispassionately reconsidered.

" *account of victories gained by him, and successes in war, the FAME OF WHICH HAD FILLED ALL LANDS,* are very ill appli-
" cable to David I." Vol. 2. p. 269.————It is painful to remark, that on this point the Noble historian seems, through inadvertency, to have expressed himself less accurately than he certainly would have wished. The passage in *Regiam Majestatem* which he alludes to, is in these words : " Quam eleganter, quam strenue, quam callide, hostium " obviando insidiis et malitiis, hostilitatis tempore armatam exercuit militiam, nemini venit in dubium." Will this passage admit the bold paraphrase of Lord Lyttelton ?—But let us hear what King David's *cotemporary*, Baldred, says on this subject. " Quoniam grassus hominis a domino diriguntur, qui *regem invictissimum*, qui tot sibi barbaras subdidit " nationes, qui de Moraviensibus et insulanis parvo labore triumphaverat." Fordoun, vol. 1. p. 304. Such are the words of a writer cotemporary with King David, addressed to a cotemporary Prince, Henry Plantagenet, King David's grand-nephew.

NOTES.

NOTE on line 1. of page 15. of the preceding INTRODUCTION.

" Videlicet, in uno fæculo continebantur 23 rotuli magni et mediocres, de compotis vicecomitum, ballivorum, " firmariorum, *thanorum*, burgorum, et aliorum, diverfis temporibus regum Scotiæ."

FORMERLY almoſt the whole kingdom of Scotland is faid to have been divided into thanedoms (*a*).
Of thoſe thanedoms about twenty-feven are mentioned in the following Index (*b*), all ſituated in thoſe provinces of Scotland which ſtretch along its eaſtern coaſt.
Of all the twenty-feven, one only, viz. that of Kinrofs, is ſituated on the ſouth ſide of the Tay, and not one of them on the ſouth of the Forth.
Thane, *Thanedom* ;—*Earl*, *Earldom* ;—*Shire*, *Sheriffdom* ;—are all terms of general and of high import, and confeſſedly of Saxon extraction.
How came thoſe terms to prevail ſo univerſally in Scotland ?—and in particular, how came *thanes* and *thanedoms* to be ſo widely diffuſed over the eaſtern provinces ſituated north of Tay ?
That that tract of country was anciently poſſeſſed by the Picts ſeems to be an agreed point. Were the Picts then a race of Saxons ?—and did their poſterity continue to poſſeſs the eaſtern provinces of Scotland, after the deſtruction of their Royal Family, and the conqueſt of their kingdom by Kenneth Macalpine, about the year 853 ?—or were the Picts either utterly extirpated or expelled from thoſe provinces, as the Britons who poſſeſſed the champaign provinces of England were by the Saxons, as the general practice of ſavages appears to render probable, and as the Scotichronicon ſeems to indicate ?—and did tribes of Saxons, driven from England by the Norman conquerors, ſeek an aſylum in Scotland, and, under the protection of the Scottiſh Monarchs, gradually inſinuate themſelves into the Pictiſh territory, rendered by the extirpation or expulſion of its former poſſeſſors in a great meaſure perhaps a ſolitary deſert ?
By whatever means it happened, there can be no doubt that thoſe countries have been for many ages poſſeſſed by a race of men deſcended of Saxon anceſtors. Their language, as different from the Celtic language of the Scots (*c*) as one language can be from another, their dreſs, their *thanedoms*, *earldoms*, and *ſhires*, without inſiſting on a variety of more minute diſcrepancies in their domeſtic manners, ſupply here the ſilence of hiſtory, and prove the fact to demonſtration.
But it is truly wonderful, that thoſe Scots and Saxons, two nations ſo diametrically oppoſite to one another in the great and prominent features of the human character, coaleſced ſo perfectly under the ſame government, that inſtead of reading of inteſtine wars between them of any material conſequence, we find them on all occaſions acting with unanimity and perfect cordiality againſt their common enemies.

(*a*) Fordoun's Scotichronicon, vol. 1. p. 231.

(*b*) Viz. Aberbuthnot, Aberkerdour, Aberlachwich (ſuppoſed to be erroneouſly written), Aberlemno, Aberluthnot, Alyth, Balhelvie, Boyne, Collie, Dingwall, Douny, Down, the ahthanedom of Dull, (ſee Fordoun, vol. 1. p. 226.), Durris, Fettercairn, Fromartin, Glammis, Glendowachy, Kinaltey, Kincardine, Kinclevin, Kinroſs, Kintore, Moniſeith, Morphy, Newdofkis, Scoon, and Tannadyce. Various thanedoms beſides theſe might be enumerated from other authorities, ſuch as thoſe of Rofs, (Fordoun, vol. 1. p. 532.), the thanedom of Fyfe, of Calder, of Cowweth, of Kinmylie, of Kalentir, &c. &c. That of Kalentir alone, in ſo far as is at preſent recollected, ſeems to be ſituated on the ſouth ſide of the Forth.

(*c*) Baldredus writes thus in his eulogium of King David I. " Et delectabatur in multitudine pacis, quam inter " barbaras gentes et *diverſitates linguarum et morum ſibi contrarias*, et propter mutuas mortes et vulnera ſibi invicem municiſ- " ſimas, tanta cautione compoſuit, tanta auctoritate ſervavit, ut inter cognatas gentes, *ejuſdemque generis et linguæ homines* " tale fœdus tanto tempore vix aliquando vidcrimus cuſtodiri." Fordoun, vol. 1. p. 300.

NOTES.

The introduction of the terms *shire* and *sheriff*, if not anterior, was probably at least coeval with those of *thanedom* and *thane*.

It is likely that *shires* comprehended at first districts of much smaller extent than the territories denoted by those terms during the last five hundred years.

In one of King Edgar's charters to the priory of Coldingham (a), we find *Coldinghamshire* mentioned.

In the chartulary of the abbey of Dunfermline we find mention made of *Dumfermlingshire*, *Delorshire*, *Newburnshire*, *Musselburghshire*, and the *shires* of *Gelland* and *Gaitmilk*. In the charter of King William in 1178 (b), founding the abbey of Aberbrothock, the *shires* of *Aberbrothock*, of *Denetbyn*, of *Kingoldrum*, and of *Athyn* occur. And in the following Index we find *Herberthshire*, and the shires of *Seoon* and *Kinghorn*. Of this many other proofs might be adduced.

In Prynne's collections, and in Mr Rymer's Fœdera (c), we find the following shires of Scotland mentioned, viz. Aberdeen, Ayr, Angus, Argyle, Banff, Berwick, Clackmannan, Crumbachy (Cromarty), Dumfries, Dunbarton, Dyngwale, Elgin, Edinburgh, Fyfe, Forfar, Forres, Haddington, Jeddeworth, Invernairn, Inverness, Kincardin, Kinross, Lanark, Linlithgow, Mernis, Oughterarder, Perth, Peebles, Roxburgh, Rotherglen, Ross (d), Selkirk, Stirling, and Wigton.

Bute seems to have been then included in Argyleshire, Renfrew in the shire of Lanark, and the stewartry of Kirkcudbright in the shire of Dumfries.

It is uncertain whether Caithness and Sutherland were then separate shires, or included in that of Ross. But whether they were then separate shires or not, we know that they, as well as Ross, were more than three hundred years after 1296 included in Inverness-shire.

Orkney and Zetland did not belong to the kingdom of Scotland till many years after 1296.

It is equally uncertain at what time the office and dignity of *Earl* was first used in Scotland.

About the year 994 we observe the name of a *Cruchne* Earl of Angus (e).—We find a *Malpedir* Earl of Mernis mentioned about the year 1095 (f).—We read of an Earl of *Gowry*, an uncle of King Edgar and King Alexander I. (g) —Of an *Angus* Earl of *Murray* (h),—and of the earldom of *Gariach* (i), in the reign of King David I. possessed by David Earl of Huntington, that King's youngest grandson.

From the time of King Malcolm IV. about 1160, downwards to the year 1286, we find the collective term *Comites* frequently used in the Scotichronicon (k).

In the same period we find mention made of different Earls of Angus (l), of Fyfe (m), of Strathern (n), of March,

---

(a) Page 135. of this Book.   (b) Chartulary of Aberbrothock.

(c) Prynne, vol. 3. from p. 649. to p. 664. inclusive, and pages 1054. and 1055. Fœdera, vol. 2. from p. 723. to 727. inclusive. See also *Rotuli Parliamenti*, vol. 1. p. 267.

(d) Were Angus and Forfar, Dingwall and Ross, Jedburgh and Roxburgh, Kincardine and Mernis, Lanark and Ruglen, then considered to be different shires? As to Lanark and Ruglen, see Fœdera, vol. 2. p. 724. at the words "Magister Militiæ Templi;" and see the penult article of the same page as to Jedburgh and Roxburgh.

(e) Fordoun's Scotichronicon, vol. 1. p. 216.   (f) Ibid. vol. 1. p. 277.   (g) Ibid. vol. 1. p. 285.

(h) Ibid. vol. 1. p. 293. 295. 304. 448. 452.   (i) Ibid. vol. 1. p. 447.; and vol. 2. p. 33. 42.

(k) Ibid. vol. 1. p. 450. 473. 474. 506. 535.; vol. 2. p. 33. 38. &c. &c. &c.

(l) Fœdera, vol. 1. p. 40. 377.; vol. 2. p. 266. 471. 555. Prynne's Collections, vol. 3. p. 652. 653.

(m) Fordoun, vol. 1. p. 297. 370. 519. 532.; vol. 2. p. 38. 58. 102. 104. 113. 127. Fœdera, vol. 1. p. 39. 428. 566. 567. 715.; vol. 2. p. 266.

(n) Fordoun, vol. 1. p. 450. 515. 529.; vol. 2. p. 109. 114. Fœdera, vol. 1. p. 39. 377. 428. 559. 565. 567. 715.; vol. 2. p. 266. 471. 555. Prynne, vol. 3. p. 649. 653.

NOTES.

or Dunbar, or *Comes Laodenfis* (a), of Rofs (b), of Caithnefs (c), of Athol (d), of Buchan (e), of Lennox (f), or Mar (g), of Menteith (h), of Carrick (i), and of Sutherland (k).

(a) Fordoun, vol. 1. p. 459. 481. 484. 492. 535. ; vol. 2. p. 59. 61. 76. 90. 131. Fœdera, vol. 1. p. 39. 377. 428. 559. 566. 567. 715.; vol. 2. p. 266. 471. 529. 555. Prynne, vol. 3. p. 652. 653.

(b) Fordoun, vol. 1. p. 480.; vol. 2. p. 61. Fœdera, vol. 1. p. 377.; vol. 2. p. 266. 471. 555.

(c) Fordoun, vol. 1. p. 512. 534.; vol. 2. p. 46. 47. 48. 59. Fœdera, vol. 2. p. 266. 471.

(d) Fordoun, vol. 1. p. 532.; vol. 2. p. 59. 72. 73. 102. 109. 110. 111. Fœdera, vol. 1. p. 377. 428.; vol. 2. p. 266. 471. 555.

(e) Fordoun, vol. 1. p. 532.; vol. 2. p. 58. 59. 85. 91. 102. 109. 113. Fœdera, vol. 1. p. 428. 566. 670. 715.; vol 2. p. 266. 471. 555. Prynne, vol. 3. p. 650. 651. 653.

(f) Fordoun, vol. 2. p. 42. Fœdera, vol. 1. p. 377. vol. 2. p. 266. 471. 555. Prynne, vol. 3. p. 563.

(g) Fordoun, vol. 2. p. 84. 85. 91. 104. 109. 113. Fœdera, vol. 1. p. 377. 428. 566. 670. 715.; vol. 2. p. 266. 471. 555. Prynne, vol. 3. p. 651. 653.

(h) Fordoun, vol. 2. p. 81. 84. 85. 91. 92. 120. Fœdera, vol. 1. p. 377. 428. 566. 670.; vol. 2. p. 266. 471. 555. Prynne, vol. 3. p. 651. 653.

(i) Fordoun, vol. 2. p. 109. 114. 115. Fœdera, vol. 1. p. 559. 566. 567.; vol. 2. p. 266. 471. Prynne, vol. 3. p. 653.

(k) Fœdera, vol. 2. p. 266. 471. Prynne, vol. 3. p. 653.

xlii

NOTICE TO THE READER.

THE Old Index is in many places a ſtrange mixture of Latin and Scots, and it abounds with errors (*a*). As even records are not exempted from miſtake, ſeveral of thoſe errors occurred no doubt in the records themſelves, and have thence been copied into the Index. But moſt of them are certainly imputable to the framer of the Index. Proper names indeed may in many inſtances puzzle the moſt ſkilful reader. Of this Prynne's Collections, eſpecially his Ragman's roll (*b*), furniſh a ſtriking proof. Nor are even the Fœdera immaculate. The lettters *i, m, n, u,* and all their combinations with one another, unleſs carefully formed, occaſion great uncertainty in reading proper names ; and *t* and *c* are generally written ſo exactly alike, that the acuteſt eye cannot diſtinguiſh the one from the other. Before an *i* this ſimilarity occaſions little inconveniency ; but before the other vowels, and the conſonants *h, r,* and *w,* it is apt to miſlead. It may be remarked, in general, that in ancient writing it is not the antiquity, but the badneſs of the character, which, to a perſon moderately converſant in old-manuſcripts, creates difficulty. The ſame is the caſe with modern writing. Many familiar epiſtles, no older than yeſterday, will embarraſs a man who could peruſe with facility a charter of high antiquity.

The contents of the 1ſt roll ſtill preſerved will be found on the bottom of page 4. the top of page 9. and on the four intermediate pages. The alterations made on the Old Index of that roll are taken from the original record itſelf, and are printed in Italics.

Of the other eleven exiſting rolls the Index is printed in a ſmaller type than that of the rolls which are miſſing ; and all the proper names in thoſe eleven rolls are corrected, and many names, not ſet down in the Old Index, are added from the rolls themſelves ; but the connecting words of the Old Index are retained, uncouth as they are. Of the firſt book of the record of charters ſtill preſerved, an index entirely new is given, for the reaſon mentioned page 70. It is printed from page 70. to page 98. incluſive, in the ſame ſmall type in which the index of the eleven exiſting rolls is printed.

Many charters contained in the Index appear to have been twice recorded, and ſome of them oftener. It is not eaſy in every caſe to conjecture the reaſon of this.

The letter *B* ſeems to ſtand for the word *blench* in ſome places, as p. 38. No. 14. 15. 22. 23. 29. 37. ;—p. 40. No. 17. ;—p. 42. No. 21. ;—p. 67. No. 3¹. 2¹.

Archidiaconus has in two or three places been erroneouſly tranſlated Arch*dean* inſtead of Arch*deacon*. The Editor is indebted for this correction to the ſuggeſtion of a learned and very reſpectable friend.

Of the 331 charters in Book 1ſt, the firſt 276 were granted by King David II. and the laſt 45 by that King's nephew, King Robert II. the firſt King of the *Stewart* family.

Such of the witneſſes to thoſe charters as are mentioned in the record are ſet down in the ſeveral entries in the Index ; and they will be found entered again in the alphabetical liſt of the *Names of Perſons.*

Of ſome of thoſe charters the places at which they were dated are not expreſſed in the record. Of the reſt about one hundred and ſixty were dated at Edinburgh, ſixty-four at Perth, ſeventeen at Aberdeen, fourteen at Scone, ten at Dundee, nine at Stirling, nine at Montroſe, ſix at St Andrew's, five at Lindores, four at Kindromy, three at Dun-

---

(*a*) The Editor is reluctantly drawn to make this remark ; for though he flatters himſelf, that the *few* to whom he is known will not impute thoſe errors to careleſſneſs or inattention on his part ; yet the *many* to whom he is unknown may poſſibly be diſpoſed to judge leſs favourably of his accuracy.

(*b*) Viz. the roll of that multitude of Scots of all ranks who ſwore fealty to King Edward I. Prynne's Collections, vol. 3. from page 648. to page 666. incluſive.

NOTICE TO THE READER.

donald, three at Melrofs, three at Spynie, two at Aberbrothock, two at Dunfermling, and one at each of the following places, viz. Coupar in Fife, Dunbartane, Drumelzier, Elgin, Invernefs, Irwine, the Foreſt of Kintore, Kinloſs, Kilwinning, Lochleven Caſtle, Linlithgow, Lochfreuch in Strathbrawn, Methuen, and Reſtennet.

Of the 276 charters by King David II. two, viz. No. 93. and 136. are dated in the 29th year of his reign; one, No. 168, in the 31ſt; two, No. 89. and 167. in the 32d; and the reſt in the 33d, 34th, 35th, 36th, 37th, 38th, 39th, 40th, and 41ſt years of his reign; and they appear in the Index pretty nearly in chronological order. The 45 charters in that book granted by King Robert II. are dated in the 1ſt and 2d years of his reign.

Of the charters in Roll 4. the index of which is printed on pages 130, 131, and 132, fix are dated at Edinburgh, thirteen at Perth, four at Scone, and one at each of the following places, viz. Coupar in Fife, Dundee, Dundonald, Kilwinning, and Lochfreuchy. The years of the King's reign in which the charters in that roll were granted, and the names of the witneſſes to the only charter in it that mentions the witneſſes, are prefixed to the index of it on page 130.

All the names contained in the firſt roll ſtill preſerved, of which the index will be found on pages 4th, 5th, 6th, 7th, 8th, and 9th, are printed there, and again in the alphabetical liſts.

Of the other ten rolls now in the General Regiſter-Houſe, the places where, and the years of the King's reign in which they were dated, together with the witneſſes named in them, are reſpectively prefixed to the index of each of them, on the following pages, viz. 115. 117. 118. 123. 125. 127. 128. 132. 134. 150. 160. 161. and 165.

A connected view is here ſubjoined of the witneſſes to thoſe charters of King David II. King Robert II. King Robert III. and of the Regent Robert Duke of Albany, viz.

WITNESSES TO THE CHARTERS OF KING DAVID II.

William, Biſhop of St Andrew's.
Patrick, Biſhop of Brechin, Chancellor.
Robert, Steward of Scotland and Earl of Strathern, King David's nephew.
John Earl of Carrick, eldeſt ſon and heir of the ſaid Robert Steward of Scotland.
George de Dunbar Earl of March.
Patrick Earl of March and of Murray.
Thomas Earl of Mar.
William Earl of Douglas.
William de Keith, Marſhall of Scotland.

Robert de Erſkine, Chamberlain of Scotland.
David de Anand.
Thomas Biſſet.
William de Diſchingtoun.
Archibald de Douglas.
John de Edmonſtoun.
Walter de Haliburton.
John Herice.
Walter de Leſlie.
Alexander de Lyndeſay.
John de Preſton.

WITNESSES TO THE CHARTERS OF KING ROBERT II.

William, and Walter, Biſhops of St Andrew's.
Walter, and Mathew, Biſhops of Glaſgow.
Patrick, Biſhop of Brechin, Chancellor of Scotland.
John de Peblys, Archdeacon of St Andrew's, and afterwards Biſhop of Dunkeld, Chancellor of Scotland.
John de Carrick, a Canon of Glaſgow, Chancellor of Scotland.
John Earl of Carrick, and Steward of Scotland, eldeſt ſon of King Robert II.
Robert, Earl of Fife and Menteith, afterwards Duke of Albany, ſecond ſon of King Robert II.
Alexander Stewart, afterwards Earl of Buchan, the third ſon of King Robert II.
George de Dunbar Earl of March.

Thomas Earl of Mar.
William Earl of Douglas and of Mar.
James Earl of Douglas and of Mar.
Archibald Earl of Douglas.
Alexander de Cockburn of Langtoun, Keeper of the Great Seal of Scotland.
James de Douglas, *Dominus de* Dalkeith.
Archibald de Douglas.
Hugh de Eglyntoun.
Robert de Erſkine.
Thomas de Erſkine.
James de Lyndeſay, a nephew of King Robert II.
Alexander de Lyndeſay.

xliv

WITNESSES TO THE CHARTERS OF KING ROBERT III.

Walter, bishop of St Andrew's.
Mathew, Bishop of Glasgow.
Gilbert, Bishop of Aberdeen.
Robert, Earl of Fife and Menteith, afterwards Duke of Albany, brother of King Robert III.
Archibald Earl of Douglas.
John Earl of March.
James de Douglas, *Dominus de* Dalkeith.

Alexander *de* Cockburn of Langtoun, Keeper of the Great Seal of Scotland.
Robert *de* Danielston.
Thomas *de* Erskine.
Robert *de* Keith.
David *de* Lyndefay of Glenesk.
James *de* Lyndefay of Craufurd.

WITNESSES TO THE CHARTERS OF THE REGENT ROBERT DUKE OF ALBANY,
ALPHABETICALLY ARRANGED.

BISHOPS.

Aberdeen, Gilbert Bishop of, Chancellor.
St Andrew's, Henry Bishop of.
Brechin, Walter Bishop of.
Dunblane, Finlay Bishop of.

Dunkeld, Robert Bishop of.
Glasgow, William Bishop of.
Murray, John Bishop of.

EARLS.

Athol and Catnes, Walter Stewart Earl of, a brother of the Regent's.
Buchan, John Stewart Earl of, a son of the Regent's.
Craufurd, David *de* Lyndefay Earl of.
———— Alexander Lyndefay Earl of.
Douglas, Archibald Earl of.
Lennox, Duncan Earl of.

Mar and Garvyach, Alexander Stewart Earl of, a nephew of the Regent's.
March, George Earl of.
Murray, Thomas Earl of.
Orkney, Henry *de Sancto Claro* Earl of.
Stratherne, Patrick *de* Grahame Earl of.

GENTLEMEN.

Abirnethy, William *de*.
———— Patrick *de*.
Achynlek, John *de*.
Allyrdas, David *de*.
Arnot, James *de*.
Beckirtoun, Henry *de*.
Berclay, David *de*.
———— John *de*.
Borthwick, William *de*, of Katkone.
———— William *de*, the father, perhaps of Katkone.
———— William *de*, the son.
Bryfbane, Thomas *de*.
Bulby, John *de*, a Canon of Murray.
Bute, Donald *de*, Dean or Deacon of Dunblane.
Cadyhow, William *de*.

Camera, William *de*, of Aberdeen, Rector of Erole.
———— John *de*, of Glasly.
———— John *de*, of Kilbride.
Campbell, Allan.
Charterys, Thomas.
Comyne, Richard *de*.
Cunynghame, Archibald *de*.
———— William *de*.
———— Humphry *de*.
Corntoun, John *de*.
Cornuel, Richard *de*, Archdeacon of Dunkeld.
Crauford, William *de*.
———— Thomas *de*, of Auchnamys.
Culrofs, John Abbot of.
Curry, Walter *de*.

WITNESSES TO CHARTERS OF THE REGENT ROBERT DUKE OF ALBANY. xlv

Dalgles, Symon *de.*
Dalmahoy, Thomas *de.*
Dalrymple, James *de.*
Douglas, James *de, locum-tenens* of the Regent.
———— Thomas *de.*
Dovery, John *de.*
———— Malifius *de.*
Drommond, John *de,* of Concraig.
Edmondftoun, David *de.*
Ercht, William *de.*
Erfkyne, Robert *de.*
Ferny, Robert *de.*
Flemyng, Malcolm, of Bygare.
Forbes, Alexander *de.*
Forfter, John of Coritorfyne.
Gardyn, Alexander *de.*
Geddes, Mathew *de,* Rector of the Kirk *de Fergha.*
Grahame, William *Dominus de,* and of Kyncardyn.
Grynlaw, Thomas *de.*
Hamyltoun, William *de.*
Hawick, Andrew *de,* Canon of Dunkeld, Rector of Liftoun, and Secretary to the Regent.
Haya, William *de,* of Nachtane.
———— William *de,* of Locherwart.
———— John *de.*
Heryng, Patrick *de.*
Home, Alexander *de.*
Howiftoun, John *de.*
Kyninmond, Elizeus *de.*
Kynros, William *de.*
Lang, William, a Canon of Abirdene.
Lawedre, Alexander *de.*
Leky, Murdak *de.*
Lefly, George *de,* of Fythkil, a *confanguineus* of the Regent's.
———— Walter *de.*
Lethe, John *de.*
Levyngftoun, Alexander *de,* of Calenter.
———— Robert *de.*
Lychtoun, Duncan *de.*
Lyndefay, Alexander *de,* fon and heir of David Earl of Craufurd.
———— William *de,* of Roffy, a brother of faid Earl.
———— Walter *de,* another brother of faid Earl.

Maxwell, Robert *de,* of Calderwood.
Mure, John.
Narne, Michael *de.*
Newtoun, Alexander *de.*
Ogilby, or Ogilvile, Alexander *de,* Sheriff of Forfar or Angous.
———— Walter *de.*
Pringil, Robert *de.*
Rollo, Duncan.
Roos, John *de,* of Hawkhede.
Rofs, Robert *de.*
Ruthven, William *de.*
Sandylandis, James *de,* of Caldore, a nephew of the Regent's.
Schaw, James *de.*
Scot, Alan, a Canon of Cambufkeneth.
Scrimzeour, John.
Setoun, Alexander *de.*
———— John *de.*
Spens, John *de.*
Stewart, John, Sheriff of Bute, a *frater naturalis* of the Regent's.
———— Alexander, of Dernle.
———— Robert, of Dernle.
———— Robert, of Fife and Kinclevyne, fon and heir of Murdak the Regent's eldeft fon.
———— Alexander, a Canon of Glafgow, a brother of the Regent's.
———— John, of Dundonald, another brother of the Regent's.
———— John, of Invermeth and Lorne, a *confanguineus* of the Regent's.
———— Robert, of Lorne.
———— Walter, of Rayliftoun, a *confanguineus* of the Regent's.
Swyntoun, John *de.*
Sympill, John, of Elyotftoun.
———— Robert.
Taillefer, Andrew.
Uchterlowny, Alexander *de.*
Walays, John of Elryfle.
Wemys, John *de.*
Wrycht, John, Conftable of Falkland.
Ydill, William.

POSTSCRIPT.

THE Editor has peculiar satisfaction in here announcing to the Public, that the printing of the following Index, aided by the manuscript alphabetical lists of the persons and places contained in it, has already, even before publication, led to a material discovery in relation to the rolls that are missing.

There is in the Library of the Faculty of Advocates at Edinburgh a large manuscript folio volume, consisting of several manuscripts, which seem to have been originally separate and detached. This large volume bears, on a blank leaf prefixed, the following words, viz.

"*A Collection of Charters, Evidents, and Antiquities, collected by E. Hadinton.*"

And it has always been regarded as a collection made by Thomas Hamilton the first Earl of Hadinton (*a*).

From an attentive perusal of that manuscript, and a minute comparison of it with the Old Index here laid before the public, it is evident, that almost all the missing rolls,—and thence probably the whole of them,—had been in the hands of the Noble Collector, and had been by him very carefully inspected.

It is likely that those rolls, as well as the other books of the record of charters passed under the great Seal, and the twelve existing rolls, from which this manuscript has been chiefly formed, came into the hands of the Earl of Hadinton in the year 1612, when he bore the office of Lord Clerk-Register.

The first 566 pages of the manuscript volume now under consideration contain copies of many curious charters taken from the 2d and 19th and all the intermediate books of the great-seal record, the 17th book only excepted.

On the top of the 567th page is written as follows, viz. " Charteris by King Robert Bruce, " King David, and subsequent Kings." From the top of page 569. to the middle of page 579. we find several titles, and many full abstracts of different charters contained in the lost rolls, and of a few in the first existing roll. From the middle of page 579 to the word " *Omissa*," near the bottom of page 582. we observe notes and short abstracts of a considerable number of charters in the 3d, 7th, 9th, 10th, 15th, 16th, 18th, and 19th books of the records of the great seal.

(*a*) This was one of the most remarkable men of the age in which he lived. He was bred to the bar, and was equally distinguished as a lawyer, as a judge, and as a Statesman. Between the years 1592 and 1636, he passed through the different offices of his Majesty's Advocate, a Senator of the College of Justice or Lord of Session, Lord President of the Court of Session, Lord Clerk-Register, Principal Secretary of State, and Lord Privy Seal; and he generally discharged more than one of those high offices at the same time. He was, for example, both principal Secretary of State and Lord President of the Court of Session, from the year 1616 to the year 1626. In the year 1595 he was named one of a celebrated junto of eight Statesmen, known in the history of Scotland by the name of *Octavians*. He first received the honour of knighthood, and was next raised to the dignity of the peerage by the style and title of Lord Binning. He was afterwards created Earl of Melrofs, and lastly Earl of Hadinton. Hence it is evident, that his abilities were of the first rate; and his various manuscripts, especially that now before us, prove, that his industry and application corresponded with his eminent abilities, and enabled him not only to execute the duties of those important public offices, but to prosecute likewise the study of different objects of law and antiquity.

POSTSCRIPT.   xlvii

Under the title "*Omiſſa*," are short abstracts, or rather perhaps full titles, of ten charters in the missing rolls. The rest of page 583. and the top of page 584. contain notes of sixteen charters in the 2d and 19th books of the great-seal record.

A manuscript of fifty pages follows next. These fifty pages consist of notes taken from a great number of charters in the 2d, and 19th, and all the intervening books of the records of the great seal.

This is followed by another short manuscript, of only four pages, entitled, "*Chartœrs Jaco-bus Primus*," containing notes from several charters in the 2d, 3d, and 4th books of the record of the great seal.

After this we find a fourth manuscript, entitled "Catalogue Minute of the Register of Dumfermeling." It is not regularly paged, but seems to contain about forty-two leaves or folios, of which two or three are blank. Of the fate of the books to which this part of the volume relates the Editor is ignorant. Many particulars contained in it seem worthy the attention of an antiquary.

Eight pages follow, entitled, "*Extractum de rotulo infeodationum Rob. Re. I.* 1324 *ante et poſt.*" On those eight pages we find full abstracts, intermixed with some shorter titles, of the charters contained in the missing roll "Rob. I. E." of which the Index is printed on the bottom of page 10. and on the four subsequent pages of this book. It is observable, that my Lord Hadinton seems to give us notes and abstracts of fourteen of the *firſt eighteen* charters in that roll, which are said in the Old Index to have been illegible, of which eighteen his Lordship omits only the first four.

After this follows another manuscript, neither paged nor titled, consisting of about twenty-six leaves, of which three or four are blank. On the first four leaves, and down to the marginal note "*begins* 1424," on the first page of the fifth, we find brief entries of many charters in the missing rolls. From that place to the end we find short entries of many charters contained in books 2d and 30th, and all the intermediate books of the records of the great seal.

We now arrive at the concluding part of this large volume, and the most important and interesting part by far. It is a manuscript of 146 pages. It contains full copies of many charters which were recorded in the missing rolls, and in the twelve rolls still preserved, and ample abstracts of many more. If therefore those missing rolls shall prove to be irrecoverably lost, this valuable collection by the Earl of Hadinton will in so far supply that great loss.

It is proper likewise to remark, that my Lord Hadinton's titles of the charters in those missing rolls, even where he inserts the titles only, are in general more particular than the titles of the same charters in the Old Index, and also apparently more accurate.

We here subjoin a brief view of most of the charters in the missing rolls which seeem to be fully copied in this precious manuscript, pointing them out by the pages of the printed Index, and the relative number on the different pages. It is judged unnecessary to insert those copied from the twelve rolls still remaining in the General Register-house.

xlviii

POSTSCRIPT.

A List of thofe Charters recorded in the miffing Rolls, of which full Copies feem to be inferted in the Earl of Hadinton's Collections.

Pag. N°
1, 5. Charter to Patrick Ogilvie.
25. ——— to Chriftian Bruce.
2, 34. ——— to William de Strabrock.
42. ——— to the burgh of Aberdeen.
45. ——— to Hugh de Rofs.
46. ——— to Mary Cuming.
48. ——— to Hugh de Barclay.
53. ——— to Roderick Alanfon or Evanfon.
3, 2. ——— to the Bifhop of Orkney.
2². ——— to the Abbey of Melros.
3². ——— to the Abbey of Kelfo.
4². ——— to the Abbey of Melros.
5. ⎫
6. ⎬ to ditto.
7. ⎪
8. ⎭
11. ——— to the Abbey of Crofragmer or Crofraguel.
20. ——— to the Abbey of Coldingham.
4, 22. ——— to the Priory of Whitehorn.
23. ⎫ to ditto.
24. ⎭
25. ——— to the preaching friars of Edinburgh.
29. ——— to the Abbey of Dunfermling.
36. ——— to the Abbey of Culrofs.
37. ——— to the Abbey of Lindores.
40. ——— to the Abbey of Scoon.
41. ——— to ditto.
42. ——— to the Abbey of Reftennet.
43. ——— to ditto.
9, 1. ——— to Thomas Ranulph.
2. ⎫
5. ⎬ to ditto.
7. ⎭
11. ——— to Walter Steward.
5, 13. ——— to ditto.
17. ⎫
20. ⎬ to James Domino de Douglas.
26. ⎭
19². ⎫ to Alexander de Setone.
22. ⎭
24¹. ——— to the burgh of Hadingtoun.
6, 26. ——— to Robert de Kethe.
41. ——— to Henry Wattil, (in the Old Index Battal).
5, 9. Reduction of a decreet concerning Meadowflat.

Pag. N°
16, 15. Charter to Gilbert de Haya.
26. ——— of liberty in favour of Adam Adamfon.
31. ——— to the burgh of Aberdeen.
17, 39. ——— to Andrew Murray, knight, and Chriftian Bruce. (This in the Old Index is entered to Andrew Knight.)
41. ——— to Malcolm Earl of Lennox.
51 ——— to Alexander Frafer.
55. ——— to ditto.
18, 67. Reduction of a decreet about Meadowflat.
70. Charter to Patrick, capitali medico noftro furgerie.
75. ——— to Donald Cambell.
76. ——— to Robert de Harkars.
77. ——— to William de Diflingtoun.
78. ——— to Galfrid de Foullertoun.
80. ——— to William Blount.
19, 90. ——— to Henry, called Buttirwambe, (in the Index Winterwambe.)
91. ——— to Robert, called Jolleiffis.
102. ——— Magiftro Mannio de Maneriis.
20, 113. ——— to William de Kingorne.
115. ——— to Nicholas Skirmefchour.
15. ——— to Thomas de Morhame, and John Giffard.
21, 22. ——— to Walter Steward.
31. ——— to ditto.
22, 1. ——— to the Abbey of Jedburgh.
2. ——— to ditto.
23, 2². ——— to the Priory of Whitehorn.
24, 3. ——— to William Beddebie.
7. ——— to Alexander Beddebie.
12. ——— to Jurdanus Williamfon.
15. ——— to the Abbey of Kelfo.
25, 2. ——— to Gilchrift Mac Ymar.
8. ——— to John Gilbertfon.
9. ——— to Richard M'Cuffok.
19. ——— to John, the fon of Gilbert M'Neill.
26, 15. ——— to John, the fon of Dunleph.
18. ——— to Colin, the fon of Neil Cambell.
30. ——— to Gillafpyk, the fon of Walter.
33. ——— to Hugh de Rofs.
27, 1. ——— to Walter, the fon of Gilbert.
4. ——— to the preaching friars of Glafgow
33, 26. ——— to the men of Galloway.
41, 4. ——— to John Carpentar.
8. ——— to the Abbey of Reftennet.

Pag.	Nº		Pag.	Nº	
41,	10.	Charter to Malcolm de Fleming.	63,	45.	Charter to William Earl of Douglas.
61,	2.	——— to John Mar.		50.	——— to John del Burgh.
	3.	——— to William Naper.		53.	——— to William Earl of Sothyrland and Margaret de Bruys, the King's fifter.
	15.	——— to the burgh of Dundee.			
	16.	——— to Alexander de Lyndefay.	65,	4.	——— to William de Difchingtoun.
62,	17.	——— to ditto.		6.	——— to Archibald de Douglas.
	23.	——— to John de Petyllock.		7.	——— to Robert de Danielftoun.
	25.	——— to Margaret Countefs of Angus.		8.	——— to the Abbey of Melros.
	26.	——— to Hugh de Crawford.		9.	——— to Thomas de Henvyle.
	27.	——— to the Abbey of Lundors.		12.	——— to James Douglas.
	31.	——— to the Bifhop of Aberdeen.		17.	——— to George Earl of March.
63,	44.	——— to John de Lyndefay.			

[To fhow the value of thofe copies taken by the Earl of Hadinton from the rolls which are miffing, the four following curious Charters, tranfcribed from the Earl's Collections, are here prefented to the Reader.]

" Renovatio Carte Comitis Moravie fuper Comitatu Moravie."

[Index, page 9. No. 1.]

"ROBERTUS Dei gratia Rex Scotorum Bernardo Abbati de Abirbrothok Cancellario fuo
" Scotiæ falutem Mandamus vobis et precipimus quatenus cartam dilecti nepotis noftri Thome
" Ranulphi comitis Moravie Domini Vallis Annandie et Moravie (certe pro *Mannie*) fuper comi-
" tatu Moravie cum pertinen. fieri et renovari faciatis in hec verba Robertus Dei gratia Rex
" Scotorum omnibus probis hominibus totius terre fue falutem Sciatis nos dediffe conceffiffe et
" hac prefenti carta noftra confirmaffe Thome Ranulphi militi dilecto nepoti noftro pro homagio et
" fervitio fuo omnes terras noftras in Moravia ficut fuerunt in manu Domini Alexandri regis Scotie
" predeceforis noftri ultimo defuncti una cum omnibus aliis terris adjacentibus infra metas et divi-
" fas fubfcript. content. incipiendo videlicet ad aquam de Spee ficut cadit in mare et fic afcendendo
" per eand. aquam includendo terras de Fouchabre Rodhenagkis (*Rethenaykis*) Rothays et de
" Bocharm per fuas rectas metas et divifas cum fuis pertinen. et fic afcendendo per dictam aquam
" de Spee ufque ad marchias de Badenach et fic includendo omnes terras de Badenach de Kyncar-
" din et de Glencarry (*Glencarny*) cum pertinen. per fuas rectas metas et divifas et fic fequendo
" marchiam de Badenach ufque marchiam de Lochabre et fic includendo terras de Lochabre de
" Mamore de Locharkerh de Glengareth et de Glenelgis cum pertinen. per fuas rectas metas et
" divifas et fic fequendo marchiam de Glenelge ufque ad mare verfus occidentem et fic per mare
" ufque ad marchias borealis Ergadie que eft comitis de Rofs et fic per marchias illas ufque
" ad marchias Roffie et fic per marchias Roffie quoufque perveniatur ad aquam de Forne
" et fic per aquam de Forne quoufque perveniatur ad mare orientale Tenend. et habend. dicto
" Thome (*et*) heredibus fuis mafculis de corpore fuo legitime procreatis feu procreandis de nobis

POSTSCRIPT.

" et heredibus nostris in feodo et hereditate in libero comitatu ac in libera regalitate cum quatuor
" querelis ad coronam nostram regiam spectantibus et cum omnibus placitis et querelis tam in com-
" munibus amerciamentis indictamentis quam in brevibus placitabilibus et cum omnibus aliis lo-
" quelis quibufcunque ad liberam regalitatem pertinentibus vel aliquo modo pertinere valentibus
" adeo libere quiete plenarie et honorifice sicut aliqua terra infra regnum nostrum in regalitate
" liberius plenius quietius aut honorificentius dari poterit aut teneri una cum magna cuftuma noftra
" burgi de Invernefs et cocketo ejufd. et libertatibus suis in omnibus excepta tantummodo parva
" cuftuma dicti burgi cum plenaria potestate attachiandi accufandi et in omnibus miniftrandi ac
" inditandi *(judicandi)* omnes illas *(illos)* dicti vicecomitatus injurias dampnis *(dampna)* feu pre-
" judicia facientes indebite cuftume predict. adeo libere in omnibus sicut nos feu aliquis miniftrorum
" noftrorum ipfos attachiare accufare miniftrare feu judicare poterimus feu poterit in premiffis Et
" quod dictus Comes et heredes fui amerciamenta efcaetas et forisfacturas inde contingentes adeo
" libere et quiete habeant et poffideant in futurum sicut nos feu aliquis predeceflorum noftrorum
" dicta amerciamenta efcaetas feu forisfacturas aliquo tempore habuimus Quare vicecomiti nostro
" de Invernefs et ballivis suis ac prepofitis et ballivis dicti burgi qui pro tempore fuerint ac ceteris
" quorum intereft firmiter precipimus et mandamus quatenus prefato Comiti et heredibus suis pre-
" dictis ac suis miniftris in premiffis fint intendentes et refpondentes confulentes et auxiliantes
" super hoc si neceffe fuerit nostra regali potentia invocata fine aliquo alio mandato nostro speciali
" interveniente Volumus quoque et concedimus quod dictus Thomas et heredes sui predicti ha-
" beant teneant et poffideant dictum comitatum cum manerio de Elgyn quod pro capitali manfione
" comitatus Moravie de cetero teneri volumus et vocari et cum omnibus aliis maneriis burgis villis
" thanagiis et omnibus terris noftris dominicis firmis et exitibus infra predict. metas contentas *(con-*
" *tentis)* cum advocationibus ecclefiarum cum feodis et forisfacturis cum silvis et foreftis moris et
" mareffis cum viis et femitis cum aquis ftagnis lacubus vivariis et molendinis cum pifcationibus
" tam maris quam aque dulcis cum venationibus aucupationibus et avium aeriis et cum omnibus
" aliis libertatibus commoditatibus et afiamentis et juftis pertinentiis suis in omnibus et per omnia
" tam non nominatis quam nominatis Quibus heredibus dicti Thome mafculis deficientibus quod
" abfit volumus quod dictus comitatus ad nos et heredes noftros libere et integre et sine aliqua
" contradictione revertatur Volumus etiam et concedimus pro nobis et heredibus noftris quod
" omnes barones et liberi tenentes dicti comitatus qui de nobis et predeceffioribus noftris in capite
" tenuerunt et eorum heredes dicto Thome et heredibus suis predictis homagia fidelitates sectas
" curie et omnia alia fervitia faciant et baronias et tenementa sua de ipfo et heredibus suis predictis
" de cetero teneant falvis tamen baronibus et libere tenentibus predict. et eorum heredibus juribus
" et libertatibus curiarum fuarum hactenus ... *(jufte)* ufitatis Volumus infuper et concedimus quod
" burgi et burgenfes fue de Elgyn de Forres et de Invernarne eafdem libertates habeant et exer-
" ceant quas tempore domini Alexandri regis Scotorum predicti et noftro habuerunt hoc folum
" falvo quod de nobis tenebant sine medio et nunc de eodem Comite tenent cum eifdem libertati-
" bus Salvo etiam nobis et heredibus noftris in hac donatione noftra burgo noftro de Invernefs
" cum loco castelli et terris ad dictum burgum pertinentibus cum pifcatione aque de Niss et cum
" molendinis burgi ejufdem cum fequela dicti burgi et terrarum ad ipfum burgum tantummodo
" pertinen. Et falvis nobis et heredibus noftris fidelitatibus Epifcoporum Abbatum Priorum et
" aliorum Prelatorum ecclefie Moravienfis et advocatione feu jure patronatus ecclefiarum eorundem
" et eorum ftatu in omnibus quem habuerunt tempore regis Alexandri predicti et aliorum prede-
" ceffiorum noftrorum regum Scotie excepto quod homines eorundem citati per nos ad defenfio-

POSTSCRIPT.

" nem regni noſtri intendant vexillo et ſequi teneantur vexillum dicti Thome Comitis et heredum
" ſuorum predictorum una cum aliis qui vexillum Moravie ſequi ſolebant antiquitus Faciendo
" nobis et heredibus noſtris dictus Thomas et heredes ſui predicti pro dicto comitatu ſervitium octo
" militum in exercitu noſtro et Scoticanum ſervitium et auxilium de ſingulis davatis debitum et
" conſuetum tantummodo ſine ſecta curie ad quamcunque curiam noſtram faciend. In cujus rei
" teſtimonium preſenti carte noſtre ſigillum noſtrum precepimus apponi Teſtibus venerabilibus
" patribus Willielmo Sancti Andree Willielmo Dunkeldenſis Henrico Abirdonenſis epiſcopis Dei
" gratia Bernardo Abbate de Abirbrothock Cancellario noſtro Malcolmo Comite de Levenax
" Gilberto de Haya Roberto de Keith Mariſcallo Scotie Alexandro de Mexnes (*Margus Mer-*
" *gus*) et Henrico de Sancto Claro militibus." (*a*)

" Carta Malcolmi Fleming de burgo de Wigtoun &c. cum terris
" regis vicecomitatus de Wigtoun erected in ane frie Erledome."

" DAVID &c. Sciatis nos &c. et hac preſenti carta noſtra confirmaſſe Malcolmo de Fle-
" ming militi dilecto et fideli noſtro pro homagio et laudabili ſervitio ſuo nobis impenſo et impen-
" dendo omnes terras noſtras de Farynes et de Rennys et totum burgum noſtrum de Wigtoun cum
" omnimodis pertinentiis ſuis ac omnes terras noſtras totius vicecomitatus noſtri de Wigtoun per
" metas et diviſas ſuas ſubſcriptas a capite vadi aque de Creeth et ſic ſequendo illam aquam quo-
" uſque perveniat ad mare ubi aqua de Creeth currit in mare et ſic per mare uſque Molorounyfuagis
" et de Molorunyfuagis per mare uſque ad antiquas metas Comitatus de Carrik et ſic per eaſdem
" metas de Carrik quouſque perveniat ad predictum caput aque de Creeth Tenen. et haben.
" omnes terras predictas una cum burgo predicto eidem Malcolmo et heredibus ſuis de corpore
" ſuo per lineam maſculinam directe deſcendentibus de nobis et heredibus noſtris in feodo et here-
" ditate in perpetuum per omnes rectas metas et diviſas ſupraſcriptas in liberum Comitatum cum
" homagiis et ſervitiis libere tenentium omnium terrarum predictarum cum feodis et foriſfacturis
" cum curiis et eſcaetis cum furca et foſſa ſok et ſak thole et theme et inſangtheiſ cum multuris
" molendinis et eorum ſequelis cum aucupationibus piſcationibus et venationibus et cum omnimodis
" libertatibus commoditatibus ayſiamentis et juſtis pertinentiis in omnibus et per omnia tam non
" nominatis quam nominatis ad liberum Comitatum ſpectantibus ſeu juſte ſpectare valentibus in ſu-
" turum una cum advocationibus eccleſiarum et cum jure ac patronatu monaſteriorum et abbacia-
" rum infra predictum comitatum exiſtentium reſervato nobis et heredibus noſtris jure patronatus
" ſedis epiſcopalis Candide Caſe cum omnibus pertinentibus et libertatibus quibuſcunque Volumus

---

(*a*) In the Library of the Faculty of Advocates there are two Duplicates, written on parchment, of the Chartulary of the Biſhoprick of Murray. The above remarkable Charter is inſerted in each of thoſe Duplicates. In the
Duplicate that appears to be the more ancient, it will be found on the *verſo* of Folio 91. In the other it is written on the
verſo of Folio 68.——My Lord Hadinton's copy has been carefully collated with both thoſe Duplicates, and ſome
apparent inaccuracies of little conſequence have by that means been corrected. The various readings adopted from the
Chartulary are printed in Italics within parentheſes.

POSTSCRIPT.

" et concedimus pro nobis et heredibus noftris quod burgenfes fui de Vigtoun eafdem libertates in
" omnibus habeant quas jufte habuerunt temporibus predecefforum noftrorum regum Scotie Et
" cum dictus locus de Vygtoun pro principali manereo totius vicecomitatus de Vygtoun habeatur
" ordinamus et perpetuo confirmamus ut ipfe Malcolmus et heredes fui predicti abinde nomen
" Comitis accipiant et Comites de Vygtoun de cetero nuncupentur Quia vero idem Malcolmus
" adjunctus (a) nofter exftitit et erga nos fe fideliter habuit in cunctis profperis et adverfis in per-
" petuam memoriam adjunctionis (a) conceffioni noftre fibi facte de Comitatu predicto quod ipfe et
" heredes fui habeant teneant et poffideant totum comitatum predictum cum pertinentiis in adeo
" liberam regalitatem ficut aliqua regalitas per totum regnum noftrum poffidetur liberius feu tenetur
" et quod dictus Malcolmus et heredes fui libere cognofcere valeant in curia fua comitatus predicti
" fuper quatuor articulis fpectantibus ad coronam Faciendo nobis et heredibus noftris predictus
" Malcolmus et heredes fui predicti Comites de Vygtoun fervitium quinque militum in exercitu
" noftro In cujus rei teftimonium &c. Teftibus &c. Apud villam de Are nono die Novembris
" anno regni noftri tertio decimo."

" Carta Libertatis de novo conceffa Galwydienfibus."

[Index, page 13. No. 80.]

" ROBERTUS &c. Sciatis nos pro nobis et fucceforibus noftris conceffiffe et hac
" prefenti carta noftra confirmaffe in perpetuum Capitaneis et omnibus hominibus Galwidie
" quod quilibet homo Galwidienfis fuper quocunque fupradicto ferjandorum Galwidie habeant
" bonam et fidelem affifam patrie et quod non teneantur ad purgationem feu acquietantiam faciend.
" fecundum antiquas leges Galwidie Exceptis tamen et refervatis nobis et heredibus noftris qua-
" tuor Loquelis fpectantibus ad coronam noftram Et refervatis etiam nobis et heredibus noftris
" articulis tangentibus proditionem et interfectionem alienarum aliorum regnorum et profecu-
" tionibus eorundem Et licet aliquis Galwidenfis per predictam affifam fuerit convictus folvet
" nobis decem vaccas pro quolibet fupradicto fuper quo fuerit convictus et non ulterius Et fi ad
" fectam noftram vel partis fuper proditione vel interfectione alienigenarum fuerit convictus erit
" in voluntate noftra de vita et membris Et fi aliquis ferjandus vel minifter Galwidie fuper aliquo
" articulo tangente officium fuum fuerit accufatus purgabit fe per integram acquietantiam Galwidie
" debitam et confuetam Et in aliis articulis ad fectam pacis (forfan pro *partis* i. e. *at the fuit of*
" *the party*) refpondebit prout alii vicini fui facere tenentur fecundum leges Galwidie fupradictas."

(a) Thefe two words are very indiftinctly written; and the word *adjecimus*, or fome fynonymous word, is evidently
omitted after the word *adjunctionis*.

POSTSCRIPT.

" Libertas Adæ filii Adam recognita coram Camerario et Justiciario."

[Index, page 16. No. 26.]

" ROBERTUS &c. Sciatis quod per bonam et fidelem affifam coram Willielmo de Lyn-
" defay tunc Camerario noftro Scotie et Joanne filio Brouingis (vel *Broningis*) Jufticiario noftro
" ad hoc fpecialiter deputat. evidenter extitit compertum et declaratum quod Ad. filius Adam
" lator prefentium non eft homo nofter ligius feu nativus quin pro voluntate fua feipfum et liberos
" fuos et eorum bona libere valeat transferre ubicunque voluerit infra regnum noftrum prout
" melius fibi viderit expedire abfque calumnia a quocunque propter quod prefatum Adam et liberos
" fuos fupradict. viz. Bethinum Joannem Reginaldum et Duncanum liberos homines noftros fore
" declaramus ac ipfos ab omni jugo et onere fervitutis quietos reddimus per prefentes in perpetuum
" In cujus rei teftimonium &c. has literas noftras perpetuo duraturas fibi fieri fecimus patentes
" apud Abirdene decimo die Septembris anno regni noftri quarto decimo."

[As connected with the fubject of *nativi homines*, a rank in fociety unknown in Scotland for feveral centuries paft, the following curious Deed, copied from an original in the Library of the Faculty of Advocates, is here laid before the reader.]

ANNO ab incarnatione Domini m° cc° xxii° facta eft hec conventio inter dominum S. (*Simonem*) priorem Sancti Andree et conventum ejufdem loci ex parte una et Gillemor Scolgo de Tarvalont hominem eorum ligium et nativum ex altera videlicet quod idem G. (*Gillemor*) tanquam eorum nativus et ligius homo de eorum licentia erit cum Domino I. (*Jacobo*) filio bone memorie M. (*Mergundi*) quondam Comitis de Mar quamdiu ipfi Priori et Conventui placuerit ita quod idem G. et ejus liberi cum tota eorum fubftantia fine alicujus contradictione vel aliquo impedimento cum dictis priori et conventui placuerit ad ipfos tanquam nativi homines fui revertentur quibus locum congruum ad habitandum bona fide affignabunt et fi idem G. vel ejus liberi per annum vel amplius cum dicto Domino I. moram fecerint annuatim folvent idem G. vel ejus liberi in recognitionem homagii fui memoratis priori et conventui unam libram cere in affumptione beate Marie et quia idem G. figillum proprium non habuit conventionem iftam figillo dicti Domini I. filii M. Comitis de Mar fecit fignari ad majorem etiam fecuritatem prefatus G. tactis facrofanctis juravit fe conventionem iftam bona fide et fine contradictione aliqua fideliter fervaturum hiis teftibus Domino D. (*Duncano*) filio M. (*Mergundi*) quondam Comitis de Mar Domino I. fratre ejus Domino P. de Malleuill vicecomite Abirdonenfi Domino R. de Stradhehin Beldin judice de Ferne Willielmo capellano de Tarvalont Adam de Cuffenin Maldouenin Mackilledored Killeferf de Rothenen.

END *of the* POSTSCRIPT.

ANE TABLE *of the* INFEFTMENTS *and* CHARTOURS *in the Rollis of* ROBERT THE FIRST, *called* KING ROBERT THE BRUCE, *King of Scottis, beginnand at the Roll marked with the letter* A, *and haveing wreatin on the back,* Rob. I. A.

1309.

In the beginning of this roll there ar thrie chartours cannot be read, bot the fourt infeftment is

In vicecom.

4 Carta Roberti Barbour, of the lands of Craigie, within the fhirefdom of Forfar, quhilk fumtym wer Joannis de Baliolo, (*a*) vic. Forfar.
5 —— Patricii de Ogiluie, de barronie de Kettenes.
6 —— Joannis Traquair, de terris de Edirdye et Henderftoun, be refignatioun of Mowbray.
7 —— Alex^{ri} Frafer, of the lands of Panbryde.
8 —— Alex^{ri} Sennifcall, of the lands and barony of Archibetoun, Forfar, de foirfaltrie of David Betoun, vic. Forfar.
9 —— to the Monks of Newbottil, of the advocatioun and donatioun of the kirk of Effye in Angus, Forfar.
10 —— Alex^{ri} Sennifcall, of the lands of Achykilbichan and Scottifbiryn.
11 —— Hugonis de Ros and his fpous, of an 18 merkis furth of the barrony of Inuerlunan, Forfar.
12 —— Willielmi Ramfay de Vchterhous, of ane dauiache of land of Ingliftoun, als meikill of Caftletown, als meikle of Walteris, blench 6s. 8d.
13 —— Valentino de Thorntoun, de terris de Thorntoun, in lie Kincardin Mernes.
14 —— Alex^{ri} Frafer, of the lands of Garuocis.
15 —— Alex^{ri} Frafer, of the lands of Strathean, de Effuly, Ballebrochy, and Auchincrofs.
16 —— Simonis Frafer, of the lands of Brortown (*b*), and ye lands in Inuerbervie, quhilks perteinit to Edmond Haftings, Kincardin.
17 —— Gilberti Johneftoune, of the lands of Hevirterrigis and Redmyre, Lanerk.
18 —— Alex^{ri} Frafer, of the lands of Culpreffache, Kincardin.
19 —— Joannis Sennifcall, of the lands of Frendraucht, Bamf.
20 —— Joannis Paige, of the ane dauoche of land in Straithbogie, called Edindovat, Aberdeen.
21 —— Willielmi de Straithbocis, of the lands of Fouern and Ardache, &c. and thrie pairts of Auchnacuy.
22 —— of the Abbacie of Der, Aberdeen.
23 —— given to the Abbacie of Der, of the advocatioun and donatioun of the kirk of Fouerne, Aberdeen.
24 —— given to the Abbacie of Der, of the kirk of Kinerward grantit be John Cumyng Earle of Buchane, Aberdeen.
25 —— given to Criftian Bruce, fifter to the King, of the land of Garviache, Aberdeen.
26 —— Gilbert de Haya de Locherward, of the lands of Auchinfichlach, &c. quhilks perteinit to Duncane Frendraucht, Knight.

A

(*a*) *viz.* contracted for vicecomitatu. (*b*) Probably contracted for Brothertown.

INDEX OF CHARTERS, &c. BY KING ROBERT I.

		In vicecom.
27	Carta grantit to the Abbot of Kinlofs, the advocatioun and donatioun of Elon,	Kinlofs.
28	—— Willielmi Lindefay, Chamberlan of Scotland, of the barrony of Sindegaitts,	Sindegaitts.
29	—— Thome Brifbane, of the lands of Little Rothy, vic. Aberdeen.	Aberdeen.
30	—— Alex^{ri} Mowbray, of the dauiache of land of Inuercabock and Lykeuyne in Strathawn.	
31	—— Patricii de Montealto, of the lands of Lofcragy and Culpedauchis.	
32	—— Roberti de Keith, Marfhell of Scotland, of the lands of Alneden and Auchidouenald (*a*), &c.	Aberdeen.
33	—— Roberti Keith Marfchell, his licence to by (*b*) fra ye Shireffcourt,	Erle Marfhell.
34	—— Willielmi de Strabrock, of the lands of Pittenweem and Drumbordathe.	
35	—— Gilberti de Haya, of the lands of Slanes,	Aberdeen.
36	—— Walteri Biffet, of the lands of Oboyn in Aberdeen,	Aberdeen.
37	—— Walteri Barclay de Thenagio de Ballhelvie,	Aberdeen.
38	—— the King's band of xx. merkis, to Joanni filio Drimyngis, furth of Lathirdaill.	
39	—— Malcolme Marifcallo, of Meikle Arveninche.	
40	—— Adame Gordoun, of the barrony of Strabogie,	Aberdeen.
41	—— Roberti Keith, of the Forreft of Kintor, except the park,	Aberdeen.
42	—— of the Burgh of Aberdein, of the Forreft of Stocket,	Aberdeen.
43	—— Thomi Gardropa, of the lands of Kincardany, Ardwell, &c. vic. Bamfe,	Bamf.
44	—— Joannis Ros, fone to the Earle of Ros, in togher with Margaret Cumyng, doghter to the Earle of Buchan, the half of the Earle of Buchan's haill lands within Scotland.	
45	—— Hugonis de Rofs, of the Thanage of Glendouachy in Bamfe,	Bamf.
46	—— Marie Cuming, fpous to Edmond Cuming, of Gillettnachis and Sauchope, with the mylne, &c. in Thanagio de Fromartin.	
47	—— Hugonis Barclay, of Fintriegafk and Balmaly in Buchaneward,	Bamf.
48	—— Hugonis Barclay, of the Thaniage of Balhelvie.	
49	—— Hugonis de Rofs and Mauld, fifter to the King, ye lands of Narne, cum burgo,	Narne,
50	—— Hugonis de Rofs and Mauld, fifter to the King, the toune of Crumbachie, with an anwell,	Crumbachie.
51	—— Angufie de Lyle, the lands of Kinbaldein and Ardnamurchin,	Inuernes.
52	—— Angufii de Lyle, of the lands of Lochabre.	
53	—— Roderici filii Alani, of Modworthe and Knodworthe, &c. cum advocatione ecclefie, &c.	Inuernes.
54	—— Angufii de Lyle, of Vnrowris and Glenogweris.	
55	—— Roberti de Monro, of Counetis in Strathfpeya, the lands of Cupermakcultis.	
56	—— Hugonis de Rofs, of the lands of Sky,	Inuernes.
57	—— Gilberti Wyfman, of the lands of Rothayis, Auchinbothe, Molben, Cardeny, &c.	
58	—— Hugonis Rofs, of Trouternes, in Sky,	Inuernes.
59	—— Hugonis Rofs, of Tarnedelle and Inuerafren.	
60	—— Hugonis de Rofs, of Straglas, Strathconan.	

(*a*) There are lands called *Auchnedan* and *Auchtidonald* in the diftrict of Buchan in Aberdeenfhire.
(*b*) Probably for *byde* : The Mufeum copy has *le*.

INDEX OF CHARTERS, &c. BY KING ROBERT I. 3

On the back of the said Roll, thir Infeftments following ar writen:

Carta. In vicecom.
1 Carta Gullielmi Irwing his infeftment of x. pund Sterling money furth of the cuftomes of
 Dundie, Forfar.
2 ——— of the Bifhop of Orkney, of thrie chalder victuall, Orkney.
3 ——— Joanni filio Brinyng, of Haltoun, Ardache, Litle and Meikle Glengleiche.
4 ——— Joannis de Rofs, ane refignatioune of his haill lands, for new infeftment.

Ane other Roll of Robert the Firft, markit on the back with this mark, Rob. I. B.

1 The firft infeftment is revin and deftroyit.
2 Carta to the Abbacie of Melros, of wards, releaves, and efcheats within Roxburgh, Melros.
3 ——— to the Abbacie of Kelkow, of the patronage of the (a) of Eglifchmalefoks in Walle
 de Cluyde, Kelcow.
4 ——— to the Abbacie of Melros, the patronage ecclefie de Wefter Ker, in Walle de Efkis, Melros.
5 ——— to the Abbacie of Melros, of that pairt of the barrony of Wefter Ker quhilk pertenit
 to L. Soullis, Melros.
6 ——— to the Abbacie of Melros, of ane 100 lib. furth of the cuftomes of Berwick, Edin-
 burᵗ, or Haddingtoune, Melros.
7 ——— to the Abbacie of Melros, of certan fifhings and tenements within Berwick, Melros.
8 ——— to the Abbacie of Melros, licence to them to byd at home the tym of the repairing
 of the walls, Melros.
9 ——— to the Abbacie of Melros, of certane lands in Kinros, Melros,
10 ——— to the Abbacie of Crofragmer (b) furth of the earledom of Carrick, be Robert his
 father and Maruce (c) his mother, or be Neill or Edward fometym Earles, Crofraguel.
11 ——— to the Abbacie of Crofragmer, of certain lands within the earldom of Carrick, Crofraguel.
12 ——— to the Abbacie of Glenlus (d), to be halden in ane frie barrony, cum furca fofsa, Glenlus.
13 ——— to the Abbacy of Glenlus, confirmatioun of yʳ liberties, Glenlus.
14 ——— to the Abbacie of Tungland, the kirk of Michis (e), within the town of Balncrofe, Tungland.
15 ——— to the Abbacie of Dundrenan, fuper terra del Polles & anni redditu qui folvere fo-
 lebant Deruorgille filio quondam Allani Domini Galliudia, Militis (f), Dundrenan.
16 ——— to the Abbacie of Newbottle, of the tua-pairt landis of Maftertoun, Newbottle.
17 ——— to the Abbacie of Newbottle, de decem mercatas argenti annuatim de pifcaria de
 Edirinche, fuper Tuedam, Newbottle.
18 ——— ane other, of Ten merkis, furth of the faid fifhing.
19 ——— to the Abbacie of Kilwinning, of a fifhing in Levin and Clyd,
20 ——— to the Abbacie of Coldinghame, of certan infeftments given by Edzear and David,
 of Lumfden, Prendergaift, &c. Coldinghame.
21 ——— Candide cafe, of Craigiltoun, quhilks perteinit to L. Soullis, Candida cafa.

(*a*) The word *Kirk* probably omitted.   (*b*) Should be *Croffraguel*.   (*c*) In the Mufeum copy it is *Margaret*.
(*d*) Something is omitted here.   (*e*) The word Michis is, in the Index, marked as contracted. Perhaps it ftands for *Michaelis*, i. e. fome kirk dedicated to St Michael; fuch as Kirkmichael or Croffmichael.   (*f*) The blunders here, as well as in
many other entries in this Index, are fo grofsly ungrammatical, that it is likely the original compiler of the Index did not under-
ftand Latin. Similar blunders are fo frequent and fo glaring, as neither to admit nor to require to be particularly pointed out.

INDEX OF CHARTERS, &c. BY KING ROBERT I.

22	Carta Prioris & Conventus Candide cafe de Malmane, que fuit quondam Deruorgille de Balliolo, et totam terram de Glenfumtault,	In vicecom. Candida cafa.
23	—— to Candide Cafe, of Wards, Relieves, and Marriadges in lie Rins & Fernis.	
24	—— Candide Cafe, of the archdeanry and kirk of Kellis, and patronage thereof,	Candida cafa.
25	—— Fratribus predicatoribus de Ed', of 5 l. Sterling furth of the miln of Libbertoun.	
26	—— to the Abbacy of Dumfermling, of ane pafturage in the muire of Erbentoly & Mukertfy,	Dumfermling.
27	—— to the Abbacy of Dumfermling, of the half of the Queensferry, fometime Mowbraye's,	Dumfermling.
28	—— to the Abbacy of Dumfermling, of ane tenement in Berwick.	
29	—— to the faid Abbacy, of the patronage of the kirk of Innerkeithing, quilk was Mowbraye's.	
30	—— to ditto, of the lands of Ferrefeild, neir Innerkeithing.	
31	—— to ditto, of certain lands within Berwick, by forfalture of ane Orfuird,	Berwick.
32	—— to ditto, of Ferryfield, neir Innerkeithing, with Regality.	
33	—— to ditto, of the lands of Kulzelauche, in barrony de Aberdour, with 40 s. furth of Mountflory, in fhira de Scoone, by Thomas Earl Murray.	
34	—— to the Abbacy of Cambufkenneth, of the patronage of the kirk of Kilmaronock.	
35	—— to the Priory of St Andrews, of the advocation of the kirk of Fordoune, in the Mearns.	
36	—— to the Abbacie of Culros, of the barony of Philpftoun, in the fheriffdome of Linlithgow,	Linlithgow.
37	—— to the Abbacy of Lindoris, with licence of peats in the muire of Kinloche and Monegoe.	
38	—— to the Abbacie of Coupar, of the lands of Aythnakethill, &c. within the Thandome of Alith,	Alith.
39	—— to the Abbacy of Coupar, the lands of Aughinlefkis.	
40	—— to the Abbacie of Scoon, an ample infeftment of many lands and liberties.	
41	—— to the Abbacy of Scoon, a ratification of their liberties.	
42	—— to the Abbey of Reftennet, ane inqueift or tryall anent their haill lands, by fundry honeft men in the country.	
43	—— to the Abbacy of Reftennet, to cut wood in the foreft of Platter.	

Ane other Roll of Robert the Firft, marked on the back with this mark, Rob. I. B. reign 16.(*a*)

This Roll has only *two charters with the dates expreffed*, viz. N° 11, dated in the 16th year of the King's reign, *and* N° 84. dated 10th July 1321. Berwick.

Memorandum. In this Roll are fix charters, whilke cannot be read, except the titles to whom they are difpened : The 2d is to James Lord of Douglas, and ficklike the 3d ; the fourth to Ade More ; the fifth to Alexander Stewart.
6 Carta to Laurence Abernethy, of the lands of Lambertoun, whilks was Ingram de Gynes, Berwick.

(*a*) This is the firft roll now remaining in the General Regifter-houfe.

INDEX OF CHARTERS, &c. BY KING ROBERT I. 5

7	Carta to Rodger Pringle, of the half lands of Quhitſum, extending to *centum ſolidat terre, que fuit Johannis de Yle (a),*	In vicecom. Berwick.
8	—— to Nicoll Fouller, of the other half of the ſaid lands, in the ſame terms,	Ibid.
9	—— to Henry Coſour, *terre in villa et territorio de Bondyngtoun, juxta Berwicum, ſuper Twed, que fuit Nicholai dicti Moyſes,*	Ibid.
10	—— to Henry Coſour, of the lands *in tenemento de Lambertoun ſuperiori, quam Williclmus de Lambertoun vendidit Rogero de Gorwyc,*	Berwick.
11	—— to Edmond Marſhall, totam terram dominicam de Ceſſeworth, whilk was Roger Mowbraye's. *Dat apud Berwicum ſuper Twed, penultimo die Martii, anno, &c. ſexto decimo,*	Roxburgh.
12	—— Jacobi Douglas, of the lands of Bethocrule, quilk was John Cuming's, *in valle de Tcuiot.*	
13	—— Jacobi Cuningham, of the lands of Haſſingdon, for ij lib. Sterling, infra vicec. de	Roxburgh.
14	—— Hugonis de le Vikers, of certain lands, burghs, and villages, of Roxburgh, Bertoun, and Maxwell, whilk was Adæ Mindrome's and Wm Daltoun,	Roxburgh.
15	—— Willielmi Maceoun, de decem libratas terræ de Mertoun, que fuerunt Ingerami Cnonut et Joannis de Weſtoun.	
16	—— Johannis de Lindſay, of the lands of Rutherford and Maxtoun, *que fuerunt Johannis de Weſtoun et Ede Gurlay,*	Roxburgh.
17	—— Henrici de Wardlaw, medietatem baroniæ de Wiltoun, whilk was Wm de Charteris *et Walteri de Pertchay.*	
18	—— Johannis *filii quond. Johannis filii* Nigelli, of lands in Mertoun, quilks were Allan le Suche, with many other lands, &c. *que fuerunt Johannis de Balliolo.*	
19	—— Abbatis et conventus de Melros, of the lands of Leſſedewyn,	Melros.
20	—— Willielmi *Barbitonſoris,* of the lands of Kirkborthewyc, with others diverſe, *que fuerunt Ade de Hodholme.*	
21	—— Willielmi Barbitonſoris duas partes terræ de Kirkborthewick, 3 partes molendini ejuſdem infra baroniam de Minthow,	Roxburgh.
22	—— Willielmi Turnebull, of that piece land by-weſt Philliphaugh,	Selkirk.
23	—— Willielmi Barbitonſoris, orientem partem de Philliphaugh Schilgreine, infra vic. de	Selkirk.
24	—— Henrici de Baliolo, militis, de terris de Branxholme, quæ fuit Ricardi Lovell, militis, in baronia de Hawick, *exceptis terris que per nos Waltero Comyn ſunt conceſſe,*	Roxburgh.
25	—— to the Abbacy of Newbottle, of ten merks ſilver furth of Berwick,	Berwick.
26	—— Johannis de Carrikis, *filii Williclmi dicti Ruſſell,* totam terram de Dorſquen, infra vicecom. de	Dumfreis.
27	—— to Richard Edgear, the place and half lands of Seneſchar, *ſicut dicta baronia inter Willielmum de Crechtoun et Iſabellam ſponſam ſuam, et ipſum Ricardum, nuper fuerat diuiſa.*	
28	—— to John Soulles, Knight, of the lands of Kirkanders and Brettalach,	Dumfreis.
29	—— to John Soulles, Knight, the barronie of Torthorald,	Dumfreis.

B

(a) The words printed in Italics in this and the ſubſequent entries of this Roll are added from the original Roll by the Editor.

INDEX OF CHARTERS, &c. BY KING ROBERT I.

                                       In vicecom.

30 Carta Willielmi de Faufyde, of the lands of Brenglefe, whilk was James Torthorald, Knight, before his forfaulture.

31 —— Johannis fil Lochlani, ane bounding infeftment of the lands of Snath, and lands of Belliferne.

32 —— Alexandri de Meyners et Egidie Sen. fponfe fue, of the barony of Dorifdeir.

33 —— to John Soullis, of the lands of Kirkandris.
   N. B. This charter is marked in the roll as delete.

34 —— to David Lindfay, of the lands of Revwans, Mefhope, Middillkauill, Blacklaw, Greenhill, *Cetis*, Ayrickftane, and Meikle Holmefyde,   Annand.

35 —— to David Lindfay, of the lands of Hawkfhaws.   Annand.

36 —— to Adæ Barbitonfori, of the lands of Brakanwra, &c. 28. (*a*), *que fuit Petri de Grame.*

37 —— to Adæ Barbitonfori, of the toft in Moffatt, *cum duabus bouatis terre adjacentibus que quondam Willielmus dictus Ingles, ad firmam tenuit de Domino vallis Annandie, avo noftro.*

38 —— to Duncan Cambell and Sufanna, fponfe fue, of the lands of Loudoun and Steuinftoun, *predictos Duncanum et Sufannam, fponfam fuam, hereditarie contingentes ratione dicte fponfe*,   Aire.

39 —— to James Stewart, *filio quondam Johannis Sen.* of the lands of *Periftoun* and Warwickhill.

40 —— to the Abbacie of Kilwinning, the lands called Le Halland, near Irwine, Aire.

41 —— to Allan Stuart, the lands of Dregerum, *que fuerunt Johannis de Balliolo, Willielmi de Ferrariis, et Allani la Suce.*

42 —— to Reginald Crawfurd, of ane annuall out of Ormifshuc, in Cunningham. Aire.

43 —— to Walter Abredalgie, of fome lands in the town of Aire, *que fuerunt Hugonis dicti Ilaiy*,   Aire.

44 —— to Adæ Hokenay, of fome tenements in Aire, *que fuerunt Henrici dicti Cyfer*, Aire.

45 —— to Edward Bruce, his brother, of the earldom of Carrick,   Aire.

46 —— to Robert Boyd, of the lands of Kilmarnock, Bondingtoun, Hertfchaw, &c. *que fuerunt Johannis de Balliolo, Godfridi de Ros, filii quondam Reginaldi de Ros, Willielmi de Mora, et Roberti de Ros*,   Renfrew.

47 —— to Robert Boyd, of Nodellefdale.

48 —— to Robert Boyd, of the lands of Hertfachw, in liberam foreftam,   Aire.

49 —— to Albino of Are, of Curenokenculrach and Autitigill,   Aire.

50 —— to Rodger Blair, of three chalders meal, *que Alanus le Suche et Willielmus de Ferrariis, milites, recipere confueverunt*, furth of the lands of Burtries, in the barony of Cuningham, *que nunc eft Jacobi Fraunces*,   Aire.

51 —— to Fergus Ardroffane, of his lands of Ardroffane, *cum tenandriis terrarum Willielmi de Porteconill, Ricardi de Boduill, Laurentii de Mora, Gilberti de Cunyngburgh, Willielmi Ker, et Ricardi de Kelcou*,   Aire.

(*a*) This No. 28. is not in the Record.

INDEX OF CHARTERS, &c. BY KING ROBERT I. 7

In vicecom.

52 Carta to Robert Sympil, of the lands of Largs, fometime John Balliol's, before his fore-
faulture, Aire.
53 —— to Robert Cuninghame, of the lands of Lambrachtoun and Grugere, in Cunninghame, *tenend. ficut Alanus la Suche et Willichnus de Fererci tenuerunt,* Aire.
54 —— to Robert Stewart, *filio et heredi Walteri Senefcalli Scotie terrarum de Cunnyngham,* Aire.
55 —— to Robert Lauder, of the lands of *Pentkatcland et de Nifbyt, que fuerunt Thome de*
Penkatcland, Edinburgh.
56 —— to Alex^r Seton, of the lands of Tranent, quilks were Allan la Suche, *una cum*
terris hufbandiis que fuerunt dicti quondam Alani in villa de Nodref, Hadington.
57 —— to William Oliphant, of the lands of Muirhoufe, *in efcambium pro quadam petia ter-*
re quam Johannes de Balliolo cepit infra claufuram parci de Kyncardin in le Merenis, Edinburgh.
58 —— to John Montfod, of that part of Trauernent quilks was William Ferrers, Knight,
et cum tenandria totius terre de Faufyde, et annuo redditu inde debito quond. Alano
la Suche, Edinburgh.
59 —— to James Douglas of Laudone, of the lands of Kincavill and Caldercleir, Edinburgh.
60 —— to John Marifcall, *filii quond. Rolandi Marifcall,* of ane anwel of x. lib. furth of
Eaft Fentoun, in Laudounia, *quem Ingeramus de Gynes, Miles, percipere confuevit,* Edinburgh.
61 —— to William Fairley, of the lands of Inuerleith, Edinburgh.
62 —— to Robert Lauder, of the lands of Colden, within the barony of Dalkeith, *que fuit*
Petri Luband, Militis, nuper de proditione erga Regem et regnum conuicti, Edinburgh
63 —— to Alexander Stuart, of the lands of Garmiltoun Dunnyng, *que fuerunt quon-*
dam Petri Luband, Militis, Edinburgh.
64 —— to Alexander Stewart, of Elvingftoun, by forfaulture of Peter Luband, Knight, Edinburgh.
65 —— to Thomas Citharift, of the forfalture of Gilloc de Camera, viz. *omnium terra-*
rum dicti Gilloc, tam infra burgum de Hadingtoun quam extra, Edinburgh.
66 —— to Alexander Senefcall, of the lands of Fifcherflatis, quilks were Peter Luband's.
67 —— to Henry de Sancto Claro, of the muire of Pentland, in liberam warennam, Edinburgh.
68 —— to Robert Lauder, of Pentketland and Nifbet, quilks were Thomas Penketland,
et quas idem Thomas forisfecit, Edinburgh.
69 —— to Thomas Sympill, of the half *of all the land which* Nicholas de Difpenfa had in
Langnidrie, *et quas dictus Nicholaus forisfecit,* Edinburgh.
70 —— to the Abbacy of Newbottle, of two parts of Maftertoun, near Neubotill, on the
refignation of Nigelli *de Carick et Mariote fponfe fue, Gilberti de Aytoun et Ade*
de Roffine fponfe fue, Edinburgh.
71 —— to Henry Cifiure, of Kilbabertone, *infra baroniam de Langbirdemannifteun et illud*
carbonarium, infra baroniam de Travernent, quod vocatur Gawaynefpot, Edinburgh.

L A N E R K.

72 Carta Walteri, filii Gilberti, the lands of Machan, in valle de Clude, *whilk belong'd to*
John Comyn, Knight.
73 —— Patricii de Moravia, of the lands of Edrftoun, in valle de Clude, *que fuit quondam*
Walteri filii Rogeri.

8   INDEX OF CHARTERS, &c. BY KING ROBERT I.

In vicecom.
74 Carta Andreæ de Dowglas, of the lands of Crefwell, *que fuit quondam Henrici de Wintoun, infra baroniam de Carnewath.*
75 —— to the Abbey of Lefmahago, of *an annual rent of Ten marks Sterling furth of the King's milns of Carnclukis.*
76 —— to Helen Quarentlay, of the lands of *Bellitftan* and *Gemilcy, in the forest of Mauldefley, in efcambium mancrii et pomerii que fuerunt dicte Elene infra burgum de Lanark.*
77 —— to James Douglas, fon to William Douglas, ane bounding infeftment of the valley of Douglas, and of Kirkmychell.
78 —— to Thomas Richartfon, of the barony of Symundftoun, in vic. de Lanerk.
79 —— to Robert Barde, of the barony of Cambufnethen, *reddendo decem celdras frumenti, et decem celdras ordei, fingulis annis, apud Rotherglen.*

DUNBRETANE.

80 Carta to Malcolme Fleming, of the land of Kirkintolach, que fuerunt quondam Johannis Comyn, Militis.
81 —— to Malcolme Fleming, of the land of Auchindonan, in the Lennox, quam Malcomus de Drumond refignavit *coram magnatibus noftris,*   Lennox.
82 —— to William Fleming of Dumbarton, of ane annual of ten merks furth of Kirkmichael, whilk is within the liberty of Dumbarton.
83 —— to Duncan, filio Morath, the feven-merk land of Racheon and Acreumonyth, in the Lennox, *and the office of ferjeandy within the fhire of Dumbretan.*
84 —— to Adæ Brunnings, of the lands of Gillanderftoun, in le Garviach, dated at a parliament holden at Perth, 10th of July 1321.

STRIUELING.

85 Carta to Henry Annand, of the lands of Salachothe and Balecharun, within the lands of Meftry.
86 —— to Alexander Frazer, of the lands of Tulchfrazer.
87 —— to William Biffet, of the lands Fuleth, Hwytemyr, Suthfield, Welcroft, Gofcroft, and Torbrokis, *and all the burgage tenements which belong'd to Henry de Malcuile within the burgh of Striuillyn.*
88 —— to William Lindfay, *omnem ftatum dominii quem Robertus de Umfrauille, miles, dudum, Comes de Anegus, habuit in baronia de Dunypas.*
89 —— to Robert Lauder, of the miln of Lethberd, *quod fuit quondam Philippi de Lyndefay, et quod Simon de Lyndefay, miles, frater ejufdem Philippi, forisfecit.*
90 —— to Malcolme Earl of Lennox, of the half of the lands of Lekkie *neareft Buchaum, in recompenfatione dominii carucate terre de Cardrofs.*

INDEX OF CHARTERS, &c. BY KING ROBERT I.

On the back of this Roll are four Charters, to wit,

In vicecom.

91 Carta to John Sulis, of the barony of Kirkanders, *que fuit quondam Johannis de Wak, militis,*   Dumfries.

92 —— *Thome Clerico, filio Johannis de Carutheris, terrarum de Muifald et de Appiltrethwaytis.*

93 —— *Thome Clerico, filio Johannis de Carutheris, medietatem totius terre que fuit Roberti de Applynden, in valle Annandie, ratione Johanne sponse sue.*

94 —— to Richard, the son of Richard, called Edgar, of the lands of Kirkpatrick.

Ane other Roll of King Robert the First, marked on the back with this mark, Ro. I. D.

1 This Roll begins with ane bounding infeftment of Thomas Earl of Murray, Lord of Annandale and Man, called Nepos Regis Roberti, of the Earldom of Murray, 19.
2 Carta to Thomas Ranulph, of the Isle of Man, and the Isle called the Calfs, 19.
3 —— to Thomas Ranulph, Earl of Murray, &c. of the half of the barony of Urre, in vicecomitatu de Dumfreis, qhilke Henry Percie forisfecit, 19.
4 —— to Thomas Ranulph, of the barony of Aberdour in Fyfe, by reason of forfaltrie, 19.
5 —— to Thomas Earl of Murray, of the new custome and coquet of Invernes, 19.
6 —— to Thomas Ranulph, &c. the barony of Morthingtoun and Langfarmacus, 19. whilk pertained to Agnes Morthingtoun, and Henry Haliburton her spouse, whilk they resigned.
7 —— to Thomas Ranulph, of the lands of Vallis Annandie, 22.
8 —— to Thomas Ranulph, &c. the gift of the forfaultry of all his vassals.
9 —— to Thomas Ranulph, of the haill lands of Vallis Annandie.
10 —— Roberti senioris filii et heredis Walteri Senescalli Scotie, of the lands of Cuninghame, tam infra burgum quam extra.
11 —— to Walter Steward, in marriage with Marjory the King's daughter, of the barony of Bathkat, the lands of Ricardtoun, the barony of Rathew, the lands of Bernys, beside Linlithgow; the land called the Brome, near the Loch of Lithgow; the lands of Bondingtoun, with the lands of Eryngaith, near Lithgow; the lands of Gallowhille, near Lithgow; ane annuall furth of the Kers of Striveling; ane annualrent of 100 shillings out of the lands of Kinpunt; and the lands of Edinhame, in vicecom. de Roxburgh (*a*).
12 —— to Walter Stewart, the barony of Kilbryde, in vicecomitatu de Lanerk, the ferme near Ruglen.

C

(*a*) In this entry as set down in the Index there are several inaccuracies: these have been, by the Editor, corrected from the original charter still remaining in the General Register House.

INDEX OF CHARTERS, &c. BY KING ROBERT I.

In vicecom.

13 Carta to Robert Stewart, fon and heir to Walter Stewart, the lands of Cefsford, in vicecom. de Roxburgh, whilk Rodger Mowbray forisfecit; the barony of Nifbitt, the barony of Langnewton and Maxtoun, the barony of Cavirtoun, in vicecom. de Roxburgh, whilk William Soullis forisfecit.

14 ——— to Robert Stewart, of the barony of Methuen, in vicecom. de Perth, the barony of Kellie, in vic. de Forfar, whilks Rodger Moubray forisfecit.

Carta Jacobi Domini de Douglas.

15 Carta to James Lord of Douglas, of the lands et tenementum de Douglas et Kirkmichaell, ane bounding infeftment thereof.

16 ——— to James Lord Douglas, of the baronie of Stabilgortoun, in Valle de Efk, John Lindfay, fon to Philip Lindfay, refigned the fame, 14.

17 ——— to James Lord of Douglas, of the mercat-town of Jedwart, the caftle thereof, Bonjedworth, and the foreft of Jedworth, with the Mains of Jedworth, 14.

18 ——— to James Lord of Douglas, of the lands of Polbuthy, in valle de Annan.

19 ——— to James Lord of Douglas, the half lands of the barony of Wefterker, in valle de Efk, whilk William Soullis forisfecit, 16.

20 ——— Jacobi Dñi de Douglas, of the lands of Botill in Galloway.

21 ——— to James Lord Douglas, of villam et tenementum de Lauder, 19.

22 ——— to James Lord Douglas, of the lands of Cockburn, whilk Patrick Luband forisfecit.

23 ——— to James Lord Douglas, of the lands of Bethocrulle, in valle de Teviot, Johannes Cuming forisfecit.

24 ——— to James Lord Douglas, the forefts of Selkirk, Ettrick, and Traquair, in ane free barony, 20.

25 ——— to James Lord Douglas, of certain lands in Berwick, lyand in the Hidgait, 20.

26 ——— to James Lord Douglas, of all his lands in ane free regalitie, and be putting on ane ring and ane emrod on the Earle and his fuccefsors fingers the day he fhould take fafine, by the King.

Ane Roll of Robert the Firft, marked on the back with this mark, E, wherein eighteen Infeftments are illegible.

19 Carta to Alexander Seton, of the lands of Seytoun, in vice. de Edinburgh, in liberum burgum,   Edinburgh.

20 ——— to Alexander Seton, of the lands of Bernes, juxta Hadingtoun, in vic. de Edinburgh,   Edinburgh.

21 ——— to Alexander Seton, of the lands of Gogar, in vic. de Edinburgh.

22 ——— to Alexander Seton, of the barony of Trauarnent, in conftabulario de Hadingtoun, et vic. de Edinburgh, whilks Wm Ferraris forisfecit, the lands of Faufyde, whilk Allan Suche forisfecit, &c.

23 ——— to Alexander Seton, of the lands of Dundas, et carucatæ terræ in Quenesferric, &c.

24 ——— to the town of Hadingtoun, of their liberties.

INDEX OF CHARTERS, &c. BY KING ROBERT I.   11

In vicecom.

25 Carta to Alexander Seton, of the lands of Elphingftoun, in vic. de Edinburgh.
26 —— to Robert Keith, of the lands of Keith Merfchell, and the office of Merfchellfchip, Keith, Symone, Colbanftoun, Alneden, in Buchan, with the new foreſt of Innerpeffer, four davache of land of Strathbogie, the foreſt of Kintoir, conteinand ane taillie.
27 —— to Walter, fon to Gilbert, of the baronie of Keneill, in vic. de Edinburgh, with the lands of Lethberd and Alcathie.
28 —— to Rannald Chene, of the land of Strathbroce.
29 —— to Murdoch Menteith, of the baronie of Dummanyn, whilk was Roger Moubray, the lands of Gilmertoun, whilk was William Soulis, in vic. de Edinburgh.
30 —— to William Murray, of the forfaultire of Hobkim de Wallinford.
31 —— to John Graham, of Duncarum, in baronia de Abercorn.
32 —— to Roger Faufyde, of ane annual of 10 l. furth of Letham, in vic. de Edinburgh.
33 —— to the faid Roger, upon the fame annual.
34 —— to Richard Hereis, of the lands of Elſtanefurd, in vic. de Edinburgh.
35 —— to William Douglas of Blacknefs, the lands of Nodringtoun.
36 —— to Reginald More, of the lands of Templeſtoun and Scheills, given to him by Rodulphus Lindſay, dudum magiſter hofpitalis S. Joh. Jerofolomitani.

BERWICK.   Berwick.

37 Carta to Adam Paxtoun, of the miln of Edringtoun.
38 —— to Alexander Seton, tenementum de Halfyngtoun, in vic. de Berwick, by Patrick Earl of March, whilks lands Maria, fponſa quondam Nicholai de Grahame, militis, et una heredum quondam Marjoriæ de Mufco Campo, comitiſſæ de Stratherne, prefato Patricio, per fuſtum et baculum furfum reddidit.
39 —— to Walter Morthingtoun, the baronie of Croſſebie, in vic. de Berwick.
40 —— to John Horneden, of the lands of Lifclefe, in vic. de Berwick.
41 —— to Henry Battall, of certain lands in the town of Berwick.
42 —— to the Earl of Murray, of Morthingtoun and Langfarmacus.
43 —— to John de Montfode, quod quondam fuit Willielmi de Orford, burgen. Berwici.

Vicecomitatus de ROXBURGH.

This roll has ane blank betwixt the 43d charter and the 49th Charter.

49 Carta to Euſtacius Maxwell, of the lands of Wefterraw, Pedynan, the lands of Park, whilk Johannes, filius Valdeui, forisfecit, et obiit contra fidem noſtram.
50 —— to Archibald Douglas, of the lands of Marbottill, whilks wer Rodger Corbet's.
51 —— to Nicoll Fouller, of the yeard of the caſtle of Roxburgh, in vic. Roxburgh.
52 —— to Roger Finlay, the lands of Cliftoune, whilks ane Rutherfurd forisfecit.
53 —— to William Maxwell and his fpoufe, of the half of the lands of Apiltrie, whilk Thomas Carnoco refigned.

12   INDEX OF CHARTERS, &c. BY KING ROBERT I.

In vicecom.

54 Carta to Robert Bruce, of the lands of Liddifdaill, whilks William Soullis erga nos forisfecit.
55 —— to Andrew Gray, of the 20 merk land of Broxmouth and Milne, whilks Thomas Ranulph Earl of Murray infeodavit Alex. Frafer, Knight.
56 —— to William Franceis, of the 20 l. land of Sprouftoun, in vic. de Roxburgh, whilks were in the King's hands by forfaulture of William Rict, Henry Drawer, Thomas Alkoats, John, Thomas, and William, filii Alani Hugo Limpetlaw, &c.
57 —— to William Sancto Claro of Hirdmanftoun, of the lands of Cefleworthe, with the miln, exceptand the lands quilk Edmond Merfhell hath lately gotten.
58 —— to Aymerus de Hauden, of ane bounding infeftment of 11 hufband lands of Sprouftoun, extendand to 20 merks lands, whilk Robert Sprouftoun and fundrie others aboue writtin forisfecit.
59 —— to the town of Jedworth.
60 —— to Bernard Hauden, of ane certain duty for keeping of the caftle of Roxburgh.
61 —— to James Cunningham, of the lands of Heffenden, in vic. de Roxburgh;
62   And to Robert Bruce, fon to the King, of the barony of Sprowftoun;
63   And Thome Carnoco, third part barony of Methyuenayn.

DUMFREIS.

64 Carta to Archibald Douglas, of the barony of Kirkcandres, infra vic. de Dumfreis, whilk fometime pertained to Sir John Wake, Knight.
65 —— to William Lindfay, channoun in Glafgow, of the barony of Kirkmichael, in Walle de Neth, whilk Roger Mowbray tint be forfalture.
66 —— to Thomas Kirkpatrick, Knight, duas denariatas terræ, in Valle de Brydeburgh, infra vic. de Dumfreis.
67 —— to Stephen Kirkpatrick, Knight, of the lands of Penefax, whilk fometime was John Penefax.
68 —— to Richard Edzear, of the penny land of Bartenonade, 1 d. land of Lobri, 1 d. land of Slochan, 1 d. land of the foreft of Glenabeukan.
69 —— to Richard Edzear, of 1 d. land in Kirkpatrick.
70 —— to Richard Edzear, of the place of Sancher, and half of the barony thereof.
71 —— to Ada: Moffat, of the lands of Knotis and Crocks, infra baroniam de Wefterker, in Valle de Efke.
72 —— to Thomas Moffat, of the lands of Glencrofts, and lands of Snegill, in the barony of Wefterker, and two cottages in the Raw thereof.
73 —— to Allan Dun, of the 1 d. land in Culfchogill, whilk Alexander Balliol forisfecit.
74 —— to John Lindfay, fon to Simon Lindfay, of the lands of Wachapilldaill and Langrigis, in Annandaill, with the 8 merk land of Scracifburt, quas Simon forisfecit, and mony mae.
75 —— to Euftachius Maxwell, of an difcharge of 32 l. Sterling, addebted furth of his owin lands for demolifhing of Carlaverok.

INDEX OF CHARTERS, &c. BY KING ROBERT I. 13

In vicecom.

76 Carta to Umphra Kirkpatrick, of the lands of Torthorwald, with the hufband-land of Roucon, Gilmorduff, and the miln of Roucan, in free foreft, bounding.
77 —— to Robert Boyd, of the lands of Duncoll and Clarkflands, in Dalfwingtoun.
78 —— to Richard Culuhach, Knight, of the lands in Kelwode, in vic. Dumfreis.
79 —— to John Kummonthe, of the lands of Kirk, in vic. de Dumfreis, whilks were John Cuming Earl of Buchan.

CARTÆ *Libertatis de novo conceffæ* GALLUIDIENSIBUS.

80 Carta anent the liberties of Galloway.
81 —— to Richard Culuhach, of the lands of Drumpullen and Aughenlo, whilk is called Glencavine, few 8 Bs.
82 —— to James Stewart, brother to Walter Stewart of Scotland, the lands of Dorifdeir, in the valley of Neith, which Alexander Meinzies refigned.
83 —— to the faid James Stewart and his fpoufe, of the barony of Enache.
84 —— to William Karlo, Knight, and Margrat his fpoufe, fifter to the King, the lands of Connyantoun and Munygip, in baronia de Kirkmichel foreft.
85 —— to William Karlo, the King's fifter's fon, the lands of Culyn, and the milne, the lands of Roucan.
86 —— to Robert Boyd, fon to William Boyd, the lands of Duncoll, and the barony of Dalfwintoun and lands of Dulgarthe, in baronia de Brdburt.
87 —— to Robert Boyd, of the lands of Glenken.
88 —— to Richard Edzear, of the land in Elietis, &c. &c.
89 —— of the foundation of ane chappel near Dumfreis, and 5l. Striveling dotted thereto by the King furth of the lands of Carlaverok, where Chriftopher Seton, his good brother, was flain in his Majeftie's fervice.

DUMFREIS.

90 Carta to Ifabell Countefs of Atholl, and Alexander Bruce her fon, the lands of Culven, et tenementum de Sannaykis, whilke was John Earl of Buchan, William de Ferrars, Allan de Souche, and John Baliol in Keltoun, forfaulted.
91 —— to Alexander Bruce, fifter to the King, Carnufmoell, Ranlifchach, &c.
92 —— to William Hurchurche, of certain lands pro termino vite fue.
93 —— to William Hurchurche, of the lands of Brigend and Tofkerton.
94 —— to Walter Stewart, of the barony of Dalfwintoun, in vic. de Dumfreis.
95 —— to John Lachlanfon, of the lands of Snache and Valifernie, &c. Kirkpatrick in Bar. Glenkarn.
96 —— to Malcolme Fleming, of the lands of Poltoun, in vic. de Wigtoun.
97 Alia Fergufio de Ardroffan, de terris de Sypeland.

D

INDEX OF CHARTERS, &c. BY KING ROBERT I.

Vicecomitatus de AIR.

In vicecom..

98 Carta to Roger Blencamſhape, of ane bounding infeftment of the lands of Laglane, in vic. de Air.
99 —— to Hew Lacy, of the 1d. land of Dundrome, Blaicklache, Barngor, Kilmechannache, &c. in vic. de Air.
100 —— to Henry Annan, the lands of Aughindraine, quas Robertus Broun forisfecit.
101 —— to William Lindſay, channon of Glaſgow, the forfalture of Adie Brown, in vic. de Air.
102 —— the gift of Adam Brown to St Michael, in eccleſia parochiali de Air.
103 —— to Reginaldo Camera, the lands of Gartgarthe.
104 —— to Robert Boyd, of the 5 l. land of Trabeache, in Kyle regis.
105 —— Ricardi de Culuhach, in Carrick, in vic. de Dumfreis.
106 —— to Nicoll, ſon of John of Kirkdolian, the lands of Workachglen, in the earldom of Carrick.
107 —— to the town of Irwing.
108 —— to Nicoll Kirkdolian, of the 1d. land of Drumnozier, in Carrick.
109 —— to Patrick Murray, of the half of the lands of Stewartoun, in Cunningham.
110 —— to Ade de Are, cf 1d. land of Smyld.
111 —— to Ade de Are, the lands of Knokingulran and Hathingill.
112 —— to Dougall Knockdolian, iijd. land Awelochis, infra comitatum de Carrik.
113 —— to Donald Are, the land Smyld.
114 —— to John Carletoun, the lands of Salmakeren, the 4th part lands of Carris, the 1 d. land of Enache, the 1d. land of Treuercrageis. The words of the charter is, *Nes intellexiſſe cartam bone memorie Domini Edwardi, Dei gratia, Regis Hibernie, fratris noſtri chariſſimi, non abolitam,* &c.; and the charter itſelf ſays, *Edwardus, Dei gratia, Rex Hibernie*; whilk teſtifies Edward Bruce to have been King of Ireland.
115 —— to Allan Montgomery, of the lands of Stahare, whilk Allan his father reſigned.
116 —— to Neill M'Thorald, of Fetherneum.
117 —— to Ade Quhyt, the lands of Stayhar, in vic. de Air.
118 —— burgenſibus burgi de Air, of the lands of Auleway, Corton, and Gorlay.
119 —— to Joannes, fil Nigelli, of the 5d. land of Molenadall, in Carrik.
120 —— to Gilbert, filio Donaldi, valeto noſtro dilecto, illum annuum redditum decem mercarum, qui nobis debetur de terra de Skeldoune, quilks lands pertaines to John Crawford of Skeldoune, in baronia de Lochmertenan, in vic. de Air,   Air.

Vicecomitatus ERGADIE

121 Carta Johannis de Menteith, militis, of the lands of Glenbecriche and Auliſaye, in Kintyre.
122 —— to Duncan Campbell, of ſundry lands in Argyle.
123 —— to Dougall Campbell alſo, of ſundry lands in Argyle.
124 —— to Arthur Campbell, of the conſtabularie of Dunſtaffage.

INDEX OF CHARTERS, &c. BY KING ROBERT I.

Ane Roll of Robert the First, markit with this mark on the back, R. I. F. reign 16.

1 Carta to Umphra Kirkpatrick, of the lands of Torthorwald, &c. — In vicecom. Dumfreis.
2 —— to Robert Bruce, son to the King, the lands of Liddifdale, whilk William Soullis forisfecit erga nos, — Roxburgh.
3 —— to Robert Bruce, filio nostro dilecto, the lands of Alexander Abernethy and Margaret his daughter, and ane of his three aires, by reason of his forfaltrie.
4 —— burgi de Peebles, super libertatem nundinarum, — Peebles.
5 —— to Andrew Gray, of the 20 merk land of Broxmouthe, given to him by Thomas Randulph Earl of Murray, — Edinburgh.
6 —— to Malisius Menteith, of the davache land of Ballygillachy, in vic. de — Forfar.
7 —— to John Lindsay, son to Simon Lindsay, Knight, of the lands of Wachopilldaill, the lands of Langriggs, quas idem Simon erga nos forisfecit.
8 —— to Alexander Seton, Knight, the lands of Elphingstoun, and the commonty of Trauernent, whilk was the Earl of Buchan's, in vic. de Edinburgh, — Edinburgh.
9 —— of reduction of ane decreit of Meadowflat, in baronie of Cowanstoun, — Lanerk.
10 —— to Dougall Campbell, of the Isle of Torsa, with many other lands in vic. de — Argyle.
11 —— to Dougall Campbell, of the lands of Menstrie, in vicecomit. de — Clackmanan.
12 —— to John le Weir, of ane annual in Ab^d, 16. — Aberdeen.
13 —— to Eustace Maxwell, of ane annuall, for demolishing the castle of Carlaverock.
14 —— to Ade, filio Alani, the lands of Moyden for 2 merks, within the barony of Cardross, — Air.
15 —— to Arthur Campbell, the constabulary of Dunstaffage, and the maines thereof, whilk Alexander Argyle had in his hands, — Argyle.
16 —— to John Brinings, of the lands of Gillanderstoun, in the Garviache, — Aberdeen.
17 —— to Walter Earl of Ross, of the lands of Dingwall, with the castle, and burgh, and liberties; the lands of Moyn, in Strathean; the lands of Ferncrosker, in Sutherland, 16. — Merns.
18 —— to Maleis Menteith, of the half davache of land of Metheleyche, and sundry other lands, 16.
19 —— to Arthur Campbell, of the 3d. land of Torrinturks, in Lorne, with many other lands, — Argyle.
20 —— to William Francis, of the lands of Sprowstoun, in vic. de — Roxburgh.
21 —— to John Crabe, of the lands called the Pudleplace, where the cock-stool stood, — Aberdeen.
22 —— to John Merser, of the foresaid lands, — Aberdeen.
23 —— to Hew Cunninghame, of the lands of Lambrathoun.

Ane Roll of Robert the First, marked on the back with this mark, G. R. I. Burnet.

1 Carta to John Logan, of the lands of Lyntoun Rotherikis, whilks extends to 10 l. land.
2 The second charter cannot be read, but it has viccecomitis Inverness above the head of the charter.

INDEX OF CHARTERS, &c. BY KING ROBERT I.

Vicecomitatus de INVERNESS.

In vicecom.

3 Carta B. Marie et Sči Gilberti de Dornoche.
4 —— to the Earl of Rofs, of the lands of Dingwall, caftle and town thereof; the lands of Movn, in Strathoun, and Farncrofcen, in Sutherland.
5 —— to the Earl of Rofs, of the lands of Tarrodall, &c.
6 —— B. Marie et S. Gilberti de Dornoche.
7 —— to the Earl of Rofs, of all his lands, with free forefts.

Vicecomitatus de BANFFE.

8 Carta Domini Murdachi de Monteith, of the lands of Rothemay.
9 —— Gilberti de Hay de Locherward, the lands of Achenus, &c.
10 —— to Andrew Clark, of the lands of Ordis, infra tenementum de Moubre.
11 —— Chriftino de Ard, militi, the third part lands of Derfkfoord, in vic. de Banff.
12 —— Chriftino de Ard, militi, the third part of the lands of Ardache, and 3d part of Skeith, in the barony of Defkford.
13 —— to Gilbert Hay of Locherward, of the foreft of Dwne, &c.
14 —— to Gilbert Chalmer, the lands of Moubreis, or Ward land.
15 —— to Gilbert Haye, of the lands of Awne, in Bouyn, with many others.

Vicecomitatus de ABERDEIN.

16 Carta Johannes de Bonevillie, militis, of the lands of Colliftoun, and two roumes de Ardenbrachtis.
17 —— to John Gardroffa, of the three merk land of Denburn, the lands of Robbiflaw, with ane fifhing in Dee.
18 —— to Maleis Monteith, of the lands of Metheleiche, the lands of Saltcoats, in Buchan.
19 —— to John Brounings, of the land in Gillanderftoun, in Garviache.
20 —— to John Crab, of the Puddleplace, where the cock-ftool ftood.
21 —— to John Merfer, of the foirfaid lands of Pudleplace.
22 —— to Ricardo Elgine, burgen. de Ab^d, of 10l. land of the cuftomes thereof.
23 —— to Ricardo Elgine, of ane annual.
24 —— to Alexander Frafer of Cluny, of the lands of Cardnye, with the fifhing of the Loch of Skeen.
25 —— to Thomas Meinzies, Knight, of the lands of Unyn, in Garioch.
26 —— libertatis Ade, fil. Aldani, recognita coram camerario et jufticiario.
27 —— to Robert Keith, Knight, of his haill lands.
28 —— to Duncan Earl of Fyffe, of the baronies of Oneill, in vic. Ab^d, baroniam de Kinncill, in vic. Perth, baronie de Caldore, in vic. de Ed^r.
29 —— Alexandri de Seton, militis, of ane tenement in Aberdeine.
30 —— Alexandri Coci, of the lands of the two Culmalows, in the thanage of Frawmartin.
31 —— to the burgh of Aberdein, anent their fifhing.

INDEX OF CHARTERS, &c. BY KING ROBERT I.

32 Carta to John Crab, of the lands of Prefcoly, Granden, and Auchmolen, and Auchter- In vicecom.
rony, in vic. de Aberdeen.
33 —— to John Brounings, of the lands of Gillanderftoun, in the Garviache, whilk Agnes Northinghame refignit.
34 —— to Walter Barclay of Kerko, Knight, of the lands of Tollie.
35 —— to Mr Roger Invernefs clark, of the lands of Fintray and Balmaly, infra vic. de Buchan, Buchan.
36 —— to Roger Chalmers, of the half of the fourth part of the weft part of Fintray.
37 —— to John Bonevill, the lands of Blairtoun, and the davach land of Many, in the thanedom of Balhelvie, in vic. de Aberdeen.
38 —— to John Bonevill, of the lands of Colftoun, the two towns of Ardendrachtis, infra comitatum de Buchan.
39 —— to Andrew Knight, of the lands of Garmauche.
40 —— to Philip Meldrum, of the lands of Crichmelade, Chreichen Ade, and Chreichen Walter, in Thanagium de Fromertein, vic. de Aberdeen.
41 —— Malcolmi Comitis de Lennox, terrarum de Strathoune, per forisfacturam Davidis de Strabogie, Militis, dudum Comitis Atholie, tempore quo Duncanus Comes de Fyfe fuit contra pacem noftram.
42 —— Joannis de Bonewill, of the lands of Blairtown, Many, &c.
43 —— Patricii de Montealto, the office of Forefterfhip de Killanell et Fromerteine.
44 —— to Elizabeth Durward, of 100s. furth of Banchory Datony, infra vic. de Aberdeen.
45 —— to Alexander Frazer, Knight, of the baronie of Kinnarde, in vic. of Ab^d, whilk Thomas Kinnarde renounced.
46 —— Hugonis de Ab^d, clerici, of the lands of Petmukftoun and Rubbiflaw, infra vic. de Ab^d.
47 —— to Sir John Broun, Knight, of the thanedome of Fromartie, in vic. de Ab^d.
48 —— to Stiven, filio Ommidi, the lands of Eafter Knokenblane, and Wefter Knokenblane, in vic. de Ab^d (*a*).
50 —— to John Bonewill, of Blairtown, Many.

Viccomitatus de KINCAIRDIN.

51 Carta to Alexander Frazer, of the lands of Auchincarny, ane bounding infeftment thereof.
52 —— to Thomas Carnoco, of ane annual.
53 —— to Alexander Burnet, ane bounding infeftment of the foreft of Drum and others.
54 —— to Alexander Irvine, of ane part of the park of Drum.
55 —— to Alexander Frazer, of the lands and foreft of Cragie, in the thanedom of Cowie.
56 —— to John Menteith, of the lands of Tarbettis and Bernis, within the thanedom of Aberbothnot.
57 —— to Alexander Burnet, of the barony of Tulliboyll, within the fherifdome of Kincardine.

(*a*) There is no No. 49, in the MS. at this place.

INDEX OF CHARTERS, &c. BY KING ROBERT I.

In vicecom.

58 Carta to Duncan Judicii, of the lands of Alrethis, in vicecom. de Kincardine.
59 —— to Colino de Garuald, the lands of Effintoyll, in the thanedom of Duris, and fherifdome of Kincardine.
60 —— to John Frazer, of the thanedom of Aberbothnet, in vic. de Kincardine.
61 —— to Alexander Frafer, of the thanedom of Cowie and Cragining, in Glafcullache.

Vicecomitatus de FORFAR.

62 Carta ane liferent-right to Mr James Carpenter, of the lands of Eafter Forfar.
63 —— to Malefius Monteith, of the lands of Ballgillachie, in vic. de   Forfar.
64 —— to William de Capella, of the difcharge of the 40 s. Sterling of his lands in Bondingtoun.
65 —— to Ifabell de Atholia, et Alexandro de Bruce, filio fuo, nepoti noftro, the lands of Balgillie, within the lands of Thanathas, and fherifdome of Forfar.
66 —— to Gilbert Hay, of the lands of Brechine, by William de Montealto of Kinblaukmonthe.
67 —— of the reduction of ane decreit of the lands of Cowaynftoun.
68 —— to Robert Young, barbitonfor, of the lands of Ardin and Thorn, in vic. de   Forfar.
69 —— quam Malifius Comes de Stratherne fecit Johanne, filie quondam Joannis de Monteith, Militis, fponfe ejufdem Comitis, of the lands of Carcathie, in vic. de   Forfar.
70 —— Patricii Capitalis medici, of the lands of Ballegillachie, in the thanedome of Monyfieth, in vic. de Forfar.
71 —— to Walter Northingtoun, of the lands of Dentrone and Balliony, in vic. de Forfar.
72 —— to William Oliphant, of the lands of Uchtertyre, whilk John Carrick refigned, whilk fometyme pertained to John Cuming.
73 —— Willielmo Ciffori, of the lands of Inuerrichti, in vic. de Forfar.
74 —— to Hew Malkarftoun, of the lands of Balclowchiris, with ane annual Monyfuthe.
75 —— to Donald Campbell, of the half of the lands of Reid Caftle, by the forfaulture of Henrie Piercie and Ingraham de Umphravile.
76 —— to Robert Harkers, of the barony of Kelor.
77 —— to William Dilhingtoun, of the lands of Ballgaffie, in the thanedom of Abberlonnoche, in vic. Forfar.
78 —— to Galfrido de Foullertoun, of the lands of Foullertoun, in vic. de Forfar.
79 —— to David Barclay, of the lands of Knocqy, in Glenefk, quas David de Brechin forisfecit.
80 —— to William Blunt, of ane bounding infeftment of the thannage of Abberlennoche, infra vic. de Forfar.
81 —— to Allan Ballmoffie, of fome lands in Dundie, and third part of Craigie.
82 —— to Robert Bruce, filio noftro chariffimo, of the lands of Fothenevin, and Caffegoueny, in vic. de Forfar.
83 —— to Ifabel de Atholia, et Alexandro de Bruce, nepoti noftro, totam terram noftram de Bagillo.
84 —— to Henry Roffie, of the lands of Inrouy, in vic. de Forfar.

INDEX OF CHARTERS, &c. BY KING ROBERT I. 19

Vicecomitatus de PERTH.

In vicecom.

85 Carta to Robert Bruce, filio fuo chariffimo, hoftilagium in villa de Scoon.
86 —— to John Gray, of ane tenement in Perth.
87 —— to Duncan Murdifone, the lands of Kurdeny and Fortuvett.
88 —— to Thomas Meinzies, of the lands of Fothergill, in Atholia.
89 —— Angufii fil. Eugenii, of the lands of Mukulyis, in vic. de Perth.
90 —— to Henry Winterwambe, of the lands of Chuluhundy and Clony.
91 —— to Robert Joliffis, of fome lands within Perth.
92 —— to Alenor Keith, of two annuals.
   To William Blunt, of ane annual.
93 —— to John Kinnynmonth, of the lands of Maleris, in vic. de Perth.
94 —— to John Aylbotis.
95 —— to Thomas de Camera, of the lands of Drumlouche, in vic. de Perth.
96 —— Willielmi de Montefixo, of the lands of Uchreardore, with the toun-duty.
97 —— to John Striveling, of the lands of Kinnedy.
98 —— to Alexander Meinzies, of the barony of Glendochyre.
99 —— to Alexander Meinzies, of the davach of land of Finlargis, in baronia de Glendoright.
100 —— to Nicoll Scarlett, of the lands of Forgund, Inchmertein, and Velachis, whilk were John Ballioll's.
101 —— Magiftro Manno de Maneris, of the lands of Kinfauns, in vic. de Perth.
102 —— Magiftro Manno de Maneris, of ane annual.
103 —— to Maria de Stratherne, fpoufe to Malis of Stratherne, of the lands of Kingkell Brechin, whilks were David de Brechin.
104 —— to John Trollop, of the lands of Fortiuolt.
105 —— Marie, fponfe Alexandri Frazer, Militis, forori noftre dilecte, et Johanni Campbell, filio fuo, nepoti noftro, pro homagio et fervitio fuo, omnes terras et tenementa que fuerunt Davidis Comitis Atholie, in comitatu Athole, quas idem David forisfecit.
106 —— to Chriftian Hair, of the lands of Wefter Foffeiche.
107 —— Roberto Bruce, Militi, dilecto filio noftro, omnia hoftilagia que fuerunt quondam Rogeri de Mowbray.
108 —— to Felanus Roche, of the lands of Petton Wathyner.
109 —— Hugonis de Erthe, officium Conftabularii de Clunye, in vic. de Perth.

Vicecomitatus de FYFFE.

110 Carta to John Weymis, the barony of Lucheris, the town of Lutheris and Bordland, the third part of the town of Prurfkis, third part of Petlouy, third part of Wallecungy, and miln of Lutheris, in vic. de Fyfe.
111 —— to Murdo Monteith, of the lands whilks were William Ferrar's, in vic. de Fyfe.

INDEX OF CHARTERS, &c. BY KING ROBERT I.

In vicecom,

112 Carta to David de Weymis, of the lands of Glafinache, in tenemento de Kinghorne.
113 —— to William Kinghorne, carucat de Sefield, terra Dromdyuan.
114 —— Ricardi de Bellomonte, of the lands of Killmumkyn de Karell.
115 —— to Nicoll Skymiefchour, officium vexillarii, terras de Hilsfield de Southborland et Marifland, in baronia de Innerkeithing, cum molendinis, quas Rogerus Moubray forisfecit.
116 —— to Robert Balcomy, of the lands of Pinkertoun.
117 —— to John Dodingftoun, of the lands of Pitcorthie, in tenemento de Kellie, quhilk Richard Syward refigned.
118 —— to William Campbell, of the lands of Glenfmanftoun and Kirkland, near Craill.
119 —— to Thomas Hay, of the third part of the lands of Lutheris, whilk the Earl of Buchan gave to Roger Cumyng.

Reigne 14.—16.—20.

Ane other Roll, marked, of Robert the Firft, on the back with this mark, H. R. I.

1 Carta to the Friars of St Johnftoun, of ane annual furth of the miln thereof,   Perth.
2 —— to the Abbacy of Dumfermling, of the patronage of Innerkeithing cuftomes, Duns, Kirkaldy, Muffelburgh,   Fyfe.
3 —— to the Priorie of St Andrewe's, of the patronage of Fordoun, in the Mearns,   Kincardin.
4 —— to the Bifhoprick of Galloway, of the archdeanry,   Wigtoun.
5 —— to Chriftian Arde, of the lands of Lickein, whilks Alexander Moubray tint by forfaulture.
6 —— to the Abbey of Lindoris, of the moor of Kinloch, given be the Earl of Wintoun, Conftable of Scotland,   Fyfe.
7 —— to Archibald Douglas, of the baronie of Kirkanders, whilks were John Soullis, in vicecom. de Dumfreis,   Dumfreis.
8 —— to William Lindfay, channon of Glafgow, of the barony of Kirkmichell, in valle de Neith, quas Rogerus Moubray forisfecit.
9 —— to Roger Blancamfchope, of the land of Laggelauer, in vicecom. de Air, ane bounding infeftment thereof,   Air.
10 —— to Hew Loocky, of the 4d. land of Sumdroun, with many other lands within the fherifdom of Air.
11 —— to Murdo Monteith, of William Ferrars, in vic. de   Fyfe.
12 —— to Stiven Kirkpatrick, of the lands of Pennifax, with the miln.
13 —— to Thomas Kirkpatrick, of the 2d. land of Braidburgis, in vicecom. de   Dumfreis.
14 —— to Ade, fon to Duncan de Mar, the lands of Balcory, Innerkerratis, Aughinftuiks, in tenemento de Murthelache,   Aberdeen.
15 —— to John Giffard, of the lands of Dunipace, in vic. de Stirling, at the earneft requeft and defire of the Earl of Murray,   Stirling.
16 —— to Murdo Monteith, of the half baronie of Rothiemay,   Aberdeen.

INDEX OF CHARTERS, &c. BY KING ROBERT I. 21

17 Carta to Murdo Monteith, of the barony of Prenbowgall, quhilk was Roger Mowbray's, In vicecom.
and the lands of Gilmertoun, quhilk Soulis forisfecit, in vicecom. de Edinburgh.
18 —— to Joannis de Bonewill, of the lands of Colliftoun, and the two Ardindrachtis, in
comitatu de Buchan, Aberdeen.
19 —— to William Predergaift, of the lands of Slamannan, and the half of Leviland, in
vicecom. de Stirling, whilk Gilbert de Malherbe forisfecit.
20 —— to William Bonkill, 20.
21 —— Oliuarii Carpentarii, of ane bounding infeftment of the lands of Edalwood, in
valle de Clyd, Lanerk.
22 —— Walteri, Senefcalli Scotie, of the lands of Eckfuird, in vicecom. de Roxburgh,
Roger Moubray forisfecit ; alfo Nifbet, (exceptand the valley of Liddell) ; the
barony of Langnewtoun and Maxtoun ; the barony of Cavertoun, in vicecom.
de Roxburgh, quas Soullis forisfecit, Roxburgh.
23 —— to Walter Stewart, of the lands of Methuen, in vicecom. de Perth, and Kellie, in
vicecom. de Forfar.
24 —— to Henry Annand, of the lands of Auchindrain, Air.
25 —— Roderico, fil. Alani, of the lands of Louchaby, the water of Loch, with the half
lands of Tulachard, in Argyle, bounding, Argyle.
26 —— to James Douglas, of the lands of Stabilgortoun, in valle de Efk, quhilk John
Lindfay refigned, 14. Annandale.
27 —— to James Lord of Douglas, the market-town of Jedworth, with the caftle thereof,
the town of Bonjedworth, with the foreft of Jedworth, Roxburgh.
28 —— to the Abbacy of Newbottill, the lands of Maftertoun, with the advocation of the
kirk thereof.
29 —— to James Lord of Douglas, the lands of Pownchic, in valle de Annand, blench, in
free foreft, Dumfreis.
30 —— to Henry Gelchedall, of the miln of Selkirk, for 2 merks argenti, 16. Selkrig.
31 —— to Walter Stewart, of the barony of Bathcat, the lands of Richardtoun, the barony
of Rathew, the lands of Bernes, the lands of Boundingtoun, Ednam, Kenpont, &c. Edinburgh.
32 —— to Walter Stewart, of the lands of Kilbride and Ferme, in vicecom. de Lanerk.
33 —— to Richard Edzar, of the 1 d. land of Kilpatrick, 14.
34 —— to Richard Edzar, of the half barony of Sanquhar.
35 —— to ditto, of the 1d. land of Barceconade, 1d. land of Lobri, 1d. land of Slochan,
&c.
36 —— to Ade Moffat, of the lands of Knocis, the lands of Crokis, the lands of Wefterker, in valle de Efke, 16. Annand.
37 —— to Thomas Mufiet, of the lands of Swegill, in Wefterker.
38 —— to William Lindfay, of ane annual in Air, 16.
39 —— to Thomas Broun, of the foundation of ane alterage of St Nicholas Kirk, in Air,
16.
40 —— to Wm de Sancto Claro of Hirdmanftoun, of the lands of Ceffeworth, Roxburgh.
41 —— to Alexander Seytoun, of the lands and town of Seatoun, in ane burgh of baronie, Edinburgh.
42 —— to Alexander Seytoun, of the lands of Bernes, near Hadingtoun, Edinburgh.

F

INDEX OF CHARTERS, &c. BY KING ROBERT I.

43 Carta to Alexander Seytoun, of the lands of Gogar,		In vicecom. Edinburgh.
44 —— to ditto, of the barony of Trauuernent, que fuit Williclmi Ferras; the lands of Fawfide, quhilk was Allan In Suche,		Edinburgh.
45 —— to the Abbacy of Kelcow, of the lands of Eglifmalefocks, in valle de Clyde,		Lanerk.
46 —— to the Abbacy of Melros, of the kirk of Wefterker, in valle de Efk,		Dumfreis.
47 —— to James Lord of Douglas, of the barony of Wefterker, quas Willielmus de Soulis forisfecit,		Dumfreis.
48 —— to Alexander Seytoun, of the fuperiority of Dundas and Weftercraigs, and fome in Quenisferry,		Edinburgh.
49 —— to William Murray, of fome lands in the burgh of Berwick,		Berwick.
50 —— of ane foundation of ane chaple, near Bamf, 16.		Bamff.
51 —— to Robert Bruce, the King's fon, of the hoftilage in Scoon,		Perth.
52 —— to Nicholas Skirmifchour, of the lands of Hillfield, and Southe Bordland, and Marifland, quhilk was Roger Moubray's, 16. blench, ane pair gilt fpurs.		
53 —— to William Aula Dunolm, the lands of Monyfothe, with the milne.		
54 —— to Adam Paxtoun, the miln of Edringtoun.		
55 —— to James Carpenter, of the lands of Eaft Forfar, in vic. de		Forfar.
56 —— to Ronnald Chalmer, of the lands of Le Rathe de Gatgirthe, 8 s. 4. argenti.		

Upon the back of this Roll there are tua Charters.

57 Carta to the Earl of Fyfe, of the lands of Oneill, in vic. de Ab^d, the barony of Kinnoul, in Perth, and Calder, in vic. de		Ab^d. Perth. Edinburgh.
58 —— to Robert Boyd, of the five penny land of Trabreche in Kill,		Air.
59 —— to John Gray, of a piece of land at the port of Perth, bounded, blench.		
60 —— to Alexander Seytoun, of Halfingtoun, in Berwick.		

Ane Roll of Robert the Firft, marked with this mark, R. I. l.

1 Carta to the Abbacy of Jedwart, of the teinds of the parochine of Jedwart, Langtoun, Nifbet, Craling, with the foundation of the chapple thereof, with fundry others, granted by David the Firft.

2 —— to the Abbacy of Jeddert, of the famen lands, and doted to the faid abbey by Henry Earl of Northumberland, and father to Malcolm and William, Kings of Scotland. In the original charter, Thomas de Londoniis is a witnefs.

3 —— to the faid Abbacy, the teinds of the parochins of the two Jedburghs and Langtoun, four oxengate of land in Langtoun, and ane croft, containing four aikers, Capella de Nifbit, with ane pleugh and ane half, with the teinds of Craling. granted by the Earls Gofpatrick, with many other lands.

4 —— of William King of Scots, to the faid Abbacy.

5 —— of Alexander King of Scots, to the faid Abbacy.

, In thir charters are contained the haill lands pertaining to the faid Abbacy, with names of the firft givers.

INDEX OF CHARTERS, &c. BY KING ROBERT I.

Ane Roll of Robert the Firſt, marked with this mark, Ro. I. K.

1 The firſt charter cannot be read.   In vicecom.
2 Carta to Thomas Ranulph, of the baronie of Mortoun, in valle de Nith,   Dumfreis.
3 ——— to Chriſtian Bruce, the King's daughter.
4 ——— to Laurence Abernethie.
5 ——— to William Iruine, of the foreſt of Drum, in Ab^d.
6 ——— to John Monteith, ſon to John Monteith, of the lands of Strugartenay, in Perth.
7 ——— to Alexander Frazer, of ane annual furth of Pendreche, in vic. de   Stirling.
8 ——— to William Douglas, ſon to umquill Sir James Douglas of Laudon, of the barony
       of Caldercleir, Kincavill, in vic. de   Edinburgh.

Anno Regni 18.

9 Carta of confirmation given by Robert the Firſt, confirmand ane infeftment given by
       King William to the town of Rutherglen, bounding,   Lannerk.
10 ——— to the Abbacey of Halyrudehouſe, of St Marieſyle.
11 ——— to Colbano de Glen, of the lands of Quilts, in vic. de Peebles, 2 merks argenti.
12 ——— to William Murray, of the half lands of Stewartoun, in Cunnynghame,   Air.
13 ——— to the Abbacey of Croſragum, of the lands of Dunegrelache.

Followes ane Roll at the end of this, whereof the firſt Charter is illegible.

1 The firſt charter illegible.
2 Carta religioſis viris priori et canonicis Candide caſe, of verie many lands, and the givers
       thereof,   Wigtoun.
3 Teſtes, Carta to Alexander Keith, of ane annuall of Recreiſts.
4 Carta to ditto, of the foreſaid annual.
5 ——— of bounding the lands of Uchterbannok to William Wallace, vicecom.   Striuiling.
6 ——— ane bounding infeftment of Uchterbannok to Robert Wallace, ibidem.

Ane other Roll is ſewed to the end of this.

1 Carta to William Blunt, of the maines of Aberlennoche, bounding,   Forfar.
2 ——— to Hew Polayn, of the lands of Fothenevin, in vicecom. de   Forfar.
3 ——— to William Blunt, of ane annual of 20 merks out of Alith,   Perth.
4 ——— to John Monteith, of the 12 merk land of Bernes, and ſundry others, 5 merks
       Ballmakuly, 4 merks Eiſter Twenethwany, 10 merks Newtoun, in thannage
       de Aberlachwich, in vicecom. de Kincardine, by eſcambion of ſome lands in
       Argyle.
5 Teſtes, Carta to the Friers of Berwick, of 40 merk Sterling out of the ſaid town.
6 Carta to the ſaid Friers, of ane annual furth of ane miln in Berwick.

INDEX OF CHARTERS, &c. BY KING ROBERT I.

                                                                                                         In vicecom.

7 Con. carta to Jean Monteith, of the lands of Cortachie, in vicecom. de Forfar, Glenlitherner, Dalkeith, half of Urwkell, in earldom of Stratherne,

8 Carta Candide cafe, of the cafualties in Farinis.

Ane Roll of Robert the Firſt, containing ane Charter of King David the Firſt, ane other of King William, marked with Ro. I. L.   Reigne.

    The Laird of Crofbie, his form of holding of his lands of Crofbie,   Air.

1 Carta to Thomas Neifbit, of ane annual of 12 merks furth of the lands of Edringtoun, in vicecom. de Peebles,   Peebles.

2 —— to John Craik, of the bounding of the half of the barony of Urde, quhilks he got in marriage frae Edward Cockburn, boundand.

3 —— con. given by Alexander King of Scotts to William Beddebie, of the lands of Menner,   Peebles.

4 —— con. given by Alexander King of Scotts to John Baddebie, of the lands of Menner.

5 —— to Adam Marfhall, of the haill barony of Mener, in valle de Tweed.

6 —— to Ade Marfhall, of ane bounding infeftment of the barony of Mener.

7 —— to Alexander Baddebie, when Ade Marfhall compearit in parliament and refigned the barony of Mener.

Da. I.

8 —— to William Kingefey and his fpoufe, of the lands of Capronftoun, in vicecom. de Peebles,   Peebles.

9 —— to William Kingefey, of the lands of Capronyftoun, in vic. de Peebles, quhilk John Melville refigned.

Da. I.

10 —— to John Monfode, of the haill barony of Skrauclyne, with the advocation of the kirk thereof, and the lands of Robertftoun, 21,   Lanerk.

Ro. I.—taxtward.

11 —— to John de Monfode, of the lands of Braidwood and Zulefheills, with the lands of Hevedis, in vic. de   Lanerk.

12 —— Jurdano, fil. Willielmi, fil. Nigelli, in excambioun, the land quhilk King Malcolm his brother, K. of Scots, gave to the faid William, in Edinhame, and the lands quhilks - - - - - - - - - - - - - had near Lanerk. William de Moruill conftable is witnefs.

Wil. R. 20.

13 —— to Michael Hart, blench, of the lands of Brakysfield, quhilk Ade Braks refignit.

Ro. I.

14 —— to Walter, filio Gilberti, of the lands of Mauchan, in valle de Clyde, quhilk John Cuming refignit.

Ro. I.

15 —— to the Abbacy of Kelcow, whilk he founded to them, of the kirk and lands of Lefmahago, anno 1ᵐ c xliiij. and of his reign the 21. Coram his teftibus Joanne Epifcopo Glafguen. Henrico filio meo, Willielmo nepote meo, Edwardo Cancellario, Bartholomeo filio Comitis, et Willielmo fratre ejus, Jordano Hayrum, Hugone de Morvilla, Odenella de Umphravill, Roberto de Bruis, Willielmo de Sommerville, David Oliphare, Willielmo de Lindfay, apud caftrum puellarum.

Da. I.

16 —— whilk Elifeus Porter gave to John Braidy, of the lands of Chawfield, in vic. de   Lanerk.

INDEX OF CHARTERS, &c. BY KING ROBERT I.   25

Ane Roll of Robert the First, marked on the back with this mark, Ro. I. M.

        In vicecom.
1 Carta to Dowgall Macfarlane, of the lands of Kindavie, Arynfchauche, &c.
2 —— Gilchreift Macymar M'Cay, of the lands of Kintyre,   Bute.
3 —— Gilberti, fil. Nigelli, terram partem terre de Cameleden, in vic. de   Drumfreis.
4 —— Fergufii de Monda Willa, the half of the lands of Stranrever, in vic. de   Wigtoun.
5 —— Donaldi Comitis de Mar, terrarum de Sawlin, in vic. de   Clackman.
6 —— Willielmi de Aughinfour, terram de Anghinfour, in Gallovidia, blench.
7 —— Nigelli M'Horrard, the lands of Kirkanders, bounding, in vic. de   Drumfreis.
8 —— Johannis, fil. Gilberti, Donald M'Kan, terras de Suchayche.
9 —— Ricardi M'Cuffocis, octo bovatas terre de Kelinfture et Cloentis, in parochia de Soureby.
10 —— Johannis, fil. Nigelli et Carriche, terre de Kellechaffe, in Gallovidia,   Wigtoun.
11 —— Willielmo Ciffori, de terris de ············ et Balmachannore, in vic. de   Forfar.
12 —— Fratrum predicatorum de Air, of ane annual furth of the milns of Air.
13 —— Fratrum predicatorum de Air, of an annualrent out of the faid milns,   Air.
14 —— to Arthour Campbell, of many lands.
15 —— Alexandri de Bruce, the barony of Din, in vic.   Forfar.
16 —— to Alexander Bruce, nepos regis Roberti, terras de Mughrum, in vic. de   Wigtoun.
17 —— to ditto, of the lands of Carnefmole, in vic.   Wigtoun.
18 —— Joannis Craigie, quarterium terre, in tenemento de Girton, &c.
19 —— Joannis, filii Gilberti M'Neill, quinque denariatas terre, in lie Rinns de Gallovidia, Wigtoun.
20 —— Willielmo de Sancto Claro, of ane annual.
21 Ane charter given by Thomas Ranulph, Comes Moravie, Drus vallis Annandie, et Cuftos Regni Scotie, Roberto de Peebles Camerario Scotie, &c. De Willielmo de Sancto Claro, of 40 l. penfion, A. D. 1329.   Annand.

Ane Roll of Robert the First, marked with this mark on the back, Ro. I. N.

2 Carta to the Abbacy of Dumfermling, of the advocation of the kirk of Kinrofs and chappel of Urwell.
3 —— to the town of Craill.
4 —— to John Strathenrie, of the lands of Bellachis, quhilk John Cuming Earl of Buchan forfaulted, in vicecom. de   Fyfe.
5 —— to John Glen, of the lands of Balmutache, extending to 10 l. land,   Fyffe.
6 —— an inquifition of the lands of Balmutache to William Locher. Mention is made of Alexander 3d, Balliol, William Wallace.
7 —— Comitis de Fyfe, of the earldom of Fyfe, in French,   Fyffe.
8 —— to Thomas de Cambow, of the lands of Grofmanftoun, in tenemento de Craill.
9 —— Willielmi de Cambow, of the lands of Cambow, in Fyfe.
10 —— to William Seward, of the barony of Kellic, in vic. de   Fyffe.

P E R T II.

In vicecom.

11 Carta to Sir Neill Campbell, and Mary his fpoufe, fifter to the King, and John their fon, all the lands quhilks were David Earl of Athole's.
12 —— to Gilbert Hay, of the office of Conftabulary of Scotland.
13 Memorandum. William de Roucaftle, his penfion of 20 l. furth of Schleples.
   Memorandum. Archibald Campbell gets the keeping of Dunftaffage.
14 Carta Angufii, fil. Eugenii, of the lands of Mucullis et de Tullenedy, in vic. de Perth, and lands of Culbarny, in Kinrofs.
15 —— Jacobi, fil. Dunflephe, of ane 7 d. land and ane half, of Kintyre, with many other lands there.
16 —— Joannis de Fortoun, of the lands of Cragie and Weft Malleris.
17 —— certain within Berwick, quhilk was John Schiltoun, given to Matilda, fpoufe to Robert Ardefh.
18 —— Colini, fil. Nigelli Campbell, of the lands of Lauchaw, Ardfcodniche.
19 —— to Andrew Gray, of the barony of Longforgound, 3d part of Cragie, 3d part of the milne of Pettarache, 3d part of Wairiftoun, and fundry other lands in Dundee, whilk was Edmond Haftings.
20 —— to Roger Cifforis, the 3d part lands of Langforgund, whilk was John Balliol's.
21 —— to William Lindfay, the lands of Letany, in vic. de   Perth.
22 —— to Thomas Ranulph, Earl of Murray, the Ifle of Man, 100 merk Sterling at Invernefs.
23 —— to Alexander younger Lord of the Ifles, of the lands of Ulks et Tyringis, with the Ifle of Mule, and other lands.
24 —— to Alexander Meinzeis, of the lands of Glendochre.
25 —— Gillefpi M'Lachlan, the 10 d. land of Schyrwaghthyne, &c.
26 —— Murthaci M'Necache, terras de Croffard.
27 —— Nigelli Oge, the lands of Killmychill, Drondrayllen, Dunnor, Keyllpoll, Reythenan.
28 —— Willielmi Oliphant, the lands of Gafkenes, in vic. de Perth, quhilk was John Cuming's,   Perth.
29 —— Abbatis et Conventus de Infula Miffarum, jus patronatus ecclefie de Killyn, in Glendochred.
30 —— Gillefpicis, filii Walteri, of the lands of Dereagis de Lachkerchen, Ardowran, &c.
31 —— Donaldi Campbell, Militis, the lands quhilk is called Venedudulocehe.
32 —— Roberti, filii Senefcalli Scotie, the lands of Kintyre.
33 —— Hugonis de Rofs, of the lands of Kinfawnis, with fifhing, in vicecom. de   Perth.

Upon the back of this Roll there are two Charters.

34 Carta to David de Barclay, of the lands of Rothmay, the lands of Brechine and Kinlo. h. , and fundry others, quhilk David de Brechin erga nos forisfecit.
35 —— to Simon Cillori, of the place called Kingafplace, in the town of Perth.

INDEX OF CHARTERS, &c. BY KING ROBERT I. 27

Another little Roll, having on the back, O, Walteri fil. Gilberti.

1	Carta Walteri, fil. Gilberti, of the lands of Mauchan, in valle de Clyde, whilk John Cuming erga nos forisfecit.	In vicecom.
2	—— Patricii de Moravia junioris, of the lands of Odiftoun, que fuit quondam Walteri, filii Regis, cum pertinentiis, in valle de Clyde,	Lanerk.
3	—— Andree de Douglas, terrarum de Creffewell, que fuit Henrici de Wintoun, infra baroniam de Carnwath,	Lanerk.
4	—— Fratrum predicatorum de Glafgow, of 20 merks Starling money, furth of the King's lands of Cadzowe, in valle de Clyde,	Lanerk.
5	—— de Lefmachutis, of 10 merks Sterling, furth of the milne of Carnelaks,	Lanerk.
6	—— Elene de Quarencele, of the lands of Beltftane.	

Upon the back of this Roll.

7	Carta Jacobi Dñi Dowglas, of the lands of Sonderland, in the barony of Hawick, ane confirmation to Douglas of Lintonrothbrekis,	Roxburgh.
8	—— Joannis Logan, of certain lands of Lintonrothbrekis, R. fol. 33. b.	
9	—— Thome, fil. Dick, the baronie of Symmonftoun, in valle de Clyde,	Lanerk.
10	—— to William Tweden, certain tenements in Striveling, quhilk Gilbert Lindfay forisfecit,	Stirling.

Thefe Charters following are on twa Leiffs of Parchments in form of ane book.

1	Carta to Alexander Seytoun, of the barony of Trauernent, in vic. Ed^r, quhilk William Ferrars forisfecit; and the lands of Fawfyde, quhilk Alan le Suche forisfecit; the lands of Mylyis, quhilk the Earl of Buchan forisfecit.	
2	—— to Alexander Seytoun, of the lands and barony of Seatoun, in liberam baroniam,	Edinburgh.
3	—— to ditto, of the town of Seatoun, in ane burgh of barony.	
4	—— to ditto, of ane mercat-day on the Sabbath day.	
5	—— to Ditto, in French, of the lands of Barns and Place Moylin, near Haddingtoun.	

In the Roll of Robert the Firft, marked on the back with this mark, ✕.

1	Carta to Thomas Edzear, of the lands of Kildonan, in the Rynes,	Wigtoun.
2	—— to Malcolme Gilmernaykie, of the lands whilk were William Touris.	
3	—— to Richard Edzear, of the barony of Kirkandres, &c.	
4	—— to Robert Wallyis, of the lands of Ballmekeran, in vicecom. de	Carrick.
5	—— to Gilchrift Tabert, of the lands of Dalkernefkane.	
6	—— to John Marfhall, of the lands of Den, in vic. de	Edinburgh.
7	—— Alani Veteri ponte, of Haknakel teldun, boundin,	Kinrofs.
8	—— to William Wifhart, the lands of Picuderlath ..h, a rofe, in vic.	Angus.

INDEX OF CHARTERS, &c. BY KING ROBERT I.

9	Carta to Hew Cunninghame, of the lands of Polearune.	In vicecom.
10	—— to William Biffet, of the lands of Merchinftoun and Dalry, in vic. de	Edinburgh.
11	—— to Gilbert Donnallfon, of the lands of Paffolet, in baronia de Hale, in vic. de	Roxburgh.

Laftly, Memorandum, To remember, that with this forefaid Roll are contained two Rolls of Decreets in Parliament.

Ane Roll, marked on the back, Rob. I. ⌧

1 Appunctuamentum inter Walterum Senefcallum Scotie et Barones Ergadie, propter interfectiones quondam Eugenii filii Fynlaii, et aliorum hominum dicti Domini Senefcalli.
2 Querela Margarete Corbet, fponfe quondam Domini Gilberti Frazer, facta Regi, quod maritus fuus effet interfectus.
3 Decretum latum per Regem, inter Andream Murray et Dominum Hugonem de Rofs, fuper baroniam de Lanach, in Rofs.
4 Concordia facta inter Dugallum Campbell, filium Colini Campbell, Militis, et Dugallum, filium Nigelli, propter viginti mercatas terrarum de Ardfcodniche, et advocationem ecclefie de Kilmartin, data 3 Augufti, A. D. 1323, apud Sconam.
5 Petitio Domini Alexandri de Badley, fuper terra de Mener, infra vicecom. de Peebles, contra Adamum Marefcallum determinata, data 4 Aug. A. D. 1323.
6 Inquifitio terrarum forrefte de Kinrofs, facta apud Kinrofs, 23 Septembris 1323, terra forrefte de Kinrofs fegregata erant a thanagio de Kinrofs.
7 Appunctuamentum parliamenti tenti apud Sconam 1323, inter Davidem de Haftyngs et Abbatem et Conventum de Dumferline, fuper terris de Molyn, Petdunedy, Petmaldue, Balcolme, PetM'Duffgyll, &c.
8 Forisfactura Roderici de Ylay, facta per Regem et Barones fuos, in parliamento tento apud Sconam, 28 Martii 1325.
9 Concordia inter Thomam Ranulphum Comitem Moravie et Dominum Willielmum Olyfant, fuper terris Willielmi de Monte Alto, ejus forisfactura, in parliamento tento apud Sanctam Crucem, 8 Martii 1326.
10 Concordia inter dictum Dominum Moravie et Helenam Siward, filiam Ricardi Siward, fponfam Ifaaci Maxwell, de terris de Kellie, in Fyfe, 12 Martii 1327.
11 Controverfia inter Hugonem Comitem de Rofs et Dominum Amleam de Moravia, fuper terris de Dromcudyn et Munlochy, &c. 3 July 1328.
12 An appointment, quhilk cannot well be read.
13 Querela Dni Willielmi Fentoun.
14 Querela Simonis Frazer et Margarete fponfe fue, fuper vicecomitem de Innernefs.
15 Querela fuper contradictione Gulielmi Graham, de terris in Stirling.
16 Super contradictione in Robertum de Alycht et Willielmum de Alycht.
17 Querela fuper contradictione judicii redditi per Comitem de Mar, inter Dominum Jacobum Douglas et Willielmum dictum Telch.

INDEX OF CHARTERS, &c. BY KING ROBERT I. 29

In vicecom.

18 Appunctuamentum parliamenti de Uchlagatis.
Appunctuamentum inter Johannem de Inchmertein et Alexandrum de Keith, super terris de Lonforgund, 1328.
19 Plegium Michaelis de Anegus, in manu custodis, quod Alanus de Pilch, subvicecomes de Innerness, non esset ab eo injuriatus.
20 Querela episcopi Aberdonensis, de decimis totius vicecom. de Ab^d, et ordinatio Cancellarii, ad faciendum ei literas de Capella, ad liberandum eidem talem seisinam.
21 Plegium Davidis Marescalli, super ter. ......
22 Renunciatio Hugonis Comitis Domino Regi, advocationis ecclesie de Philorth, in Buchan, data apud Perth, 29 Martii 1330.
23 Plegium Abbatis et Conventus de Aberbrothok, Scottistoun, Haltoun, Coneueth, &c.
24 Querela Simonis Frazer et Margarete sponse, et unius heredis Comitis de Caithnes, super comitatu de Caithnes, apud Kinross, 4 Decembris 1330.
Appunctuamentum parliamenti tentum apud Sconam, die Martis proxime post festum Sctē Katherine, A. D. 1331.
Super contradictione judicii Air inter Joannem de Moravia de Drumfingard et Dominum Arthurum Campbell, de terris de Glenscanchell superiori,   Air.
Super contradictione judicii inter Thomam Mosti et Dominum de Wardlaw,   Lanerk.
Super contradictione judicii inter Oliverum Carpenter et Walterum filium Gilberti,   Lanerk.
Super contradictione judicii inter Duncanum Comitem de Fyfe et Abbatiam de Dumfermline.
Amerciatus est Thomas Erch, ab omni comparatione parliamenti,   Fyfe.
Querela Willielmi Hay, quod non devenit cautionarius pro Edwardo Moravie.
Statutum in parliamento, penes victualia.
Querela Dni Skirling, super Willielmum de Twedy, quod non faceret ei sectas et servitia.

H

INDEX OF CHARTERS, &c. BY KING DAVID II.

Ane Roll of David the Second, marked on the back with this mark, D. 2. A. X.

	In vicecom.
1 Carta, Confirmatio generalis facta Johanni Kennedy,	Carrick.
2 —— to John Lorn, of all his lands in Lorne, whilk were Alexander of Lorne's, within Lorne.	
3 —— ane bounding infeftment to Walter Ciffori, of the lands in Gleneche, Lorne, with the half of the miln of Gloreth, in vicecom. de	Stirling.
4 —— to Ade Couffor, of the office Cronarie, in vicecom. de	Berwick.
5 —— to Gilbert de Infula, of the ane half of the lands of Gloret and milne, whereof Walter Ciffor hath the other half.	
6 —— to Malcolme Fleming of Biggar, the lands of Leigne, whilk were John Kennedie's, whilk the faid John Kennedy forisfecit.	
7 —— blank.	
8 —— to John Preftoun, of all the lands in Fyfe and Perth which were John Kinbuck's, by reafon of forfaltire.	
9 —— to Elizabeth de Mongall, of all the lands whilks pertained to Alexander her father, except the lands of Aldmanyn, belonging to Robert Wallace.	
10 —— Confirmationis of ane infeftment given by Malcolm Fleming Earl of Wigtoun, to John Danielftoun, of the Ifle of Inchkalleche, in lacu de Lochlounne, with the advocation of the kirk thereof, with the lands of Kilmaronock,	Lennox.
11 —— by David Earl of Levenache to Andrew Cunningham, of the lands of Afcohome, with the milne and fifhing thereof, the 4th part lands of Leurache, the half lands of Gartheyre, the lands of Dromccairne, the lands of Bromchean, infra comitatum de Lennox.	
12 —— to John Monteith and Marjorie de Striveling, daughter to John Stirling, vic. de Clackmanan, et dominum de Cars de Striveling et Alucthe, of the faids lands, by refignation of his faid fpoufe in the King's hands, in favour of her fpoufe.	
13 —— to Dowgall M'Dowgall, of the lands of Twinhame, with the lands of Worg, in vic. de Dumfreis.	
14 —— Con. to the Abbacie of Glenluce, of their haill lands,	Wigtoun.
15 —— to Robert Rouloche, of the lands of Threepwood, in vic. de	Lanerk.
16 —— to Roger Greenlaw, the lands of Butlerland, in the town of Crawmond, quhilk William Bartlemow refigned.	
17 —— to William Baillie, of the barony of Lambirtoun, in vic. de Lanerk,	Lanerk.
18 —— to Alexander Lindfay, of the barony of Byris, in conftab. de Hadingtoun, in vic. de Edinburgh.	
19 —— to Merchato de Glacefter, of Logyumchauche, in vicecom. de	Fyfe.
—— to William Colvill, of the half lands of Quhytfum, in vic. de	Berwick.
21 —— to John Bradie, of the lands of Shawfield, in vic. de	Lanerk.

INDEX OF CHARTERS, &c. BY KING DAVID II.

22	Carta to John Mairtine, burgefs of Ed^r, of all his lands,	In vicecom. Edinburgh.
23	—— to Adam Tore, burgefs of Ed^r, of exchange in all Scotland.	
24	—— to Adam Tore forefaid, and James Mulekin in Florence, the exchanging of all money in Scotland, and the cuinzie-houfe and liberties,	Edinburgh.
25	—— to the Abbacy of Tungland, of the advocation of the kirk of Sanaigh, within the diocefe of Galloway,	Wigtoun.
26	—— to William Robertfon and John Reidheuche, of the lands of Loch-houfe, whilks were William Mairis, and gave them with his daughters to the forefaid perfons, in vicecom. de	Linlithgow.
27	—— to William Fradrighay, of the half of the lands of Conwathe, in vicecom. de Banff,	Banff.
28	—— to the Abbacy of Dundrenan, of the lands of Culyn, Davach, and Rungiftoun, in vic. de	Drumfreis.
29	—— to Roger Kirkpatrick, of the lands of Glenefkene, in vic. de	Drumfreis.
30	—— Herberto Murray, of the half of the barony of Pedynane, in vicecom. de Lanerk, whilk Herbert Maxwell forisfecit,	Lanerk.
31	—— to Robert Rolloche, of fome lands in Perth,	Perth.
32	—— to the Abbacy of Newbottell, of their haill lands in ane barony,	Edinburgh.
33	—— to William Broun, of the lands of Greenhead, whilk William Greenhead forisfecit, in vicecom. de	Selkirk.
34	—— to Thomas Earl of Mar, of the lordfhip of Garviache,	Aberdeen.
35	—— to William de Sancto Claro, of the lands of Mertoun, of Merchingftoun, in vic. de Ed^r, whilk William Biffet refigned,	Edinburgh.
36	—— to Gillefpi Campbell, of all lands pertaining to Colcin Campbell, by reafon of forfaultry.	
37	—— to James Blair, of the lands of Kilkennet, in comitatu de Lenox, in vicecom. de Dumbarton, whilk Gilbert Norie forisfecit,	Dumbarton.
38	—— to the Abbacy of Newbottill, of the advocation of the kirk of Clerkingtoun, and ane annual of Keringtoun,	Edinburgh.
39	—— to Alexander Maitland, of all the lands whilks pertained to John Burnard, whilk he loft by forfaultrie.	
40	—— to John, goldfmith burgefs of Ed^r, of the feying of all the money,	Edinburgh.
41	—— to Margaret M'Dowgall, of the lands of Culken, Keltoun, Bowbey, &c. with many mae, in vic. de	Drumfreis.
42	—— to the Earl of Douglas, and his creation, apud Ed^r, 4to Februarii, anno regni 28.	
43	—— to the Earl of Douglas, of Strathurd, Logy, Strabran, in vic. de	Perth.
44	—— to Alexander Haliburtoun, of the lands of Dreme, in vicecom. de Ed^r, William More refignit,	Edinburgh.
45	—— to John Crichtoun, of the keeping of the caftle of Lochlevin, and the Sherifship of Kinrofs-fhire,	Lennox, Kinrofs.

INDEX OF CHARTERS, &c. BY KING DAVID II.

Ane Roll of David the Second, marked on the back with this mark, ⌧

	In vicecom.
1 Carta to Philip of Meldrum, of the foreſt of Awne.	
2 —— to Thomas Lipp, the lands of Netherdull, of Drumbeth, Pettinbruynache, with the office of Conſtabulary of Culan, in vicecom. de	Aberdeen.
3 —— to John Dun, of the lands of Ardache and Schethe, in vicecom. de	Banff.
4 —— to Henry Cheyne, of ane annual of Straloche and Achſtuckis, in vicecom. de	Aberdeen.
5 —— to William Earl of Sutherland, and Margaret the King's ſiſter, the earldom of Sutherland in ane regalitie,	Sutherland.
6 —— to Laurence Gowan, of ane annual of Eaſter Hopkillow, in vicecom. de	Peebles.
7 —— to Richard Meinzies, of ane annual furth of Newbie, in vicecom. de Peebles,	Peebles.
8 —— to Neſome Ramſay, of the North Barnes, in the barony of Craill, in vicecom. de Fyfe,	Fyfe.
9 —— to Donald Piggotis, of all lands whilk pertained to John Crab, in vicecom. de Berwick, et de Ab^d, infra burgos et extra	Berwick, Aberdeen.
10 —— to John Piggotis, of the lands of Littlegurdie, in vicecom. de Perth,	Perth.

ABERDEIN.

11 Carta to Richard Rolpott, Thomas Ligerwood, John Craigie, John Gardropa, and John Abernethy, of ane tenement in Ab^d,	Aberdeen.,
12 —— to Henry Ramſay, of the lands of Balbartane, Orkvenay, Petkenny, in ſchira de Kinghorne, in vic. de Fyfe, with the comontie of Carewyne,	Fyfe.
13 —— to William Earl of Sutherland and Margaret the King's ſiſter, of the barony of Cluny, in vic. de Ab, with the advocation of the kirk,	Aberdeen.
14 —— to John Gray, of five chalder of victuall furth of the thanage of Morphie,	Kincardin.
15 —— to David Fleeming, of ane annuall furth of the thanage of Meikle Morphie, in vic. de Kincardine, with the lands of Dorſhan and Weſt park of Kincardine,	Kincardine.
16 —— to James Sandilands, in compenſation of the lands of Craiglokart and Stenypath, of ane annualrent out of Horſeburgh and Heſteſkrews, in Pillein,	Edinburgh.
17 —— to Robert Dalzell, the lands of Croykſtoune, in vic. de Peebles,	Peebles.
18 —— to William Abernethy, of the lands of Rothemay, whilks David of Strathbogie forisfecit, in vicecom. de	Aberdeen.
19 —— to Roger Crawfurd of Cumnok, of annualrents out of Kyle, in vicecom. de	Air.
20 —— to Dougall M'Dougall, of the lands of Sannacks, Twinhame, Kiltown, in	Drumfreis.
21 —— to Fergus M'Dougall, of the Conſtabulary of Kirkubry, with ane three merk land in	Drumfreis.
22 —— to Fergus, fil. Mathei, of the lands of Netherwood, Cuvnathiſrigis, in vic. de	Drumfreis.
23 —— to Thomas, fil. Michael, of the lands of Bondingtoun, in vicecom. de	Peebles.

INDEX OF CHARTERS, &c. BY KING DAVID II.

	In vicecom.
24 Carta to Alexander Stewart, of ane annual furth of the barony of Cambufnethan, in vic. de	Lanerk.
25 ——— to William Baillie, of the lands of Alloway, in vicecom. de Clackmannan, 10 merk Sterl.	Clackm.
26 ——— to the men of Galloway, anent their laws and liberties,	Galloway.
27 ——— to ———————— of the baronie of Robertftoun, in vic. de Lanerk,	Lanerk.
28 ——— to William de Gardino, of the lands and baronie of Hertishuyde, in vic. de	Lanerk.
29 ——— Mauritio de Moravia Comiti de Strathern, of the barony of Hawick, in vic. de	Roxburgh.
30 ——— to Hew Blair, of the lands of Auchintelketye, in vicecom. de Kinrofs, 40s. Starling,	Kinrofhyre.
31 ——— to John Drummond, of all lands quhilks pertained to Marie Montefixo.	
32 ——— to Patrick Eicharift de Carrick, &c. of lands in comitatu de Carrick, vic. de	Air.
33 ——— to Malcolme Dalnieftoun, of all lands whilk pertained to Geill Somervell and Thomas Awmfrayis, whilk they loft by forfaulture.	
34 ——— to Edward Keith, of the foreft of Kintore and barony of Alneden, the foreft of Cardenauche, in Buchan, in vic.	Aberdeen.
35 ——— to John Ramfay, of the lands of Lumquhat, in vic. de Fyfe, quhilk Thomas Brechin forisfecit,	Fyfe.
36 ——— to Gilbert M'Lelan, of his lands.	
37 ——— to Ronald Chene, of the thaynedome of Newdofkis, in vic. de	Kincardin.
83 ——— to John Mautimer, of certain lands in Lanerk, whilk Ade Roger forisfecit,	Lanerk.
39 ——— to William Galbraith, of the lands of Buchany, in comitatu de Monteith, in vic. de Perth, and Portmelen, in Dumbartan,	Perth. Dumbartan.
40 ——— to Ade de Argenti, of the lands of Borland, in vic. de Clackmannan, Stulecherbert Shiells, in vicecom. de	Edinburgh.
41 ——— to Edward Keith, of his lands and offices.	
42 ——— to William Wifeman, of the barony of Dun, in vic. de Forfar, whilk David Strathbogie forisfecit,	Forfar.
43 ——— to Robert Glen, and Margaret Bruce, the King's fifter, the lands of Nether Pittedye, in fchira de Kinghorn,	Fyfe.
44 ——— to Margaret Abernethy Countefs of Angus, ane annual whilk the King has furth of Abernethy.	
45 ——— to Robert Maitland of Thirleftone, the lands of Ladytoun, Lagbie, and Boltoun, juxta aquam de Tyne.	
46 ——— to John Valeyis, of the ferjandrie of Carrick,	Carrick.
47 ——— Con. to William Barrowman, of the lands of Fortrie, in vic. de	Banff.
48 ——— Con. to Walter Turnbull, of the lands of Mintow.	
49 ——— to the Earl of Sutherland and his fpoufe, of the lands of Dunoter.	
Ane grant to the Abbot and Convent of Newbottill, to be free from appearance at the courts of jufticiary within Edr or Lowthian,	Edinburgh.

INDEX OF CHARTERS, &c. BY KING DAVID II.

Ane Roll of David the Second, marked on the back, Da. II. A. A.

		In vicecom:
1	Carta to John Innerpeffer, of the lands of Coneuache, in vic. de Banff,	Banff.
2	—— of ane penfion to David Foulartoun.	
3	—— to William Difhingtoun, of the lands of Balmany, and Aberlenoche, and Tolligdonache,	Forfar.
4	—— to Walter Spittell, of the lands of Kinninmonthe, in vicecom. de	Fyfe.
5	—— to Bryce Wichtis, of ane annual.	
6	—— to Gilbert M'Nable, of the lands of Bothmachan, in vicecom. de	Perth.
7	—— to Henry Lithgow, of the lands of Lochflatts, Wellflatts, and Braddall.	
8	—— to Alice Randelftoun, of ane pleuch of land in Otterftoun, in vic. de	Perth.
9	—— to Ifabel Countefs of Fyfe, of the barony of Glefcluue, in vic. de Perth, with Airth and Slomanno, in Striveling, and Richitdraw.	
10	—— to Alexander Strathechin, of the lands of Morphie Wefter, in vic. de	Kincard.
11	—— to Gilbert Kennedy, of the lands of Crogiltoun and Polltoun, in vic. de Wigtoun, twa Bruchtounes, and Kythreull Wigtoun,	Wigtoun.
12	—— to Alexander Ricklingtoun, of the lands of Eafter Spott.	
13	—— to the Abbacy of Halyroodhoufe, of their liberties.	
14	—— to Andrew Murray, of the lands of Kepmad, in vic. de	Stirling.
15	—— to Alexander Lindfay, of the lands of Newdofkis, in vic. de	Kincard.
16	—— to Robert Dalzell, of the town and lands of Selkirk,	Selkirk.
17	—— to Margery Chene, of the lands of Strathbrok, and half of Catnels,	Aberdeen.
18	—— to John Ker, of ane tenement in Ab^d.	

Ane other Roll fixed to the end of this Roll, whereof the firft is made to Alexander Lindfay, and cannot be read.

2	Carta to the Abbacy of Cambufkenneth, of ane annual.	
3	—— to Thomas Fleming Earl of Wigtoun, of the earldom of Wigtoun.	
4	—— to John Kennedy, of the 2d. land of ········ lying in vicecom. de	Aire.
5	—— to Robert Erfkine, of the barony of Kinnoul, apud	Perth.
6	—— to William Suppyld, of the lands of Lumlethan and Craigolt, in vicecom. de	Forfar.
7	—— to Allan Frifkine, of the barony of Inchture,	Perth.
8	—— to Allan Frefkine, of the lands of Crambreth, in vic. de	Fyfe.
9	—— to John Melville, of the barony of Glenbervie, in vic. de	Kincardin.
10	—— Con. to Thomas Papedy, of the lands of Manderftoun,	Berwick.
11	—— Con. to James Douglas, of the lands of Aberdour, in vicecom. de	Fyfe.

INDEX OF CHARTERS, &c. BY KING DAVID II.

All the rest of this Roll gotten marked

	In vicecom.
12 Carta to Donald Bannerman, of the lands of Clintertoun and Watertoun.	
13 —— of ane tenement in Ed', and tells not to whom.	
14 —— to Richard Cuming, of the lands of Dovellie, with forest of Tarnway in Murray, in vicecom. de	Inverness.
15 —— to Walter, filio Gilberti, of the lands of Cadyow and Eddelwood, in vic. de Lanerk, ane ample charter,	Lanerk.
16 —— to John Abernethy, of the lands of Baglillie, in vicecom. de	Fiffe.
17 —— to Robert Bruce, of the lands of Rate, in vicecom. de	Perth.
18 —— to Alexander Stratoun, of the lands of Glenchungall, &c. near Innerbervie.	
19 —— to Walter Leslie, of the barony of Philorth.	
20 —— to Adam Urquhart, of the lands of Fohestery, in Buch. cum Fortyre.	
21 —— Con. to Ade Urquhart, of Combrathie, given by Hugh Ross, ut supra.	
22 —— to Walter Pitcarne, of the barony of Moneythin, in vicecom. de	Kincardin.
23 —— to Patrick Ramsay, Knight, of some lands of Keringtoun, in vicecom. de	Edinburgh.

Ane Roll of David II. marked D. II. B. ✗

1 The first charter cannot be read.	
2 Carta to John Lorne, of the lands of Lorne.	
3 —— to Walter Cissorie, of ane bounding infestment of the half lands of Gloret, within the earldom of Lennox, and vicecom. de	Striveling.
4 —— to Ade Cosour, of ane liferent of the office of Coronarship, in vicecom. de	Berwick.
5 —— to Gilbert de Insula, of the other half lands of Gloret,	Striveling.
6 —— to Malcolm Fleming of Biggar, of the lands of Lainzie,	Lanerk.
7 —— blank.	
8 —— to John Prestoun, of the lands of Kinbuk, in vic. de	Fife.
9 —— to Elizabeth Mongaile, of the lands of Alderminnyn.	
10 —— to John Dalnielstoun, of the Isle of Lochlowmond, with the advocation of the kirk of Inchekalloche,	Lennox.
11 —— to Andrew Conynghame, of the lands of Eshom, with the miln and fishing, and Drumcarne, with sundry others, in vic. de	Lennox.
12 —— to John Monteith and his spouse, of the lands of Kerse and Aluethe, and sheriffship of Clackmannan,	Clackm.
13 —— to Dougall M'Dougall, of the lands of Evinhame, the lands of Worgar, in vic. de	Drumf.
14 —— Con. to the Abbacy of Glenluce, of ane 5 merk land of the earldom of Wigtoun, and ane 5 merk land of Carmole,	Wigtoun.
15 —— to Malcolm Earl of Wigtoun, of the 5 merk land of Carmnole and Knoclucbirvan.	
16 —— to Robert Rowlock, of the lands of Threepwood, in vic. de	Lanerk.
17 —— to Robertson and Redheuche, of certain lands in the town of Linlithgow.	

INDEX OF CHARTERS, &c. BY KING DAVID II.

	In vicecom.
18 Carta to William Sodrighay, of the lands of Conwache, in vicecom. de Banf, and	Banff.
Lochyardoche, in vic. de Ab{d},	Aberdeen.
19 —— to the Abbacy of Dundrenan and Cullindach, in vic. de	Drumf.
20 —— to Roger Kirkpatrick, of the lands of Gleneflam, in vicecom. de Drumfreis, quhilk John Marfhell forisfecit,	Drumf.
21 —— to Herbert Murray, of the lands of Pedenan, in vicecom. de Lanerk, quhilks Herbert Maxwell forisfecit,	Lanerk.
22 —— to Robert Rowloch, of certain lands in Perth,	Perth.
23 —— to the Abbacy of Newbottill, of all their lands in a free barony,	Edinburgh.
24 —— to William Brown, of the lands of Greinhead, in vicecom. de	Selkirk.
25 —— to the Earl of Mar, of the lands of Garviache.	
26 —— to William Sinclair, of the lands of Merchingftoun and Mortoun, in vicecom. de	Edinburgh.
27 —— to Roger Greinlaw, of Butterland, in Cramond.	
28 —— to William Baillie, of the lands of Lambingtoun,	Lanerk.
29 —— to Alexander Lindfay, of the barony of Byres, in vicecom. de	Edinburgh.
30 —— Morthaci Glocefter, of the lands of Logymurtach, in vicecom. de	Fife.
31 —— to William Colvill, of the lands of Quhitfom, in vic. de	Berwick.
32 —— to John Braidye, of the lands of Shawfield, in vic. de	Lanerk.
33 —— to John Mairtein, of the haill lands he conqueffed.	
34 —— to Adam Torr, of the keeping of exchanges of money, and liberties thereof.	
35 —— to Ade Torrie, of the Deputrie of the exchange and Mulekin of Florence.	
36 —— to the Abbacy of Tungland, of the patronage of the church of Sanaigh.	
37 —— to Gillefpie Campbell, of Dougall Campbell's forfaulture.	
38 —— Jacobi Blair, of the lands of Kilvynet, in vicecom. de	Dumbart.
39 —— to the Abbacy of Newbottill, of the patronage of the kirk of Clarkingtoun, of 5 marks out thereof, and 2s. out of Ballwood,	Edinburgh.
40 —— to Alexander Maitland, of the forfaulture of John Burnard.	
41 —— to John Goldfmith, of the fey of gold and filver.	
42 —— to John M'Dougall, of the lands of Sennark and Culven, Keltoun, Bondby, fet by Corbetfon.	
43 —— to the Earl of Douglas, of Strathurd and foreft of Brenan, &c.	
44 Obligatio Regis pro Comitatu de Douglas.	
45 Carta to Alexander Halyburton, of the lands of Drem, blench.	
46 —— to John Creichtoun, of the keeping of Lochlevin,	Lennox.

Ane Roll of David the Second, marked with this mark, D. II. B. B.

1 Carta to William Ramfay, of the lands of Innerleith, in vicecom. de Ed{r},	Edinburgh.
2 —— to Mauld Bruce, fifter to the King, of the lands of Fromerteine, and thanage of Kintore,	Aberdeen.
3 —— to Henry Ramfay, of the lands of Balbyertane, Balberdy, the lands of Corveny, the lands of Pitkenny, with the commontie of Carewne, in fchira Kinghorne, vic. de Fyfe,	Fyfe.

INDEX OF CHARTERS, &c. BY KING DAVID II.

		In vicecom.
4	Carta to William Maitland, of the bondage-lands of Traquair, and fundry others, Innerletham, Ormhuchftane, by refignation of Edward Keith,	Peebles.
5	—— to William Chalmers, of the lands of Caftlefield, in vic. de	Banff.
6	—— Con. to Strathaqhun of Carmylie, of the lands of Carmyle, Drummayeth, Hackmangerum, Achyclare, Moncur, by Henry Maulea of Panmore.	
7	—— to Walter Bur, clerk, of ane annual in the lands of Tyrie and Sefield, in the conftabulary of Kinghorne.	
8	—— to Henry Kinghorne, of the meafure and gage.	
9	—— to Allan Fawfyde, of ane forfaulture of ane Coupland, herauld quhetamter, in the time of Edward Langfhanks and Edward Balliol ufurped the Crown.	
10	—— to Margaret Murray, of the cuftoms of Bamfe for her lifetime,	Banff.
11	—— Bartholino Kingorne, of the conftabularie of Kinghorne,	Fyfe.
12	—— to Herbert Maxwell, of the difcharge of the duty of Carleverock.	
13	—— to Margaret Murray, of ane penfion.	
14	—— to John Murray, of all his lands, after the deceafe of Chriftian the King's fifter.	
15	—— to Murray and Liddell, of the ward of Allardes.	
16	—— to Margaret Murray, of the burrow-maills of	Edinburgh.
17	—— Con. of the lands of Tulliecravan and Dronan, to Malcolme Drummond, in vic. de	Perth.
18	—— Con. to William Lefk, of the lands of Lefkgoroune.	
19	—— to the Abbacy of Scoon, of the thanage of Scoon.	
20	—— to the Abbacy of Scoon, anent their liberties.	

Ane Roll of David the Second, marked with C on the back.

1	Carta to Malcolme Dalnielftoun, of the lands of Glenhargie, in vic. de Cloginfheach, four lib. land of Glens.	Air.
2	—— to Nicoll Striveling, of the lands of Stockertoun, in vic. de	Drumfreis.
3	—— to Simon Gourlay, of the lands of Adokftoun, Caprounflats, in the conftabulary of Hadington,	Edinburgh.
4	—— to Alexander Lambie, of the lands of Bernes, in the barony of Craill, in vic. de Fyfe,	Fyfe.
5	—— to John Stewart, of the half of the lands of Ferdill, in vic. de Perth,	Perth.
6	—— to the Abbacy of Cambufkenneth, of ane annual furth of Bothkenner.	
7	—— to Rannald Crawfurd, of the lands of Tollyouchy and Drumgarnade, for 13s. 4d. in vic. de	Kinrofs.
8	—— to Allan Stewart, father to John Stewart of Dernly, of the lands of Croffewell, Drochdreg, 8 part of Glengary, called commonly Knokill, in Rinns of Galloway, &c.	Air. Galloway.
9	—— to John Wighame, of the lands of Over Libbertoun, in vic. de Ed^r, quhilk Allan Baroune refigned,	Edinburgh.
10	—— to John Battayll, of all his lands.	
11	—— to Margaret Bruce, of the lands of Caftlefield, in vic. de Banff, quhilk Henry Culane refigned,	Banff.

INDEX OF CHARTERS, &c. BY KING DAVID II.

		In vicecom.
12	Carta to Roger Greinlaw, of the forfaulture of Thomas Meldrum.	
13	—— to Hew Blair, of the lands of Maler eift, paying 5 chalders of victuall yearly, in vic. de	Perth.
14	—— to John Lyll, of the new wark in Ab^d, B. for gilt fpurs,	Aberdeen.
15	—— to William Sempill, of the lands of Raice, in vic. de Perth, B.	
16	—— of ane annual furth of the Petrevy, in vic. de Fyfe, to the Lady Chappell, near Dumfermling, doted by Andrew Murray,	Fyfe.
17	—— to William Chalmer, of the lands of Thanftoun and Foullertoun, in vicecom. de	Aberdeen.
18	—— to the Abbacy of Dryburgh, furth of Pencatland, doted by John Maxwell of Pencatland,	Edinburgh.
19	—— to Patrick Earl of March.	
20	—— of ane annual to the Virgin Chapple, near Dumfermling, given by Andrew Murray, brother to the King.	
21	—— upon the priviledges granted to the Carmalite Friers.	
22	—— to Ade Chicharifte, of the lands of Balveny, Tolecandalantum, in the thanedom of Abrelenno, in vicecom. de Forfar, B.	Forfar.
23	—— to John Lyll, of ane voyd in Ab^d, near the cock-ftool, B.	Aberdeen.
24	—— to Richard Greinhuid, of certain lands in Roxburgh, by the forfalture of William Waldefield,	Roxburgh.
25	—— to William Levingftoun, of the lands of Callenter, by forfaultrie of Patrick Callentyre,	Linlithgow.
26	—— to William Pittillock, of the half lands of Gillaftoun, quhilk John Scot refigned, in vicecom. de	Fyfe.
27	—— to Malcolme Ramfay, of the lands of Maines and 4 part of Coull, in vicecom. de	Forfar.
28	—— of difcharge to Alexander Stirling, of ane difcharge of the caftle wards furth of his lands, in vicecom. de	Roxburgh.
29	—— to William Chalmer, of the lands of Thanftoun and Foullertoun, and of the duty of Kinkeld and Dys, B.	Forfar.
30	—— to the Abbacy of Reftennet, to cut wood in the foreft of Platter.	
31	—— to Laurence Killebrand, of the lands of Toulchmaler, Toulcheadame, in vicecom. de Striveling, blench, 1 pair fpurrs,	Stirling.
32	—— to Robert Glen, of the lands of Gafgow foreft, in the thanedome of Kentore, in vic. de	Aberdeen.
33	—— to Margaret Bruce, of the lands of Morphie, in vic.	Kincardin.
34	—— to William Ramfay, of the lands of Nether Libbertoun, in vicecom. de	Edinburgh.
35	—— to Patrick Ramfay, of the lands of Over and Nether Crakneftoun, in vicecom. de	Kincardine.
36	—— to Henry Ramfay, of the lands of Balbertan, Balberdy, Petkeny, in vic. de	Fiffe.
37	—— Waltero Difpenfa, of the half of the lands of M'ftoun, B. in vicecom. de	Edinburgh.
38	—— to James Sandilands, of the baronie of Wiftoun, quhilk William Levingfton refigned, in vic.	Lanerk.
39	—— of the difcharge of Caftlewards, to James Sandylands, furth of the baronie of Wiftoun, in vicecom. de	Lanerk.
	—— to Maurice Murray, Earl of Strathern, of ane jufticiary.	

INDEX OF CHARTERS, &c. BY KING DAVID II. 39

41	Carta to ditto, of the right of Donypais,	In vicecom. Linlithgow.
42	—— to the Earl of Sutherland and his fpoufe, of Lyncarem, Fetterkairn, Aburbuchnock, and half of Foirmartein and Kintore, of the thandome, in vic. de	Forfar.
43	—— to David Weems and his fpoufe, of the lands of Weft Rires, given by Duncan Earl of Fyfe,	Fyfe.
44	—— to William Peebles, of certain lands in vicecom. de Forfar, viz. Lumlethin, Craggock,	Forfar.
45	—— to John Ranulph, Earl of Murray, of the office of jufticiarie in Annandale and Man, for all the dayes of his lifetime.	
46	—— to Robert Glen, of the lands of Glafgow Forreft, in vicecom. de	Aberdeen.
47	—— to Rannald Chene, of the lands of Duffus.	
48	—— to David Weems, of the lands of Ballalie.	
49	—— to Alexander Frazer, of the fheriffhip of Abⁿ,	Aberdeen.
50	—— to Malcolme Drummond, of the Coronarfhip, in vicecom. de	Perth.
51	—— to William Menzies, of the keeping of the foreft of Alyth, vicecom.	Kincardine.
52	—— Joanni Mafculo, of the miln of Douny, in vicecom.	Forfar.
53	—— to William Chalmer, of the keeping of the water-port of	Berwick.
54	—— to Donald Edzear, of the Captainfhip Clanmacgowin.	
55	—— to Walter Rowlin, of ane fifhing upon Tay, called the Weft Halfe.	
56	—— to Peter Prendergaift, of the thanedom of Thannades.	
57	—— to Malcolme Pagainfon, of the keeping of the King's gardens in Edr,	Edinburgh.
58	—— Con. to Gilbert Carrik, of the lands of Buchan, in vic. de	Strivling.

Ane Roll of David Second, marked on the back with this mark, Da. II. D.

1	Carta to William Lord Douglas, younger, of the lands of Efkdale and Euifdale, whilk William Lovell forisfecit.	
2	—— Johannis filii Margarete, of the barony of Wiltoun, whilk William Maxwell forisfecit, in vicecom.	Roxburgh.
3	—— To William Lord Douglas, of the lands of Lyddall, whilks William Soulls forisfecit.	
4	—— to Thomas Carnock, the lands of Grinbifhuide, whilk Thomas Rofs forisfecit, in vicecom.	Roxburgh.
5	—— to the Abbacy of Kelkow, of ane free market.	
6	—— to Michael Angus, of the lands of Weft Lummifdaine, in vicecom. de Berwick, whilk Robert Lummifdaine forisfecit.	
7	—— to Walter Haliburtoun, of Eaft Lamberton, in vicecom. de Berwick,	Berwick.
8	—— to Gillefpie Campbell, of the forfaulture of all Dowgall Campbell, his brother's lands in general.	
9	—— to Jeffray Touris, of the forfaulture of Thomas Weftown, in general.	
10	—— to Gillefpi Campbell, of the barony of Melfirthe, by reafon of forfaltrie.	

INDEX OF CHARTERS, &c. BY KING DAVID II.

EDINBURH.

	In vicecom.
11 Carta to William Lord Douglas younger, of the baronie of Dalkeith, in vicecom. de	Edinburgh.
12 —— to John Preftoune, of the barony of Gouirtown, in vicecom. de	Edinburgh.
13 —— to William More, of the barony of Abercorn, by the refignation of John Graham.	
14 —— to William Logtoune, of the lands of Logtoune, in vic.	Edinburgh.
15 —— to Henry Pigot, of the lands of Dechment, in vic.	Edinburgh.
16 —— to the Abbot of Halyrudhoufe, to be mafter of the King's chappell.	

PEEBLES.

17 Carta to Thomas Nifbet, of the lands of Edringtoun, in vic. de Peebles, B. with thirle to Peebles milne,	Peebles.
18 —— to Henry Kinghorne, of the gadge in all burghs.	
19 —— to Thomas Baxter, of the lands of Barncleuche, in baronia of Caidzou, in vicecom. de	Lanerk.
20 —— to Maurice Murray, of the barony of Strathevin, in vicecom. de	Lanerk.
21 —— to Robert Stewart, of his haill lands, (except Bathcat and Ratho), given in parliament, the 14th year of the King's reign, at Aberdeen. Memorandum, A parliament holdin at Aberdeen.	
22 —— to John Mauteland, of the lands of Leghmure, in Colbowfton, in vic. de	Lanerk.
23 —— to John Gilchomedy, of the lands of Morintoun, in vic. de	Lanerk.

ARE.

24 Carta to John Troupe, of the lands of Glennope, bounding	
25 —— to John Somerlede, filio Johannis de Carrik, the lands of Garnache, Glencairethe, Erfknamerchin.	
26 —— to John, filio Nigelli, the lands of Culhornlethe, Clerigenache, &c. in	Carrick.
27 —— to John, filio Somerlede, of 4 d. land of Barleythe.	
28 —— to Thomas Boyd, of the forfaultry of William Carpentar.	

DRUMFREIS.

29 Carta to Gilbert Carrick, of the lands of Kenmore, bounding, in vic. de	Drumfreis.
30 —— to Malcolm Conhethe, of the lands of Culnhethe, Burland, and Kellwood, in vic. Drumfreis, and Foullartoun, in vic. de Roxburgh.	
31 —— to Robert Corbet, the lands of Barchar, quhilk John Barkar forisfecit, in vicecom. de Drumfreis,	Drumfreis.
32 —— to Lachlan Edzear, of the lands of Bomby, whilk were Lindfay's, in vicecom. de	Drumfreis.
33 —— to Fergus M'Dowgall, of the lands of Borgis, whilk John Mowbray forisfecit, in vic. de	Drumfreis.

INDEX OF CHARTERS, &c. BY KING DAVID II.   41

                                           In vicecom.

34 Carta to the monaftry of Dundrennan, the lands of Dungernok, in the water of Dee,
  in Galloway, in vic. de   Dumfreis.
35 —— to the Bifhop of Galloway, of the lands of Dermore, in the Rins, within the town
  of Innermeafan.
36 —— to Thomas Crawford, of the ten merk lands of Twinghame, in vic. de   Dumfreis.
37 —— to William Lord Douglas, younger, of the lands in general whilks were John
  Moubray's, fon to Roger Moubray, flaine traitors.
38 —— to Andro Buthergafk, of the half lands of Ure, in vicecom. de   Drumfreis.
39 —— to ditto, of the half lands of Pettie, in vic. Forfar, blench, John Maxtoun refigned.
40 —— to Ade Buthergafk, of the lands of Lothurmure, in vicecom. de   Banff.
41 —— to Roger Chalmer, of the lands of Dalrufcoun, on Dee, in   Dumfreis.

On the back of this Roll.

42 Carta to Gilbert Carrick, ane liferent of the office of Coronerfhip betwixt the waters of
  Air and Doue.

Ane Roll of David II. marked on the back, Da. II. D. D.

1 Carta to John Preftoun, of the lands of Gouiertoun, in Lothian,   Edinburgh.
2 —— to William Livingftoun, of the barony of Wiftoun, in vic. de   Lanerk.
3 —— to Walter Bickartoun, of the barony of Lufnes,   Haddingtoun.
4 —— to John Carpentar, of ane penfion during his lifetime.
5 —— to the Abbacy of Saulfyde, in Galloway, of the lands of Skeagmorchky, Tyber,
b. I. &c.
6 —— to James Boyd, of the lands of Gauyliftoun, in Galloway, quhilk John Gauil-
  ftoun forisfecit.
7 —— to Angus, of the Ifles ; the Ifle of Ila, Kintyre, the Ifle of Gythy, the Ifle of
  Dewre, the Ifle of Coluynfay, the 24 merk land of Moror, near the lands of
  Mule.
8 —— to the Abbacy of Reftennat, of certain liberties.
9 —— to John Urwell, of the lands of Urwell, and milne.
10 —— ane bounding infeftment of the earldom of Wigtoun, to Malcolme Fleming.
11 —— to Robert Walleyis, of the lands of Drumferne, in King's Kyll, in vicecom. de
  Air, 5 s. Sterl.   Air.

Defunt.

12 Carta to Ade Hepburn, of the lands of Trepren and Southall, Earl of March.
13 —— to Ade Dumbar, of the forfaltrie of John Gros, in   Berwick.
14 —— to the Abbacy of Kelcow, of ane regality.
15 —— to the Abbacy of Lefmahagu, of their liberties.
16 —— to William Balford, of the lands of Balledone, in vic. de Fyfe, by gift of the
  Earl of Fyfe,   Fyfe.

		In vicecom.
17	Carta to Maurice Murray, of the barony of Strathevin, by refignation of Alexander Stewart,	v. Lanerk.
18	—— to Philip Meldrum, of the foreſt of Aune.	
19	—— to the Earl of March, of all the caſtlewairds within his lands, during his lifetime.	
20	—— by the Earl of March, to Ade Hepburn, of the lands of Merſingtoun, and ſome in Colbrand's-path, bounding.	
21	—— to Ade Hepburn, of the lands of Southalls and Northalls, whilk Hew Gourlay of Beinſtoun foriſfecit, at the Earl of March's diſpoſition, with the lands of Rollandſtoun, B.	

Ane other charter on the back of this roll, whilk cannot be read.

Ane Roll of David the Second, marked on the back with this mark, D. II. E.
Alexander de Elphinſtoun, Dominus ejuſdem.

1	Carta to Andrew Saryn, of ane tenement in Ab^d.	
2	—— to Andrew Erſkine, of the lands of Raplach, near Strivling.	
3	—— to Hew Dumbar, chanon in Aberdeen, of ane penſion of the cuſtoms of Ab^d,	Aberdeen.
4	—— to John Craig, of Ribbiſlaw, in vicecom. de	Aberdeen.
5	—— to William Levingſtoun and Chriſtian Callenter, his ſpouſe, of the lands of Kilſythe, in vic. de	Dumbarton.
6	—— to William Ramſay, of ane penſion.	
7	—— to Neill Cuninghame, of xj l. furth of Carlaverock.	
8	—— Waltero, fil. Auguſtini, burges of Edinburgh, of the lands of Nidrie, in vic. de Edr, quhilk John Bannatyn of Corrokis reſigned.	
9	—— to Allan Grahame, of the lands of Mertoun, quhilk William Sinclair reſigned.	
10	—— to the kirk of Ab^d, of the patronage of Logy, in	Buchan.
11	—— to William Cuninghame, of the earldom of Carrick.	
12	—— to our Lady kirk in Ab^d, of the lands of Ealchull, in vic. de Banff,	Banff.
13	—— to our Lady kirk in Ab^d, of the park of Ealcholl, in vicecom. de	Banff.
14	—— to Gilbert Glencharnie, of the lands of Glencharnie, in vicecom. de	Inverneſs.
15	—— to John Reid, of the lands of Pelainſlatt, in the park of Cardroſs, and Dalguhorne, in vic. de	Dumbarton.
16	—— to John Hay of Tulliboyll, of the lands that lye betwixt Spey and Tynot, and foreſt of Awne.	
17	—— by John Ranulph Earl of Murray to John Urwell, of the lands of Shangwer, Talache, and Drome, with the foreſt thereof.	
18	—— to the cathedral kirk of Ab^d, of the patronage of the kirk of Philorth.	
19	—— Con. by the Earl of March, to William de Wallibus, of the Sheriffſhip and Conſtabulary of Elgine.	
20	—— Con. by Thomas Earl of Mar, to John Roſs, of Gilcomſtoun, in vic. de	Aberdeen.
21	—— by William Keith Marefchall and Andrew Garmache, of the lands of Enot and Gelechan to Ade Pringle, in the barony of Strathaghin, in vic. Kincardine, and of Badcaſs, in the barony of Rothynorman, in vic. de	Aberdeen.

INDEX OF CHARTERS, &c. BY KING DAVID II.   43

In vicecom.

22 Carta for Margaret Logy, to the Friars of Ab^d, of ane annual of 1 ᶜ s. Starling furth of the barony of Banchire, Davinnie.

23 ——— by Robert, Steward of Scotland, Earl of Stratherne, to Walter Murray of Tullibardine, of the lands of Tulliebardine, Pitvar, Aldy, Dundovan, Glencoy, Nethergaſk, and Dalrywath, in comitatu de Strathern ; and alſo the charter given by Alexander Abernethie, of the lands of Petcarlingis, in baronia de Banbreiche, in vicecom. de Fyfe.

24 ——— by William Fenton, of the lands of Lunroſs to the chappel of Baky.

25 ——— to Alexander Cockburn, of ane annual furth of the cuſtomes of Haddingtoun.

26 ——— to John Riddell, of the lands of Cranſtoun, in vic. Edinburgh.

27 ——— to Robert Stewart of Scandlochtie, of the lands of Daliell and Moderwill, in vic. de Lanerk, by reaſon of Robert Dewell, Knight, againſt the King's faith, byding in England, Lanerk.

28 ——— given by Margaret Cronfod, of ane annual furth of the lands of Hochkello, be James Twedy, and of the lands of Scraling.

29 ——— given by Thomas Earl of Mar, to John Johnſton, of ane annual furth of the barony of Cloueth, in vicecom. de Forfar.

30 ——— by William Earl of Sutherland, to Nicoll Sutherland, of 16 davachs of land lying within the earldom of Southerland, bounding, in ane free barony of Thorboll.

31 ——— containing an agreeance between Margaret ſpouſe to Rannald Chene and Alexander Fraſer, anent the lands of Duffus.

32 ——— given by John Bannatyn, in Corrocks, in vic. de Lanerk, to Henry Nuddrie, of the three part lands of Nudriemerſchell, in vicecom. de Edinburgh.

33 ——— by Thomas Earl of Mar, to William Chalmer, of the lands of Eiſter Ruthven, in Cromar.

34 ——— to the Biſhop of St Andrews, of the great cuſtoms of St Andrews, Fife.

35 ——— to the Abbacy of Dumfermling, of the lands of Gartneker, in vicecom. de Clackman.

36 ——— to the ſaid Abbacy, of the lands and milne of Tillecultry, in vicecom. de Clackman.

37 ——— Con. given by Margaret and Marjorie Montgomeries, of the lands of Caſtlys, to John Kennedy, in vicecom. de Air.

38 ——— to John Pitſcottie, of ſome lands in Perth.

39 ——— to Walter Leſly, of ane penſion furth of the cuſtomes of Dundee.

40 ——— to Margaret Sinclair Counteſs of Angus, of ane penſion furth of Tollie, in vicecom. Kincardin.

41 ——— of excambion betwixt Alexander Livingſtoun of that Ilk and Ade More, Knight.

42 ——— of a penſion to Patrick Earl of March.

43 ——— to George Dumbar, of the half of the barony of Tibris, and Mortoun, in vicecom. de Drumfreis.

44 ——— of ane annual of ſix merks furth of Newbie, in vicecom. de Peebles.

45 ——— to Marion Cumming, relict of umquhill John Langlands, of the lands of Milfaſtoun and Ochterhuyd, with the milne thereof, which came in the King's hand by recognition.

46 ——— given by the Earl of March to Alexander Rickietoun, of certain lands in Duns and Milnhauch, and Muſhulane in Drumly, and Home.

INDEX OF CHARTERS, &c. BY KING DAVID II.

In vicecom.
47 Carta to Robert, fon to the Earle of Athole, of the half lands of Ferdill, in vicecom. de Perth.
48 —— to William Wardlaw of - - - - - - - - - of the lands of Crofgate, in the barony of Coldinghame, by reafon of Raulf Eklis his forfaulture; 1 pleugh land in Blenherne, by forfaultrie of Henry Ellane; 2 pleughs of land in Hiltoun, pertaining fometyme to John Hiltoun, quhilk he loft by forfaultrie.
49 —— given by John Grahame of Dalkeith, to John Grahame, of the lands of Elvinftoune.
50 —— to Thomas Durance, of the Crounerfhip, in vic.   Drumf.
51 —— given by William Fentoun, of the lands of Lunrofs, to the Chappell of Baky.
52 —— to Adam Forreft, of the Juftice-clerkfhip, by-north Forth.
53 —— to James Mulekin of Florence, of the cunzie-houfe.
54 —— given by Thomas Earl of Mar, to Alexander Lindfay, of the lands of Ballindolloche and Ruthven, in vicecom. de   Forfar.
55 —— of ane appointment betwixt Robert, Great Steward of Scotland, Earl of Stratherne, on the one part, and the Abbot of Halyruidehoufe, anent the annual awand to them furth of the Kerfs of Striveling.
56 —— to Henry Afkirk, of the forfaultry of Ade Glendoning, within   Roxburgh.
57 —— of ratification to John of the Ifles, of all his lands.
58 —— to Robert Erfkine, of the lands of Malerby, and 13s. annual furth of Pitfcottie, his lands, for the lands of Adametoun, in barony of Kyll, whilk James Blair refigned,   Perth.
59 —— to Thomas Biffet, of the earldom of Fyfe. Tenet.

Ane Roll of David the II. marked on the back, F, fovernc.

1 Carta to William Ramfay, of the earldom of Fyfe.
2 —— to Robert Hebborne, of the lands of Kingftoun, in vic. de   Peebles.
3 —— to Robert Ruffell, of the lands of Sympleland, in vic. Drumfreis, by refignation of Fergus Ardroffane,   Drumfreis.
4 —— to Elizabeth Crichtoun, of the forfaultry of Margaret Saluan.
5 —— to Andrew Buthergaik, of the lands of Petty, in vic.   Forfar.
6 —— to Walter Panilleyner, of ane tenement in Abd, and the South Brae of the Caftle.
7 —— to Margaret Glenurchy, and to John Campbell her fpoufe, of the lands of Glenurchy.
8 —— to Roger Hog, burgefs of Edr, of ane annual furth of Dalry.
9 —— to James Blair, of the lands of Corfchogill, in the barony of Drumlanrig, in vic. de Drumf.
10 —— to Thomas Webfter, of ane land in the Weftbow, in   Edinburgh.
11 —— to Thomas Halywoll, of the Hoftillarie in Traquhair, by forfaulture of John Craik, vicecom. de   Peebles.
12 —— to Adame Difpenfa, of the Conftabularie of Kinghorne, in vicecom. de Fyfe, with the Smithieland and Marifland,   Fyfe.
13 —— to Robert Hebburne, of the forfaultrie of Ade Moffat in generall.

INDEX OF CHARTERS, &c. BY KING DAVID II.

In vicecom.

14 Carta to Hew Abernethy, of all the lands quhilk Laurence his father tint by forfaulrie in general, except Lambertoun.
15 ——— to Thomas Foullartoun, of ane twentie pound land in the earldom of Carrik, viz. Glennopper, Garfer, Akthynfore, Akencarne, Crcholloch.
16 ——— to William Cunnynghame, of the earldom of Carrik, except Thomas Fullartoune's.
17 ——— to Thomas Murray, of the barony of Hawick and Sprouftoun, in vicecom. de   Roxburgh.
18 ——— to Ade Buthergafk, and his fpoufe, of the barony of Desforde, Ardache, Skeythis, in vicecom. de   Banff.
19 ——— of remiffion to Henry Monimufk, and ane new gift of all his lands within the fherifdome of Banff and Ab^d.
20 ——— to William Toryn, of the barony of Foverne, in vic. de Aberdeen, by recognition fra Henry Strabrok.
21 ——— to Thomas Ker, of the lands of Steinftoun, in vic. Peebles, whilk Chriftian Liddell forisfecit.
22 ——— to William Ramfay Earl of Fyfe, of the erection of Coupar in ane free burgh.
23 ——— to the Priorie of Elcho, of their liberties.
24 ——— to David Kernok, of the lands of Kincairny and Salveneich, in baronia de Innerkeithing, in vicecom. de   Fyfe.
25 ——— anent the liberties of the kirk of Kinnellour.
26 ——— to Adam Erefkine of Barrowchan, of the forfaultrie of John Striveling in general.
27 ——— to Ade Urquhart, of the fheriffdome of Crombathie and fherifship thereof, whilk William Earle of Rofs refignit.
28 ——— to Walter Durrand, of the lands of Maybie in Galloway, in vicecom. de   Drumf.
29 ——— to Nicoll Smerles, of all John Smerles his lands.

On the back of this Roll are fome Charters; the three firft cannot be read.

33 Carta given by John Ranulph Earl of Murray, to Walter Stewart, Knight, father to John Stewart of Dalfwintoun, of the lands of Garleyis, Glenmannache, Corffoche, and Kirkormock, in vicecom. de   Drumf.
34 ——— to John Murray, of the lands of Cranftounriddell.
35 ——— given by Marion Dunmore, to Robert, Steward of Scotland, of the lands of Dunmore, in Fyfe, in favour of Roger Mortimer.
36 ——— to William Difpens of Dumbarrie, of the lands of Bondingtoune, in the conftabulary of Haddingtoun, in vicecom. de Ed^r, given be William Earle of Dowglas.
37 ——— to William Waux, of the keeping of the foreft of Buyne and Awne.
38 ——— to John Grant, of ane penfion of 40l.
39 ——— to Robert, Stewart of Scotland, Earl of Stratherne, of ane penfion of 40l.
40 ——— to Mr Richard Kilvintoun, of ane penfion.
41 ——— of refignation in Robert Great Steward of Scotland's lands, Governor of Scotland in the King's abfence in England, by Jhone Carrik, who refigned the three part lands of Roflyn to Andrew Volouns.

INDEX OF CHARTERS, &c. BY KING DAVID II.

	In vicecom.
42 Carta given by John Lyll of Ducholl, to Andrew Watson burgess of Ab⁴, of ane tenement near the cock-stool.	
43 —— to Alexander Geleel, of the keeping of the Cockatt.	
44 —— to John Gray, of all his lands, and of Craigie, in vic. de	Kincardin.
45 —— to John Lindsay of Thorstoun, of the Sheriff ship of	Air.
46 —— to John Drummond, of the office of Baillierie of Abthain of Dull, in Atholl.	
47 —— to Norman Lesly, of ane pension induring the ward of Ballinbreich.	
48 —— to William Earl of Douglas, to Thomas Roseins, of the lands of Bothrull, in vicecom. de	Roxburgh.
49 —— of the conjunct fee of Elizabeth Stewart, daughter of the Great Steward of Scotland, Earl of Strathern, spouse to David Hay Great Constable, son to Thomas Great Constable of Scotland.	
50 —— given by William Bishop of St Andrews, to Mr Henry Stowpie, of the lands of Abthane, in Kinghorne.	
51 —— given by William Earl of Douglas, to Richard Ker, of the lands of Salmestoun, in vic. de	Edinburgh.
52 —— given by John Leane, to Gilbert Carrik, of the lands of Buchan, in vic. de	Strivling.
53 —— by Thomas Earl of Mar, to John Crab burges of Ab⁴, of the land of Quhilt, in vic. de	Aberdeen.
54 —— given be John Weems of that Ilk, to Alexander Nisbet, of the lands of Glasmouth, near Kinghorne, in vicecom. de	Fyfe.
55 —— to John Crab, of twa tenements in	Aberdeen.
56 —— given by William Fedderesse of that Ilk, to William Cumming and Helen Fedderesse, of the lands of Fedresse.	
57 —— confirmand the liberties and rights of the lands and kirks in the Garuiauche, to the Abbacy of Lindoris. Tenet.	

Ane Roll of David II. marked on the back, Da. II. G.

1 Carta to James Sandoks, of the lands of Craiglockhart and Stonypethe, vicecom. de	Edinburgh.
2 —— to Maurice Murray, of the town of Branxholme, in the barony of Hawick, in vicecom. de Roxburgh, quhilk John Baliol forfaulted.	
3 —— to Maurice Murray, of the twa Lethams, with the lands of Carmulache, quhilk Alexander Moubrey forisfecit, with the lands of Ogilvee, in es. William Hamiltoun, Englishman.	
4 —— to Maurice Murray, of the lands of Gosfoord and Bissetland, in vicecom. de	Edinburgh.
5 —— to Gilbert Kerr, of the lands of Kenmore, in vic.	Drumf.
6 —— to Laurence Gillibrand, the lands of Southaiks, in vic.	Drumf.
7 —— to William Gallerei, of the forfaulture of John Strathawry, clerk, in general.	
8 —— to David Chalmer, the lands of Petsethik and Balnerosk, in baronia de Monimusk, in vic. de Ab⁴, quhilk Henry Monimusk forisfecit.	

INDEX OF CHARTERS, &c. BY KING DAVID II.   47

                                                                                             In vicecom.

9 Carta to Philip Meldrum, of the lands of Lafingiftoun, in the barony of Kargill, in vi-
      cecom. de   Perth.
10 ——— to Thomas Terry, of the lands of Glenefclane, in the valleys of Nithe, in vice-
      com. de   Drumf.
11 ——— to John Stewart, fon of John Stewart, of the 40s. land of Warekewry, in the
      barony of Culven, in vicecom. de   Drumf.
12 ——— to John Kerrict, fon of Thomas Kerrict, 1d. land of Corfetrechache, in comitatu
      de Carrik.
13 ——— to William Shaw, of 20 l. land, quhilk was William Kirkofwald's, in vicecom. de   Drumf.
14 ——— to John Sommerledi de Carrick, 1d. land of Delrenache, forling Linach, 4d.
      land of Killcrenache, 4d. land of Dencleache, in comitatu de Carrik.
15 ——— to John Turnbery, of the lands of Lefynarne, in comitatu de Carrik.
16 ——— to Adam Johnftoun, of the lands of Cronanton, Molyn, Monykipper, Rahill,
      in the barony of Kirkmyell, in vicecom. de Drumf. quhilk William Carlioll
      wadfet, by the claufe of reverfion pertains to the King,   Drumf.
17 ——— to David Annand, of the forfaultire of Margaret Lovell, in the barony of Inner-
      kyn.
18 ——— to Ifabell of Atholl, the lands of Barinne heurie, whilk Gilbert Culquhen, He-
      rauld, forisfecit, in vicecom. de   Drumf.
19 ——— of Patrick M'Culache, his lands granted to John Carrik in liferent.
20 ——— to John Crawfurd of Cumnock, of the forfaulture of John Sommerled.
21 ——— to John Crawfurd, of the 40 merk land in Sanquhar, in vicecom. de   Drumf.
22 ——— to Maurice Millar, of his libertie.

F Y F E.

23 Carta to David Chalmer, the lands of Balgochrie, in the barony of Fethill, in vicecom.
      de Fyfe, with the fifhing of Taye, called the Sandie water,   Fyfe.
24 ——— to David Annand, of the town of Pettacherache, with the north part of the ba-
      rony of Innerkeithing, with the coldcheughe and milne of Graggefood, by for-
      faulture of Margarett Lovell.
25 ——— William Difpenfa, of the keeping of the foreft and moor of Cardenenie, in the
      barony of Kinghorn, in the conftabulary of Kinghorn.
26 ——— to Ade Difpenfa, of the keeping of the King's door.

P E R T II.

27 Carta to Duncan Naper, of the lands of Petfour and Drumgran, in vicecom. de Perth,
      by forfaultrie of Dornagill Moffet,   Perth.
28 ——— to Adam Blancradock, of the lands of Craigie and Weftmaler, in vicecom. de
      Perth, quhilk John Fortune forisfecit,   Perth.

INDEX OF CHARTERS, &c. BY KING DAVID II.

29 Carta given by William Douglas Earl of Athol, at Ab^d, the 16th of February 1341 yeirs, to Robert Stewart, Great Stewart of Scotland, of the earldome of Athole. — In vicecom.
30 —— to William Touris, of the forfaultrie of John Fortoune, in vicecom. de — Perth.
31 —— to the faid William, of the famen lands.

FORFAR.

32 Carta to William Douglas younger, of the lands of Reidcaftle, whilk Eve Moubray and John Moubray her fon forisfecit, in vicecom. — Forfar.
33 —— to Andrew Burr, of the lands of King's Lour, Drumgethe, Godfraiftoune, whilk John Innerpeffer refigned, in vicecom. de — Forfar.
34 —— to Donald Strathechin, and Annabell his wife, of the lands of Kingflour, Langlevis, Godefrayftoune, in vicecom. Forfar, whilk Andrew Burr refigned in the King's hands, at Barbrothe, 1343 years, 16th April; the lands of Cardenbarclay, and annual furth of the miln of Panmure, in vicecom. de Forfar; the barony of Monycabbok, Tullimaddin, and Craig, in vicecom. Ab^d, whilk the King gave him alfo.

On the back of this Roll.

35 The office of the Sheriffship is granted to William Lord Dowglafs for his lifetime. — Lanerk.

Ane Roll of David II. marked on the back, D. II. E. E.

1 Carta to John Lord of the Ifles, of the Ifle callit Ylle, Geday, Jura, Colonfay, Ifle of Mule, Ifle of Tirade, Ifle of Colla, Ifle of Leges; the lands of Moruar, Lochaber, Durdoman, Glenchomure, with all the little ifles adjacent.
2 —— to Rannald Roifoune of the Ifles, of 10d. land of Kenneaill, in North Argyle.
3 —— to Rannald, of the Ifles of Yweft, Barra, Egghee, Rune, ane part of the lands of Garrow, Morwarne, Mudworthe, Mordhowar, Arefayis, Cundewithe.
4 —— to Malcolme, fon to Tormode M‘Cloyde, twa parts of Glenegle, in vicecom. de — Innernes.
5 —— to Alexander M‘Nacht..n, of the forfaultry of John, fon to Duncan, fon to Alexander of the Ifles.
6 —— to Torkyll M‘Cloyd, of the 4 penny land of Affeynkt, with the fortalice in the ifle thereof.
7 —— to the kirk of Bangore, of fome lands given by the Earl of Carrick, whilk I cannot read.
1 —— to Andrew Moncur, of the lands of Corfelflat, containing the bounding thereof.
2 —— to Walter Biffet, of the lands of Clerkingtoun, in vic. de Ed_r, and Kinbrakmonth, in vic. de Fyfe.
3 —— of ane contract betwixt Biffet and Ker anent marriage, and the lands of Coulter, with revocation, in vic. de — Lanerk.

INDEX OF CHARTERS, &c. BY KING DAVID II.

In vicecom.

4 Carta to William Earl of Dowglas, of the lands of Balmachothlie, Logibryde, Blabolg, within the barony of Schathurd, to the Abbay of Dumfermling.
John Lindsay laird of Craigie, Hew Lord Eglingtoun, Godfrey Lord Ardrossane, Allane Campbell, Hew Blair of that Ilk.
1 Carta, where John Monteith gave to the Abbacy of Kilwinning, in Cuninghame, the patronage of the kirk of Brigide, in Arran. This John Monteith is stiled John Monteith Lord of Arran and Knapdaill. In this charter also, John Laird of Maxwell grants and dispones to the Abbacy of Kilwinning, the patronage of the kirk of Libbertoun.
2 —— to the burgh of Kinghorne, and erection thereof, by Alexander King of Scots, dated at Largauche, the 26th June, anno regni 36, &c.
1 —— to John Lang.
2 —— given by Thomas Stewart Earl of Angus, to Robert Erskine, of the lands of Adametoun, in vic. de Air, Air.
3 —— to Robert Erskine, of the lands of Kintillache, in vicecom. Perth.
4 —— to Robert Erskine, of the lands of Quilt, in vicecom. Fyfe.
5 —— to Robert Erskein, of the lands of Erskeine.
6 —— to Thomas Strathachin, of the lands of Knok, in vic. de Kincardin.
7 —— given be Robert, Great Stewart, to Michael Butler, of the baronie of Kinboyscher.
8 —— given by William Keith, Marischall of Scotland, to Ade Strathachin, of the lands of Augherthyne and Scarry, in vicecom. de Aberdeen.
9 —— to Thomas Carnoco, of the half of the lands of Kinfawns.
10 —— be the Earl of Fyfe, to John Skeen, of the lands of West Ferny, in marriage.

On the back of the Roll.

Ane charter to William Earl of Sutherland, of the barony of Urquhard, in Invernefs, in excambion for all the lands in Kincardine, which he got in marriage with Margorie the King's sister.

Ane Roll of David the Second, marked on the back with this mark, D. II.

1 Carta to the Abbacy of Aberbroth, granted by William King of Scotts, of the foundation, confirmed by King David, Forfar.
2 —— to Robert Colvill, of the baronie of Wchiltrie, in vicecom. de Air.
3 —— to Thomas Bisset, of the lands of Obeyn, in vic. Aberdeen.
4 —— to the Abbacy of Arbroth, anent their customes and liberties, Forfar.
5 —— to John Stewart, son to Walter Stewart, of the customes of Ed^r. Tenet.

INDEX OF CHARTERS, &c. BY KING DAVID II.

Ane Roll of David II. marked on the back of the Roll with this mark, Da. II. I.
Oboyn.

Willielmus Dominus Gordoun, terrarum de Balmont.　　　　　　　　　　　　　In vicecom.

Vic. F Y F E.

1 Carta to Duncan Wallace, of the lands of Oxinhame, whilk Robert Colvill, Knight, forisfecit, in vic.　　　　　　　　　　　　　　　　　　　　　　　　　　Roxburgh.
2 —— to Malcolm Wallayis, of the lands within the fherifdome of Drumfreis, refigned by Marjorie Fleeming, fofter-fifter to the King, Countefs of Wigtoun, pertaining to Robert Colvill, and quhilk he loft by forfaultrie.
3 —— to Roger Hog, of ane annual furth of the lands of Eiftfentoun, in the conftabulary of Hadingtoun, vic. de　　　　　　　　　　　　　　　　　　　Edinburgh.
4 —— to Allan Erfkine, of the office of the Crownarfhip of Fyfe and Fothryf.
5 —— to Laurence Gillebrand, of ane 20l. penfion out of Balhelvie, in Ab¹,　Aberdeen.
6 —— to Finlay Keiris, of all his lands in general.
7 —— to Roger Cochran, of the lands of Pitfour and Drumgran, in vic. de Perth ; and Kilnamhew, with the chappel, in vicecom. de　　　　　　　　　　　Dumbarton.
8 —— to Alexander Cockburn, of the lands of Buryfield, in the conftabulary of Hadingtoun, vic. de　　　　　　　　　　　　　　　　　　　　　　Edinburgh.
9 —— to Robert Lage, of the lands of Neatherholme, Auldtounayle, four oxgate of land in Moffat, and twa cottages, whilk was ane Wᵐ Wezage and John Plegnans forisfecit.
10 —— to Malcolme Ciffore, of ane annual furth of Leydlovane, vic. de　　　Dumbarton.
11 —— to James Douglas, fon to John Douglas, of the lands of Garmiltoundunyngs, in vicecom. de Edʳ, whilk fell in the King's hands by the baftardie of John Echlis.
12 —— to Ifabel Toulch, fifter to Henry Toulch, of the lands of Toulch, in vic. de　Aberdeen.
13 —— to William Keith, Marifhall of Scotland, and Walter Moygne, of the arrearage and annuels of Oboyn, in vicecom. de　　　　　　　　　　　　　　Aberdeen.
14 —— to William Baillie, of ane annual furth of the cuftomes of Edʳ.
15 —— to our Lady Altar of Dundee.
16 —— given by Margaret Mowbray, to William Wifhart, of the lands of Pitkery.
17 —— to Robert Balbreny of Innercchtie, the office of Mair, and lands of Innerechtie, in vicecom. de Forfar.
18 —— to John Cairns, the place called the Peill of Lithgow, within the burgh of Lithgow, he being obliged to build it for the King's coming.
19 —— to Malcolme Urwell, Chaplain, the keeping of St Leonard's, near Perth.
20 —— given by William Landells Bifhop of St Andrew's, of the advocation and donation of the kirk of Inchore, and chappel of Kinnard annexed thereto, and kirklands thereof,

INDEX OF CHARTERS, &c. BY KING DAVID II. 51

		In vicecom.
21	Carta to John Iles, the reverſion of the barony of Lundie, in vic. de Forfar, after the deceaſe of Jean Counteſs of Stratherne.	
22	—— to the Prior of Inchmahome, of ane annual of 700 s. Sterling furth of the Sheriff's offices of Fyfe and Perth.	
23	—— to Walter Oliphant, of the baronie of Kellie, in vicecom. de Fyfe, by reſignation of Helen Maxwell, daughter and heir of Richard Siward, Knight.	
24	—— of the dotation of the lands of Pitravie, in vic. de Fyfe, to St Nicholas Altar, in the paroch-kirk of Edr, by Roger Hog burges of Edr,	Fyfe.
25	—— to the Prior of Craill, of the ſecond Teinds betwixt the waters of Neithe and Neth.	
26	—— to Stevin More, of the lands of Tullicultrie, in vic. de	Clackman.
27	—— to John of Lorne, and his ſpouſe, of the lands of Glenlyon, in comitatu Atholie.	
28	—— to Thomas Culluchache, of the lands of Barbe, in vic. de	Air.
29	—— to Michael Simorledy, of the lands of Larglane, Blarſkeache, Colonlopagache, Ballemontyre, Coultan, in comitatu de Carrik, in vicecom. de	Air.
30	—— to Sircatho, of ſeven acres of land of Raudilitoun, in vic. de	Edinburgh.
31	—— to the Whyte Friars of Aberdein, of their haill rights.	
32	—— to the Whyte Friers of St Johnſtoun, to the Whyte Friers of Luſnethe, and to the reſt of that order.	
33	—— to James Douglas, of the lands of Croynantoun, Molyn, Rahill, Monygaip, in vicecom. de	Drumfreis.
34	—— of the contract and marriage betwixt Maliſius Earl of Stratherne, Cathneſs, and Orkney, and William Earl of Roſs.	
35	—— given by William More of Abercorn, to William Touris and Helenor Bruce Counteſs of Carrik, of the lands of Dalry, in vic. de	Edinburgh.
36	—— to Ade Irwine, of the lands of Maynes, and fourth part of Coull, in vic. de	Forfar.
37	—— to Alexander Strathaquhin, of the Coronarſhip of Forfar and Kincardine, with 4 l. land out of the ſheriff's offices.	
38	—— to Walter Moygne, of the office of Sherifſhip of Abd ad vitam.	
39	—— to John Craigie, of the lands of Butland, in vic. Edr, by forfaultrie of William Roull,	Edinburgh.
40	—— to Ade Corſour, meſſer, of certain lands in Aymuthe, in Coldinghame, quhilk Margaret Turnbull foriſfecit.	
41	—— to Nicoll Malcolme, of ane tenement in Stirling.	
42	—— by the Bp of Brechine, of the chapple of Bothe, and of the lands of Carncorthie, by William Mauld of Panmore, to the kirk of Brechine.	
43	—— to Andrew Spring, burges of Ab, of ane baſtardie.	
44	—— to Iſabel Fortoun and Thomas Roſs, of the milne of Craigie, in vicecom. de	Edinburgh.
45	—— to John Kennedy, of the lands of Garvan, and ane annual of B ll. ıs lonochans, in comitatu de Carrick, vicecom. de	Air.
46	—— by Robert, ſon of Duncan Earl of Atholl, to Alexander Jeinzeis of Fothergill, upon the marriage of Jean, daughter to the ſaid Robert, one of the heirs of Gleneſk.	

INDEX OF CHARTERS, &c. BY KING DAVID II.

	In vicecom.
47 Carta given by Duncan Earl of Fyfe, to Duncan, fon to Andrew Earl of Athole, of the lands of Difchener and Twehener, in the barony of Strathurde.	
48 —— to John Brown, fon to David Brown, of the lands of Cumerpolftoun, in the conftabularie of Hadingtoun, vic. de	Edinburgh.
49 —— anent the King's revocation.	
50 —— of a penfion to Hew Rofs.	
51 —— to John Murray, of the lands of Innerlethan, in vic. de	Peebles.
52 —— by William Lord Gordoun, to Mr Thomas and Alexander Gordouns, his fons, of the lands of Ballmonth, in vicecom. de Fyfe,	Fyfe.
53 —— given by Elizabeth Auldburgh, of the lands of Braid, Baulay, Colmanftoun, and Ravinifnuick, to John Burgens, Virgin.	
54 —— to Duncan Chapman, burgefs of Ab^d, of the lands of Rotherftoun, near Dee, and the fifhing, in vic. de Ab^l, whilk was John Buchan's, and, by forfaultrie of the faid Duncan, to pertain to William Leith burgefs of Aberdeen,	Aberdeen.
55 —— to William Fodringhay, of the lands of Balhelvie, in vic. Aberdeen, 20l. Stirling, co. by Sir Thomas Murray, to William Batyftoun, of Over and Nether Lachopes, in barony of Bothwell, anno 2do, vicecom. de	Lanerk.
	Tenet.

Ane Roll of David the Second, marked on the back, Da. II. K.

The firft cannot be weill read.

2 Carta to Thomas Erfkine, of the lands of Culnaltoun and Tulchgorne, in vicecom. de	Strivling.
3 —— to Thomas Allards, of ane penfion.	
4 —— to John Dunbar and Ifabell Countefs of Fyfe, of the earldom of Fyfe.	
5 —— to Thomas Culnache, of the lands of Kellwood and Brulane, in vicecom. de Drumfreis,	Drumfreis.
6 —— anent the liberties of Brechine.	
7 —— to James Lindfay, fon to James Lindfay, ane penfion of the cuftomes of Dundee.	
8 —— of refignation, by William Earl of Dowglafs, of the lordfhip of Dalkeith, to Mary Dowglafs, daughter to umquhill William Earl of Douglafs.	
9 —— of refignation, by William Earl of Rofs, of the foreft of Platter, lands of Fincvin, and advocation of the kirk thereof, and of ane new infeftment to the faid Earl.	
10 —— to the inhabitants of the town of Brechine.	
11 —— anent the liberties of Montrofs, for 16 l. Sterling.	
12 —— to Thomas Rait, of the baronie of Urees, in vic.	Kincardin.
13 —— to Alexander Lindfay, of the baronie of Innercaritie, by refignation of Margaret Abernethie Countefs of Angus.	
14 —— to Walter Lefly, of the thanage of Abrekerdor, in vic. Banff, of the thanadge of Kincardine, Fothercardine, and Abrelouchmoir, in vic. de	Kincardin.
15 —— to Alexander Porter, of the new park of Stirling.	
16 —— to John Hering, of the lands of Glafclune, in vicecom.	Perth.

17 Carta to Robert Stewart Earl of Stratherne, of the barony of Methven, v. 100 kowes and 300 sheep going out of Balmonth.   In vicecom.
18 —— Alexandri de Monteith, of a pasturage of the muires of Craill.
19 —— to Richard Cuming, of ane annual furth of the baronies of Carnowsies, in vicecom. Banff, quhilk John Burnard, measser, resigned,   Banff.
20 —— to William Earl of Ross, of the earldom of Ross and lordship of Sky, with ane taillie to Walter Lesly.
21 —— to Donald M'Nayre, of the lands of Easter Fossache, with the Abthanrie of Dull, in vic. de   Perth.
22 —— to Duncan Walleyeis, of the lands of Somdrome, and Drounferne, and Swild, in vicecom. de   Air.
23 —— to Duncan Walleyis, of the lands of Ochterbannak, in vic. de   Stirling.
24 —— to ditto, of ane annuell furth of the lands of Barres, in vicecom. de   Kinkardine.
25 —— to Robert Erskine, of the keeping of the castle of Stirling, and sherifship of Stirling, with 14 chalders of wheat, 12 chalders of oats out of Bothkenner, with 200 marks Sterling out of the lordship.
26 —— to John Bothwell, of the lands of Garrowoll, in vic. de   Banff.
27 —— to David Stewart, son to Robert Stewart Earl of Strathern, of the lands of Kinloch, in vicecom.   Perth.
28 —— to John Barclay, son to David Barclay, of the lands of Colcarny, in vic. de Kinros,   Kinross.
29 —— to Robert Dalnielstoun, of the barony of Glencarne.
30 —— to John Wallayis of Richartoun, of the lands of Moorlecere, in vic. de Forfar. Nota. John Lindsay of Thuirstoun resigned the superiority.
31 —— Bricio Wight, of the lands of Ballachaye and Balloche, in vicecom. de   Kinross.
32 —— to Agnes Dumbar, of ane annual furth of the customes of Ab^d and Hadingtoun.

Ane Roll of David II. marked on the back, Da. II. L.

1 Carta to Robert Meinzies, Knight, of the barony of Enache, in the valleys of Neiche, quhilk Robert Meinzies, his father, resigned in Robert the Great Stewart his hands, for new infestment to be given.
2 —— to Ingrahame Cullan, of the lands of Ochtereny, Auchmyln, Prostoli, and Graindud, and all the lands in Ab^d whilks were John Crabbe's.
3 —— to Andrew Buttergask, of the barony of Troupe, in vic. de Bamfe,   Bamfe.
The half lands of Currokis, in vic. de   Lanerk.
4 —— to the Abbacy de Dumfermling.
5 —— given be John Grahame of Torboltoun, to ——
6 —— to Rannald More, Chalmerlan, of the lands of Formerteine, Akinter, Oboyn, Meikle Morfy, Douny, and Caverays, whilk was Isabel Balliol's, heir to Thomas Balliol.

INDEX OF CHARTERS, &c. BY KING DAVID II.

In vicecom.

7 Carta given by Chriſtian Bruce, of the lands of Edindurnache, in the Garrioch, 100 s. Sterling furth of the lands of Gilberthill, in the Garrioche, to our Lady's chappel in the Garrioch.

8 —— of the erection of Innerbervie in ane free burgh, without prejudice to Aberdeen, Monrofs, and Dundee, Aberbrothock.

9 —— of the kirk of St Qwyntein, of Kirkmacho, in the diocie of Glafgow, to the Abbacy of Arbroth.

10 —— to William Roll, of the forfaulture in general of John Ulmſtoun.

11 —— to Malcolm Fleming, of the baronie of Leigne, Kilmarnnock, the barony of Dallicll, in liberam warennam.

12 —— of ane licrent to Helen, fpoufe to William Mowat. Tenet.

Ane Roll of David II. marked on the back, Da. II. M. M.

1 Carta to William Douglafs, of the lands of Kilbothok and Newlands, by refignation of John Graham of Dalkeith.

2 —— to William Douglafs elder, of the lands of Reidcaſtle, in vic. Forfar, be the forfaultrie of Henry Peircie.

3 —— to Maurice Murray, of the barony of Sprouſtoun, in vicecom.   Roxburgh.

4 —— to Maurice Murray, of the waird of Walter Cuming of Rowallan, in the barony of Hawick, in vic. de Roxburgh, with the lands thereof.

5 —— to Alexander Ramfay, of the land of Hawthorndean, in the barony of Conyrtoun, vic. de Ed', quhilk Laurence Abernethy forifsecit.

6 —— to John Lilly, of ane annual of 30 s. furth of the lands of Smeithfield, in vicecom. de Peebles,   Peebles.

7 —— given by Andrew Murray, pantrieman, and Chriſtian Bruce his fpoufe, to Bernard Spence, of the lands of Vnthank, in the regality of Garrioch, quhilk John Dundenie forisfecit.

8 —— to Simeon Gourlay, of the crownerſhip of Fyfe.

9 —— to John Cowperii, of the Caſtlebank of Abd.

10 —— to Ade Buttergaſk, of the park of Gilchill, in vicecom. de   Banff.

11 —— given by Chriſtian Bruce, Ladie Garviache, to Andrew Buttergaſk, of the lands of Meiklewardurs, Inneralmeſſie, Knokinglafs, within the lordſhip of Garioche, &c.

12 —— given by John Ranulph Earl of Murray, of the lands of Schanquhar, Tullache Drome, with the keeping of the foreſt thereof, to John Wrwell.

13 —— to Ingraham Ardlar, of the lands of Balcorie, whilk William Marſ; ill refigned, in vicecom.   Forfar.

14 —— to John Somerledy of Carrick, 1d. land of Larglan, Blearflach, Culenchopagache, in comitatu Carrick, vicecom.   Air.

15 —— to Archibald Wefchell, of the lands of Ouyn, in the lop. of Garrioch, by refignatioun of Meinzies of Fothergill.

INDEX OF CHARTERS, &c. BY KING DAVID II. 55

In vicecom.

16 Carta blench to Robert Wallayis and his heirs-male only, of the lands of Somdrome and Quyltoun, in baronia de Kyll, and vicecom. de   Air.

17 —— to John Stewart, of the barony of Kellie, by resignation of James Stewart.

18 —— to William Lord Douglas, by resignation made at Ab^d the 26th day of May 1342, by Hew Lord Douglas, and brother and heir to James Lord of Dowglafs, in favour of the said William Lord Douglafs, who was son to Archibald Dowglafs, who was brother to the said James Lord Dowglafs, of the lands of Dowglafdale, Carmichell, the forest of Selkirk, Lauderdale, Bothroull, Efkdaill, Stabilgortoun, Bottill in Galloway, Ramertrak, and ferme of Rutherglen, (with all the liberties of the famen lands, given to James umquhill Earl of Douglas, for his great labours and pains taken in defence of the country), to the said William.

19 —— to Andrew Buttergafk, of the forest of Buyn, in vicecom. de Banff, in excambion for the lands Quhuhame, in vicecom. de   Drumfreis.

20 —— to Andrew Buttergafk, of the lands of Sannak, Culven, and Keltoun, in vicecom.   Drumfreis.

21 —— to Thomas Hill, of the lands of Hill, in vicecom.   Edinburgh.

22 —— to William Reidwall, clark, of the clerkship of the Cockett, in Ab^d. Tenet.

Ane Roll of David II. marked on the back, Da. II. N. Ane bounding Infestment of the Town of Air granted by King William and Alexander.

1 Carta Con. given by Gofpatrick Earl of March, of the kirks of Nifbit and Edrehame, to the Abbacy of Coldinghame, with ane certain annual of Evehame.

2 —— to Simeon Chapman, of the Bauds and Breriebanks, in vicecom. de Lanerk, whilk John Livingftoun wodsett to him,   Lennerk.

3 —— to John Craigie, of the lands of Merchingftoun, in vicecom. de Ed^r, whilk John Crichtoun resigned.   Edinburgh.

4 —— to Simeon Chaklok, of the lands of Fawfide, and Bervor, and ane part of Slanes, in vic. de   Kincardine.

5 —— to the Abbacy of Newbottill, of the lands of Lethame, with the forest thereof.

6 —— given by Walter Biffet, of the half baronie of Culter, in Lanerk, to William Newbiggin Laird of Dunfyir, for his good, commendable, laudable service, except the lands of Nifbet, within the said barony.

7 —— to Ade Pringle, of lands of Langforgound, quhilk Eupham Dumfermling resigned,   Perth.

8 —— to John Binning, of the lands in Ed^r, whilk John Slingifbie forisfecit,   Edinburgh.

9 —— to the burgh of Aire, anent their bounding, granted by William and Alexander Kings of Scotland. Tenet.

INDEX OF CHARTERS, &c. BY KING DAVID II.

Ane Roll of Da. II. marked on the back with this mark, DJ. II. ⊙

In vicecom.

1 Carta to Maurice Murray, of the carldom of Stratherne, whilk Malifius Earl of Stratherne lately overgave and renunced to the Earl of Warran, Englifhman, the haill carldom of Stratherne.

2 —— to Duncan Naper, of the lands of William Ed^r, within the town of Ed^r, by reafon of the forfaultrie of the faid William, who was flain by Robert Ciflore, burgefs of Innerkeithing,   Edinburgh.

3 —— to Duncan Earl of Fyfe, of the coquet of the burgh of Coupar in Fyfe, 15th year of the King's reign.

4 —— to Chriftian Bruce, of the lands of Peteclache, in the 4 part of Paulkland, whilk Duncan Earl of Fyfe refigned, in vicecom. de   Fyfe.

5 —— to Mary Meldrum, fpoufe to Philip Meldrum, of the lands of Logyardoch and Craigie, in vicecom. de   Aberdeen.

6 —— to William Pittilloche, of the forfaultrie of Roger Pringill, of his lands in Whitfome, in vicecom.   Berwick.

7 —— to Ade Buttergafk, of the barony of Weftfuird, whilk Gilbert Maxwell refigned, in vicecom.   Banff.

8 —— to Alexander Craigie, of the lands of Ardlowry, whilk Adam Reidhall refigned, in vicecom. de   Kinrofs.

9 —— to Gilbert Carrik, of the lands of Kenmore, bounding, in vic.   Drumf.

10 —— to Gilbert Clerk of Dumbartan, of the lands of Sehenyllis, whilk Patrick M'Gillen forisfecit, in vicecom. de   Aire.

11 —— to Maurice Murray Earl of Stratherne, of the faid earldom, whilk Malifius Earl of Stratherne gave to the Earl of Warrane, and he tint the famen by forfaultrie.

12 —— of excambion, to Andrew Buttergafk, of the lands of Stormond and Cluny, in vicecom. Perth, to him, for the lands of Ballgillie, in vicecom.   Forfar.

13 —— to Thomas Fawfide, of the lands of Powis and Craigs, of the lands of Plain, vicecom.   Striveling.

14 —— to Bryce Blair, of the lands Myirhall, in vicecom. Peebles, quhilk Laurence Abernethie forisfecit,   Peebles.

15 —— to William Pittillok, of the half lands of Gibliftoun, in vicecom. Fyfe, quhilk John Scot loft by forfaultrie.

16 —— to Nicholas Chicharift, of the forfaultrie of Alexander Cruiks, in conftabulario Lithgow, vic. de   Edinburgh.

17 —— to William Ramfay, of the lands of Eaft Fentoun, quhilk Thomas Hay forisfecit, in vicecom. de   Edinburgh.

18 —— to Laurence Gilliebrand, of the lands of Suthayk, in vicecom. de   Drumfreis.

19 —— to William Murray, fon to Maurice Murray, the forfaultrie of Godfred Rofs, within the baronie of Stanchoufe, vicecom.   Lanerk.

INDEX OF CHARTERS, &c. BY KING DAVID II.

		In vicecom.
20	Carta to John Martenfone, of the lands of Dalwelache, with the fifhing upon the water of Efk, att the earneft defire of the Queen of Scotland,	Efk.
21	—— to Ferquhard Johnftoun, of the lands of Eafterfordy, in vicecom. de	Aberdeen.
22	—— to Alexander Craigie, of the forfaultrie of his father in liferent.	
23	—— to Alexander Meinzies, of the barony of Fothergill, in vicecom. de	Perth.
24	—— to William Herwart, of the office of keeping the King's muire in Craill, and cunningare, in liferent.	
25	—— to John Crawfurd of Cumnock, of keeping of the new foreft of Glenkenne.	
26	—— to Richard Halywall, of the hoftillarie of Traquair, whilk John Craig tint by forfaultrie, 15 Jan. Ann. 15, in vicecom. de	Peebles.
27	—— anent the Clan of Clenconnan, and who fhould be captain thereof,	Galloway.
28	—— anent the Clan of Kenelman.	
29	—— anent the Clan of Muntercafduff, John M'Kennedy Captain thereof.	
30	—— anent the ordaining of John Ranulph Earl of Murray, commendator of the fhirriffdome of Drumfreis.	
31	—— to William More, of the lands of Laftounfcheills.	
32	—— to John Trumble, of the lands of Humdallwalfchop, in the barony of Mener, in vicecom. de	Peebles.
33	—— to Robert Widow, of the lands of Ardkegy, in the barony of Innerlunan, quhilk William Mowat refigned, in vicecom. de Forfar,	Forfar.
34	—— to William Bartillmow, of ane bounding infeftment of the lands called the Quarrellpottis, upon the fouth fide of	Edinburgh.
35	—— to Walter Haliburtoun, of the lands of Nether Lambertoun, in vicecom. de Berwick, quhilk Laurence Abernethie forisfecit,	Berwick.
36	—— by Allan Auldwell, to John Spens, of the lands of Balnkell and Coldoun, in vic. de	Kinrofs.
37	—— to Hew Eglingtoun, of the lands of Bondingtoun and half lands of Nortoun, in the barony of Rathow, in Lothian; ane annual furth of Wefthall.	
38	—— to the Abbey of Reftennet, of ane annual furth of the cuftomes of Dundee, extending to 20 marks Sterling.	
39	—— to Robert Joy, burgefs of Perth, of the forfaultrie of Ade Fouftoune, Englifhman.	

Tenet, except three.

Ane Roll of Da. II. marked on the back, Da. II. Buchanan.

1	Carta Con. given be the Earl of Dowglas, to Laurence Govan, of the lands of Pollinfiche, within the Earldom of Dowglas, in vicecom. de	Lanerk.
2	—— by the Abbacy of Kinlofs, to Donnald Bonnyman, of ane tenement in Theifsgate of Ab^d,	Aberdeen.
3	—— by Alexander Seton, to Ade Forreft, of two pleughs land in the town of Nidderie, in vicecom. de	Linlithgow.

INDEX OF CHARTERS, &c. BY KING DAVID II.

		In vicecom.
4	Carta by John Guildbrune of Balhelvie, to Walter Moygne, Knight, the lands of Auchluchty, within the lordſhip of Ardendrathe, in vicecom. de Ab^d,	Aberdeen.
5	—— by Thomas Biſſet, to William Kergill, of the lands of Brambaine, vic. de	Perth.
6	—— by Adam Salter, to Marjory his ſpouſe, of the lands of Lethbertſcheills.	
7	—— by Margaret Abernethie Counteſs of Angus, to Patrick Innerpeffer, of the lands of Bondingtoun and Newtoun, in vicecom. de	Forfar.
8	—— by James Lindeſay younger, to William Tailzefer, of the lands of Hairclouche. vic. de Lanerk, with a rent of 13 s. 4 d. out of Mudelob,	Lanerk.
9	—— to Andrew Rait, burgeſs of Ed^r.	
10	—— given by Hew Roſs laird of Philorthe, to Alexander Sinclare, ſon of Thomas Sinclare, of the lands of Eiſtertyrie, in vicecom.	Aberdeen.
11	—— by William Earl of Roſs, to the ſaid Alexander Sinclare, of the lands of Bray, within the Mares of Fornwyre, in vicecom.	Innerneſs.
12	—— by Donald Earl of Lennox, to Maurice Buchannan, of that pleugh of land called commonly Buchannan, &c. containing the bounding.	Tenet.

Ane Roll of David the Second, marked on the back, Da. II. C. S. X.

1	Carta Con. given by the Abbacie of Kelcow, of the kirk of Ingliſchmalholks, in valle de Clyde,	Lanerk.
2	—— by Richard Edzear, to John Crawfurd in Togher, the lands of Kilpatrick Nether,	Drumfreis.
3	—— by Patrick Callenter, to Henry Dowglas and his ſpouſe, of the lands of Callentar, in vicecom. de Striveling,	Striveling
4	—— by Robert Keith Mariſchall, to John Maitlane, his ſiſter's ſon, the lands of Cowanſtoune.	
5	—— by Robert, Steward of Scotland, to William Liddell, of the lands of Lochullike, in the barony of Bathcat,	Lenlithgow.
6	—— by Henric Braid of that Ilk, to Henry Multra, of the lands of Greenhill, of the conſtabulary of	Edinburgh.
7	—— to Thomas Lumiſdaine, of the lands of Drum, Condland, in vicecom. de Fyfe, and Eaſter and Weſter Maler, in Ab^d, by the Earl of Fyfe,	Fyfe.
8	—— to Robert Keith, of the lands of Keith Mareſchall, the office of Mareſchallſhip of Scotland, Keith Symon, Colbanſtoun, Alneden, in Buchan, with the new foreſt of Innerpeffer, four davach of land in Strathbogie, the foreſt of Kintore, by reſignation of Robert Keith his father.	
9	—— by David Hay of Erroll, to William Spens burgeſs of Perth, of the lands of Glaſbany, in the baronie of Erroll,	Perth.
10	—— anent the liberty and conſuetude of Ab^l.	
11	—— by Thomas Hay, to Thomas Monypenny of Pitmillie, of his part of the lands within the barony of Lucheris, in vic.	Perth.
12	—— to Alexander Ramſay, of the barony of Kernock, in vicecom. de Fyfe,	Fyfe.

INDEX OF CHARTERS, &c. BY KING DAVID II. 59

In vicecom.
13 Carta to John Monypenny of Pitmillie, of the lands of Drumranet, in the baronie of
 Craill, in vic. de   Fyfe.
14 —— by Walter Maule of Panmore, to John Monypenny, of Skonie, Ballefchane of
 Cambingftoun, Greenford, Carncorthie, Petcouran of Witfield, with the Maynes
 thereof, the baronie of Balhoufie, in vicecom.   Forfar.
15 —— by Alexander Stewart of Strathawin, to Patrick Gourlay, upon the half lands of
 Blanne.
16 —— by Chriftian Bruce, to Ade Buttergafk, of the lands of Wichcrofs, within the regality of Garrioche.
17 —— to the Abbacy of Kelcow, of all the forfaultries of all the rebels within Berwick.
18 —— by Edward Hadden, to his fpoufe, in conjunct fee, of the lands of Brochtoun, in
 vicecom. de   Peebles.
19 —— to James Tweedie, of Drummellier, in vicecom. de   Peebles.
                                                                                                                                 Tenet.

Ane Roll of Dav. II. R. Thanedom of Cluny to the Frazer.

1 Carta to Hew Dalnielftoune, of his lands in general whilk belonged to Margaret
 Mufchett, one of the heirs of William de Montefixo, whilk fhe loft by forfaultrie.
2 —— to Hew Blair, of the forfaultrie of Euftace Lorane in generall.
3 —— to the Abbacy of Dryburgh, of the advocation of the kirks of Beate Marie Virginis, in Ettrik foreft.
4 —— to William Flemying, fon to Symon Flemyng, of the lands of Kirkmichell, with
 the multure, with licence to him to big ane milne upon Leven for to ferve his
 lands,   Dumbarton.
5 —— to William Pettillok, herauld, the three hufband lands of the town of Bonjedward,
 by forfaultry of Roger Pringill, in vic. de Roxburgh, with the reft of his for-
 faultrie,   Roxburgh.
6 —— to Walter Halyburtoun, of the lands of Segey, Craiginfermer, Ledlewnewle, Lade-
 glafchun, with the bounding of the pafture of Oyglethe, in vicecom. de   Kinrofs.
7 —— to Robert Cuninghame younger, of the lands of Garvard, the lands called 5 pen-
 ney land, in vicecom. Argadie, blench, ane pair of gloves.
8 —— to Hew Danyelftoun, of the forfaultrie of David Marfhall, Knight, except Danyelftoun, which Thomas Carno gat by gift, and the lands of Corftorphing, whilk
 Malcolm Ramfay got.
9 —— to Thomas Meinzeis, of the lands of Weft and North Cultnachy, Burliche, Ballingall Eifter, Teminynane, extending to a 40 marks land, pays 6 s. 8 d. Sterling,
 in vicecom. de   Kinrofs.
10 —— to Gilbert Gacefter, of the lands of Edderlings, Cambyfenew, Garvald, 1 (2)
 Canrenis, Craigeneneur, (2) Oywalds, Calkilkeft, whilk John Ewinfon loft by
 forfaultrie, in vicecom. de   Argyle.

INDEX OF CHARTERS, &c. BY KING DAVID II.

	In vicecom.
11 Carta to Margaret Corbet Lady M'Craftoun, of annual of M'Creftoun, quhilk William Beaton forisfecit.	
12 —— to Thomas Carnok, of his lands within Selkirk, and the miln thereof, with ane narration of his father's fervice and his awin, and the lands in Kinghorne whilk he poffefied, blench, leporarium,	Selkirk.
13 —— to Bartall Loen, and Philippa Moubray his fpoufe, of the lands of Barnbowgill, in vicecom. de Ed^r, whilk John Grahame Earl of Monteith and his fpoufe refigned.	
14 —— to William Frazer, and Margaret Murray his fpoufe, of the thanedome of Durris and thanedom of Collie, whilk thanedome of Collie was Alexander Frazer's, his father, with lands of Efkyltuh, in	Kincardine.
15 —— to Ailan Fawfide, of the lands of Balmakewin, Altoun, Abreluthnok, in vicecom. de	Kincardine.
16 —— to John Doun, of the lands of Ardache, Skeithis, in vicecom. de	Banf.
17 —— to John Reyntoun, of the forfaultrie of Thomas Riddle, in the town of	Berwick.
18 —— to Godfray Rofs of Conynghameheid, the miln of Craigie, in vicecom. de	Perth.
19 —— to John Bruce, the toun of Kinrofs, the lands of Enachrache, Coftigorer, Welew, Wallachan, Macoiche, Wroclache, the miln of Quorthie, Tochintollie, Macherderrly, and Larache.	
20 —— to Roger Purvoyis, of the Ifle of Arry and Slepeles, with the fifhing pertaining thereto upon Taye.	
21 —— to Walter Halyburtoun, Knight, and John Hume, the forfaultrie of John Stratherne in general.	
22 —— to Margorie Chalmer, of ane cuftom in Perth,	Perth.
23 —— to John Spence, of the lands of Eifter Tollumache, Cultbuy, fourth part Balleleneche, in vicecom. de Kinrofs, blench, 4s. argenti,	Kinrofs.
24 —— to Chriftian Lundy and her fifter, of the lands of Sheks, in the conftabulary Lithgow, vic.	Edinburgh.
25 —— to John Tennand, of the lands of Laureftoun, with 40 creills of peitts in Crawmond, in vic. de Ed^r, pays 33s. 4d. Sterling to the King, and 33s. 4d. Sterling to the Bifchop of Dunkeld,	Edinburgh.
26 —— to William Rofs, of twa rude of land in the town of Innernefs, bounded,	Innernefs.
27 —— to Nicoll Enokdolian, of ane penny land near his land, and Dalfupin, upon the fouth fide of Garvan, vic. de	Air.
28 —— to Hew Danielftoune, of the difcharge of the caftlewards in the barony of Glencardine, in vicecom. de	Drumfreis.
29 —— to John Aytoune, of the lands of Over Pettedie, in the fhyre of Fyfe, halfe boll for every chalder at Kinghorne,	Fyfe.
30 —— to Robert, Great Stuart of Scotland, of the lands of Kyntire, with the advocation of the kirks thereof in fee; and to John Stewart, his fon, gotten betwixt him and Elizabeth More, daughter to Adam More, Knight, and failzeing of John, to Walter, his fecond brother,	Kintire.

INDEX OF CHARTERS, &c. BY KING DAVID II. 61

		In vicecom.
31	Carta be Malcolm Fleming Earl of Wigtoun, to Robert Dumbartan, clerk of regifter, of the lands of Hallys and Letbernard, in vicecom.	Edinburgh.
32	—— by Hew Giffard, Laird Zefter, to John Douglas, fon to James Lord Douglas, viz. the barronies of Zefter, Morhame, Duncanlau, in vicecom. de Ed^r; Te- lin, in vicecom. Forfar; Polgavite, vicecom. Perth; Herbertfhire, in vicecom. Stirling,	Forfar, Perth, Forfar, Stirling.
33	—— to Edward Keith, of fome lands, given to him by Edward Keith Marefchall.	

Ane Roll of Da. II. marked on the back, S, Dundie, Gafk.

1 Carta to the Abbot of Coupar, of the kirk of Erroll, given by Gilbert Hay of Erroll, Conftable of Scotland.
2 —— to John Marr, Channon of Ab^d, and Prebendary of the kirk of Innernauchty, of the lands of Cruterftoun, in the Garrioch, vic. de Ab^d, given by Thomas Earl of Marr, Lord Garrioche and Cavers, una cum Lege Flemynga dicitur Fleming Lauche; Liddell, then fheriff of Ab^d, is witnefs.
3 —— to William Nepar, of the half lands of Petfour, Perknoe, vic. Perth, the half lands of Killmahew, where the chappel is fituate, vic. Dumbartan, by forfaltrie of Dornagill Montefixo.
4 —— to Sir William Forrefter, and Elizabeth Mungall his fpoufe, of all the lands whilk pertained to William Falkirk, except Alderrumny, whilk Robert Wallace got.
5 —— to Malcolm Culchone, of the lands of Gafk, and 13s. 4d. furth of the lands of Balmalyn, vic. — Aberdeen.
6 —— to Margaret Abernethy Countefs of Angus, of 16 l. furth of the lands of Aberne- thie in liferent, in vicecom. de — Perth.
7 —— to Chriftian Anderfon, of the lands of Alice Lundie and Edward Lettam, by for- faultrie.
8 —— to Patrick M'Cowrache, for the coronnarfhip by-north the water of Creiche.
9 —— to John Wygun, of ane tenement in Ed^r, whilk was Birkin Meiks, — Edinburgh.
10 —— to the Abbacy of Cambufkenneth, of ane certain duty furth of Tullimuchache, vic. — Stirling.
11 —— to Robert Stuart, of the barrony of Stanboithie, (by Thomas Murray Lord of Bothwell), vic. de Clackmannan, ward — Clackmannan.
12 —— to Janet Monypenny, of the 3d part of Leuchars, in vicecom. de Fyfe, — Fyfe.
13 —— to Thomas Cranftoun, of the barony of Stobbs, within the barony of Caueris, vicecom. de Roxburgh, by the Earl of Marr, — Roxburgh.
14 —— to John Balnhard, of the lands of Carnagie, in the barony of Panmuire, in vice- com. de Forfar, given by Walter Mauld, — Forfar.
15 —— to the town of Dundee.
16 —— to Alexander Lindfay, fon to Sir David Lindfay, Lord of Crawfurd, and Kath- rine Stirling his fpoufe, ane of the heirs of Sir John Stirling of Glenefk, of all their lands in vicecom. de Inuernefs and — Innernefs, Forfar.

INDEX OF CHARTERS, &c. BY KING DAVID II.

	In vicecom.
17 Carta to Alexander Lindfay, of the barony of Byres, given by Sir James Lindfay, his brother, in vicecom. de	Edinburgh.
18 —— to Alexander Lindfay, of the lands of Achibeton, given by Thomas Earl of Angus,	Forfar.
19 —— to Robert Glen, of the lands of Glafgow le Foreft, in the thanedome of Kintor, blench,	Aberdeen.
20 —— to Thomas Nefbit, of the lands of Edrintoun, by refignation of Andrew Clarky, blench,	Peebles.
21 —— to Allan Lawder, of 10 l. furth of the jufticiary by-fouth Forth.	
22 —— to Ranald Chene, of the fourth part of Kathnefs, given by William Fedrey,	Innernefs.
23 —— to John Petillock, of the forfaultrie of Roger Pringle, Mem. in Parliamento apud Scoon, 6 Novembris, anno regni regis 28, David the Second makes a general revocation.	
24 —— to Marjory Murray, of the lands of Morphie, Cantuly, in vicecom. de	Kincardin.
25 —— to Margaret Countefs of Angus, fpoufe to umquil Sir John Sinclare, of 20 l. Starling furth of the duties of Colley.	
26 —— to Hew Crawford of Clyddifdale, of ane pleugh of land in Heffilden, in the barony of Stanehoufe, vic. de Lanerk, of the lands of Blancaurig, in the barony of South Channan, given be Flemming of Biggar,	Lanerk.
27 —— to the Abbot of Lindoris, of the kirk of Aughtermuchty, given by Duncan Earl of Fyfe. Mention is made here of the battle of Durhame.	
28 —— to Robert Lord Erefkine, of the barony of Kinoull, by refignation of Ifabel Fyfe, heir to Duncan fometime Earl of Fyfe, in vic. de	Perth.
29 —— to ditto, of the cuftomes of Dundee and 3d part of Pettarache, blench, vic. Forfar, quhilk fometime pertained to John Campbell Earl of Athol,	Forfar.
30 —— to the Prior of Man, of 5 merks furth of Perth.	
31 —— to the Bifhop of Ab^d, of his fecond teinds, in vic. de	Banff and Ab^d.
32 —— of ane donation, by John Scot burgefs of Innernefs, to Lady Chappel,	Innernefs.
33 —— to William Touris, of certain land in Ab^d, (general).	
34 —— to the Vicear, of ane net's fifhing in Forth, and four aikers of land,	Stirling.
35 —— to the Earl of Carrik, of his liberties,	Air.
36 —— to Chriftian Johnftoun, of the lands of Wefter Fondowy, given by William Earl of Douglas, in vic.	Perth.
37 —— to William Sincler, of the lands of Balgorthy, by refignation of William Earl of Rofs, in vicecom.	Fyfe.
38 —— to Sir Robert Erfkine, and Chriftian Keith his fpoufe, of Walyftoun and Elgereth, given by Thomas Murray of Bothuel, in	Lanerk.
39 —— to Margaret Seaton, daughter to umquill Sir Alexander Seaton, of her togher of the 20 l. land of Lamingtoun,	Lanerk.
40 —— to Robert Meinzeis, of the barony of Enach, in Niddifdale, viccecom. de	Drumfreis.
41 —— to Thomas Hill, of the lands of Sandhaugh and half of Auchinbedy, given by Thomas Earl of Marr, in vic. de	Banff.
42 —— to John Ifaac, of ane penfion.	

INDEX OF CHARTERS, &c. BY KING DAVID II. 63

	In vicecom.
43 Carta to John Mercer, of the lands of Pettland, in Strathurd, by the Earl of Dowglas.	
44 —— to John Lindfay of Thor, of the lands of Murletyre, wherein is mention of the burning of Failliekyll, in vicecom. de	Forfar.
45 —— to William Earl of Dowglas, of the fheriffship of	Lanerk.
46 —— to Robert Dalzell, of the ferjandfhip of Lanerk, by refignation of Andrew Starheved,	Ibidem.
47 —— to William Giffard, of the clerkfhip of the cockquet.	
48 —— to David Libbertoun, of the office of fergandrie of the overward of the conftabulary of Ed^r, with the lands of Over Libbertoun pertaining thereto, in vicecom. de Ed^r,	Edinburgh.
49 —— to Allan Lauder, of ane penfion furth of the jufticiarie be-fouth Forth.	
50 —— to John Burgh, maiffer, paffagium babellæ aque de Forth, juxta	Stirling.
51 —— to John Hefwell, of the lands of Kingifland, in	Peebles.
52 —— to Ade Cofour, maiffer, of the lands of Otterburn,	Berwick.
53 —— to William Earl of Sutherland, and umquill Margaret Bruce, fifter to the King, of the barony of Downy, vic. Forfar, baronies Kincardin, and Aberluthnok, and Fettercardin, vic. Kincardin, half of Formartein, half of the thandome of Kintore, in vic. de	Aberdein.
54 —— to Thomas Harkars, of the baronie of Preftoun, vic. Drumfreis, by refignation of Bartilmo Loon and Philippa Moubray, holden of the Earl of Douglafs, in vic.	Drumfreis.
	Tenet.

KELCOW.

Ane little Roll, containing three Charters.

1. Carta to the Abbacy of Kelcow, being burnt by England, to cut wood in Selkirk and Jedwart forefts for reparation,   Selkirk.
2. —— to the Abbacy of Kelcow, making the town of Kelcow, Bolden, and Reverden in ane regalitie.
3. —— to Lefmahago, difcharging them of all impofts.

Ane Roll of Da. II. markit on the back, S. (a)

1. Carta Con. of Alex^r King of Scots, to the Abbacie of Aberbrothe, of the barrony of Nig, and confirmit be the faid David,   Forfar.
2. —— Con. to the Abbacie of Aberbrothe, grantit be Robert the Firft, of the lands of Dollandaldftoun, Dronfled, Culbakie, Monbodok, Blenferkin, Fafdauache, the half of Tuberache, tua pairt of Kinkell, Petmagarterache,   Forfar.

                        Ane of A.
                        Tent.

(a) This Roll is omitted in the Mufeum copy.

INDEX OF CHARTERS, &c. BY KING DAVID II.

Ane Roll of Da. II. marked on the back, Da. II. T.

1 Carta anent the liberties of Lindoris, and of the lands of Craigie, Mylntoun, Claypotts, Balmow. — In vicecom.
2 —— to Alexander Cockburn, of the lands of Carriddin, in vic. de — Edinburgh.
3 —— by David Lord of Crawford, to the Abbacy of Lindoris, ane quantity of walx furth of the lands of Cairnye.
4 —— by Thomas Earl of Marr, to Eugene Fergufon, of the lands of Uchtererne, in Cromar, — Aberdeen.
5 —— to John Herice, of the barony of Traucriglis, by refignation of Thomas Earl of Marr, in vicecom. — Drumfreis.
6 —— to Robert Bruce, the King's coufin, of the lands of Germainftoun, of Canetgaitifend, Petfouldoun, Germanftoun, Kerfs, Park, Medowis, Grogary, Gartindoe, Dryfield, in vicecom. de Clackmannan, taillie, — Clackman.
7 —— to William Fawfide, and Marion Fleming his fpoufe, of the milne of Talligartis, called the Lynd Miln, in vicecom. de — Clackman.
8 —— to the Abbacy of Cambufkenneth, of ane penfion forth of the lands of Plain, vic. de — Stirling.
9 —— to William Spence, burges of Perth, — Perth.
10 —— to the Abbacy of Lindoris, of the half lands of Eafter Craigie, in the barony of Barnbowgall, — Edinburgh.
11 —— to Ade Forrefter, of the half lands of Whytburne, in conftab. of Linlithgow, vic. de — Edinburgh.
12 —— to William Dalzell, of fyve pund Starling furth of the town and fheriffdom of Lanerk, as ferjand, either out of the fheriff compt or juftice air, — Lanerk.
13 —— to Robert Muterer, burges of Ed^r, of the lands within the barony of Reftalrig whilk pertained to John Colti, — Edinburgh.
14 —— to our Lady altar in the kirk of Ed^r, of the lands of Rayliftoun, — Edinburgh.
15 —— to Robert Bodefield, by Sir William More, of all his lands in Drumfreis, and fourtie acres in Traquair.
16 —— to Fergus Edinghame, burges of Ed^r, of ane tenement of land in Ed^r, on the fouth fide of the croce of Ed^r, wadfet to him by Moffat, — Edinburgh.
17 —— by William Cunningham Earl of Carrick, to James Likprevick, of the half lands in Polkarne, in Kingfkyll, vic. de — Air.
18 —— to the Abbacy of Lindoris, of the half lands of Eaft Craigis, in the barony of Barnbowgall, vic. de Ed^r, by refignation of Bartilmo Loon and Philippa Moubray his fpoufe.
19 —— by John Conftable, burgefs of Abdy, to the Carmelite Friers in the Abbay, four mark Sterling money forth of ane annualrent out of the thieff's gate of Aberdeen, the fouth fide thereof.
20 —— to Robert Eviot, of the half lands of Caffindole, the lands of Balguhcraignen, the lands of Talling, the miln of Sheres.

INDEX OF CHARTERS, &c. BY KING DAVID II.

	In vicecom.
21 Carta by Dowgall M'Dowgall, to John Turnbull, of the 4 mark lands of Litlegrewy, within the lordſhip of Kirkaſſudie, in vicecom. de Drumfreis, and 20 l. land of Glengarg and Glencraig,	Drumfreis.
22 —— to the town of Ldr, of ane piece land within the town, and bounded, near to the caſtle.	
23 —— to William Gladſtones, of the lands of Wodgrenyntoun, Winkyſtoun, Acomfield, in vic. de Peebles, whilk Patrick Maxwell reſigned,	Peebles.
24 —— to ditto, of the annual furth of Wynkiſtoun, Woodgrenyntoun, in vicecom.	Peebles.
	Tenet.

Ane Roll of David II. marked on the back with this mark, Da. II. IV.

1 Carta to Andrew Murray, of the lands of Tulchadame, Tulchmaler, in vicecom. de	Sterling.
2 —— to Alexander Frazer, of the thanedome of Doris,	Kincardin.
3 —— to Ar^d Douglas, of the lands of Clerkingtoun, half barony of Culter, in vicecom. de Lanerk, which Walter Biſſet reſigned,	Lanerk.
4 —— to William Diſhingtoun, of the lands of Kinbrackmont, vic. de Fyfe, quhilk Walter Biſſet reſigned,	Fyfe.
5 —— to Henry Douglas, of the 3d part of the lands of Logtoun, in vic. de Ed^r, quhilk Thomas Watſon reſigned,	Edinburgh.
6 —— to Ar^l Douglas, of the earldom of Galloway, containing the bounding,	Galloway.
7 —— to Robert Danielſtoun, of the lands of Treipwood, in vicecom. de Lanerk, by the forfaultrie of ane Haiſlie,	Lanerk.
8 —— Con. to the Abbacy of Melros, for the wards, reliefs, marriages, eſcheats, annualrents of ſheriff-courts and juſtice-courts within the ſheriffdome of Roxburgh,	Roxburgh.
9 —— to Thomas Heuwyll, of the lands of Coulyn and Roucan, in vicecom. de	Drumfreis.
10 —— to Thomas Raythe, of the lands of Balgillachie, in vic. de	Forfar.
11 —— to William Ramſay of Dalhouſie, of the lands of Nether Libbertoun, with the 8th part called King's park,	Edinburgh.
12 —— to James Douglas, ſon to James Douglas, of the barony of Dalkeith, with ane taillie, blench, for ane pair of gloves att the caſtle of Dalkeith, if it be ſought ; taillie inviolable, in vic. de	Edinburgh.
13 —— to Fergus Ayrth, of all his lands in general.	
14 —— to Alexander Lindſay, of the barony of Innerratie, by reſignation of Margaret Abernethy Countefs of Angus, in vic. de	Forfar.
15 —— to Walter Lefly, of the reverſion of the thanedome of Kincardine, Abrecouthnot, Fetherkern, from William Earl of Sutherland, vic. de	Kincardin.
16 —— to ditto, of the thanedome of Abrekeldoure, the lands of Blairfenache, in vic. de	Banff.
17 —— to the Earl of March, of the erection of the town of Dumbare in a free burgh.	
18 —— to William Earl of Douglas, of the lands of Balmonth, quhilk John Gordon reſigned, in vic. de	Fyfe.

R

INDEX OF CHARTERS, &c. BY KING DAVID II.

	In vicecom.
19 Carta to Thomas Spring, of the lands of Gatkin, in vicecom. de Ab^d, by refignation of M'Guffock.	
20 —— anent the protection and liberties of Halyroodhoufe.	
21 —— to John Areler, of the lands of Ardber, Baldowrie, in vic. de	Forfar.
22 —— to John Latoren, of his freedom.	
23 —— to John Hereice, of the lands of Achray, and ane annuall of 20 merks furth of the lands of Skeok, in vic. de Stirling, blench,	Stirling.
24 —— of the liberties of Halyruidhoufe betwixt Alvyn and Colbrandefpath.	
25 —— to John Hereice, of 20 marks furth of Skeok, viceeom. de	Stirling.

Ane Roll of David II. marked on the back, Da. II. X. X.

1 Carta by William Keith Marefchall, who married Margaret Frazer, heir to Frazer of Stratherhin, to Ade Pringle and his fpoufe, of the lands of Knoc and Galachan, in the barony of Stratherhin,	Aberdeen.
2 —— to William Earl of Sutherland, of the half of the barony of Formartein, vic. de	Aberdeen.
3 —— to John Bothwell, of eleven pund Sterling, with four chalder of victual of the thanedom of Doun, in vicecom. de	Banff.
4 —— to Brice Wacht, of the lands of Ballachache, in vic. de	Kinros.
5 —— to Walter Maxwell, of the lands of Capringftoun,	Peebles.
6 —— to Marthaco Rind, of four oxengate of land of Cafs, and four oxengate of land in foreft of Platter, in vicecom. de 23.	Forfar.
7 —— to Walter Lefly and his fpoufe, the new foreft of Drumfreis.	
8 —— given by Philip Arbuthnet, to the Carmalite Friars of Ab^d, of 13 s. Sterling forth of his lands of Arbuthnet.	
9 —— to Robert Sincler, of the lands of Finlater, in vic.	Banf.
10 —— to the Abbacy of Reftennet, furth of the lands of Memmure.	
11 —— to the Lady Altar St Geills, of ane tenement in Ed^r, given by William Hare burgefs of Ed^r,	Edinburgh.
	Tenet.

Ane Roll of Da. II. marked on the back, Da. II. Y.

1 Carta to the Coronarfhip of Ed^r, given to John Edmanftoun.	
2 —— given by Margaret Monfode, to Walter ············ her fpoufe, of the lands Hebeddees, vic.	Lanerk.
3 —— Con. given by Margaret Abernethie Countefs of Angus, to William Monfode, of the lands of Balmedy.	
4 —— to Alexander Lindfay, of ane annual of 9 merks furth of Glenefk, in vicecom. de Forfar.	
5 —— to John Mercer, of ane tenement in Perth.	

INDEX OF CHARTERS, &c. BY KING DAVID II. 67

In vicecom.
6 Carta to David Spring, of ane annual of 20 marks furth of Meikle Morfie, 100 s. furth of Durfclume.
1 —— Con. given by Patrick Dumbar Earl of Murray, to John Hepburne, of the lands of Over and Nether Merkill.
2 —— to Alexander Ruclintoun, of ane tenement in   Edinburgh.
3 —— to John Gray, clerk of regifter, of ane penfion.
4 —— to Ade Page, of ane penfion.
5 —— to Robert Lauder, juftice by-north the water of Forth, of ane penfion.
6 —— to Roger Hog, burgefs of Edr.
7 —— by John Hay, to John Young vicar of Fordyis, of the lands of Rowbaiky, in Doun, in vicecom.   Banff.
8 —— to William Sommer, of ane annual furth of Baldevie, with the miln thereof, vic. Banff.
9 —— of a penfion to Andrew Kirkaldie.
10 —— ane penfion to the Vicar of Lithgow, in all time coming, by the King, of eleven pund Stirling furth of the cuftoms of Lithgow.
11 —— to Robert Corrie, and Eupham his fpoufe, daughter to Thomas Torthorwald, who was flain at the battle of Durham. The Lady of Cowlyn and Buchan, in vic. Drumfreis.
12 —— Con. given by William More of Abercorne, to David Meldrum, of the half of the lands of Weft Byres, within the barony of Abercorn.
—— ane penfion to Walter Lefly furth of the cuftoms of Dundee.
1 —— Con. by Rodger Mortimer of Foullis, to his wife.
2 —— Con. by the faid Rodger, to his fpoufe, called Margaret Monteith, daughter to Alexander Monteith, of the lands of Cuthillmyre.
3 —— to John Logie (perhaps for Lion) of that Ilk, of the thanedom of Thanades, and the reverfion of the thanedom of Glamis, B.
4 —— to Agnes Kelouer, of the lands of Kepancnate and the new park of Stirling.
5 —— to William Barnes, of the lands of Eafter and Wefter Quhyburne.
6 —— to James Dowglafs, of the annuals of Efchelis, Horfbrukis, Eafter Hopkillow, and Newbie, in vicecom.   Peeble.
1 —— to Malcolme Fleming, of the lands of Rinns of Wigtoun, bounding.
2 —— to ditto, of the lands of Sthboger, in the barony of Leinzie, whilk Thomas Balcafky forisfecit, B.

STIRLING.

3 Carta to Maurice Murray, of the lands of Atheren, in vic.   Stirling.
4 —— to Henry Marfhell, of the forfaultrie of Hoffewell.
5 —— to Hew Urrye, of the forfaultrie of Ofbert, within the vic. of Stirling, with the ferjeandrie of the faid fhyre.
6 —— to Walter Moygn, of the foreft of Drymnie, in vic.   Kincard.
7 —— to Ade Argente, of the lands of Lethbertfheills, whilk William Lundie forisfecit, in vicecom. &c   Sterling.

INDEX OF CHARTERS, &c. BY KING DAVID II.

		In vicecom.
8 —— to Robert Wallayis, of 10 merks annual furth of the lands of Durris, in vic. Kincardine, quhilk John Earl of Buchan forisfecit,		Kincardine.
9 —— to Hew Urry, of the forfaultrie of Osbert Stirling, within the sherifdom of Stirling, and the 100s. land of Sallochill, quhilk Adam except Chalmer had in poffeffion.		
10 —— to Gilbert Carrik, Knight, of the lands of Buchannan, for 8 mark Stirling, in vicecom. de		Stirling.
11 —— to David Chalmer, of the lands of Breirtoun, in vic. Kincardine, with the half lands of Polmais, in vic. Stirling, quhilk John Urwell refigned at Kaldrome.		
12 —— to Hew Blair, of the lands of Easter Maler, for 10l. Stirling, in vicecom. de		Perth.
13 —— given by John Inchtour, to Gilbert Innerlunan, of Balgallie.		
14 —— to John Dun, of the lands of Ardache and Skethis, in vic.		Banff.
15 —— by Duncan Earl of Fyfe, of the lands of Thomaftoun, to Roger Mortimer, in vic.	Fyfe.
16 —— Con. given by John Cambroun, to Roger Mortimer, of the lands of Lochtoun, in vic.		Perth.
17 —— to Rennald Chene, of the lands of Carnfewald, Landis of Ardenly.		
1 —— to Arthur Campbell, quod nulli fubjicitur, pro terris nifi regi.		
2 —— to Dougall Conynghame, quod nulli fubjicitur, pro terris nifi regi.		
3 —— given by Robert Erfkine, of the erection of the kirk of Kinnoul to the Abbacie of Cambufkenneth.		
1 —— given by Alexander Meinzies of Reidhall, to John Biffet, of the lands of Swanftoun and Pillmoorie, with 6s. annuitie of Reidhall.		
—— to Robert Stewart of Stanebothie, of the half lands of Reidcaftle, in vic. Forfar, quhilk Andrew Campbell refigned,		Forfar.
2 —— given by Andrew Campbell, to Robert Stewart, of the lands of Withitonn and Ballendallache, within the barony of Reidcaftle, vic.		Forfar.
3 —— to the Abbacy of Newbottle, the lands of Lathan, with free foreft.		
4 —— to the Abbacy of Lindoris, Meadow Spot, with the meadow and yard called Stodfald, with power to caft fewall in the muire of Braid.		
5 —— to John Hereice, of the lands of Kirkunying, with the place where the monaftrie of Holme ftude, in vic. de		Drumfreis.
6 —— to Duncan Fras, (probably for Frafer), of the lands of Brounemeky, Mullbyne, Ordycheyes, in comitatu Moravie, and of Orehnefy, Balmariot, Auchmore, vic.	Banff.
7 —— to William Boyd, of the lands of Anchmar, quhilk Duncan Lufs forisfecit,		Dumbarton.
8 —— to John Reid, conftable of the caftle of Edr, of the lands and foreft of Lochindorbe, in vic. Innernefs, quhilk John Cuming forisfecit. This is found to be eiked to this roll of Y.		

Ane Roll of Da. II. marked on the back with this mark, Da. ∞

1 Carta to John Gray, clerk of regifter, of the burrow maills of Peebles.
2 —— to William Chalmer, of the juftice-clerkfhip by-north Forth.
3 —— to John Innerpeffer, of the fhereffship of Banff.

INDEX OF CHARTERS, &c. BY KING DAVID II.

4 Carta to Bryce Wyght, of the lands of Balloche, in vicecom. de   In vicecom. Kinrofs.
5 ——— to Robert Annand, of ane annual furth of the cuftomes of Ab^d.
6 ——— to Hew Rofs, of the lands of Doun, in vic.   Banff.

Tenet.

Ane Book in Parchment.

Carta to John Grahame de Dalkeith, de terris de Elvingftoun,   Edinburgh.
    The reft of the firft fide cannot be read.
Carta Domini Willielmi de Wallibus, of the offices of the fherifship and conftabulary of Elgine.
——— Andree Spring, of a piece of land within the town of Aberdeen.
——— Andree de Erfkine, of the lands of Raplache,   Sterling.
——— Hugonis de Dumbar, of 10 marks Sterling of the cuftomes of Ab^d,   Aberdeen.
——— Willielmi de Levingftoun, of the lands of Kilfyth,   Dumbarton.
——— donatio Willielmo de Ramfay, of 20 l. Sterling, to be paid by the Chamberlain of Scotland.
——— Walteri, fil. Auguftini, of the lands of Nidrie,   Edinburgh.
——— Allani de Grahame, of the lands of Mertoun.
——— capituli Aberdonenfis, of the right of the patronage of the kirk of Logie.
——— ejufdem capituli de parko de Garquhill.
——— Gilberti de Glencharnye, of the barony of Glencharnye,   Invernefs.
——— Joannis Reid, for his lifetime, of the lands of Pellynflott.
——— Joannis de Haya, of the haill lands betwixt the water Spey, &c.
——— Joannis de Urgwell, of the lands of Stanquhar, Tulloch, and Drum.
——— of the right of the patronage of the kirk of Philorthe to the Bifhop of Ab^d.
——— Joannis de Rofs, of the lands of Gilcolmiftoune.
——— Ade Pringle, of the lands of Knock and Gilftoune,   Kincardine.
——— fratrum predicatorum de Ab^d, of 100s. Starlings out of the barony of Banchrie de Devenie.
——— Waltero de Moravia, of the lands of Tullibardin, &c.   Perth.
——— Alexandri Cockburne, of 20 l. Stirling out of the cuftoms of the burgh of Haddingtoun.
——— Joannis de Riddell, of the lands of Cranftoun,   Edinburgh.
——— Roberti, Senefcalli, of the lands of Dalyell and Modrall,   Lanerk.
——— Joannis, filii Joannis, of a 10 l. land in the barony of Eldenethe.
——— Michaelis de Sutherland, of the lands of Therboll,   Sutherland.
——— Willielmi de Camera, of the lands of Eafter Rothnein.
——— epi et fuorum civium civitatis S. Andree.
——— Joannis Kennedy, de terris de Caffills, Dalmortoun, et Schauven,   Carrick.
——— Alexandri More, de terris de Kynchubr.
——— Willielmi Wardlaw, de terris de Corfgoatt.

INDEX OF CHARTERS, &c. BY KING DAVID II.

In vicecom.

Carta Roberti, fil. Duncani de Atholia, de terris de Ferdill.
Officium coronarie vicecom. de Ed^r, conceditur Johanni de Edmiftoun, pro tempore vite.
Carta Walteri de Cragy, de terris de Hebiddys.
—— Dn̄e Marie le Chien, de terris de Duffus.
—— Willielmi de Faffingtoun, de terris de Balmedy.
—— Con. Henrici de Nudrie, of fome aikers in Nudrie.
—— Monafterii de Dumfermling, de terra de Gartneker.
—— ejufdem Monafterii, de terra de Tullicutrie.
—— Johannis de Petfcoty, de certis terris infra burgum de Perth.
—— Comitiffe de Angus, de 20 l. Sterling percipiend. de thanagio de Colly.
—— Georgii de Dunbar, de dimidietate baroniarum de Tibris et de Mortoune.
—— Marjorie Cumyn, fponfe Johannis de Langlands, de terris de Milfaliftoun, &c.

Ane Book in Parchment, containing the Charters following, granted by King David.

The firft page cannot be read. N. B. *This is the firft Book now in the General Regifter-Houfe.*

THE Old Index, in fo far as it refpects this Book, is far from being accurate. The Editor, therefore, as, from the original Book of Record itfelf, formed an Index entirely new, which he lays before the Public, as a fpecimen of the manner in which he propofes to print an Index of all the Books of the Record of the Great Seal, if fuch an undertaking fhall receive the Public approbation.

IN this firft Book of Charters, as well as in the twelve Rolls now in the General Regifter-Houfe, the Witneffes to the Royal Charters, which were not then fo uniform as they became afterwards, are feldom inferted. Where they are inferted, their Names are given in the Index. The Names too of the Refigners, in Charters of Refignation, are given. And in Charters of Confirmation, the Names, as well of the Granters of the Charters confirmed, as of the Witneffes to thofe Original Charters, are fet down. This, with the two Alphabetical Indexes of Lands and of Perfons fubjoined to the whole, will exhibit an Hiftorical View, as Ufeful as it will be Curious, of the Property and Families of Scotland, by means of which both Lands and Perfons may be traced with accuracy and eafe.

IT is true, as is faid in the Old Index, that the firft page of this firft book of record is almoft totally illegible.

1 The title of the 1ft charter is, " Confirmatio carte Johannis de Grahame," and its conclufion is, " nri xxxiii°;" which probably denotes its having been granted in the 33d year of King David's reign.
2 The fecond deed begins, " Officium coronatoris," and it concludes, " xxvit^o die Martii, anno regni nri xxxiii°."
3 The title of the 3d charter is, " Confirmatio capellanie fundate, per Willielmum de," and from the body of the deed, the name of the founder feems to have been " Fentoun ;" the commencing word " David" is legible and at the end, the figures " xxxiii°" are hardly legible.
4 The 4th begins " Officium," and after two or three decayed words, " parte auftrali aque de Forth," may be read.
5 The 5th has for title, " Lra" litera) " data Jacobo Mulekyn monetario." The word " David" at its beginning is legible, and the grantee is, in the body of the deed, defigned " De Florence."

INDEX OF CHARTERS, &c. BY KING DAVID II.

6 Not a single word of the 6th deed is legible on the first page of the book; but the greater part of the two concluding lines engrossed on the top of the second page are plain enough, viz. (com-) " potis suis annuis, " visis ipsius Nigelli literis de recepto, plene volumus allocari et hoc nullo" - - - - - - - - - - " rei testi- " monium, &c. apud Kyndromy, septimo die Septembris, anno regni nostri xxxiii°."

7 Carta Confirm. donationis per Patricium Comitem Marchie et Moravie, officii vicecomitis, et constabularie de Elgyne, Willielmo de Vallibus. Carta Confir. data est apud Spyny, 5to Januar. an. reg. 33°.

8 —— Andree Spryng, tenementi in burgo de Abirden; testibus Willielmo Episcopo Sancti Andree, et Patricio Episcopo Brechinensi cancellario nostro, Roberto Senescallo Scotie, Comite de Stratherne, nepote nostro, Willielmo de Keith, Mareschallo nostro Scotie, et Archebaldo de Douglas, - - - - - - - apud Abirden, 10 Sept. an. reg. 33.

9 —— Andree de Eskyne, terre de Raplach juxta Strivelyne; dat. apud castrum de Levyn, 25to - - - - - - - - an. reg. 33.

10 —— Hugoni de Dunbarr, Canonico Abirdonensi, decem marcarum Sterlingorum annuatim de custuma burgi de Abirden; dat. apud Abirden, 14 Septem. an. reg. 33.

11 —— Confir. donationis per Dominum de Rubyflaw, Johanni de Crab, burgensi de Abirden, cujusdam petie terre in dominio de Rubyflaw; apud Abirden, xii. Septem. an. reg. 33.

12 —— data, ad instantiam Roberti de Erskyne, Militis, Willielmo de Levynsloun, et Christiane de Kalentar, filie quondam Patricii de Kalentar, sponse dicti Willielmi, terre de Kyllynsith, in vic. de Dunbretane, quam quondam Malcolmus Flamyngi Comes de Wygtoun dederat quondam Roberto de Vall, (sortase pro *Vallibus*), cujus filia et heres Margareta, nata de Anglicana, sine heredibus in regno Scotie, in fata decessit; dat. apud Kyndromy, 13. Octob. an. reg. 33.

13 —— Willielmo Ramesay, Militi, viginti librarum Sterlingorum annuatim; dat. apud Abirden, 9. Septemb. an. reg. 33.

14 —— Waltero, filio Augustini, burgensi de Edynbourgh, terre de Nudrie, in vic. de Edynburgh, quam Johannes de Bennachtyne de le Corrokys resignavit; apud Kyndromy, 19. Septemb. an. reg. 33.

15 —— Confirm. donationis concesse per Willielmum de Sancto Claro, terre dominice de Mertoun (excepto tantum manerio ejusdem) Alano de Grahame. Carta Confirm. Regis data est apud Abirden, 1. Novembris, an. reg. 33.

16 —— capitulo et collegio canonicorum de Abirdon, juris patronatus ecclesie de Logy in Buchania, in episcopatu Aberdonensi; apud Abirden, 12. Septemb. an. reg. 33.

17 " David, Dei gratia, Rex Scottorum, omnibus, &c. Scitis nos dedisse, concessisse, et hac presenti carta " nostra confirmasse, dilecto consanguineo nostro Willielmo de Cunynghame, Militi, totam comitatum " nostrum de Carrik."—Cetera desunt.

18 Carta Alexandro Episcopo et Capitulo Abirdonensi, terre parci de Gairhull, (sic), in vic. de Banff; apud Abirden, 12. Sept. an reg. 33.

19 Litera et concessio capitulo et collegio canonicorum de Abirdon, " quod hi omnes et singuli, qui in parco de " Galechell, (f.e), infra vic. de Banff, secare, dolare, venari, cum animalibus pasturare, aut injustis viis uti " sine ipsius capituli aut ipsius deputati licentia presumpserint, amerciamenta sive escaeta ejusdem parci " ab antiquo consueta, viz. sex vaccas, eidem capitulo vel ejus ad hoc assignato sine diminutione qua- " cunque persolvent. In cujus rei, &c. Testibus, &c. apud forestam de Kyntor, in festo Sancti Cle- " mentis, anno regni nostri tricesimo tertio."

20 Carta Gilberto de Glencharny, baronie de Glencharny, in vic. de Invernefs et comitatu Moravie, quam ipse Gilbertus resignavit; tenende dict. Gilberto et heredibus masculis de suo corpore, quibus deficientibus, Duncano Frazer, et Cristiane, sponse ejus, sorori dicti Gilberti, et heredibus masculis de eorum corporibus, &c.; apud Abirden, 18. Januarii, an. reg. 33.

21 —— Johanni Reid, terrarum vocat. Pelanyslat, jacen. intra parcum regis de Cardrofs, et terram de Dalgworne, in vic. de Dunbertane; apud Spyny, 28. Novemb. an. reg. 33.

22 —— Johanni de Haya de Tolyboyll, " quod possit redigere in culturam totam terram que jacet inter aquam " de Spee et rivolum de Tynet, in foresta del Awne, et ipsam terram habere, cum omnibus liberta- " tibus," &c.; apud Abirden, 16. Januarii, an. reg. 33.

INDEX OF CHARTERS, &c. BY KING DAVID II.

23 Carta Confirm. donationis quam quondam Johannes Ranulphi Comes Moravie fecit quondam Johanni Urewell et Andree filio ejus, de terris de Stanqwar, Tulach, et Drom, cum cuftodia foreftarum earundem; apud Kynlofs, 24. Decemb. an. reg. 33.

24 —— Alexandro Epifcopo et Capitulo Aberdonenfi, juris patronatus ecclefie de Filorth, ad fuftentationem duorum capellanorum; apud Abirden, 20. Januarii, an. reg. 33.

25 —— Confirm. donationis quam Patricius Comes Marchie et Moravie fecit Willielmo de Vallibus, de officio vicecomitis et conftabularie de Elgyne; apud Spyny, 5. Januar. an reg. 33.

26 —— Confirm. donationis quam Thomas Comes de Marr fecit Johanni de Rofs, de terra de Gilcolmyftoun, in vic. de Abirden; apud Abirden, 16. Novemb. an. reg. 33.

27 —— Confirm. donationum quas Willielmus de Keth, Marefcallus Scotie, ac Andreas de Garvyach fecerunt Ade Pyngle, (forfan pro *Pryngle*), de terris de Knoc et de Geleftan, in baronia de Strathechyn, infra vic. de Kyncardon; et de terris de Badcafs, in tenemento de Kynbeoun, in baronia de Rothynormam, infra vic. de Abirden; apud Abirden, 15. Januarii, an reg. 33.

28 —— fratribus predicatoribus de Abirden, centum folidorum annuatim ex baronia de Banchorydeveny, in vic. de Abirden, " pro falute anime noftre, et anime Margarete de Logy, dilecte noftre ;" apud Abirden, 20. Januar. an reg. 33.

29 —— Confirm. donationis quam Robertus, Senefcallus Scotie, Comes de Stratherne, fecit Waltero de Moravia de Tullibardine, de terris de Tullibardyne, Petvet. Aldy, Dundovane, terra dominicali de Glendovane, Glencoy, Nethyrgafky, et Dalrivach, in comitatu de Stratherne; et donationis quam Alexander de Abirnethy, Miles, fecit Johanni de Moravia de Tullybardyne, Militi, de terris de Pekerlyngi, in baronia de Ballynbrech, in vic. de Fiff; apud Elgyne, 7. Decem. an. reg. 33.

30 —— Confirm. donationis quam Willielmus de Fentoun fecit uni capellano, in capella fua de Baky, de terra de Kinrofs; apud Edynburgh, 26. Februar. an. reg. 33.

31 —— Alexandro de Cokburne, viginti librarum Sterlingorum de magna cuftuma burgi de Hadyngtoun; fine data.

32 —— Refig. Johanni de Rydall, terrarum de Cranftoun, in vic. de Edynburgh, fuper refignatione dicti Johannis; apud Edynburgh, 25. Januar. an. reg. 33.

33 —— Roberto, Senefcallo de Scandbothchy, terrarum de Daleel et de Modyrwall, in vic. de Lanerk, " nos " contingen. pro eo quod heredes quondam Roberti Delwall, (fortaffe pro *Del Wallibus*), Militis, con- " tra pacem et fidem noftram in Anglia commorantur ;" tenend. ficut quondam Malcolmus Flemyng et predictus Robertus Delvall eas tenuerunt; apud Edynburgh, 23. Martii, an. reg. 33.

34 —— Confirm. donationis uni capellano in ecclefia de Dunmanyne, de annuo redditu novem marcarum Sterlingorum debito de terris de Hopkelloch, per Jacobum de Tuedi ; et de duabus marcis Sterlingorum annuatim de dicte Margarete terris de Scraline; 9. Martii, an. reg. 33.

35 —— Confirm. donationis quam Thomas Comes de Marr fecit Johanni, filio Johannis, burgenfi de Linlitheu, de decem libratis terre, in baronia de Cloveth, in vic. de Forfar; 4. Februar. a. r. 33.

36 —— Confirm. carte conceffe per Willielmum Comitem de Sothirlande, fratri fuo Nicholao de Sothirlande, fexdecim davatarum terre, in comitatu de Sothirlande, in baronia que dicitur Thorboll : teftes in carta Comitis non inferuntur in regiftro : Carta Regis data eft apud Edynburgh, 17. Octob. a. r. 34.

37 —— Confirm. carte conceffe per Thomam Comitem de Marre, Willielmo de Camera, terre de Eftirrothnem, in Cramarr; teftes in carta Comitis non inferuntur in recordo : Carta confir. data eft apud Strivelyne, 26. Maii, a. r 33.

38 —— Confirm. Willielmo de Laundelys, Epifcopo Sancti Andree, et fuis fucceffforibus in eo epifcopatu, antiquorum privilegiorum conceffforum predeceffforibus fuis, et hominibus eorum civitatis Sancti Andree ; 5. Junii, a. r. 33.

39 —— Confirm. Johanni Kenedy, de terra de Caftlys, in vic. de Are, vendita illi per Marjoriam de Mungumry feniorem, et Marjoriam de Mungumry, filiam Johannis de Mungumry; et de terra de Dalmorton, in comitatu de Carrik, et vic. de Are, illi vendita per Johannem de Turnebery; et de terra de Schauven, illi vendita per Murthacum filium Somerlady ; fine data et teftibus.

INDEX OF CHARTERS, &c. BY KING DAVID II. 73

40 Carta Confirm. carte conceſſe per Alexandrum de Elfynſtoun, Dominum ejuſdem, Alexandro More, filio quondam Ade More, Militis, terre de Kychumbr, in baronia de Stanhous, (quam Dominus Godfridus de Roos dedit Alexandro de Elfynſtoun, patri dicti Alexandri, in excambio pro quadam petia terre in Erthbeg): teſtes in originali carta non inferuntur in recordo ; carta confirm. data fuit apud Edynburgh, 4 Junii, a. r. 33.

41 ——— Willielmo de Wardlaw, duarum bovatarum terre in villa de Corſgat, in baronia de Coldyngham, ad Regem " contingentium ratione forisfacture quondam Randulphi de Eklys, qui obiit ad fidem et pacem " Regis Anglie;" item unius carucate terre jacentis in Blanhern, ad Regem " ſpectantis ratione eſcaete " pro eo quod heredes quondam Henrici de Ellame ad fidem et pacem Regis Anglie nunc exiſtunt;" et ſimiliter duarum carucatarum terre " que fuerunt quondam Ade de Hiltoun, in villa de Hiltoun, " nos contingentium ratione eſchaete pro eo quod dictus Adam ad pacem et fidem Regis Anglie nunc " exiſtit ;" 24. Martii, a. r. 33.

42 ——— Roberto, filio Duncani de Atholia, medietatis terrarum Regis de Ferdill, in vic. de Perth : teſtibus Willielmo Epiſcopo Sancti Andree, et Patricio Epiſcopo Brechinenſi Cancellario ; Roberto Seneſcallo Scotie Comite de Stratherne nepote Regis ; Roberto de Erſkyne Camerario Scotie, et Thoma Byſet, Militibus ; apud Perth, 24. Maii, a. r. 33.

43 " Officium coronarie vic. de Edynburgh conceditur Johanni de Edmondiſtoun, pro toto tempore vite ſue ;" apud Abirden, 5. Novem. an. reg. 33.

44 Carta Confirm. donationis quam Margareta de Munſode in ſua legitima viduitate fecit Waltero de Cragi, filio ſuo juniori, de terris de Hebeddys, in vic. de Lanark ; 9. Martii, a. r. 33.

45 ——— Confirm. donationis quam Margareta de Abirnethy, Comitiſſa de Anegus, fecit Willielmo de Faſſyngtoun, et Margarete ſponſe ſue, de terra de Balmady ; 6. Febr. a. r. 33.

46 ——— Confirm. carte conceſſe per Robertum Regem, ſuper terra de Duffhous, contenta in certis conventionibus, inter Dominam Mariam, ſponſam quondam Reginaldi le Chen, Militis, et Alexandrum Fraſer ; carta Regis Roberti data fuit apud Elgin, 6. Novem. an. reg. 7°; carta confirm. Regis Davidis, apud Edynburgh, 18. Octob. a. r. 34.

47 ——— Confirm. carte conceſſe per Johannem de Benauchtyne de Corrokes, Henrico de Nudre, quarundam partium terrarum de Nudre-Mareſcall: Teſtes in originali carta non nominantur ; carta Regis datur apud Edynburgh, 20. Oct. a. r. 34.

48 ——— Abbati et conventui de Dunfermelyne, terre de Gartneker, in vic. de Clacmanane, tenende in libera regalitate ; 4. Auguſti, a. r. 34.

49 ——— iiſdem, terre de Tolycultre, cum molendino, in vic. de Clacmanane, in libera regalitate ; 4. Aug. a. r. 34.

50 ——— Confirm. Johanni de Petſcoty, burgenſi de Perth, omnium terrarum, tenementorum, annuorum reddituum, &c. que habuit in burgo de Perth ; 28. Julii, a. r. 34.

51 ——— Margarete de Sancto Claro Comitiſſe de Anegus, viginte librarum Sterlingorum annuatim ex thanagio de Colly ; apud Sanctum Andream, 13. April. a. r. 34.

52 " Memorandum, quod 3. Julii, a. r. 34. Quadraginta libre Sterlingorum conceduntur Domino Patricio Co- " miti Marchie et Moravie," &c. " pro regis libito voluntatis duratur."

53 Carta Georgio de Dunbar, medietatis baroniarum de Tibris et Mortoun, in vic. de Drumfres, quas Patricius Comes Marchie et Moravie, et Agnes ſponſa ſua, reſignaverunt ; 28. Junii, a. r. 34.

54 " Memorandum, quod annuus redditus ſex marcarum de terra de Newby, in vic. de Peblis, conceditur David " Broune, pro tempore vite; 1. Julii, a. r. 34."

55 Carta Mariote Cunyne, ſponſe quondam Johannis de Langland, terrarum de Mylſalliſtoun et Ochterheuyd, cum molendino de Mylſalliſtoun ; 3. Julii, a. r. 34.

56 ——— Confirm. donationis facte per Patricium Comitem Marchie et Moravie, armigero ſuo, Alexandro de Reclyntoun, de terris dominicis dicti Comitis de Duns et Mylchaulch, aliarumq. ; 2. Julii, a. r. 34.

57 ——— Conf. donationis quam Thomas Comes de Marr fecit Alexandro de Lyndeſay, baronie de Balwyn Joloch et Rothven, in vic. de Forfar ; 3. Julii, a. r. 34.

INDEX OF CHARTERS, &c. BY KING DAVID II.

58 Carta Conf. conventionis facte inter Robertum Senefcallum Scotie Comitem de Stratherne, et Abbatem et Conventum Sancte Crucis, fuper folutione annui redditus e terris de la Carfs, in vic. de Strivelyn ; 16. Julii, a. r. 34.

59 —— Henrico de Afkirk, terre que fuit Ade de Glentoun, in burgo de Roxburgh, et cuftodie omnium menfurarum dicti burgi ; 20. Julii, a. r. 34.

60 —— Confirm. omnium donationum et conceffionum factarum per quofcunq. vel quafcunq. Johanni de Infulis, de quibufcunq. terris, tenementis, annuis redditibus, et poffeffionibus ; 4. Julii, a. r. 34.

61 —— Roberto de Erfkyne, Militi, terre de Malerbe, in vic. de Perth, et annuo redditu trefdecim folidorum et quatuor denariorum Sterlingorum, de particula terre que fuit Johannis de Petfcoty, quam terram Jacobus de Blare refignavit ; 15. Aug. a. r. 34.

62 —— Thome Bifet, Militi, totius comitatus de Fif ; tenendi eidem Thome, et heredibus mafculis inter ipfam et Yfabellam de Fif procreandis ; quibus deficientibus, " volumus quod totus predictus comitatus ad " nos et heredes noftros libere revertatur ;" 8. Junii, a. r. 34.

63 —— Confir. donationis quam Patricius de Dunbarr Comes Marchie et Moravie, fecit alumpno fuo Johanni de Hibburne, et heredibus mafculis de corpore fuo, quibus deficien. Patricio Hibburne, fratri fuo, et heredibus de corpore ejus, de terris de Ovirmerkhill et Nehirmerkhill, in vicecomitatu Marchie ; 9. Junii, an. reg. 34.

64 —— Alexandro de Reelyntoun, cujufdam tenementi in burgo de Edynburgh, 3. Julii, a. r. 34.

65 —— Johanni Gray, clerico rotulorum, centum folidorum Sterlingorum, ex finibus, amerciamentis, feu efcaetis itineris camerarie, et totidem folidorum de exitibus jufticiarie ex parte boreali aque Forth, per annum, pro tempore vite.

66 —— Ade Page, fervienti Regis, centum folidorum Sterlingorum annuatim, percipiendorum per manus camerarii, pro toto tempore vite fue ; 7. Julii, a. r. 34.

67 —— Roberto de Lawedre, Militi, annue penfionis 20l. de exitibus jufticiarie ex parte boreali aque de Forth ; apud Dunfermelyne, 1. Oct. a. r. 34.

68 —— Rogero Hog, burgenfi de Edynburgh, tenementi et omnium terrarum et annuorun reddituum ejus in dicto burgo ; 23. Aug. a. r. 34.

69 —— Confirm. Johanni Yung, vicario ecclefie de Fordys, affedationis illi facte per Johannem de Haya, vic terra de Robe Buky, in le Awne, in vic. de Banff ; 14. Oct. a. r. 34.

70 —— Willielmo Somer, annui redditus 40 folid. de terra de Baldavie, et molendino ejufdem, in vic. de Banff; apud Perth, 28. Maii, a. r. 33.

71 —— Andree de Kirkaldy, capellano, 5 marcarum Sterlingorum annuatim de cuftuma civitatis Sancti Andree, " quoufque per Dominum Regem ad aliquod beneficium ecclefiafticum fuerit promotus ;" 25. Aug. a. r. 34.

72 —— Ade, perpetuo vicario de Lynlithcu, capellano Regis, 10l. Sterlingorum de cuftuma regia burgi de Lynlithcu, annuatim, pro toto tempore vite ejus ; 7. Sept. a. r. 34.

73 —— Roberto de Corry, et Sufanne fponfe ejus, filie et heredi Thome de Torthorwald, " in mea prefentia, " ad fidem et pacem noftram, apud bellum commiffum apud Durhame defuncti, terrarum de Coulyn " et Ruchane, que fuerunt quondam Willielmi de Carliolo," in vic. de Drumfres ; 18. Oct. a. r. 34.

74 —— Confirmationis Davidi de Melgdrum, medietatis terre de Weftbins, in baronia de Abircorn, data illi per Willielmum More de Abircorn ; apud Melros, 28. Oct. a. r. 34.

75 —— Waltero de Lefly, Militi, pro toto tempore vite fue, 40l. Sterl. annuatim, de magna cuftuma burgi de Dunde ; 14. Oct. a. r. 34.

76 —— Johanni de Logy, Domino ejufdem, thanagii de Thanadas, in vic. de Forfar, et reverfionis thanagii de Glaumes, in eodem vic. ; apud Perth, 4. Apr. a. r. 34.

77 —— Alexandro de Lyndfay, annui redditus 9 marcarum de terris de Glenefk, in vic. de Forfar ; 25. Aug. a. r. 34.

78 —— Johanni Mercer, burgenfi de Perth, particule terre in burgo de Perth ; apud Perth, 27. Sept. a. r. 34.

INDEX OF CHARTERS, &c. BY KING DAVID II.

79 Carta Davidi Flamyng, annui redditus 20 marcarum de Magno Morfy, et 100 folidorum de Durfchine, cum parco de Durfchine, et refidui de occidentali parco de Kyncardyn ; " quoufque de quadraginta marcis " terre hereditarie alibi per nos fibi fuerit provifum ;" apud Melros, 27. Oct. a. r. 34.

80 —— Confirm. donationis quam Rogerus de Mortuo Mari, Miles, fecit Margarete de Meneteth, fponfe ejus, filie Alexandri de Meneteth, de terris de Foulys, in vic. de Perth, " in liberam dotem antequam ma- " trimonium inter eofdem in facie ecclefie fuerat celebratum," pro toto tempore vite dict. Margarete ; 14. Julii, a. r. 35.

81 " Confirmatur etiam dictis die loco ac anno donatio illa quam idem Rogerus fecit dicte fponfe fue ante- " quam matrimonium, ut fupra, inter eofdem factum fuerat", de terra de Cuthilmyre.

82 " Apud Drumfres, 27. Junii, a. r. 35. Conceduntur Bricio Wych, ad tempus vite, pro feodo annuatim 100 folidi Sterl. per manus Camerarii Scotie."

83 Carta Agneti de Kelor, quod terre de Kepnemad non teneantur nifi tantum in tribus fectis curie faciendis an- nuatim ad tria placita capitalia apud Stricvlyn, " aliis articulis et conditionibus in carta progenitoris " noftri terrarum novi et antiqui parcorum juxta Strivelyne, ac dict. terre de Kepnemad, in fuo robore " duraturis ;" apud Strivelyne, 6. Julii, a. r. 35.

84 Conceffio Willielmo de Carnys, et Duncano, filio ejus et heredi, quod pro terris fuis de Eftirwytburne et Wefterwytburne, de cetero teneantur tantum in tribus fectis per annum ad tria placita in curia con- ftabularie de Lynlithcu ; 26. Sept. a. r. 35.

85 Carta Jacobo de Douglas, filio quondam Johannis de Douglas, Militis, annui redditus de Effchlis, Horfbruk, Efterhopkeliouch, et Newby, in vic. de Peblys ; 27. Sept. a. r. 35.

86 —— Confir. duarum cartarum Abbati et Monachis de Kylwynnyne, prioris per Johannem de Meneteth, Do- minum de Arane et Knapdall, juris patronatus ecclefiarum Sancte Marie, et Sancte Brigide, infule de Arane ; hiis teftibus, Domino Beano rectore ecclefie Sancte Marie de Arane, Willielmo de Fou- lartoun, Chriftiano M'Nawych, Comedino Medico, Hugone filio Johannis, Buano Weir, Roberto Boyman, Thoma de Infirmitorio, et multis aliis ; date in monafterio predicto, 12. Octob. anno Do- mini 1357 ; alterius carte conceffe per Johannem de Maxwell, Dominum ejufdem, juris patronatus ec- clefie de Libertoun, cum una acra terre juxta terram ecclefie, " quam ego coram pluribus perambulavi " et eifdem affignavi, falvo jure Domini Roberti de Glene, rectore ejufdem, quoufque cedat vel de- " cedat ;" teftibus Domino Roberto Senefcallo Scotie, Mauricio de Moravia, Johanne Senefcallo Domino de Periftoun, Johanne de Lyndefay Domino de Cragine, Hugone Domino de Eglyntoun, Militibus ; Godfrido Domino de Ardroffane, Alano Cambell, Hugone del Blare, et Johanne fratre fuo, et multis aliis ; caret data ; et carta Regis caret et teftibus et data.

87 —— Confir. carte per Alexandrum Regem Scottorum, burgenfibus et communitati burgi de Kyngorne, forum in dicto burgo omni die Jovis tenendi ; teftibus Nicholao de Haya, Andrea de Moravia, David de Leveftoun, Militibus, apud Largauch, 26. Junii, an. reg. 36°. Carta confir. Regis Davidis fuper- addit quedam alia privilegia, teftibus Willielmo Epifcopo Sancti Andree, et Patricio Epifcopo Brechi- nenfi Cancellario, Roberto Senefcallo Scotie Comite de Stratherne, Willielmo Comite de Douglas, Roberto de Erfkyne Camerario, Archebaldo de Douglas, Johanne Herice, Militibus ; apud Perth, 2° Julii, an. reg. 35.

88 —— Confir. carte conceffe per Alexandrum dictum conftabull. burgenfem de Abirdene, fratribus ordinis de Monte Carmeli apud Abirdene, quatuor marcarum Sterlingor. annui redditus ex terra in vico caftri dicti burgi ; 14. Maii, 1350 : Carta confir. Regis data eft apud Edynburgh, 5. April. a. r. 35.

89 —— Johanni de Kenedy, duarum denariatarum terre ex parte boreali aque de Gervane, cum annuo redditu decem marcarum de Ballichlewnekan, et annuo reditu quinque marcarum de Dahewacht, in comitatu de Carrik, et vic. de Are, " quoufque nos, vel heredes noftri, eundem Johannem, vel heredes fuos, de " viginti libratis terre infra vic. de Are, vel de quadraginta marcatis terre extra dictum vicccomitatum, " infeodavimus ;" apud Dunbretane, 18. Septem. a. r. 32.

INDEX OF CHARTERS, &c. BY KING DAVID II.

90 Carta Confir. carte conceffe per Johannem de Moravia de Newtoun in Fyf, Henrico de Lychtoun carucate terre, cum Lochflat, Welflat, et Bradvale, et tenementi de Innerdovet, quas Cecilia Trymblay, filia et heres quondam Roberti de Trymblay, refignavit apud Sandford ; dictus vero Henricus, et heredes ejus, &c. debent ad molendinum de Newtoun unam firlotam cujuflibet bladi de qualibet celdra quam molabunt ad molendinum predictum ; teftibus Dominis Johanne de Kyndelouch, et Nicholao de Ramefay, Militibus, W. de Sancto Claro Domino de Dyferth, Alexandro de Lyndfay de Glenefk, Matheo Sibald, et aliis ; carta confirm. Regis data eft apud Perth, 20. Novemb. a. r. 34.

91 —— Confirm. carte conceffe per Patricium de Dumbarr Comitem Marchie et Moravie, Alexandro de Ryklyntoun, dimidii terre de Eftfpot, cum tenandria in villa de Qwytfoum, que fuit quondam Scirce Frefer, et " quas Patricius de Ramefay, Miles, Dominus de Dalufy, refignavit, in plena curia noftra " apud Qwytyngeham ;" teftibus, in carta Comitis, W. et A. de Halburtoun, Patricio de Polworth, W. de Diffyngtoun, Militibus, W. de Erch, Alexandro de Kokburne, Adam de Nefbit, et multis aliis ; carta Regis data eft, 8. Aprilis, a. r. 35.

92 —— Confir. carte Alexandri Regis Scottorum, Abbati et Conventui de Londors, omnium terrarum quas tenuerunt a prima fundatione domus fue, et eos eximentis ab auxiliis, exercitibus, et aliis forinfecis fervitiis de terris fuis ; teftibus, in carta Alexandri Regis, Willielmo filio Alani Senefcalli jufticiario Scotie, Willielmo Olifant jufticiario Laodonie, Bernard Frafer, Waltero Byfeth, Johanne de Haya ; apud caftrum Puellarum, 12. Novem. an. reg. 33tio ; carta confir. Regis Davidis nominatim eximit a predictis fervitiis terras de Cragy, Miltoun, Claypottys, et Balmaw ; et data eft apud Dunde, 20. Sept. an. reg. 36.

93 —— Alexandro de Cokburne, baronie de Caredyn, in vic. de Edynburgh, " que nos contingit ratione efcaete " pro eo quod Johannes de Veteri Ponte dictam baroniam injufte alienavit, noftra licentia non optenta;" apud Sconam, 1o. Novem. an. reg. 29º.

94 —— Confir. donationis fex petrarum cere Abbati et Conventui de Londors, facte per Davidem de Lyndefay Dominum de Crauford, folubilium per ballivum vel firmarium de Carny, et emendarum duobus marcis dicto Davidi debitis annuatim de terra de Pethfour juxta Carny ; 19. Novem. an. Dom. 1355 ; carta confirm. Regis data eft apud Lundors, 3. Aug. an. reg. 36.

95 —— Confir. carte conceffe per Thomam Comitem de Marr, Egoni filio Ferguffi, terre de Huchtererne, in comitatu de Marr ; apud caftrum de Kyndromy, teftibus Dominis Waltero Moygn, Johanne le Graunte, et Laurentio Gilibrand, Militibus ; Magiftris Johanne de Cromdole decretorum doctore canonico Roffenfi, Gilberto Armeftrang canonico Moravienfi, Domino Johanne de Marr canonico Abirdonenfi, Thoma et Alexandro Brifbane fratribus, et multis aliis ; carta conf. Regis data eft apud Kyndromy, 9 Septem. an. reg. 36.

96 —— Johanni Herice, Militi, baronie de Triuereglys, in vic. de Drumfres, que fuit Thome Comitis de Marr, et quam " idem Comes coram pluribus regni noftri prelatis et proceribus" refignavit, cum quibufdam privilegiis obfervatione digniffimis ; 17. Octob. a. r. 36.

97 —— Roberto de Bruys, terrarum de Gerfmanyftoun, la Canet, Gatyfende, Petfouldoun, Gerfmanyftoun Carfs, la Perkmedow, Gragory, Garyncloe, et Dryfeld, in vic. de Clacmanan ; excepto molendino vocat le Lyndmill " quoufq. pro dicto Roberto aut heredibus ejus de equivalentia dictarum terrarum " alibi duximus providere ;" 20. Octob. a. r. 36.

98 —— Willielmo de Fawfyd, et Marjorie Flemyng, fponfe ejus, molendini in terris de Tolygart vocat. le Lyndmill, in vic. de Clackmanan, pro tempore vite dict. Marjorie ; declaran. etiam quod terra de Tolygart antea conceffa, libera fit pro eodem tempore ab arreagiis et carriagiis ; 18. Octob. a. r. 36.

—— " pro falute anime noftre, et anime Margerete Regine Scotie noftre focie," &c. ecclefie et canonicis de Cambufkyneth annui redditus decem librarum argenti de terris de le Planc, in vic. de Strivelyne ; apud Perth, 25. Aug. a. r. 36.

INDEX OF CHARTERS, &c. BY KING DAVID II. 77

100 Carta Confirm. conventionis facte inter aldermannum, ballivos, et communitatem burgi de Perth, et Willielmum de Difpenfa, burgenfem de Perth, qua dicti aldermannus, &c. ad feodifirmam dimiferunt dicto Willielmo " cuftumam pontis de Perth, que per communitatem ville de Perth affedari con-
" fuevit annuatim tholoneario pontis, falvis tamen terris firmis et redditibus, tam in villa quam extra,
" tam ex antiqua infeodatione quam nova predicto ponti conceffis vel concedendis, in difpofitione
" predicte communitatis ville de Perth in perpetuum remanfuris; pro quaquidem cuftuma deponenda
" et in perpetuum interpellanda ita, viz. quod omnes tranfeuntes pauperes et divites a preftatione
" dicte cuftume fint liberi et quieti in perpetuum, predictus Willielmus dedit, conceffit, &c. ad fa-
" bricam et fuftentationem predicti pontis tres libras Sterlingorum annuatim de terra fua de Gilgir-
" gyftoun," &c. parti hujus fcripti penes dictum Willielmum refidenti figilla Johannis Bifapifman, tunc aldermanni, et Michaelis Fiffer, Ricardi de Balcolmy, et Criftiani de Aula, tunc ballivorum de Perth, funt appenfa; teftibus, in dicta conventione, Dominis R. Senefcallo Scotie, D. de Haya Conftabulario Scotie, Andrea de Buthurgafk tunc vicecomite de Perth, Johanne Cambrin de Balgrigernach, Rogero de Mortuo Mari, Andrea de Douglas, Militibus, quibufdam burgenfibus, et multis aliis; apud Perth, die Martis, in fefto Apoftolorum Petri et Pauli, an. Dom. 1344: Carta conf. Regis data eft apud Edynburgh, 6. Novem. a. r. 36.

101 —— Abbati et Conventui de Londors, medietatis terre de Efter Cragy, in baronia de Parnbogall, in vic. de Edynburgh, pro falute anime Regis et animarum Bartholomei Loone, (forfan pro Lorne), et Philippe de Moubray, fponfe ejus, filie et heredis quondam Philippi de Moubray, Militis; quam terram predict. Bartholomeus et Philippa coram pluribus regni magnatibus refignaverunt; apud Lundors, 3. Aug. an. reg. 36.

102 —— Ade dicti Forefter, medietatis terre de Qwhitburne, in conftabularia de Linlitheu, et vic. de Edynburgh, quam Johannes Yung, burgenfis de Lynlitheu, refignavit; 17. Aug. a. r. 36.

103 —— Willielmo de Dalyell, ferjando de feodo vicecomitatus de Lanerk, quinque librarum Sterlingor. annuatim pro feodo fuo, five de exitibus curiarum dicti vicecomitatus, five de exitibus itineris jufticiarii; 13. Aug. a. r. 36.

104 —— Roberto Multrer, burgenfi de Edynburgh, terrarum que fuerunt Johannis Colti, in baronia de Laftalryk; 22. Junii, a. r. 36.

105 —— Confirm. donationis quam Willielmus More, Miles, fecit in perpetuam elemofinam altari Sancte Marie Virginis, in ecclefia parochiali de Edynburgh, terre de Raylifloun, in vic. de Edynburgh; 18. Septem. a. r. 34.

106 —— Rogero Wodyfeld, omnium ejus tenementorum, &c. in burgo de Drumfres, et viginti librarum terre, cum uno burgagio, in villa de Traqwayre, quas Joneta, filia Walteri de Moffet, et Ricardus Duchti, maritus ejus, eidem Rogero impignoraverunt, " ficut carte, litere, vel evidentie, viva voce vel in
" fcriptis, quas exinde habet in fe jufte plenius continent et proportant;" 6. Decem. a. r. 36.

107 —— Fergufio de Edinhame, burgenfi de Edynburgh, et Margarete de Strivelyne fponfe ejus, terre que fuit Willielmi Bertholmew, in burgo de Edynburgh; 6. Decem. a. r. 36.

108 —— Confirm carte Willielmi de Conynghame Domini de Carrik, Jacobo de Leprewyk, medietatis terre de Polkarne, in Kyle-regis, et in vic. de Are; teftibus, Dominis David filio Walteri, Johanne de Daniellyftoun, Alexandro Senefcallo, Militibus; Johanne filio Domini Valteri, Johanne de Nefbith, Johanne de Robardiftoun, et multis aliis; carta confir. Regis data eft 5. Decem. a. r. 36.

109 —— Confirm. donationis quam Margareta Ovyot, filia et una heredum David Ovyot, Militis, fponfa Roberti de Meygneris, Militis, fecit Ricardo Ovyot, confanguineo fuo, de dimidia parte terre de Caffyndoly, de tota terra de Balqwy et de Cragueir, de Calange, et tota parte fua molendini de Syres, in vic. de Fyff; apud monafterium de Lundors, 7. Aug. a. r. 36.

110 —— Confirm. donationis quam Dugallus M'Dowalle, Miles, fecit Johanni Trapont, nunc dicto Carric heraudo, de quatuor marcatis terre de Litilgretby, in dominio de Kyraffalde, in vic. de Drumfres, et de viginti folidatis terre de Glengarg et Glenerag, in dominio de Curwen, in vic. predict; 5. Decem. a. r. 36.

INDEX OF CHARTERS, &c. BY KING DAVID II.

111 Carta burgenſibus et communitati de Edynburgh, petie terre " in dicto burgo in vico communi ex parte oc-
"cidentali veteris tholonei aſcendendo verſus caſtrum, continentis centum pedes in longitudine, et
" triginta duos pedes in latitudine, ubi novum tholoneum ſibi conſtruere valeant et edificare ;" 3. Decem. a. r. 36.

112 ——— Willielmo de Gladſtanes, filio et heredi Willielmi Gladſtanes, Militis, terrarum de Wodgrenyntoun, Wynkieſtoun, et Acolmefield, in vic. de Peblys, quas Patricius Mallevill reſignavit ; 18. Decem. a. r. 36.

113 ——— Willielmo de Gladſtanes, annui redditus de terris de Wynkiſtoun et Wodgrenyntoun, in vic. de Peblys;
apud Perth, 25. Januarii, a. r. 36.

114 ——— Alano de Erſkyne, baronic de Inchture, in vic. de Perth, quam Johannes de Inchture reſignavit, "apud
" Perth, coram pluribus regni noſtri magnatibus ;" 2. Octob. a. r. 36.

115 ——— Alano de Erſkyne, terre de Crambeth, in vic. de Fyf, quam Alexander de Crambeth reſignavit, apud
Perth, coram pluribus regni magnatibus, 2. Octob. a. r. 36.

116 ——— Confirm. carte conceſſe per Criſtianam de Malavilla, Dominam de Glenbervy, Johanni de Malavilla,
conſanguineo ejus, terrarum de Legevyn, Curmyr, Coldon, Blarernach, Hardiwod, et Radynauane,
in baronia de Glenbervy, et vic. de Kyncardyn ; et concedentis quod dict. Johannes et heredes ſui
poſſint molare, apud molendinum de Glenbervy, pro viceciſmo quinto vaſe multure ; teſtibus, Adam
Epiſcopo Brechinenſi, ac Dominis Willielmo de Monte Alto, David de Berclay, Malcolmo de Rameſay vicecomite de Agnegus, (ſic), Militibus, Johanne de Stratoun, Johanne Judice, Waltero de Al-
lardas, Samuele de Wyltoun, Thoma de Strathechyn juniore, et multis aliis ; carta conf. Regis data
eſt apud Perth, 6. Aprilis, a. r. 36.

117 ——— Confirm. carte conceſſe per Willielmum de Keth Mareſcallum Scotie, et Margaretam ſponſam ejus,
neptem et heredem Alexandri Fraſer, Militis, Domini baronie de Strathekyn, Ade Pyngle, et Marjorie ſponſe ejus, filie et heredi Willielmi dicti Ingeramiſman, terrarum davate del Knoc et Gelac-
bane, in dict. baronia, cum molendino de Camby ; apud manerium noſtrum foreſte de Kyntor, 12.
Maii, an. Dom. 1361 ; carta Regis confirm. data eſt apud Perth, 6. Aprilis, an. reg. 36.

118 ——— Confirm. carte conceſſe per Andream Dempſter et Johannem de Cullas, priori et canonicis de Roſtynot,
quatuor librarum Sterlingorum, ratione decimi denarii de terris de Menmar ; teſtibus Willielmo et
Patricio Epiſcopis Sancti Andree et Brechinenſi, et Domino David de Grahame, Domino de Ald-
monros, et Roberto de Ramefay Vicecomite de Forfar, 8. Aprilis, an. Dom. 1360 ; carta confirm.
Regis data eſt apud Sconam, 3. Auguſti, an. reg. 36.

119 ——— Johanni de Innerpeſſir, et Criſtiane de Sancto Michaele, ſponſe ejus, medietatis terre de Conevath, in
vic. de Banff, et terrarum de duabus Logy Ardachis, in vic. de Abirdene, ſicut Philip de Melgdrum,
Miles, pater, et Andreas de Melgdrum frater predicte Criſtiane, eas tenuerunt ; apud Munros, 31.
Martii, an. reg. 36.

120 ——— "fioliolo noſtro David Fauconer, quem de Sacro fonte levavimus, octo librarum Sterlingor. ad
" ſuſtentationem ſuam annuatim percipiendarum de itineribus Camerarie ;" apud Munros, 2. April.
a. r. 36.

121 ——— Willielmo de Diſſchyntoun, Militi, terre de Balmany, molendini de Aberlennach, terre de Tolyqwon-
lach, et annui redditus de Flemyngtoun, in thanagio de Aberlennach, et vic. de Forfar, " quouſq.
" nos, vel heredes noſtri, dictum Willielmum, vel heredes ſuos, per cartam noſtram infeodaverimus
" de viginti marcatis terre in loco aliquo competenti ;" 18. Feb. a. r. 36.

122 ——— Waltero de Spetall, decime partis terrarum de Kynynmunth, in quarterio de Fortheryf, in vic. de Fyf,
quam Adam de Moncur, et Agnes de Ramſay, ſponſa ſua, reſignaverunt ; apud Perth, 6. April.
a. r. 36.

123 ——— " Bricio Wych, ſervienti noſtro, pro feodo ſuo, centum ſolidorum Sterlingorum annuatim percipiendo-
" rum de terris de Ballachach," in ballia de Kynroſs ; apud Abirbrotnock, 8. April. a. r. 36.

124 ——— Confirm. donationis quam Alicia de Randalyſtoun fecit Waltero de Hoſpith, de uno toſto et croſto
in villa de Eſtriſtoun, et de tribus acris terre adjacentibus ibidem ; 25. Febr. a. r. 36.

INDEX OF CHARTERS, &c. BY KING DAVID II.

125 Carta Confirm. carte conceſſe per Thomam Byſet, Militem, Yſabelle de Fyf Domine ejuſdem, " ante matrimonium inter me et ipſam in facie eccleſie celebratum," baronie de Glaſclune, in vic. de Perth, partis terre de Erth et Slamanane, in vic. de Strivelyne, dicto Thome pertinentis, et terre ejus de Cuthyldrayne, in vic. de Fyf, pro toto tempore vite dicte Yſabelle; apud Sanctum Andream, 10. Januar. an. Dom. 1362; his teſtibus, venerabilibus Dominis Willielmo, Johanne, et Patricio, Sancti Andree, Dunkeldenſi, et Brechinenſi, Epiſcopis; Domino Roberto Seneſcallo Scotie et Comite de Stratherne, Patricio Comite de Marchia et Moravia; Dominis Roberto Erſkyne, Willielmo de Diſſcyntoun, Andrea de Valonis, et Johanne de Kundeloch, Militibus; Michaele de Balfour, David de Barclay, et multis aliis; carta confirm Regis data eſt apud Perth, 17. April. an reg. 36.

126 ——— Aſſedationis Alexro de Strathachyne, terrarum de Morfy Inferiori, in vic. de Kyncardin, pro vita dict. Alexti; apud Aberbrothoc, 6to Aprilis, an. reg. 36to.

127 ——— Confir. carte conceſſ. per Johannem Kenedy, filio ſuo et heredi Gilberto Kenedy, de terris de Srogiltoun, de Poltoun, et de duabus Brochtounis de Leythyrdall, in vic. de Wigtoun; apud Perth, 22do Martii, an. reg. 36to.

128 ——— Protectionis in favorem Abbatis et Conventus Sancti Nemoris; 8vo Maii, an. reg. 36to.

129 ——— Confir. donationis conceſſ. per Agnetem Koullor, Andree de Moravia, terrarum de Kepmade, in vic. de Strivelyn; 10mo Maii, an. reg. 36to.

130 ——— Alexro de Lyndeſay, omnium terrarum Regis in thanagio de Newdoſk, in vic. de Kyncardyn; 10o Maii, an reg 36to.

131 ——— Roberto de Dalyell, terrarum Regis de Selkyrk, exceptis firmis Regis de burgo de Selkyrk; 15o Maii, an. reg. 36to.

132 ——— Mariote Chene, ſponſe quond. Johannis de Douglas, medietatis baronie de Strabrock, in conſtabulario de Lynlitheu, in vic. de Edynburgh, et quarte partis comitatus Cathanie, in vic. de Invernels; ſuper reſignatione ipſius Mariote facta Edynburgi, in preſentia diverſorum procerum et baronum regni, 25to die Maii, anno Domini 1366 .

133 ——— Johanni Ker, burgenſi de Strivelyne, particate terre in vico furcarum burgi de Abirdene; 1o Junii, an. reg. 36to.

134 ——— Malcolmo de Fauſide, filio et heredi quondam Rogeri de Fauſyde, Militis, terre de Lathhame, in coaſtabularia de Hadyngtoun, in vic. de Edynburgh, " contingentis Regi ratione eſcaete, ex eo quod " dictus Malcolmus ad raptum cujuſdem mulieris perſonaliter exiſtebat;" alias conceſſe per Regem Johanni de Lyle Militi, et nunc reſignate per dictum Johannem; teſtibus Willielmo Epiſcopo Sancti Andree, et Patricio Epiſcopo Brechinenſi Cancellario, Roberto Seneſcallo Comite de Stratherne nepote noſtro, Patricio Comite Marchie et Moravie, Willielmo Comite de Douglas, Roberto de Erſkyne, Willielmo de Dyſſchintoun, Militibus, apud Edynburgh, 25to Novembris, ann. reg. 37mo.

135 ——— Confirmationis carte conceſſe per Malcolmum de Fauſide antedict. Alexro de Cocburn, preſcripte terre de Lethhame; teſtibus (in carta Malcolmi) Patricio Comite Marchie et Moravie, Waltero de Halyburton, Thoma de Fauſide, et Patricio de Hebburn, Militibus; Johanne de Sancto Claro Domino de Hirdmanſtoun, Willielmo Mautalent, Symone de Preſton tunc vicecomite de Edynburgh, Adam de Neſbyth, et Willielmo de Fauſyde, conſanguineis meis, et multis aliis; teſtibus (in carta Regis) iiſdem perſonis quorum nomina inſcribuntur in carta precedente, (No 134.), cum Archibaldo de Douglas, cujus nomen ſcribitur inter Comitem de Douglas et Robertum de Erſkyne; apud Perth, 13to Januarii, an. reg. 37mo.

136 ——— Alexo de Cocburn, baronie de Caredyn, in vic. de Edynburgh, regi contingentis pro eo quod Johannes de Veteri Ponte dictam baroniam injuſte alienavit licentia Regis non optenta; teſtibus ut in N 135to, excepto Willmo de Dyſſchingtoun; apud Sconam, 10. Novemb. a. r. 29.

137 ——— Confir. trium cartarum, quarum 1ma conceſſa per Willielmum Regem Scottorum, Willielmo de Veteri Ponte, terrarum de Boulton, Caredyn, et Langtoun, in Warennam; teſtibus (in carta Regis Will.) David fratre meo, W. de Bid. Cancellario, Roberto de Quincy Juſticiario, Hugone Riddell, Jo-

INDEX OF CHARTERS, &c. BY KING DAVID II.

hanne de London, Bern. filio Briant, apud Jedworth: 2da conceffa per Robertum Regem Scot. Willielmo de Veteri Ponte, omnium feodorum et forisfacturarum baronie fue de Caredyn; teftibus (in dicta 1ma carta Regis Roberti) Roberto de Keth, David de Berkeley, Jacobo de Lyndefay, Militibus, Waltero Senefcallo Scotie, Willielmo de Lyndefay Camerario Scotie, Henrico de Anandia, et aliis: 3^{tia} conceffa per eundem Regem Robertum, Willielmo de Veteri Ponti, Militi, baroniarum de Bolton et Langtoun, data apud Dunftaffynch, fub figillo dicti Regis Roberti, 20° Octobris, an. reg. 4to; teftibus in carta Regis Davidis iifdem qui infcribuntur in N° 136to; apud Perth, 16. Apr. a. r. 36.

138 Carta Alex° de Stratoun, molendini in burgo et territorio de Inverbervy, et quarterii de Glenchungole, valen. fecundum antiquum extentum decem marcas Sterlingorum; data apud Monros, 17° Januarii, an. reg. 39no.

139 —— Johanni de Leftalrik, molendini de Inftrothir, in vic. de Fyf; apud Perth, 10mo Martii, an reg. 39no.

140 —— Confir. carte conceffe per Thomam Senefcallum, Comitem de Anegus et Dominum de Bonkyll, Andree Parker, burgenfi de Dunde, terrarum de Kyngenny et Carntoun, et duarum marcarum annui redditus ex terris de Wymachy, in baronia de Athy; teftibus (in carta Comitis) Hugone Abbate de Balmerynach, Domino Laurentio Archidiacono Brechinenfi, Roberto de Erfkyne, Roberto de Ramefay, Roberto de Chefholme, Militibus, Waltero de Lefly, Alexandro Skynnech, et aliis; carta Regis data eft apud Perth, 10. Martii, an. reg. 39.

141 —— Johanni de Loorne, terre de Glenlion, in Athol; apud Perth, 12. Martii. an. reg. 39.

142 —— Johanni del Yle, et Margarete de Vaus fponfe ejus, terre de Buchane, in vic. de Strivelyne; apud Perth, 15. Martii, a. r. 39.

143 —— Jacobo de Blare, omnium terrarum et annuorum reddituum que fuerunt quondam Ade Chiry, in vic. de Are: 3^{tio} Februarii, an. reg. 39°.

144 —— Johanni de Edmounftoun, Militi, terrarum thanagii del Boyen, in vic. de Banff, cum annuo redditu quatuor librarum exeunte de villa de Banff; apud Perth, 17. Martii, an. reg. 39.

145 —— Johanni de Abirnethy, Militi, terrarum de Balgeuery, Cragynkat, Balglaly Wefter, et Balglaly Efter, in conftabularia de Kynghorne, et vic. de Fyff; apud Perth, 15to Martii, an. reg. 39.

146 —— Thome Foreft, particate terre in burgo de Edynburgh que fuit quondam Alexandri Fairley baftardi; apud Perth, 16. Martii, an. reg. 39.

147 —— Waltero de Newbyggyng, medietatis baronie de Cult, refignate per Willielmum de Newbyggyng; 22. Aprilis, an. reg. 39°.

148 —— Andree de Conynghame, annui redditus duarum marcarum ex terra de Kyndevy, in vic. de Perth; 22. Aprilis, an. reg. 39.

149 —— Confir. donationis per Alexandrum Regem Scottorum, fratris predicatoribus de Elgyne, duarum celdrarum frumenti, duarum celdrarum ordei, et unius celdre brafci, annuatim, ex firmis vicecomitatus de Elgyne; teftibus (in carta Regis Alex.) Alexandro Comyne Comite de Buchane Jufticiario et Conftabulario Scotie, Donaldo Comite de Marr, Ingeramo de Gynys, Reginaldo le Chyne, Militibus; apud Kyntor, 29° Martii, an. reg. 36to: Carta conf. Regis David data eft 20. Aprilis, an reg. 39.

150 —— Nicholao de Erfkyne, terrarum de Kynnoule, in vic. de Perth, refignatarum per Robertum de Erfkyne, Militem, patrem predicti Nicholai, cum confenfu Criftiane de Keth ejus fponfe, coram magnatibus regni, apud Perth, 14to Januarii, anno Domini 1366to, tenendarum in liberam baroniam et warrennam adeo libere, &c. ficut prediCtus Robertus, et Criftiana fponfa ejus, aut aliquis Comes de Fyf, Dominus baronie predicte, eam tenuit, faciendo inde Regi fervitium de dicta baronia debitum et confuetum; " vero tamen volumus et concedimus, pro nobis et heredibus noftris, quod heredes Nicholai, &c. per-
" maneant liberi et penitus exempti quoad baroniam predictam, de warda, relevio, et maritagio quo-
" tiefcunque et quandocunque contigerint in futurum;" teftibus Will. Epifcopo Sancti Andree, et Pat. Epo. Brechinen. Cancel. noftro, Roberto Senefcallo Scotie Comite de Stratherne nepote noftro, Patricio Comite Marchie et Moravie, Willielmo Comite de Douglas, Archebaldo de Douglas, et Willielmo de Dyffchyngtoun, Militibus, apud Perth, 18vo Januarii, an. reg. 37°.

INDEX OF CHARTERS, &c. BY KING DAVID II.

151 Carta Confir. carte per Margaretam de Lefly, relictam quondam Domini Normanni Lefly, Militis, Willielmo Guppyld, partium terrarum quondam Alexandri de Lambirtoun, viz. Lumlathyn et Cragoe, in vic. de Forfar, et Afdory, in vic. de Fyfe; testibus (in carta Margarete) Laurentio Archidiacono Brechinensi, Nobili Domina Margareta Comitissa Angufie; Nobilibus viris et Dominis Waltero de Lefly et Alexandro de Lyndefay, Militibus; discretis viris Johanne Gill. Domino de Torfopy, Johanne de Monte acuto, et multis aliis; carta Regis David data est $11°$ Februarii, an. reg. $37°$.

152 —— Willielmo de Lyndefay, terre de Byrys, in constabularia de Hadyngtoun, et vic. de Edynburgh, quam Alexander de Lyndefay refignavit, " apud Perth, 16. Januar. an. Dom. 1366, coram pluribus regni " noftri prelatis et proceribus tunc ibidem in confilio noltro congregatis;" teftibus Epifcopis Sancti Andree, et Brechinenfi Cancellario, Comitibus de Stratherne, Marchie, et Moravie, et de Douglas, antedictis, Roberto de Erfkyne et Waltero de Haliburtoun, Militibus; apud Perth, 17. Januar. a. r. 37.

153 —— Abbati et Conventui de Cambufkyneth, annui redditus 40 folidorum de terris de Erfch, aliorum 40 folidorum de terris de Cambufbarun, cum dimidio firme dict. terrarum de Cambufbarun, in vic. de Strivelyne, " in recompenfationem 8 librarum 5 denariorum Sterlingorum eifdem antiquitus debitorum " de vicecomitatu noftro de Strivelyne nomine annue penfionis; 30. Novemb. a. r. 37.

154 —— Thome Flemyng Comiti de Vyngtoun (certe pro Wygtoun) comitatus de Wygtoun, ficut Malcolmus Comes de Vygtoun, avus dicti Thome, eum tenuit; apud Perth, 26. Januar. a. r. 37.

155 —— Confirm. carte Patricii Comitis de Dunbarr, Thome Papedy, filio Johannis Papedy, terre de Mandredeftoun, conceffe dicto Thome per Stephanum fratrem fuum; teftibus in carta Patricii, " me tunc " exiftente apud Dunfs," Domino Waldevo rectore ecclefie de Dunbarr, Rogero de Merley, David de Graham, Roberto filio Comitis, Philippo Pether Senefcallo dicti Patricii Comitis, Alano de Harkers, Henrico filio Waldewy, et multis aliis; carta confirm. Regis data eft 10. Feb. a. r. 37.

156 —— Confirm. carte Willielmi Douglas, Militis, Domini Vallis de Ledell, nepoti fuo Jacobo de Douglas, terre de Abirdowyr in vic. de Fyff; teftibus Abbatibus Sancte Crucis de Edynburgh et de Newbotill, Andrea de Douglas " avunculo meo," Willielmo de Douglas feniore fratre meo, Ricardo Small rectore ecclefie de Rathewe, Johanne de Abirnethyn, Martino Lytill, et multis aliis, apud Dalkeith; carta confirm Regis data eft apud Drummellyer, 14. Decemb. a. r. 37.

157 —— Willielmo Comiti Sutherlandie, et heredibus mafculis de corpore fuo, medietatis thanagii de Fermartine, in vic. de Abirden, " quam eidem alias conceffimus pro tempore vite fue;" apud Dunde, 30. Julii, a. r. 37.

158 Donatio Johanni de Bothuill, decem librarum Sterlingorum et quatuor celdrarum frumenti annuatim de thanagio de Doune, in vic. de Banf, pro tempore vite ejus; apud Dunde, 31. Julii, a. r. 37.

159 —— Bricio Wych, terrarum de Ballachach, in vic. de Kynros, nomine fui feodi pro tempore vite ejus; apud Strivelyne, 19. Julii, a. r. 37.

160 Carta Confir. Regis Roberti, Johanni de Mallevil, Waltero filio fuo et heredi, et Margarete filie Johannis Ayr fponfe dicti Walteri, et Symoni fratri dicte Margarete, et heredibus mafculis de corporibus dictorum Margarete et Symonis fucceffive, terrarum de Capronneftoun, in vic. de Peblys, et infeodationis *talliate* prefcripte conceffe per Robertum Regem; 5. Julii, a. r. 37.

161 —— Murthaeo del Rynd, quatuor bovatarum terre arabilis in forefta de Plater, propinquius adjacentium terris ejus del Cafs, in vic. de Forfar, reddendo unum par cirothecarum albarum vel duos denarios argenti, nomine albe firme, fi petatur tantum, " apud mancrium noftrum de Forfar; et vo- " lumus quod animalia infra foreftam noftram de Plater ubi et quum animalia foreftaria dicte forefte " noftre pafturam habeant;" apud Dunde, 31. Julii, a. r. 37.

162 —— Waltero de Leffely, Militi, et Eufamie de Rofs fponfe ejus, *confanguinee noftre*, nove forefte, in vic. de Drumfres, tenende in bofcis, &c. " cum bondis, bondagiis *nativis*, et eorum fequelis," &c.; apud Perth, 13. Septemb. a. r. 37.

X

INDEX OF CHARTERS, &c. BY KING DAVID II.

163 Carta Confirm. donationis per Philippum de Abirbothnot Dominum ejufdem, Fratribus Carmelitanis burgi de Abirdene, ad emendationem fabrice ecclefie eorum, annui redditus 13 folid. et 4 denar. Sterlingor. de terra de Abirbuthnot; carta Philippi data eft apud Abirdene, 25. April. an. Dom. 1355°; et carta confir. Regis data eft apud Abirdene, 17. Aug. a. r. 37.

164 —— Ricardo de Sancto Claro, terre de Fynleter, in vic. de Banf, que fuit Joanne de Fynleter, et quam eadem Joanna, apud Dunde, 31. Julii 1366, refignavit; tenende dict. Ricardo et Joanne in vitali redditu, heredibufque inter ipfos legitime procreandis; quibus deficientibus, heredibus dicte Joanne quibufcunque; carta Regis data eft apud Dunde, 31. Julii, a. r. 37.

165 —— Confirm. donationis facte per Willielmum Hare, burgenfem de Edinburgh, Altari Beate Marie, in ecclefia Sancti Egidii de Edynburgh, terre in vico boreali dicti burgi; 26. Octob. a. r. 37.

166 —— Confirm. carte Regis Alexandri 2di, burgo de Ayr, quorundam privilegiorum et quarundam terrarum particulariter bondat. Carta Regis Alexandri verbatim in hac carta confirmationis tranfcribitur, et finitur his verbis, " ficut carta Domini Regis Willielmi patris mei teftatur; teftibus Waltero filio " Alani Sen: f:alli, W. Olyfard Jufticiario Laudonie, Ingelramo de Balliol, H. de Balliol Came" rario, H de Strevelyn filio Comitis David, Duncano filio Gilberti, Johanne de Maxweyll, Regi" naldo de Crawford Viccecomite de Ayr, Waltero Byfed; apud Are, 9. Maii, an. reg. 9°;" carta conf. Regis Davidis data eft 10. Maii, a. r. 37.

167 —— Ade Coffour, bovate terre in tenemento de Aymouth, in baronia de Coldyngham, que fuit Margarete Trymbill, et per illam forisfacta; teftibus Patricio Epifcopo Brechinenfi Cancellario, Roberto Senefeallo Scotie Comite de Stratherne, Willielmo Comite de Douglas, Waltero de Haliburton et Johanne Herice, Militibus; 6. Decem. an. reg 32do.

168 —— Alexandro de Cokburn, terre de Bouryfelde cum pertinen. tam in burgo de Hadyngton quam extra, in conftabularia ejufdem, in vic. de Edynburgh, quam Johannes Lang, burgenfis de Edynburgh, " co" ram prelatis et proceribus regni" refignavit; teftibus Epifcopo et duobus Comitibus in immediate precedente carta infertis, cum Roberto de Erfkyne et Johanne de Prefton, Militibus; apud Perth, 17. April. a. r. 31.

169 —— Confirm. carte facte per Patricium de Dunbarr Comitem Marchie et Moravie, Priori et Conventui Dunelmenfi ac Monachis in cella de Coldyngham, ville et ecclefie de Edreham et ville de Nefbyt; in carta Patricii Comitis verbatim inferitur antiqua carta predeceforis ejus Gofpatricii Comitis fratris Dilfun, earundem villarum et ecclefie, Sancto Cuthberto et monachis ejus, " pro anima Malcolm Regis et fi" liorum ejus regum Edgari et Alexandri, et pro Rege David et filio ejus Henrico," &c.; teftibus (in carta Gofpatricii) Willielmo Dun. Gofp. filio ejus, Ulkil filio Meld, Rand.'de Lynd, S. prefbitero, Johanne capellano filio ejus, Gofp. filio Cryne et Alex. fratre ejus, et Lambert Dap. Val.; carta Patricii Comitis finitur his verbis: " In cujus rei teftimonium, figillum noftrum magnum huic " prefenti carte noftre f. cimus apponi, apud caftrum noftrum de Dunbarr, 24to die Maii, an. Dom. " 1367m, hiis teftibus, Domino Patricio Hebhorn Domino de Halis, Georgio de Dunbar confan" guineo noftro, Alexandro de Ramefay, Alexandro Rikklyntoun tunc conftabulario noftro de Dun" barr, Roberto Leche Senefcallo noftro, et Ricardo de Ellum, et multis aliis; quam quidem car" tam nos Agnes Comitiffa Marchie et Moravie, in omnibus punctis fuis, articulis, et circumftan" tiis, modo pariter et forma fupra dictis, approbamus, ratificamus, et in perpetuum confirmamus; " in cujus rei teftimonium, figillum noftrum, cum figillo Reverendi Domini mei Comitis prefentibus " eft appenfum, die, loco, et anno fupradictis; carta conf. Regis Davidis data eft ------ die Au" gufti, an reg. 38."

——— Confirm. impignorationis facte per Johannem de Lyvyngftoun de Drumry, Symoni Chepman burgenfi de Lanark, duarum partium terrarum de Bankes et del Brerybankes, in territorio de Lanark, et quarundam acrarum, pro duodecim libris Sterlingorum; apud Lanark, an. Dom. 1364, " tefte com" munitate de Lanark cum figillo fuo communi prefentibus appofito;" carta conf. data 22. Aug. a. r. 2d.

INDEX OF CHARTERS, &c. BY KING DAVID II. 83

171 Carta Johanni de Cragy, terre de Merchanſtoun, in vic. de Edynburgh, quam Johannes de Creychtoun reſignavit apud Dunde, 12. Aug. 1367; carta Regis data eſt apud Dunde, 14. Aug. a. r. 38.

172 —— Confirm. Symoni Schaklok, terrarum de Faufyd, Reccor. et medietatis terre de Slanys, in vic. de Kyncardin, difpoſitarum dicto Symoni per Criſtianam de Monteforti, filiam et heredem Johannis de Monteforti de Kyneff, et Agnetem de Monteforti; apud Monrofs, 8. Aug. a. r. 38.

173 —— Abbati et Conventui de Neubottill, " quod habeant et poſſileant terras ſuas vallis de Lethane in libe-
" ram foreſtam," &c.; " quare firmiter prohibemus ne quis in eiſdem terris fecet, aucupet, aut ve-
" netur, ſeu in lacubus, vivariis, in ſtagnis ſuis vel aquis piſcari preſumat fine licentia dictorum re-
" ligiorum ſpeciali, ſuper noſtram plenariam forisfacturam decem librarum;" apud Sconam, 28.
Septem. a. r. 38.

174 —— Confirm. carte conceſſe per Walterum Byſet dominum medictatis baronie de Culter, in vic. de Lanark, Willielmo de Newbygzyng Domino de Dunfyar, medietatis dictæ baronie de Culter; teſtibus W. de Wardlaw Epiſcopo Glaſguenſi, Patricio Epiſcopo Brechinenſi, Adamo Epiſcopo Candide Caſe, Dominis Waltero de Erſkyne, Archebaldo de Douglas, David filio Domini Walteri, Militibus; Domino Roberto de Glen rectore eccleſie de Libertoun, Johanne de Graham, Patricio de Lumley, Adam de Lanark clerico burgenſi, et multis aliis; carta conf. Regis data eſt apud Sconam, 30. Septr, a. r. 38.

175 —— Ade Pingle, terre de Longforgund, in vic. de Perth, " que fuit Alexandri de Dumſermelyne, et
" quam Eumia de Dunfermelyne, confanguinea et heres ejuſdem quondam Alexandri, nobis, in par-
" liamento noſtro tento apud Sconam, coram pluribus regni noſtri, 28vo Septem. a. D. 1367, &c.
" reſignavit;" apud Sconam, 2. Octob. a. r. 38.

176 —— Johanni de Benyne, terrarum que fuerunt quondam Ade de Slyngyſby infra burgum de Edynburgh; 12. Novem. a. r. 38.

177 —— Roberto Seneſcallo de Schanbothy, medietatis terrarum Rubei Caſtri, in vic. de Forfar, quas Andreas Cambell, apud Strivelyne, 4. Martii, a. D. 1367, reſignavit; apud Perth, 8. Martii, a. r. 38.

178 —— Confirm. donationis quam Andreas Cambell, Miles, fecit Roberto Seneſcallo de Schanbothy, quinque denariatarum terre de Wychietoune et de Ballandolach, in baronia Rubei Caſtri, et vic. de Forfar; apud Perth, 8. Martii, a. r. 38.

179 —— Abbati et Conventui de Neubotill, quod habeant et poſſideant terras ſuas Wallis de Lethane, in liberam foreſtam, " cum modo parcandi et pena pargagii, et cum omnibus aliis et ſingulis conſuetudinibus et
" juribus libere foreſte; quare firmiter prohibemus ne quis in eiſdem terris fecet," &c. ut in N° 173. " fine licentia dictorum religioforum ſpeciali, ſub pena libere foreſte;" apud Edynburgh, 17° Febr. a. r. 38°.

180 —— Eccleſie Sanctæ Marie de Neubotill, donationum iis factarum per Henricum de Brade, et Elizabeth de Alburgh filiam ejus et heredem, " incrementi et ayſamenti terre eorum de Crag, viz. totius prati
" quod vocatur Medenſpot, et fontis qui eſt in eodem prato, et orti qui vocatur Stodfald, cum com-
" munia in mora et petaria infra terram de Brade, ad querendum focale pro ſuſtentatione hominum
" ſuorum infra dictam terram de Crag commorantium;" 17. Feb. a. r. 38.

181 —— Duncano Fraſer, et Criſtiane ſponſe ſue, partium terrarum de Brouuemoldy, Mulbynne, et Ordichoys, in comitatu Moravie, de Creebyjoſy, Balmariot, et Auchynmare, in vic. de Baniff, et de Ballyntraile, in vic. de Perth, quas Margareta Gelibrand, ſponſa quondam Laurentii Gelybrand, Militis, et mater dictæ Criſtiane, reſignavit; apud Strathurd, 18. Januar. a. r. 38.

182 —— Willielmo Boyd, terre de Auchmarr, in vic. de Dumbretane, " que fuit Duncani de Luſs, et que, ra-
" tione forisfacture ejuſdem Duncani, nos contingit;" 18. Decem. a. r. 38.

183 —— Symoni Reed conſtabulario caſtri de Edynburgh, foreſte de Lochyndorbe, in vic. de Inverneſs, " que, ratione forisfacture quondam Johannis Comyne, Militis, nos contingit;" 16. Novem. a. r. 38.

184 Carta Confirm carte Alexandri de Lyndesay de Ormyftoun facte ad implendam " conventionem inter eum
" et Alexandrum de Cokburn, de utriufque eorum amicorum et parentum confilio et confenfu, fuper
" matrimonio inter Johan em fil'um dicti Alexandri de Cokburn, de prima uxore fua genitum, et
" Johnetam filiam et heredem dicti Alexandri de Lyndefay," terraru a de Ormyftoun, cum tenandria
terre de Murhous, et terrarum de Templifhall et Paftoun, in conftabularia de Hadyngton et vic. de
Edynburgh; teftibus Dominis Thoma et Hugone monafteriorum Sancte Crucis et Neubotil Abbatibus, Domino Archebaldo de Douglas, Domino Jacobo de Douglas, Domino Waltero de Haliburt-
ton, Domino Georgio de Abirnythy, Domino Patricio de Hebburn, Domino Alexandro de Haliburt-
ton, Militibus; Johanne de Sancto Claro, Willelmo de Creichton Domino ejufdem. Symone de
Preftoun tunc temporis vicecomite Laudonie, Alexandro de Ryclintoun, Adam de Nefbith Domino
ejufdem, Th ma de Oppringvl, Johanne de Spottyfwod Domino ejufdem, et multis aliis; teftibus,
in carta conf. Regis, Willelmo Epifcopo Sancti Andree, Patricio Epifcopo Brechinenfi Cancellario,
Roberto Senefcallo Scotie Comite de Strathern, Willelmo Comite de Douglas, Roberto de Erfkyne,
Waltero de Lefsley, et Alexandro de Lyndefay, Militibus; 23. Febru. a. r. 39.

185 —— Confirm. omnium conventionum factarum inter Alexandrum de Lyndefay de Ormyftoun ex parte una,
et Alexandrum de Cocburn ex parte altera, fuper maritagio contrahendo inter filium Alexri de Cocburn et filiam Alexri de Lyndefay; teftibus, quinque prioribus in precedenti carta, N° 184, cum
Waltero de Haliburton, David de Anand, et Johanne de Edmundfton, Militibus; 23. Feb. a. r. 39.

186 —— Johanne Herice, Militi, terrarum de Kirkgunyane, que fuerunt Abbatis et Conventus de Holme, in
vic. de Drumfres, cum annuorum reddituum earundem arreragiis, et le Saltcotis, " quoufque con-
" cordia inter regnum noftrum et Angliam fuerit reformata, et licentiamus eundem militem quod
" licite componere valeat cum dictis religiofis et convenire de jure quod eifdem competit in dictis
" terris;" apud Dunfermeling, 7. Junii, a. r. 39.

187 —— " Dilecto medico noftro Donnald Bannerman," terrarum duarum Clyntreys et duarum Auchranys,
viz. Le Watertoun et le Weltoun, " ita quod idem Donnaldus, et heredes fui, perficiant illam ca-
" pellam Beate Marie, in eadem terra fituatam, et faciant unam miffam celebrare femel in ebdomada
" pro anima Reverendiffimi patris noftri Domini Roberti Regis Scotie," &c.: " infuper concedimus,
" quod licet donationes et conceffiones noftras generaliter vel fpecialiter revocare nos contigerit,
" omnes et fingule terre predicte de Clyntreys et de Auchrynys, cum pertinen. pro noftra fanitate
" noftro mediante confilio fibi date et conceffe, penes prefatum Donaldum et heredes fuos perpetuo
" remaneant;" apud Sconam, 21. Junii, a. r. 39.

188 —— Johanni (forfan *Wygmer*) burgagii tenementi in burgo de Edynburgh, inter terram Johannis Wygmer
ex orientali, et terram Walteri Curry ex occidentali, Regi contingentis forisfactura Willielmi Bertill-
mew; apud Londors, 24. Decem. a. r. 39.

189 —— Ricardo Comyne, terrarum de Develly, cum officio foreftarii forefte de Ternway, in comitatu Moravie,
et vic. de Invernys; apud Dunde, 6. Januar. a. r. 39.

190 —— " Cum recolende memorie Dominus progenitor nofter per cartam fuam hereditarie ad firmam conceffit
" quondam Waltero filio Gilberti, Militi, patri David filii Walteri, Militis, baroniam de Cadyou
" cum pertinen. infra vic. de Lanark, pro 80 l. Sterlingorum, 22 celdris frumenti et 6 celdris ordei
" annuatim inde folvendis, prout in dicta carta Domini progenitoris noftri plenius dinofcitur contineri;
" nos attendentes, prout (in) prefenti noftro confilio tento apud Perth, 9. die Decem. fuper hoc fui-
" mus informati, quod dicta baronia, tam per guerras quam per varias peftilentias que ab aliis tem-
" poribus contingebant, adeo diminuta extitit et deftructa quod ipfius firme et redditus afcendere
" non poffunt ad totam fommam pecunie et bladorum per annum, dedimus, conceffimus, et ex de-
" liberatione dicti confilii noftri hac prefenti carta noftra confirmavimus, prefato Davidi predictam
" baroniam de Cadyou cum pertinen. et terram five tenandriam de Edelwod, cum fervitio tenendo-
" rum ejufdem, una cum annuo redditu quatuor marcarum nobis inde debito in augmentum baronie
" de C. fupradicte;" Reddendo, &c. 80 l. Sterlingorum, apud Rucbglen, ad teftum dedicationis ec-

INDEX OF CHARTERS, &c. BY KING DAVID II. 85

"elefie Glafguenfis; et " ex deliberatione dicti confilii noftri remittimus eidem David et heredibus
" fuis predictam fommam bladorum," &c.; " conceffimus etiam eidem David et heredibus fuis, quod
" cum aliquis heres ejufdem poft deceffum fui progenitoris de dicta baronia cum pertinen. fupra
" nominatis faifinam debitam receperit, non teneatur ad aliquam duplicationem firme predicte, fed
" quod folvat nobis et heredibus noftris illo anno introitus fui infra dictam baroniam, nomine dicte
" duplicationis, ultra debitam firmam dicte baronie, decem marcas Sterlingorum, unum palefri-
" dum pretii decem marcarum tantum, pro omni alio onere," &c.; apud Londors, 27. Decem.
a. r. 39.

191 Carta " dilecto bachillario noftro Johanni de Abirnethy," terre de Balgynery, Cragynkat, Balglaly Wefter et Efter, in baronia de Kyngorne, in vic. de Fyf, tenend. dicto Johanni " in extentam viginti li-
" brarum terre ufque ad terminum decem annorum ;" 15. Febr. a. r. 39.

192 —— "Confanguineo noftro Roberto de Bruys," terrarum de Rate, in vic. de Perth; apud Roftynot, 17. Januar. a. r. 39.

193 Altera carta confirmationis carte (184) Alexri de Lyndefay, his verbis in Tenendis additis, " quibus forte de-
" ficientibus," (heredibus, viz. inter Alexandrum Cokburne et Johnetam de Lyndefay mafculis vel
feminins), " Willielmo de Lyndefay Domino del Byris, et heredibus fuis de corpore fuo legitime
" procreatis feu procreandis; quibus forfan deficientibus, heredibus dicte Johnete quibufcunque ;"
in ceteris due carte concordant, fed in hac pofteriore teftes carte Regis non inferuntur in recordo.

194 Carta Confirm. carte Regis Roberti, fratribus predicatoribus de Invernys, in dotationem ecclefie fue, decem
librarum Sterlingorum ex firmis burgi de Invernys; teftibus Edwardo Bruyfs Comite de Carric,
Thoma Ranulph Comite Moravie, Johanne de Meneteth, Roberto de Keth Marefcallo Scotie, Gilberto de Haya, et Henrico de Sancto Claro, Militibus; apud Dunde, 21. Octob. an. reg. 8vo; carta
confir. Regis Davidis data eft 20. April. a. r. 39.

195 —— " Confanguineo noftro Georgio de Dumbarr," terrarum de Cumnok, in vic. de Are, de Blauntyre, in
vic. de Lanark, et de Glenken et Mochrum, in vic. de Drumfres, quas Patricius Dunbarr Miles ultimus Comes Marchie refignavit; apud Strivelyne, 25° Julii, a. r. 39.

196 —— " Confanguineo noftro Georgio de Dunbarr," comitatus Marchie, quem predictus Patricius ultimus
Comes ejufdem refignavit; apud Strivelyne, 25. Julii, a. r. 39.

197 —— Willielmo de Diffcyngtoun, confanguineo et heredi Johannis Burnard, tertie partis medietatis baronie
de Ardrofs, in vic. de Fyf, et tertie partis baronie de Curry, in vic. de Edynburgh, que fuerunt dicti
Johannis Burnard; quia " ex deliberatione noftri confilii in pleno Parliamento noftro tento apud
" Sconam alias extiterit declaratum," quod dictus Johannes Burnard apud foreeletum de Lydal,
Rege Davide ibidem perfonaliter exiftente, lethaliter vulneratus, et poftea receptus in caftrum de Roxburgh, priufquam redditum fuit Anglis per Euftachium de Loren, ibi finaliter ex dicto vulnere de-
ceffit, et quod antequam de jure dicti Willielmi Regi conftabat, pre dictas terras conceffterat Alexandro Mautelent; " fed habita fuper hoc deliberatione noftri confilii matura in Parliamento noftro
" tento apud Perth," terre antedicte nunc finaliter conceffe funt dicto Willielmo de Diffyngtoun
Militi; " apud Perth, in pleno Parliamento noftro tento ibidem," 17. Martii, a. r. 39.

198 —— Johanni Gray Clerico Rotulorum, omnium firmarum et exituum burgi de Peblys, illis que ad iter Camerarie pertinuerunt duntaxat exceptis, pro toto tempore vite fue, " per fe, vel affignatum feu de-
" putatum fuum ad hoc literatorie conftitutum ;" 31. Maii, an. reg. 40°.

199 —— Willielmo de Camera, officii Clerici Rotulorum Jufticiarie ex parte boreali aque de Forth, ad voluntatem Regis; apud Abirdene, 27. Octob. a. r. 40.

200 —— Johanni de Innerpefir, officii Vicecomitis de Banff, pro toto tempore vite fue; apud Invernys, 16. Novemb. a. r. 40.

201 —— Bricio Wych, terre de Ballech, in vic. de Kynros, pro toto tempore vite fue, cum bondis, bondagiis,
et *nativis* dicte terre, que declaratur libera ab omnibus cariagiis et multuris durante tempore predicto; apud Perth, 15. Decem. a. r. 40.

Y

INDEX OF CHARTERS, &c. BY KING DAVID II.

202 Carta Hugoni de Roos, et Margarete de Berclay sponse sue, ac eorum diutius viventi pro toto tempore suarum vitarum, annui redditus decem librarum et quatuor celdrarum frumenti de terris de Doune, in vic. de Banff; apud Perth, 16. Feb. a. r. 40.

203 —— Roberto de Anandia, quatuor marcarum Sterlingorum annuatim de firmis burgi de Abirden, pro toto tempore vite sue; apud Abirdene, 5. Decem. a. r. 40.

204 —— Confirm. carte concesse per Walterum Lesley, Militem, Dominum de Filorth, Johanni de Urchard, filio Ade de Urchard, Vicecomitis de Crombathy, terre de Fohesterdy in Buchania, in valle de Kynedore, cum le Fortyre ejusdem quod dicitur Clochorby; testes in carta Walteri non in recordo inscribuntur; carta data est apud Invernes, 8. Novem. a. Dom. 1369: Testes in carta confir. Regis sunt iidem duo Episcopi et duo Comites, quorum nomina exprimuntur in carta N° 184, una cum Roberto de Erskyne et Willielmo de Disschyngtoun, Militibus; apud Monros, 8. Decem. a. r. 40.

205 —— Confirm. carte per Hugonem de Rofs Dominum de Fylorth, filium quondam Domini Hugonis Comitis de Rofs, concesse Ade de Urchard Vicecomiti de Crumbathy, predicte terre de Fohesterdy, cum le Fortyre ejusdem quod dicitur Clochorby; testes in carta Hugonis non in recordo nominantur; carta ejus data est apud Owlenys, 1° Julii, a. D. 1365 : carta conf. Regis data est apud Monros, 8. Decem. a. r. 40.

206 —— Confirm. donationis quam Duncanus Norri fecit Waltero de Petearne, terrarum de Moneyethyn, in baronia de Moneyethyn, in vic. de Kyncardyn; exceptis aula, orto pomerio, uno orreo, cum una acra terre propinquius adjacenti ad partem orientalem, pro habitatione dicti Duncani reservatis; apud Perth, 15. Decem. a. r. 40.

207 —— Confirm. donationis quam Patricius de Ramesay, Miles, Dominus de Keryntoun, fecit Johanni filio Mathei, terrarum que vocantur le Mamylcroft, cum le Cotland ejusdem, jacen. in villa et territorio de Keryntoun, in vic. de Edynburgh; 20. Aug. a. r. 40.

208 —— Capellanis Sancti Monani in capella quam Rex David de novo fundavit, terrarum de Estbernys, in vic. de Fyf, et terrarum de Den, in vic. de Edynburgh; 3. Apr. a. r. 40.

209 —— Thome de Erskyne, Militi, et Johanne de Berclay sponse ejus, feodi et reversionis totius terre de Culcuchone et de Tulchgorme, in vic. de Strivelyne, quarum liberum tenementum in manibus Johannis de Burch, Militis, pro tempore vite sue, tunc exstabat; apud Strivelyne, 16. Apr. a. r. 40.

210 —— Thome de Allirdas, annui redditus viginti solidorum de terris de Litilbaras, in vic. de Kyncardyn; 7. Apr. a. r. 40.

211 —— Thome de Culnchach, et Malcolmo filio ejus, terrarum de Keldewod et Bourland, in vic. de Drumsres, quas dictus Thomas resignavit; 6. Maii, a. r. 40.

212 —— Patricio Episcopo Brechinensi, quod omnes mercatores villam de Brechyn inhabitantes liberum introitum habeant et exitum in aquas de Tay et Southesk, infra vic. de Forfar, cum suis mercandiis, in batellis, navibus, et falcoftis, solvendo cuftumas confuetas; non obstante aliqua assedatione facta burgensibus de Dunde et Monros per Regem vel Camerarium; 4. April. a. r. 40.

213 —— Jacobo de Lyndesay, filio et heredi quondam Jacobi de Lyndesay, Militis, centum marcarum Sterlingorum de magna cuftuma burgi de Dunde, sicut David de Lyndesay, Miles, avus dicti Jacobi, eas percipere confuevit tempore quo magna cuftuma rega unius facci lane extendebat ad dimidiam marcam Sterling. excepta tertia parte dict. 100 marc. Egidie de Lyndesay matri dicti Jacobi ratione tertie sue; 3. Ap. a. r. 40.

214 " David, &c. Sciatis, quod alias Willielmus Comes de Douglas, apud Edynburgh, in presentia nostri et
" plurium nobilium regni nostri, resignavit, &c. quondam Marie de Douglas, filie et heredi quon-
" dam Willielmi de Doug'as, et heredibus suis, omnes terras, &c. quas habuit in baronia de Dal-
" keth, infra vic. de Edynburgh, &c. et hoc omnibus quo:um interest notum facimus ;" 6. Apr.
a. r. 40.

215 —— Willielmo Comiti de Rofs, omnis juris quod dictus Comes habuit in foresta de le Plater, in terris de Fytherevynt, et in advocatione ecclesie ejusdem; quod dictus Comes alias resignaverat in favorem Regis, sed non proprio metu ad illud inductus; 6. Maii, a. r. 40.

INDEX OF CHARTERS, &c. BY KING DAVID II. 87

216 Carta inhabitantibus villam de Brechyn, liberi introitus in, et exitus ab aquis de Southesk et Tay, in vic. de Forfar, cum bonis suis et mercandiis, in batellis, navibus, et falcostis, solvendo custumas consuetas; et quod nullo modo impediantur per burgenses burgorum de Dunde et Monros, propter quamcunque assedationem illis vel dictis eorum burgis factam; 4. Apr. a. r. 40.

217 —— Burgensibus et communitati burgi de Monros, totius dicti burgi de Monros ad feodam firmam sive in feodum, cum territorio et communi pastura dicti burgi eidem adjacente, cum piscariis in aquis de Northesk et Southesk in croisyairs et retibus antiquitus consuetis, cum molendinis, sive ad ventum sive ad aquam, cum tholoneo, parva custuma, curiis, et earum exitibus; reddendo annuatim sexdecim libras Sterlingorum; 1. Maii, a. r. 40.

218 —— Thome de Rate, terrarum in baronia de Ures, in vic. de Kyncardin, que fuerunt Duncani Walay, Militis, et quas idem Duncanus resignavit; 2. Maii, a. r. 40.

219 —— Alexandro de Lyndesay, Militi, baronie de Inveraritie, in vic. de Forfar, quam Margareta de Abirnethy Comitissa de Anegus resignavit; 4. Maii, a. r. 40.

220 " David, &c. Licet alias infeodavimus Walterum de Lesly, Militem, de thanagio de Abirkyrdore, in vic.
" de Banff, et de thanagiis de Kyncardyn; tamen quia forte heredes thanorum qui dicta thanagia
" antiquitus ad feodam firmam tenuerunt, recuperare poterint dicta thanagia, tenenda prout ipso-
" rum predecessores ipsa tenuerunt; concessimus, quod si dicti heredes vel aliquis eorum dicta thana-
" gia vel aliquod ipsorum recuperaverint, idem consanguineus noster et heredes sui habeant servitia
" heredum vel heredis dictorum thanorum vel thani, et feodifirmas antiquitus debitas de thanagiis
" prenotatis;" 6. Mai, a. r. 40.

221 Carta Alexandro Porter, et Johnete sponse ejus, terre de Novo Parco, in vic. de Strivelyne, reservatis Regi viridi et venatione ejusdem prati; reddendo unum arcum cum uno circulo pro alaudis annuatim nomine albe firme; 15. Julii, a. r. 41.

222 —— Roberto de Erskyne, Militi, pro toto tempore vite sue, custodie castri de Strivelyne, cum officio Vicecomitis ejusdem, cum potestate constituendi alium vicecomitem loco suo, ac constabularium et janitorem; et pro sustentatione dicti castri annuatim 14 celdrarum frumenti et 12 celdrarum farine avenarum de terra de Bothkenere, in vic. de Strivelyne, et 200 marcarum per manus Camerarii de terris firmatis et annuis redditibus Regi pertinentibus in vic. de Strivelyne, et wardis, releviis, et escaetis que Regem contingere poterint in dicto vic.; apud Strivelyne, 16. Apr. a. r. 40.

223 —— Confirm. donationis facte per Thomam Byseth de Glasclune, Willielmo de Kergyll, terre de Breynbeyn, in vic. de Perth; 2. Maii, a. r. 40.

224 —— Confirm. donationis quam Adam de Argento fecit Marjorie sponse sue, terre de Lethberdschelis; 30. Apr. a. r. 40.

225 —— Confirm. donationis quam Margareta de Abirnethy Comitissa de Agnegus fecit Patricio de Inverpefir, et Margarete de Fallingtoun sponse ejus, terrarum de Bondyngtoun et Newtoun, in vic. de Forfar; 3. Maii, a. r. 40.

226 —— Confirm. donationis quam Jacobus de Lyndesay, filius et heres quondam Jacobi de Lyndesay, Militis, fecit Willielmo Tailfer, terre de Hareclouch, in vic. de Lanark, et annui redditus tresdecim solidorum et quatuor denariorum de firmis terre de Mudelok, in baronia de Crawford Lyndesay in eodem vic.; 3. Apr. a. r. 40.

227 —— Confirm. donationis quam Ricardus de Roxburgh fecit, et Eviota, filia et heres eius, ratificavit, Andree Bet burgensi de Edynburgh, terrarum et burgagiorum dicti Ricardi in burgis de Edynburgh et Strivelyne; 2. Maii, a. r. 40.

228 —— Andree de Moravia, terre de Tulchadam et Tulchmaler, in vic. de Strivelyne; " revocatione nostra " generali in parliamento nostro ultimo facta de terris nostris dominicis non obstante;" 28. Aug. a. r. 40.

229 —— Alexandro Fraser, terrarum thanagii de Durrys, in vic. de Kyncardyn; 4 Sept. a. r. 40.

230 —— Archebaldo de Douglas, Militi, terrarum de Clerkyntoun, in v c. de Edynburgh, et medietatis baronie de Cultir, in vic. de Lanark, quas Walterus Byset de Clerkyntoun resignavit; 1. Aug. a. r. 40.

231 Carta Willielmo de Dyſſchyntoun, terrarum de Kynbrachmound, in vic. de Fyff, quas Walterus Byſet de Clerkyntoun reſignavit ; iiſdem teſtibus qui nominantur in carta N° 184. una cum Archebaldo de Douglas.

232 —— Henrico de Douglas, terrarum de Logtoun, in vic. de Edynburgh, quas Thomas filius Walteri reſignavit ; 20 Sept. a. r. 40.

233 —— Archebaldo de Douglas, Militi, omnium Regis terrarum Gallovidie inter aquam de Creth et aquam de Nyth, ſicut Edwardus de Bruys Regis avunculus eas poſſedit ; 18. Sept. a. r. 40.

234 —— Roberto de Danyelſtoun, terrarum de Trepwod, in vic. de Lanark, foriſfactarum per quoſdam cognominis Horſſely ; apud Perth, 19. Octob. a. r. 40.

235 —— Confirm. donationis per Robertum Regem facte Abbati et Conventui de Melros, ad fabricam eccleſie monaſterii de Melros de novo conſtruende, duorum millium librarum Sterlingorum, levandarum ex wardis, reliviis, maritagiis, eſcaetis, finibus, amerciamentis, exitibus, et perquiſitis curiarum, tam juſticiarie quam vicecomitatus, infra vicecomitatum de Roxburgh, quouſque totalis ſumma dict. 2000 l. fuerit ſoluta ; Jacobus Dominus de Douglas nominatus eſt ſuperauditor levationis et receptus per dicti Regis Roberti cartam, que data eſt in pleno Parliamento apud Sconam, 26° Martii, a. r. Roberti Regis viceſimo, teſtibus Willielmo, Johanne, et Willielmo, Epiſcopis Sancti Andree, Glaſguenſi, et Dunkeldenſi, Bernardo Abbate de Abirbrothok Cancellario, Duncano Comite de Fyff, Thoma Ranulph Comite Moravie Domino Vallis Anandie et Mannie nepote Regis, Waltero Seneſcallo Scotie, et Jacobo Domino de Douglas, Militibus ; carta confir. Regis Davidis declaratur quod dicte warde, &c. remaneant in manibus dictorum religioſorum donec dicte 2000 l. plene fuerint levate ; et Archebaldus de Douglas, Miles, conſtituitur ſuperauditor et executor ſpecialis ſuper receptis et expenſis ; et carta confirm. data eſt 16. Sept. a. r. 40.

236 —— Thome de Henvyle, et Evane ſponſe ejus, terrarum de Cowlyn et Rowean, in vic. de Drumfres, que reverſe ſunt ad Regem, Suſanna ſponſa Roberti de Corry mortua ſine herede inter dictum conjugem et ipſam procreato, quia dicte terre conceſſe fuerant dicto Roberto et Suſanne, et alteri eorum diutius viventi, et heredibus inter illos procreandis ; quibus deficientibus, reverſure ad Regem, ſalvo dicti Roberti de Corry ad eaſdem jure ; 6. Octob. a. r. 40.

237 —— Thome de Rate, terrarum de Balgillachy, in vic. de Forfar, quas Gilbertus medicus, frater et heres Ectoris medici, apud Monros, 23. Octob. a. D. 1369, coram pluribus regni reſignavit ; tenend. ſicut quondam Patricius M'Beth pater dicti Gilberti infeodatus fuit in eiſdem ; apud Monros, 23. Octob. a. r. 40.

238 —— Willielmo de Rameſay de Dalwolfy, Militi, et Agneti ſponſe ejus, terre de Nether Libertoun, excepte prato quod vocatur Pratum Regis, " quouſque dictum Willielmum et Agnetam de quadraginta mar-
" catis terre infeodavimus hereditarie in loco aliquo competenti ;" apud Monros, 24. Octob. a. r. 40.

239 —— Jacobo de Douglas, Militi, baronie de Dalketh et caſtri ejuſdem, in vic. de Edynburgh, per dictum Jacobum reſignate ; tenende dicto Jacobo, et heredibus maſculis de ſuo corpore ; quibus deficientibus,
" propinquioribus ſemper heredibus maſculis dicti Jacobi cognomen de Douglas habentibus, ſic
" quod dicta baronia et caſtrum cum pertinen. ad heredem femellarum quamcunque propinquam
" vel remotam non deſcendat aut pertineat ullo modo, niſi forte contigerit omnes hujuſmodi heredes
" maſculos prenominatos cognomen de Douglas habentes totaliter deficere," &c. " Volumus etiam
" et concedimus, quod non ſit licitum alicui heredum ejuſdem militis predictorum aliquam donatio-
" nem, conceſſionem, et aſſignationem ſeu reſignationem quamcunque facere aliquo tempore in futu-
" rum de dictis baronia et caſtro cum pertinen. vel aliqua parte earundem, per quas ſeu quam pre-
" ſens noſtra infeodatio talliata adnichilari, diminui, vel frangi valeat, ſed quod ipſa preſens infeo-
" datio in omnibus et per omnia ut premittitur imperpetuum permaneat plena, integra, et illeſa ;"
apud Monros, 9. Decem. a. r. 40.

240 —— Ferguſio de Erch, et Beatrice ſponſe ejus, et Willielmo filio eorum, omnium terrarum et reddituum que fuerunt dicti Ferguſii infra regnum, et que ipſe Ferguſius reſignavit ; apud Strivelyne, 4. Octob. a. r. 40.

INDEX OF CHARTERS, &c. BY KING DAVID II.   89

241 Carta Alexandro de Lyndefay, Militi, baronie de Inveraryte, in vic. de Forfar, cum bondis, bondagiis, *nativis*, &c. refignat. per Margaretam de Abirnethy Comitiffam de Anegus; 15. Jan. a. r. 40.

242 ——— Waltero de Lefley, Militi, et Eufamie fponfe ejus, feodi et reverfionis thanagiorum de Kyncardyn, Abirlouthnot, et Fethirkern, in vic. de Kyncardyn, quorum liberum tenementum in manibus Willielmi Comitis Suthirland.e nunc exiftit; apud Perth, penultimo die Febr. a r. 40.

243 ——— Waltero de Lefley, et Eufamie fponfe ejus, thanagii de Abirkyrdor et terre de Blarefenach, in vic. de Banff; apud Perth, penultimo Febr. a. r. 40.

244 " David, &c. Quia ad aures noftras pervenerit, quod mercatores de Anglia, ac de Berwyco, et Roxburgh,
" qui funt ad fidem Regis Anglie, emunt et de regno noftro abducunt lanas et coria, ac alia bona et
" mercimonia de quibus cuftuma nobis debetur, nullam cuftumam nobis inde folvent., ex eo forte
" quod burgus nofter de Hadyngtoun, et cuftumarii ejufdem funt a marchiis regni noftri plus quam
" hiis diebus expediret remoti, Nos fuper hoc de remedio providere volentes, ac contemplatione dilecti
" confanguinei noftri Georgii Comitis Marchie, conceffimus, &c. quod dictus Comes, et heredes fui
" Comites Marchie, apud Dunbar liberum burgum habeat, ac liberos burgenfes incolas dicti burgi ple-
" na burgenfium libertate gaudentes, emendo coria, pellas, lanas, et alia quecunque mercimonia in
" aliis burgis noftri regni emi et vendi confueta; quodque crucem fori publici habeant, &c. ac forum
" ibidem omni die lune teneant, et cuftumarii noftra et heredum noftrorum auctoritate ftatuantur, ad
" (forfan pro *ac*) tronum ad ponderandum lanas, et Coketam, ac liberum portum apud le Bellehaven
" habeant, cum libero introitu et exitu navium et mercimoniorum," &c. &c. " Volumus infuper quod
" dictus burgus de Dunbar habeat pro bondis fuis totum Comitatum Marchie, fic tamen quod liceat
" burgenfibus burgi noftri de Hadyngtoun infra dictum Comitatum Marchie emere lanas, pelles, coria,
" et alia mercimonia que fupra, folventes inde cuftumariis noftris in dicto burgo de Dunbarr, ut fupra
" conftituendis, cuftumam et alia divoria, capiendo Coketam fuam apud Dunbarr; quoque fimili
" modo liceat burgenfibus de Dunbarr emere infra bondas dicti burgi de Hadyngtoun, lanas, &c.
" folvendo fimiliter cuftumam et alia divoria in talibus confueta, apud eundem burgum de Hadyng-
" toun, et ibidem Coketam fuam capiendo ;" 8. Febr. a. r. 40.

245 Carta Willielmo Comiti de Douglas, terre occidentalis de Balmonth, in vic. de Fyff, quam Johannes de Gordon, 14. Januar. a. D. 1369. refignavit; carta refig. Regis data eft 14 Januar. a. r. 40.

246 ——— Thome Spring, terre de Gafk, in vic. de Abirden, et annui redditus duarum marcarum de terra de Dalmalyne, refignat. per Elenam M'Guffok, 24. Decem. a. D. 1369; carta Regis eft ejufdem datæ.

247 " David, &c. Sciatis, nos religiofos viros Abbatem et Conventum monafterii Sancte Crucis de Edynburgh,
" terras fuas, homines fuos, et univerfas eorundem poffeffiones, ac omnia bona fua mobilia et im-
" mobilia, ecclefiaftica et mundana, fub firma pace et protectione noftra jufte fufcepiffe," &c.
" Conceffimus etiam eifdem religiofis quod nullus namos fuos, aut hominum fuorum, capiat pro ali-
" cujus debito, plegiagio, vel forisfacto, nifi pro eorundem proprio debito, plegiagio, vel forisfacto ;"
apud Perth, 24. Februarii, a. r. 40.

248 Carta Johanni de Ardlere (forfan pro *Ardblere*) et heredibus de corpore ejus, quibus deficientibus, Patricio de Blare fratri ejus, &c. terre de Ardlere (forfan pro *Ardblere*) et de Baldowry, in vic. de Forfar, una cum uno burgagio in burgo de Inverkethyne, refignat. per dictum Johannem; apud Perth, 2. Martii, a. r. 40.

249 " David, &c. Sciatis nos, Willielmum filium Johannis, latorem prefentium, qui, ut a quibufdam diceba-
" tur, *nofter fervus et nativus kone erat de thanagio noftro de Thanadus*, infra vic. de Forfar, noftrum
" hominem liberum feciffe, fcilicet et omnes qui de eodem Willielmo exierunt; ita quod ipfe, et
" omnes exeuntes ab eodem, cum tota fua fequela, fine clameo noftro vel heredum noftrorum, quoad
" aliquam notam fervitutis, libere morari valeant infra regnum noftrum ubicunque fibi melius vide-
" rit expedire; quare volumus et concedimus quod predictus Willielmus, et omnes exeuntes ab eo-
" dem, liberi fint et quieti ab omni fervitute nativa imperpetuum," &c.; " In cujus rei teftimonium,
" prefentibus literis, penes ipfum Willielmum et fequelam fuam perpetuo remanfuris, figillum noftrum
" precepimus apponi; apud Perth, ultimo Feb. a. r. 40."

Z

INDEX OF CHARTERS, &c. BY KING DAVID II.

250 Carta Johanni Herice, Militi, terrarum de Achray, cum annuo redditu viginti marcarum de terris de Skeok, in vic. de Strivelyne; " quem quidem annuum redditum, alias Johanni M'Kelly per cartam noftram " conceffum, pretextu et virtute generalis revocationis facte in noftro Parliamento de terris noftris " dominicis, ad manus noftras alias recepimus revocatum;" 14 Martii, a. r. 40.

251 —— Confirm. Abbati et Conventui Sancte Crucis de Edynburgh, decime partis lucrorum, efcaetarum, et firrum, de quibufcunque placitis, tam Camerarie et Jufticiarie, quam curiarum vicecomitum, et prepofitorum burgorum, feu aliquo quocunque modo contingentium inter aquam de Avyn et Colbranncepeth; " ficut carte five litere quondam progenitoris noftri, et aliorum predeceffurum regum " Scotie, dictis religiofis inde facte in fe plenius continent et proportant;" 26° Julii, a. r. 40.

252 —— Johanni Herice, Militi, annui redditus viginti marcarum de terris de Skeok, in vic. de Strivelyne, &c. ut in N° 250; 2. April. a. r. 40.

253 —— Alexandro Porter, et Johnete fponfe ejus, terre Novi Parci, in vic. de Strivelyne, ut in N° 221; apud Edynburgh, 15. Julii, a. r. 41.

254 —— Johanni Heryng, juris five recti terrarum baronie de Glaflune, in vic. de Perth, quod jus five rectum Thomas Byfet, filius et heres quondam Thome Byfet, Militis, " per literas fuas patentes figillo fuo " et figillo Venerabilis Patris Abbatis Sancte Crucis de Edynburgh, ac figillo Georgii de Dunbarr " Comitis Marchie confanguinei noftri fignatas, furfum reddidit, pureque et fimpliciter refignavit;" 18° Septem. a. r. 41.

255 —— Roberto Senefcallo Scotie Comiti de Stratherne, et Eufamie Comitiffe Moravie fponfe fue, baronie de Methfen, in vic. de Perth, refignate per dictum Senefcallum; 17. Septem. a. r. 41.

256 —— Alexandro de Meneteth, Militi, communis pafture pro centum bobus et vaccis et trecentis ovibus infra moras de Carale, in vic. de Fyf, exeuntium de terra de Balmonthe, infra eundem vicecomitatum; 8. Maii, a. r. 41.

257 —— Ricardo Comyne, annui redditus decem marcarum Sterlingorum de terris de duabus Carnoufiis, in vic. de Banff, quem Johannes Burnard claviger Regis refignavit; 15. Septem. a. r. 41.

258 —— Willielmo Comiti de Rofs, " Comitatus de Rofs et dominii de Sky, ac omnium aliorum dominio- " rum et terrarum que fuerunt ipfius Comitis ubicunque infra regnum, exceptis dominiis " illis et terris que fuerunt dicti Comitis infra vicecomitatus de Abirdene, de Drumfres, " et de Wygtoun; quem quidem comitatum, terras, et dominia idem Comes non vi, &c. fed " mera et fpontanea voluntate fua, nobis apud Perth in pleno Parliamento noftro tento ibidem, 23. " Octob. a. D 1370, in prefentia Roberti Senefcalli Scotie Comitis de Stratherne nepotis noftri, " Willielmi Comitis de Douglas, Georgii Comitis Marchie, Johannis Senefcalli Comitis de Carryk, " Archebaldi de Douglas, Roberti de Erfkyne, Alexandri de Lyndefay, Willielmi de Diffchyng- " toun, Militis, et aliorum plurium Baronum et Nobilium regni noftri, per fuas literas patentes, et " etiam cum fufto et baculo, per manus procuratorum fuorum, fufficientem ad hoc commiffionem " habentium, furfum reddidit, pureque et fimpliciter refignavit, &c. Tenend. et habend. dicto Co- " miti, et heredibus fuis mafculis de corpore fuo legitime procreandis; quibus deficientibus, Waltero " de Lefley, Militi, et Eufamie fponfe fue, et eorum diutius viventi, et heredibus de dicta Eufamia " procreatis feu procreandis, ita, videlicet, quod fi heres mafculus de ipfa Eufamia non exierit, et " plures forte de fe habuerit filias, fenior femper filia, tam ipfius Fufamie quam fuorum heredum de " fe excuntium, deficientibus heredibus mafculis, habeat totum jus et integrum dictum comitatum, " dominia, et terras, cum pertinen. exceptis fupra exceptis, fine divifione aliquali, et ipfis Waltero, " et Eufamia fponfa fua, et heredibus de ipfa Eufamia legitime procreandis, fortaffe deficientibus, " Johanna junior filia dicti Comitis, et heredes fui; et quando ipfi heredes femelle fuerint, femper " fenior heres femella, fine divifione et participatione aliqua, totum et integrum dictum comitatum, " dominia, et terras predictas, cum pertinen. exceptis fupra exceptis, teneat et teneant, de nobis " et heredibus noftris, in feodo et hereditate," &c.; apud Perth, 23. Octob. an. reg 41.

259 —— Dovenaldo M'Nayre, terre de Eftir Foffach, in Abthania de Dull, in vic. de Perth, quam Hugo de Berclay de Kyppok, apud Perth, 24. Octob. a. D. 1370, refignavit; apud Perth, 24. Octob. a. r. 41.

INDEX OF CHARTERS, &c. BY KING DAVID II. 91

260 Carta Duncano Walays, Militi, et Elianore de Bruys fponfe ejus, terrarum de Sundrome, de Drumferne, et de Sywyld, in vic. de Are, quas idem Duncanus, apud Are, 11. Augufti, a. D. 1370, refignavit; apud Perth, 22. Octob. a. r. 41.

261 —— Duncano Walays, Militi, et Elianore fponfe ejus, terrarum de Ochtirbannok, in vic. de Strivelync, quas idem Duncanus refignavit; apud Perth, 22. Octob. a. r. 41.

262 —— Duncano Walays, Militi, et Elianore de Bruys fponfe fue, annui redditus decem marcarum de terris de Barres, in vic. de Kyncardin, quem ipfe Duncanus refignavit; apud Perth, 22. Octob. a. r. 41.

263 —— Johanni de Botheuill, pro toto tempore vite fue, terre parci de Garqwoll, in vic. de Banff; 19. Apr. a. r. 41.

264 —— Davidi Senefcallo, filio Roberti Senefcalli Scotie Comitis de Stratherne, annui redditus de tenemento de Kyndeloch, in vic. de Perth; apud Perth, 27. Octob. a. r. 41.

265 —— Johanni de Barclay, filio Davidis de Barclay, partis de Colcarny, in vic. de Kynros, quam idem David refignavit; apud Perth, 9. Novemb. a. r. 41.

266 —— Roberto de Danyelftoun, baronie de Glencarne, in vic. de Drumfres, quam Johannes de Danyelftoun, pater dicti Roberti, refignavit; cum bondis, bondagiis, *nativis*, et fequelis eorundem; 31. Decemb. a. r. 41.

267 —— Johanni Walays de Ricardtoun, terrarum de Murletter, in vic. de Forfar, et fuperioritatis terre quondam Johannis de Kinros, Militis, quas Johannes de Lyndefay de Thuriftoun, Miles, refignavit; apud Edynburgh, 26. Januarii, an. reg 41.

268 —— Bricio Wych, terrarum de Ballachach et Ballech, in vic. de Kynros; " conceffimus etiam quod dicte " terre libere fint et immunes ab omnibus carriagiis et multuris;" apud Edynburgh, 29. Januarii, an. reg. 41.

269 —— Confirm. donationis quam Willielmus Comes de Douglas fecit Laurentio de Govane, terrarum de Pollynfeych, in comitatu de Douglas, et vic. de Lanark; apud Melros, 9. Septemb. a. r. 41.

270 —— Confirm. donationis quam Abbas et Conventus de Kynlos fecit Donaldo Banerman, terre fue jacentis in vico furcarum burgi de Abirdene, ex occidentali parte ejufdem vici; apud Perth, 18. Octob. a. r. 41.

271 —— Confirm. donationis quam Willielmus de Setoun fecit Ade Foreft, duarum carucatarum terre in villa de Nudreff, in conftabularia de Lynlithcu; apud Perth, 23. Octob. a. r. 41.

272 —— Confirm. donationis quam Johannes de Bona Villa de Balhelvy fecit Waltero Moygne, Militi, de terra de Ochluchry, jacente in dominio de Ardendrauch, et vic. de Abirdene; apud Perth, 23° Octob. a. r. 41.

273 —— Confirm. donationis quam Hugo de Rofs de Felorth fecit Alexandro de Sancto Claro, filio quondam Thome de Sancto Claro, de terra de Eftirtyry, in vic. de Abirdene; apud Dunde, 1. Novemb. a. r. 41.

274 —— Confirm. donationis quam Willielmus Comes de Rofs fecit Alexandro de Sancto Claro, filio quondam Thome de Sancto Claro, de tota davata terre de Bray infra Marefium de Fornewyr, in vic. de Invernys; apud Dunde, 1. Novemb. a. r. 41.

275 —— Confirm. carte conceffe per Dovenaldum Comitem de Levenax, " Mauricio de Bouchannane, filio et " heredi quondam Mauricii de Bouchannane, terre que vocatur Bouchannane, una cam Sallechy er " has divifas, a Kelyn ufque Aldinarr, ficut defcendit infra aquam de Hanerch," (vel Ha erch), " et " illam terram de Saliechy per has fimiliter divifas, a Sallechy ufque Kelg, et ficut defcendit in Bagno " de Lougchlomneid, &c. cum curia vite et membrorum habenda et tenenda in dictis terris quotifcunque voluerit, et exitibus earundem gaudendi. ita tamen quod fi aliquis fit accufatus de huj " " di querela, quod fit judicatus ad curiam dicti Mauricii et heredum fuorum, et quod ponatur ad " mortem ad furcas noftras" (viz. Comitis de Levenax) " del Cathyr," &c. Reddendo " inde no- " bis et heredibus noftris in communi exercitu Domini noftri Regis, quando contigerit, unum cafeum " de qualibet domo in qua fit cafeus in dictis terris," &c.; " falvis nobis et heredibus noftris ab

"hominibus fuis in predictis terris manentibus, oftenfionem armorum (fic) fuorum;" teftibus, in carta Comitis, Dominis Malcolmo Flemyng Comite de Wygtoun, Willielmo de Lewynftoun, Militibus, et Domino Gilberto de Carrik, Milite, Waltero de Foflane, Ewaro Cambell, Finlao filio Roberti de Camfy, Keffano clerico noftro, et multis aliis; carta confirm. Regis data eft apud Edynburgh, 26. Januar. a. r. 41.

276 " David, Dei gratia, Rex Scottorum. Notum facimus univerfis, quod licet ex confuetudine ab antiquis in-
" troducta temporibus, et continuata ufque prefens per nos et predeceffores noftros extiterit, tan-
" quam pro privilegio fpeciali, fervatum, quod bona quaecunque mobilia epifcoporum regni noftri tem-
" pore mortis ipforum regiis fic applicata fuit ufibus, quod ab ipfis epifcopis in fuis teftamentis con-
" dendis, fuper bonis difponendis hujufmodi omnino fuerit hactenus adempta facultas; quia tamen,
" tam per Cleri noftri quam aliorum de noftro confilio prudentiam fuimus jam veris et lucidis ratio-
" nibus informati quod confuetudo hujufmodi ceffit hactenus, et in pofterum cedere manifefte di-
" nofcitur in indecentiam honeftatis ecclefie et in opprobrium ftatus Cleri; Nos, ob reverentiam divini
" nominis, et ad inftantiam prelatorum fuper hoc nobis inftanter fupplicantium, et de confenfu et
" affenfu Roberti Senefcalli Scotie nepotis noftri, et liberorum fuorum, necnon aliorum baronum
" et procerum, ac trium communitatum regni noftri in pleno noftro Parliamento tento apud Perth,
" pro nobis, noftrifque heredibus, et fucceffibus de gratia noftra fpeciali concedimus, et prefen-
" tium literarum ferie confirmamus, quod omnes et finguli epifcopi regni noftri, tam pofteri quam
" prefentes, de quibufcunque mobilibus fuis, tempore mortis fue, fua teftamenta condere valeant,
" et pro fua voluntate difponere, fine aliquo objecto, contradictione, vel impedimento, dicta confue-
" tudine, five ufu longevi temporis in contrarium non obftante; terris tamen, redditibus, dominiis,
" et fervitiis quibufcunque ipforum epifcopatuum, cum pertinentiis, necnon juribus patronatuum ec-
" clefiarum, que ad regaliam noftram pertinere confueverunt, et adhuc pertinent fede vacante, et
" omnibus et fingulis aliis, preter expreffa fuperius, juri regio, voluntatique et difpofitioni noftri,
" heredum et fucceffurum noftrorum, in omnibus et per omnia refervatis; et fi contingat ali-
" quem epifcoporum regni noftri, aliquo unquam tempore, quod abfit, ab inteftato decedere, volu-
" mus, et tenore prefentium concedimus, pro nobis, et noftris heredibus et fucceffibus in per-
" petuum, quod amici et propinquiores dictorum epifcoporum, de univerfis fuis bonis mobilibus,
" abfque quocunque impedimento per nos aut miniftros noftros faciendo, difponant pro fue libito
" voluntatis, prout pro falute animarum ipforum epifcoporum melius videant expedire," &c.; " tef-
" tibus, Roberto Senefcallo Comite de Stratherne nepote noftro fupradicto, *Johanne Senefcallo Co-*
" *mite de Carryk filio fuo primogenito et herede,* Thoma Comite de Marr, Georgio de Dunbarr Comite
" Marchie, Willielmo Comite de ―――." Cetera defunt.

HERE *the Record of King David's Charters ends :――――The reft of this firft Book of Record confifts of Charters by King Robert II.*

INDEX OF CHARTERS, &c. BY KING ROBERT II.

BOOK I.

277 Carta Confir. carte conceffe per Regem dum fuerat Senefcallus Scotie. Carta originalis verbatim inferitur in carta confirmationis, et incipit his verbis, viz. "Robertus Senefcallus Scocie Comes de Stratherne, " falutem in Domino fempiternam. Noverit univerfitas veftra Nos de confenfu et affenfu dilecti primo- " geniti noftri et heredis Johannis Senefcalli Comitis de Carrik, dediffe, &c. Alano de Lawedre tenenti " noftro de Whytflad, wardas, maritagia, relevia, annuos redditus, albas firmas, et earum dupli- " cationes, cum curiarum efchaetis, et fervitiis libere tenentium de tenendria de Birkyfyd, Lygeard- " wode, et Mouftoun, que de nobis tenentur in capite, infra vic. de Berwyco fuper Tweydam, te- " nend. de nobis et heredibus noftris baronibus de Renfrue in feodo ; homagio vel fidelitate Comitis " Marchie, fi nobis debetur de tenendria de Birkyfide, duntaxat exceptis ;" carta originalis data eft apud Renfrewe, hiis teftibus, Dominis Roberto de Erfkyne, Johanne de Danielftoun, et Adam de Fowlertoun, Militibus ; carta confirmationis data eft apud Sanctum Andream, 13. Junii, an. reg. primo ; teftibus, Willielmo et Patricio, Sancti Andree et Brechinenfi Epifcopis, *Johanne primogenito noftro Comite de Carryc Senefcallo Scotie*, Roberto Comite de Meneteth, Alexandro Senefcallo, filiis noftris kariffimis ; Willielmo Comite de Douglas, Johanne de Carric Canonico Glafguenfi Cancellario noftro ; Alexandro de Lyndefay, et Roberto de Erfkyn, Militibus, confanguineis noftris.

278 —— Confirm. donationis quam Malcolmus, filius Johannis, filii Nigelli de Carrik, fecit Alano de Lawedre, de terra de Mertoun, que fuit quondam Alani le Suche, de medietate terre dominice de Lawedre, cum medietate molendini fullonis ejufdem, que fuit quondam Domini Johannis de Balliolo, et de terra de Newbyggyng, in conftabularia de Lawedre, infra vic. de Berwyk fuper Twedam ; apud Sanctum Andream, 13. Junii, an. reg. 1mo.

279 —— Confirm. donationis quam Hugo de Eglyntoun, Miles, fecit Alano de Lawedre, de terra de Nortoun, in baronia de Rothew, in vic. de Edynburgh ; apud Sanctum Audream, 13. Junii, an. reg. 1.

280 —— Confirm. donationis quam Willielmus Comes de Douglas fecit Alano de Lawedre, de terra de Urmotftoun, in regalitate de Lawedre ; apud Sanctum Andream, 13. Junii, an. reg. 1.

281 —— Confirm. donationis " quam nos fecimus dum nos eramus Senefcallus Scotie," Alano de Lawedre, et Alicie Cambell, et eorum diutius viventi, de duabus carucatis terre in villa de Nortoun, in baronia de Rathew, in vic. de Edynburgh, que fuerunt Ibbok et Minote de Nortoun antiquorum tenentium earundem, et quas Fynlaus filius Henrici refignavit ; apud Sanctum Andream, 13. Junii, an. reg. 1mo.

282 —— Confirmans fundationem capelle juxta cimiterium ecclefie parochialis de Mayboyl, in comitatu de Carric, per Johannem Kenedy Dominum de Dounouure, et donationem per eundem 18 marcarum terre de terris fuis vicinis ecclefie de Mayboylle et capelle predictis, et 18 bollarum farine de ficca multura de dicta terra percipi confucta, ac 10 marcarum Sterlingorum annuatim de terra ejus de Balmaclewhane, et 5 marcarum terre de Barrecloych, et 6 marcarum terre de Freuchane, et 5 marcarum terre de Barrelach, ad fuftentationem ipfius capelle, unius clerici et trium capellanorum divina ibidem celebraturorum : " In cujus rei teftimonium, figillum meum, una cum figillo Domini Gil- " berti Kenedy, Militis, filii mei et heredis, ac etiam cum figillo Walteri Epifcopi Glafguenfis, cum " figillo communi capituli ejufdem ad majorem fecuritatem, prefenti litere, et uni alteri ejufdem te- " noris eft appenfum ;" data apud Dounouur, 29. Novemb. an. Dom. 1371 ; carta confir. Regis data eft apud Doundovenald, 4to Decemb. an. reg. 1 .

283 —— Confirm. donationis quam ballivi et communitas ville de Hadyngtoun fecerunt Hugoni de Selkyrk burgenfi de Edynburgh, parve petie terre in dicto burgo ; apud Perth, 2. Julii, an reg. 1mo.

284 —— Confirm. donationis quam Anna de Keloch fecit Altari Sancte Crucis in ecclefia parochiali de Strivelyne, et Nicholao de Torboltoun Vicario dicte ecclefie, pro tempore vite ejus, de uno tofto in terra de Veteri Parco prope Strivelyne ; apud Strivelyne, 26. Februar. a. r. 2do

INDEX OF CHARTERS, &c. BY KING ROBERT II.

285 Carta Johanni Kenedy, medietatis baronies e Dalrimpill, in vic. de Are, quam Malcolmus, filius Gilcristi, filii Ade de Dalrimpill, resignavit; testibus Sancti Andree, Glasguensi, et Brechinensi Episcopis, Johanne *primogenito nostro* Comite de Carrik et Senescallo Scotie; Thoma Comite de Marr, Willielmo Comite de Douglas consanguineis nostris; Roberto Comite de Meneteth filio nostro; Archibaldo de Douglas, Alexandro de Lyndesay, Roberto de Erskyne, Militibus, consanguineis nostris; et Johanne de Carrik Canonico Glasguensi Cancellario nostro; apud Sconam, 30. Maii, an. reg. 1.

286 —— "Carissimo filio nostro Alexandro Senescabili," (certe pro *Senescalli*), 60 davatarum terre de Badennach, una cum castro de Lochyndorbe, et terris ac forestis eidem castro annexis, in vic. de Invernes, Tenend. eidem Alexandro, et heredibus de corpore suo procreandis; quibus deficientibus, David Senescallo filio nostro Comiti de Stratherne, et heredibus de corpore suo exeuntibus, adeo libere, &c. sicut quondam Johannes Comyn, vel aliquis predecessorum suorum, dictas terras et castrum tenuit; apud Sconam, 30. Martii, an. reg. 1mo.

287 —— Thome de Rate, medietatis baronie de Oures, in vic. de Kyncardyn, quam Matheus de Eychles, filius et heres quondam Willielmi de Eychles et Beatricis de Carletoun sponse ejus, apud Sconam resignavit, 30. Martii, a. Dom. 1371; apud Perth, 31. Martii, an. reg. 1mo.

288 —— Thome de Rate, medietatis baronie de Oures, in vic. de Kyncardyn, quam Duncanus de Walays, Miles, resignavit; apud Perth, 1mo Aprilis, a. r. 1mo.

289 —— Roberto de Erskyne, Militi, 20 librarum Sterlingorum annui redditus ex baronia de Cadyou, in vic de Lanark, in excambium terre de Bondyngtoun, et annui redditus quatuor marcarum de terris de Westhall, in baronia de Ratheu, in vic. de Edynburgh; apud Edynburgh, 4. Maii, an. reg. 1mo.

290 —— Hugoni de Eglyntoun, Militi, terre de Allirtoun, in baronia de Kylbryd, in vic. de Lanark; 5. Maii, a. r. 1.

291 —— Hugoni de Eglyntoun, Militi, terre de Bondyngtoun, et annui redditus quatuor marcarum et octo solidorum de terris de Westhall, in baronia de Rathew, in vic. de Edynburgh; 6. Maii, a. r. 1°.

292 —— Hugoni de Eglyntoun, Militi, terre de Gyffeyn, in baronia de Kyle-Senescalh, in vic. de Are; 4. Maii, a. r. 1°.

293 —— "Dilecto filio nostro David Senescallo, Militi, Comiti de Stratherne," castri de Urchard et baronie ejusdem, in vic. de Invernys; tenend. dicto David, et heredibus de corpore ejus procreandis; quibus deficientibus, " dilecto filio nostro Alexandro Senescallo, Militi," et heredibus de corpore ejus procreandis; 19. Junii, a. r. 1mo.

294 —— "David Senescallo, Militi, Comiti de Stratherne, filio nostro karissimo," comitatus de Stratherne; tenendi sibi et heredibus suis in omnibus et per omnia sicut quondam Malisius Comes de Stratherne, vel aliquis alius Comes ejusdem, ipsum comitatum tenuit; " cum additione subscripta, quod ipse et " heredes sui ipsum comitatum habeant, teneant, et possideant in libera regalitate, cum feodis et foris-" facturis, et cum placitis quatuor punctorum corone nostre, libere et quiete; et cum omnibus aliis " libertatibus, commoditatibus, et aisiamentis, et justis pertinentiis quibuscunque que ad liberam " regalitatem pertinent, seu debent, secundum regni leges et consuetudines, pertinere;" apud Perth, 3. Julii, a. r. 1mo.

295 —— Andree de Clapham, terrarum de Tornakyders, in constabularia de Carale, et in vic. de Fyff, quas Mariota de Wardrobe resignavit; apud Perth, 2. Julii, a. r. 1mo.

296 —— Confirm. donationis quam Matheus de Crake fecit Ade de Foulertoun, Militi, et Marjorie sponse ejus, de duabus marcis Sterlingorum annui redditus debiti ex molendino de Corsby: Item alterius donationis quam Cuthbertus de Mortoun fecit dicto Ade, de duabus marcis Sterlingorum annui redditus debiti ex medietate terre de Corsby, que fuit quondam Johannis filii Gilberti; apud Doundonnald, 4. Decemb. a. r 1. (*a*)

---

a Here the old Index very unaccountably concludes, omitting no fewer than thirty-five Charters in the end of this Book.

INDEX OF CHARTERS, &c. BY KING ROBERT II. 95

297 Carta Confirm. donationis quam Jacobus Senefcallus Scotie, *avus nofter*, fecit Ade de Foulertoun, Militi, filio quondam Alani de Foulertoun, terre de Foulertoun, in Kyle-Senefcalli, in vic. de Are, et terre de Gaylis et Pifcar e de Irwyne, et 4¾ marcarum annui redditus de terra de Shualtoun ; carta confirm. Regis caret et data et teftibus.

298 —— Confirmans donationem quam Matheus de Crake fecit Ade de Foulertoun, Militi, et Marjorie fponfe ejus, duarum marcarum annui redditus debiti ex molendino de Corfby ; item donationis quam Cuthbertus de Mortoun fecit prefato Militi, viginti-fex folidorum et octo denariorum Sterlingorum annui redditus ex medietate terre de Corfby, que fuit quondam Johannis filii Gilberti, 4. Decemb. a. r. 1.

299 —— Andree de Conynghame, terre de Kyndevy, in tenemento de Fortevyot, in vic. de Perth, quam Malcolmus filius Mordaci refignavit ; apud Strivelyn, 16to Januarii, a. r. 1mo.

300 —— Confirm. donationis quam " nos, dum eramus Senefcallus Scotie, et antequam ad regie dignitatis cel- " fitudinem fuimus fublimati, fecimus" Marjorie de Foulertoun, de annuo redditu viginti folidorum exeunte de terra de le Trone, in vic. de Are ; apud Irwyn, 7. Decemb. a. r. 1mo.

301 —— Confirmans donationem quam " primogenitus nofter kariffimus Johannes Comes de Carrik Senefcallus " Scotie" fecit Johanni de Foulertoun, filio et heredi Ade de Foulertoun, Militis, de terris de Lachis Orientali et Occidentali, et de terris de Harparlande, in baronia de Kyle-Senefcalli, et vic. de Are, Tenendarum " de prefato Johanne primogenito nofiro et heredibus fuis in feodo ;" apud Sconam, 5to Marcii, a. r. 2do.

302 —— Burgo et burgenfibus de Irwyne, declarans quod per inquifitonem de mandato Regis factam per ballivum de Cunynghame fuper contraverfia mota inter burgenfes de Are et dictos burgenfes de Irwyne, de limitibus et libertatibus dictorum burgorum, fuit clare compertum, quod dicti burgenfes de Irwyne " fuerunt a 30, 40, 50, et 60 annis et ultra et citra, et a tempore et per tempus de cujus " contrario memoria hominum non exiftit, in poffeffione finium, limitum, et bondarum totius baronie " de Conynghame, et baronie de Largis, dicti burgi de Irwyne libertatibus annexarum, pro fuis tan- " tum mercandifis et mercimoniis in eifdem exercentibus ;" confirmans itaque illa privilegia, et concedens quod burgenfes de Irwyne tenant illud burgum in liberum burgum, " abfque exactione cujuf- " cunque tollonei, feu alterius cujuflibet fervitutis," et quod gaudebunt Gylda, et omni Gylde liberate qua alii quicunque regni burgenfes hactenus funt gavifi ; teftibus Willielmo et Patricio Sancti Andree et Brechinenfis Ecclefiarum Epifcopis ; primogenito noftro Johanne Comite de Carrik et Senefcallo Scotie, Roberto Comite de Fyf et de Meneteth, filio noftro dilecto, Willielmo Comite de Douglas ; Johanne de Carrik Canonico Glafguenfi Cancellario noftro ; Hugone de Eglyntoun, et Roberto de Erfkyne, Militibus ; apud Edynburgh, 8vo Aprilis, a. r. 2do.

303 —— David Senefcalli, Militi, comitatus de Stratherne, tenendi ficut quondam Malifius Comes de Stratherne, vel aliquis alius Comes ejufdem eum tenuit, " cum additione fubfcripta, quod ipfe et heredes fui " dictum comitatum, *ac omnes alias et fingulas terras, tenandrias, et tenementa, cum pertinentiis, que tene-* " *tur et tenebantur antiquitus de ipfo comitatu ubicunque infra regnum noftrum*, (a) habeant in integra re- " galitate, cum feodis, forisfacturis, et cum placitis quatuor punctorum corone noftre ;" teftibus Willielmo et Patricio Sancti Andree et Brechinenfi Epifcopis, Johanne primogenito noftro Comite de Carryk Senefcallo Scotie, Roberto Comite de Meneteth, Alexandro Senefcalli, filiis noftris kariffimis ; Willielmo Comite de Douglas, Johanne de Carryk Canonico Glafguenfi Cancellario, Alexandro de Lyndefay, et Roberto de Erfkyne, Militibus ; apud Perth, 3. Julii, a. r. 1.

304 —— " David Senefcalli, Militi, filio noftro kariffimo," comitatus de Stratherne, ejufdem tenoris cum immediate precedenti N° 303, hac claufula addita, " Reddendo ipfe David, et heredes fui, nobis et he- " redibus noftris, de dicto comitatu, cum pertinen. unum par calcarium deauratorum nomine alba

---

(a) The words printed in Italics are omitted in the preceding N° 294. This probably was the reafon of the Charter being recorded here anew

INDEX OF CHARTERS, &c. BY KING ROBERT II.

" firme, apud Dulye, ad feftum Nativitatis Beati Johannis Baptifte annuatim, fi petatur tantum, pro
" warda, relevio, maritagio, ac omnibus aliis et fingulis fervitiis, fecularibus exactionibus, feu de-
" manda, que de dicto comitatu exigi poterit aut requiri;" teftibus, feptem primis in N 303, una
cum Roberto de Erfkyne, et Hugone de Eglyntoun, Militibus; apud Methfen, 19. Octob. a. r. 2.

305 Carta Archebaldo de Douglas, Militi, et heredibus ejus, omnis juris in terris, redditibus, officiis, wardis, releviis, maretagiis, efcaetis, forisfacturis, reverfionibus terrarum, et aliis quibufcunque, quod per mortem Johanne de Moravia uxoris dicti Archebaldi, abfque herede de corporibus eorundem procreato fuperftite et permanente, Regi devolvere poterit: apud Sconam, 31. Marcii 1371, et an. reg. 1; teftibus, " Willielmo et Waltero Sancti Andree et Glafguen," &c.; nomina aliorum teftium defunt.

306 —— Burgo et burgenfibus de Irwyne; Hec eft carta N° 302 fupra notata, rurfum regiftrata.

307 —— Alexandro de Lyndefay. Militi, thanagii de Douny, in vic. de Forfare; cum bondis, bondagiis, nativis et eorum fequelis, &c.; apud Perth, 8. Junii, a. r. 2.

308 —— Willielmo de Kergyll, carrucate terre, partis de Balhevy, (vel Balheny), in baronia de Banff, et vic. de Perth, quam Johannes Herice refignavit; apud Perth, 3. Februar. a. r. 1.

309 —— " Dilecto filio noftro Johanni de Dunbar, et Marjorie fponfe ejus, filie noftre cariffime," et eorum diutius viventi, ac heredibus inter ipfos legitime procreatis feu procreandis; quibus forte deficientibus, Georgio de Dunborr Comiti Marchie, et heredibus fuis legitimis quibufcunque, totius comitatus Moravie, exceptis dominiis et terris de Lochabir et de le Baydenach, et caftro de Urchard et baronia ejufdem, necnon magna cuftuma Regi contingente per totum comitatum predictum et de ipfo comitatu; tenendi in unum integrum et liberum comitatum et in pura et libera regalitate, cum curiis, tam quatuor punctorum ad coronam fpectantium, quam aliis, cum earundem curiarum exitibus, &c.; et quotiefcunque relevium de dicto comitatu per mortem Comitis deberi contigerit, ducente libre Sterlingorum, et non amplius, pro relevio perfolventur; apud Sconam, in pleno Parliamento tento ibidem, 9. Martii, an. reg. 2do.

310 —— " David Senefcallo, Militi, Comiti de Stratherne, filio noftro cariffimo," comitatus de Stratherne, in libera regalitate; apud Edynburgh, 19. Junii, a. r. 1.

311 —— " Thome de Aula furrigico, (forraffe pro chirurgico), pro fideli fervitio fuo," quatuor carrucatarum terre in tenemento de Staneley, in baronia de Renfrew, et vic. de Lanark; faciendo Senefcallo Scotie tres fectas ad curiam de Renfrew ad tria placita capitalia annis fingulis ibidem tenenda; apud Dundonald, 1. Decemb. a. r. 1.

312 —— Roberto de Maxwell, filio et heredi Johannis de Maxwell de Carlaverok, Militi, omnium terrarum que fuerunt ejufdem Johannis tent. in capite de Rege, " et quas ipfe Johannes nobis, apud Kylwy-
" nyne, die 18vo Septemb. coram pluribus regni noftri proceribus," refignavit; libero tenemento earundem dicto Johanni refervato pro tempore vite, " et in cafu quod Chriftiana fponfa ipfius vivere
" contigerit poft mortem dicti Johannis, volumus quod tertia pars dictarum terrarum penes eandem
" Chriftianam remaneat pro toto tempore vite ejus;" apud Kylwynyne, 19. Septemb. a. r. 1°.

313 —— Willielmo Byloune, medietatis terre de Ferrygtounfeld, viz. trefdecim acrarum juxta burgum de Forfare; tenend. pro fervitiis debitis manerio de Forfare, " quoufque heredes dicte terre, fi qui fuerint,
" ipfam terram a nobis feu heredibus recuperaverint in forma juris;" apud Cuprum in Fyff, 5. Januar. a. r. 1°.

314 —— Thome de Rate, medietatis baronie de Oures, in vic. de Kyncardyn, quam Matheus de Eychles, filius et heres quondam Willielmi de Eychles, et Beatricis de Carltoun fponfe ejus, apud Sconam, 30. Martii, an. Dom. 1371, refignavit; apud Perth, 31. Martii, a. r. 1°.

315 —— Johanni Lyon, omnium terrarum thanagii de Glammyfs, in vic. de Forfar: " Volumus infuper, quod
" quandocunq. heredes dicti Johannis relevium pro dictis terris" (aliquid hic deeft) " tenebuntur
" folvere decem libras Sterlingorum tantum de ufuali moneta;" apud Lochfreuch in Strabrawn, 18. Marc i, a. r. 2do.

INDEX OF CHARTERS, &c. BY KING ROBERT II.

316 Carta " dilecto filio nostro Johanni del Yle, omnium et singularum terrarum trecentarum marcarum qu\=
" fuerunt quondam Alani filii Roderici," viz. terrarum de Modoworth, Arrassag, Moreobyr, Knode-
worte, Ouiste, Barrech, Rume, Eggeh, et Heryte, tam infrà partes insularum quam in magna terra ;
" apud Sconam, tempore Parliamenti nostri ibidem tenti, nono die Martii, anno regni nostri se-
" cundo."

317 —— " Mariote de Cardny dilecte nostre," terrarum de Tolyry, de Burelly, de Estirbalnegall, et de Schen-
vall, et molendini de Milnethort, in vic. de Kynrofs ; tenend. eidem Mariote et proli inter nos et
ipsam procreate seu procreande, et ipsa prole forte deficiente, heredibus ipsius Mariote de corpore ipsius
" alias procreandis legitime ;" apud Perth, 27. Martii, a. r. 2do.

318 —— " Karissimo nepoti nostro Jacobo de Lyndesay, Militi," dominii de Wygtoun, cum burgo ejusdem,
(excepta baronia de Carnyfmul,) quod Thomas Flemyng, nepos quondam Malcolmi Flemyng, antea
apud Glasgu, tempore Regis David avunculi Regis Roberti, resignaverat ; et quod idem Thomas
iterum resignavit in presentia Regis Roberti, apud Perth, 19. Aprilis, an. Dom. 1372, " coram
" pluribus regni nostri proceribus et nobilibus assistentibus nobis ibidem ;" apud Perth, 20. April.
a. r. 2.

319 —— Confirmans cartam Regis David avunculi Regis Roberti, Jacobo de Douglas, Militi, terrarum de
Wodefeld, Tyry, Sefelde, duarum Balbretanis, cum molendino ad dictas terras pertinen. in constabularia de Kyngorne, et vic. de Fyff ; declarans dict. ter. as exoneratas et exemptas de annuis redditibus sequentibus, viz. uno quatuor marcarum debito monasterio de Aberbrothok, altero duodecim
solidorum monasterio infule Sancti Columbe, alio quadraginta solidorum pro feodo constabularii de
Kyngorne, et ultimo duarum celdrarum et dimidii celdre frumenti, duarum celdrarum et dimidii
celdre ordei, et quinque celdrarum avenarum, Episcopo Dunkeldensi ; qui omnes annui redditus in
posterum solvendi sunt per possessores residui terrarum dicte constabularie ; apud Edynburgh, 3. Februar. an. reg. dicti Regis David 39 ; carta confir. Regis Roberti data est apud Perth, 27. Junii, an.
reg. 2.

320 —— Willielmo de Somervill, medietatis baronie de Manuel, in vic. de Strivelyne, quam Christiana Crousar
resignavit ; apud Perth, 27. Junii, a. r. 2.

321 —— " Dilecto fratri nostro Hugoni de Eglyntoun, Militi, et carissime sorori nostre Egidie de Lyndesay
" sponse ejus," terre de Bonyngtoun, medietatis terre de Nortoun, cum dominio terrarum de Westhallis et del Cotraw, et quatuor marcarum et octo solidorum annui redditus ex dictis terris de
Westhallis et Cotraw, in vic. de Edynburgh ; apud Perth, 28. Junii, an. reg. 2do.

322 —— Confirmans donationem quam Johannes de Lyndesay de Toristoun fecit Hugoni de Rath, de officio
coronatorie vicecomitatus de Are pro tempore vite dicti Johannis ; concedens etiam dictum officium dicto Hugoni pro toto tempore vite ipsius post mortem dicti Johannis ; carta confirm. caret
data.

323 —— Johanni Cragy, 40 marcarum Sterlingorum annuatim, " quousq. dictus Johannes et heredes sui de 40
" marcatis terre in loco competenti hereditarie infeodati fuerint et sasiti ;" apud Dunde, 14. Martii,
a. r. 2.

324 —— Johanni Walays, Militi, terrarum Tah Unystoun, in baronia de Inverwyk, in vic. de Edynburgh, 20
marcarum annui redditus de terra de Thornyle, in baronia de Renfrew, in vic. de Lanark, 8 marcarum annui redditus de terris de Inglynstoun de Annottouris, in baronia de Doryfder, in vic.
de Drumfres, et omnium terrarum de Retre, in comitatu Buchanie, et vic. de Abirdene ; que omnia
Johannes de Lyndefay de Cragy Miles resignavit ; carta est sine data.

325 —— Ade Wawayne, carrucate terre que fuit quondam Johannis Scroupe, in vic. de Roxburgh, cujus
una medietas jacet in tenemento de Somerstoun, in baronia de Uvyrerelyne, et altera medietas in
baronia de Farnydoune ; sine data.

B b

326 Preceptum directum vicecomiti et ballivis suis de Perth, quod faciant folvi conventui de Scona *fecundas decimas* de firmis terrarum de Rate et Kynfaunys, in quarum pacifica poffeffione dictus conventus fuerat temporibus Regum Roberti et Davidis avi et avunculi Roberti Regis 2di; 8. Maii, a. r. 2.

327 Carta confirmans cartam per Willielmum Comitem de Rofs Dominum de Sky, conceffam Paulo M'Tyre, et heredibus inter ipfum et Mariam de Grahame; quibus deficientibus, legitimis heredibus dicti Pauli, terrarum de Gerloch infra partes Ergadie; tenend. adeo honorifice, &c. "ficut aliqua terra infra dominium noftrum (i. e. Comitis de Rofs) plenius poffidetur;" reddendo unum denarium argenti nomine albe firme annuatim pro omni alio fervitio, "excepto fervitio forinfeco Domini Regis, cum regia voluntas fupervenerit;" fcript. fub figillo noftro, apud Delghem, 5. April. a. D. 1366; teftibus, Alexandro Epifcopo Roffenfi, Hugone de Roffe fratre Comitis Willielmi, Henrico Senefcalli, Johanne de Tarale, Edmondo de Wytona, cum multis aliis; carta confir. Regis data eft 8. Maii, an. reg. 2; teftibus, Willielmo et Patricio Sancti Andree et Brechinenfis Ecclefiarum Epifcopis, primogenito noftro Johanne Comite de Carryk Senefcallo Scotie, Roberto Comite de Fyff et de Meneteth, filio noftro dilecto, Willielmo Comite de Douglas, Georgio de Dunbarr Comite Marchie, Johanne de Carryk Canonico Glafguenfi Cancellario noftro, Hugone de Eglyntoun, et Roberto de Erfkyne, Militibus.

328 —— "Cariffime Socie noftre *Eufamie Regine Scotie*, et Davidi Comiti de Stratherne filio noftro et suo, "caftri noftri lacus de Levyn, cum pertinen.; et ad fuftentationem ejufdem, terrarum de Enachre, "Cafkygoure, Glaflochy, Bondland de Kynrofs, cotagiorum et molendinorum, ac annuorum reddituum "hoftilagiorum ville de Kynrofs; necnon terre de Cultbuy, duorum Tulyochys, Maucuyth, Latheirich, Tomenaygne, Drumgarlet, Techyntulchy, Achteveny, Mauearler, et medietatis ville de Veldelle, Croftmartyn, Bracmam, Brochlach, et annui redditus de Culcarny, cum pertinen. in vic. "de Kynrofs; pro toto tempore vite dictorum Socie noftre, et David filii noftri et fui, cujuflibet "eorum;" apud Edynburgh, 8. Maii, an. reg. 2do.

329 "Evidentie Alano de Lawedre alias conceffe, que funt feptem numero, cum una protectione perpetua, renovate funt, de data, 10. die menfis Martii, an. reg. Regis 2do."

330 "Officium vicecomitis vicecomitatus de Kynrofs conceditur Roberto Haket pro tempore vite, apud Edynburgh, 8. die menfis Maii, anno predicto."

331 "Officium coronatoris infra vic. de Are approbatur et ratificatur Hugoni de Rath, tanquam fubftituto Domini Johannis de Lyndefay de Thoriftoun; Militis, ad tempus vite dicti Domini Johannis, et poft "obitum ejus, conceditur predicto Hugoni pro tempore vite ipfius, fi illum fuperftitem effe contigerit;" apud Edynburgh, 9. Aprilis, anno——

Chartarium, ane Parchment Book, togidder with Parliaments.

Carta Johannis de Infulis que vocantur Ifles Geday, Jura, Colinefay, cum aliis infulis eidem pertinen. viz. Tirayd et Colla, Lewes, Morimarie, Louchabre, terra de Durdoman, Glenchonyre, caftra de Kernorborgh, Ifeleborgh, Dungeuall.

—— Reginaldi filii Roderici, de terris de Kintale in Ergadia Boreali, data per Dominum Rofs.

—— dicti de certis infulis, viz. Yweft, Barra, Fgghe, Romme, terris de Garrw Moybarne, Myndewith, Mordhowar, Arefayg, Cundeworth, cum omnibus pertinentiis.

—— Malcolmi filii Turmode M'Clyde, de duabus partibus tenementi de Glenelgenie, viz. octo douatis et quinque denariatis terre, cum pertinentiis, infra vic. de Invernes.

—— Alexandri M'Naughtan, de omnibus terris que fuerunt Johannis, filii Duncani, filii Alexandri de Yle, et omnibus terris, cum pertinentiis, que fuerunt Johannis Dornagilli ratione forisfacture.

—— Torkyle M'Cloyde, de terris de Afkynkte, una foircelata infule ejufdem.

Par. Rob. III.

Carta burgi de Coupar.
—— burgi de North Berwick.

This " CHARTARIUM, ANE PARCHMENT BOOK, TOGIDDER WITH PARLIAMENTS," *as it is intitled in the old Index, appears to be the Book of Record recovered in November 1793 from the State-Paper Office at London, by Lord Frederick Campbell, in his official character of Lord Clerk-Regifter for Scotland, as is more particularly mentioned above in the Introduction.*

THE Framer of the old Index has only taken notice of the few Charters contained in this important Record, without troubling himfelf either about the other very curious deeds which it contains, or about the Parliamentary Proceedings inferted in it, one Parliament only being briefly mentioned by him, viz. " *Par. Rob. III.*" *and that erroneoufly; for none of the Parliaments entered in the book in queftion are of that King. It is proper, therefore, to give a particular Index of this Book.*

INDEX OF CHARTERS, &c. BY KING DAVID II.

A Quarto Manuscript on Vellum, delivered by his Majesty's Command, from his State-Paper Office at London, to Lord Frederick Campbell, as Lord Clerk-Register for Scotland, in November 1793.

The Volume, before being Bound in its present Form, appears to have consisted of seven or eight, or perhaps more different Parts; and either before being Bound, or since, it seems to have suffered some Mutilations. In the Binding too, either from ignorance, or carelessness, or both, some of the Leaves have been misplaced. It still consists of 74 Folios, or 148 Pages, of a Quarto Size, very closely written.

We proceed to give a particular Index of this valuable Record. It contains as follows, viz.

Folio.
1. Carta Regis Davidis 2^{di}, Johanni de Yle, infularum de Yle, Geday, Jura, Colinfey, Mule, Tiryad, Colla, Lewes, et terrarum de Morimare, Louchabre, Durdomon, Glenchomyr, cum cuftodia caftrorum de Kernoborgh, Ifelcborgh, et Dunchouall, cum terris et minutis infulis ad dicta caftra pertinentibus; apud Are, 12° Junii, anno regni 15to.
do. Carta ejufdem Regis, confirmans cartam conceffam per Willielmum Comitem de Rofs, filium et heredem quondam Hugonis Comitis de Rofs, Reginaldo filio Roderici de Infulis, decem davatarum terre de Kennetale, in Ergadia Boreali; data apud caftrum dicti Comitis de Urcharde, 4to Julii, an. Dom. 1347, teftibus, Johanne et Rogero Moravie et Roffie Epifcopis, Dominis Roberto de Lawedre, Jacobo de Kerdale, et Willielmo de Mowbray, Militibus; Domino Thoma de Lichtoun Canonico Moravienfi, Johanne de Berclay, Adam de Urcharde, Johanne Yong de Dyngvale, et multis aliis Clercis et Laicis; carta Regis eft fine data.
2. —— ejufdem Regis, Reginaldo filio Roderici de Infulis, infularum de Yweft, Barra, Egghe, et Roumme, et octo unciatarum terre de Garw Morwarne, videlicet, Mudeworth, Mordhowor, Arefayg, et Cundeworth, faciendo tam per mare quam per terram fervitia confueta; apud Are, 12° Junii, an. reg. 15to.
do. —— ejufdem Regis, Malcolmo filio Turmode Maclode, duarum partium tenementi de Glenelg, viz. octo davatarum et quinque denariatarum terre, in vic. de Invernys; faciendo fervitium unius navis viginti et fex remorum quum fuper hoc requifitus fuerit.
do. —— ejufdem Regis, Alexandro Macnauchtane, omnium terrarum que fuerunt quondam Johannis, filii Duncani, filii Alexandri de Yle, et omnium terrarum que fuerunt quondam Johannis Dungalli parfonne; terre non nominantur, et carta caret data.
do —— ejufdem Regis, Torkile Maclode, quatuor davatarum terre de Affeynkte cum forcelata infule ejufdem; faciendo fervitium navis viginti remorum quum dictus Torkile vel heredes fui fuper hoc fuerint premuniti; carta eft fine data.

TREATIES, PARLIAMENTS, &c.

3. A Bull of Pope Boniface VIII. fent to Edward I. King of England, afferting the independency of the kingdom of Scotland, dated 5. Kalend. Julii, pontificatus noftri anno quinto, (i. e. 27th June 1300.)
4. An embaffy from King Robert II. of Scotland to King Charles V. of France, dated 31ft January 1374, (i. e. 1375), foliciting the French King's interpofition with the Pope and Cardinals, to procure a favourable decree in a fuit profecuted before the Papal Judicatory, at the inftance of Margaret Logy Queen of Scots, and demanding reparation for depredations on Scots traders by Norman pirates.

INDEX OF CHARTERS, &c. BY KING DAVID II.

Folio.

The deed is in the form of a notorial inftrument, in which King Robert's letter, and the anfwer by King Charles, both in the French language, are *verbatim* inferted. King Robert's Ambaffadors were, Mr Adam de Tynnynghame Dean of Aberdeen, Sir Duncan de Waloys, and Sir John de Edmondftoun, Knights.——This deed is evidently mifplaced in the binding; and after it, two leaves appear to have been cut away.

7 " Factum Norvagie." (This is the original title in the record: what follows here, printed in Italics, is written in a character three centuries at leaft more modern, viz.) *" Concordia inter Alexandrum Regem Scotie et Magnum ejus nominis 4, super infulis regni Scotie."* This is a confirmation by King Robert I. of Scotland and Haquin V. King of Norway, executed at Invernefs, the firft Sunday after the feftival of Symon and Jude, (28th of October), in the year 1312, of a prior treaty, dated at Perth, in the church of the Preaching Friars, on the Friday firft following the feftival of the Apoftles Peter and Paul, (6th of July) 1266, between King Alexander III. of Scotland, " ibidem cum clero et proceribus regni fui majoribus perfonaliter comparente," and King Magnus IV. King of Norway, by his Ambaffadors; by which King Magnus ceded for ever in favour of the King of Scots, " Manniam, cum ceteris infulis Sodorenfibus, et omnibus aliis infulis ex " parte occidentali et auftrali magni Haff," &c. " exceptis infulis Orcadie et Yhetlandie, quas idem " Rex Norwagie fpecialiter refervavit ;" in confideration of which ceffion, the King of Scots, and his heirs for ever, were to pay to the King of Norway, and his heirs, 100 marks yearly, " bonorum " et legalium Sterlingorum, fecundum modum et ufum curie Romane, ac regnorum Francie, Anglie, " et Scotie," within St Magnus church in Orkney, " terra fcilicet Domini Regis Norvagie ;" together with 4000 marks Sterling more, within the fpace of four years then firft following; the payment of the firft 1000 marks to be made about the 24th of June 1267, and the fourth and laft 1000 at the fame term in the year 1270. To the duplicate of the original treaty, which was to remain in poffeffion of the King of Norway, was appended the feal of the King of Scots, together with the feals of Gamelinus and of John Bifhops of St Andrew's and Glafgow, and of Alexander Comyn Earl of Buchan, and of Patrick, William, and Adam, Earls of Dunbar, Marre, and Carric, and of Robert de Meygneris, a Baron. The forefaid treaty is, as obferved above, confirmed by King Robert and King Haquin; and King Robert binds himfelf and the kingdom of Scotland, to pay King Haquin and the kingdom of Norway, 100 marks Sterling yearly. King Robert's feal, together with the feals of Henry, David, Thomas, and Ferquhard, Bifhops of Aberdeen, Murray, Rofs, and Caithnefs, and of William, David, and Thomas Ranulphi, Earls of Rofs, Athole, and Murray, were appended to the duplicate of this confirmation, which was to remain with King Haquin.

8 An acquittance by the commiffioners of faid King Haquin to King Robert, for the 100 marks due for the year 1312, in terms of the above confirmation, and for 500 marks more due for the five years preceding, dated on the Thurfday immediately before the feftival of the Annunciation (25th of March) 1312.

9 " Collo, fic. Tractatus pacis firmate." This deed is in French. It is a ratification by King Edward III. of England, " et totum confilium," dated at Northamptoun, the 4th of May, in the 2d year of that King's reign, viz. 1328, of a treaty, which is *verbatim* tranfcribed in the ratification, concluded at Edinburgh on the 17th of March 1327, (i. e. 1328), between Robert King of Scots and the Plenipotentiaries of faid King Edward III. viz. Henry Bifhop of Lincoln, William Bifhop of Norwich, Henry de Percy, William de la Souche de Afheby, and Geofry le Scrop (*a*). By this treaty it is agreed, 1mo, That a marriage fhould be folemnized as foon as poffible between David, eldeft fon and

C c

(*a*) The original duplicate of this treaty left with the King of Scots is among the Archives in the General Regifter-Houfe at Edinburgh, with the feals of the three lay Plenipotentiaries ftill pretty entire, thofe of Percy and Scrop efpecially.

INDEX OF CHARTERS, &c. BY KING DAVID II.

Folio.

heir of the King of Scots, and Johanna, sister of the King of England, both being then under age; that the King of Scots should assign, in name of dowry, during her life, to the said Johanna, lands within Scotland to the amount of L. 2000 of yearly rent, with the knights-fees, patronages of churches, and other pertinents; but reserving to the King of Scots, and his successors, the patronages of Abbies, Priories, and Hospitals, and his regal rights; providing, That although David should die before the solemnization of the marriage, Johanna should nevertheless enjoy her said dowry, of which the King of Scots is bound to grant her charter and *seisin* before the festival of the Ascension then next; that if Johanna should die before solemnizing the marriage, in that event, the King of England should have the power of marrying David with the Lady nearest to him, the King of England, by blood, who is to have the same dowry; that if David should die before solemnizing the marriage, the King of England should have the heir-male of the King of Scots for husband to Johanna, or failing her, to the Lady nearest by blood to the King of England; that Johanna should be put into the hands of the King of Scots, or his Commissioners, at Berwick-upon-Tweed, on the 15th of July then next; but if David should die before the marriage should be solemnized, Johanna should be at liberty to abide with and to return (*a*) to her brother the King of England, unless she should be with child (*b*), in which event, she should not be at liberty to depart without consent of the King and Barons, ("*sans congee du Roi et du Barnage*"). 2do, That the said Kings, their heirs, and successors, should be faithful allies, and as such, should assist each other, saving, on the part of the King of Scots, his alliance with the French King; but declaring, That if, in consequence of that alliance, the King of Scots should make war on the King of England, the latter should likewise be at liberty to make war on him, the King of Scots; and that in case war should be levied in Ireland against the King of England, or in the Isle of Mann, or the other islands, against the King of Scots, neither of those Kings should assist the enemies of the other. 3tio, It is covenanted and agreed, That all writings, obligations, instruments, and other muniments touching the subjection of the people or country (*terre*) of Scotland to the King of England, (which were, by a written deed (*lettre*) of the King of England, declared null and void); and all other instruments and deeds touching the freedom of Scotland that might be discovered, should be delivered, as soon as they could be found, to the King of Scots, according to a special indenture or inventory to be made of the same; but in case the writing or deed granted by the King of England, annulling those instruments, should become ineffectual and void (*c*), the instruments and other deeds so to be delivered to the King of Scots, should be by him given back to the King of England by a similar indenture or inventory. 4to, That the King of England should endeavour to obtain any suits instituted in the Court of Rome or elsewhere, by the Pope's authority, against the King of Scotland, his kingdom, or subjects, to be dismissed, recalled and annulled. 5to, That the King of Scots and his kingdom, and the prelates and other inhabitants (*gens*) thereof, should be obliged to pay to the King of England L. 20,000 Sterling in the space of three years, by three termly payments, at Tweedmouth; in relation to which payments, the King of Scots his prelates, and other subjects, should grant a public instrument in writing, subjecting themselves to the Pope's jurisdiction. 6to, That the laws of the marches should be well and faithfully kept, and contraventions thereof by the subjects of either kingdom justly redressed; and that if any case not clearly provided for by those laws should occur, the same should be referred to the said Kings themselves, and their respective councils, or to commis-

---

(*a*) "*Demourer et retourner.*"

(*b*) If David died before the marriage should be canonically solemnized, it was indelicate to suppose that Johanna could be with child.

(*c*) This is explained by a relative deed executed by King Edward, of the same date with this ratification; of which relative deed, an abstract will be found on the following page.

INDEX OF CHARTERS, &c. BY KING DAVID II.

Folio

fioners to be specially appointed by them. *7mo*, The plenipotentiaries of the King of England become bound to procure letters-patent from that King, under his seal, approving and ratifying the said treaty in all its circumstances, and to deliver the same to the Mayor of Berwick at the festival of the Ascension then next ; declaring likewise, That by the said treaty, no prejudice was, by either King, intended to Holy Church. *8vo*, and finally, Hugh Earl of Rosse, and Robert de Lawedre Justiciary of Lothian, in presence of, by the special command, and on the soul of the King of Scots, swore on the Holy Gospels, to the faithful performance of the stipulations relative to the marriage, and all the other articles of the treaty ; and Henry de Percy took a similar oath, by the authority of and on the soul of the King of England ; and the King of Scots immediately approved and ratified the treaty.

11 Discharge by King Edward III. of England, " Domino David, Dei gratia, Regi Scottorum, illustri fratri nostro karissimo," for 10,000 marks Sterling, in full payment of 30,000 marks, due to King Edward by the treaty of peace between him and Robert King of Scots, father to King David ; the discharge is dated 10th January, an. reg. Edwardi 4to, i. e. 1331 (*a*).

11 Confirmation and ratification by King Edward III. of England, dated at Northamptoun, the 4th of May, an. reg. sui 2do, (i. e. 1328), of a treaty concluded at Edinburgh, the 17th of March 1327, (i. e. 1328), between Robert King of Scots, with consent of the Prelates, Earls, Barons, " aliorumque procerum" and Commons (*communitatum*) of the kingdom of Scotland, in Parliament, on the one part, and Henry Bishop of Lincoln, William Bishop of Norwich, Henry de Percy, William la Zouche de Asseby, and Geoffry le Scrop, Commissioners and Ambassadors of said Edward King of England, on the other part ; by which treaty, in the *1st* place, The King of Scots obliged himself to pay, at the term of Michaelmas, in the year 1328, at Tweedmouth, to the King of England, L. 100,000 Sterling (*b*) ; and in case he should fail, then he the said King of Scots, with consent foresaid, grants and agrees, That the deed or letters-patent (*litere patentes*) of the King of England, dated at York, the 1st of March, in the 2d year of his reign, (i. e. said year 1328), which are *verbatim* transcribed in the said treaty, should be null and void, and should be given back to the King of England, and the matters mentioned in those letters-patent in relation to the kingdoms of England and Scotland should return to the same state and condition in which they were before the granting of those letters-patent by the King of England, and the obligation for paying the said L. 100,000 should in like manner become null and void. In the 2d place, It was agreed, That if a marriage should take place between David, eldest son and heir of the King of Scots, and Johanna, sister of the King of England, within six months after they should arrive at marriageable age ; or if such marriage should fail and not take place through any other cause than the fault of said David, then the obligation for payment of the L. 100,000 should be null and void, and should be given back to the King of Scots within the space of six months, and yet the letters-patent of the King of England should remain in full force and effect ; and the Ambassadors of King Edward further become obliged to get the said indenture or treaty ratified and confirmed by King of England, under his great seal ; and that the ratification should be, about the festival of the Ascension then next, put into the hands of the Mayor of the town of Berwick-upon-Tweed, to be by him delivered to the King of Scots. The letters-patent of said King Edward, made the basis of and inserted in the above treaty, bear, That as the attempts made by him, King Edward, and by some of his predecessors, Kings of England, to attain the *superiority (jura regiminis dominii, seu superioritatis)* of the kingdom of Scotland, had been productive of severe misfortunes to the inhabitants both of England and Scotland, by grievous wars, slaughter,

---

(*a*) This deed is evidently misplaced in the book.

(*b*) This confirmation seems to refer, not to the principal treaty mentioned above, but to a different treaty of the same date, meant as a counterpart of the principal treaty.

Folio.

and devaſtations; therefore, in order to avoid ſimilar calamities for the future, and to eſtabliſh a ſolid and durable peace between the two kingdoms, he King Edward, with the advice and conſent of the Prelates, Nobles, Earls, Barons, and Commons of his kingdom in Parliament, agreed and declared, That the juſt limits (*recte marchie*) of the kingdom of Scotland ſhould be held and preſerved to the ſaid Robert King of Scots, and his ſucceſſors, the ſame as they were in the time of Alexander King of Scots, who laſt deceaſed, and ſhould ever remain ſeparate in all reſpects from the kingdom of England, entire, quit (*quietus*), and free from every claim of ſubjection or dependence; and King Edward, for himſelf and his ſucceſſors, renounces, in favour of King Robert and his ſucceſſors, every claim of right to which he or his anceſtors had made pretenſions; and he declares all obligations, agreements, and ſtipulations made and granted at any times bypaſt by any kings, or inhabitants of Scotland whether clergy or laity, in relation to the ſubjection of the kingdom of Scotland, altogether invalid and ineffectual: And King Edward ſays, That by ſeparate letters-patent, he had ſpecially authoriſed the ſaid Henry de Percy and William la Souche of Aſſeby, or either of them, to ſwear on his, King Edward's ſoul, to the faithful performance of the premiſſes.

12. The Letters-patent or commiſſion, mentioned in the concluſion of the laſt deed, by King Edward, proceeding on the narrative, That he had granted letters-patent in favour of Robert King of Scots, declaring, That he, King Robert, was to poſſeſs the kingdom of Scotland according to the ſame boundaries by which it had been poſſeſſed in the time of Alexander King of Scots, who laſt deceaſed; and that he had made a renunciation to the ſame King Robert of every pretenſion of right to the kingdom of Scotland acclaimed by him, King Edward, or any of his predeceſſors: Therefore, in order to confirm and corroborate the premiſſes, he authoriſed Henry de Percy and William la Souche of Aſſeby, or either of them, to ſwear on his, King Edward's ſoul, for the faithful performance of the ſame; dated at York, the 1ſt of March, in the 2d year of King Edward's reign.

72 " Remiſſio ſeu abolitio criminis conceſſa Roberto Duci Albanie et Archibaldo Comiti Douglas, propter mor-
" tem illatam Davidi filio primogenito Roberti III. Regis Scotie." ———This is the title prefixed to the deed in the book. But the character in which that title is written is later, by two centuries, than the character in which the deed is recorded. Nor is the title perfectly juſt; becauſe the deed, inſtead of being a remiſſion of the crime, is more properly a declaration that the parties were guiltleſs of the crime: For after mentioning that Prince David had been arreſted by command of the Duke of Albany and Earl of Douglas, and committed priſoner to the caſtle of St Andrew's, and afterwards removed from thence to Falkland, and detained in confinement there, it has theſe words: " Ubi ab hac luce divina providentia et non aliter migraſſe dinoſcitur." It then mentions, that the conduct of the Duke and Earl in this buſineſs had been arraigned, at the King's inſtance, and tried before the King and a general council or Parliament, holden at Edinburgh the 16th May 1402, and that, for certain reaſons touching the public utility, judged improper for inſertion in the deed, the arreſt of the Prince had appeared juſtifiable. The deed is dated the 20th of that month of May, and it was authenticated by the Great Seal.

N. B. The above deed appears to be recorded on a blank page of the book, and far out of its proper place, according to the chronological order of the tranſaction and of the date of the writ.

13 A declaration by King Richard I. of England, That he had reſtored to William King of Scots the caſtles of Berwick, Roxburgh, Edynburgh, and Strivilyn, as belonging to King William by hereditary right; and that he had likewiſe diſcharged all conceſſions and compacts which King Henry (II.), the father of King Richard, had extorted from King William in conſequence of King William's captivity; that King William was to perform to King Richard what William's brother, King Malcolm, had been obliged to perform for his lands in England to King Richard's predeceſſors; that King Richard was in like manner to perform to King William, and his ſucceſſors, whatever King Richard's anceſtors had been, by ancient uſage, obliged to perform, in relation to the treatment of the Kings of Scots

INDEX OF TREATIES, &c. BY KING DAVID II. &c. 10,

Folio.
while going to the court of England and returning home again, and during their residence at court, as should be ascertained by four English Noblemen to be chosen by King William, in conjunction with four Scots Noblemen to be chosen by King Richard; that all usurpations by Englishmen within Scotland posterior to the time when King William was made prisoner, should be restored; and that King William and his heirs should possess all his estates within England, as well his demesne lands as those holden under him in vassallage, *(seu dominicis vel feodis)*, either in the earldom of Huntingtoun or elsewhere, in the same manner as King Malcolm, the brother of William, had possessed them; that King Richard had renounced to King William the allegiance of his subjects, and had delivered back all the writs which King Henry had received from him in consequence of his captivity, and if any were omitted and should be afterwards found, they were to be altogether invalid and ineffectual; and finally, that King William had become the liege-man of King Richard, and had sworn fealty to him for all the lands within England, for which King William's predecessors had been the liege-men of King Richard's predecessors. " Teste meipso, anno regni nostri primo (a)."

Here again a leaf appears to have been cut away.

(a) This deed, as recorded here, differs in some circumstances from the copy printed by Mr Rymer in the Fœdera, vol. 1. p. 64. In this record, King Richard, among his other titles, has that of " *Dominus Hibernia*," which is not in Mr Rymer's copy. Here too the restoration of the castles of Edinburgh and Stirling is mentioned, as well as of Berwick and Roxburgh, which two last only are inserted in Mr Rymer's copy. Here again, after the words " et a " quatuor proceribus Regni Scotie a nobis electis," these words are added, viz. " *postquam Willielmus Bastard, Conquestor* " *dicti regni Anglie, et heredes sui re num Anglie optinuerunt ;*" a palpable interpolation, not superfluous only, but even utterly unconnected with the tenur of the deed. Lastly, instead of the " teste meipso," copied above, the telling clause in Mr Rymer's copy is full and complete, and such as a transaction so solemn demanded. It is thus expressed, " Ut autem " ratum et firmum sit illud in perpetuum, presenti carta et sigillo nostro id roboravimus, testibus Baldewino Cantuar. " et Waltero Rothomag. et J. Dublinen. Archiepiscopis; et Hugone Dunelmen. Hugone Lincolnien. Godefrido Win- " tonien. Huberto Sarisberien. Reginaldo Bathonien. Episcopis; et Domino Johanne fratre nostro; R. Comite Leicef- " trie, Hugone Comite de Waren. H. Bardol. Stephano de Longo Campo, dapifero nostro, et aliis multis; quinto die " Decembris, dat. per manum W. Elyen. electi cancellarii nostri, apud Cantuar. regni nostri anno primo." And Mr Ryman subjoins the following remark, which proves the seal to have been still entire when he made the copy, viz. *Sigilum integrum pendet de serico, filis aureis et argenteis intertexto.* From these last words it is evident, that the deed copied by Mr Rymer was truly the original deed itself; and this question obviously results, How came this writ, which belonged to the King and kingdom of Scotland, to be found among the English archives? To this the Editor is enabled to give a satisfactory answer, namely, that the deed in question was one of those carried off from the castle of Edinburgh by the orders of King Edward I. of England, and lodged at Berwick on the 23d of August, in the 20th year of that King's reign, i. e. 1292, previously to his giving judgement about the succession to the Crown of Scotland. This is established by a roll still preserved in the Chapter-house at Westminster, perused by the Editor on Friday the 20th of September 1793, and again on the 26th and 27th of April 1796, and printed in the book, intitled, *Calendars of Ancient Charters*, published by Sir Joseph Ayloffe, anno 1774, page 327, under the article " Catalogus munimentorum que capta fuerunt " in Thesauria de Edynburgh," &c. The fifth article of which munimenta is, *Litera Richardi Regis Anglie de restitione castrorum de Rokesburgh et Berwick.* On page 340. article second, it occurs again in these words: " *Carta ejusdem Richardi* " *Regis de restitutione jurium, et castrorum, libertatum, et literarum Regis Scotie.*" But the same deed is more fully entered on the 287th page of that book, under the head of " Tractatus pacis et treugarum," &c. copied from an index of papers in the Chapter-house, made up between 1603 and 1625, by Mr Agarde, who, from that index, which was likewise carefully perused in the Chapter-house by the Editor, appears to have been a man of uncommon fidelity and accuracy. In that 287th page of the *Calendars of Ancient Charters*, the instrument under consideration is entered in these words, viz. " A. D. " 1189. Litera Regis Ricardi Primi de redditione castrorum de Rokesburgh et de Berwick, et de restitutione omnium liber- " tatum quas habuerunt Reges Scotie, ante captionem Regis Willielmi, et de literis restitutis et restituendis si que fuerint " invente, et quod litere invente et non restitute omnino non valeant, dat. 5. Decembris, 1. Ric. I " —It is, on the whole, sufficiently clear, that the deed in this book has been recorded posterior to 1292, when the original charter by

D d

INDEX OF TREATIES, &c. BY KING DAVID II.

Folio.

14 A treaty of alliance between King Robert I. of Scotland and King Charles IV. of France, called *Charles le Bel*, dated at Corbeuil in April 1326. The following expressions on the part of King Charles, in the preamble, are remarkable, viz. " Et voulenz croiftre l'amitie et la beneveuillance *qui a efte de* " *longs temps* entre nos predeceffeurs Roys de France et notre royaume, et entre les Roys d'Efcoce " et le dit royalme d'Efcoce." The commiffioners for King Robert were, his nephew Thomas Ranulph Earl of Murray and Lord of Annandale and of Mann, Robert de Keth Marifchall of Scotland, with three churchmen, Mr James Beu Archdean of St Andrew's, Adam Murray, and Walter de Twynham a canon of Glafgow; but the Marifchall does not feem to have gone to France.

After this deed, two leaves feem to have been cut away.

15 A letter from King John of France, addreffed to the clergy, earls, barons, *et communitatibus villarum et partium regni Scotie* (a), thanking them for having, at a recent conference with the Englifh, rejected the folicitations of the latter to break their old alliance with France, and promifing to make a powerful diverfion in favour of the Scots. King John's letter is dated at Paris, the 8th of Auguft 1352.

— Another letter from the fame King John to the Bifhop of St Andrew's, commending, in ftrong terms, the fidelity of the Bifhop in particular, and of the Scots nation in general, in perfifting in their alliance with France; intimating a truce between the French and Englifh, concluded in the hope of a peace; and affuring the Bifhop, that if a peace fhould take place, the interefts of the kingdom of Scotland fhould be by him as faithfully confulted in the treaty as thofe of the kingdom of France. This letter has no date.

— A declaration or remiffion by the faid King John in favour of Edward Balliol, Knight, bearing, that although on account of the war carried on againft the Scots, the allies of him King John, by the faid Edward, at the inftigation of the Englifh, Edward's eftates within France had been *per gentes noftras*, (viz. King John's), fequeftrated and annexed to King John's domains; yet as Edward was reported to have an intention of returning to his allegiance to King John, and to the friendfhip of the Scots; therefore King John promifes, in that event, to reftore Edward's eftates, or to confer on him fomething more valuable in their ftead; dated at Paris, 28th September 1361.

— Another letter of King John of France, addreffed to the Regent, and to all the prelates, chiefs, (*principibus*) barons, and nobles of the kingdom of Scotland, expreffing, in ftrong religious terms, his forrow for the late flaughters and devaftations inflicted on Scotland by the Englifh; and exhorting them to perfift in their refiftance; but in cafe their efforts fhould finally prove ineffectual, and their country fhould be fubdued, he affures them of a kind reception in the kingdom of France.

16 Another letter from the fame King John, expreffing the deepeft forrow for the fufferings and misfortunes of the Scots, his faithful allies, in confequence of the repeated advantages obtained over them by the

---

King Richard was carried out of Scotland by the command of Edward I.; and that in recording it an inaccurate copy has been followed. It appears, too, to have been, like the *Remiffio* laft noticed, recorded on a blank page, and ftill much farther out of its proper place, according to its date; for, according to chronological order, it ought to have been the firft in the book. In all the material points, however, the deed, as here recorded, agrees with the original charter as printed in the Fœdera.

Poftfcript. The charter itfelf is ftill in the Chapter-houfe at Weftminfter, where it was carefully perufed by the Editor, and collated with the printed copy in the Fœdera, on Tuefday and Wednefday the 26th and 27th of April 1796. The feal is ftill perfectly entire, hanging by the filken cord defcribed by Mr Rymer; but the writing is in a rapid ftate of decay, though ftill legible, excepting a few words here and there in the folds. In Mr Rymer's printed copy there are fome inaccuracies, but not of any material importance.

(*a*) David King of Scots is not here mentioned, becaufe, having been made prifoner at the battle of Durham in October 1346, he was at this time detained in captivity in England, where, about four years after, King John of France arrived in the fame unfortunate fituation.

INDEX OF TREATIES, &c. BY KING DAVID II.

Folio.

more numerous forces of their enemies the English, and promising to send to their aid 500 armed knights, and an equal number of archers, on his own expence.

16 A writ by the said King John, directed to his Admiral and all his officers of justice, informing them, that he had taken under his special protection all Scotsmen, particularly Scots merchants trading to the ports of France, and therefore commanding those officers to act accordingly: and as it was reported that a Scots trading vessel had been seized and plundered by some French pirates, he directs restitution to be made of such of the effects as could be recovered, under pain of severe punishment.

> These three last entries seem, from the record, to have been all of the same date with the fourth preceding, viz. 28th September 1360.
>
> *After this last writ, another leaf of the book has evidently been cut away.*

17 "*Cōpia alligantie Regis Francie facte cum Anglicis in nostri prejudicium.*" Such is the title prefixed to this deed in the record. The deed itself is an engagement of alliance by King John of France in favour of the King of England, by which all the treaties between France and Scotland are expressly declared to be annulled and retracted by King John, under the sanction of the Pope's authority, obtained at his instance and that of the King of England; and King John obliges himself, and his heirs and successors, to assist the King of England against all his enemies, saving his alliances with the Pope and the Emperor. It is remarkable, that nothing reciprocal is stipulated to be performed in return by the King of England, whose name is not once mentioned in the whole instrument; and it is plain, that the principal object was to break off King John's connection with the Scots; and that King John's concessions were the effect of mere compulsion. The instrument is witnessed by many of the first nobility of France, and is dated at Boulogne, the 26th of October 1360.

19 "*Prima treuga et liberatio regis.*" This is the treaty for liberating King David from his captivity in England, where he had been now detained prisoner eleven years, ever since the battle of Durham. His ransom was, by this treaty, fixed at 100,000 marks Sterling, payable, by equal portions, in the space of ten years, at the rate of 10,000 marks each year; and twenty hostages, for the more sure payment, were to be sent to England, of whom the first named is *Johan Seneschal*. Three of the following seven noblemen were always to be of the number of those twenty hostages, viz. the Steward of Scotland, the Earls of March, Marr, Ross, and Sutherland, the Lord Douglas, and Thomas de Murray; that in the mean time, during the whole period of the said ten years, an inviolable truce should subsist between the two kingdoms and the isle of Man; in which truce were to be included, *Monsieur Edward de Balliol et Johan des Isles, et tous autres aliez et adherans* of the King of England; and that John, eldest son and heir apparent of the Steward of Scotland, (*Jolan, aynsne fitz et heir-apparant du Seneschal d'Escoce*), one of the foresaid hostages (a), should remain in the company of the Lord of Percy or of Neville till the first payment should be made, after which, the immediate younger brother of said John should come and remain as hostage in his brother's place until the next annual payment of 10,000 marks should in like manner be made. The treaty is dated at Berwick-on-Tweed, the 3d day of October 1357. It is in the French language, and in various respects highly curious.

22 A confirmation by King David of the preceding treaty, containing a personal obligation on him, King David, to fulfil the same in all its articles.

23 A ratification of the same treaty by the bishops of Scotland, containing an obligation on them to enforce the performance of the same by ecclesiastical censures, particularly by the sentence of greater excommunication; and containing likewise a subsidiary obligation on them and their sees for payment of the

---

(a) This of itself alone is the most satisfactory and decisive proof, that John, afterwards King Robert III. was universally known to be the legitimate son of Robert the Great Steward, afterwards King Robert II. more than thirteen years before his father's accession to the Crown of Scotland.

INDEX OF TREATIES, &c. BY KING DAVID II.

Folio.

ranfom. By this ratification, the following earls and barons appear to have become bound to compel King David to perform the conditions incumbent perfonally on him, viz. Patrick Earl of March, Thomas Earl of Angus, and William Earl of Sutherland, Thomas de Murray, James de Lyndefay, David de Grahame, Robert de Erfkyne, William de Levyngftoun, David de Wemys, Thomas Byfet, William de Vaux, and William de Ramefay, Knights, and Roger de Kyrkpatrick *Domicellus*, dated at E. y burgh, the 26th of September, and at Berwick-on-Tweed, the 6th of October 1357.

25 A fimilar ratification by Patrick Earl of March, Thomas Earl of Angus, William Earl of Sutherland, Thomas de Murray, *Panetarius* of Scotland, William de Levyngftoun, and Robert de Erfkyne, Knights, for themfelves, as well as for the other great barons, in virtue of fpecial powers from them for that effect; by which too, they, like the prelates, oblige themfelves and their heirs fubfidiarily in payment of the ranfom. Of this deed the date is not fet down in the record.

— A bull from Pope Innocent VI. dated at Avignon, 11. kalend. of July, (21ft of June), in the 6th year of his Pontificate, addreffed to King David, declining to give his fanction to the obligation for paying the ranfom, to which the bifhops, abbots, priors, and other ecclefiaftics of Scotland had fubjected themfelves, their effects, fees, chapters, and monafteries.

26 Proceedings of a parliament holden at Scone, the 6th of November 1357. Here, apparently with a view to levy money for paying the King's ranfom, a general account is ordained to be taken of the true value of all the lands and revenues, both of the ecclefiaftics and laymen, throughout the whole kingdom, and of all corns, cattle, and other goods, of whatever kind, *ex. eptis albis ovibus, equis domitis et bobus, domorum utenfilibus, et bladorum decimis*; in relation to which, very particular directions are given. Here too all grants by the King, of lands and revenues belonging to the Crown, and of wards and other royal cafualties, are revoked. On the whole, the proceedings of this Parliament are very remarkable and interefting.

27 An inftrument, dated at Invernefs, 15th November 1369, by John of Yle Lord of the Ifles, by which, in confideration of the pardon of his former tranfgrefftions, granted by King David, he becomes bound to make fatisfaction for all injuries or damages done by him to the King's fubjects, to give obedience to the laws himfelf, and to oblige his fons, and his vaffals, and all the inhabitants of his eftates, to do the fame, and to anfwer rea'ily to the King's officers for all taxes and contributions impofed or to be impofed. For fulfilling the premiffes, he engages to deliver as hoftages, within the caftle of Dumbarton, his fon by a daughter of the Steward of Scotland, named Donald, a grandfon named Angus, being the fon of his deceafed fon John, together with a natural fon of his own, named Donald; and further, the Earl of Stratherne Steward of Scotland becomes furety for him, and appends his feal to the inftrument, along with the feal of the faid John Lord of the Ifles.

28 A renewal of the truce by King Edward III. for four years certain, dated 20th of June 1365. The inftrument expreffes a penal fum of L. 100,000 Sterling, payable by the Scots on account of the arrears of the ranfom; but declares, that the payments to be made by the Scots fhall be imputed towards the extinction of 80,000 marks, the balance of ranfom ftill really unpaid. The inftrument is in French.

29 An inftrument by King David to the fame effect, dated at Edinburgh, 12th of June 1365. This deed too is in the French language.

Here another leaf feems to have been cut away.

30 A convention, dated 1ft September 1367, at Muirhouflaw, and from thence adjourned to Roxburgh, relative to the affairs of the marches, between Thomas de Beauchamp Earl of Warrick Marifchall of England, the Lord Percy, and Henry Piercy his eldeft fon, on the one part, and the Bifhops of St Andrew's and Glafgow, Patrick Earl of March and of Murray, William Earl of Douglas, Robert de Erfkyn, Walter de Lefley, Walter de Haliburton, and Hugh de Eglintoun, Knights, on the other part.

INDEX OF PARLIAMENTS, &c. BY KING ROBERT II.   109

Folio.
31 A prolongation of the truce, containing an obligation for payment of 56,000 marks, the balance of the ranfom ſtill due, at the rate of 4000 marks each year; on complete payment of which 56,000 marks, all former obligations in relation to the ranfom, particularly that for the penal fum of L. 100,000 above mentioned, were to become null and void.

Here another leaf, on which the concluding part of this deed was recorded, has been cut away.

32 Commiſſion by King Edward, dated 13th June, in the 45th year of his reign, i. e. 1371, to certain perfons to receive 4000 marks Sterling, which was to be paid him at the feaſt of St John the Baptiſt then next, 24th of June, by Robert King of Scots, as part of 52,000 marks, the balance of ranfom ſtill unpaid.

33 Another commiſſion by King Edward, dated 13th June, in the 46th year of his reign, 1372, to the perfons contained in the preceding commiſſion, to receive 4000 marks more, to account of 48,000 marks, the balance of the ranfom then due.

34 A receipt and difcharge by King Edward for the laſt-mentioned 4000 marks, dated 26th of faid month of June 1372, at Weſtminſter.

— Another receipt for the fame fum by King Edward's commiſſioners, dated at Berwick-on-Tweed, the 23d of June 1372.

— A very formal proteſtation by the commiſſioners of King Robert, in relation to certain alledged informalities in the receipts for the partial payments of the ranfom then and formerly made, dated at Berwick-on-Tweed, 23d of June 1372.

36 An indenture relative to the fame informalities between William and George Earls of Douglas and March, the Scots wardens of the eaſt marches, and the Biſhop of Durham and Henry Lord Percy, the Engliſh wardens, date ? at Lylyet-crofs, the 18th October 1372.

— Two commiſſions of wardenry by King Edward, the one for the eaſt, the other for the weſt marches, both dated at Weſtminſter, the 16th of October, in the 43d year of his reign, i. e. 1369.

37 Another commiſſion of wardenry for the eaſt marches by King Edward, dated at Weſtminſter, the 25th of June, in the 45th year of his reign, 1371.

After this, two leaves appear to have been cut away.

39 A parliament holden at Scone, 4th of March 1363-4. Here the three eſtates gave a flat negative to certain propofals, not particularifed in the minute, which had been agitated between King David and fome perfons prefent with him at London, and the council of the King of England, of which the tendency may be eaſily perceived from the words of the minute: " Et refponfum fuit expreſſe per tres com-
" munitates ibidem, quod ea quæ petita fuerant per Regem Angliæ et fuum confilium, ut prenotatum
" eſt, nullo modo voluerunt concedere, nec eis aliqualiter aſſentiri; veruntamen ad omnia quæ poſſent
" fieri pro bona pace habenda, *perpetuo ſtatu Regio, libertate et integritate Regni, ſervatis et illæſis*, li-
" benter et unanimiter exponerent," &c.

40 A parliament holden within the houſe of the Preaching Friars at Perth, on the 13th of January 1364-5. The attention of this parliament feems to have been entirely employed about eſtabliſhing either a folid peace with England, or a long truce, and about paying the balance of the King's ranfom, of which 20,000 marks had been already paid. The different inſtructions prefcribed by this parliament to the ambaſſadors employed in the negotiation are here fet down, and are very remarkable, particularly the propofal of giving to a younger fon of King Edward *mille libratas terræ* within Galloway, which had been the property of the deceafed Edward Bailiol, together with the iſland of Mann, eſtimated at 1000 merks more.

42 An act of a parliament holden at Perth, the 14th of January 1365-6, in relation to the weighing of wool, intitled, " *De trona et tronariis.*"

— A parliament holden at Perth, 24th July 1365, within the houſe of the Preaching Friars. Here an additional inſtruction is given to the ambaſſadors fent into England to negotiate a peace, in relation to

E e

INDEX OF PARLIAMENTS, &c. BY KING DAVID II.

Folio.

assistance to be reciprocally given by the two kingdoms to each other in case of invasion; viz. that the Scots would agree to assist the English in Ireland.

43 Another parliament holden within the monastery of Holyroodhouse, the 8th of May 1366. Here we find a resolution relative to the negotiations with King Edward III. of England, which contains the following remarkable clause, viz. " In primis cum super quatuor punctis, videlicet, *homagio, successione, regni de-* " *membratione*, ac subsidio gentium armorum perpetuo per regnum Scotie, regno Anglie, et modo infra " propria duo regna, et ultra per regnum Scotie extra regnum Anglie impendendo, fuisset aliquam- " diu tractatum, *finaliter refutatis primis tribus punctis tanquam intollerabilibus;* deliberatum extiterit, " fore super quarto puncto tractaudum," &c.——Subjoined, we find an act in relation to a new coinage of money of the same fineness with the money then current in England.

44 Proceedings of a parliament holden at Scone, the 20th of July 1366. This part of the record is highly curious. In order to levy equally, from persons of every description, money for paying the expences and debts of the King, the expences of the ambassadors employed in England, and the balance of the King's ransom still due, a return had been laid before parliament, in consequence probably of the directions of the parliament 1357, both of the old extent and of the true worth, *veri valoris*, of all the revenues of the church, and of all the lands within the kingdom; but the directions of that parliament relative to moveable (*a*) or personal property not having been complied with, therefore an account of all the effects of the inhabitants of the boroughs and of the country, " *omnia bona burgensium* " *et husbandorum*," is appointed to be reported against the festival of the Nativity of the blessed Virgin, (the 8th of September). Then is subjoined in the record a state of the values of the bishopricks, specifying the general amount of each, both according to the old extent, and likewise according to the *verus valor* or present value; and this is followed by a similar state of the values of the different shires. To show the proportion between the old extent and the present worth, the following particulars are here exhibited, omitting the shillings and pence, viz.

BISHOPRICKS.

Whithorn, old extent, L. 368   Aberdeen, old extent,   L. 1480   Brechin, old extent, L. 441
           present worth,   143   present worth,   1358   present worth,   321
Argyll,   old extent,   280   Murray,   old extent,   1418   Dunkeld, old extent,   1206
           present worth,   133   present worth,   559   present worth,   653

SHIRES.

Fyfe, old extent, L. 3465   Aberdeen, old extent, L. 4448   Roxburgh, old extent, L. 1133   Are, old extent, L. 4057
      present worth, 1555   present worth, 2588   present worth,   524   present worth, 1396
Perth, old extent,   6192 Dumfries, old extent,   1666   Berwick, old extent,   622   Edinburgh, with the con-
       present worth, 3067   present worth,   880   present worth,   372   stabularie, old extent, 4029
Forfar, old extent,   3370 Dumbarton,old extent,   1442   Stirling, old extent,   1749   present worth, 3030
        present worth, 2240   present worth,   96   present worth,   687

47 A parliament holden at Scone, in the month of September 1367. Here is given a state of royal casualties and domains granted away by the King, and still remaining in the hands of those to whom they had been granted, notwithstanding the revocation by the parliament 1357; and this parliament passes various resolutions in relation to such grants.——Here we have a proclamation by the King, under the authority of parliament, relative to the coin; and a statute directing how sasine of lands within such

---

(*a*) *Moveable* property is a Scots law-term, signifying every species of effects unconnected with land or tenements.

INDEX OF PARLIAMENTS, &c. BY KING ROBERT II. &c.

Folio.

parts of the country as were still possessed by the English, should be given to the heirs of the former proprietors, who had deceased loyal subjects. This act proves, that at this early period *saisine* was attended with the same symbolical ceremonies with which it is attended at the present moment.

52 A parliament holden at Perth, the 6th of March 1368-9.

54 A parliament holden at Scone, 20th of June 1368.

55 A parliament holden at Perth, 18th February 1369-70. A variety of regulations enacted by this parliament are inserted in the record.

58 Here the coronation of King Robert II. the first King of the family of Stewart, is particularly mentioned. It appears to have been performed at Scone, the 26th of March 1371, being the 32d day after his uncle's death, which happened on the festival of St Peter's cathedral, viz. 22d February 1370-1.

— The names of the prelates, earls, and barons, who did homage next day, 27th March 1370-1.

— Ordinance by the King and Privy Council in relation to the *living* or economy of the King and Queen, and the keeping and support of the royal houses and castles, conceived in very general terms, 3d May 1371.

— A parliament holden at Scone, " secundo die mensis Marcii anno gratie millesimo trecentesimo septuagesimo " *secundo*, et anno regni ipsius Regis *primo*." (a)

60 Further proceedings of the same parliament, 2d of March 1371-2, in the second year of the reign of King Robert II.

61 A renewal of the league between France and Scotland, by King Charles VI. of France and Robert Duke of Albany Regent of Scotland, dated 9th February 1406-7. In corroboration of this treaty on behalf of the King of France, Louis King of Jerusalem and Sicily, Duke of Anjou, and Count of Provence, Forcalquier, Maine, Pimont, and Roucy; together with John son of the King of France, Duke of Berry and Auvergne, Count of Poitou, Destampes, Boulogne, and Auvergne, swear on the soul of the King of France to the faithful observance of the same.

This treaty, the deed of the latest date in this book of record, appears to have been recorded in a character different from that of all the rest of the book, on three pages originally left blank.

In this part of the book again, two, if not three leaves have evidently been cut off.

63 Settlement of the succession to the Crown of Scotland by King Robert II. with consent of a parliament holden at Scone, the 4th of April 1373, in the 3d year of his reign.

— Obligation by William Earl of Douglas to resign the privilege of a port at North Berwick, granted him by King Robert II. if the same should be found detrimental to the King, or to the community in general, or to the burrows in particular, dated 26th April 1373.

64 Renewal, in the French language, between King Robert II. of Scotland and King Charles V. of France, *Charles le Sage*, of the ancient league between their two kingdoms. The duplicate by King Robert is dated at the castle of Edinburgh, the 28th of October 1371; that by King Charles, at the castle of the wood of Vincennes, near Paris, the last of June 1371.

68 Obligation by King Charles relative to the same treaty, and of the same date with the duplicate executed by him, viz. last of June 1371, by which he engages to advance 100,000 nobles of gold, to enable King Robert to pay the balance of King David's ransom, still due to the King of England, or a greater sum, if a greater balance should be found to be due; and in case King Robert should not be found obliged to pay that balance, then he, King Robert, was to employ those 100,000 gold nobles in levying war against the English, provided the Pope should absolve the King, Prelates, and Lords (*Seigneurs*) of

---

(a) In the record, the date of this parliament seems to be erroneously entered, by a transposition of the words *secundo* and *primo* out of their proper places into the places of one another; for instead of being written as in this place, it ought to have been written as we find it on the *verso* of folio 60. viz. " Anno gratie millesimo trecentesimo septuagesimo " *primo*," (i. e. 1371-2) " et anno regni ipsius Regis *secundo*."

INDEX OF PARLIAMENTS, &c. BY KING ROBERT II.

Folio.

Scotland from the oaths they had sworn to keep the truce with England, and should declare the truce itself null and void. King Charles further obliged himself, prior to the commencement of hostilities by the Scots, to send armour for 500 knights and squires, and also for 500 *serjeans*; and to be at the charge of a certain number of soldiers for a certain period, as is particularly mentioned in the obligation.

69 A renewal, in general terms, of the same treaty, by King Charles VI. of France, son to King Charles V. dated 8th April 1383.

— Confirmation by the same King, of the obligation by his father relative to the subsidy, in case the Scots should make war on the English, dated 15th June 1383.

70 Relative obligation by King Robert II. on the subject of the war to be prosecuted in consequence of that treaty of subsidy, dated 20th August 1383.

Here another leaf appears to have been cut away.

71 " Quedam ordinatio facta in consilio Regis super diversis articulis et punctis confiderandis et fervandis in exer-
" citu faciendo per Gallicos et Scotos similiter."

The instrument itself is in French, although its title be in Latin. It is an indenture, dated at Edinburgh, in the beginning of July 1385, between King Robert II. of Scotland, his eldest son John Earl of Carrick, and several other earls and barons of Scotland, on the one part; and a noble *seigneur*, John de Vienne Admiral of France, *Lieutenant du Roi de France*, in Scotland and England, together with several other noble and brave knights and *seigneurs* of the kingdom of France, sent, for the special purpose contained in the indenture, by the King of France, to his ally the King of Scotland, on the other part. Its tendency is to regulate all matters that might occur in the course of an invasion of England on the side of the marches, to be prosecuted by an army composed of Scots and French soldiers in conjunction. Several of the articles are singular and remarkable.

72 A parliament holden at Edinburgh in April 1385.————And finally,

73 A parliament holden at Edinburgh in June 1385.

INDEX OF CHARTERS BY KING ROBERT II.

The Table of the Infeftments of Robert II.

		In vicecom.
1	Carta to Robert Appiltoune, of ane tenement of land in	Innernefs.
2	—— to James Winchburgh, of ane annual furth of a tenement in Ed^r.	
3	—— Con. given by Robert Earl of Fife and Monteith to Patrick Graham, of half a pleugh of land in Aughinrofs, in vic. de	Lennox.
4	—— to John Kinneir, of the barony of Kinneir,	Fife.
5	—— to Patrick Innerpeffer, of the 3d part of the lands of Craigie, near Dundee, called Bruis lands, quilk was Walter Balmoffie, and the Co. fuperiority Alexander Scrymgeors conftable of Dundee refigned, in vic.	Forfar.
6	—— to Hew Rofs of Kinfauns, of 10 l. Stirling, 14 Chalder of victual furth of Doun, in vicecom. de	Banff.
7	—— to Thomas Rate, of the half lands of Arroche, within the barony of Brechine, by Walter Stewart, fon to Robert King of Scots, and Margaret Barclay, daughter to David Barclay of Brechin, his fpoufe, in vic.	Forfar.

Ane Roll of Robert II. marked on the back, Ro. II. B. Fleming of Biggar, Fleming of Leinzie.

N. B. *This is the fecond Roll now in the General Regifter-Houfe.* The Editor has, from the original roll, corrected the inaccuracies in the old index; and from the charters of confirmation, he has added the names of the original granters of the charters confirmed, together with the names of the witneffes to thofe charters. The old index contains the names of moft of the refigners in the charters of refignation.

The witneffes to only four of the charters by King Robert II. in this roll are inferted in the record, viz. No. 4, 10, 64, and 65. The following perfons are witneffes to all the four, viz. William Bifhop of St Andrew's, Patrick Bifhop of Brechin, John, the King's eldeft fon, Earl of Carrick and Steward of Scotland, Robert Earl of Fyfe and Menteith another fon of the King's, William Earl of Douglas, and John de Carric, a canon of Glafgow, Chancellor: Hugh de Eglyntoun, Knight, is a witnefs to No. 4, 64, and 65: James de Lyndefay, a nephew of the King's, is a witnefs to No. 64, and 65: Robert de Erfkyne, Knight, is a witnefs to No. 4, and 10: And Alexander Stewart, another of the King's fons, with Alexander de Lyndefay, Knight, are witneffes to No. 4.

The charters in this roll are dated in the 1ft, 2d, 3d, 4th, and 5th years of the reign of King Robert II. as follows, viz. No. 1, 2, 4, 5, 6, 7, 8, 9, and 24, in the firft year of his reign: No. 3, 10, 11, 12, 13, 14, 20, 23, 44, 45, 46, 47, 48, 49, 53, and 56, in the fecond: No. 15, 16, 17, 18, 19, 21, 22, 25, 26, 27, 29, 37, 38, 39, 40, 41, 42, 43, 58, 59, 60, and 64, in the third: No. 28, 30, 31, 32, 33, 34, 35, 36, 50, 51, 52, 54, 55, 57, 61, 62, 63, 65, 66, 67, in the fourth: And No. 68, 69, 70, 71, 72, 73, 74, and 75, in the fifth year of his reign.

In this roll, the charters are, like thofe in Book I. dated at a variety of different places, namely, fourteen of them at Edinburgh, fourteen at Perth, eight at Stirling, feven at Dunfermling, four at St Andrew's, four at Scone, three at Kirkofwald, two at Aberdeen, two at Dunbretane, two at Are, two at Kilwynnine, two at Methfen, two at Kinghorn, two at Inverkethyne, one at Doundovenald, one at Clony, one at Kyndrochit, one at Arncle, and one at Cumbray; and in two of them, the places at which they were granted are not mentioned.

F f

INDEX OF CHARTERS BY KING ROBERT II.

In the old index, the charters in this roll are numbered as if it had confifted of five different parts. This peculiarity, if adopted in the printing, might have been productive of confufion in forming the indexes of the perfons and lands; and therefore the numbers of the charters are printed in a continued feries from 1 to 75, as they certainly ought to have been in the old index.

1 Carta, the foundation of the college-kirk of Mayboill, (Page 93. No. 282.)
2 —— by the town of Haddingtoun, to Hew Selkirk, (—— No. 283.)
3 —— foundation of the altar of Holyrood, in the kirk of Stirling, (—— No. 284.)
4 —— to Allan de Lawedre, of the lands of Birkyfide, &c. (—— No. 277.)
5 —— to ditto, by Malcolm fon of Neil de Carrick, of the lands of Mertoun, &c. (—— No. 278.)
6 —— to ditto, by Hugh de Eglyntoun, of the lands of Nortoun, (—— No. 279.)
7 —— to ditto, by William Earl of Douglas, of the lands of Urmotftoun, (—— No. 280.)
8 —— to ditto, by the King when Steward, of part of the lands of Nortoun, (—— No. 281.)
9 —— confirming a charter granted by William de Setoun to John de Faufyde, of the lands of Wefter Fawfyde, in the barony of Tranent.
10 —— confirming a charter by William Earl of Rofs *Dominum de* Sky, to Paul M'Tyre, of the lands of Gerloch, (Page 98. No. 327.)
11 —— to Allan de Lawedre, (—— No. 329.)
12 —— of the office of Sheriff of Kinrofs to Robert Haket, (—— No. 330.)
13 —— of the office of Coroner of Ayrfhire to Hugh de Rath, (—— No. 331.)
14 —— to Queen Eupham, and David Earl of Strathern her fon, of Loch-Leven caftle, &c. (—— No 328.)
15 —— to John M'Kelly, of the lands of Byngane, in the barony of Methven, and fhire of Perth.
16 —— confirming a grant by the deceafed Ifabel Countefs of Fyff, to Margaret Hog, wife of John de Peblys, and John Hog, fon and heir of the deceafed Roger Hog burgefs of Edinburgh by faid Margaret Hog, of an annualrent of 4 marks Sterling out of the lands of Over and Nether Sydferff, in the barony of North Berwick.
17 —— to John Frafer, fon of Alexander Frafer, of the lands of Wefter Effintoly, which John de Dalgarrock refigned, in vic. de Kincardin.
18 —— confirming to the kirk of Methelak, in the diocefe of Aberdeen, a piece of ground particularly bounded, given by Walter Menteith.
19 —— to James de Lindfay, of the New Foreft in Galloway, which Walter Lefly refigned.
20 —— Con. of a charter by Robert Earl of Fife to Robert Stewart of Schanbothy, of the lands of Gerpet, Craigy, 3d part Kulbak, Fordell, &c. in the barony of Luchnys, in vic. de Fyfe.
21 —— of a penfion of 20 marks Starling to Andrew de Cunynghame.
22 —— to John de Edmanftoun, Knight, of an piece of land in Haddingtoun.
23 —— to John de Maxwell and Ifabel de Lindfay his fpoufe, of the lands of Akynheuid, in viceconi. de Lanerk, by refignation of John de Maxwell.
24 —— given by James de Lindfay to John de Maxwell, of the lands of Hackfhaws, Glengonvir, and Fynglen, in vic. de Peebles.
25 —— to Patrick Gray, of the 3d part of the lands of Langforgund, in vic. de Perth, whilk Chriftian Kidd refigned, doing fervice for the third part of a knight's fee, by and attour the Scots fervice due in the time of the laft King Alexander.
26 —— given by Andrew de Lefly to Bernard de Kergyll, of the lands of Culmellie and Auld Culmellie, in the barony of Cuffeny, in viceconi. de Aberdeen.
27 —— given by William de Lindfay, Knight, to Margaret de Abernethy Countefs of Angus, of an annual of 10 l. furth of the lands of Byrys, vic. Edinburgh.
28 —— to Simon de Preftoun, of the lands of Craigmiller, in vic. de Edinburgh, whilk William de Capella refigned, fufteinnand an archer in the King's army.
29 —— to Allan de Lauder, juftice-clerk by-fouth Forth, of a fallary of 10 l. Sterling.

INDEX OF CHARTERS BY KING ROBERT II.

30 Carta to Robert Stewart of Innermaith, of the barony of Dorifdeir, in vic. de Drumfreis, whilk Alexander de Meygners of Redhall refigned.

31 —— Con. of a leafe by Alexander de Meygners of Redhall to Robert Earl of Fyfe and Monteith, of the barony of Reidhall, vic. Edinburgh, except Dreghorne and Woodhall; and of the barony of Glendochyr, in vic. de Perth, during the faid Earl's life.

32 —— to Fergus M'Dougall, of the barony of Macarftoun, refigned by Margaret Frafer, his mother.

33 —— to ditto, of the baronies of Yhethame and Crifloun, whilk Margaret Frafer his mother refigned in his favour, ward, vic. de Roxburgh.

34 —— to Gilbert de Glacefter, of the lands of Glacefter, in vic. Ergadie, and all his lands in the fhires of Forfar and Perth; and failleing of heirs-male of his own body, to Alexander Skyrmechur.

35 —— to John Earl of Carrick, the King's eldeft fon, Stewart of Scotland, and Annabella his wife, and the heirs to be begotten between them, of the earldom of Carrick, on the refignation of faid John.

36 —— to James de Blair, of the lands of Heroud, and all the lands in general of Euftace Lorreyn, vic. Roxburgh, Drumfreis, Air, by his forfaultrie.

37 —— to Duncan Wallace, Knight, and Elenor de Bruys Countefs of Carrik, his fpoufe, of the barony of Dalzell, and Modirvale, in vic. Lanerk; the barony of Oxinhame, and Hetroun, and Maxtoun, vic. Roxburgh; the lands of Erthbyfet, Slawmaoane, and Wefter Bannok, in vic. Strivling; an annual of 10 marks furth of the barony of Barras, vic. de Kincardine; to them and the heirs of faid Duncan's body; quilks failing, to James Sandilands, and the heirs of his body; whom failing, to Allan Cathcart, and the heirs-male of his body; whilks failing, to Robert Colquhoun, and the heirs-male of his body; whom all failing, to Duncan's heirs whatfomever.

38 —— to ditto, and his fpoufe above named, and the heirs of Duncan's body, the baronies of Sondrom and Dallmellingtoun, in vic. de Air; which failing, to Allan Cathcart, and the heirs-male of his body; which failing, to Robert de Culquhone, and the heirs-male of his body; which failing, to the heirs whatfomever of faid Duncan.

39 —— Con. of a grant by Thomas Fleming, grandfon and heir to umquill Malcolme Fleming Earl of Wigtoun, to Gilbert Kennedy, of the lands of Kirkyntullach, ward.

40 —— Con. of a grant by Allan de Erefkine to John M'Kelly, of the lands of Crambeth.

41 —— to Hew de Eglyntoun, of the forfaultrie of Michael de Lardener.

42 —— to John de Maxwell, of the lands of Softlaw, in the barony of Maxwell, vic. Roxburgh, forfaulted by William Stewart, by his refiding under the peace and allegiance of the King of England.

43 —— to the Abbay of Scoon, of L. 5 : 3 : 4 Sterling yearly out of the feu-duties of the burrow of Perth.

44 —— to John de Maxwell, and Ifabel de Lyndfay his wife, of the lands of Lyandcors, in the barony of Renfrew, in vicecom. Lanerk, whilk John de Burgh refigned, holding of the Steward, ward.

45 —— to Henry Coftour, fon of John Coffour, of the lands of Otterburne, vic. Berwick, ward.

46 —— Con. of a grant by George Earl of March *Dominus* of Annandale, to Neill Ewar, of the lands of Smallgyllis and Svftynghowys in Annandale.

47 —— to William Earl of Douglas, of the foreft of Cabrauche, the half davache of Auchmayre, the fuperiority of the other half, whilk is called Clenech, which David Brown of Glandriftoun refigned.

48 —— to John de Keith, by refignation of William de Keith Marefchall, and Margaret Frazer his fpoufe, of all his lands and offices.

49 —— to William de Fenteun, of ane penfion of 40 l. Sterling.

50 —— Con. to William Boyd, of the baronie of Leinzie, by wadfet of Thomas Fleming of Fulwood, formerly Earl of Wigtoun, for 80 l. Sterling; and an affignation thereof by faid William Boyd to Malcolm Flemyng of Biggar.

51 —— Con. to William Hunter, of the lands of Arncle, by refignation of Andrew Campbell, blench, for a penny upon the ground of the lands.

52 —— to James de Blair, of the lands of Corfhogil, in the barony of Drumlanrig, in viccom. de Drumfreis.

INDEX OF CHARTERS BY KING ROBERT II.

53 Carta Con. of a grant by Malcolm Campbell, fon of Dugald Campbell, to Dugall Campbell his brother, of the three farthing lands of Gannay, one-farthing land of Glencre, four-penny land of Glenhiferne more, in Argyll.

54 —— to William de Lyndefay, Knight, of the lands of Borthwickfchelys, in the barony of Chambirlayne-newton, and fhire of Roxburgh, which Laurence de Abrenethy, Knight, loft by forfaulture.

55 —— to John de Roos, of the lands of Eafter Cardny, refigned by John de Johnftoun, with the privilege of taking wood from the King's foreft of Clony, for fupporting the houfes on faid lands, and of fifhing in the loch of Cardny.

56 —— confirming a charter by Archibald de Douglas *Dominus* of Galloway, with confent of Walter Bifhop of Glafgow, founding a hofpital and chapel; and for the fupport of the fame, endowing them with the lands of Corfinychell and Fregvere.

57 —— to Arthur Cambell, fon of Ewar Cambell, of the lands of Strachur, in the fhire of Argyll, refigned by faid Ewar.

58 —— confirming a charter by his uncle King David, (it fhould have been *King Robert his grandfather*, as the names of the witneffes clearly prove), to the Abbay of Crofragmer, of the lands of Dungrelach; witneffes in the original charter, the Bifhops of St Andrew's and Dunkeld, Bernard Abbot of Aberbrothoc, Chancellor, Walter Steward of Scotland, James *Dominus de* Douglas; Alexander Frafer Chamberlain, and Malcolm Flemyng, Knights; at Berwick-upon-Tweed, the 4th June, *an. reg* 18vo. The charter of confirmation by King Robert II. is dated at Kirkofwald, 14th November, in the 3d year of his reign.

59 —— confirming a charter by King Robert I to the Abbay of Crofragmer, of all its lands within the earldom of Carryk, viz. the lands of Crofragmer, Suthbarne, Clenacheth, Balcerillen, Lorkane, Dunnehyne, the kirk-land of Kircoifwald, and all the lands belonging to their parifh-kirks; with the lands of Dalthorane, Corral, and Hachethnevach, given to the Abbay by the deceafed Edward, brother of King Robert; witneffes to King Robert's charter, the Bifhops of St Andrew's and Dunkeld, Bernard Abbot of Aberbrothoc, Chancellor, Walter Steward of Scotland, and James *Dominus de* Douglas; at Berwick-on-Tweed, in the 18th year of King Robert I.'s reign.

60 —— confirming a charter of King Robert I. to the Abbay of Crofragmer, of all the kirks, lands, rents, and poffeffions beftowed on it by Duncan, Neill, and Edward, Earls of Carric, and by Robert de Bruys and Marjory, the father and mother of him King Robert I. and by all other perfons, as fully and freely as it had enjoyed them in the time of King Alexander III.; witneffes to the charter of King Robert I. William, John, William, and Gilbert, Bifhops of St Andrew's, Glafgow, Dunkeld, and Mann, the Abbot of Aberbrothoc, Chancellor, Thomas Ranulphi Earl of Murray, *Dominus vallis Anandie et Mannie*, the King's nephew, Walter Steward of Scotland, James *Dominus de* Douglas, Gilbert de Haya Conftable, and Robert de Keth Marifhall; at Cambufkyneth, the 20th July, in the 21ft year of the reign of King Robert I.

61 —— to John Earl of Carrick, and Annabella his wife, and the heirs of their bodies, of the earldom of Carric.

62 —— to Alexander de Lindfay, of the lands and barony of Baltrody, in vic. de Perth, by refignation of Margaret de Abernethie Countefs of Angus.

63 —— confirming a grant by the King's eldeft fon John Earl of Carrick, to John Sympill, of the lands of Glafford, with the advocation of the kirk thereof; with the tenendrie of Croliragwell, of Ridren, and Blackfuird; and the park of Clounqwarn, and the lands of Knokglafs, Clonfkeath, Clayanyfs, Torranys, and Ardachrys, in the barony of Kilbryde, vicecom. de Lanark.

64 —— confirming a charter given by Robert de Erfkyne of that Ilk, Knight, to Patrick Fleming, fecond fon to Malcolme Fleming of Biggar, of all his lands within the barony of Leygnch, viz. the lands of Bord, Tweouris, Wefter Croy, Eafter Croy, Smethelloun, Balloch, and Ardre, in excambion for the lands of Dalnotir and Garfeaden, whilk were Patrick Fleming's, in comitatu de Lennox, vic. de Dum-

INDEX OF CHARTERS BY KING ROBERT II. 117

barton. The charter by Robert de Erſkyn is dated at Edinburgh, 18th April 1369; witneſſes, Robert Steward of Scotland, John Stewart of Kyle Earl of Carric, Patrick de Grame, ſon and heir of David de Grame Lord of Dundaf, William de Galbrath, Murdach de Levenax, and others.

65 — Carta confirming a grant by Thomas Fleming late Earl of Wigtoun to William Boyd, ſon of the deceaſed Thomas Boyd of Kelmarnock, on account of ſervice to be performed by ſaid William Boyd during all the days of his life, of ane penſion of 12 marks Sterling, till the ſaid Earl or his heirs ſhould infeſt the ſaid William or his heirs heritably in 12 merks worth of land, either in the ſhire of Dumbarton or in that of Lanark.

66 —— to John de Danyelſtoun, of the lands of Mauldiſley, Law, and Kylkadyow, in the barony of Carluk, in the ſhire of Lanark.

67 —— to the aldermen, burgeſſes, and community of Perth, of the ſaid burgh of Perth, with its milns, multures, and pertinents, and with the iſlands called the Law, Incheeret, Incharry, and Sleples, in the river Tay, with the fiſhings all around thoſe iſlands, for payment of 80 l. Sterling yearly.

68 —— to William Strang, of the paſturage of 60 oxen and cows, 300 ſheep, and 4 horſes, belonging to his lands of Kynaldy and Petardy, upon the moor of Carale, with 40 cart-loads of turffs, and 10 cart-loads of broom from the ſaid moor.

69 —— confirming a grant by John M'Wrenan to William Rede, of the lands of Bairſkemyn, within the barony of Kingſkyll, and ſhire of Are.

70 —— to Alexander de Lindſay, of ane annual of 10 s ſhillings Sterling furth of the burrow-maills of Craill, whilk John de Balcolmi had of before, and Alexander de Cambok before him; and which the ſaid John de Balcolmi reſigned.

71 —— to Alexander de Lindſay, of 10 marks Sterling furth of the burrow-maills of Forfar.

72 —— to Robert de Keth, ſon of William de Keth Mareſchall, of the forreſt of Colly, the forreſt called the Forreſt of the Month, the lands of Ferachy, Glaſtolach, Cragy, Clochnahule, whilk of old was of the thanedom of Colly, and viceom. Kincardin.

73 —— Con. to Robert de Keth, of the baronie of Strathechin and the forreſts thereof, viz. Coulperſauch and Corlethny, in vic. de Kincardin, by reſignation of his father and mother, viz. William de Keth Mareſchal and Margaret Fraſer.

74 —— to Walter de Moravia of Drumfargard, of the half lands of Ardormy, in the barony of Banf, vic. Perth, by diſpoſition of Robert Hull, under reverſion.

75 —— to William de Lindſay, of the lands of Drem, in the conſtabulary of Hadingtoun, vic. de Edinburgh, whilk pertained to Johanna de Erth of Wauchtoun, and which William de Gourlay her ſon and heir reſigned.

Ane Roll of Robert II. marked on the back with Ro. II. C.

N. B. *This is the fifth Roll of Royal Charters now in the General Regiſter-Houſe.*

It conſiſts of 126 charters granted by King Robert II. during the firſt eleven years of his reign, viz. No. 3. and 4. in the 1ſt year; No. 1. in the 2d year; No. 2. and 53. in the 3d year; No. 5, 6, 7, 51, 52, 54, 55, 56, 57, 58, 61, 62, 64, 73, and 74, in the 4th year; No. 8, 59, 60, 63, 65, 66, 67, 68, 69, 70, 71, 72, and 75, in the 5th year; No. 10. and 50. and all the intermediate Nos. (except No. 36. which has no date), are in the 6th year; No. 95, 96, 98, and from 101 to 116, incluſive, are in the 7th year; No. 94, 97, 99, 100, and 110, are in the 8th year, No. 86, 87, 90, 93, and from 117 to 126, incluſive, are in the 9th year; from No. 76. to 84, incluſive, with No. 88, 91, and 92, are in the 10th year; and No. 85. and 89. are in the 11th year.

Of thoſe charters, forty are dated at Perth, twenty at Methfen, thirteen at Edinburgh, ten at Scoon, eight at Stirling, ſeven at Dundee, three at Lynlithcu, three at Kyndrochit, two at Inverkethyne, two at Cambuſkyneth, Two at St Andrew's, two at Rothſay, two at Kylwynyne, and one at each of the following places, viz. Inver-

INDEX OF CHARTERS BY KING ROBERT II.

bervy, the Monaftery of Coupar, Irwyne, Glenfchee, Are, Nude in Badenach, Laundors, Glenqwhouglas, Renfrew, and Dunkeld; in No. 36. and 72. the places where they were granted are not mentioned.

Only fourteen of the Royal charters in this roll bear the names of the witneffes, viz. No. 3, 4, 8, 73, 74, 76, 91, 101, 103, 105, 106, 109, 110, and 117. William Bifhop of St Andrew's, John Earl of Carrick and Steward of Scotland, Robert Earl of Fife and Menteith, William Earl of Douglas, and the Chancellor, are witneffes in all the fourteen; but in No. 76, 91, 105, 106, 109, 110, and 117, the Earl of Douglas has the additional title of Earl of Marr; and in No. 3, 4, 8, 73, and 74, John de Carrick, a canon of Glafgow, is named as Chancellor; in No. 101, 103, 105, 106, 109, and 110, John de Peblys Archdean of St Andrew's is mentioned as Chancellor; and in No. 117, John Bifhop of Dunkeld, (the fame John de Peblys, then promoted to that See), is called Chancellor; James de Lyndefay, a nephew of the King's, is a witnefs in No. 8, 73, 74, 76, 91, 101, 103, 105, 106, 109, 110, 117; Alexander de Lyndefay is a witnefs in No. 3, 4, 76, 91, 101, 103, 105, 106, 109, 110, and 117; Robert de Erfkine is a witnefs in No. 3, 4. 8, 73, 74. and 101; Archebald de Douglas is a witnefs in No. 3, 73, and 105; Hugh de Eglyntoun is a witnefs in No. 8. 73, and 74; Patrick Bifhop of Brechin and Thomas Earl of Marr are witneffes in No. 3. and 4; and Walter Bifhop of Glafgow is a witnefs in No. 3.

1 Carta to Alexander Stewart of Badenach, the King's fon, of the office of Lieutenancy from the confines of the earldom of Murray to the Pentland frith.
2 —— to ditto, of the relieff of the earldom of Lennox.
3 —— to ditto, of the lands of Badennach, and the caftle of Lochyndorbe.
4 —— to ditto, of the barony of Strathawn, in vic. de Banff.
5 —— to Thomas a Carfane, of a penfion of 10 l. Sterling.
6 —— to Thomas a Carfane, of a tenement in Lynlithcu.
7 —— to Robert Earl of Fyfe and Monteith, a fon of the King's, of the barony of Reidhall, vic. de-Edinburgh, and the barony of Glendochwere, vic. Perth, whilk Alexander de Moygners refigned.
8 —— confirming a charter by Lawrence de Haya *Dominus de* Erfkyndy, with confent of Findlay de Hay his fon, to John Clark, in togher with Margaret his daughter, of the lands of Lonyanys, vic. de Invernys. The original charter confirmed is dated at Perth, 30th November, an. Dom. 1376: " Hiis teftibus, " David de Grahame Milite, Thoma de Haya Domino de Erroll Conftabulario Scotie, Magiftro Ro- " berto Gatmylk, Magiftro Johanne Sommervill, Johanne Rollo, Nicholao de Haya, Willielmo de " Kergill, Hugone de Abrenythy, Willielmo de Lytheu, et multis aliis."
9 —— to Thomas de Erfkyne, of the barony of Dun, in the fhire of Forfar, refigned by Robert de Erfkyne his father.
10 —— confirming a charter by William More of Abrecorn to John M'Kolly, of 4 aikers of land, in the Cars of Bothkenner, the territory of the Grange, and the Stodfauld, vic. de Stirling.
11 —— to John de Gordoune, of the lands of Strathbolgy, in the fhire of Abreden, whilk Robert, fome time King of Scots, gave to Adam de Gordoune, great-grandfather of faid John, for the forfaultrie of David de Strabolgy, who, though pardoned and reftored to his eftate by Andrew de Murray, Regent in the minority of King David II. had again revolted to the Englifh, had died under the allegiance of the King of England, and had been again forfeited.
12 —— to John del Yle, and his heirs by his wife Margaret, a daughter of the King's, of the ifle of Colowfay.
13 —— to ditto, of all the lands of Lochabre, in vic. Invernys.
14 —— to ditto, of the lands of Kintyr, and the half of Knapdaill.
15 —— to Walter de Tulach, of the lands of Bondyngtoun, in vic. Forfar, which John de Capella refigned.
16 —— to Robert Earl of Fyfe and Monteith, of the lands of Leithbertfcheills, in the conftabulary of Lithgow, and fhire of Edinburgh.
17 —— confirming a grant by Malcolm de Ramfay of Ouchterhoufe to Hew Lyell, of the lands of Morthyll, vic. de Forfar.
18 —— to Robert de Roos, fon of Hugh de Roos, of the lands of Kyldmethane, quilk Marjory de Kyldmethane refigned, in vic. de Fyfe.

INDEX OF CHARTERS BY KING ROBERT II. 119

19 Carta to John Alanſon, of the lands of Kyllenane, in the barony of Cowall, in Argyle.
20 —— to John de Roos and John Lyoun, of the forfaultrie of Ade de Paxtoun and Richard Brown within the ſhiriffdom of Berwick, and alſo the lands of Bondyngtoun of Lethame, the carucate of land called Reid Plewland, the miln of Edringtoun, the fiſhing of New Water, Hundwatter, Colle, and Abſtele, and one net's fiſhing in Tutyngford, in vic. de Berwick.
21 —— to John de Maxwell, of the New Foreſt in Galloway, by reſignation of James de Lindſay, the King's ſiſter's ſon.
22 —— confirming a grant by William de Ruthven to John Peny, of the walkmilne of Ballernach, and five aikers of arable land, with the graſs of five oxen and one horſe within the ſaid William's lands.
23 —— to David de Fowlertoun, of the two Methlaykys, in vic. de Aberdeen, whilk were evicted frae William de Melgdrum, by ſentence of a jury, in the King's preſence, at Kyncardyn, in le Mernys, 11th of December 1375.
24 —— to William de Camera, uſher of the King's chappell, of the lands of Erolly, annexed to that office of uſher, by reſignation of John de Capella.
25 —— to Murthac, ſon of Malcolm, of the half lands of Leckie, lyand near Buchanan, vic. de Stirling, reſigned by Malcolm his father.
26 —— to ſaid Murthac, ſon of Malcolm, of two fourth-parts of the land called Racheon and Akrenmoneyth, in the Lennox, with the office of ſerjeandry in the ſhire of Dumbretane, on the reſignation of Malcolm his father.
27 —— to John Earl of Carric Steward of Scotland, of the lands of Preſtisfeld, Grange of St Giles, and Spittletoun, in the ſhire of Edinburgh, forfaulted by the Friars of Harehop, on account of their living under allegiance to the King of England.
28 —— to John Gray clark of regiſter, of ane tenement in Leith.
29 —— to Hew de Eglingtoun, Knight, of certain annuals within the ſheriffdom of Air, whilk Robert de Bruys reſigned, viz. 50 s. out of Drumdow, 8 s. 4 d. out of Stayre, 33 s. 4 d. out of Cars, and 40 s. out of Monyhagane.
30 —— to Robert de Meigners, of the barony of Enache, within the valley of Neith, reſigned by John Meygners his father.
31 —— to Walter de Sancto Claro, of the barony of Ceſſeworth, except the lands which Edmond Marſhall got, on the reſignation of John de Sancto Claro.
32 —— to Patrick Fleming, of ane annual of 20 s. out of the lands of Over and Nether Grynyſcaſtle.
33 —— to Marion Cygrym, of ane annual of 4 l. Sterling.
34 —— to John Tay, of the lands of Foulſcheills, and an annual of half a mark out of the lands of Polkamet, in the ſhire of Edynburgh, on the reſignation of John Ferguſon.
35 —— to James de Lindſay, of the lands of Kirkmychell, vic. de Drumfreis, whilk Roger de Moubray foriſfecit in the time of King Robert I.
36 —— to David de Hamyltoun, *filius et heres David filii Walteri,* of an annual of 40 marks Sterling out of the barony of Cadiou, in the ſhire of Lanark, in excambion for the lands of Clonyſchenach, Bernys, and Auldlandys, in the barony of Renfrew, conveyed by ſaid David to Robert de Erſkyne.
37 —— to William de Aynyſlay, of the lands of Dolphingſtoun, by forfaultrie of John de Aynyſlay his father.
38 —— to Neil de Conynghame, of the lands of Weſt Barns, viz. Weſtfield, Seeflat, Templeland, Galowſeſyde, vic. Fyfe, by reſignation of Patrick de Polworth.
39 —— to the Friers of Air, called *Fratres predicatores,* of 20 l. Stirling furth of the milns of Air.
40 —— to John de Roos, of the office of Juſticiary of the forreſts of Cluny and Alyth, in vic. de Perth.
41 —— to John de Roos, of the keeping of the caſtle of Cluny, and for upholding the ſame, of the King's annuals furth of Muchlyner, Coneragy, and the miln and meadow of Cluny, in vic. de Perth.
42 —— to William filio Willielmi, of the Brewland of Methven, by reſignation of Roger filio Patricii.
43 —— to William Naper, of the lands of Eaſtergarmyltoun, in the conſtabulary of Hadingtoun, vic. de Edinburgh, reſigned by William Naper, ſon of John Naper of Garmyltoun.

INDEX OF CHARTERS BY KING ROBERT II.

44 Carta to William de Newtoun, of the barony of Newtoun, in the conſtabulary of Hadingtoun, vic. de Edinburgh, on the reſignation of Robert de Swyntoun, and Margaret his wife.
45 —— to Alexander Stuart *Domino de* Badenache, of two davachs of land of Invercabock, in the barony of Strathoune, vic. de Banff, quilk Alexander del Airde reſigned; blench, for a pair of ſpurrs.
46 —— to ditto, of three davachs of lands of Garthyes, within the earldom of Sothyrland, by reſignation of Alexander de Aird; and blench.
47 —— to Thomas de Haya Conſtable of Scotland, of the 100 l. land of Slaines, vic. Aberdeen; blench, for a pair of ſpurrs.
48 —— confirming a grant by Alexander de Stratoun to Ade Forſter, of the lands of Caſtlecary, in vic. de Edinburgh.
49 —— confirming a grant by William More of Abrecorne to Adam Foreſter burgeſs of Edinburgh, of the Mains of Corſtorfine, vic. de Edinburgh.
50 —— confirming a grant by Robert Earl of Fyfe to Arthur Cambell, of certain lands within the barony of Glendocher, vic. de Perth.
51 —— to Hew de Eglintoun, of the lands of Lochlebogfyde, in the barony of Renfrew; few for 10 l. Sterling.
52 —— to John Mercer, of ane tenement in Perth.
53 —— to John de Maxwell, of the north part of Bardre, and north part of Bardynghathe, in the earldome of Stratherne, vic. de Perth.
54 —— to David de Dunbar, of the barony of Blantyre, vic. Lanerk; and Cumnok, with the advocation of the kirk thereof, vic. Air, by reſignation of George Earl of Marche.
55 —— to James de Lindſay, of the lands of Abirbothrie, *necnon locum caſtri de Invercuych*, whilk John de Welhame and John de Balcaſky reſigned, in vic. de Perth.
56 —— to John Heryng, of all the lands whilks pertained to Thomas Biſſet in general.
57 —— confirming to Margaret de Abirnethy Counteſs of Angus a grant by Alexander de Lindſay, of the barony of Baltrodie, in vic. de Perth.
58 —— confirming a grant by Andrew de Valloniis to John M'Kelly, of the lands of Byniane, in the barony of Methuen, vic. de Perth.
59 —— to David Stewart Earl of Stratherne, of the lands and caſtle of Brathewell, with all other lands in the earldom of Caithneſs whilk pertained to Alexander del Aird, by his reſignation.
60 —— to David Earl of Stratherne, of the earldom of Stratherne, whilk Alexander de Ard reſigned.
61 —— containing ane contract betwixt Hew de Eglingtoun, brother to the King, on the one part, and Hew de Aldeſtoun, on the other part, by which ſaid Hew de Aldeſtoun impignorates the lands of Cambuſbarron, Inraloun, and of Schephalch, in vic. de Stirling.
62 —— to Alexander de Lindſay, of the lands of Cambow, by reſignation of John de Balcolmy, vic. de Fyfe.
63 —— to Alexander de Lindſay, of the lands of Fothnevyn, with the office of forreſter of the forreſt of Plater, whilk David de Annandia reſigned, in vic. de Forfar.
64 —— confirming a grant by William Earl of Roſs to Hew de Roſs his brother, of the lands of Balnagown, Achanyii, and Corty, and of an annualrent of 4 l. out of Tarbard, within the earldom of Roſs, and ſhire of Inverneſs.
65 —— to John de Cappella, keeper of the King's chappell, of the lands of Erolly, whilk Simon de Preſtoun reſigned, he John performing the ſame ſervice in the King's chapel that his predeceſſors uſed to perform, for the third part of Craigmillar, in vic. de Edinburgh.
66 —— confirming a grant by Walter de Leſly to William de Lindſay, of the lands of Abirkyrdore, vic. de Banff.
67 —— confirming a grant by David de Pennycuik to William de Crechtoun, of the lands of Braidwood, in vic. de Edinburgh.
68 —— to William Herewart, of the office of Mairſhip of the eaſt quarter of Fife, with the land called the Mairtoun, whilk William Mair reſigned.
69 —— confirming a grant by King David II. to Allan de Erſkyne, of the lands of Incheture, vic. Perth, whilk John de Inchture reſigned.

INDEX OF CHARTERS BY KING ROBERT II.

70 Carta confirming a grant by Andrew Bet to his fpoufe, of ane tenement in Edinburgh.
71 —— to John Wynd, of the office of Mairfhip Principal, vic. Aberdeen, with the lands of Petmukftoun, whilk land and office Robert de Keith, fon to William de Keith Marfhal of Scotland, refigned.
72 —— to John de Dunbar Earl of Murray, and Marjory his wife, and the heirs of their bodies; whom failing, to George Earl of March, of the thanedome of Kintore; referving the tenandries, free tenants, the lands of the free tenants, *et canis.*
73 —— to James de Douglas of Dalkeith, by refignation of James de Douglas his father, of the barony of Kincavile and Calder-cleir, in the conftabulary of Lithgow, vic. de Edinburgh; the barony of Prefloun, vic. Drumfreis; barony of Kilbothok and Newlands, and the barony of Lyntounrotheryk, in vic. Peblys; William, Francis, and Thomas, brothers of James the father are mentioned.
74 —— legitimation to Patrick Innerpeffer burgefs of Dundee.
75 —— to James de Lindfay, of the lands of Aberbothry, vic. de Perth; and alfo the Caftleftead of Innercuych, in the thanedom of Alyth, vic. Perth, by refignation of John de Welhame and John de Balcafkie; together with the lands within the faid thanedome of Alyth, which belonged to Bernard de Hawden, Richard de Bekyrtoun, Robert de Setoun, and Thomas de Rettre.
76 —— confirming a grant by James de Douglas of Dalkeith to David filio Petri, of the lands of Garmyltoundunyng, in the conftabulary of Haddingtoun, vic. de Edinburgh.
77 —— to Malcolm Fleming, of ane tenement in Crawmond, in the fhire of Edinburgh, refigned by Marjory Flemyng.
78 —— to Gaffrid de Strathechyn, fon of John de Strathechyn, of an annuelrent of 10 marks out of the lands of Petgarvie, in the thanedom of Abirluthnott, in Kincardinefhire.
79 —— confirming a grant by David Earl Palatine of Stratherne and Earl of Caithnefs, with confent of the King his father and his Council, to John Rollo, of the lands of Findony, and park of Douny, Drumcroube, and Ladcathy, in the earldom of Stratherne, vicecom. de Perth.
80 —— to Thomas de Walchope, of ane penfion of 20 marks Sterling.
81 —— confirming a grant by James de Lyndefay to William de Lyndefay, of the lands of Chambyrlayn-newtoun, vic. de Roxburgh.
82 —— confirming a grant by William Earl of Dowglafs and Mar to John de Turribus, of the lands of Garmiltounnobill, in the conftabulary of Hadingtoun, and vic. de Edinburgh.
83 —— confirming grants to Thomas de Cranyftoun, of the lands of Foulleryfland in Denun, and Little Rulwod near Denun, in the barony of Cavers, vic. Roxburgh, by William Earl of Douglas and Mar, with other lands given him by John Mautalent, John de Payinftoun, William de Setoun, and Thomas de Symondftoun.
84 —— to William de Strathy, of ane tenement in Stirling.
85 —— to Patrick Gray, of a penfion of L. 26 : 13 : 4 Sterling.
86 —— to Allan de Erfkyn, of the lands of Inchmartyn, in the barony of Langforgund, in vicecom. de Perth, by refignation of John Lyon Chamberlain of Scotland.
87 —— to Allan de Erikyn, of the lands of Banchory, in the conftabularie of Kinghorne, in vic. Fyfe, quilk John Lyon, the King's fon-in-law and Chamberlane of Scotland, refigned.
88 —— to William de Cockburn, fon to Alexander de Cockburn, and Margaret de Monfode his fpoufe, of the barony of Seraling, vic. de Peebles, by refignation of John Stewart and Margaret Cragy his fpoufe, with the patronage of the church of Seraling; and the lands of Heuidis, formerly in the barony of Bradwod, in vicecom. Lanerk, now united to Seraling, in vic. de Peebles; blench, for three broadheaded arrows.
89 —— to Margaret de Caplochy, of the lands of Caplochy, in vic. de Fyff, refigned by David de Caplochy her father.
90 —— of an annual of 6 marks Sterling to a chaplain in the chappell of Cambuflang, furth of the lands called the Eaft Ferme of Rutherglen, by refignation of William de Dalyell, Militis.
91 —— to James de Douglas, of Lydalifdale, fon to William Earl of Douglas and Mar, of ane penfion of 200 marks Sterling furth of the great cuftom of the burgh of Hadyngtoun.

INDEX OF CHARTERS BY KING ROBERT II.

92 Carta confirming a charter granted by the Abbacy of Dumfermling to John de Swyntoun *Domino* of Litle Swintoun, of the lands of the whole *dominii* of Great Swyntoun. The witneffes in the original charter confirmed are, William Bifhop of St Andrew's, John Earl of Carric Steward of Scotland, Robert Earl of Fyfe and Menteth, William Earl of Douglas and Marr, George Earl of March " *Domino vallis Annandie et Mannie,*" John Earl of Murray, James de Douglas " *Domino vallis de Laydalyfdal,*" and Archibald de Douglas " *Domino Galwydie.*"

93 —— to Alexander de Lindfay, of ane penfion of 40 l. Sterling forth of the cuftoms of Aberdeen.

94 —— to Robert de Apletoun, of fome lands in the town of Innernefs.

95 —— to James de Winchburgh, of two annualrents furth of tenements in the burgh of Edinburgh.

96 —— confirming a grant by Robert Earl of Fyfe and Menteth to Patrick de Grahame, of half ane pleugh of land in Auchinros, in the earldom of Lennox.

97 —— confirming a charter granted by Walter Stewart, a fon of the King's, and Margaret his fpoufe, daughter and heir of David de Barclay of Brechyn, to Thomas Raite *Domino de Ovores*, of the half lands of Arroch, in the barony of Brechyn, vicecom. de Forfar. The ftyle of the charter confirmed is particular. It is dated at Scone, *in pleno parliamento Domini Regis*, holden there 19th October 1378, the 8th year of the reign of King Robert II.; and the original charter bears to have been authenticated by the feals of the Queen and of John Earl of Carrick, as well as by the feals of Walter Stewart and his faid wife.

98 —— to John de Kinneir, of the lands of Kinneir, vic. de Fyff.

99 —— to Hew de Roos of Kinfaunys, of ane annual of 10 l. Sterling and four chalders of wheat furth of the lands of Doun, vic. de Banff.

100 —— to Patrick de Innerpeffer, of the third part of the lands of Craigy, with the fifhing, in the barony of Dunde, vic. de Forfar, called Le Bruyfpart, the property of which had belonged to Walter de Balmoffy, and the fuperiority to Alexander Scrymchur conftable of Dunde.

101 —— to Margaret de Cragy, of the lands of Ardlery, vic. de Kinrofs.

102 —— confirming a grant by James de Douglas of Dalkeith to Andrew de Ormyftoun, of a 10 l. land in the territory of Drumcorfs, in the barony of Bathgate, and conftabulary of Lithgow, vic. de Edinburgh.

103 —— to William Marfhall, of the lands of Effilmonth and Meikle Arnyuche, in Buchan, vic. Aberdeen, by refignation of Malcolm Marfhall his father.

104 —— to Allan de Lauder, of the town and lands of Haltoune, in the barony of Rathow, vic. de Edinburgh, whilk John de Haltoun refigned.

105 —— to John Kennedy, of half of the barony of Dalrumple, vic. de Air, by refignation of Hew the fon of Roland de Dalrumple.

106 —— to John Meygners, of ane annual of 8 s. due for caftleward out of the land of Vogry, in the fhire of Edinburgh.

107 —— confirming a charter by King David II. to John de Allintm Clerk, of the forfaultrie of Richard de Rothirford, fon of William de Rothirford, lying within the barony of Craufurd-Lindfay, in vicecom. de Lanark. The witneffes in the charter of King David II. confirmed, are, William Bifhop of St Andrew's, and Patrick Bifhop of Brechin the Chancellor, Robert Steward of Scotland Earl of Stratherne, Patrick de Dunbar Earl of March and Murray, Thomas Earl of Marr, William Earl of Fyff, and John de Preftoun; and it is dated at Edinburgh, 12th April, an. reg. Davidis 28vo.

108 —— to Richard de Monte Alto chancellour of the church of Brechine, and William de Monte Alto his baftard fon, of the barony of Ferne, vic. Forfar.

109 —— to Thomas de Fodringhay, of the lands of Balewny, in vic. de Forfar.

110 —— to Andrew Mercer, of the lands of Ballayach and Balleve, vic. Kinrofs, blench.

111 —— confirming a grant by David Stewart Earl Palatine of Stratherne and Earl of Caithnefs, to William de Rofs, of the lands whilks were Walter de Murray's, within the earldom of Caithnefs, except Thomas Scarlat his lands of Weiter Clith and Nether Greneland.

INDEX OF CHARTERS BY KING ROBERT II. 123

112 Carta confirming a grant by Thomas Stewart Earl of Angus to Thomas Reidpath, of fifteen hufband-lands and feven cottage-crofts, lying in the toun of Preftoun, and barony of Bonkill, vic. de Berwick.

113 —— confirming a grant by James de Douglas of Dalkeith, of the lands of Qwylt and Fethane, in vic. Peebles, for fuftentation of a chaplain in the chapel of Dalkeith.

114 —— to Alexander Stewart, the King's fon by Marion de Carduy, of the lands of Inverlownan, whilk Richard de Monte Alto chaplain refigned, in vic. de Forfar; and failing Alexander and the heirs of his body, to John his brother uterine; whom failing, to James, another fon of the King's by the fame Marion.

115 —— to Richard de Monte Alto chancellor of the church of Brechin, and William his baftard fon, of the barony of Kynblachmond, in the fhire of Forfar.

116 —— to Richard de Monte Alto chancellor of Brechine, of a yearly penfion during his life of L. 20 Sterling out of the great cuftom of the burrow of Dunde.

117 —— confirming a grant by Thomas de Haya conftable of Scotland to Richard de Kynnard, of the lands of Chethynrawach and Kynnynmond, in the barony of Slaines, and fhire of Aberdeen.

118 —— to Thomas de Londrys, of the lands of Haucfland, being a 6s. and 8d. land, within the Mains of Innerkip, in the barony of Renfrew.

119 —— to Alexander Stewart *Domino de* Badanach, of the lands of Curr, Cluthry, with the twa towns called Tullachgorme, vic. Innernefs, John de Innerpeffer refigned, blench.

120 —— to faid Alexander Stewart of Badenach, of the lands of Munge, Rene, and Cragy, by efcheat of William *filii Walteri*.

121 —— to ditto, of the lands of Tempar, Laffintulach, Tullachrofkie, Kenachan, Gart, Bufrak, 3d part of Lychnoch, in vic. Perth; blenfch, 1d. argenti.

122 —— to ditto, of the lands of Balhelmy, by refignation of William de Fodringhay, in vic. Aberdeen.

123 —— to ditto, of the half lands of Conwath, in vic. de Banff, and the half lands of Logyardach, in vic. de Aberdeen, by refignation of William de Fodringhay; blench, for 1d. argenti.

124 —— to John Lyoune, fon-in-law to the King, of ane 10l. land in the town of Thurifton and Woodhall, and a cottage-land in Wodoley, in the conftabulary of Hadingtoun, and fhire of Edinburgh, by refignation of Margaret de Eklys.

125 —— to Patrick de Innerpeffer burgefs of Dundee, of the lands of Balmaledy, Balmethnach, Smythyhill, Haltoun, and Abirluthnot, whilk Walter de Lefly refigned, in the fhire of Kyncardyn.

126 —— to Ade Forfter burges of Edinburgh, of ane penfion of 20 marks Sterling money furth of the burrow-maills of Edinburgh.

Ane Roll of Robert II. marked on the back, Ro. II. D. Cranftoun, Riddell.

N. B. *This is the feventh Roll of Royal Charters now in the General Regifter-Haufe.*

The charters in this roll, being thirty-four in all, are dated in the 7th, 11th, 12th, and 13th years of the reign of King Robert II. viz. No. 1, and 28, in the 7th year; No. 8, and 9, in the 11th year; No. 2, 3, 4, 5, 13, 14, 15, 16, 17, 18, 19, 20, 22, 23, 24, 25, 26, 27, and 29, in the 12th year; and all the reft, (except No. 21, in which the year is illegible), in the 13th year of his reign.

They are dated at various places, viz. nine at Edinburgh, five at Perth, four at Invernefs, four at Kilwinning, three at Kyncardyn, two at Kyndrochit, and one at each of the following places, viz. Arnell, Cumbray, Scone, Strivelyn, Methfen, Glafgow, and Dunbrettan.

Only the laft charter in the roll, i. e. No. 34, has witneffes, viz. William Bifhop of St Andrew's, John Bifhop of Dunkeld Chancellor, John the King's eldeft fon Earl of Carrie, Robert Earl of Fife and Menteith, the King's fon, William Earl of Douglas an Mar; Archibald de Douglas, and Robert de Erfkyne, Knights.

All the material words of No. 1 are either torn away, or are rendered illegible by the decay of the ink. We only fee that it was dated at Perth, the 8th of October, an. reg 7mo.

INDEX OF CHARTERS BY KING ROBERT II.

2 Carta to John de Dunbar Earl of Murray, *filio nostro*, of the lands and thanedom of Kintore, except the lands of Thaynstoun.
3 —— to David de Fullartoun, of ane pension of 10 l. Sterling.
4 —— to Thomas de Rate, of the lands of Ures, Clathok, Hiitoun, and Katerlyne, the brewhouse of Denhouse, Lumgerr, the miln of Dunnotter, and part of the lands of Dunnotter, whilk Matthew de Glacester forisfecit.
5 —— to John de Retre, and Margaret de Mygill his spouse, of the lands of Logymigill, by resignation of John Mygill her father, in vic. de Perth.
6 —— to Uchtred M'Dowell, of a pension forth of Malcarstoun, given by his father Fergus M'Dowell.
7 —— to Andrew Mercer, of an annual furth of the King's custom or the burrow-mailis of Perth, of 40 marks Sterling.
8 —— to Allan de Lauder, of the lands of the Burrow Moor of Edinburgh, by resignation of Richard Broun.
9 —— to Thomas Lamb, of the office of serjeandrie, by resignation of John Brown of Burrowmoor.
10 —— to John de Ardler, of ane annual of 6 merks furth of the two towns of Kelor, in vic. Forfar, on the resignation of John Kelor.
11 —— to Peter de Cockburne, of the lands of Henriland, lands in Bothill, and the kirk-land of Kirkhuird, in vic. Peebles; with the lands of Sunderland, with the place thereof, vic. Selkirk, resigned by Peter de Cockburne his father.
12 —— to William Watson, of the lands of Cranstoun Riddell, in vic. Edinburgh; failing of heirs of his body, to Alexander de Murray, and George de Murray brother of Alexander.
13 —— to John Stewart son to the King, gotten by him upon Marion Cardny, the lands of Kinclevin, Ervyntoly, Tulibeltyn, and Little Dulmernok, in the thanedom of Kinclevin, in vic. Perth; blench, for 1 d.
14 —— to James Stewart, gotten betwixt the King and Marion Cardny, the eist half of the lands of Kinfawns, the lands of Rate, the lands and miln of Forteviot, in vic. Perth; blench, for 1 d.
15 —— to Alexander Stewart son to the King and Marion Cardny, the lands of Lounan, in vic. Forfar, whilk Richard Mowat resigned; and the lands of Petfour, vic. Aberdeen; blench, for 2 d.
16 —— to Ade Forrester, of ane tenement of land in Edinburgh.
17 —— to ditto, of the hostilary of Traquair, in vic. Peebles.
18 —— to John Lyon, of the thanedom of Glendowachy, in vic. de Banff.
19 —— to Alexander de Strathechyn of Carmyly, of the office of coronership of the sheressdome of Forfar and Kincairdine, by resignation of Alexander de Strathechyn of Auchintoly.
20 —— confirming a grant by Eupham *Domina de* Rofs to Alexander Stewart Earl of Buchan, of the earldom of Rofs.
21 —— to Alexander Stewart *Domino de* Badenach, of the baronie of Kynnedward, by resignation of Eupham Domina de Rofs.
22 —— to John Lyon, of an annualrent of four chalders of victual, and 10 l. Sterling, furth of Dounn, in the shire of Banff, fallen to the King by escheat, because Hugo de Rofs had alienated it to Andrew de Berclay without the King's leave.
23 —— to Ade Forrester, of two parts of the lands of Wrights houses near Edinburgh, by resignation of Henry Wintoun and Amy Brown.
24 —— to Malcolm Fleming of Biggar, of the baronie of Leinzie, in the shire of Dunbretane, whilks Thomas Fleming resigned.
25 —— to the King's son Alexander Stewart Earl of Buchan, and Eupham *Demine de* Rofs, of the thanedom and castle of Dingwall, by resignation of the said Eupham.
26 —— to ditto, of the baronies and lordship of Sky and Lewes; lands in Caithness and Sutherland, in the shires of Innerness and Nairne; certain lands in Athol, in Perthshire; the barony of Fythkill; lands in Galloway; Forgrundtheny and Kinfauns in Perthshire; the thanedom of Glendowachie; and the lands of Deskfuird, in Banffshire, by resignation of the said Eupham.

INDEX OF CHARTERS BY KING ROBERT II.

27 Carta to Walter Stewart " *nepoti nostro,*" of the superioritie of the wester half of the lands of Kinfauns, by resignation of Eupham Ross, daughter to William Earl of Ross, in her viduity.
28 —— to John Lyon, of the lands of Langforgrund, called Le Bruys part, in Perthshire, on the resignation of Agnes, the widow of Robert de Ramsay; also the lands of Adam Pingle and Thomas Scarlot, in the same barony; with the superiority of Monorgrund; blench, for ane penny.
29 —— to John Stewart, gotten betwixt the King and " *dilectam nostram Moram,*" of the lands of Ballachys, Invernate, Mukirsly, in the thanedom of Kynclevyn, in Perthshire; failing John, and the heirs of his body, to James, the King's son by Marion de Cardny, and the heirs of his body; whom failing, to Alexander, another of his sons by the said Marion, and the heirs of his body; whom failing, to John, a third son of the King's by said Marion, and the heirs of his body; whom failing, to return to the King and his heirs, Kings of Scotland.
30 —— to John Corss burgess of Lithgow, of the lands of Hill, near Lynlithcow, resigned by Thomas de Hill.
31 —— to Ade Forrester, of ane annual of 20 marks furth of the burrow-mailis of Edinburgh.
32 —— to John Corss, of the lands of Hilclyff of Over Prestoun, and two parts of the Mains thereof; wadset by John de Malavilla.
33 —— to John de Lindsay of Dunrod, of the barony of Killbryde, in Lanarkshire, the lands of Rogertoun, Half Kittokfyde, Thorntoun, Bogtoun, Hasthrepland, Carnduff, Facfield, Brousterland, except a piece of land called Philphill.
34 —— to Henry de Douglas, of several annualrents furth of certain lands, viz. Corscunyngfelde, Hucheounfelde, and Wynkystoun, in the shire of Peblys.

Ane Roll of Robert II. marked on the back, Ro. II. E.

This is the ninth Roll of Royal Charters in the General Register-House.

This roll contains twenty-six charters. The nine first are granted by King Robert II. in the 19th and 20th years of his reign, viz. No. 1, 2, and 3, in the 19th year; and No. 4, 5, 6, 7, 8, and 9, in the 20th year.

Five of those nine are dated at Lynlithgow, and one is dated at each of the following places, viz. Dundee, Aberdeen, Perth, and Arnelle.

Walter Bishop of St Andrew's, Robert Earl of Fife and Menteith, Archibald Earl of Douglas *Dominus Galwydie*, James de Douglas *Dominus de Dalkeith*, and Thomas de Erskyne, are witnesses to all the nine; John Earl of Carrick Steward of Scotland, the King's eldest son, is a witness to No. 1, 2, 3, 4, 5, 6, 7, and 9; John Bishop of Dunkeld, the Chancellor, is a witness to No. 1, 2, 3, 4, and 5; Alexander de Cocburne de Langtoun, Keeper of the Great Seal, is a witness to No. 4, 5, 6, 7, 8, and 9; and Mathew Bishop of Glasgow is a witness to No. 6, 7, 8, and 9.

1 Carta to Alexander de Lindsay, of the superioritie of Oures, of Lumgerr, and of Hiltoun, in vic. Kincardineshire, and Balgillow, in Forfarshire, which had belonged to Thomas de Rate.
2 —— to John de Tullach, of ane tenement in Aberdeen.
3 —— confirming a charter by Christian daughter of Hugh de Benhame, to Allan Lundie, of the half of ane davach of land of Benhame, in Kincardineshire, and a charter by William de Monte Alto, to Thomas the son of Adam, of the lands of Hamtoun, in the barony of Kynblachmon I, in Forfarshire.
4 —— to Henry de Douglas, of the barony of Logtoun, in the shire of Edinburgh, on his own resignation.
5 —— to Henry de Douglas, of the Castlestead and Castle of Lochlevyne, with the lands of Achynker, Caskygour, Glaslochy, Eister and Wester Tulyochchy, Cultbuy, the town of Kynros, Mawcuyth, Mawardlary, Thomynan, the half of Urwell, Blacklach, Drumgerloc, Achteveny, Colcarny, Croft Martyn, and Theyntulchy, all in the shire of Kynros, on his own resignation.

6 Carta to Henry de Douglas, of the lands of Longnewton, in Roxburghshire, on his own refignation.
7 —— confirming a charter granted by William de Faffyngtoun, to John de Douglas burgefs of Edinburgh, of the lands of Malcolmyftoun, in the shire of Edinburgh, lying between the lands of Ricardtoun on the south, and Hirdmanyftoun on the north; the witneffes to the original charter are, John Young a bailie of Edinburgh, Andrew Bet, John the son of Henry, John Frafer, William de Benyn, and Martin de Benyn, burgeffes of Edinburgh. The charter of confirmation is granted by the King as Steward of Scotland.
8 —— to John de Rofs, of the lands of Auchinbak, in the barony of Renfrew, and shire of Lanark, whilk John de Robertun in Ernockfahunfoy refigned ; blench, for ane pair of gloves, or two pennies.
9 —— to George de Dunbar, son and heir of George Earl of March, of his ward, releiff, and marriage, for the earldom of March, and for Annandale; and failing faid George, to his brothers, Wawan, Colin, Patrick, and John.

Here endeth King Robert II. his Charters. In the samen Roll follows of Robert III.
" *Hic incipit Regiftrum Domini Roberti Tertii Regis Scotorum, tempore Alexandri*
" *de Cocburne Cuftodis Magni Sigilli ejufdem Domini Regis.*"

10 —— to Henry de Preftoun, for the redemption of Sir Ranulph de Percy, Knight, Englifhman, of the lands and barony of Fermartyn, in Aberdeenshire ; the town of Fyvie, and place thereof ; the town of Meikle Gurdnies, and five-merk land of Parkhill ; refigned by James de Lyndefay.
11 —— to St Patrick's chappell in the caftle of Dunbartan, of 10 marks Sterling yearly out of the burrow-maills of Dunbarton.
12 —— confirming a grant by King Robert II. to Robert Archibald chaplain, of the hofpital of Roxburgh.
13 —— A precept directed to the Baillies of Dunbretan, commanding them to pay to the chaplain of St Patrick's chapel, in the caftle of Dunbretan, the 10 marks yearly, doted by the preceding grant, No. 11.
14 —— to the monaftery of Halyrudchoufe, of divers lands, and kirks, and privileges granted to the said monaftery and channons by David King of Scots, fon to St Margaret, founder of the kirk. This charter by King Robert III. confirms the original charter by King David I. and two charters, one by King Robert I. and another by his fon King David II. confirming said original charter. The witneffes to the charter of King David I. are, Robert Bifhop of St Andrew's, John Bifhop of Glafgow, Henry King David's fon, William his grandfon, Edward his Chancellor, Herbert his Chamberlain, Gillemychel *Comite*, Gofpatrick the brother of Dolfyn, Robert de Monte Acuto, Robert de Burneville, Peter de Bruys, Norman the Sheriff, Oggu Leifeng, Gillife, William de Grame, Turftan de Crectune, Blenius the Archdean, Aelfrinus the Chaplain, and Waleranus the Chaplain. The witneffes to the charter of King Robert I. are, William Bifhop of St Andrew's, and William Bifhop of Dunkeld, Bernard Abbot of Abirbrothoc the Chancellor, Thomas Ranulph Earl of Murray *Dominus* of Annandale and Mann, Walter Steward of Scotland, James *Dominus* de Douglas, John de Menceteth, Gilbert de Haya Conftable of Scotland, Robert de Keth Marifhal of Scotland, and Alexander de Setoun. The charter of King David II. is dated at Dunfermelyne, 30th December, an. reg. 14to, before thefe witneffes, William Bifhop of St Andrew's, Robert Steward the King's nephew, Duncan Earl of Fife, John Ranulph Earl of Murray *Dominus* of Annandale and Mann, Patrick de Dunbar Earl of March, Mauricius de Moravia, Malcolm Fleming, and Thomas de Carnoco Chancellor.
15 —— confirming a charter by King Robert II. which again confirms a grant by King David I. to the Abbey of Holyroodhoufe, of the tenth of all the efcheats, fines, &c. of the chamberlain, jufticiary, sheriff, and burrow courts between the river Awyne and Colbrandifpeth, in the shire of Edinburgh ; and of the half of the tenth of certain royal cafualties within Kentyre and Erregyle. The charter of King

INDEX OF CHARTERS BY KING ROBERT III. 127

Robert II. is dated at Edynburgh, the 25th of June, an. reg. 12°, before thefe witneffes, viz. William Bifhop of St Andrew's, John Bifhop of Dunkeld the Chancellor, John the King's eldeft fon Earl of Carric and Steward of Scotland, Robert Earl of Fyfe and Menteith, William Earl of Douglas and Marr; James de Lyndefay and Robert de Erfkyne, Knights.

16 Carta to the faid Abbaey anent the feu-duty of their barony of Kars, in Stirlingfhire.

17 —— to Norman de Leflie, of the barony of Balnebrech, in Fifefhire; the barony of Lowr, and the lands of Dunlopy, in Forfarfhire; and the baronies of Cufchene and Rothynorman, in Aberdeenfhire; with ane taillie.

18 —— to the Abbacy of Halyrudhoufe, of the barony of Kars, in Stirlingfhire, for Co L Sterling of annual feu-duty.

19 —— to Thomas Moffat, of ane annual of 10 l. furth of the great cuftom of Edinburgh.

20 —— to David de Lindfay of Gleneik, in liferent, of an annuity of 40 l. Sterling furth of the great cuftom of Aberdeen.

21 —— to David de Lindfay of Glenefk, in liferent, of an annuity of 40 marks Sterling out of the great cuftom of Aberdeen, for his fervice to David Earl of Carrick, the King's eldeft fon.

22 —— to William de Laurdelis, of the lands of Swynfide and Raynaldiftoun, in Roxburghfhire, fallen to the Crown by the forfeiture of Robert Burell.

23 —— confirming a charter by John Turnebull of Myntow, to Sir William Stewart of Jedworth *nepoti fuo*, of the lands of Myntow, in Roxburghfhire. The original charter is dated at Myntow, the 8th of December, a. D. 1390, before thefe witneffes, Robert Colvyll of Oxenhame, Richard de Ruthirfurde of that Ilk, William de Gledftanys, Adam de Glendonewyn, Thomas Colvyll, William de Laundelis of Swynyfhede, Adam Turnebull of Quhytthope, Adam Turnebull of Foultoun, Thomas Turnebull, and John de Wellis.

24 —— to Alexander Sibbald, of the third part of the lands of Cukiftoun, lyand in the quarter of Crale, in Fifefhire.

25 —— to William Fleming, of the office of Mair-of-fee of the barony of Carale, with the land of Martoun, and the acre called Pulterland, belonging to faid office.

26 —— confirming a charter by King David II. to the Abbey of Calkow, erecting their toun of Calkow, the barony of Boldene, and the lands of Reveden, into a regality. King David's charter is dated at Abirdene, the 23d of April, an. reg. 1410, before thefe witneffes, William Bifhop of St Andrew's, William Bifhop of Glafgow; Galfrid Abbot of Abirbrothoc, William Abbot of Melros, and John Abbot of Jedworth; Robert Steward of Scotland, the King's nephew; Duncan Earl of Fyfe, and John Earl of Murray; Thomas de Carnoco the Chancellor; David de Haya Conftable; Philip de Melgdrum and David Flemyng, Knights.

The feventeen charters of King Robert III. in this roll, are all dated in the firft year of his reign. Ten of them are dated at Edinburgh, three at Scone, two at Dundonald, one at Logirate, and one at Dunfermelyn.

In No. 12. there are no witneffes inferted. To all the remaining fixteen, Walter Bifhop of St Andrew's, Mathew Bifhop of Glafgow, Robert Earl of Fyfe and Menteith, Archibald Earl of Douglas *Dominus Galwydie*, Thomas de Erfkyne, and Alexander de Cocburne de Langtoun Keeper of the Great Seal, are witneffes; James de Douglas Dominus de Dalkeith, is likewife a witnefs in all thofe fixteen, except No. 10; and John Earl of March, David de Lyndefay of Glenefk, and Robert de Keth, are witneffes to No. 10.

INDEX OF CHARTERS BY KING ROBERT II.

Ane Roll of Robert II. marked on the back with this mark, F.

This is the sixth Roll now in the General Register-House.

This roll contains five-and-thirty charters by King Robert II. dated in the 3d, 4th, 5th, 7th, 8th, 11th, and 12th years of his reign, viz. No. 22, in the 3d year: No. 20, 21, 23, 24, 25, 26, 30, 31, and 32, in the 4th: No. 27, 28, 29, 33, and 34, in the 5th: No. 3, 4, and 5, in the 7th: No. 2, 6, 7, 8, and 9, in the 8th: No. 10, 13, 14, 15, 16, 17, 18, and 19, in the 11th: And No. 11, and 12, in the 12th year. Neither No. 1, nor No. 35, have date or place.

The other thirty-three are dated at a variety of different places, viz. thirteen at Perth, five at Edinburgh, three at Scone, two at Methfen, two at Dundee, and one at each of the following places, viz. Stirling, Glenquhouglas, Arncle, Are, Edebredfcheels, Nude in Badenach, Longdors, and Linlithcu.

William Bifhop of St Andrew's, John Bifhop of Dunkeld the Chancellor, John Earl of Carrie Steward of Scotland, Robert Earl of Fife and Menteith, William Earl of Douglas and Marr, James de Lyndefay, and Alexander de Lyndefay, are wineffes to No. 9. None of the reft have any witneffes.

1 Carta confirming a donation by John Crab burgefs of Aberdeen, to the Carmelite Friers in Aberdeen, of fundry lands and annualls.———In this charter, mention is made of the Denburn, Robbiflaw, the Gallowgate, the Upper and Nether Kirkgates, the Grene, and the Caftlegate.———The original charter is dated at Abreden, an. Dom. 1382, and was authenticated by the granter's feal, and by the common feal of the burrow, and the feals of Adam Pyngle the father, and Alexander the fon of William, two of the burgeffes.

2 ——— to Robert de Appiltoun, of a vennel in the Kirkgate, and a part of the Caftlchill of Invernefs.
3 ——— to James de Winchburgh, of two annualrents furth of two tenements in Edinburgh.
4 ——— confirming a charter by Robert Earl of Fyfe and Menteth, to Patrick de Grahame, of half a pleugh of land in Aughinrofs, in the earldom of Levenax.
5 ——— to John de Kynneer, of the barony of Kynneer, in Fifefhire, on his own refignation.
6 ——— to Patrick de Innerpeffer, of the third part of the lands of Craghil, in the barony of Dundee, in Forfarfhire, called Bruys part, which belonged to Walter de Balmoffy, and of which the fuperiority was refigned by Alexander Schirmechour conftable of Dunde.
7 ——— to Hew de Roos of Kinfauns, of ane annual of 10 l. Sterling, and 4 chalders victual, furth of the lands of Doun, in Banffhire.
8 ——— confirming a charter to Thomas de Rate, of the half lands of Arroch, in the barony of Brechine, vic. Forfar, granted by Walter Stewart fon to the King, and Margaret his fpoufe, daughter and heir to David de Berelay de Brechyn, Knight.
9 ——— to John de Migghil, of the barony of Mygghil, in Perthfhire, by refignation of John Mygghil his grandfire.
10 ——— to Patrick de Innerpeffer burgefs of Dundee, of 52 foot in length and 14 in breadth in the Ilie-ftreet of Dundee.
11 ——— to Laurence Cowan, of the caftle wards of Roxburgh.
12 ——— to John Lyon, of the lands of Killdonwhan, in Fifefhire, by refignation of Robert de Roos, fon and heir of Hugh de Roos of Kynfaunis.
13 ——— to John de Fairley, of the lands of Bavillay, in Edinburghfhire, on the refignation of William de Fairley of Braid, his father.
14 ——— to Henry de Douglas, of the lands of Logtoun, in Edinburghfhire, on his own refignation.
15 ——— to James de Lindfay, Knight, as Baron of Crawforde-Lindefay, of the fuperioritie of Ley, Fulwood, Cairtland, and Bondyntoun, in Lanarkfhire.

INDEX OF CHARTERS BY KING ROBERT II.

16 Carta to William More, Knight, of the barony of Abercorn and Dean, in the conflabulary of Lithgow, and fhire of Edinburgh; and the lands of Airth, Cambufbarron, Craigorth, Skeok, and Torwood, in Stirlingfhire, on his own refignation.
17 ——— to Richard de Sancto Claro, of the lands of Finlettre, and of the Grievefchip of Culane, in Banffshire.
18 ——— to John Lyon, of the lands of Altermonie and Dalrevach, in Stirlingfhire, fallen to the King by the forfeiture of William Clerc of Faukirk.
19 ——— to John de Swyntoun, Knight, of ane penfion of 20l. Sterling.
20 ——— to Hew de Eglintoun, Knight, and Egidia his wife, fifter of the King, of the lands of Lochlebogfide, in baronia de Renfrew.
21 ——— to John Mercier, of a piece of land at the north end of the bridge of the Caftlegayle of Perth.
22 ——— to Sir John de Maxwell, of the eaft part of Bardre, and the eaft part of Bardinhathe, in the earldom of Stratherne, and fhire of Perth, granted to Sir John by David the King's fon, Earl of Stratherne.
23 ——— to David de Dunbar, of the baronies of Blauntyre, in Lanarkfhire, and of Cumnok, in Ayrfhire, with advocation of the kirk, by refignation of George de Dunbar Earl of March.
24 ——— to James de Lyndefay, Knight, of the lands of Abrebothry, in Perthfhire, on his own refignation; and of the Caftle-ftead of Invircuych, and all the lands which belonged to John de Welhame and John de Balkafky, in the thanage of Alicht, and fhire of Perth.
25 ——— to John Heryng, of his haill lands, by refignation of Thomas Biffet.
26 ——— to John Makkelli, of his haill lands of Byniane, in the barony of Methfen, and fhire of Perth, by refignation of Andrew de Valoniis.
27 ——— to David Stewart Earl of Stratherne, fon to the King, of the caftle of Brathwell, and haill lands thereof, and all other lands, as well in Caithnefs as in any other part within Scotland, whilk Alexander de le Arde inherited, in right of Matilda de Stratherne his mother; on the refignation of faid Alexander de le Arde.
28 ——— to David Earl of Stratherne, of the earldom of Stratherne, by refignation of Alexander de le Arde.
29 ——— confirming an indenture, dated the 21ft of March 1374, at Ardroffan, betwixt Hew de Eglingtoun, Knight, and Hew de Auldiftoun, by which the latter wadfets to the former the lands of Cambufbarron, Inviraloun, and Schiphaulch, in Stirlingfhire, for L. 80 Sterling.
30 ——— to Alexander de Lindfay, Knight, of the lands of Cambow, in Fifefhire, by refignation of John de Balcolmy.
31 ——— to Alexander de Lindfay, of the lands of Fothenevin, with the office of forreftrie of the foreft of Plater, in the fhire of Forfar, on the refignation of David de Annandia, Knight.
32 ——— confirming a grant by William Earl of Roffe, to Hugh de Roffe his brother, of the lands of Balnagowne, Achavill, and Corty, and an annual duty of 4l. furth of Tarbet, within the earldom of Rofs, and fhire of Invernefs.
33 ——— to John de Capella, of the lands of Eroly, in Forfarfhire, by refignation of Sir Simon de Preftoun, Knight.
34 ——— to William de Lindfay, Knight, of the lands of Abrekerdore, in Banffhire, difponed by Walter de Lefley, Knight.
35 ——— to William de Crechtoun, of the lands of Bradewod, in the fhire of Edinburgh, difponed to faid William by David de Penicuke.

K k

INDEX OF CHARTERS BY KING ROBERT II.

In ane Roll newly come to my knowledge, viz. upon the 21st day of January 1629,. marked on the back, A. Ro. II.

Terra de Douny.

This Roll is only of the first and second years of the King's reign.
The two first charters cannot be read.

This is the fourth Roll now in the General Register-House.

The 1st charter is illegible.

The 2d is in favour of William de Kergyll, of lands in the barony of Banff, on the resignation of John Herrice, dated in the 1st year of King Robert II.'s reign. No witnesses are inserted. The names of the lands and of the shire are illegible.

This roll consists of three-and-thirty charters, granted by King Robert II. Seventeen of those charters are dated in the first year of that King's reign, viz. No. 2, 4, 7, 8, 9, 10, 11, 12, 13, 14, 15, 16, 17, 18, 19, 20, and 28; eleven are granted in the second year of his reign, viz. No. 3, 5, 6, 21, 22, 24, 27, 29, 30, 32, and 33; neither the place nor year are legible in No. 1; and in No. 23, 25, 26, and 31, the places where and years when they were granted are not inserted.

Only one charter in this roll has the names of the witnesses, viz. No. 7. The witnesses to it are, William Bishop of St Andrew's, Walter Bishop of Glasgow, Patrick Bishop of Brechin; John the King's eldest son Earl of Carrick and Steward of Scotland; Thomas Earl of Mar, William Earl of Douglas, Robert Earl of Menteith; Archibald de Douglas, Alexander de Lyndesay, Robert de Erskyne, and John de Carrick the Chancellor.

3 Carta to John de Dunbar, and Margory, daughter to the King, his wife, of the earldom of Murray, except Lochaber, Badenach, the castle and barony of Urchard, &c. payand for the relief thereof, when it should fall due, 200 l. Sterling; failing heirs of their bodies, the earldom is made descendible to George Earl of March, and his heirs; dated in a full parliament at Scone, in the 2d year of King Robert II.'s reign.

4 —— to David Senescall Militi Comiti de Stratherne, filio nostro, de Comitatu de Stratherne, in libera regalitate; anno regni primo.

5 —— Jacobo de Lindsay, de dominio de Wigtoun, cum burgo ejusdem, except the barony of Carnysmul, whilk Malcolm Fleming had first resigned in the hands of King David II. and which Thomas Fleming his grandson and heir had again resigned the day before the date of this charter, viz. 20th April, an. reg. 2do, i. e. 1372. See p. 97. No. 318.

6 —— confirming a charter by King David II. to James de Douglas, Knight, of the lands of Wodefelde, Tyry, Sefelde, the two Balbertans, and the miln thereof, in the constabulary of Kinghorne, and shire of Fyfe. See p. 97. No. 319.

7 —— Johanni Kennedy, de dimidio baronie de Dalrumple, in vicecom. de Are, by resignation of Malcolm de Dalrumple, the grandson of Adam de Dalrumpill.

8 —— Alexandro Senescalli, " filio nostro," Militi, de sexaginta davatis terre de Badennach, cum castro de Lochindorbe, cum forrestis eidem castro annexatis, in vicecom. de Invernefs.

9 —— Thome de Rate, de dimidio baronie de Oures, in vicecom. de Kyncardyn, by resignation of Matthew de Eychles, son of William de Eychles, by Beatrix de Caritoun his wife.

10 —— to the said Thomas de Rate, of the other half of the said barony of Oures, on the resignation of Duncan Walays. N. B. This charter is omitted in the old index.

INDEX OF CHARTERS BY KING ROBERT II. 131

11 Carta to Robert de Erſkyne, of 20 l. Stirling of the annualrent due out of the lands of Cadzow, in Lanarkſhire, in excambion for the lands of Bondingtoun; and four marks furth of the lands of Weſthall, in baronia de Rathow, vicecom. Edinburgh.

12 ——— Hugoni de Eglyngtoun, Militi, de terris de Allertoun, in baronia de Kilbryde, et vicecom. de Lanark.

13 ——— to ditto, de terris de Bondingtoun, et annuo redditu quatuor marcarum et octo ſolidorum de terris de Weſthall, in baronia de Rathew, et vicecom. de Edinburgh, on the reſignation of Robert de Erſkyne.

14 ——— to ditto, de terris de Gyffeyn, in baronia de Kyle Seneſcalli, in vicecom. de Ayr.

15 ——— Davidi Seneſcalli Militi Comiti de Stratherne, caſtri et baronie de Urchard, in vicecom. de Inverneſs.

16 ——— Davidi Seneſcalli Militi Comiti de Stratherne, filio noſtro chariſſimo, de comitatu de Stratherne, in liberâ regalitate   Vid. p. 94. No. 294.

17 ——— Andree de Clapham, of the lands of Tornakyders, in Fifeſhire, on the reſignation of Mariota de Wardrobe N. B. This charter too is omitted in the old index.

18 ——— Thome de Aula, de quatuor mercatis terre in tenemento de Staneley, in baronia de Renfrew, et vicecom. de Lanark.

19 ——— Robert de Maxwell, filio et heredi Johannis de Maxwell de Carlaverock, Militis, de omnibus terris ſuis quas ſe de nobis tenuit in capite."

20 ——— Willielmo Lydoun, de medietate terrarum de Feryngtounfeld, viz. 13 acris terre, jacen. juxta burgum de Forfar, devent. in manus regis propter defectum heredum.

21 ——— Willielmo de Somervill, de dimidietate baronie de Manuell, in Stirlingſhire, by reſignation of Chriſtian Crouſar.

22 ——— Hugoni de Eglingtoun Militi, et Egidie de Lyndiſay ſorori Regis ſponſe ſue, de terris de Boningtoun, dimidio terre de Nortoun, et dominio terrarum de Weſthall et Cotraw, cum annuo redditu 4 marcarum et 8 ſolidorum de Weſthall et Cotraw, in vicecom. de Edinburgh, tenen. de Rege et heredibus ſuis Seneſcallis Scotie.

23 ——— Hugoni de Rath, de officio coronatoris, vicecomitat. de Air, illi diſpoſit. per Johannem de Lyndeſay de Toriſtoun. Vide p. 98. No. 331.

24 ——— Joanni de Cragy, de annuo redditu 40 marcarum.

25 ——— Johanni Wallays, de terris de Thurryſtoun, in baronia de Innerweek, et vicecom. de Edinburgh; et viginti mercatarum annui redditus de terris de Thornyle, in baronia de Renfrew, et vicecom. de Lanark; octo marcarum annui redditus de terris de Inglyſtoun et Annottouris, in baronia de Doryſder, et vicecom. de Drumfres; et omnium terrarum de Retre, in comitatu Buchanie, et vicecom. de Abirdene; omnibus reſignatis per Johannem de Lyndeſay de Cragy Militem.

26 ——— Ade Wawayn, de carrucata terre, in vicecom. de Roxburgh, cujus una dimidietas jacet in tenemento de Somerſtoun, in baronia de Overcrailling, et altera dimidietas in baronia de Farnydoun, forfeited by John Scampe.

27 ——— Johanni Lyon, de thanagio de Glammyſa, relevium taxatur ad 10 l. Sterling tantum.

28 ——— Thome de Rate, de dimidio baronie de Ouris, in vicecom. de Kyncardyn, reſignat. per Matheum de Eychles. Vide No. 9. hujus rotuli.

29 ——— Johanni del Yle, de trecentis mercatis terrarum que fuerunt quondam Alani filii Roderici, vic. Modeworth, Araſlag, Moreovyr, Knedeworte, Ovyſte, Barrah, Rume, Eggeh, Hyrte. Vide p. 97. No. 316.

30 ——— Mariote de Cardne, de terris de Tolyre, Burelle, Eiſterbalnegall, et Shenvall, cum molendino, que vocatur Milnethort, in vicecom. de Kinreſs. Vid. p. 97. No. 317.

31 ——— confirming ane contract made betwixt George de Dunbar Earl of March, and Agnes de Dunbar his ſiſter, and James de Douglas Dominus de Dalkeith; by which the ſaid Earl becomes bound to give, in liberum maritagium with his ſiſter, to ſaid James de Douglas, 100 l. land in the iſle of Man, how ſoon it can be recovered either by wars or by peace.

32 Carta to Robert Earl of Fyfe and Menteith, of the keeping of the caftle of Stirling, with 14 chalders of wheat, 12 chalders of oat-meal, out of Bothkenner, in Stirlingfhire, with 200 l. yearly to be paid by the chamberlain, for fupport thereof.

33 —— confirming a charter by William Bifhop of St Andrew's to John Cragy, of the lands of Kyldeleth, for a yearly duty of 10 l. Sterling, and giving fuit at the Bifhop's courts at Liftoun.

Ane Roll of Robert II. marked on the back with G, Rutherglen, 13 l. Sterling.

This is the eighth Roll now in the General Regifter-Houfe.

It contains one-and-forty charters, granted by King Robert II. in the 8th, 9th, 11th, 12th, 13th, 14th, 16th, 17th, 18th, and 19th years of his reign.

Nine of thofe charters are dated at Edinburgh, five at Perth, three at Glafgow, three at Stirling, three at Lynlithgow, two at Dundee, two at Kylwyning, two at Arnele, and one at each of the following places, viz. Scone, Logyrate, Kyndrocht, Ayr, and Methfen ; the other feven do not mention the places at which they were granted.

Only five of the charters in this roll mention the witneffes, viz. No. 2, 3, 4, 5, and 28. William Bifhop of St Andrew's, John Bifhop of Dunkeld the Chancellor, John Earl of Carrick and Steward of Scotland the King's eldeft fon, and Robert Earl of Fyfe and Menteith, are witneffes to all the five ; James Earl of Douglas and Marr is witnefs to No. 2, 3, 4, and 28 ; Archibald de Douglas and Robert de Erfkyne are witneffes to No. 2, 3, 4, and 5 ; and James de Lyndefay and Alexander de Lyndefay are witneffes to No. 28.

1 Carta of the burgh of Hadingtoun, to the burgeffes and community thereof, for payment of 15 l. Sterling yearly.

2 —— to William de Douglas, fon of Archibald de Douglas, Knight, of a penfion of 40 l. Sterling yearly.

3 —— to William de Douglas, and his fpoufe Egidia the King's daughter, of a yearly penfion of 300 l. Sterling furth of the burrow-maills of Edinburgh, Litheu, Dunde, and Abirdene.

4 —— to Patrick de Innerpeffer, of the lands of Balmaledy, Balmachennach, Haltoun, and Smithiehill, in Kincardinefhire, whilk Walter de Lefly and Euphemia his wife refigned.

5 —— to St Laurence Altar, in the kirk of Stirling, of a paffage-boat on the river Forth, with a croft of land annexed to the fame, and of certain annual duties particularly mentioned in the charter ; " faciendo " inde dicti capellani, pro falubri ftatu noftro liberorumq. noftrorum, necnon pro anima *quondam* " *cariffime confortis noftre Euphamie Regine Scotie,*" &c. This proves Queen Eupham to have been dead before this charter was granted, viz. 28th February 1388-9. Fordoun fays fhe died in the year 1387, Book 14. chap. 50.

6 —— of the burgh of Ruglen, to the burgeffes and community thereof, for payment of 13 l. Sterling yearly.

7 —— given by the King, with confent of his eldeft fon John Earl of Carrick, to Walter de Ogilvy, of ane annualrent of 29 l. Sterling furth of the thanedom of Kyngaltvy, in the fhire of Forfar.

8 —— to Andrew Dempfter, of the office of Dempfter in parliament, and juftice-airs, and in the fheriff-court of the fhire of Forfar, to him and his heirs, with the ufual fees belonging to the fame.

9 —— to James de Sandilands, of the barony of Dalzell and Modervale, and the barony of Wyftoun, in the fhire of Lanark ; the lands of Arthbifet, Ochterbannok, and Slomannane more, in Stirlingfhire, to be holden by the faid James and Joanna the King's daughter his fpoufe, and their heirs.

10 —— to John Palmer, of certain lands within the burghs of Stirling and Dunbretan, and the city of Glafgow, difponed to him by his father Gregory, called Chepman.

11 —— to David de Lindfay, of the fuperioritie of Cambow, in Fifefhire.

12 —— to faid David de Lyndefay, of the lands of Strathnarn, in vicecomitatu de Invernefs ; 40 l. Sterling out of the burrow-maills of Aberdeen ; the lands of Glenefk and Futhenevin, with the forreft of Platar, in Forfarfhire.

INDEX OF CHARTERS BY KING ROBERT II.

13 Carta to James de Lindsay, of the castle and barony of Crawforde, except the lands of Holeluch, Buchowys, Poltrayll, and Hertop, in vicecomitatibus de Lanark et Annandale; and Kirkmichell, in vic. de Drumfreis; ane annual of 100 marks Sterling furth of the customs of Dundee; the patronage of the kirk of Faill, in vic. de Air; and the thanedom of Alith, in vic. de Perth, on his own resignation: to said James de Lyndesay, and the heirs-male of his body; whom failing, to David de Lyndesay, " filio nostro (Roberti 2di, viz.) dilecto," and the heirs-male of his body; whom failing, to Alexander, William, and Walter, brothers-german of said David, and the heirs-male of their bodies respectively; whom failing, to the nearest heirs of said James bearing the name and arms of Lyndesay.

14 ——— confirming an agreement betwixt David de Lyndesay the King's son-in-law and John Earl of Murray, in relation to the superiority of the lands of Strathnarne, in the shire of Inverness.

15 ——— of ane pension of 100 l. Sterling, to John Earl of Murray, furth of the customs of Elgine and Forres.

16 ——— to ditto, of another pension of 100 l. Sterling furth of the customs of Aberdeen.

17 ——— to the burgesses and community of Ruglen, of the said burgh, for payment of 13 l. Sterling yearly.

18 ——— to William de Dunbar burgess of Aberdeen, a bastard, authorising him to dispose of his subjects at his pleasure, his bastardy notwithstanding

19 ——— to James Scrymgeor, of the lands of Innerkeithing and the miln, in Fifeshire, on his own resignation.

20 ——— to William de Douglas, son to Archibald de Douglas *Domini Galwidie*, of 100 l. land in Roxburghshire, to be given him by his said father. No lands are mentioned.

21 ——— to ditto, of ane pension of 40 l. Sterling.

22 ——— to William Stewart of Jedworth, of the lands of Fynlawys, in the barony of Oxinhame, quas Thomas de Rydall forisfecit.

23 ——— to Robert Stewart of Innermaith, of ane pension of 20 merks furth of the customs of Innerkeithing.

24 ——— to Alexander de Irwyne, of the lands of Park of Drum, in Kyncardineshire, and annuals pertaining thereto, whilk John Moigne resign'd.

25 ——— to the kirk of Holyrood of Peebles, of the meadow near the burgh of Peebles called *Pratum Regni*.

26 ——— to the burgesses and community of Lynlithgw, of that burgh and the harbour of Blacknes, for payment of five pounds Sterling yearly.

27 ——— to Robert Brown, of the cockquet of Perth.

28 ——— to William de Mygill, of the barony of Mygill, in Perthshire, on the resignation of John de Mygill his grandfather.

29 ——— to Patrick de Innerpesser, of ground in Dundee.

30 ——— to Laurence de Goven, of an annual duty of 100 shillings out of the castleward of Roxburgh.

31 ——— to John Lyon, of the lands of Keklonquhane, in Fifeshire, by resignation of Robert de Roos, son and heir of Hugh de Roos of Kinfaunis.

32 ——— to John de Fairly of Braid, and Helen de Dowglas, daughter natural to Sir Henry de Douglas, of the lands of Bavillay, in the shire of Edinburgh.

33 ——— to Sir Henry de Douglas, of the lands of Logtoun, in the shire of Edinburgh, on his own resignation.

34 ——— to James de Lindsay, of the superiority of Ley, Cartland, Foulwood, and Bondingtoun, in Lanarkshire, to be holden of him as Baron of the barony of Crawford-Lyndesay.

35 ——— to William More, of the lands of Abercorne and Dene, in the constabulary of Linlithgow, and shire of Edinburgh, and others, as in No. 16. p. 129.

36 ——— to Richard de Sinclair, of the lands of Findlater, &c. as in No. 17. p. 129.

37 ——— to Sir John Lyon, of the lands of Altermony and Dalrevach, in Stirlingshire, by forfaultrie of William Clerk of Fal'kirk. See p. 129. No. 18.

38 ——— to John de Swyntoun, of ane pension of 20 l. Sterling.

INDEX OF CHARTERS BY KING ROBERT II.

On the back of this Roll are three Charters.

39 Carta to Alexander Earl of Buchan, of half ane devach of land of Invirnorſyn, with the park, one fourth-part of Blary, ane fourth-part of Inchbrenys, 4th part of Lochlettre, and 4th part of Dalſtanghy, in Invernefs-ſhire, by reſignation of Robert de Cheſhelm.

40 —— to Alexander Earl of Buchan, of the lands of Abernethy, in Invernefs-ſhire, by reſignation of John Comyn.

41 —— to David de Ramſay, of the lands of Inverleith, in the ſhire of Edinburgh.

Ane Roll of Robert II. marked on the back, H.

This is the third Roll now in the General Regiſter-Houſe.

It contains twenty charters granted by King Robert II. The firſt is illegible, and the ſecond and eighth do not expreſs either the place where or date when they were granted. The remaining ſeventeen bear to have been granted in the ſecond year of that King's reign.

Eight of thoſe ſeventeen charters are dated at Edinburgh, three at Are, and one at each of the following places, viz. St Andrew's, Stirling, Glammys, Methfen, Dunbretane, and Arnele.

None of the royal charters contain the names of the witneſſes.

1 The firſt charter cannot be read.

2 Carta to William Earl of Douglas, of the lands of Tillieculrie, in the ſhire of Clackmannan, by reſignation of Thomas Earl of Mar.

3 —— confirming a grant by Mary Counteſs of Monteith, to John de Drommond, of the lands of Roſenethe, in the earldom of Lennox, diſponed by ſaid John de Drommond to Alexander de Meneteth.

4 —— to Marion de Cardny, and the iſſue procreated or to be procreated between the King and her; whom failing, to the heirs of Marion's body lawfully to be begotten, of the twa Clyntres, Weltoun, and Watirtoun, in Aberdeenſhire, cum *nativis " et eorum ſequelis,"* &c.

5 —— confirming a charter by Thomas Flemyng formerly (*alias*) Earl of Wygtoun, to Archibald de Douglas Knight, *Domino Galwydie ex orientali parte aque de Creth*, of the earldom of Wygtoun, in conſideration of a large ſum of money; the ſaid Thomas having been induced to ſell it on account of grievous feuds that had ariſen between him and the more powerful of the ancient indigenous inhabitants of the earldom, (" majores *indigenas* comitatus prediċti"). The original charter is dated at Edynburgh, the 8th of February 1371-2; witneſſes, Walter Abbot of Holywood, William Monypeny rector of the church of Cambuſlang, Neil de Conyghame, Thomas de Rath, and Nicolas Smerles, burgeſſes of Drumfres.

6 —— confirming a charter of confirmation by King Alexander II. of a grant by Neil Earl of Carryk, to Roland de Carryk and his heirs, conſtituting them head of their tribe or clan (*progeniei ſue*), in all matters pertaining to the *Kenkynoll,* " tam in calumpniis quam aliis articulis et negotiis ad Kenkynoll " pertinere valentibus," with the office of Bailliary of the foreſaid country (Carryk), and of leading the men thereof, under the Earl. King Alexander's charter is dated at Strivelyne, the 20th of January, in the 27th year of his reign, before theſe witneſſes, Alexander Steward of Scotland, James his ſon, and Richard de Setoun.

INDEX OF CHARTERS BY KING ROBERT II. 135

7 Carta confirming the above-mentioned original charter itself by Neil Earl of Carryk, to Roland de Carryk. Earl Neil's charter has neither place nor date; but it has for witnesses, " Domino Alano Hoft. Jufti-
" ciario Scotie, Domino Colino fratre ejufdem, Dominis Bartholomeo Flamens, Ricardo Mafculo,
" Thoma de Conyngifburgh, Waltero Marefcallo, Militibus, Henrico M'Kynbethy, et Willielmo C:-
" pellano."

8 —— apparently intended as a confirmation of a remiffion by King Robert I. in favour of Gilbert de Carryk, Knight, for furrendering the caftle of Louchdone to the Englifh, and for delivering (probably to the Englifh too) Criftofer de Setoun that King's fon-in-law. King Robert's charter has neither place nor date; but it has the following witneffes, viz. " Edwardo de Brwys, Jacobo Senefcallo Scotie, Tho-
" .... Ranulphi, Johanne de Meneteth, Nigello Cambell Militibus; Jacobo Domino de Douglas, A-
" lexandro Frafer, Waltero de Uykyrtoun, Henrico de Anandia clerico, et multis aliis." Here the record ftops there, and of courfe the ufual *confirming* claufe is omitted.

N. B. Each of the three immediately preceding charters, viz. No. 6, 7, and 8, has on the margin of the roll thefe words in an ancient character, " Confirmatio Johannis Kenedy;" and all the other charters in this roll have fimilar marginal titles written by the fame hand.

9 —— to Thomas de Haya Conftable of Scotland, " dilecto filio noftro," and Elizabeth his wife, " filie " noftre dilecte," and the heirs of their bodies, of an annual duty of 18 merks Sterling out of the lands of Inchetuthyle, in Perthfhire.

10 —— to Forfith clerk, of ane annual duty of 100 fhillings out of the land of Polmas Marefchell, in Stirlingfhire.

11 —— confirming a grant by King David II. to Alexander Porter, of the New Park in the fhire of Stirling.

12 —— " Robertus, &c. Cum Johannes filius Williehni, et Criftiana fponfa fua, ratione dicte fpohfe, et he-
" redes ipfius Chriftiane, nobis, et heredibus noftris Regibus Scotie, reddere teneantur annuatim, apud
" manerium noftrum de Forfar, trecentos plauftratus petarum, pro terris de Balmofchenore et de
" Tyrebeg, infra vic. de Forfar; nos, quod apud Forfar totiens ficut predeceffores noftri refiden-
" tiam hiis temporibus non faciamus, conceffimus dicto Johanni, de gratia noftra fpeciali, *ac de con-*
" *fenfu et voluntate Johannis primogeniti noftri Comitis de Carryk Senefcalli Scotie,* quod predictus Jo-
" hannes," &c. " pro dictis trecentis plauftratibus petarum, tantum nobis et heredibus noftris inve-
" niant, quotiens nos et ipfos apud Forfar venire contigerit, focale ad fufficientiam pro mora noftra
" et heredum noftrorum ibidem facienda," &c. " apud Glaumys, 28vo Octobris, an. reg. fe-
" cundo."

13 —— confirming a grant by Ingeram M'Gillelan, to Robert Stewart of Schanbothy, of ane davach of land of Caftletoun, Hogeftoun, Wefter Balblayn, the half of the milne thereof, and the fourth part of Morehufe, in the barony of Reid Caftle upon Lownan, in the fhire of Forfar.

14 —— to Robert de Erfkyne, Knight, of ane annuall duty of 20 l. and 10 marks Sterling forth of the barony of Cadyow, in viceeom. de Lanark, in excambion for the lands of Bondingtoun, and an annual duty of four marks out of Wefthall, in the barony of Rathew, and fhire of Edinburgh.

15 —— confirming a charter by James de Douglas de Dalketh, Knight, to William de Croffevyle, of the different of 20 marks of land, viz. the lands of Robertftoun and of Horthornchill, in the fhire of Lanark. The original charter confirmed is dated at Dalketh, 10th July 1372.

16 —— confirming a grant by John de Wemys, to Andrew de Valoniis, of the half of the miln of Lochore, in Fifefhire.

17 —— to James Stewart, a fon of the King's, and the heirs of his body; whom failing, to his brother-uterine John Stewart, of the reverfion of ane annual duty of 16 l. Sterling, liferented by Margaret Countefs of Angus, out of the barony of Abirnethy, in Perthfhire.

INDEX OF CHARTERS BY KING ROBERT II.

18 Carta confirming a grant by the King's fon (in-law) John de Yle, to Reginald de Yle his fon, of the land of Mudewort, and caftle of Elantirym; the lands of Arrafagk, Morowore, and Cundeford; the iflands of Egge, Rume, Huwyfte, with the caftle of Vynvawle; the iflands of Barre and Hert, and the fmall iflands adjacent; the lands of Swynwort, Lettirlochletle, Ardegowar, Hawlafte; and 60 mark lands in Lochabre, viz. Loche, Kylmald, and Locharkage.

19 —— confirming a charter given by George de Dunbarr Earl of March " Dominus vallis Annandie et " Mannie," to James de Dowglafs Dominus de Dalkeith, and Agnes his fpoufe, fifter to the faid Earl, of the lands of Mordingtoun, in the fhire of Berwyck. The Earl of March's charter is dated at Dunbar, 21ft November 1372, before thefe witneffes, viz. his brother John de Dunbar Earl of Murray; Walter de Halyburton, Patrick de Hebburne, and John de Edmondftoun, Knights; Gilbert Heryng, Alexander de Ryclyntoun, Philip de N. fbyt, John de Wardlaw, and John del Yle.

20 —— to James de Douglas, and Agnes his fpoufe, of the lands of Whittinghame, within the earldom of March.

INDEX OF CHARTERS BY KING ROBERT III.

Ro. III. ✗

Ane Roll of Robert III, marked on the back, Ro. III. A.

	In vicecom.
1 Carta Con. given by William of Abernethie, Knight, Lord Saltoun, to John Abernethy, of the lands of Kynnaltie, in the barony of Rethy, with ane taillie, blench,	Forfar.
2 —— to Neill Sutherland, of the town of Auldwick, in Caithnefs, with ane burgh of barony, and ane taillie.	Innernes.
3 —— to John Park, of a penfion furth of the burrow-maills of Lithgow.	
4 —— to Archibald Cuming, of the Weft Barnes of Craill, vic.	Fyfe.
5 —— to John Ramorgny, of ane penfion furth of the cuftomes of St Andrewe's.	
6 —— Con. given by Alexander Irvine of Drum, to Robert Bell burgefs of Dundee, of the wodfet of the lands of Inchftare, and of the annual furth of Owris,	Forfar.
7 —— to James Frafer, of ane annual of 20 marks furth of the lands of Carnowne and Oulmefli, in the barony of Frendraught,	Aberdeen.
8 —— given by William Mauld of Panmure, to Alexander Aughterlony, and Janet Mauld his fpoufe, of the lands of Greinford,	Forfar.
9 —— to William Naper, of the lands of Wrightshoufes, ane part thereof by refignation of Ade Forrefter, blench, for ane penny; and fheills of the miln of Peebles, blench,	Edinburgh.
10 —— to Alexander.———The Old Index leaves this entry unconcluded.	Peebles.
11 —— to William Meldrum, of the 3d part lands of Cleis, 3d part of the milne of Cleis, third part of Wefter Cleis, third part of Bordland, third part of Newiftoun, third part of the town and miln of Newftoun, in the barony of Cleis,	Fyfe.
12 —— of a new infeftment of the town of Drumfreis, for 20l. in few.	
13 —— to Robert Hall, of the lands called Caftlevallie of Rutherglen, and the King's Ifles, blench,	Rutherglen.
14 —— to Robert Knock, of the lands of Knock, within the liberty of Renfrew, whilk William Cunyngame, fon to the Sheriff of Air, refigned,	Renfrew.
15 —— to the town of Perth, anent the fheriffship within burgh.	
16 —— to Sir William Ruthven, of the fheriffship of St Johnftoun.	
17 —— to Arthur Campbell, of the lands of Monfluie,	Clackman.
18 —— to Sir William Inglis, of the barony of Maner, blench, vicecom. Peebles, for the flaughter of Thomas Struther, Englifhman, in fingle combat; refervand the lands poffeft by William Gladftanes, Knight, in the faid baronie, and superiority thereof.	

138 INDEX OF CHARTERS BY KING ROBERT III.

		In vicecom.
19	Carta to Malcolme Drummond Earl of Marr, of ane penſion of 20 l. money, furth of Innerneſs, in recompence and ſatisfaction of the third part of the ranſom of Sir Randolph Piercy, which exceeded ſix hundred pounds money. This Drummond is called the King's brother.	
20	—— of certain liberties granted to the Abbacy of Aberbrothock.	
21	—— of Mortification, by Mr John Barbour, Archdean of Ab^d, of twenty ſhilling to the cathedral of Ab^d.	
22	—— to John Ogſtoun, of the lands of Schithun, by reſignation of John Maxwell of Pollock.	Aberdeen.
23	—— to the Monaſtery of Paiſley, of their haill lands in Renfrew, Air, Roxburgh, Peebles, in ane free barony, with ane regalitie; Mott, Huntlaw, lying in Haſfeldane, Ords in Peebles.	
24	—— to Andrew French, of the lands of Bondingtoun, within the barony of Cuninghame,	Air.
25	—— to Gilchriſt More, of the lands of Kintumer, in the barony of Stanehouſe,	Lanerk.
26	—— to Sir John Hamilton of Roſs, of ane penſion of 29 marks Sterling, furth of the barony of Mauchan, by John Hamilton of Cadzow, Knight,	Lanerk.
27	—— to John Edmond, Knight, the King's brother, and Elizabeth Sinclair his ſpouſe, daughter to the Earl of Orkney, of the lands of Murlache, vic. Banff, by reſignation of the Earl of Orkney.	Banff.
28	—— to Douglas, herauld to the King, of the lands of Putterlane,	Edinburgh.
29	—— to John Weems, of the third part of the barony of Luicheris ; the lands of Skathachy, Pettincreiff; half lands of Wolmanſtoun, Bredles ; third part of Bowlands ; third part of Purſke, Petlowny, Baloyngy, with the miln, Brekmoune, Logie, Weſter Cruvy ; third part of Struburne, Fordall, Weſterfothey, Kulbakie ; in the barony of Lucheris.	Fyfe.
30	—— to John Dalzell, of the lands of Kinmonth, Bouchtanis, half lands of Clune, by reſignation of Alexander Keith,	Banff.
31	—— to William Cunynghame, of the barony of Reidhall, by reſignation of Murdo Stewart,	Edinburgh.
32	—— to Walter Tullach, of the town and lands of Ratray, within the earldom of Buchan, by reſignation of Hew Wallace,	Aberdeen.
33	—— Con. to William Danielſtoun, of ane penſion furth of the barony of Mauldſley, in vic.	Lanerk.
34	—— to St John's chappell, in the north ſide of St Geylli's kirk,	Edinburgh.
35	—— to John Chalmer burgeſs of Ab^d, of ane penſion furth of the burrow-maills in	Aberdeen.
36	—— to Walter Hamilton, of ane tenement of land in	Edinburgh.
37	—— to John Weems, of the third part of the barony of Lucheris, vic. Fyfe, whilk was John Hayi's of Tullibothe; the third part of the ſaids lands ; the lands of Pettincreife, Seathochy, Wolmeſtoun, Burdles, and Craill ; by reſignation of John Weems, ſra infeftment,	Fyfe.
38	—— to Walter Stewart the King's brother, Lord of Brechine, of ane penſion furth of the burrow-maills of	Edinburgh.

INDEX OF CHARTERS BY KING ROBERT III.

39 Carta Con. by Walter Stewart of Raylſtoun ſheriff of Perth, to Robert Earl of Fyfe, of the barony of Fothergill. — In vicecom. Perth.
40 —— to George Dalzell, of the barony of Dalzell, by reſignation of James Sandilands the King's good-brother.
41 —— anent our Ladie's altar in the kirk of Stirling.

Ane Roll of Robert III. marked on the back, Rob. III. B.

The infeftments in this Roll are betwixt the eight and fifteen years of the King's reign, incluſive.

1 Carta to James Hamiltoun, of the barony of Kinneill, 8, — Edinburgh.
2 —— to David Lindſay, of the barony of Mogill, — Perth.
3 —— to James Hamiltoun, of the baronies of Caidzow, Machan, Lanerk, vic. — Lanerk.
4 —— to Gilchriſt More, of the barony of Stanehouſe, — Lanerk.
5 —— to John Mowat, of the lands of Syandford, in the barony of Ferne; the lands of Gilharne, in the barony of Kinblackmonth, vic. de — Forfar.
6 —— given by David Lord Lindſay, to Thomas Sibbald of Balgony, of five pound furth of Craill, 8, — Fife.
7 —— Con. of ane infeftment granted by James Sandilands, to George Earl of Angus, brother to Iſabel Counteſs of Marr and Garrioch, of the lands of Cavers, with the ſheriffſhip, and keeping of the caſtle of Roxburgh; the town, caſtle, and forreſt of Jedburgh; the lands of Bonjedworth; the lordſhip of Liddell, vic. Roxburgh; the haill town of Selkirk; the ſervice and ſuperiority of the barony of Buttill, Drumlanrigg, vic. Drumfreis; the annualls furth of the burgh of Hadingtoun, vic. Ed^r; the lands of Dounbouk, Calbrache, and Clenaghe, vic. de Banff; the ſucceſſion of the barony of Tillieculthrie, vic. Clackmannan; Eiſter Hurdories; anno regni 8vo.
8 —— to George Douglas Earl of Angus, and Mary Stewart his ſpouſe, daughter to the King, of all the lands within the ſheriſdom of Forfar; the barony of Abernethy, vic. Perth; barony of Bonkill, vic. Berwick; in a free regality, with advocation of kirks, — Forfar. Perth. Berwick.
9 —— to the Earl of Angus, his and their heirs-male, of all the amerciaments of court of his lands, within vic. — Forfar.
10 —— to Agnes Peebles, ſpouſe to John Reed burgeſs of Ed^r, of ane tenement in Ed^r, — Edinburgh.
11 —— to William Lindſay of Logie, of the fourth part of Culcarny, — Kinroſs.
12 —— to Thomas Monetar, maſter of the office of Coinzieing, — Edinburgh.
13 —— to George Leſly, of the barony of Carny, — Perth.
14 —— to William Barclay, of the lands of Tuich and Bolgy, — Fyfe.
15 —— to the toun of Renfrew.
16 —— to John Lyill, of the barony of Lundy, — Forfar.

INDEX OF CHARTERS BY KING ROBERT III.

		In vicecom.
17	Carta to the Abbacy of Arbrothe, of ane chalder of victuall furth of Benholme,	Forfar.
18	—— to Duncan Kirkpatrick, of the barony of Torthorwald,	Drumf.
19	—— to Walter Stewart the King's brother, Earl of Caithnefs, of the earldom of Atholl,	Perth.
20	—— to Robert Earl of Fyfe, of the earldom of Atholl,	Perth.
21	—— Con. to the Abbacy of Lindores, anent their liberties, granted by Alexander King of Scots.	
22	—— granted by Archibald Earl of Angus, to Adam Forrefter, of the barony of Clerkingtoun, blench,	Edinburgh.
23	—— to Adam Gordon, of the lands of Gordon and Fogo, vic. Berwick, the fuperiority whereof pertains to the King, by forfaultrie of the Earl of March,	Berwick.
24	—— to John Levingftoun, of ane penfion furth of the cuftoms of Lithgow.	
25	—— to Robert Maxwell of Pollo, fon to Sir John Maxwell, of 20l. furth of the cuftoms of Dundee,	Forfar.
26	—— to David Fleming of Biggar, of the lands of Auchlan, in the barony of Kinnedward,	Aberdeen.
27	—— to James Lord of Dalkeith, of a penfion furth of the cuftoms of Edr.	
28	—— to Duncan Lichtoun, of ane penfion furth of the lands of Kinnettill,	Forfar.
29	—— to James Stewart fon naturall to the King, of the lands of Kilbryde, with ane taillie,	Lanerk.
30	—— to John Barclay, of the lands of Kippo, Lochtoun, and Morfktoun,	Fyfe.
31	—— to Walter Earl of Caithnes, of the lands of Brechin, Ruthuen, Nethvar,	Forfar.
32	—— to ditto, of the baftardie of Simon Cattill, within	Monrofs.
33	—— to John Stewart, fon to Marion Carney, of a penfion furth of the cuftomes of Dundee.	
34	—— to William Cunynghame, of the fuperioritie of Perftoun, Warwikhill, Drummore, Caprinftoun, Warwicks, in the barony of Cunningham,	Ayr.
35	—— to Alexander Laverock, of ane tenement in	Perth.
36	—— to Andrew Lockhart, of the lands of Bar, Gallartlands, Makifwodeis, and Newtoun, in the barony of Walter's Kyll, vic.	Air.
37	—— to John Lockhart, of the lands of Dalry, Auchinbert, in the barony of Walterskyll,	Air.
38	—— to Michael Mr, of ane annual rent furth of Finlater, Netherdull, Pettindreich, Balleynch, and the town of Perth.	
39	—— to John Dalzell, of ane tenement in Edr.	
40	—— to Thomas Ethingtoun, of the lands of Kinbrakmonth, vicecom. Fyfe; Langhirdmanltoun, Currie, Reidhewis, Kilbabertoun, vic. Edr; Balglaffie, Balvany, Tulliwhenland, with the common pafturage in the Moor Month, the lands of Flemingtoun, vic. Forfar; Cafdughly, vic. Kinrofs,	Kinrofs.
41	—— to Thomas Difhingtoun, of the lands of Ardroffe, blench,	Fyfe.
42	—— to the Abbacy of Kilwinning, of the advocation of the kirk of Rofay, by James Stewart, grandfon to the King,	Bute.
43	—— by Andrew Lefly, to Thomas Gardin, of the lands of Bad, whilk is in the barony of Rothynermand,	Aberdeen.

INDEX OF CHARTERS BY KING ROBERT III.

		In vicecom.
44	Carta Con. given to Thomas Gardin, of the lands of Fulbakater, in the barony of Kinnedward,	Aberdeen.
45	—— to James Douglas of Strathbrok, of the lands of Buteland, vic. Ed^r, whilk Robert Rouk resigned.	Edinburgh.
46	—— to John Stane, of the lands of Glenbervie, by Melvill of Glenbervie.	
47	—— to Thomas Duncanson of Athol, of the lands of Strathloche or Easter Davache, and Thomcury, Dekarwand, Dalacharmy,	Perth.
48	—— to Thomas Duncanson of Athol, of Strowane, ane ratification of all his lands, with a taillie.	
49	—— to Alexander Nisbit, of the lands of Tuyndsheills, Hertfollings, twa Chyrnsides, quilk Agnes Twyndsheills, spouse to - - - - - - - - Lindsay, resigned,	Berwick.
50	—— to Findlay Bunting, of the lands of Mylnetelame, and six marks of the barony of Cardross,	Dumbart.
51	—— to the Monastery of Cambuskenneth, of the hospital called St James Hospital.	
52	—— to John Stewart of Ardgowane, of the lands of Ardcowan, in the barony of Innerkip, and barony of Renfrew.	
53	—— Con. given by Isabel Countess of Marr and Garrioche, to Alexander Keith of Grandoun, of the lands of Glendowachy, blench,	Banff.
54	—— to Alexander Ogilvy sheriff of Angus, of the barony of Neve, vic. Forfar, by resignation of William Cuningham of Kilmawris,	Forfar.
55	—— to Bernard Rossie, of the barony of Rossie, and the lands of Inene, in the samen sheriffdom,	Forfar.
56	—— to Dugal Carnagy, of the half lands of Kinnaird, by the wadset of Margaret Kinnaird,	Forfar.
57	—— to John Dolas, of the lands of Herbertsheills, half lands of Blacklawis, 4th part lands of Fisheartoun, in the barony of Kinell,	Kincardine.
58	—— to ditto, of the lands of Elstandsurde, in the constabulary of Hadingtoun,	Edinburgh.
59	—— to John Chirnsyde, of the lands of Fowllerland, in the toun of Quhitsome, by resignation of John Nisbit,	Berwick.
60	—— to Thomas Monipenny, and Christian Keith his spouse, of the third part of the barony of Leuchars,	Fife.
61	—— to David Duff, of the lands of Maldakatu and Baldavy,	Banff.
62	—— to Alexander Ogilvy sheriff, of ane pension of 20 l.	
63	—— to Alexander Keith of Grandoun, of the keeping of the castle of Banff,	Banff.
64	—— to David Earl of Crawfurd, of the barony of Crawfurd, with ane regalitie,	Lanerk.
65	—— to David Hay, of the place of Cullen,	Banff.
66	—— to Robert Cairncors, of the lands of Feres, whilks were John Meinzeis.	
67	—— to William Douglass, of the place and loch of Lochlevin, viz. Thross, Clasleuchan, Suneereech, Cassigwar, Weltertulachy, Mawcloych, Darrgarlat, Thentulchy, Aughteveny, Thonynun, Brokloucht, and Themalw, Croftmartyn, Martardlery; the half of Urwell, Cultvoy, Lathrocht, the town and hostlary of Kinross, cottages, and milnes; the annualls of Cultcarny, vic. Kinross.	

INDEX OF CHARTERS BY KING ROBERT III.

		In vicecom.
68	Carta to Walter Ogilvie, of the lands of Garlet, in the barony of Kinnell, vic. Forfar, 15.	
69	—— to the Abbacy of Croffragwell, of all their lands to be in a free regalitie, at length contained in the charter; Aliffay iſle.	
70	—— to William Abernethy, of the baronie of Rethy and Kylzalany,	Forfar.
71	—— to Archibald Douglas, ſon to the Earl of Douglas, of the lordſhip of Douglas, and regalities of the foreſt of Etrik, Lauderdaill, and Romannoch, and all the reſt in general, with a taillie. This Archibald married Margaret daughter to King Robert III. as this charter declares.	
72	—— to David Fleming of Biggar, of the ane-penny land of Barbethe, the lands of Caſlis, twa-merk land of Galnethe, ane-penny land of Glentall, in the parochine of Stratoun.	
73	—— to Murdoch Leckie, of two fourth-parts of Bathewnu and Altremony, blench,	Lennox.
74	—— Con. to Duncan Briſbane, of the lands of Bulincard,	Perth.
75	—— to William Scot, of the lands of Nemphlar, by reſignation of Janet Lockhart his mother, 24. Auguſti 1404,	Lanerk.
76	—— to Coline Campbell of Lochaw, of certain lands in Neather Cowell, whilk pertained to John Stewart of Aughingowne, ſon natural to the King.	
77	—— to Thomas Mellvill, of the office of Cuinzie ſtriking,	} Air.
78	—— to Galfur Goldſmith cunzier,	
79	—— to William Lindſay of the Byres, of the office of ſheriffſhip of Edinburgh, and office of conſtabulary of Haddingtoun, in liferent,	Hadington.
80	—— to the Abbacy of Paiſley, given by John Wallace of Craigie, of the lands of Thornley, in the barony of Renfrew,	Lanerk.
81	—— to the Monaſtery of Paiſley, given by Adam Fullartoun, of ane annualrent furth of Ruſſelland, in the barony of Corſbie; by Hew Boyll, out of Ryiſholme; by Kelſoland, out of Langbank, in Cunningham.	
82	—— by Iſabel Douglas Counteſs of Marr, of the lands of Tullicurran, Stratharbus, vic. Perth, and the Kirktoun of Eſſye, vic. Forfar, to Walter Ogilvie,	Perth. Forfar.
83	—— to David Earl of Crawfurd, of the baronie of Megill, by reſignation of William Megill,	Perth.
84	—— Con. to David Earl of Crawfurd, of the barony of Melginche, vic. Perth, and Cloveth, vic. Forfar, given by Iſabell Counteſs of Marr,	Perth. Forfar.
85	—— given by John Dolas to ditto, of the lands of Herbertſheills, half of Blacklawis, 4th part of Fiſcheantoun, in the barony of Bamf,	Kincardin.
86	—— to ditto, of Alicht Baltrody.	
87	—— to ditto, of the barony of Downy, Achebetoun, Innerraratic, Clova, Guthrie, Ecclis, Ruthven, Gleneſk, to be in a barony, to anſwer to the ſheriff of Forfar,	Forfar.
88	—— by David Earl of Crawfurd, to Thomas Earl of Murray, of the ſheriffſhip of	Banff.
89	—— to William Touris, of the lands of Berntoun,	Edinburgh.
90	—— to the Abbacy of Deer, of the cuſtom of all the wool growing within the ſheriffdom, and parochines of the ſaid Abbey,	Aberdeen.

INDEX OF CHARTERS BY KING ROBERT III.

In vicecom.

91 Carta given by John Allerdes, to Walter Ogilvie of Calcare, of the lands of Innercarrewchie, in the barony of Kerymure,   Forfar.
92 —— by John Ogftoun, to Walter Ogilvie, of the lands of Kinbredy, Breky,   Forfar.
93 —— to the bridge of Perth, of 2 l. Sterling furth of the cuftoms of Perth.
94 —— to Walter Ogilvie, of the lands of Eafter Keillour, whilk John Barclay of Kippo refigned,   Forfar.
95 —— to Thomas Hay Conftable of Scotland, of Galbrydftoun, and the barony of Capet.
96 —— to William Touris, of the fuperiority of King's Crawmond,   Edinburgh.
97 —— given by William Auldftoun, to David Fleming of Biggar, of the lands of Cambufbarron, Blaregis,   Stirling.
98 —— to William Wardlaw of Wiltoun, of the lands of Uchterfeatmylne, Sametoun, Todfhaw, in the barony of Wiltoun,   Roxburgh.
99 —— by Katherine Rofs of Paxtoun, to .... Stewart of Cardny, of the lands of Petye,   Forfar.
100 —— to our Lady Altar in the kirk of Dundee, of ane annual of five lib. Starling furth of the cuftomes thereof; anno regni 16.
                        Tenet.

Ane Roll of Robert III. marked on the back with this mark, C, Pinkertoun.

The firft infeftment cannot be read.
2 Carta to John Nudrie and his fpoufe, of certain lands in Crawmond,   Edinburgh.
3 —— to Hew Rofs of Kinfawns, of the barony of Craigie and Maler, with the miln thereof, with ane tallie,   Perth.
4 —— to St Leonard's, near Edr, of the barony of Brochtoun,   Edinburgh.
5 —— to Adam More of Rowallan, and .... Danielftoun his fpoufe, of the lands of Polnekill, Grey, Dumblay, Clunche, Clony, Herber, Darlache, Balgram, in the barony of Cuningham, vic. Air; the lands of Ayntflare; by refignation of Janet Danielftoun,   Air. Lanerk.
6 —— Con. to Alexander Lindfay, of 40 marks Sterling of the cuftoms of Montrofs,   Forfar.
7 —— to John Seytoun, of the lands of Bernes and Wintoun,   Edinburgh.
8 —— to Robert Dyckifon, of the lands of Hethonfields,   Peebles.
9 —— Con. by Thomas Hay Lord of Erroll, Conftable, &c. to Thomas Annand, of the lands of Gurdy, in the barony of Capet,   Perth.
10 —— to John Ramfay, of the lands of Morfemulun,   Kincardin.
11 —— to Laurence ...., ane annual furth of the barony of Maxtoun,   Edinburgh.
12 —— to Thomas Balcomy, of the lands of Pinkertoun and Randelftoun, with lands in Craill and Kingaldifcrofts,   Fyfe.
13 —— to William Landallis, of Landis in Oxenhame, whilk John Wyllie forisfecit,   Roxburgh.
14 —— to William Stewart of Jedworth, of the 3d part lands of Mintow,   Roxburgh.

INDEX OF CHARTERS BY KING ROBERT III.

		In vicecom
15	Carta to John Barclay, of Kippow and Arncorſt,	Fyfe.
16	—— to William Lindſay, of the lands of Pettindreiche, by reſignation of William Keith, and - - - - - - - Fraſer his ſpouſe,	Stirling.
17	—— to ditto, of ane annuall of 8 l. Sterling furth of the lands of Dunnottar, whilk the ſaid William has preſently reſigned in favour of William Keith Mariſhall,	Kincardin.
18	—— to Ade Wain, of the lands of Stevinſtoun, whilk Maklare reſigned,	Edinburgh.
19	—— to William Keith, of the barony and caſtle of Dunnotar, by reſignation of William Lindſay, with ane taillie,	Kincardin.
20	—— given by George Earl of March to James Sincler, of Lochirmagus,	Berwick.
21	—— given by James Sandilands of Calder, to George Lauder of Haltoun, the lands of Sorneſawlache, Greinhill, of the barony of Wiſtoun, by reſignation of Marion Pettendreich,	Lanark.
22	—— to Alexander Lindſay of Bachber,	Banff.
23	—— to William Diſhingtoun, of the lands of Hirdmanſtoun, vic. Ed^r; Balglaſſie, vic. Forfar; Duglyn, vic. Kinroſs,	Ed^r. Forfar. Kinroſs.
24	—— to William Ruthven, of the lands of Ruthven, vic. Perth; Ballernoch, vic. Ed^r,	Perth. Edinburgh.
25	—— to Duncan Talzeor, of ane tenement in Dundee,	Dundee.
26	—— to the Abbacy of Scoon, of the patronage of St Geill's kirk, in Ed^r,	Perth.
27	—— to the toun of Lanerk, for ſex marks Stirling, and three marks to St Leonard's, near Lanerk,	Lanerk.
28	—— to David Grahame, of the lands of Mukler,	Perth.
29	—— to James Dowglas of Dalkeith, of the lands of Hawthornfyke, of the conſtabulary of Linlithgow; himſelf witneſs,	Edinburgh.
30	—— to the toun of Forfar, for L. 8 : 13 : 4 Sterling in few.	
31	—— to John Tait, of the lands of Pren, vic.	Peebles.
32	—— to John Pettinweyme channon, of the milne of Anſtruther,	Fyfe.
33	—— Con. to Robert Haſwell, of the lands of Etteribinfchap, Hepop,	Roxburgh.
34	—— Con. to the Abbacy of Kilwinning and Beith, of ane regality, with the lands of Brimmerlands and Lyand croſs, by Sir John Maxwell of Pollok.	
35	—— to Thomas Baird, of the lands of Podaw, Langhail, and Kirkhope, Coverhill, half lands of Glaſs, Glenraith, Lettels, in the barony of Moner,	Peebles.
36	—— to the Abbacy of Halyroodhouſe, of the lands of Kers,	Stirling.
37	—— to Richard Broun, of the eaſt half lands of Otterſtoun, by reſignation of John Lambertoun,	Fyfe.
38	—— to David Lindſay, of the ſuperiority of Carnbie, whilk pertained to James Melvill; the ſuperiority of Balcomy, whilk pertains to Nicoll Hay; the ſuperiority of Cambock, vic. Fyfe; 15. Jan. anno regni 4to,	Fife.
39	—— to David Bruce, of the lands of Rate,	Perth.
40	—— to Thomas Murray of Culbyne, Janet Maxwell, daughter to Maxwell of Pollock, his ſpouſe, of ane pleugh of Sandſo d, the lands of Clauk, the milne of Semell, the paſſage and fiſhing of Seſſel in the barony of Nauhame, and lordſhip of Newtoun, the lands of Badſod, all vic.	Aberdeen.

INDEX OF CHARTERS BY KING ROBERT III. 145

Ane Roll of Robert III. marked on the back, D.

                                                                                              In vicecom.

1 Carta to Patrick Caldwall.
2 —— of ane foundation of a chappel att Chryftfwell.
3 —— to James Stewart of Kinfauns, of the difcharge of annual, taillie.
4 —— to Hew Wallayis, of the lands of Craigin and Richardtoun, vic. Air ; the lands of Thurftoun, Thornwell, vic. Ed', taillie.
5 —— to John Sempill, of ane annual of 20 l. ufual money.
6 —— given by David Moore of Abercorn, to David Fleming, of the foreft of Torwood, Stirling.
7 —— to the Monaftery of Melros, of ane tenement in Leith,
8 —— to ditto, of ane tenement in Ed',
9 —— to William Broun of Colftoun, of the lands of Malcolmftoun, Whytlaw, Litle Currie, in the barony of Rathew, by refignation of William Faffingtoun,   Edinburgh.
10 —— to the burgh of Innerkeithing, of their liberty to be betwixt Levin's mouth and Dovan's mouth, and the middis of the water, few 100s.   Fyfe.
11 —— to James Stewart of Kilbryde, his heirs-male, quilks failing, to John Stewart of Ardgowan, of ane annual furth of the cuftoms of Ed'.
12 —— to William Fairlie, of the lands of Braid,   Edinburgh.
13 —— of St Nicholas chappel in Duncanlaw, vic. Ed', of the lands quilk were John Stratoune's,   Edinburgh.
14 —— to Walter Gladftanes, of ane annual of Winkiftoun and Wodgrainningtoun, Peebles.
15 —— Con. to John Gladftanes, of the lands of Hundwallefhape, vic. Peebles ; the lands of Robertoun and the town of Selkirk, vic. Selkirk ; by refignation of Peebles. Margaret Glaidftanes his mother,   Selkirk.
16 —— given by Archibald Douglas Lord of Galloway and Bothwell, to the college of Bothwell, of the lands of Ofbarnyftoun, in the barony of Bothwell, vic. La- Lanerk. nerk ; the lands of Netherurd, vic. Peebles ; dated 10. Oct. 1398,   Peebles.
17 —— to Thomas Erefkine, of the barony of Alloway and forreft of Clackmannan, with ane taillie and regality,   Clackman.
18 —— to Ronnald Dalmahoy, of the ferjand land of Skyok,   Stirling.
19 —— to William Lindfay of Logie, of the 4th part lands of Culcarny,   Kinrofs.
20 —— to Ronnald Kinnaird, and Marjory Kirkaldie his fpoufe, of the barony of Inch- fture,   Perth.
21 —— to Thomas Blair of Bothyok, of the lands of Ardlare, Kylldowry, Balgillochie, Forfar.
22 —— to the Monaftery of Lefmahago, of 20 marks furth of the milnes of Carlouk.
23 —— to the Abbacy of Kilwinning, of the advocation of St Briged kirk, in Arran, Bute.
24 —— of the foundation of the chaplandrie of the paroch-kirk of Lanerk, by ane John Simpfone burges of Lanerk.
25 —— to St Duthei's Altar, in the paroch-kirk of   Edinburgh.
26 —— to John Stewart, fon to the Duke of Albany, of the barony of Cowll and O'Neill,   Aberdeen.

INDEX OF CHARTERS BY KING ROBERT III.

		In vicecom.
27	Carta to William Cuninghame, of the lands of Killmawers, the lands of Lambrachtoun, the lands of Killbryde, the lands of Skelmurly, the lands of Polquharne, vic. Air; the lands of Reidhall, vic. de Ed'; the lands of Neve, vic. Forfar; the lands of Haffenden, vic. Roxburgh; Rainfarnly, baronia de Renfrew, with ane taillie,	Air. Edinburgh. Forfar. Roxburgh.
28	—— to John Stewart of Aughingowne, the lands of Stron, in the barony of Cowall, with ane taillie.	
29	—— to George Lefly, of the lands of Fithkill, by refignation of Alexander Lefly Earl of Rofs; blench, for ane pair of gloves,	Fyfe.
30	—— to Walter Tullach, of the fifhing of the half net of the raik upon Dee, by refignation of Alexander Frazer fheriff of Ab^d,	Aberdeen.
31	—— to David Mowat, of the lands of Robertfon, in the barony of Cuninghame,	Air.
32	—— to William Lauder, of his lands in Borrow Moor,	Edinburgh.
33	—— to John Melvill, of the lands of Petachruch, in the barony of Innerkeithing, whilk Henry Ramfay forisfecit,	Fyfe.
34	—— Con. by David Fleming of Biggar and Leinzie, to the Abbacy of Holyrudehoufe, of ane annual of 20 marks Stirling, in the barony of Kers,	Stirling.
35	—— Con. to John Stewart of Bute, of ane annual of 20 marks furth of the barony of Abrenethy, with ane taillie,	Perth.
36	—— of St James's Altar, in the paroch-kirk of	Edinburgh.
37	—— to Patrick Fleming, of lands of Honemener, Glenruftok, within the baronie of Olvier Caftle, vic. Peebles.	
38	—— to William Preftoun, of the lands of Wefter Bindingtoun,	Edinburgh.
39	—— Con. by William King of Scots, to the burgh of Perth, anent their liberties; Alexander Vicecomes de Stirling is witnefs,	Perth.
40	—— Con. to the town of Perth, anent the breaking bouk of the lading of all fhips coming within Drumlaw,	Perth.
41	—— to Andrew Wardlaw, of the lands of Prieftfield and St Glie grange,	Edinburgh.
42	—— to David Duke of Rothfay, and Mary Douglas, daughter to the Earl of Douglas, of ane annual furth of the burrowis be fouth Forth,	
43	—— Con. by Robert Bruce of Rate and Clackmannan, to Thomas Bruce his fon natural, of the lands of Wefterkennet,	Clackman.
44	—— Con. by John Lauchlanfon of Niddifdale, Laird of Durydarach, to Duncan Dalrumpill, of the office of Tothia Daroche, in Niddifdale.	
45	—— Con. to the Abbacy of Dumfermling, of the patronage of the kirk of Innerkeithing, whilk Roger Moulray forisfecit, and the great cuftom of Innerkeithing, Mufſelburgh, Kirkaldie, and the Queensferry.	
46	—— Con. by Ronnald Fullarton of Crofbie and Dreghorne, of fix marks ten fhillings to the Whitefriers, near Irvine, furth of his lands,	Air.
47	—— to John Stewart, brother to the King, of the twa Cardnys,	Perth.
48	—— to John Crichtoun, of the barony of Crichtoun,	Edinburgh.
49	—— by David Fleming, the chappels of Kirkintullach, the lands of Drumtablay, with the miln thereof,	Dumbart.

INDEX OF CHARTERS BY KING ROBERT III.   147

	In vicecom.
50 Carta by Margaret Countefs of Mar and Angus, to William Borthwick, of the lands of Ludniche and Wefter Drumcanchy, in the barony of Kirimoor,	Forfar.
51 —— Con. by King William, to the burgh of Innerkeithing and their liberties,	Fyfe.
52 —— by Chriftian Airth, to Walter Burntoun, of the third part of the lands of Lufnes,	Hadington.
53 —— to Walter Burntoun, of the lands of Lufno, with the fuperiority thereof,	Edinburgh.
54 —— to the Earl of Dowglas, of the keeping of the marches, with ane taillie.	
55 —— to John Gordon, of the lands of Strathbogy,	Aberdeen.

Ane Roll of Robert III. marked on the back, F, O, Airlie, Perth, Ogilvie, Alexander Dñus Forbes, Ifabella Comitiffa de Mar.

1 Carta Con. by Alexander Murray, of Coubin and Newtoun, in Fyfe, to Mr Walter Forrefter fecretary, of ane annual of Innerdovat,	Fyfe.
2 —— Con. by Robert Turnbull, to Gregorie Kingiffone, of certain aikers in the fluires of Innerdovat.	
3 —— to John Turnbull, of the lands of Wauchopheid, in the baronie of Roxburgh, by the forfaultrie of John Bour,	Roxburgh.
4 —— to the Monaftery of Culrofs, of the cuftome of Woll.	
5 —— to Thomas Frefkine, of the lands of Ellem and teind-fheaves, within the earldom of March, and fheriffdom of Berwick, by the forfaultrie of the Earl of March.	
6 —— by David Fleming of Biggar, to John Rofs of Halkhead, of the lands of Cambufbarron,	Stirling.
7 —— by Ifabell Countefs of Mar, called Douglas, to Alexander Stewart, fon to Alexander Earl of Buchan, of the earldom of Mar and Caftelldrummy, of the lordfhip of Garviauch, with the advocation of the kirks pertaining thereto, the barony of Strathalvecht, vic. Banff; the barony of Cremond, in Buchan; ij. c. marks furth of the cuftoms of Haddingtoun; the foreft of Jedworth, and part of the barony of Cavers,	Aberdeen. Banff. Roxburgh.
8 —— to Walter Tullach, of the lands of Polnave, of fome lands in Balhelvies, given to him by John Lyon of Glamis,	Stirling. Aberdeen.
9 —— to Gilbert Wauchop, of the lands of Niddery,	Edinburgh.
10 —— to Laurence Spot, of ane tenement in	Edinburgh.
11 —— to William Boyd of Badinhach, of the lands of Galvan and Rafk, 'in the barony of Renfrew.	
12 —— anent the chaplain of St John Altar in the kirk of Stirling, by Sir Alexander Porter,	Stirling.
13 —— Con. by Ifabell Douglas Countefs of Mar, to Alexander Halyburtoun, of the barony of Sawline, vic. Fyfe, taillie,	Fyfe.

INDEX OF CHARTERS BY KING ROBERT III.

		In vicecom.
14	Carta to David Mowat, of the barony of Stanhoufe, vic. Lanerk; the barony of Brochtoun, Winkiftoun, Burelfield, vic. de	Lanerk. Peebles.
15	—— to Laurence Crichtoun, of the lands of Newhall, in the barony of Pennycook,	Edinburgh.
16	—— to John Spittell, of the lands of Kinninmond,	Fyfe.
17	—— to Robert Wintoun, of certain lands in the town of Crombie and Auchindald, in the barony of Cromby, the lands and town of Clefe,	Fyfe.
18	—— by Robert Maitland, to Robert Wintoun, of the barony of Hirdmanftoun, called Curry,	Edinburgh.
19	—— to Robert Franx, of the lands of Thornydyke, vic. Berwick; the lands of Petceks, vicecom. Edinburgh, whilks Ade Franx forisfecit,	Berwick. Edinburgh.
20	—— by John Dallas, in wadfet to Gilbert Graham of Morphie, of the lands of Blacklawis, and his part of the Fifhertoun, in the barony of Kinneff,	Kincardin.
21	—— by Walter Haliburtoun of Dirletoun, to John Chalmer burges of Perth, of the lands of Segie,	Kinrofs.
22	—— to William Cockburn, of ane annual of 10l.	
23	—— to the Bifhop St Andrew's, of the cuftoms of St Andrew's for ever,	Fyfe.
24	—— by Adam Forrefter of Corftorphin, to William Muirhead, of the lands of Quhytburn, vic. Ed'r, in the conftabularie of Lithgow,	Edinburgh.
25	—— to David Fleming, of the lands of Wodland and Meiklegall, in the barony of Monycabow,	Aberdeen.
26	—— to David Fleeming of Biggar, of the lands of Cavers, and thereffhip of Roxburgh, by reafon of recognition, by difpofition of Ifabel Countefs of Mar, to Archibald Earl of Dowglas,	Roxburgh.
27	—— to Archibald M'Dougall, of the lands of M'Carftoune, Yhethame, and Elyftoun, taillie,	Roxburgh.
28	—— to David Earl of Craufurd, of the barony of Kinneff, taillie,	Kincardin.
29	—— by David Earl of Craufurd, to John Dolas, of the lands of Bondingtoun, Newtoun, Balgerfchache, in the barony of Innerearity,	Edinburgh. Forfar.
30	—— to the Earl of Orkney, of his caftle wards of Pentland and Rofline, and their pendicles,	Edinburgh.
31	—— to John Crawfurd, of the lands of Braidfhaw, Brykinhead, Nethertoun, with the pafturage of 12 oxen and ane horfe in Millarland, in the barony of Cuninghame,	Air.
32	—— to William Butter, of the lands of Gormall, the twa Tullynedyis,	Perth.
33	—— Con. to John Nudrie, of the lands of Eaft Quarter of Pentland muire, the half lands of Erneeraig, in Pentland, and in the barony of Rofline, given by Henry Earl of Orkney, in excambion with the place and yeards of Kinkerawmond,	Edinburgh.
34	—— to Alexander Earl of Buchan, of the caftle hill of the toun of Innernes, with ane taillie,	Innernes.
35	—— Con. by Archibald Earl of Douglas, &c. to William Graham of Kincardine, the lands of Logyachray,	Stirling.
36	—— Con. by Thomas Colvill of Oxenhame, to Henry Preftoun, of his part of Fromertein, viceeom. Ab'd, with the caftles and tolls of the burgh of Fyvie,	Aberdeen.

INDEX OF CHARTERS BY KING ROBERT III.

37	Carta Con. by John Herries Lord or Laird of Tarriglis, to Sir Henry Preftoun, of his part of the barony of Fromertein, with the caftle and tollis of the burgh thereof,	In vicecom. Aberdeen.
38	—— Con. by Colin Campbell of Lochow, to Maurice M'Naughtane, of fundrie lands in Over Lochow, with ane taillie, which are evill to be copied,	Argyle.
39	—— Con. by William Mauld of Panmoor, to John Strathachane of Carmyllie, of the lands of Carmyllie, Drumadicht, Hakwrangdrum, Achlare, with the park and Whythill, with the milne and brew-houfe of Strathes, Copprofhill, Moncur.	Forfar.
40	—— to Alexander Strathaquhin of Carmylie, of ane annual out of the lands of Ingliftoun, Brigtoun, Kinnettlis,	Forfar.
41	—— of the foundation of ane chappellan within the kirk of Brechin, by Alexander Ogilvie fheriff of Angus, of 10 marks Sterling furth of the barony of Effie,	Forfar.
42	—— by Alexander Ogilvie, of 10 merks Sterling of the ferm of the town of Neva, in the barony of Effie, to the foundation of ane chaplan in the kirk of Uchterhoufe,	Forfar.
43	—— to James Spalding, of the lands of Fermall and Fornachty, by Walter Haliburton of Dirltoun,	Forfar.
44	—— of the revocation of the recognition of the Reid Friars lands.	
45	—— to the burgh of Perth, of all efcheatts and forfaultries fallen within the fame burgh,	Perth.
46	—— by James Frazer of Frendraught, to the White Friers of Aberdene, the lands of Little Glenfache, vic. Kincardine, in the Mearnes,	Kincardin.
47	—— to John Letham, of the lands of Letham, by the forfaultrie of Patrick Earl of March,	Berwick.
48	—— to William Douglas of Niddifdale, of the weft part of the town of Drumfreifs.	
49	—— to Gilbert Kennedy, of the land of Caffells, Giletre, two Kilmoris, within the earldom of Carrick, vicecom. de Air, taillie,	Air.
50	—— to James Kennedy, and Mary Stewart, daughter to the King, of the baronie of Dalrumple, in Kingfkyle, taillie,	Air.
51	—— to James Kennedy, and his heirs-male, of the capitanfhip, head, and commandment of his kin,	Air.
52	—— by John Stewart, brother to the King, of 20 marks of the cuftoms of Innerkeithing,	Fyfe.
53	—— Con. by Walter Leflie Earl of Rofs, to Alexander Frazer, in general.	
54	—— Con. by John Stratoun, to John Cuthris, of the half lands of Errolly,	Forfar.
55	—— to William Touris, of the lands of Barntoun, in Crawmand,	Edinburgh.
56	—— Con. by Ifabel Douglas Countefs of Mar, to Alexander Forbes, fon to John Forbes, Knight, of the lands of Edinbanchorie and Craiglogy, blench, for 1d. Sterling, at Kylldromys, fi petatur tantum,	Aberdeen.
57	—— to Walter Stewart Lord of Brechine, of the earldom of Caithnefs, and regalitie thereof, by refignation of the Countefs Palatine, called Eupham Stewart Countefs Palatine of Strathern; blench, for a reid haulk.	

P p

INDEX OF CHARTERS BY KING ROBERT III.

		In vicecom.
58	Carta Con. by Sir John Weymes of Reres, of the foundation of a chappell at Reres, with fix marks money furth of his lands of Logymurtache, fix marks furth of the lands of Purfk, in the barony of Leuchars,	Fyfe.
59	—— to Adam Forrefter, of 40s. of caftlewards furth of the barony of Dalhouffie and Cockpen, with ane confirmation of Clarkingtoun, and remiffion of the caftlewards of Clarkingtoun for ever,	Edinburgh.
60	—— by Archibald Earl of Douglas, fon-in-law to the King, to William Stewart of Teviotdale or of Jedworth, the lands of Abercorne, and caftle thereof, blench,	Edinburgh.
61	—— Con. by John Glen, to Walter Ogilvie, in marriage, the lands of Ballhawell,	Forfar.

Ane Roll of Robert III. marked on the back, ✗ *Weymis, Cambufnathan.*

This is the tenth Roll of Royal Charters now in the General Regifter-Houfe.

It contains fifty-fix charters, granted by King Robert III. in the firft, fecond, and third years of his reign, viz. No. 1, 2, 3, 4, 5, 6, 8, 9, 12, 13, 14, 15, 16, and 17, in the firft year; No. 7, 10, 11, 18, 19, 20, 22, 23, 24, 25, 28, 32, 33, 34, 35, 36, 37, 40, and 43, in the fecond year; and No. 26, 29, 30, 38, 39, 41, 42, 44, 45, 46, 47, 48, 49, 50, 51, 53, 54, and 55, in the third year: No. 21, 27, 31, and 56, have no dates.

No. 10, 30, 54, and 56, have no witneffes. Mathew Bifhop of Glafgow, and Robert Earl of Fife and Menteith, the King's brother, are witneffes to all the charters in the roll, excepting thofe four; James de Douglas *Dominus de Dalkith*, and Alexander de Cokburne of Langtonne, Keeper of the Great Seal, are likewife witneffes in them all, thofe four and No. 21. only excepted; Archibald Earl of Douglas *Dominus Galwidie*, is alfo a witnefs in them all, excepting No. 10, 21, 30, 38, 54, and 56; Thomas de Erfkyne is a witnefs in them all, except No. 10, 21, 27, 30, 54, and 56; Walter Bifhop of St Andrew's is a witnefs in them all, excepting No. 10, 18, 19, 20, 21, 22, 25, 26, 29, 30, 31, 32, 33, 34, 40, 54, and 56; Gilbert Bifhop of Aberdeen, is a witnefs to all the charters laft enumerated where the name of Walter Bifhop of St Andrew's is not inferted; and finally, James de Lyndfay de Crauforde, and Robert de Danyelftoun, are among the witneffes to No. 11.

Eleven of thofe charters are dated at Perth, nine at Dunfermlyne, feven at Edinburgh, feven at Scone, five at Irwyne, four at Lynlithqu, two at the caftle of Rothfay, two at Strivelyne, and one at each of the following places, viz. Fynlauftoun, Gervelane, Dundonnald, Dunde, Bute, and Dunbretane.

1 Carta to Alexander de Keith, fon natural to William Keith Marefchall, of the lands of Grandowne, Auchmoyln, Profly, Crabiltoun, and Balmady.

  N. B. Nearly one half of this charter, No. 1. is now torn away. The part torn off contained the *defignation* or defcription of Alexander de Keth, to whom the charter was granted, as well as of the refigner. The names of the lands ftill remain.

2 —— confirmation of a charter by David de Lindfay of Glenefk, to Walter de Ogilby fheriff of Angus and Dominus de Cuglterhous, of ane annual penfion of 20 l. Sterling furth of the lands of Newdofk, Glenefk, and Blacokmoor, within the fhires of Forfar and of the Mernys, to be enjoyed by the faid Walter and his heirs, till they fhould be, by the faid David or his heirs, feifed heritably in a 20 l. land within one or other of thofe fhires. The original charter is dated at Dunde, 9th March 1390; witneffes, Alexander de Lyndfay, Patrick Gray, John de Lyndfay, Malifeus de S ens, Knights; Alexander de Ogilby, Philip de Lyndefay, William de Ochteriowny, and Patrick de Blare.

INDEX OF CHARTERS BY KING ROBERT III.

3 Carta Con. of a charter by King Robert II. to David de Foullertoun, of 8l. Sterling furth of the customs of Aberdeen. The original charter is dated at Meffen, 15. February, an. reg. Rob. 2di 15to; witnesses, Walter *Sedis Apostolice Cardinali*, John Bishop of Dunkeld Chancellor, John Earl of Carric, and Steward of Scotland, Robert Earl of Fyfe and Meneteth, and James Earl of Dowglas, Archibald de Dowglas " Domino Galwydie," and Thomas de Erskyne.

4 —— to Andrew Mur, uncle to the King, of ane pension of 20l. Sterling furth of the great customs on both sides of Forth, until said Andrew or his heirs should be heritably seised in a 20l. land in some convenient place.

5 —— Con. of a charter by King Robert II. to William Naper, of certain lands in King's Crawmund, by resignation of John Rede, son of Simeon Rede. King Robert II.'s charter is dated at Edinburgh, 8. December, ann. reg. 18vo; witnesses, Walter Bishop of St Andrew's, John Bishop of Dunkeld Chancellor, John Earl of Carric Steward of Scotland, Robert Earl of Fyfe and Meneteth, George Earl of March, Archibald de Douglas " Domino Galwidie," and Thomas de Erskyn.

6 —— to John Earl of Murray, brother to the King, of the escheat of the barony of Deskfurde, in the shire of Banff, which had belonged to the deceased John de Sancto Claro, who had died at the King's horn, (*ad cornu positi et defuncti*); and the escheat also of the lands of Fynletter, in the same shire, which had belonged to Richard de Sancto Claro, then at the King's horn, (*ad cornu existentis*); and granting him 20l. Sterling yearly besides, out of the great custom of the burgh of Inverness.

7 —— Con. of a charter by David de Sancto Claro Earl of Orkney and *Dominus de* Roslyne, to Henry de Sancto Claro his brother, of the lands of Newburgh and Auchdale, in Aberdeenshire, in exchange for all interest he, Henry, had to any lands in Orkney or Schetland, in right of his mother Isabell de Sancto Claro. The original charter is dated 23d April 1391; witnesses, Sir Walter de Bochane Archdean of Schetland, Sir Symon de Papay, Sir Thomas de Kirknefs, Sir John Punkyne, Sir Michael de Westray, and Sir Haquin, Knights; Richard de Sancto Claro, Thomas de Layik, Alexander de Claphame, and Thomas de Leth.

8 —— Con. of a charter by Walter de Murray of Tulliebairdine, to the Abbacy of Culross, of the lands of Auldtoun, of Pethwer, Cuthilduran, and Castleberg. The witnesses to the original charter, (which has no date), are, Walter Bishop of Dunblane, John Abbot of Dunfermlyn, Thomas Byseth Do- " mino de Fif," Robert de Erskyn " Domino ejusdem," and Andrew de Valonis, Knights; Alan de Erskyn, Robert Stewart of Invermeth, Michael de Balfour, and Robert Hakegth.

9 —— Con. of a charter by King Robert II. to St Margaret's chappell within the castle of Edinburgh, of 8l. Sterling yearly furth of the customs of Edinburgh. King Robert II.'s charter is dated 14th February, an. reg. 19; witnesses, Walter Bishop of St Andrew's, and John Bishop of Dunkeld Chancellor; Robert Earl of Fife and Meneteth, Archibald Earl of Douglas " *Domino Galwidie*;" James de Douglas *Domino de* Dalketh, and Thomas de Erskyne.

10 —— to Laurence Landallis macer, of 10l. Sterling a-year for his fee

11 —— to Thomas de Somerville of Cumbusnethen, (son and heir of William de Somerville, Knight), and Joneta Stewart his wife, of the barony of Cambusnethane, in Lanarkshire, on the resignation of Alexander Stewart of Dernley, Knight, and Johanna his wife; but reserving the liferent thereof to said Alexander and Johanna.

12 —— Con. of a grant by Malcolm de Drummond, the King's brother, to John de Swyntoun, Knight, of 200 merks Sterling of ane annual pension, during the life of said John.

13 —— to Andrew de Keth, son and heir of John de Keth of Inverogy, and his wife, of the lands of Strathbrok, in the constabulary of Lithgow, vic. Edinburgh, by resignation of Mary Chene, mother of him, Andrew.

14 —— to St Salvator's altar, in the paroch-kirk of Dundee, of the third part of the lands of the Milntoun of Craigie, and the third part of Westfield, in the barony of Dundee, vic. Forfar, on the resignation of James Skirmechour constable of Dundee.

15 —— to the Abbacy of Dryburgh, of the rents of the priorie of South Berwick.

INDEX OF CHARTERS BY KING ROBERT III.

16 Carta to David Fleming, of 50 l. Sterling furth of the rents of Holyrudehoufe, due for the lands of Cars in Stirlingfhire.

17 —— Con of a charter by Alexander de Murray of Culbyn, to Patrick Forfter burgefs of Dundee, of lands in the town and territory of Inverdubet and barony of Newtoun, Fifefhire, on the refignation of Walter Forfter, the brother of Patrick. The charter confirmed is dated 11th March 1390-1; witneffes, Alexander Abbot of Scone, Sir James Skyrmichour conftable of Dundee, and Alexander his brother, Walter de Lychtoun, Richard de Spalding, and David de Abrekerdor.

18 —— to Adam More of Rowalane, of the lands of Rowalane, in the barony of Cuninghame, and fhire of Ayr, on the refignation of faid Adam.

19 —— to John de Crawfurd of Ardacht, of the lands of Ardacht, within the *dominium* of Rowalane, the barony of Cuninghame, and fhire of Ayr, to be holden blench of the Lairds, (*Dominis*), of Rowalane.

20 —— to Sir Robert de Danyelftoun, of the lands of Stanele, in the barony of Renfrew, and fhire of Lanark.

21 —— Con. of a grant by James de Lindfay, Knight, to the Trinity Friars in Dundee, of ane tenement in Dundee; and the King fuperadds a grant from himfelf, of the kirk of Ketnes. This charter is incomplete.

22 —— to the Abbacy of Coldinghame, confirming three evidents by Edgear King of Scots, ane other by David I. with their haill lands at length, whilks were given to the Abbacy of Durhame of old (*a*).

(*a*) Six charters founding and endowing the priory of Coldingham, on the coaft of Berwickfhire, and annexing the fame to the fee of St Cuthbert or Durham, are the moft ancient Scots deeds now known, with certainty, to exift.

The firft of thofe charters was granted by King Duncan II. a fon of King Malcolm III. denominated *Canmore*. This Duncan filled the throne of Scotland eighteen months only, viz. from about May 1094 till towards the end of the year 1095. He is faid to have been illegitimate, and is regarded as an ufurper.

The other five charters were granted by King Edgar, a legitimate fon of the fame Malcolm. Edgar reigned in Scotland from October 1098 till January 1106-7.

Thofe fix charters, together with a progreffive chain of pofterior deeds by fucceeding Kings and fome Noblemen of Scotland, in relation to the fame priory, are preferved among the archives of the Deanry of Durham, to which the priory was annexed. Thus depofited in England, thofe ancient deeds efcaped the ruin in which the papers, as well as the edifices themfelves, of the religious houfes in Scotland, were involved by the deftructive phrenzy of our ruffian Reformers.

Fac-fimilies of King Duncan's charter, and of two of King Edgar's, are exhibited in the *Diplomata Scotiæ*, by Mr Anderfon.

The above charter of confirmation, No. 22. which gives occafion to the prefent note, contains a *verbatim* tranfcript of three of Edgar's charters, of which thofe engraved in the *Diplomata* are two.

In the beginning of October 1793, the Editor, on his way from London to Edinburgh, halted a few days at Durham, where, in confequence of introductory letters from Lord Frederick Campbell, to the now deceafed Dr Hinchliffe Bifhop of Peterborough, then Dean of Durham, and to fome of the Gentlemen of the Chapter, he was received with the moft obliging politenefs, of which he will ever entertain a grateful recollection, and was indulged with free and unconfined accefs to the archives of the Deanry.

The Editor, by thefe means, had an opportunity of perufing, among a great number of other curious ancient deeds, thofe fix Scots charters, and of infpecting and confidering them with the moft careful deliberation. Not having it then in his power to confult either the charter of confirmation or the *Diplomata*, he could not difcover which of thofe charters were engraved, or which of them were ingroffed in the charter of confirmation. But being pretty certain, that neither the *Diplomata* nor the charter contained all the fix, he, at a venture, tranfcribed, with his own hand, the charter by King Duncan, and three of Edgar's;—and, by fingular good fortune, he happened to copy the two charters by Edgar which are not inferted in the charter of confirmation.

Hence he is enabled to infert, in this place, copies of all thofe fix charters;—and the reader, it is hoped, will not be difpleafed to fee fubjoined a few fhort obfervations, made by the Editor, on the four copied by him, when the originals were before his eyes. The points and the capital letters ufed in the original charters are retained in the printing. But thofe who wifh to be acquainted with the written characters ufed in the originals, muft have recourfe to the *Diplomata*.

INDEX OF CHARTERS BY KING ROBERT III. 153

23 Carta Con. of a grant by James de Douglas of Dalkeith, to James de Douglas his son and heir, of the castle and town of Dalkeith, in the shire of Edinburgh, and of lands to the extent of 500 marks not specified in the confirmation.

The COPIES *made by the* EDITOR.

1. *ECO duncanus filius regis Malcolumb constans hereditarie rex scotie: dedi in elemosina Sancto Cuthberto & suis scruitoribus Tiningebam. Aldeham. Scuchale. Cnolle. hatheruuich. & de Broccesmuthe omne seruitium quod inde habuit fodanus episcopus. & hec dedi in tali quitantia cum saca & soca. qualem unquam meliorem habuit sanctus Cuthbertus. ab illis de quibus tenet suas elemosinas. Et hoc dedi pro me ipso. & pro anima patris mei. & pro fratribus meis. & pro uxore mea. & pro infintibus meis. Et quum uolui quod istud donum stabile esset. sancto cuthberto. feci quod fratres mei concesserunt. Qui autem istud uoluerit destruere. uel ministris sancti cuthberti aliquid inde auferre : maledictionem dei. & sancti Cuthberti. & meam : habcat. amen.*

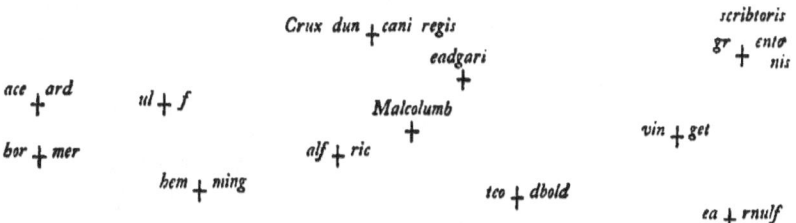

N. B. It has a seal appended at the right-hand corner, on brownish wax, with the impression of a ⟨man?⟩ on horseback; and there has been a circumscription, of which the greater part is now crumbled off; but " ⟨Sign...⟩ " " orum," is still legible.— On the whole, there cannot, in my humble opinion, be the least doubt as to the authenticity of this most curious charter.

2. *Eadgarus rex scottorum. Omnibus in regno suo scottis & Anglis. salutem. Sciatis quod ego concedo & dono domino meo Sancto Cuthberto & monachis eius Paxtun ita sicut ego eam habui cum hominibus. terris & aquis. & monachi eam possideant ita libere & quiete sicut Coldingham ad uoluntatem suam. valete.*

There is a seal appendent at a tag on the left-hand corner, having the figure of a King seated on his throne. There has been a circumscription, of which a few letters only are now legible, the rest being worn away. .... " E .... m bs."

3. *Eadgarus dei gratia rex scottorum. Omnibus suis fidelibus per regnum suum scottis & anglis salutem. Sciatis quod ego dono in elemosinam deo & Sancto Cuthberto et monachis eius fiscwic tam in terris quam in aquis. & cum omnibus sibi adiacentibus. & nominatim illam terram que iacet inter horu.rdene & Cnapadene. pro anima patris & matris mee. & pro salute anime mee & fratrum meorum & sororum liberam & quietam tenendam & habendam & ad uoluntatem monachorum Sancti Cuthberti domini nei disponendam. Valete.*

There is a seal, on brownish wax, at a tag on the left-hand corner, representing a King sitting on his throne, with a sceptre in his right hand, and a sword in his left. The circumscription is much decayed. These letters are still legible, ... " Edga .... otiorum basilei."

N. B. All the three seals above mentioned have been on a whitish wax, now become brownish; and none of them have had any reverse.

154   INDEX OF CHARTERS BY KING ROBERT III.

24 Carta to the Monaſtery of Melros, of the cuſtom of 50 ſacks of wool, granted by David de Bruyſe King of
    Scots, and confirmed by King Robert II.
25 ——— to William Stewart of Jedworth, of 40 merks of annual penſion during his life out of the cuſtoms of
    Edinburgh and Linlithqu.

---

    4. *Eadgarus, rex ſcottorum Omnibus ſuis hominibus ſcottis & anglis, ſalutem. Sciatis quod ego do in ele-
moſinam deo omnipotenti & Sancto Cuthberto domino meo. & eccleſie dunelmenſi & monachis in eadem
eccleſia deo ſeruientibus & in perpetuum ſeruituris pro animabus patris mei & matris mee. & pro ſalute
corporis mei & anime mee & fratrum meorum & ſororum mearum. & pro omnibus anteceſſoribus & ſuc-
ceſſoribus meis. manſionem de Coldingaham. & cum iſta manſione has ſubſcriptas manſiones. ſcilicet Aldcambus Lummeſdene Regnintun. Riſtun. Swinewde farndun Eitun Aliam Eitun Prenegeſt. Crammeſ-
muthe. Has ſuperſcriptas manſiones concedo deo & Sancto predicto & monachis eius cum omnibus terris,
ſiluis, & aquis, & teloneis, & fracturis nauium. & omnibus conſuetudinibus que pertinent ad predictas
manſiones. & quas pater meus in eis habuit quietas & ſolidas ſecundum uoluntatem illorum inperpetuum
libere diſponendas.*

    At the left-hand corner, there is a tag, at which a ſeal has evidently been appended, as ſome remains of the wax
are ſtill adhering to the parchment tag.

    N. B. The above charters were copied from the originals, belonging to the Chapter-Houſe of Durham,
at Durham, Thurſday morning, the 3d of October 1793, by me,

                                                      WILLM ROBERTSON.

The CHARTER of CONFIRMATION, N° 22.

    N. B. The firſt charter recited in the charter of confirmation, is the laſt of the three printed above. Some im-
material diſcrepancies, (in the orthography of the names of the lands eſpecially), between the preceding copy and
the charter of confirmation, will not eſcape the reader's obſervation.

    Robertus, Dei gratia, Rex Scottorum, omnibus probis hominibus totius terre ſue, clericis et laicis, ſalutem ; Sciatis
(nos) inſpexiſſe quandam confirmationem David quondam Regis Scottorum, non raſam, non cancellatam, nec in aliqua
ſui parte vitiatam, tenorem qui ſequitur continentem ; David, Dei gratia, Rex Scottorum, omnibus probis hominibus
totius terre ſue, clericis et laicis, ſalutem, Sciatis nos inſpexiſſe, ac veraciter intellexiſſe, cartam venerabilis patris noſtri
Roberti Regis Scottorum in hec verba ; Robertus, Dei gratia, Rex Scottorum, omnibus probis hominibus totius terre
ſue, clericis et laicis, ſalutem, Sciatis nos inſpexiſſe, ac veraciter intellexiſſe, tres cartas Edgari, et quartam cartam David, regum Scotie, ac quintam cartam Comitis de Dunbarre, non cancellatas, non abolitas, nec in aliqua ſui parte vitia-
tas, in hec verba ; *Edgarus, Rex Scottorum, omnibus ſuis hominibus, Scottis et Anglis, ſalutem, Sciatis quod
ego do in clemoſinam Deo omnipotenti, et Sancto Cuthberto Domino meo, et eccleſie Dunelmenſi, et monachis in
eadem eccleſia Deo ſeruientibus et in perpetuum ſervituris, pro animabus patris (mei et matris) mee, et pro
ſalute corporis mei et anime mee, fratrum meorum et ſororum mearum, et pro omnibus anteceſſoribus et ſuc-
ceſſoribus meis, manſionem de Coldynghame, et cum iſta manſione has ſuperſcriptas manſiones, ſcilicet, Aldecambus, Lummyſden, Rayntoun, Piſtoun, Swynwodde, Farnedoun, Eytoun, aliam Eytoun, Prendregeſt, Cramſ-
muth, has ſuperſcriptas manſiones* (con-) *cedo Deo et Sancto predicto et monachis ejus, cum omnibus terris,
ſilvis, et aquis, et toleneis, et fracturis navium et omnibus conſuetudinibus que pertinent ad predictas manſiones, et quas pater meus in eis habuit, quietas et ſolidas, ſecundum voluntatem illorum imperpetuum libere
diſponendas : Item Edgarus, Dei gratia, Rex Scottorum, omnibus probis per regnum ſuum, Scottis et Anglis, ſalutem ; Sciatis me dediſſe omnipotenti Deo, et ejus Sancto Confeſſori Cuthberto, et monachis ejus,*

INDEX OF CHARTERS BY KING ROBERT III. 155

26 Carta to the Abbacy of Halyroodhoufe, of the lands and barony of Kers, the lands of Fawkirk, Lathame, and Ogillface, in the fhire of Stirling; and the lands of Caldcoats and Freirtoun, in the fhire of Edinburgh, in ane regalitie.

---

pro animabus patris mei et matris mee, et pro falute anime mee, et fratrum et fororum mearum, Coldyngbame, et omnes illas terras quas habent in Laudonio, ita liberas et quietas, cum omnibus confuetudinibus, ficut eas ego ipfe habui in mea propria manu: Et volo et precipio omnibus meis hominibus, ut nullus illorum ammodo eis aliquam moleftiam vel injuriam inde faciat, vel hanc meam donationem infringat; fit in pace, et quiete, et honorifice imperpetuum habeant eas et teneant: Item Edgarus, Rex Scottorum, omnibus per regnum fuum, Scottis et Anglis, falutem; Sciatis me ad dedicationem veniffe ecclefie Beate Marie apud Coldyngbame, que quidem dedicatio ad Dei laudem et ad meuum placitum quieta omnibus et accepta honorabiliter eft adimpleta; et ego eidem ecclefie fuper altare optuli in dotem, et donavi villam totam de Swyntoun, cum divifis fuis, ficut Lyolf habuit, liberam et quietam imperpetuum habendam ab omni calumpnia, et ad voluntatem monachorum Sancti Cuthberti difponendam, pro animabus patris mei et matris mee, et pro falute anime mee, et fratrum et fororum mearum; donavi etiam monachis predictis viginti quatuor animalia ad reftaurandam illam eandem terram, et conftitui eandem pacem in Coldyngbame, eundo, et redeundo, et ibidem morando, que fervatur in Eland et in Nercham; infuper etiam ftatui hominibus in Coldyngbamefchire, ficut ipfi eligerunt, et in manu mea firmaverunt, ut unoquoque anno de unaquaque caruca dimidiam marcam argenti monachis perfolvant; Teftibus Alfa, Thorleng, et Alfric pinccrna, et Algaro prefbitero, et Oferno prefbitero, et Knut, Corls, et Ogga, et Lefing, et Sweni, Ulfkilf, et Ligulf de Bebbonburgh, et Uchtir felaniffunc, etiam Binet, Qhwite, et Tigerne: Item, David, Dei gratia, Rex Scottorum, omnibus per regnum fuum in Scotia et Laudonio conftitutis, Scottis et Anglis, falutem; Sciatis me conceffiffe et dediffe Deo, et Sancto Cuthberto, et monachis ejus de Dunelmo, in elimofina, has terras in Laudonio, fcilicet, Coldyngbame, Aldecambus, Lummefden, Reftoun, Rayntoun, Swynwaade, Prendregeft, Lytoun, et aliam Eytoun, et Cramimouth, Lambirtoun, et aliam Lambirtoun, Paxtoun, Fifhewike, et Swyntoun; necnon has fuperfcriptas terras ego do et concedo Deo, et Sancto predicto, et monachis de Dunelmo, cum facca et focca, et tol et theam, et infangandihef; et cum omnibus terris, et filvis, et aquis, et fracturis navium; et cum omnibus confuetudinibus, liberas et quietas ab omni opere et fervitio, pro falute anime mee, et filii mei Henrici, et pro animabus patris et matris mee, et fratrum et fororum mearum, precipio etiam et defendo ne aliquis de hac mea donatione aliquam injurium vel moleftiam aut calumpniam monachis Sancti Cuthberti amodo faciat, quia volo ut hec mea elimofina libera et quieta ab omni calumpnia in perpetuum remaneat; hec carta firmata eft anno ab incarnatione Domini, Milleftmo centefimo vicefimo fexto, tertio anno regni mei, apud Peblis, tefte et confenfu Henrici filii mei, et illi alii funt inde teftes, Johannes Epifcopus, Robertus de Bruys, Herbertus Cancellarius, Adelmus Archidiaconus, Paganus de Braiola, Hugo de Brito, Berengarius, Ingana, Gofpatricius Vicecomes, Avarus: Item, omnibus fancte matris ecclefie prefentibus et futuris, Patricius Comes, filius Waldevi Comitis, falutem; Sciatis me conceffiffe, et prefenti carta confirmaffe, Deo, et Sancto Cuthberto, et monachis ejus de Dunelmo, in perpetuam elemofinam, villam de Edirhame, et ecclefiam ejufdem ville, cum capella de Erfeldona, et aliis capellis fuis et pertinentiis, et aliam villam que dicitur Nefbit, liberas et quietas imperpetuum poffidendas, cum omnibus que ad eafdem villas in terris, in aquis, et pratis, et pafcuis, et molendinis, pro anima patris et matris mee, et pro anima Malcolmi Regis, et filiorum ejus Regum Edgari Alexandri David, et illi ejus Henrici Comitis,

INDEX OF CHARTERS BY KING ROBERT III.

27 Carta Con. of a charter given by Andrew de Murray of Ballynbruch, to Janet Kirchalche, of the lands of Tuchadam, in Stirlingshire, in liferent. The charter confirmed is dated at Manuell, 14. May 1392; witnesses, John de Hamyltoun *Domino de* Cadyow, Alexander de Hamyltoun *Domino de* Inverwick, Knights; William de Hamyltoun, Andrew de Hamyltoun, Robert Lovele, and Aleyander Lyowne.

---

et Malcolmi Regis, et pro Domino meo Rege Willielmo, et David fratre ejus, et pro meipso et uxore mea, et heredibus meis, et pro animabus omnium parentum meorum; et si aliquis huic elemosine mee contradicere voluerit, Deus sibi et hanc vitam et regnum celorum auferat; hiis testibus, Domino Hugone Cancellario, Magistro Willielmo Malo Vicino, Ricardo de Prebenda, Hugone de Sigillo, Willielmo de Bosco, Magistro Ricardo de Coldinghame, Magistro Angusio, Galfrido de Ancroft, Gilberto Withing, Roberto de Muschamis, Ricardo de Merleia, Stephano Papedy, Adam filio Alden. Patricio filio ejus, Nees de Waletoun, Roberto de Burneville, Roberto filio ejus, Gilberto de Home, Gilberto filio Walteri, Rolando Senescallo, Willielmo filio Edgari, Henrico de Prendregest, Edwardo de Aldecambus, Alano de Swyntoun, Willielmo de Nesbit, et aliis multis; quas quidem cartas, donationes, et concessiones, et confirmationes, in omnibus et singulis punctis, articuli, circumstantiis, et conditionibus suis, forma pariter et effectu, per omnes libertates, commoditates, et consuetudines suas, approbamus, ratificamus, ac presenti carta nostra imperpetuum confirmamus, adeo libere et quiete, plenarie, pure, et honorifice, sicut eisdam cartis suis usi sunt tempore bone memorie Domini Alexandri, Dei gratia Regis Scottorum, predecessoris nostri ultimo defuncti; in cujus rei testimonium, presenti carte nostre sigillum nostrum precepimus apponi, teltibus venerabilibus in Christo patribus Willielmo Sancti Andree, Johanne Glasguensis, Johanne Muraviensis ecclesiarum, Dei gratia, Episcopis; Bernardo Abbate de Abirbrothoc Cancellario nostro, Thoma Ranulphi Comite Moravie Domino vallis Anandie ac Mannie nepote nostro carissimo, Jacobo Domino de Douglas, Gilberto de Haya Constabulario nostro, Roberto de Keth Marescallo nostro, Alexandro de Setoun, Roberto de Lawedre, et Roberto de Meygnerya, Militibus, apud Edynburgh, sexto decimo die Marcii, anno regni nostri vicesimo secundo, (*End of King Robert I.'s charter*); quam quidem cartam, donationes, concessiones, et confirmationes, in omnibus et singulis punctis, articulis, circumstantiis, et conditionibus suis, forma pariter et effectu, per omnes libertates, commoditates, et consuetudines suas, approbamus, ratificamus, et presenti carta nostra imperpetuum confirmamus; in cujus rei testimonium, presenti carte nostre sigillum nostrum precepimus apponi, hiis testibus, Domino Willielmo Comite de Douglas consanguineo nostro, Roberto de Erskine Milite confederato nostro, Magistro Waltero de Warthelaw Archidiacono Laudonie Secretario nostro, Magistro Gilberto Armestrang preposito Sancti Andree, Domino Johanne Heriee Milite, Jacobo de Douglas, et multis aliis; dat. apud Edynburgh, primo die Januarii, anno regni nostri tricesimo quarto, (*End of King David II.'s charter*); quam quidem cartam confirmationis, donationesq; et concessiones in eadem contentas, in omnibus punctis suis, et articulis, conditionibus, et modis ac circumstantiis suis quibuscunq; forma pariter et effectu, per omnes libertates, commoditates, et consuetudines suas, in omnibus et per omnia, approbamus, ratificamus, et presenti carta nostra, pro nobis et heredibus nostris, ut premissum est, imperpetuum confirmamus, salvo servitio nostro; in cujus rei testimonium, presenti carte nostre confirmationis nostrum precepimus apponi sigillum; testibus venerabilibus in Christo patribus Matheo et Gilberto Glasguensis et Abirdonensis ecclesiarum episcopis, Roberto de Fif et de Meneteth fratre nostro carissimo, Archebaldo de Douglas Domino Galwidie consanguineo nostro, Comitibus; Jacobo de Douglas Domino de Dalketh, Thoma de Erskine, consanguineis nostris dilectis, Militibus; et Alexandro de Cokburne de Langtoune Custode Magni Sigilli nostri; apud Lynlithqu, vicesimo sexto die Januarii, anno regni nostri secundo.

Of late the authenticity of the charter by King Duncan has been called in question, and it has been represented as a forgery.

But as every forgery must have an object, it may be asked, For what purpose was the charter in question fabricated?

The granter, real or pretended, has always been regarded as illegitimate, and as an *usurper*; and his reign was but of eighteen months duration. Now, although usurpers give away lands and offices, and execute all other acts of administration just as if they were lawful Sovereigns, yet as their deeds are, by succeeding Kings, ever deemed illegal and ineffectual, to forge charters or grants by such usurpers appears to be highly preposterous.

But if so absurd a fabrication could be at all attempted, it surely could be attempted only during the actual reign of the usurper, not after his dethronement or death.

INDEX OF CHARTERS BY KING ROBERT III.

28 Carta to Allan de Erefkine, and his fpoufe, of ane annual rent of ten marks ten fhillings eight pence Sterling furth of the lands of Crambeth, in Fifefhire, on his own refignation.

29 —— to William Dubrell, of all the lands and tenements in the burgh of Inverkethine, which belonged to Elene Tollare ; on Elene's refignation.

30 —— to the Abbacy of Holyrude houfe, of the barony of Broughtoun, in the fhire of Edinburgh, in ane regalitie.

31 —— Con. of infeftments granted by Thomas Mautalent of Halfyntoun, to William Mautalent his fon, and Elizabeth Watfon, William's fpoufe, of the lands of Scheylynlaw, Traquair, and Inverlethane. In the roll the date of this charter is omitted.

32 —— to William de Lindfay, of 40 marks Sterling out of the cuftoms of Edinburgh and Hadingtoun, redeemable by paying him 400 marks Sterling, or by infefting him heritably in 40 marks of land any where in the Lowlands.

33 —— to William Stewart of Jedworth, of ane pairt of the toun and lands of Mintow, with the advocation of the kirk thereof, by refignation of George Abernethie.

34 —— to William de Cochran, of 40 s. Sterling furth of the burrow-maills of Ruglen.

35 —— Con. of a charter of wadfet, given by William de Angus Abbot of Lindores, to David de Abirkerdor, of feven marks furth of various tenements in the town of Dunde.

36 —— to William de Camera burgefs of Aberdeen, of ane annualrent of 40 s. Sterling furth of the barony of Fyndoun, in the fhire of Kyncardyn, on the refignation of John Crabb.

37 —— Con. of a charter by Norman Lefly of Balnabreich, to John Ramfay of Colluthye, of the lands of Balmadyfide and Pettachop, blench, to be holden of Leflie. This charter proceeds on a verdict pronounced at Glenduky, 5th July 1390, by the following jury, viz. Andrew de Ramefay de Redy, John de Kynnere, William de Berclay, John de Camera, Alan de Lochmalony, Walter de Ramefay, Malifeus de Kynynmond, John de Kyndeloch, William Stirk, William de Ferny, John de Ramefay, William de Lochmalony, Robert Lyel, Andrew de Camera, and John de Arous.

38 —— to Hew Wallayas, of ane annual rent of 40 s. out of a tenement in Edinburgh.

The charter, therefore, by King Duncan, if really forged, muft be prefumed to have been forged during Duncan's ufurpation, that is, between 30th April 1094, and 1ft November 1095.

If fo, it feems to follow, 1ft, That Duncan was in the practice of giving charters ; 2d, That the fabricator would not fail to imitate fome true and genuine charter.

This confideration, it is humbly thought, tends powerfully to obviate the objections to the authenticity of this charter, derived from its form and tenor.

The words " *conftans hereditarie Rex Scotie,*" are by the objectors judged improper, and are therefore ftated as indications of a forgery.

One cannot eafily affent to this conclufion. It is far from being improbable, that Duncan, fenfible of labouring under a defect in point of birth, would employ an expreffion calculated to difavow the imputation of illegitimacy, and to imprefs pofterity with a different belief. But to a forger, unlefs, as hinted above, he was at the moment following a genuine charter as a model, fuch an expreffion could hardly have occurred.

The objection to the feal, as having an impreffion on one fide only, appears, with fubmiffion, to be equally inconclufive. If Duncan's feal has no reverfe, neither has Edgar's ; and it is generally admitted, that Edgar's brother and fucceffor, King Alexander I. was the firft King of Scotland whofe feals had an impreffion on both fides.

Duncan, it is true, appears on his feal in the figure of an armed warrior, whereas Edgar is reprefented on his, fitting on a throne, and crowned. But what inference unfavourable to the authenticity of the deed can reafonably refult from this ? At that early period, Kings, it is likely, were in this matter influenced more by fancy than by precedent.

More might be advanced on this fubject ; but for the prefent further enlargement feems neither neceffary nor proper.

The charter, on the whole, may perhaps warrant this conclufion, That whether forged or genuine, it was framed during the fhort reign of King Duncan II. and confequently, that that Prince was in the practice of giving charters.

INDEX OF CHARTERS BY KING ROBERT III.

39 Carta to William de Danyelftoun, of 20 marks Sterling out of the great cuftom of Dunbar, to continue until the King fhould grant to him or his heirs ten marks of land in fome competent place.

40 —— to Marion de Wardlaw, and Andrew de Wardlaw her fon, of the lands of Riccardiftoun and Warynftoun, with the pertinents, in the barony of Currie, and fhire of Edinburgh.

41 —— Con. of a charter by King Robert II. to Roger de Crawfurd, of a milne, and piece of land adjacent thereto, refigned by Allan Stewart, fon of Allan Stewart, Knight, " confanguinei noftri" (i. e. of King Robert II.) " dilecti." The charter confirmed was dated at Are, 4th Auguft, an. reg. Rob. 2di 19no.

42 —— Con. of a charter of King Robert II. to Roger de Crawfurd, of the lands of Schyvilt, in Ayrfhire, by refignation of Reginald, the fon of Reginald Awbyne.

43 —— to Walter Stewart *Domino de* Brechin, of the fuperiority of Menmore, in Forfarfhire, with an annualrent of 6s. 8d. Sterling furth of the faid lands.

44 —— to John de Erefkine, of the barony of Dun, in Forfarfhire, on the refignation of Thomas de Erfkyne his father.

45 —— to Duncan Earl of Lennox, and the heirs-male of his body, whilks failing, to Murdo Stewart " con-" fanguinco noftro," and Ifabel his wife, daughter to the faid Earl, and the heirs of their bodies, of the earldom of Lennox, on the faid Earl's refignation.

46 —— to the Monaftry of Arbroth, of the cuftom of half a merk for every fack of wool growing within the regality thereof, &c.

47 —— to John de Dalzell, and to his fons, Walter, Adam, and Robert, and the heirs-male of their bodies refpectively and fucceffively, of St Leonard's hofpital at Lanerk, with the lands pertaining thereto.

48 —— to John de Buchannane, and Jonet de Lany, daughter and heir of John de Lany, of the lands of Petquhonardy, in Perthfhire, on the refignation of faid Jonet de Lany.

49 —— to Duncan Cambell, fon and heir of Colin Cambell, of the lands of Menftry, in the fhire of Clackmannan, on the refignation of faid Colin.

50 —— to Robert de Danyelftoun, of the lands of Danyelftoun and Fynlawyftoun, in the barony of Renfrew, and fhire of Lanark, on his own refignation.

51 —— to Murdo Stewart, of 100 mark Sterling furth of the great cuftom of the burgh of Aberdeen, during all the days of his life.

52 —— to Robert Earl of Fyfe and Menteth, of 200 merks Sterling furth of the great cuftoms of the burghs of Lithgow and Coupar, during all the days of his life.

53 —— Con. to John de Weemes, Knight, of the lands of Rires, and all others whilks he holds of the Earl of Fife, in the barony of Rires; the lands of Myrearny, Newtoun of Markinche, Nether Cameroune, Welter Tarvate, and Tulybrek; and alfo the lands of Kyncaldrum, whilks Alexander de Abernethy conveyed to John de Wemys, Knight, grandfather of faid John; and likewife the lands of Rate, Glennyftoun, and Polgulde, which Alan de Erfkyne, Robert de Levyngiftoun, and John de Bofevil, Knights, conveyed to faid John de Wemys.

54 —— to the faid Sir John de Wemys, empowering him to build a caftle with turrets on his lands of Reres.

55 —— to James de Valence, of the lands of Crambethe, by refignation of Allan de Erefkine and Alexander de Crambeth.

56 —— to the Queen of Scotland, of an annual allowance of 2500 marks Sterling during her life, out of the great cuftom of certain burghs, for fupport of her ornaments and flate. This grant is founded on an act of a parliament holden at Scone, in March, the firft year of King Robert II.'s reign.—The charter is incomplete.

ROBERT DUKE OF ALBANY HIS REGISTER.

Ane Roll of Robert Duke of Albany, marked Scott.

In vicecom.

1 Carta granted by the Lord of Baluerie, to his brother William Scott, of his part of the lands of Sireyis, blench of him, and ward of the King,   Fyfe.
2 —— Con. to Alexander Frazer, and Elizabeth Keith his spouse, of the lands of Kinnell, ward,   Forfar.
3 —— to Thomas Glaidstouns, of the lands of Withnyhope, ward,   Selkirk.

Another Roll, marked Abrecorne.

1 Carta to John Sibbald of Balgonie, of his lands of Ward, Rossyve, and Crambeth, ward.
2 —— to Malcolme Fleming of Biggar, of the lands of Torwood, by resignation of William Lindsay of Byres, ward,   Hadington.
3 —— Con. impignorationis terrarum de Oliver castell pro Roberto Dickson, per Malcolmum Fleming de Biggar, redeemable upon 100 l.   Peebles.
4 —— to Malcolm Fleming of Biggar, of the barony of Biggar, vic. Lanerk, with the annuals furth of the kirk of Stirling pertaining to the Abbacie of Halyroodhouse, waird,   Lanerk. Stirling.
5 —— Con. given by William Lindsay of Crambeth, to John Spens burgess of Perth, of the lands of Fruchie, in the barony of Crambeth,   Fyfe.
6 —— to David Barclay, son to .... Barclay of Culch, of the baronies of Craimbeth and Cleish, by resignation of Dornagild Stirling and John Spittell of Kynmonth, ward,   Fyfe.
7 —— to John Lindsay of the Byres, of the baronie of Byres, the Dreme, constabulary of Hadingtoun, vic. Ed^r; the barony of Chalmernewtoun, vic. Roxburgh; barony of Airth, vic. Stirling; the barony of Abercorne, with the dean thereto annexed, constabulary of Lithgow, vic. de   Edinburgh. Roxburgh. Lithgow.
8 —— to Robert Cunningham, of the lands of Killmawers, Lumbrachtoun, vic. Kilbryd; Skellmorle, Polquharne, vic. Air; Reidhall, vic. Ed^r; Hassindean, vic. Roxburgh; Ranfarncle, in the barony of Renfrew, waird,   Air. Edinburgh. Roxburgh.
9 —— to Eupham Leslie Countess of Ross, of the earldom of Ross, of the lands of Stroglashe, of the town of Nairne, and castle thereof, vic. Innerness; the lands of Kincardine, vic. ejusdem; the right of the barony of Fithkill,

INDEX OF CHARTERS BY ROBERT DUKE OF ALBANY.

vic. Fyfe; with ane taillie to John Stewart Earl of Buchane; whilks failing, to Robert Stewart his brother; quilks failing, to the King, waird; wit. Jo. Steuart, - - - - - - - - fon naturalis.

10 Carta to John Stewart Earl of Buchan, of the baronie of Kinnedwart, by refignation of Eupham Lefly Countefs of Rofs, waird,   Aberdeen.

11 —— to William Hay of Erroll Conftable of Scotland, of the barony of Collie, by refignation of Frazer of Philorth,   Kincardin.

Robertus Dux Strathbogie.

Ane Roll, marked on the back, Strathbogie.

This is the eleventh Roll of Charters now in the General Regifter-Houfe.—It contains 48 charters granted by Robert Duke of Albany, as Regent of Scotland, in the 1ft, 2d, 3d, and 4th years of his Regency. Of thofe charters, two-and-twenty are dated at Perth, feven at Fawkland, four at Strivelyne, two at Dunde, two at Doune in Menteth, two at Edynburgh, and one at each of the following places, viz. the Monaftry of Paifley, Dunblane, the Monaftry of Culros, Inchgale, the caftle of Rothefay, *Portus Regine*, (Queensferry), Setoun, Are, and Hadyngtoun.

In two of thofe charters, viz. No. 16. and 31. no witneffes are inferted. The remaining 46 charters contain an unufual variety of witneffes. Gilbert Bifhop of Abirdene the chancellor, is a witnefs in all the 46: Andrew de Hawyk (fometimes defigned Canon of Dunkel, fometimes Rector of Lyftoun) Secretary to the Regent, is witnefs in them all, excepting No. 1, 2, 10, 11, 12, 18, 32, 37, and 45: John Stewart, a fon of the Regent's, is a witnefs in 1, 2, and 15, under the defignation *of Coul*; in No. 32. under that of Earl of Buchane; and under the title " *Dominus de Buchane,*" in 4, 5, 6, 7, 8, 9, 13, 17, 22, 24, 25, 26, 27, 28, 29, 34, 37, 38, 39, 42, 43, 45, 46, 47, and 48: Robert Stewart of Fif, fon and heir of Murdac, the Regent's eldeft fon and heir, fometimes defigned of Kinclevyne, is witn fs in 19, 20, 21, 22, 24, 25, 26, 27, 28, 29, 32, 34, 38, 47, and 48: Walter Stewart Earl of Athole and Catnes, a brother of the Regent's, is a witnefs to 10, 11, 12, 32, and 35: Alexander Stewart Earl of Mar and Garvvach, a nephew of the Regent's, is a witnefs to 3, 4, 5, 6, 7, 8, 9, 18, 22, and 25: Alexander Stewart, a Canon of Glafgow, and John Stewart of Dundonald, brothers of the Regent's, are witneffs in 27: John Stewart, *frater naturalis* of the Regent, and fheriff of Bute, is a witnefs to 1, and 36: Robert and Alexander Stewarts of Dernle are witneffes to faid No. 1: John Stewart of Lorne, a *confanguineus* of the Regent's, is a witnefs to 10, 11, 12, 14, 17, 19, 20, 23, 25, 26, 29, 30, 32, 34, 38, 39, 40, 45, and 47: Walter Stewart of Rayliiloun, another *confanguineus* of the Regent's, is a witnefs to 26, 28, 37, and 47: John Stewart of Invermeth is a witnefs to 37: Henry Bifhop of St Andrew's is a witnefs to 32: William Bifhop of Glafgow, to 45: Robert Bifhop of Dunkeld, to 32, and 35: Finlay Bifhop of Dunblane, to 14, and 35: Walter Bifhop of Brechin, to 35, and 45: And John Bifhop of Murray, to 32: David de Lyndefay Earl of Crawfurde, to 3: Alexander de Lyndefay, fon and heir to faid Earl, to 4, 5, 6, 7, and 42: William de Lyndefay of Roffy, and Walter de Lyndefay, brothers to faid David Earl of Crawfurde, to 3, 4, 5, 6, 7, and 9: And faid Walter de Lindefay, to 18: Thomas Earl of Murray, nephew to the Regent, to 10, and 11: Patrick de Grahame Earl of Stratherne, to 10, 11, 12, 35, 37, and 47: Duncan Earl of Lennox, to 36: Henry de Sancto Claro Earl of Orkney, to 32: William de Grahame, defigned fometimes of Kyncardyn, fometimes *Dominus de Grahame*, to 10, 11, 12, 17, 19, 20, 25, 26, 29, 30, 32, 34, 38, 39, and 40: John de Achynlek, to 36: David de Perclay, to 3, 14, 15, 21, 26, 27, 28, 30, 33, 34, 38, 40, 42, 43, 44, 46, 47, and 48: John de Berclay, to 15: Donald de Bute Dean of Dunblane, to 21, 22, 23, 29, and 40: Henry de Beckirtoun, to 33: Thomas de Bryfbane, to 37: John de Bufby, a Canon of Murray, to 44: William

INDEX OF CHARTERS BY ROBERT DUKE OF ALBANY.   161

te Bortlowic de Katkone, to 47: Thomas de Craufurde de Auchnamys, to 1: Archibald de Conynghame, to 3, 17, 26, 27, 33, 38, 40: Richard de Comyne, to 13, 15, 19, 20, 34, 41, 43: John Abbot of Culros to 18: William de Camera of Abirdene, rector of the kirk of Erole, to 21, and 23: William de Conynghame, to 30: Richard de Cornwell Archdean of Dunkeld, to 30: Humphry de Conynghame, to 36, and 46: Alan Cambell, to 36: Thomas Charterys, to 37: Walter de Curry, to 46: John de Dovery, to 13, and 15: Malifius de Dovery, to 15: John de Drommond of Concrag, to 14: James de Dalrympill, to 27: James de Douglas, *locumtenens* of the Regent, to 28: Symon de Dalgles, to 39: Thomas de Dalmehoy, to 42: Robert de Erskyne, to 18: William de Ercht, to 17, 21, 22: Alexander de Forbes, to 3: John Forster of Corstorfyne, to 18, 42, and 45: Malcolm Flemyng of Bygare, to 24, and 29: Robert de Ferny, to 28, and 48: Thomas de Grynlaw, to 44: Mathew de Geddes, rector of the kirk *de Foresta*, to 47: John de Howistoun, to 1: William de Haya de Nachtane, to 15: John de Haya, to 21: William de Hamyltoun, to 25: Patrick de Heryng to 47: Alexander de Home, to 47: George de Lefly of Fythkil, a *consanguineus* of the Regent's, to 10, 11, 13, 19, 20, 23, 25, 26, 28, 30, 32, 38, 39, and 40: Walter de Lefly, to 39: William Lang, a Canon of Abirdene, to 21: Alexander de Levyngstoun of Calenter, to 24, and 29: John de Lethe, to 33: Murdak de Leky, to 39: John Mure, to 27: Robert de Maxwell, to 46: Michael de Narne, to 13, 17, 19, 20, 34, and 43: Alexander de Newtoun, to 39: Alexander de Ogilvile (or Ogilby, as it is written in No. 8, 9, and 42.) sheriff of Forfore or Angous, to 4, 5, 6, 7, 8. and 9: Walter de Ogilby, to 9, and 42: John de Roos, to 2: Robert de Ros, to 37: William de Ruthven, to 29: John Symple of Eliotstoun, and Robert Symple, to 1, and 2: James de Schaw, to 23: James de Sandylandis of Caldore, a nephew of the Regent's, to 24, and 46: Alexander de Setoun, to 25, and 39: John de Setoun, to 44: John de Spens, to 37: Alan Scot, a Canon of Cambuskyneth, to 41: John Schirmezour, to 46: John Walays of Elryfle, to 1: John Wrycht constable of Falkland, to 19, and 20: John de Wemys, to 25, 35, and 40: and William Ydill, to 23.

1 Carta to William Cunninghame of Reidhall, of ane annual of ten marks furth of the barony of Uchiltrie, by refignation of Alexander Stewart, fon and heir to John Stewart of Craigy.

2 ——— Con. of a charter by Thomas Mautalent of Halfyngtoun, William Mautalent his fon and heir, and Margaret, wife of faid Thomas, to Thomas de Melvill burgefs of Edinburgh, of the lands of Halfyngtoun, within the earldom of March. The telling claufe in the original charter is in thefe words, viz.
" In cujus rei teftimonium, figilla noftra prefenti fcripto funt appenfa, et ad majorem hujus rei evi-
" dentiam figillum magnifici et potentis viri et Domini noftri Jacobi de Douglas, fratris Domini Ar-
" chebaldi de Douglas Comitis ejufdem, huic fimiliter apponi procuravimus; prefentibus David
" de Crauforde Priore Monafterii Sanctae Crucis de Edynburgh, et Johanne dicto Wan Canonico re-
" gulari ejufdem, et Alexandro de Cokburn filio quondam Willielmi de Cokburn de Hadyngtoun."

3 ——— Con. of a grant by Archebald Earl of Douglas, to Walter de Ogilvy, of the lands of Curdabow, Purgevy, Galoucht, and Glenquharady, in the barony of Lintrethin, vic. Forfar.

4 ——— Con. of a charter by David de Lyndefay Earl of Craufurde, with confent of Alexander de Lyndefay his fon and heir, to the chaplandrie of our Lady in the paroch-kirk of Dundee, of 12 marks annually furth of the lands of Dunfynd and Downycane, in the barony of Downy, and fhire of Forfar. The charter confirmed is dated at Dunde, 10th December 1406; witneffes, William and Walter de Lyndefay, brothers of the faid Earl, Alexander de Lyndefay, his eldeft fon and heir, John Montymer, Adam Clerk, and William Man the Earl's Secretary.

5 ——— Con. of a charter by the fame Earl, with confent of his faid fon, to a chaplain in the paroch-kirk of Dundee, of 12 marks annually furth of the lands of Kirktoun and Haltoun, of the barony of Inverarite.

6 ——— Con. of another charter by the fame Earl and his fon, to a chaplain in the paroch-kirk of Dundee, of 12 marks a-year furth of the lands of Abberbothrie, in the fhire of Perth.

7 ——— Con. of a fourth charter by the faid Earl and his fon, to a chaplain in the parifh-kirk of Dundee, of 12 marks annually furth of the lands of Melgynche, Bagraw, and the miln thereof, in Perthfhire. Thefe laft three charters have the fame date and the fame witneffes with No. 4.

S f

8 Carta Con. of a charter by the said Earl and his eldest son, to David de Lyndesay, a younger son of the said Earl of Crawfurd, of the lands of Newdoske, in Kincardineshire, to said David, and the heirs-male of his body; whom failing, to Gerrard de Lyndesay, another son of the said Earl, and the heirs-male of his body; whom likewise failing, to return to the said Earl, and his heirs whomsoever. The Earl's charter is dated at Dunde, 12th February 1406-7; witnesses, William de Grahame of Kyncardyne, William and Walter de Lyndesay of Rossy, Patrick Gray of Broxmouth, William de Haya of Nachtane, Knights; Alexander de Ogilvile sheriff of Angous, Walter de Ogilvile, John Mortymer, and William Man the Earl's Secretary.

9 —— Con. of another charter by said David Earl of Craufurde, to David de Lyndesay his son, of ane annual pension of 40 merks due the Earl out of the great custom of the burgh of Monros. The destination is the same with that in the last charter, No. 8. The Earl's charter is dated 12th February 1406-7; witnesses, William de Grahame, William and Walter de Lyndesay, Knights; Alexander de Ogilvile sheriff of Angus, Walter de Ogilvile, John Mortymer, Adam Clerk, and William Man the Earl's Secretary.

10 —— Con. of a charter dated at Abirdene, 20th September 1406, (which contains no witnesses), by William de Keth, Knight, Marishal of Scotland, and Margaret his wife, to Robert de Keth, Knight, *Domino de* Troupe, their son, of the office of sheriff of Kyncardynshire.

11 —— Con. of a charter, without witnesses, dated like the last charter, No. 10. by the same William de Keth, to the foresaid Robert de Keth, his son and heir, of the barony of Keth, in the constabulary of Hadyngtoun, and shire of Edinburgh, with the office of Marishal; the lands and church of Colbanystoun, in the shire of Lanark; the barony of Aldene, and forrest of Kyntor and Carnbrowys, "ad "taxationem quatuor davatarum de Strabolgy," in the shire of Abirdene; with the superiority of one *davata* of the land of Drumhane, and of another *davata* of the land of Auchnahamper, in Banffshire; to be holden of the King *in capite*, in terms of a charter granted by King Robert I. by authority of parliament, to Robert de Keth, Marishal of Scotland, uncle of said William de Keth.

12 —— Con. of a charter by John Forster of Corstorfyne and Nether Libertoun, to his brother Thomas Forster, of the lands of Drylaw, in the shire of Edinburgh. The charter confirmed is dated at Corstorfyne, 20th August 1406; witnesses, Gilbert Bishop of Aberdeen Chancellor of Scotland, Mr William de Lawedr Archdean of Lothian; George de Prestoun, William de Lyddale, Knights; William Currour and Duncan Rollo, burgesses of Edinburgh.

13 —— Con. of a charter granted by the Regent himself, in his private character, to John de Ramesay, son of William de Ramesay of Culuthy, of the Regent's castle and lands in the barony of Luchrys, Fifeshire, in excambion for the lands of Balnefery, Mundole, Balnegetht, and Tarress, in Invernefs-shire. Several Ramsays of the families of Culuthy and Kernock are inserted in the destination. The charter confirmed was dated at *Manerium nostrum de Fawkland*, 14th November 1398; witnesses, Walter Bishop of St Andrews, and Gilbert Bishop of Aberdeen Chancellor, David Stewart Duke of Rothesay Earl of Carrick and of *Athoyle*, Archebald Earl of Douglas *Domino* Galwydie, Murdac Stewart, son and heir of the Regent, justiciary of Scotland north of Forth, Richard Comyne, James de Walence, and John de Duvery.

14 —— to Alexander de Ramorgny, of the lands of Pitglassy, in Fifeshire, on his own resignation.

15 —— founding a chaplainry in the kirk of Inverkethine, and endowing the same with the third of the lands of Rossythe, in Fifeshire.

16 —— of the office of Chamberlainrie of all Scotland to John *Domino de* Buchane, son to Robert Duke of Albany, for all the days of his life.

17 —— Con. of a charter by Johanna de Keth *Domina de* Gallystoun, to her son Andrew de Hamyltoun, of her lands of Gallystoun, in the barony of Kyle, and shire of Are, viz. Tholoch, Uvermomunde, Langfyde, Bryntwod, Serne, Kirktoun, and Dundivane. The original charter is dated at Dalserff, the 11th December 1406; witnesses, William de Conynghame, then sheriff of Are, William Baille *Domino de* Barnburne, William de Dalyell *Domino ejusdem*, and William de Hamyltoun, a son of said Jo-

INDEX OF CHARTERS BY ROBERT DUKE OF ALBANY. 163

hanna, Knights; Hugh Cambell *Domino de* Lowdoun, John Stewart, a son of said Johanna, *Domino de* Crukystoun, James de Conyngham, and John Cambell of Gallystoun.

18 Carta to Walter de Lightoun, of ane annual duty of two marks furth of the lands of Campsy, with the superiority of the same lands, lying in the barony of Lintrethine, and shire of Forfar, on the resignation of Thomas de Strathechyne.

19 —— Con. of a charter by William de Ketht Marischall of Scotland, and Margaret Fraser his wife, to John Stewart *Domino de* Buchane, and the heirs-male of his body; whom failing, to his brothers-german, Andrew and Robert Stewarts, and the heirs-male of their bodies respectively; whom failing, to Robert de Ketht, son of said William, and the heirs-male of his body, &c. of the lands of Tulchfraser and Drippis, in Stirlingshire, with the office of Sheriff of that shire. The original charter is dated at Abirdene, 2d May 1407, but has no witnesses.

20 —— Con. of a charter dated at Abirdene, 2d May 1407, granted by the said William de Keth and his spouse, to John *Domino de* Buchane, Great Chamberlain, and the other substitutes contained in last charter, (No. 19.), of the barony of Obeyn, in Aberdeenshire. The charter confirmed has no witnesses.

21 —— to David de Gardyne, of the lands of Kininmonth, Buchrommys, and the half of the lands of Clune, in Banffshire, on the resignation of William de Dalyell.

22 —— of 10 marks furth of the lands of Craigorthe, in Stirlingshire, to an chaplan in St Michael's chappell, in the castle of Stirling.

23 —— to David Paneter of Monrofs, of the lands of Cragoch and Ardoch, in the barony of Logy, in Forfarshire, by resignation of David de Logy of Cragoch, waird.

24 —— Con. of a grant by William de Ruthven of Balernach, to Walter de Haliburtoun of Dryltoun, of 40 l. of annualrent furth of the barony of Ballernach, in the shire of Edynburgh.

25 —— Con. of a wadset by William de Setoun, with consent of John de Setoun his father, to the said Walter de Haliburtoun, of ane annual of 50 marks furth of the barony and coalieries of Tranent.

26 —— Con. of a grant by John de Drommond of Cargill, Knight, to John Forster of Corstorfyne, of the lands of Uchtertyre, in the barony of Kyncardyne, in Stirlingshire.

27 —— Con. of a charter by Walter de Halyburtoun de Dryltoun, to Adam de Hoppringile, son of William de Hoppringile, of the lands of Faunys, in the earldom of March; witnesses to the original charter, (which has no date), John Setoun, William de Haya, Walter de Bickirtoun; Alexander, George, Fergus, and John de Haliburtoun; and William de Spens.

28 —— Con. of a sale by Thomas Mautalent of Halsyngtoun, to William Watson of Cranystoun, of the lands of Trakware and Sheringlaw, vic. Peebles.

29 —— Con. of a wadset of twelve marks Scots out of the barony and coallieries of Difart, in Fifeshire, granted by Henry de Sancto Claro Earl of Orkney, to John Ferster of Corstorfyne, in consideration of 300 " nobilibus boni et sufficientis auri monete Anglicane," advanced by said John to him the Earl of Orkney.

30 —— Con. of a charter by John de Dolas of Estir Leky, to Murdoch de Leky, of the lands of Estir Leky, in the shire of Stirling. The original charter is dated at Leky, 12th February 1406-7; witnesses, Duncan Earl of Levenax; John Gourlay and Alexander Post, burgesses of Stirling; Patrick Lyndesay, and John Naper *Domino de* Kilmehew. The charter of confirmation is dated in the first year of the regency.

31 —— Con. of a grant by the said John de Dolas, to the said Murdoch de Leky, of the foresaid lands of Estir Leky.—*This charter is omitted in the Old Index, and is dated in the second year of the regency.*

32 —— to Alexander de Setoun, son to Sir William de Setoun, and Elizabeth de Gordoun, daughter and heir to umquill Adam de Gordoun, Knight, and the heirs to be begotten between them; whom failing, to the heirs whomsoever of said Elizabeth, of the lands and baronies of Huntly and Gordoun, vic. Berwick; also the lands of Fogow, of Fawnys, and of Mellowristanes, and all other lands which belonged to said Adam within the said sherifsdom; the lands of Strabolgie and Beldygordoun, and all

INDEX OF CHARTERS BY ROBERT DUKE OF ALBANY.

other lands whilk belonged to the said Adam, within the sheriffdom of Aberdeen; on the resignation of said Elizabeth; apud Perth, 20th July 1408, in the 3d year of his government.

33 Carta to David Wattystoun, son and heir of John Wattystoun, of the half of the lands of Wattystoun, in the shire of Forfare, with an annual duty of eight marks surth of the thanedom of Thanethays; on his own resignation.

34 —— Con. of a grant by John de Sancto Michaeli, to Patrick de Sanquhare, of the lands of Murecrofte, lyand in the barony of Polgowny, and shire of Aberdeen, to be holden of the Baron of Polgowny.

35 —— to Alexander de Gairdyne, of the lands of Borowfield, in the shire of Forfare, by resignation of William *Dominus de* Grame.

36 —— to John Cambell of Lowdounhill, of the lands of Chalachbrek, extending to a ten-mark land, in the earldom of Carrick, and shire of Are, on the resignation of Thomas M'Dowell.

37 —— to Walter Stewart Earle of Athole and Caithness, the Regent's brother, of the barony of Cortoquhy, with the advocation of the kirk thereof, in the shire of Forfare, by resignation of Archibald Earl of Douglas.

38 —— Con. of a grant by Janet de Ketht *Domina de* Gallystoun, during the time of her widowity, to William de Hamyltoun, Knight, her son, of the lands of Bathcat, in constab. Linlithgow, vic. Edinburgh.

39 —— to John de Hawdene, of the lands of Hawdene and Zethame, in vic. Roxburgh; the lands of Brochtoun, vic. Peebles; on the resignation of William de Hawdene his father.

40 —— Con. of a grant by Margaret de Cragy, with consent of Herbert de Maxwell her husband, and of Alexander Stewart her son and heir, to William Currour Forster burgess of Edinburgh, of the lands of Ardlory, in Kinross-shire.

41 —— to Christian and Janet, daughters to William, son of Robert burgess of Dumfermling, of the fourth part of the lands of Milnflatt, and third part of Westoun, in the constabulary of Hadyngtoun, and shire of Edinburgh, on the resignation of John de Echlyne vicar of Kinneff.

42 —— to Alexander de Lauder, and Elizabeth Forster his spouse, daughter to Jo. Forster of Corstorphyne, of the lands of Plat, Westhall, and North Raw, in the barony of Rathow, and shire of Edinburgh, on the resignation of said Alexander, holden of the Prince.

43 —— Con. of a sale by Patrick Gray, Knight, to Robert de Seres burgess of Dunde, of a part of the commoun meadow at the north of the burgh of Dunde.

44 —— to David de Ferne burgess of Perth, of the lands of Mukelere, in the barony of Cluny, and shire of Perth, by resignation of David de Grame.

45 —— to Thomas de Corsby, of the lands and barony of Bowne, in Berwickshire, on the resignation of Thomas de Corsby his father.

46 —— to Thomas de Kirkpatrick, of the lands and barony of Kyllosbarne and Brygburgh, in Dumfries-shire, on his own resignation.

47 —— to Archibald Earl of Douglas *Domino* Galwidie, and the heirs-male of his body; whilks failing, to the Earl of March, and his heirs-male, " Dominii vallis Anandie," by resignation of George Earl of March, and George de Donbare his son and heir.

48 —— Con. of a grant by Thomas Mautalent, with consent of William his son, to Mariot de Crag, and William Watson her son, of the lands of Quhylta and Gresshloun, in the shire of Peblys.

INDEX OF CHARTERS BY ROBERT DUKE OF ALBANY. 165

Ane Roll of Robert Duke of Albany, marked thus on the back, Henricus Comes Orkadiæ Dñus de Sto Claro.

This is the twelfth and laſt Roll of Charters now in the General Regiſter-Houſe.

It conſiſts of nine-and-twenty charters, granted by Robert Duke of Albany as Regent of Scotland, in the ſecond, fourth, fifth, ſixth, ſeventh, and eighth years of his regency.

Eight of thoſe charters are dated at Perth, ſix at Edynburgh, three at Doun in Menteth, three at Inverkeithing, two at Strivelyng, two at Falkland, one at Are, one at Coupar in Fyfe, and one at Dunfermeling: In two, viz. No. 16, and 17, the place is not mentioned.

No. 15, 16, 17, and 19, have no witneſſes. Gilbert Biſhop of Aberdeen is a witneſs to all the reſt: Andrew de Hawyk, the Regent's Secretary, is witneſs to all the twenty-five that have witneſſes, except No. 3: Robert Stewart of Fyfe, the Regent's grandſon, is a witneſs to 1, 2, 3, 10, 14, 18, 21, 22, 23, 25, and 28: John Stewart, ſometimes ſtyled *Dominus*, ſometimes Earl of Buchan, is witneſs to 1, 2, 3, 4, 5, 7, 8, 9, 11, 13, 14, 18, 20, 21, and 22: John Stewart *Dominus de* Lorn, to 4, 5, 7, 8, 9, 11, 14, and 20: Robert Stewart of Lorn, to 5, and 6: Alexander Stewart Earl of Marr, to 18: Walter Stewart Earl of Athol and Catnes, to 20: Henry Biſhop of St Andrew's, and William Biſhop of Glaſgow, to 11: Walter Biſhop of Brechin, to 9, 22, and 23: Patrick Earl of Strathern, to 6: Archibald Earl of Douglas, to 7, 8, 9, 10, 11, 27, and 28: George Earl of March, to 7, 8, and 10: Alexander Earl of Craufurd, to 20: William *Dominus de Graham*, to 5, 6, 7, 8, 9, 20, and 22: Robert de Maxwell, John Roos de Hawkhede, and John Skyrmezour, to 1: David Berclay, to 1, 2, 3, 5, 6, 12, 13, 14, 22, and 24: William de Kynros, to 2: Elizeus de Kyninmond, Duncan de Lychtoun, and Alexander de Gardyn, to 3: George de Leſly, to 3, and 5: William de Haya of Lochorwart, and John Sympill of Elyotſtoun, to 4: Michael de Narne, to 5, and 13: Alexander de Uchterlowny, to 6: Robert de Ferny, to 6, and 12: William de Abirnethy, and William de Crawforde, to 10: Richard Comyne, to 12, and 13: John de Camera of Glaſly, to 12, and 23: John de Camera of Kilbride, to 29: Walter de Curry, to 14, 22, and 23: Robert de Maxwell of Caldorwod, to 18, 21, 22, and 23: John Forſter of Corſtorfine, to 18, and 21: Alexander de Ogilby ſheriff of Forfar, to 18: James de Arnot, and David de Allyrdas, to 23: William de Lyndeſay de Roſſy, William de Borthwic the ſon, and Robert de Pringil, to 24: William de Borthwic the father, to 24, 26, 27, and 28: Duncan Rollo, to 24, 26, and 27: David de Edmondſtoun, John de Swyntoun, and Patrick de Abirnethi, to 25: William de Cadyhow, to 26, 27, and 28: Andrew Taillefer, to 26: Robert de Livingſtoun, to 28: Alexander de Lawedre, John de Corntown, and Thomas de Douglas, to 29.

1 Carta Con of a grant by William de Cunningham, to John Turnebule, ſon of Adam Turnebule of Quhithope, of the lands of Haſſyndenebank, in Roxburghſhire.

2 ——— Con. of a charter by Hugh Fraſer *Dominus de Lovet et de Kynnell*, to Peter de Strivelyne, and John his ſon, of the lands of Eſtir Breky, in the barony of Kynnell, and ſhire of Forfare; the original charter is dated at Kynnell, 30th March 1407; witneſſes, Alexander de Ogilby ſheriff of Forfare, Walter de Ogilby *Dominus de* Carcary, William de Camera *Dominus de* Fyndoun, Thomas Lyell rector of the kirk of Kynnell, and Alexander de Gardyne.

3 ——— to Duthac de Carnegy, of the half tewn of Kynnard, with the ſuperiority of the brewhouſe thereof, by reſignation of Mariot de Kynnard.

T t

INDEX OF CHARTERS BY ROBERT DUKE OF ALBANY.

4 Carta to Dungall M'Dowale, of the baronies of Yhester, Doncanlaw, Morhame, Telyne, and Polgavy, in vicecom. de Edinburgh, Forfare, and Perth, by refignation of Eupham Giffart, daughter and one of the heirs of Hew Giffart.

5 —— Con. of a grant by Alexander de Strathechine of Ledynturk, to David Berclay of Durn, of ane annualrent of five merks out of the lands of Pettgarvic, in the fhire of Kincardyne.

6 —— to William Idell of Murebrakis, of the 3d part of the baronies of Balcaly and Kyngerok, in the barony of Seres, and fhire of Fyfe, by refignation of Robert de Carncors.

7 —— to William de Borthwic, of the lands of Borthwic and Thoftcotys, in Selkirkfhire, by refignation of Robert Scott.

8 —— Con. of a wadfet by William de Monte Alto of Loferagy, to John his fon, of the lands of Frefwick and Ochyngill, in Caithnefs.

9 —— to William Watfon, fon to William Watfon of Cranyftoun, of the lands of Trekware and Schelynglaw, in the fhire of Peblys, on the refignation of faid William Watfon.

10 —— Con. of a charter by Henry de Sancto Claro Earl of Orkney, to his brother John de Sancto Claro, of the lands of Sunellifhope and Loganhoufe, in the moor of Pentland, and fhire of Edinburgh. The original charter is dated at Roflyne, 12th September 1410; but it has no witneffes.

11 —— Con. of a charter by James de Douglas *Dominus de* Dalketh, to his fon James de Douglas of Robertoun, of the lands of Stanypeth and Baldwynyfgill, now in the barony of Dalkeith, formerly in the barony of Lintoun. The original charter is dated at Dalketh, 10th of July 1411; witneffes, James de Douglas, fon and heir of faid James de Douglas of Dalketh, William Monypeny, James Watfon Archdean of Tevidale, Alexander de Grahame, Adam de Corry, and Alexander Giffard.

12 —— Con. of a charter by King Robert III. to the Abbay of Jedworth, of the hofpital of St Mary Magdalen's chappel of Ruthirfurde, in the fhire of Roxburgh. King Robert's charter is dated at Glafgu, 2d May, an. reg. 6to; witneffes, Walter Bifhop of St Andrew's, Mathew Bifhop of Glafgow, Archibald Earl of Douglas *Dominus Galwidie*, James de Douglas *Dominus de* Dalketht, Thomas de Erfkyne, and Alexander de Cockburne Keeper of the Great Seal.

13 —— Con. of a charter by Walter de Haliburtoun of Dirkton, to George de Haliburtoun his brother, of the lands and miln of Gogare. The original charter is dated at Dryltoun, 8th June 1409; witneffes, George de Dunbarr Earl of Marche, Henry de Sancto Claro Earl of Orkynnay, William de Lyndefay, William de Sancto Claro, Robert de Lawedre, Walter de Haliburtoun, Alexander de Haliburtoun, John de Haliburtoun, William Bonvile, William de Cranyftoun, and William de Hafwell.

14 —— Con. of a grant by Alexander Stewart Earl of Marr and Garviach, and *Dominus de Dufte* in Brabant, to his brother Andrew Stewart, of the lands of Sandhalch, in the barony of Monblary, and fhire of Banf; and the lands of Tulquhorfk, in the earldom of Marr, and fhire of Aberdeen.

15 —— Con. of a charter by Patrick de Grahame Earl of Strathern, with confent of Eufamia his wife, to Eufamia de Lindefai, daughter of Alexander de Lindefai of Glenefk, of ane annualrent of 5 l. Scots furth of the two towns of Kinkell, in the fhire of Perth. The original charter is dated at Perth, 6th December 1406; but contains no witneffes.

16 —— Con. of ane annualrent granted by Alexander de Lyndefay Earl of Crauforde, to the faid Eufamia during her life, out of the lands of Wefter Brichtey, in the fhire of Forfare.

17 —— Con. of an annualrent of five marks granted by William de Lyndefay, to his fifter the faid Eufamia, out of his two towns of Rofly, in Fyfefhire.

18 —— Con. of a charter by Robert de Keth Marifchal of Scotland, to his fon John de Keth, of the barony of Troup, in the fhire of Banf. The original charter is dated at Aberdene, 2d June 1413; witneffes, Gilbert Bifhop of Aberdeen Chancellor of Scotland, Alexander Earl of Marr and Garviach, Henry de Preftoun, Alexander de Keth, William de Keth, and Alexander de Irwine *Dominus de* Drum.

INDEX OF CHARTERS BY ROBERT DUKE OF ALBANY.

19 Precept to the sheriff of Kincardyn, ordering him to cause to be paid to the Bishop of Brechin the second teinds, *secundas decimas*, of wardis, reliefs, marriages, fines, and escheats within that shire.

20 Carta Con. of a grant by Walter de Ogilvile of Carcary, to St George's altar in the kirk of Brechine, of 10 marks annually furth of the lands of the kirktoun of Essie, Kelore, and Fingask, in the shire of Forfar.

21 —— Con. of ane indenture betwixt William de Fentoun of Baky, on the one part, and Margaret de le Ard of Ercles and Thomas de Cheselhelme, her son and heir, on the other part, dividing between them the lands of which they were heirs portioners, viz. the barony of Rethy, in Forfarshire; the lands of Culase and Buthergask, in Perthshire; the lands of Quodquen, in Lanarkshire; the barony of Gask, in Forfarshire; the town of Kinrossy, and miln thereof, and the lands of Strathy and Pronny, in the earldom of Strathern; the barony of Drumblate, the two Tollis, and Culquhork, in the earldom of Marr; the two Arketys and Craigtown, in the barony of Crouden, and shire of Aberdeen; and the lands of the Ard, in Inverness-shire. The indenture is dated at Kinrossy, 25th April 1403, but has no witnesses.

22 —— Con. of a grant by William Crab burgess of Aberdene, to the Carmelite Friars of Aberdene, of various subjects and annualrents.—Mention is here made of the Denburn, the Stokrude, St Mary's well, Clayhills, the croft called the Cuttyng, the Loch of Dee, and the Milns of the Justiciary; and of the following streets, viz. the Shipraw, the Gallowgate, the Green, Futy, and the Key.—*This charter is omitted in the Old Index.*

23 —— Con. of a grant by John Monypeny of Petmoly, to Thomas Monypeny his son, of the lands of Balbot, in the constabulary of Craill, vic. Fyfe.

24 —— to John Stewart Earl of Buchan, the Regent's son, and Elizabeth de Douglas his spouse, daughter to Archibald Earl of Douglas, of the lands of Stewartoun and Ormishuch, in the barony of Cunningham, and shire of Ayr, resigned by the said Archibald Earl of Douglas.

25 —— to the same persons, of the lands of Dunlop, in the barony of Conynghame, and shire of Air, by resignation of the said Earl of Douglas.

26 —— to the said Earl of Buchan, and his spouse, of the lands of Trabuyage, in the earldom of Carryke, and shire of Are, on the resignation of the said Archibald Earl of Douglas.

27 —— to the said Earl and his spouse, of the lands of Tulchfraser, in the shire of Strivelyne, on the resignation of said John Earl of Buchan.

28 —— to the same persons, of the barony of Tulicultre, in the shire of Clackmanane.

29 —— to Margaret de Abirnethy, daughter of William de Borthwic, of the lands of Buteland, in the shire of Edinburgh, on the resignation of Archibald Earl of Douglas *Dominus Galwidie et vallis Anandie.*

F I N I S.

INDEX to the Religious Houses, Corporations, &c. to which the Charters are granted, and to all the Persons, excepting those Witnesses to the Royal Charters and to the Charters by the Regent Robert Duke of Albany pointed out in a separate Arrangement subjoined to the Introduction.

THE figures followed by commas denote the pages; the figures following the commas, and divided from one another by points, denote the entries in the different pages.

When the same numerical figures occur more than once, prefixed to different entries, in the same page, (as in page 23. where each of the figures 1, 2, 3, 4, 5, and 6, occurs thrice), the second and subsequent entries of each figure is pointed out by the small figures 2, 3, 4, &c. placed at the upper right-hand corner of the figures so repeated, like the figures indicating the square and cube roots, &c. in algebraical notation. Thus, in page 23. the figures 3² after the name *Keith* shews, that *Keith* is mentioned in the second marginal entry marked by the figure 3; and 3³ after *Blunt* shews, that the name *Blunt* will be found in the third marginal entry marked by figure 3.

Some entries in different pages of the book have no marginal figures prefixed. Such entries are here referred to by the number of the line in which they occur, the letter *l* being prefixed to the figure. Thus, under *Aberbrothock Abb.* will be found 156, *l.* 20. which shews that the Abbot of Aberbrothock is mentioned in the 20th line from the top of the 156th page.

Instead of copying all the varieties in which the same *name*, either of person or place, is written or spelt in different places of the book, the most usual orthography is adopted.

When the Latin word *filius* is added to a Latin Christian name, as *filius Duncani, filius Donaldi, filius Willelmi, filius Walteri, filius Roberti, filius Petri,* &c. the name is here given in English as it is used in modern writing, viz. *Duncanson, Donaldson, Williamson, Watson, Robertson, Paterson,* &c.

A

Aberbrothock Abbey and Abbot, 29. 23.—49, 1¹. 4¹—54, 9—63, 1². 2¹.—88, 235.—97, 319.—116, 58. 59. 60.—126, 14.—127, 26.—138, 20.—140, 17.—156, *l.* 20.—158, 46.
Aberbrothock burrow, 54, 8¹.
Aberdeen, 1⁰, 46.
Aberdeen, Bishop and Chapter, 29. 20.—62, 31.—69, 1. 15. 1. 16. 1. 21. —71, 16. 18. 19.—72, 24.—101, 7. —156, l. 34.—162, 12. 13.—166,18.
Aberdeen burrow, 2, 42.—16, 22. 31. —42, 10. 12. 13. 18¹, —43, 21⁰.—51, 52.—53, 31.—58, 10⁴.—66, 8.— 69, l 24.— 72, 28.—75, 80.—82, 161.—128, 1.—138, 21.—149, 46. —167, 22.
Abernethy, 4, 6.—15, 3.—23, 4.—32, 11. 18.—33, 44.—35, 16.—42, 23. —45, 14.—52, 13.—54, 5.—56, 14. —57, 35.—58, 7.—61, 6.—65, 14. —69, 3².—72, 29.—73, 45.—80, 145.—81, 116. 84, 184.—85, 191. —87, 219. 225.—89, 241.—114, 27. 116, 54. 62.—118, 8.—120, 57.— 137, 1.—142, 70.—157, 33.—158, 53.—167, 29.
Abredalgy, 6, 48
Abrekerdour, 152, 17.—157, 35.

Adam, a chaplain of King David II. 74, 72.
Adamson, 125, 3.
Aelfrinus, a chaplain to King David I. 126, 14.
Alano Hostiario, justiciary of Scotland, 135, 7.
Duke of Albany, 124, 12¹.—111, 61. —162, 13. 10.
Alexander I. II. and III. Kings of Scotland, 22, 5.—24, 3. 4.—25, 6¹ —49, 2.—55, 9.—63, 1.—82, 169. —101, 7.—15, 1. 42.
Alkoats, 12, 56
Alian of Galloway, 3, 15.
Alian of Galloway, 3, 15.
Allanson, 2, 53.—14, 5²—15, 14.— 16, 26.—21, 25.—110, 19.
Allardes, 52, 3.—78, 116.—80, 210.— 143, 91.
Allintoun, 122, 107.
Alycht, 28, 16.
Amarus, 155, l. 36.
Ancroft, 156, 10.
Anderson, 61, 7.
St Andrew's Bishop, 43. 34.—46, 50. 69, l. 34.—71, 8.—72, 38.—73, 42. —75, 87.—78, 118.—79, 125. 134. 135.—80, 150.—81, 152.—84, 184.

185.—88, 235.—101, 7.—109, 3. —16, 58. 5, 60.—122, 92. 127. — 125, 14.—137, 15. 26.—132, 35. — 148, 23.—151, 3. 5. 9.—156, l. 19. —162, 13.—166, 12.
St Andrew's burrow, 43, 34.—63, l. 54 —72, 38.—74, 71. 137, 5.—148, 23.
St Andrew's Priory, 4, 35.—20, 3. Angus, 2, 19.—32, 6.—156, l. 9.— 157, 35.
Angus of the Isles, 41, 7.
Angus, Earl and Countess of, 8, 88.— 38. 44.—43, 40.—49, 2².—52, 13. —58, 7.—61, 6.—62, 18. 25.—65, 14.—66, 3².—70, l. 11.—73, 45. 51. —80, 140.—81, 151.—87, 219. 225. —88, 241.—108, 24. 25.—114, 2². —115, 92.—121, 57.—123, 112.— 135, 17. 133, 7. 8. 9.—140, 22 — 147, 5.
A nand, 8, 85. 14, 100.—21, 24.— 47, 17. 24.—69, 5.—80, 137. 84, 185.—89, 203.—120, 3.—129, 31. —135, 8. 14. 9.
Applete n, 113, .—122, 94.—128, 2.
Applynden, 9, 93.
Arbuthnott, 66, 8.—82, 163.
Archibald, 20, 12.
Ardblair, 89, 243.

INDEX TO THE RELIGIOUS HOUSES, PERSONS, &c.

Arde, 16, 11. 12.—20, 5.—26, 17.—
  120, 45. 46. 59. 60.—129, 27. 28
  —167, 21.
Ardlere, 54, 13.—66, 21.—89, 248.—
  124, 10.
Ardrollan, 6, 51.— 13, 97.—44, 3.—
  49, l. 3.—75, 86.
Are, 6, 4,—14, 110. 111. 113.—81,
  160.
Archer, 65, 21.
Argyle, 15, 15.
Argyll, the Barons of, 28, 1.
A..strang, 76 95.—156, l. 28.
Arcus, 157, 3.
Afkirk, 44, 56.—4, 69.
Affelmus, an Archdeacon tempore R.
  David. (?), 155, l 34.
Athole, Earl of, 13, 60.— 17, 41.— 18.
  65. 83. · 19, 105.—26, 11.—44, 4.
  —48, 29.—51, 46. · 52, 47.—52, 29.
  —101, 7.—162, 13.—164, 37.
Atholia, de, 18, 65. 83.—47, 18.
Auchterlony, 137, 8.—150, 2.
Aughinfour, 25, 6.
Auldburgh, 52, 53.—83, 180.
Auldiftoun, 120, 61.—123, 29.—143,
  97.
Auldwell, 57, 36.
Auftin, 42, 8.—69, l. 13.—71, 14.
Awbyne, 148, 42.
Awmfrayis, 33, 33.
Aylbotis, 19, 94.
Aynflay, 119, 3.
Ayr burrow, 14, 118.—25, 12. 13.—
  55, 9.
Ayrth, 19, 109.—29, l. 23.—65, 12.
  —76, 91.— 88, 240.— 117, 75.—
  147, 52.
Aytoun, 7, 70.—60, 29.

B.

Badley, 28, 5.
Baillie, 30, 17.— 33, 25.— 36, 28.—
  50, 14.—162, 17.
Balbreny, 50, 17.
Balcafky, 67, 2¹.—120, 55.—121, 75.
  —120, 24.
Balcolmy, 20, 116.—77, 100.— 117, 70.
  —129, 30.—143, 12.
Balfour, 41, 16.—79, 125.—151, 8.
Balliol, 1, 4.— 4, 22.— 5, 1⁸. 24.—
  6, 41. 46.— 47, 52. 5.— 12, 73.—
  —13, 90.—19, 100.— 25, 6².—26,
  20.—37, 9¹.—46, 2.— 53, 6.—82.
  166.—93, 278.—107, 19.—109, 40.
Balmerynack Abbot, 80, 140.
Balmoffy, 18, 81.—113, 5.—122, 100.
  —128, 6.
Balnhard, 61, 14.
Bannatyne, 42, 8.—43, 32.—71, 14.—
  74, 47.
Bannerman, 35, 12¹.— 84, 187.—91,
  2.
Barbour, 1, 4.—5, 20. 21. 23.—6, 36.
  37.— 138, 21.
Barclay, 2, 37. 47. 48.—17, 34.—18,

79.—26, 34.—53, 28. — 78, 116.—
  79, 125.—80, 137.—86, 102. 2 ,).—
  90, 259.—91, 265.—100, 1 .— 1 3,
  7.—122, 97.— 124, 22 —128, 8.—
  139. 14.—140, 30.—143, 94.—144,
  15.—157, 37.—159, 6.—166, 5.
Barde, 8, 79.— 144, 35.
Barkar, 40, 31.
Barnes, 67, 5².
Baron, 37, 9².
The Barons of Argyll, 28, 1.
Burrowman, 13, 47.
Bartholomew, an Earl's fon, temp. Reg.
  David. 1ᵐⁱ, 24, 15.
Bartholomew, 3, 16. — 57, 34.—77.
  107.—84, 188.
Battall, 11, 41.—37, 10⁸.
Batyftoun, 52, 55.
Baxter, 40, 19.
Beanus, Rector of St Mary's in Arra-
  75, 86.
Heauchamp, Earl of Warwick, 108, ...
Bediebie, 24, 3. 4. 7².
Bell, 137, 6.
Bellomonte, (Beaumont), 20, 114.
Beuhame, 125, 3.
Benyne, 83, 176—126, 7.
Berengarius, 155, l. 35.
Ber, 87, 227.—121, 70.—126, 7.
Beroun, 1, 8.—6c, 11.
Beu, 108, 14.
Bickartoun, 41, 3.—121, 75.—135, 8.
  —162, 27.
Bidun, Walter de, Chancellor to King
  William, 79, 137.
Binning, 55, 8.
Bifapiftoun, 77, 100.
Biffet, 2, 36.— 8, 87.— 28, 10¹.—31,
  35.—44, 59.—48, 2². 3⁵.—49, 1¹
  —55, 6.—58, 5¹.—65, 3.—68, 1¹.
  —73, 42.—14, 62.— 76, 92.—79,
  125.—82, 166.—83, 174.—87, 221.
  230.—88, 231.—50, 254.—107, 23.
  —120, 56.—129, 25.—151, 8.
Blair, 6, 50.—31, 3⁰.—33, 30.— 36,
  38.—38, 13.—44, 58. 9.—49, l. 4.
  —56, 14.—59, 2.—68, 12.—74, 61.
  —75, 86.—80, 143.—89, 248.—115,
  36, 52.—145, 21.—150, 2.
Blaneraddock, 47, 28.
Blencamfchape, 14, 98.—20, 9.
Blenius, an Archdeacon, temp. Regis
  Dav. 1ᵐⁱ, 126, 14.
Blunt, 18, 80.—19, 92.—23, 1¹.
Bochane, 151, 7.
Pope Boniface VIII. 100, 3.
Bonkill, 21, 20.
Bonneville, 16, 16.—17, 37. 38. 42 50.
  —21, 1⁸.—91, 272.—166, 13.
Bonnyman, 57, 2.
Borthwick, 147, 50.—166, 7.—167, 29.
Bofco, 156, l. 9.
Bofevil, 158, 53.
Bothwell, 6, 5.—53, 26.—66, 3¹.—
  81, 158.—91, 263.
Bour, 147, 3.

Boyd, 6, 46 47. 48.—13, 77. 86. 87.
  — 4, 104.—22, 58.—40, 28.—41,
  6.—68, 7. — 83, 182.— 115, 50.—
  117, 65.—147, 11.
Boy'l, 142, 81.
Boyman, 75, 86.
Brade, 58, 6².—83, 180.
Braidy, 24, 16.—30, 21.—36, 32.
  taiols, 155, l 35.
  ake, 24, 13.
Brechin, 18, 79.—19. 103.—26, 34.—
  33, 55.
Brechin, Archdeacon of, 80, 140.—31,
  151.
  chin, Bifhop of, 51, 42.—71, 8.—
      12.— 75, 82.—78, 116. 118.—
  9, 125 134. 13 .— 80, 150.—51,
  15 .—52, 167 168.—83, 174.—84,
  184. 185.—86, 212.— 22, 107.—
  157, 19.
  ient 79. 137.
Brinyngs or Brounyngs, 2, 38.—3, 3¹.
  .8, 84.—15 16.—16, 19.—17, 33.
Bifbane, 2, 29.—36, 95.—142, 74.
Britu, Hugo de, 155, l. 35.
Brown, 14, 100. 101. 102.—17, 4⁰.—
  21, 39.—31, 33.—36, 24.—52, 48.
  —73, 54.—115, 47.—119, 20.—134,
  8. 9. 23.—133, 27.—144, 37.—145,
  177, 19.
Bruce, 1, 25.—2, 49. 10.—6, 37. 45.
  —12, 54. 62.—13, 90. 91.—14, 114.
  —15, 2¹. 3.—18, 65. 82. 83.—19,
  85. 107.—22, 51.—13, 3¹ —24, 15.
  —25, 15. 16. 17.—27, 1. —28, 33.—49,
  36, 2.—37. 14 11⁸.—38, 33.—49,
  l. 26.—51, 35.—54, 7¹. 7⁸. 11⁸.—
  56, a.—59, 16.—0, 109.—53, 53.
  64, 6.—76, 97.—85, 192. 144.—88.
  214.—91, 260. 261. 262.—115, 37.
  38.—116, 6.—119, 29.—125, 14.
  —135, 8.—144, 39.—146, 43.—154,
  74.—155, l. 34.
Buchan, 52, 54.
Buchan, Earl of, 1, 24.—2, 44.—13,
  79. 90.—15, 8.—10, 119.—25, 4¹.
  —27, 1¹.—68, 8¹.—80, 149.—101,
  7.—124, 20. 25. 26.—134, 34. 42.—
  147, 7.— 148, 34.— 150, 9. 10.—
  162, 16.—163, 19. 20.—167, 24. 25.
  26. 27. 28.
Buchannan, 58, 12¹.—91, 275.—158,
  4⁸.
Bunting, 141, 50.
Burell, 127, 22.
Burgenfs, 52, 53.
Burgh, 63, 50.—86, 209.—115, 44.
Burnard, 31, 39.—36, 40.—53, 19.—
  85, 197.
Burnett, 17, 53. 57.
Buroeville, 126, 14.—156, l. 11.
Burntown, 147, 52. 53.
Burr, 37, 71.—48, 33. 34.
Butler, 49, 7.
Butter, 148, 32.

INDEX TO THE RELIGIOUS HOUSES, PERSONS, &c.

Buttergalk, 41, 3⁹, 39, 40.—44, 5.—45, 18.—52, 3.—54, 10¹, 11².—55, 19, 20.—56, 7, 12.—59, 16.—77, 100.
Bydoune, 96, 313.—131, 20.

C.

Cairncors, 141, 66.—166, 6.
Cairns, 50, 18.—75, 84.
Caithnefs, Bifhop of, 101, 7.
Caithnefs, Earl of, 29, 24.—51, 34.—121, 79.—122, 111.—140, 19, 31, 32.—154, 37.
Caldwall, 145, 1.
Callentar, 38, 25.—42, 5.—58, 3.—71, 12.
Cambow, 25, 8¹, 9².—117, 70.
Cambrin, 77, 100.
Cumbrown, 68, 16.
Camhufkenueth Abb 4, 34.—34, 2³.—37, 6².—61, 10.—64, 8.—68, 3¹.—76, 99.—81, 153.—141, 51.
Campbell, 6, 38.—14, 122, 123, 124.—15, 10, 11, 15, 19.—18, 75.—19, 105.—118.—25, 14.—26, 11, l. 5, 18, 31.—28, 4.—29, l. 18.—31, 36.—36, 37.—39, 8, 10.—44, 7.—49, l. 4.—62, 29.—68, 1¹, l. 23, 2².—75, 86.—83, 177, 178.—92, 275.—93, 281.—115, 51.—116, 53, 5².—120, 50.—135, 8.—137, 17.—142, 76.—149, 38.—158, 49.—163, 17.—164, 36.
Camfy, 92, 275.
Capella, 18, 64.—114, 28.—118, 15.—119, 24.—120, 65.—129, 33.
Caplochy, 121, 89.
Cardny, 97, 317.—123, 114.—124, 13, 14, 15.—125, 29.—131, 50.—134, 4.—145, 33.
Cargill, 38, 5¹.—67, 223.—69, 308.—114, 26.—118, 8.—130, l. 8.
Carlile, 47, 16.—74, 73.
Carlton, 14, 114.—94, 287.—96, 314. 130, 9.
Carnegie, 141, 56.—165, 3.
Carmcu and Carnock, 11, 53.—12, 63.—17, 52.—39, 4.—45, 24.—49, 9.—59, 8.—60, 12.—126, 14.—127, 26.
Carpenter, (Wright), 18, 62.—21, 21.—22, 55.—92, l. 20.—40, 40, 28.—41, 4.
Carrick, 5, 26.—7, 70.—18, 72.—25, 10¹.—33, 32.—39, 58.—40, 19.—41, 42.—45, 41.—46, 52.—47, 12. 14, 19.—50, 9.—68, 10.—92, 275.—93, 277, 278.—114, 5.—134, 6.—135, 7, 8
Carrick, Earl of, 3, 10.—48, 7.—51, 35.—62, 35.—64, 17.—7¹, 108.—85, 194.—90, 258.—92, 276.—93, 277.—101, 7.—112, 71.—115, 35, 37, 38.—116, 60, 61, 63.—117, 64.—119, 27.—122, 92, 97.—127, 15. 21.—132, 7.—134, 6.—135, 7, 12.—151, 3, 5.—162, 13.
Carrikis, 5, 26.

Carrutheris, 9, 92. 93.
Carfan, 118, 5, 6.
Cathcart, 115, 37, 38.
Cattill, 140, 32.
Chacklock, 55, 4.
Chalmer, (Camera), 7, 65.—14, 103.—16, 14.—17, 36.—19, 95.—22, 56.—37, 5¹.—38, 17, 29.—39, 53.—41, 41.—43, 33.—46, 8.—47, 23.—60, 22.—68, 9, 11, 2¹.—69, l. 33.—72, 37.—85, 199.—119, 24.—138, 55.—148, 21.—157, 36, 37.—165, 2.
Chapman, 52, 54.—55, 2.—82, 170.—132, 10.
King Charles IV. of France, 106, 14.
King Charles V. of France, 100, 4.—111, 64, 68.
King Charles VI. of France, 111, 61.—112, 69.
Charteris, 5, 17.
Chene, 11, 28.—32, 4.—33, 37.—34, 17.—39, 47.—43, 31.—62, 22.—68, 80, 149.—151, 13.
Chefchelme, 80, 140.—134, 39.—167, 21.
Chirnfyde, 141, 59.
Chiry, 80, 143.
Clapham, 94, 295.—131, 17.—151, 7, 17.
Clarky, 62, 20.
Cliffor, 6, 44.—7, 71.—18, 73.—25, 11.—26, 20, 25.—30, 3, 5.—35, 4.—50, 10.—56, 2.
Citharift, (Harper), 7, 65.—33, 32.—38, 22.—56, 16.
Clenconnan, 57, 27.
Clerk, 9, 92, 93.—16, 10.—56, 10.—113, 8.—129, 18.—133, 37.—161, 4, 5, 6, 7.—169, 13.
Clerk of Register, 61, 31.—67, 5¹.—68, 11.—74, 65.—85, 198.
Cnount, 5, 15.
Coci, (Cook), 16, 30.
Cockburn, 24, 2.—43, 25.—50, 8.—64, 2.—69, l. 27.—72, 31.—76, 91, 93.—79, 135, 136.—84, 184. 185, 193.—121, 88.—124, 11.—126, l. 15.—148, 22.—156, l. 38.—161, 26, 12.
Coldingham, 156, l. 9.
Coldingham Priory, 3, 20.—55, 1.—82, 169.—152, 22.
Cochran, 50, 7.—157, 34.
Colquhoun, 47, 18.—61, 5.—115, 37, 38.
Colti, 64, 13.—77, 104.
Colville, 30, 20.—36, 31.—49, 2¹.—50, l. 2.—127, 23.—148, 36.
Comedious, the phyfician, 75, 86.
Conhethe, 40, 10.
Conftable of Scotland. See Hay, and 24, 12.
Copland, 37, 9¹.
Corbet, 11, 50.—28, 2.—36, 42.—40, 31.—60, 11.

Corbetfon, 36, 42.
Corrie, 67, 11.—74, 73.—88, 236.—166, 11.
Corsby, 164, 45.
Corfs, 125, 30. 32.
Coffour, 5, 9, 10.—30, 4.—35, 4.—51, 40.—63, 52.—82, 167.—97, 320.—115, 45.—131, 21.
Coupar Abb. 4, 38, 39.—61, 1.
Coupar burrow, 56, 3.
Cowan, 128, 11.
Cowper, 54, 9¹.
Crab, 15, 21.—16, 20.—17, 32.—32, 9.—46, 53, 55.—53, 2.—71, 11.—148, 1.—157, 36.—167, 22.
Craig, 42, 4.—57, 26.—164, 48.
Craigie, 25, 18.—32, 11.—55, 3.—56, 6.—57, 22.—70, l. 4.—73, 44.—83, 171.—97, 323.—121, 88.—122, 101, 131, 24.—132, 33.—164, 40.
Craik, 24, 2.—44, 11.—94, 296.
Crail Priory, 51, 25.
Crambeth, 78, 115.—158, 55.
Cranftoun, 61, 13.—121, 83.—166, 13.
Crawfurd, 6, 42.—14, 120.—32, 19.—37, 7¹.—41, 36.—47, 20, 21.—57, 25.—58, 2.—62, 26.—82, 166.—148, 31.—152, 19.—158, 41.—42, 161, 2.
Crawfurd, Earl of, 141, 64.—142, 83, 84, 88.—148, 28, 29.—161, 4, 5, 6.—147, 162, 8, 9.—166, 16.
Crichton, 5, 27.—31, 45.—36, 46.—44, 4.—55, 3.—87, 171.—84, 184.—85, 193.—120, 67.—126, 14.—129, 35.—146, 48.—148, 15.
Crumdule, 76, 95.
Cronfod, 43, 28.
Crooks, 50, 16.
Croffevile, 135, 15.
Croffragwell Abb. 3, 10, 11.—23, 13.—116, 58, 59, 60.—142, 69.
Croufur, 97, 320.—131, 21.
Culchone, 47, 18.—61, 5.—115, 37, 38.
Culfs, 78, 118.
Cullen, 37, 11².—53, 2.
Cluehach, 13, 78, 81.—14, 105.—51, 28.—52, 5.—86, 211.
Culquhen, 47, 18.
Culrofs Abb. 4, 36.—147, 4.—151, 8.
Cuming, 1, 24.—2, 44, 46.—5, 12, 24.—7, 72.—8, 80.—10, 23.—13, 9.—18, 72.—20, 119.—24, 14.—25, 4¹.—26, 28.—27, 1¹.—35, 14¹.—43, 45.—46, 56.—53, 19.—54, 4.—58, 8.—70, l. 13.—80, 149.—83, 183.—84, 188.—97, 257.—94, 286.—101, 7.—134, 40.—137, 4.—162, 13.
Cunyne, 73, 55.
Cunyngburgh, 6, 51.—135, 7.
Cunyngham, 5, 13.—7, 53.—12, 61.—15, 42.—19, 37.—30, 11.—53, 11.—42, 7, 11.—45, 14.—50, 7.—64, 17.—68, 2¹.—71, 17.—77, 108.—80, 148.—95, 299.—114, 21.—119.

INDEX TO THE RELIGIOUS HOUSES, PERSONS, &c.

3⁸.—134, 5.—137, 14.—138, 31.—140, 14.—14¹, 54.—146, 27.—150, 8.—161, 1.—162, 17.—163, 17.—165, 1.
Currour, 162, 12.—164, 40.
Curry, 84, 18ll.
Cuthris, 149, 54.
Cygryin, 119, 33.
Cyfer, 6, 44.

D.

Dalgarnock, 114, 17.
Dalmah·y, 14⁵, 18.
Dalrymple, 94, 285.—122, 105.—130, 7.—146, 44.
Daltoun, 5, 14.
Dalziel, 32, 17.—34, 16.—63, 46.—64, 12.—77, 103.—79, 131.—121, 90.—138, 30.—139, 40.—140, 39.—158, 4².—162, 17.—161, 21.
Danielſtoun, 30, 10.—33, 33.—35, 10.—37, 1.—53, 29.—59, 1. 8.—60, 28.—65, 7.—77, 108.—88, 234.—91, 266.—93, 2⁸⁷.—117, 66.—118, 31.—143, 5.—152, 20.—158, 19. 50.
King David I. 3, 20.—22, 1.—82, 169. 155. l. 2. l. 42.
Earl Divid, the brother of King William, 70, 137.—136, l. 5.
King David II. 43, 1².—62, 23.—107, 19.
David Duke of Rothſay, eldeſt ſon of King Robert III. his death, 104, 12¹.
Deer Abb. y, 1, 12, 23, 24.
Delwill, ⁷2, 33.
Dempſter, 78, 118.—132, 8.
Dervorgilla, daughter of Allan of Galloway, 3, 15.—4, 22.
Dewell, 43, 27.
Dickſon, 27, 9.—150, 3¹.
Diſchingtoun, 18, 77.—84, 3¹.—65, 4.—76 91.—78, 121.—79, 125, 134, 136.—80, 150.—85, 19².—88, 231.—90, 25².—142, 40, 41.—144, 21.
Diſpenſa, ⁷, 69.—38, 37.—44, 12.—45, 3¹.—47, 25, 26.—⁸⁷, 100.
Dolas, 141, 57, 58.—142, 85, 86, 87.—148, 20, 29.—161, 30, 11.
Dolfyn, the brother of Gofpatrick, 126, 14.
Donaldſon, 14, 120.—2³, 11¹.
Dornagill's ſon John, 59, l. 11.
Douglas, 4, 8, 37.—5, 12.—7, 59.—8, 74.—77.—10, 15, 16, 17, 18, 19, 20, 21, 22, 23, 24, 25, 26.—11, 35, 50.—12, 64.—20, 7.—21, 26, 27, 29.—22, 47.—23, 8.—27, 3¹. 7¹.—28, 17.—34, 11².—39, l. 3.—40, 11.—41, 37. 4⁸, 29, 32, 35.—5¹, 11.—51, 3.—52¹, 11.—54, 2.—55, 18.—58, 3.—61, 32.—65, 3. 5. 6, 12.—67, 6.—71, 8.—75, 85, 87.—77, 100.—79, 132, 135.—80, 150.—81, 156.—83, 174.—84, 184.—85, 193. 86, 215.—87, 230.—88, 232, 233.

235, 239.—90, 258.—97, 319.—116, 5⁶. 58, 59, 60.—121, 73, 7¹. 91.—122, 92. 102.—123, 11.—125, 34. 4. 5.—126, 6, 7, 14.—128, 14.—130, 6.—131, 31.—132, 2, 3.—133, 20, 21, 32, 33.—134, 5.—135, 8, 15.—136, 19, 20.—138, 2⁸.—139, 8.—140, 27.—141, 45, 6.—142, 71, 82.—144, 29.—145, 16, 146, 42.—147, ⁹.—149, 48, 56.—151, 3, 5, 9.—153, 23.—156, l. 2 l. 29, l. 36, l. 37.—161, 2.—166, 11. 12.—167, 24, 25, 26, 27, 28.
Douglas, Earl of, 31, 42, 43.—36, 43, 44.—45, 36.—46, 4⁸, 31.—49, 4¹.—52, 8.—55, 18.—57, 1.—62, 36.—63, 43, 45, 54.—65, 18.—75, 87.—79, 134, 135, 136, 137.—80, 150.—81, 152.—82, 167, 168.—84, 184.—185.—86, 204, 215.—88, 231.—89, 245.—90, 258.—91, 269.—92, 236.—93, 280.—104, 12³.—108, 30.—109, 36.—111, 63.—114, 7.—115, 4⁵.—121, 82, 83, 91.—122, 92.—127, 15.—134, 2.—142, 71.—146, 42.—147, 54.—148, 26, 35.—150, 155, 15¹, 9.—156, l. 2.—161, ·· 3.—162, 13.—164, 37, 47.—166, 12.—167, 24, 25, 26, 29.
Drawer, 12, 56.
Drimyngis's ſon, 2, 38.—3, 3¹.
Drummond, 8, 81.—83, 31.—37, 17.—30, 50.—40, 46.—115, 35.—116, 61.—134, 3.—138, 19.—151, 12.—164, 2¹¹.
Dryburgh Abb. 38, 18.—59, 3.—151, 15
Dubrell, 157, 29.
Duchti, 77, 126.
Duddingſtoun, 20, 117.
Duff, 141, 61.
Dumbartan, 61, 31.
Dumblane, Bifhop of, 151, 8.
Dun, 12, 73.—32, 3.—6, 6.—68, 14.—70, l. 12.—71, 10.—73, 53.—76, 91.—81, 155.—82, 169.—85, 195. 1, 6.—90, 234, 92, 276.—96 300. 1, 1, 7.—120, 54.—121, 72.—122, 1, 7.—124, 126, 9, 14.—129, 13 130, 3.—131, 31.—133, 18.—136, 139, 164, 47.—166, 13.
Duncan the Judge, 18, 58.
Duncanſon of Atholl, 30, l. 1.—73, 42.
Duncanſon, 141, 47, 48.
Dundenie, 54, 7².
Dundrennan Abb. 3, 15.—31, 28.—36, 19.—41, 34.
Dunfermelyne, 55, 7.—83, 175.
Dunfermling Abb. 4, 26, 27, 28, 29, 30, 31, 32, 33.—20, 2.—25, 2².—28, 7.—29, l. 21.—43, 35, 36.—40, 4¹.—53, 4.—70, l. 8. l. 9.—73, 43, 49.—146, 45.—151, 8.

Dunkeld, Bifhop of, 60, 25.—79, 125.—88, 235.—116, 58, 59, 60.—216, 14.—127, 15.—151, 3, 5, 9.
Dunmore, 45, 35.
Dunſtephe's ſon, 26, 15.
Durance, 44, 50.
Durham, 27, 53.—82, 169.
Durham, Bifhop of, 109, 36.
Durrand, 45, 28.
Durward, (Uſtiarius), 17, 44.
Duvery, 162, 13.
Dyckiſon, 143, 8.

E.

Echlyne, 164, 41.
King Edgar, 3, 20.—82, 169.—155, l. 42.
Edgar, 5, 27.—12, 68, 69, 70.—131, 88.—21, 33, 34, 35.—27, 1³, 3¹.—39, 54.—40, 32.—58, 2.
Edgar's ſon, 156, l. 12.
Edinburgh, 56, 2
Edinburgh city, 4, 25.—54, 14.—73, 111.
Edingham, 64, 16.—77, 107.
Edmond, 138, 27.
Edmonitoun, 66, 1³.—70, l. 2.—73, 41.—80, 144.—84, 185.—101, 4.—114, 22.—136, 19
King Edward I of England, 37, 9¹.—103, 2.
King Edward III. of England, 101, 9.—103, 11¹, 11³.—136, 28.
Edward, Chancellor to King David I. 24, 15.—126, 14.
Eglingtoun, 49, l. 3.—57, 37.—76, 86.—93, 279.—94, 290, 2, 91, 292.—97, 121.—108, 30.—114, 6.—115, 41.—119, 29.—120, 51, 61.—129, 20, 29.—131, 12, 13, 14, 22.
Eicharft (probably for Citharift) of Carrick, 33, 32.
Eklys, 44, 4⁸.—50, 11.—73, 41.—123, 124.—94, 287.—96, 314.—130, 9, 13, 28.
Echo Priory 45, 25.
Elgin, 16, 22, 23.
Elcin burrow, 80, 149.
Ellam, 44, 4⁸.—73, 41.—82, 169.
Elphinſton, 73, 40.
Erch or Erth, 19, 109.—29, l. 23.—5, 13.—76, 91.—88, 240.—117 75.—147, 52.
Erſkyne, 34, 5². 7². 8².—42, 2.—44, 58.—46, 26.—49, 1¹. 3. 4². 5.—50, 4.—52, 2.—5¹, 25.—62, 28.—88, 6⁶, 3.—69, l. 8.—71, 5, 12.—73, 42.—74, 61.—75, 8⁸.—78, 114, 115.—79, 125, 140, 135.—86, 140, 150.—91, 152.—82, 1⁵⁸.—3, 174.—84, 184.—156.—86, 20⁹.—8⁸—92, 25⁸.—93, 277.—94, 289, 108, 23, 25.—26, 115, 40.—116, 64.—118, 9.—119, 36.—20, 69.—121, 86.—12⁷, 15.—131, 11, 13.—135, 14.—145, 17.—147, 5.—151, 3, 5, 8, 9.

INDEX TO THE RELIGIOUS HOUSES, PERSONS, &c. 173

156, l. 27. l. 36,—157, 28. — 158, 44, 53, 55,—166, 12.
Erth or Erch, 19, 109 — 29, l. 23.— 65, 13. — 76, 91.—88, 240.—117, 75.—147, 52.
Ethingtoun, 140, 40.
Eupham Queen of Scotland, 98, 328. —114, 14.—132, 5.
Eviot, 64, 20.—77, 109.
Ewanson or Ewinson, 19, 89.—26, 14. —59, 10.
Ewar, 115, 46.
Eychles, 94, 287.—96, 314.—130, 9. —131, 28.

F.
Faffingtoun, 70, l. 6. — 73, 45. — 87, 225.—126, 7.—145, 9.
Fairlie, 7, 61.—80, 146.—128, 13.— 133, 32.—145, 12.
Falconar, (*Fauconer*), 78, 120.
Falkirk, 61, 4.
Fawfyde, 6, 30.—11, 32. 33.—37, 9¹. —56, 13.—60, 15.—64, 7.—76, 98. —79, 134, 135.—114, 9.
Feddereffe, 46, 56.—62, 22.
Fedrey, 62, 22.
Fentoun, 28, 13.—43, 24.—44, 51.— 70, 3.—72, 30.—115, 49.—167, 21
Fergufson, 64, 4.—76, 95.—119, 34.
Ferne, 164, 44.
Ferny, 157, 37.
Ferrars, 6, 41. 50. — 7, 53. 58. — 10, 22⁸.—13, 90.—19, 111.—20, 11.— 22, 42.—27, 1³.
Findlater, 82, 164.
Finlay, 11, 52.
Finlayson, 28, 1.
Fifher, 77, 100.
Fleming, 8, 80. 81. 82.—23, 96.—30, 6. 10.—32, 15.—34, 3². — 35, 6.— 41, 10.—50, 2.—54, 11.—59, 4.— 61, 31.— 62, 26.—64, 7.—67, 1². 2¹.—71, 12.—72, 33.—75, 79—76, 98.—81, 154.—92, 275.—97, 318. —115, 39. 50.—116, 58. 64.—118, 65.—119, 32.—121, 77. — 124, 24. —126, 14.—127, 23. 26.—130, 5. —134, 5.—135, 7.—140, 26.—142, 72.—143, 9⁸.—146, 34. 37. 40.— 147, 6.—148, 25. 26.— 152, 16.— 159, 2². 3⁴. 4.
Fodringhay, 31, 27.—52, 55.— 122, 129.—123, 122. 123.
Forbes, 149, 56.
Forrett, 44, 52.—57, 3.—80, 146.— 91, 271.
Forrester, 61, 4.—64, 11.—77, 102.— 120, 48. 49.—123, 126.—124, 16. 1⁸. 23.—135, 31.— 137, 9. — 140, 22.—147, 1.—148, 24.—150, 59.— 152, 17.—162, 12.—163, 16. 29.— 164, 42.
Forfyth, 135, 10.
Fortune, 26, 16.—47, 28.—48, 30. 31. —51, 44.

Foslane, 92, 275.
Foustoune, 57, 39.
Fowler, 5, 8.—11, 51.
Francis, 6, 50.—12, 56.—15, 20.
Franx, 148, 19.
Fraser, 1, 7. 14. 15. 16. 18.—8, 86.— 12, 55.—17, 45. 51. 55.— 18, 60. 61.—19, 105.—23, 7.—28, 2. 14.— 29, 24.—39, 49.—43, 31.—62, 14. —65, 2.—66, 1.—68, 6.—71, 20.— 73, 46.—76, 91. 92.—78, 117.—83, 181.—87, 229.—114, 17.—115, 32. 33. 48.—116, 58.—117, 73.—126, 7.—135, 8.—137, 7.—144, 16.— 146, 30.—149, 46. 53.—159, 2.— 160, 11.—163, 19.—165, 2.
Frendraught, 1, 26.
French, 138, 24.
Friars, 20, 1.—23, 5¹. 6¹.—43, 22.— 119, 27.
Friars of the Carmelite order, 38, 21.— 64, 19.—66, 8.—75, 88.—82, 163. —128, 1.—157, 22.——Preaching Friars, 4, 25.—25, 12. 13.—27, 4. —69, l. 24.—92, 28.—90, 149.—85 194.—119, 39.——Trinity Friars, 152, 21.——White Friars, 51, 31. 32.
Fullartoun, 18, 78.—24, l. 6.—34, 2. —45, 15. 16.—75, 86.—93, 277.— 94, 296.—95, 297. 298. 300. 301.— 119, 23.—124, 3.—142, 81.—146, 45.—151, 3.
Fyfe, 62, 26.—74, 62.—79, 125.
Fyfe, Earl of, 16, 28.—17, 41.—22, 57.—25, 7¹.—29, l. 21.—34, 9.— 39, 43.—41, 16.—45, 22.—52, 6². 4.—5², 3. 4.—58, 7².—62, 27. 28. —68, 15.—80, 150.—88, 235.—113, 3.—114, 16. 20.—115, 31.—118, 7. 16.—120, 50.—122, 92. 96. 107.— 126, 14.—127, 15. 25.—128, 4.— 132, 31.—139, 39.—140, 20.—151, 3. 5. 8. 9.—156, l. 36.—156, 52. 53.

G.
Galbraith, 35, 39.—117, 64.
Gallerei, 46, 7.
Galloway, Allan of, 3, 15.
Galloway, Bishop of, 20, 4.—41, 35.
Galloway, the men of, 33, 26.
Garden, 35, 28.—140, 43.— 141, 44. —163, 21.—164, 35.—165, 2.
Gardrop, 2, 43.—16, 17.—32, 11.
Garmache, 42, 21¹.
Garvald, 18, 59.
Garviach, 72, 27.
Gatmilk, 118, 8.
Gauhiloun, 41, 6.
Gelchedall, 21, 30.
Geleel, 46, 43.
Giffard, 20, 15.—61, 32.—63, 47.— 166, 4. 11.
Gilbert, the phyfician, 88, 237.
Gilbert's fon Walter (Hamilton), 7, 72.

—11, 27. — 24, 14. — 27, 1. — 29, l. 20.—15, 15.—84, 19².
Gilbert's fon Duncan, 82, 166.
Gilbert's fon John, 25, 8.—94, 276.— 95, 298.
Gilchomedy, 40, 23.
Gillebrand, 38, 31.—45, 6.—50, 5.— 56, 18.—76, 95.—83, 181.
Gillemycholl, 126, 14.
Gillile, 126, 14.
Gilmernaykie, 27, 2¹.
Glacester, 30, 19.—36, 30.—59, 10.— 115, 34.—124, 4.
Gladstanes, 65, 23. 24.—78, 112. 113. —127, 23.—137, 18.—145, 14. 15. —159, 2.
Glasgow, Bishop of, 24, 15.—83, 174. —88, 235.—93, 232.—101, 7.— 108, 30.—116, 56. 60.—125, 14.— 127, 26.—156, l. 19. l. 34.—166, 12.
Glasgow city, 27, 4¹.
Glasgow, preaching friars of, 27, 4¹.
Glen, 23, 11.—25, 5¹.—33, 43.—38, 32.—30, 46.—62, 19. — 75, 86.— 83, 174.—152, 61.
Glencharny, 42, 14. — 69, l. 17.—71, 20.
Glendoning, 44, 56.—127, 23.
Glenluce Abb. 3, 12. 13.—30, 14.— 35, 14¹.
Glentoun, 74, 59.
Glenurchy, 44, 7.
Goldfmith, 31, 40.—36, 41.—142, 78.
Gordon, 2, 40.—50, l. 3.—52, 52.— 65, 18.—89, 245.— 118, 11.—140, 24.—143¹, 55.—163, 32.
Gorwyc, 5, 10.
Gofpatrick, an Earl, 22, 3. — Gofpatrick, brother of Dolfyn, 126, 14.— Gofpatrick, a Sheriff, tempore David, Reg. 1™, 155, l. 35.
Gourlay, 5, 16.—37, 3.—42, 21.—54, 8².—59, 15.—117, 75.—163, 30.
Govan, 32, 6.—57, 1.—12, 269.—133, 30.
Graham, 6, 36.—11, 31. 38.—28, 15. —40, 13.—42, 9.—44, 49.—53, 5. —54, 1.—60, 23.—69, 1. 4. l. 14. 70, 1.—71, 15.—78, 119.—81, 155. —83, 174.—78, 327.—108, 23.— 113, 3.—117, 64.—118, 8.—122, 96.—126, 14.—128, 4.—144, 28. —148, 20. 35.—162, 8. 9.—164, 35. 44.—166, 11. 15.
Grant, 45, 38.—76, 95.
Gray, 12, 55.—15, 5.—17, 87.—22, 59.—26, 19.—32, 14.—46, 44.— 67, 1.—68, 1².—74, 65.—85, 19². —114, 25.—119, 28.—121, 65.— 152, 2.—162, 8.—164, 43.
Greenhead, 31, 33.—38, 24.
Greenlaw, 30, 16.—36, 27.—38, 12.
Guldbrune, 58, 4.
Guppyld, 81, 151.
Gynes, 4, 6.—7, 60.—20, 149.

X x

INDEX TO THE RELIGIOUS HOUSES, PERSONS, &c.

H.

Hadden, 50, 18.
Haddingtoun burrow, 10, 24².
Hair and Hare, 19, 106.—82, 165.
Haiftie, 65, 7.
Haliburton, 9, 6.—31, 44.—36, 45.—39, 7.—57, 35.—59, 6.—60, 21.—76, 91.—79, 135.—81, 152.—92, 167.—84, 184, 185.—85, 197.—108, 30.—126, 10.—147, 13.—14¹, 21.—140, 43.—163, 24, 25, 27.—166, 13.
Halket, 68, 320.—114, 12.—151, 8.
Hall, 22, 53.—77, 100.—96, 311.—131, 18.—137, 13.
Haltoun, 122, 104.
Halywall, 41, 11.—57, 26.
Hamilton, 7, 72.—11, 27.—24, 14.—27, 1.—46, 3.—77, 108.—83, 174.—84, 190.—119, 36.—138, 26, 36.—139, 1, 3.—156, 27.—162, 17.—164, 28.
Haquin V. King of Norway, 101, 7.
Haquin, 151, 7.
Hare, 66, 11.
Harkars, 18, 76.—63, 54.—91, 155
Harper, 7, 65.—33, 32.—38, 22.—56, 16.
Hart, 24, 13.
Haftings, 1, 16.—26, 19.—28, 7.
Hafwell, 63, 51.—67, 4¹.—144, 33.—166, 15.
Hawden, 12, 58, 60.—121, 75.—164, 30.
Hay, 1, 26.—2, 35.—6, 43. — 16, 9. 13, 15.—18, 66.—20, 119.—24, 15.—26, 12.—29, l. 24.—42, 16.—46, 49.—56, 17.—58, 9¹, 1.² —61, 1.—67, —69, l 19.—71, 22.—74, 69.—75, 8¹.—76, 92.—77, 10¹.—85, 194.—116, 60.—118, 8.—12c, 4¹.—123, 117.—126, 14.—127, 26.—135, 9.—138, 3¹.—141, 65.—143, 95.—144, 3¹.—156, l. 2c.—160, 11.—162, 8.—163, 27.
Hayrum, 24, 15.
Hector the phyfician, 8º, 237.
Henryfon, (Henderfon), 93, 281.—126, 7.
Henry Earl of Northumberland, the fon of King David I. 22, 2.—24, 15.—82, 16.—126, 14.—155, l. 2. l. 41.
Henvyle, Heuwyll, 65, 9.—88, 236
Hepburn, 41, 12.—42, 20, 21.—4¹, 2.—13.—57, 1.—74, 63.—79, 135.—2, 169.—84, 184.—136, 19.
Herbert, chamberlain to King David I. 126, 14.
Herbert, chancellor to King David I. 155, l. 24.
Hering, 52, 16.—92, 254.—120, 5¹.—129, 25.—136, 16.
Herowart, 57, 24.—62, 68.
Herries, 11, 34.—64, 5.—66, 23, 25.—68, 5.—75, 87.—76, 96.—82, 15.

16º.—84, 186.—90, 250, 252.—96. 308.—149, 37.—156, l. 29.
Hill, 55, 21—62, 41.—125, 30.
Hiltoun, 44, 48.—73, 41.
Hudholme, 5, 20.
Hog, 44, 8.—50, 3.—51, 24.—67, 6¹.—74, 68.—114, 16.
Hokenay, 6, 44.
Holme Abb. 84, 186.
Holyroodhoufe Abb. 23, 10.—14, 13.—4¹, 16.—44, 55.—74, 58.—81, 156, 84, 184.—85, 193.—89, 24. 90, 251, 254.—1.6, 14, 15.—127 16, 18.—44, 36.—146, 34.—152, 16.—153, 26.—157, 30.—159, 4.
Holywood, 70, 12.—134, 5.
Hume, 60, 21.—1.6, l. 12.
Hoppringle, 84, 114.—85, 193.—163, 27.
Horneden, 11, 40.
Horfeley, 88, 234.
Hofpitfi, 78, 124.
Hoftiario, 135, 7.
Hugh, chancellor to King William, 155, l. 8.
Hull, 117, 74.
Humphries, 13, 33.
Hunter, 115, 51.
Hurchurche, 13, 92. 93.

I.

Idel, 166, 6.
Jedburgh Abb. 22, 1. 2. 3. 4. 5.—127. 26.—166, 12.
Jedburgh burrow, 12, 59.
Inchaffray Abb. 26, 29.
Inchmahome Prior. 51, 22.
Inchmertein, 29, l. 2.
Inchtour, 68, 13.—78, 114.—120, 69.
Infirmitorio, Thomas de, 75, 86.
Ingama, 155, l. 35.
Ingeramifman, 78, 117.
Inglis, 6, 37.—137, 18.
Innerpeffer, 34, 1.—48, 33.—58, 7.—68, 3¹.—78, 119.—¹5, 2cc.—87, 225.—113, 5.—121, 74.—122, 15¹.—123, 119, 125.—128, 6, 1c.—132, 4.—133, 29.
Pope Innocent VI. 108, 25¹.
Inverlunan, 68, 13.
Invernefs, 17, 35.—85, 193.
Johanna, Queen of King David II. 101, 9.
John, a Bifhop, tempore R. David. 1ᵐⁱ 155, l. 34.
St John's chapel, 130, 34.
John King of France, 106, 15. 15¹. 15¹. 15². 16.—167, 16¹. 1.
John, the Judge, 78, 116.
John, Margaret's fon, 39, 2.
John, eldeft fon and heir apparent of the Steward, 107, 19.
Johnfton, 1, 17.—43, 29.—4¹, 16.—51, 11.—67, 36.—6, l. 31.—2, 75.—75, 86.—89, 24.—93, 278.—116, 55.
St Julufton, 51, 32.

Ioliffis, 19, 91.
Joy, 57, 39.
Ireland, Edward Bruce King of, 14, 114.
Irwine, 3, 1.—17, 54.—23, 5.—51, 36.—133, 24.—137, 6.—166, 18.
Irwine burrow, 14, 107.
Ifaac, 62, 42.
Ifles, Ifle, Ifla, Ylea, Yle, Yla, 26, 23.—30, 5.—35, 5.—48, 1, 5.—51, 21.
Juftice-Clerk, 85, 199.

K.

Karlo, 13, 85.
Keith, 2, 32. 33. 41.—11, 26.—16, 27.—19, 92.—23, 3¹, 4².—29, l. 7.—33, 34, 41.—37, 4.—42, 21¹.—49, 8.—50, 13.—5", 4² 8¹.—61, 3¹.—62, 38.—66, 1.—71, 8.—72, 27.—78, 117.—80, 137.—50.—55, 194.—106, 14.—115, 48.—116, 50.—117, 72, 73.—121, 71.—126, 14.—138, 30.—141, 53. 60. 63.—43, 9.—144, 16. 17. 19.—150, 1.—151, 13. 156, l. 22.—159, 2.—162, 10. 11. 17.—163, 19. 20.—164, 38.—166, 18.
Keiris, 50, 6.
Keloch, 93, 284.
Kelor, 67, 4².—75, 83.—79, 129.—24, 10.
Kelfo, 6, 51.
Kelfo Abb. 3, 3².—22, 45.—24, 15. 30, 5.—41, 14.—58, 1.—59, 17.—63, 1.—127, 26.
Kenelman clan, 57, 28.
Kennedy, 30, l. 6.—34, 11. 4².—43, 37.—51, 45.—69, l. 35.—72, 39.—75, 89.—79, 127.—93, 282.—94, 285.—115, 39.—122, 105.—130, 7. 134, 6.—135, 7. 8. l. 14.—149, 49. 50, 51.
Kerdale, 100, 1².
Kernock, 45, 24.
Kerr, 6, 51.—34, 18.—45, 21.—46, 51, 5.—48, 3¹.—79, 133.
Keffan, the clerk, 92, 275.
Kidd, 114, 25.
Killebrand, (probably for Gillebrand), 38, 31.
Kilvintoun, 45, 40.
Kilwinning Abb. 3, 19.—6, 40.—49, —75, 86.—140, 42.—144, 34.—145, 23.
Kinbuck, 30, 8.
Kinpefey, 24, 8². 9.
Kinghorne, 20, 113.—37, 8. 11.—40, 18.
Kingiffone, 147, 2.
Kinlofs Abb. 2, 27.—57, 2.—91, 270.
Kirnarde, 17, 45.—13. 117.—141, 56.—145, 10.—165, 3.
Kinneir, 113, 4.—122, 96.—128, 5.—157, 37.
Kinnellour, kirk of, 45, 25.
Kinninmonth, 13, 79.—19, 93.—157, 37.
Kinrofs, 91, 267.

INDEX TO THE RELIGIOUS HOUSES, PERSONS, &c. 175

Kirchalche, 156, 27.
Kirkaldie, 67, 9.—74, 71.—145, 20.
Kirkdolian, 14, 106. 108.
Kirknefs, 151, 7.
Kirkofwald, 47, 13.
Kirkpatrick, 12, 66. 67.—13, 76.—15, 1.—2°, 12. 13.—31, 29.—36, 20.—108, 23.—140, 18.—164, 46.
Knight, 17, 39.
Knock 12°, 14.
Knockdolian, 14, 112.—60, 27.
Kyldmethan, 118, 18.
Kyndclouch, 76, 90.—79, 125.—157. 37.

L.

Lacy, 14, 99.
Lady-Chapel, near Dunfermling, 38. 16. 20.
Lage, 50, 9.
Lamb, 124, 9.
Lambertoun, 5, 10.—81, 151.—144, 37.
Lambie, 37, 4¹.
Lanark, 83, 1⁻⁴.
Lanark community, 82, 170.
Lang, 49, 1³.
Langlands, 43, 45.—70, l. 13.—73, 55.
Lardener, 115, 41.
Latoren, 66, 22.
Lauchlanfon, 6, 31.—13, 95.—146, 44.
Lauder, 7, 55. 62. 68.— 8, 89.— 62, 21.—61, 49.—67, 5.—74, 67.—93, 277. 278. 279. 280. 281.—98, 329. —100, 1³.—103, 9.—114, 4. 5. 6. 7. 8, 11. 29.—122, 104.—124, 8.— 144, 21.—146, 32.— 156, l. 22.— 162, 12.—164, 42.—166, 13.
Laundelys, 50, 20.—72, 38.—127, 22. 23.—143, 13.—151, 10.
St Laurence Altar, 132, 5.
Laverock, 140, 35.
Leane, 46, 52.
Leafk, 37, 18.—151, 7.
Lcche, 82, 169.
Leckie, 142, 73.—163, 30. 31.
Leifing, 126, 14.
Leith, 52, 54.—151, 7.
Lennox, 117, 64.
Lennox, Earl of, 8, 90.—17, 41.—30, 11.—58, 12.—91, 275.—15°, 45.— 163, 30.
Leny, 158, 4⁰.
St Leonard's, near Edinburgh, 143, 4.
Leprevick, 64, 1°.—77, 108.
Lefmachutis, (Lefmahagow), 8, 75.— 27, 5.—41, 15.—68, 3.—145, 22.
Leflie, 35, 19.—43, 30.—46, 47.—52, 14.—53, 20.—65, 15 16.—66, 7.— 67, l. 21.—74, 75.—80, 140.— 81, 151. 162.—84, 184.—86, 204.—87. 210.—88, 231.—89, 242. 243.—90. 258.—108, 30.—114, 19. 26.—120, 66.—122, 125.—127, 17.—129, 34 132, 4.—139, 13.—140, 43.—146, 29.—149, 53.—157, 37.—159, 9.— 160, 10.

Leftalrik, 80, 139.
Letham, 61, 7.—149, 47.
Libbertoun, 63, 48.
Lichtoun, 76, 90.—100, 1³.—140, 28. 152, 17.—163, 18.
Liddell, 37, 15.—45, 21.— 58, 5¹.— 61, 2.—162, 12.
Ligertwood, 32, 11.
Lilly, 54, 6.
Limpetlaw, 12, 56.
Lincoln, the Bifhop of, 101, 9.—101, 11².
Lindores Abb. 4, 37.—20, 6.—46, 5°.— 62, 27.—64, 1. 3. 10. 18.—68, 4.— 76, 92. 94.—77, 121.—157, 35.
Lipp, 32, 2.
Lithgow, 34, 7.—118, 8.
Little, 81, 156.
Livingftoun, 38, 25. 38.—41, 2.—42. 5.—43, 41.—55, 2.—69, l. 10.— 71, 12.— 75, 87.—82, 170.— 92, 275.—108, 23. 25.—140, 24.—158, 53.
Locher, 25, 62.
Lochmalony, 157, 37.
Lockhart, 140, 36, 37.—142, 75.
Logan, 15, 1³.—27, 8.
Logie, Margaret, Queen of Scots, 100, 4. 76.—163, 23.
Logie, 43, 22.—67, 3³.—72, 28.—74, 76.—163, 23.
London, de, 22, 2.—80, 137.
Londrys, 123, 118.
Loocky, 20, 10.
Loon, 60, 13.—63, 54.—64, 18.—77, 101.
Lorain, 59, 2.—85, 197.—115, 36.
Lorn, 30, 2.— 35, 2.— 51, 27.— 80, 141.
Lovel, 5, 24.— 39, l.—47, 17. 24.— 156, 27.
Luband, 7, 62. 63. 64. 66.—10, 22.
Lugtown, 40, 14.
Lumby, 83, 174.
Lunifden, 39, 6.—58, 7².
Lundie, 60, 24.—61, 7.—67, 7³.— 125, 3.
Lufs, 67, 7.—83, 182.
Lyell, 118, 17.—139, 16.—157, 37.— 2³.—149, 38.
Lyle, 2, 51. 52. 54.—38, 14. 23.—46, 42.—79, 134.
Lyndefay, 2, 28.— 5, 16.—6, 34.— 8. 89.—10, 16.—11, 36.—12, 65. 74.—14, 101.—15, 7.—2°, 8.—21. 26. 38.—24, 15.—2¹, 21.—27, 10. —30, 18.—41, 15.—36, 29.—40. 32.—44, 54.—46, 45.—49, l. 2. 52, 7. 13.—53, 30.—58, 8.—61, 1². —62, 17, 18.—63, 44.—64, 5, l. 7. 14.—66, 4°.—73, 57.—74, 77.— 5, 86.—76, 94.—79, 13°.— 8¹. 137.—81, 151. 152.—84, 184. 185 —85, 193.—86, 213.—87, 219 216. —89, 241.—90, 258.—91, 2⁻ 7.— 96, 307.—97, 318. 321 322. 324.— 98, 331.—108, 23.—114, 19. 23. 24.

27.—115, 44.— 116, 54. 62.— 117, 70. 71. 75.—119, 21. 35.—120. 55, 57. 62. 63. 66.—121, 75, 81.—122, 93.—125, 33. l.—126, 10.—12°, 5. 20. 21.—128, 15.—129, 24. 30. 31. 34.— 130, 5.—131, 22. 23. 25.— 132, 11, 12.—131, 13. 14. 34.— 39, 2. 6. 11.—141, 49.—142, 79.— 43, 6.—144, 16 17. 19. 22. 38.—145, 19.—150, 2.—152, 21.—15°, 32.— 159, 2³. 5. 7.—161, 4. 5. 6. 7.— 162, 8. 9.—163, 30.—166, 13. 15. 16, 17.
Lynlithgow burrow, 153, 26.
Lyon, 67, 3³.—96, 315.—119, 20.— 121, 86. 87.—123, 124.—124, 18. 22.—125, 28.—128 12.— 129, 18. 131, 27.—133, 31. 37.— 147, 8.— 156, 27.
Lythcu, 118, 8.

M.

M'Beth, 88, 237.
M'Cay, 25, 2.
M'Cowrache, 61, 8.
M'Culloch, 47, 19.
M'Dowal, 77, 110.—124, 6.—164, 36. —166, 4.
M'Dowgall, 30, 13.—31, 41.—32, 20. 21.—55, 38.— 36, 42.—40, 33.— 65, 21.—115, 32. 33.—148, 27.
M'Farlane, 25, 1.
M'Gillelan, 135, 13.
M'Gillen, 56, 10.
M'Guffock, 25, 9.—66, 19.—89, 246.
M'Horrard, 25, 7.
M'Kan, 25, 8.
M'Kelly, 90, 250.—114, 15.—115, 40. 118, 10.— 2¹, 58.—129, 26.
M'Kennedy, 57, 29.
M'Kynbethy, 135, 7.
M'Lauchlan, 26, 25.
M'Lellan, 33, 36.
M'Leod, 4⁸, 4. 6.— 99, l. 8. l. 13.— 100, 2³ 2¹.
M'Nable, 24, 6¹.
M'Nauchtan, 4⁸, 5.—99, l. 10.— 100, 2¹.—149, 38.
M'Nawych, 75, 86.
M'Nayre, 53, 21.—90, 259.
M'Nenache, 26, 26.
M'Neill, 29, 19.
M'Thorald, 14, 116.
M'Tyre, 98, 32³.—114, 10.
M'Wrenan, 117, 69.
Maceoun, 5, 15.
Macymar, 25, 2.
Magnus IV. King of Norway, 101, 7.
Mair, 31, 26.— 2, 63.
Maitland, 31, 39.—32, 45.—36, 40.— 47.—40. 72.—5°, 4¹.—125. —85, 197.—121, 83.— 14, l. 10.— 159, 31.— 61, 2.—163, 28.—164, 4⁰.
Maklare, 144, 18.
Malcolm III. King of Scots, 82, 169, —155, l. 42.

INDEX TO THE RELIGIOUS HOUSES, PERSONS, &c.

Malco'm IV. King of Scots, 24, 12.—
 15⁶, l. 5.
Malcolm, 51, 41.
Malcolm's fon, 19, 25, 26.
Malherbe, 21, 19.
Maſkarſtoun, 18, 24.
Maleticino, 15⁶, l. 8.
Man, 161, 4. 5. 6. 7.—162, 8. 9.
Maneris, 19, 101. 102.
Mann, the Biſhop of, 116, 60.
Mann, the Prior of, 62, 30.
March, the Earl of, 11, 38.—72, 3.—
 38, 19.—47, 12.—42, 19. 20. 21.
 19².—43, 42. 46.—55, 1.—65, 17.
 —71, 7.—72, 25.—72, 52. 53. 56.
 —74, 63.—76, 91.—79, 125. 134.
 135.—80, 150.—81, 152. 155.—82,
 160.—85, 165.—89, 244.—9⁰, 25.
 258.—92, 276.—93, 277.—96, 309.
 —101, 7.—108, 23. 25. 30.—109,
 36.—115, 46.—120, 54.—121, 72.
 —122, 92. 107.—126, 9. 14.—129,
 23 —130, 3.—131, 31.—136, 19.—
 1.0, 23.—144, 20.—147, 5.—149,
 47.—151, 5.—155, l. 36. l. 37.—164,
 4².—166, 13.
St Margaret Queen of Scots, 126, 14.
Margaret Logie Queen of Scots, 76, 99
 —100, 4.
Marr, 20, 14.—61, 2.
Marr, Earl of, 25, 5.—28, 17.—31,
 34.—36, 23.—42, 20².—43, 29. 33.
 —44, 52.—46, 83.—61, 2. 13.—
 62, 41.—64, 4. 5.—72, 26. 35. 37
 —73, 57.—76, 95. 96.—80, 149.—
 92, 276.—101, 7.—121, 82. 83. 91.
 —122, 92. 107.—127, 15.—138, 2.
 —138, 19.—139, 7.—141, 53.—142,
 82. 84.—147, 50. 7. 13.—148, 26.—
 149, 5⁶.—166, 11. 18.
Marſhall, 2. 39.—5, 11.—7, 60.—12,
 57.—24, 5. 6. 7².—27, 6².—28, 5,
 —29, 21.—36, 20.—54, 13.—59, 8.
 —6⁶, 4¹.—119, 31.—122, 103.—
 136, 7.
Marſhall of Scotland. *See Keith.*
Martenſon, 57. 29.
Martin, 31, 22.—36, 33.
Mathieſon, 32, 22.—86, 207.
Maule, 37, 6.—39, 52.—51, 42.—59,
 14.—61, 14.—135, 7.—137, 8.—
 149, 39.
Maxwell, 11, 42. 53.—12, 75.—15, 13
 —28, 107.—31, 3.—36, 11.—37, 12.
 —38, 18.—39, 2.—49, 1.—51, 23.—
 56, 7.—65, 23.—66, 5.—75, 86.—
 82, 156.—9⁶, 312.—114, 23. 24.—
 115, 42. 44.—119, 21.—120, 53.—
 129, 22.—131, 19.—138, 2.—140,
 25.—144, 84. 40.—164, 40.
Meek, 61, 9.
Megill, 124, 5.—128, 9.—133, 28.—
 142, 83.
Lichrum, 17, 40.—32, 1.—3⁰, 12.—
 42, 18.—47, 9.—56, 5.—67, 12.—
 74, 74.—78, 119.—119, 23.—127,
 26.—127, 11.

Melroſs Abb. 3, 2². 4¹. 5. 6. 7. 8. 9.
 —5, 19.—22, 46.—55, 8.—88, 235.
 —127, 26.—145, 7. 8.—154, 24.
M.lville, 8, 87.—24, 9.—25, 4.—34,
 9¹—78, 112. 116.—81, 160.—126,
 32.—141, 46.—142, 77.—144, 38.
 —146, 33.—161, 2.
Menteith, 11, 2).—14, 121.—15, 6.
 18.—16, 8. 18.—17, 56.—18, 63.
 69.—19, 111.—20, 11. 16.—21, 17.
 —23, 6. 4¹.—24, 7.—30, 12.—35,
 12¹.—40, 1.—53, 18.—67, 2¹.—
 75, 80. 81. 86.—85, 194.—90, 256.
 —114, 18.—126, 14.—134, 3.—
 135, 8.
Menteith, Earl of, 60, 13.—113, 3.—
 115, 31.—118, 7. 16.—122, 92. 96.
 —127, 15.—128, 4.—132, 32.—
 144, 3.—151, 3. 5. 9.—156, l. 36.
 158, 52.
Menzies, 13, 82.—16, 25.—19, 88. 98.
 99.—26, 24.—32, 7.—39, 51.—51.
 46.—53, 1.—54, 1 5.—57, 23.—59,
 9.—62, 40.—68, 1².—141, 66.
Mercer, 15, 22.—16, 21.—63, 43.—
 66, 5¹.—74, 78.—120, 52.—122,
 110.—112, 7.—129, 21.—140, 38.
Merley, 81, 155.—156, l. 10.
Meyners, Meygneris, 6, 32.—19, 101.
 102.—77, 109.—101, 7.—115, 30.
 31.—118, 7.—119, 30.—122, 106.
 —156, l. 22.
De Sancto Michaeli, 164, 34.
Michael's fon, (perhaps Mitchelſon), 32,
 23.
Millar, 47, 22.
Milliken, 31, 24.—36, 35.—44, 53.—
 70, 5.
Mindrome, 5, 14.
Moffat, 12, 71.—21, 36. 37.—44, 13.
 —47, 27.—64, 16.—77, 106.—127,
 19.
Moncur, 48, 1².—78, 122.
Monda villa, 25, 4.
Monetar, 139, 12.
Monfod, 7, 58.—11, 43.—24, 10. 11.
 —66, 2². 3¹.—73, 44.—121, 88.
Mongail, 30, 9.—35, 9.—51, 4.
Monimail, 45, 19.—46, 8.
Monro, 2, 55.
Montacute, 81, 151.—126, 14.
Monte-alto, (probably *Mowat*), 2, 31.
 —17, 43.—28, 9¹.—78, 116.—122,
 108.—123, 114. 115. 116.—125, 3.
 —166, 8.
Monte-fixo, (Muſchet), 19, 96.—59, 1.
 61, 3.
Montfort, 83, 172.
Montgomery, 14, 115.—43, 37.—72,
 59.
Monypenny, 58, 11¹.—59, 13. 14.—
 61, 12.—134, 5.—141, 60.—166,
 11.—167, 23.
Moram, 125, 29.
Morath's fon, 8, 83.
More, 4, l. 38.—6, 46. 51.—11, 36.—
 31, 44.—40, 13.—43, 41.—51, 26.

35.—53, 6.—57, 31.—60, 30.—64,
 15.—67, 12.—69, l. 38.—73, 40.—
 74, 74.—77, 105.—118, 10.—120,
 49.—125, 29.—129, 16.—133, 35.
 —138, 25.—139, 4.—143, 5.—145,
 6.—151, 4.—152, 18.
Mortimer, 33, 38.—45, 35.—67, 1².
 2¹.—68, 15. 16.—75, 80. 81.—77,
 100.—161, 4. 5. 6. 7.—162, 8. 9.
Morthingtoun, 9, 6.—11, 39.
Mortoun, 94, 296.—95, 298.
Morville, 24, 12. 15.
Moſſi, 29, l. 19.
Mowat, (See *Monte-alto*), 54, 12.—57,
 33.—124, 15.—139, 5.—146, 31.—
 148, 14.
Mowbray, 1, 6.—2, 30.—4, 27. 29.—
 5, 11.—10, 13. 14.—11, 29.—12,
 65.—19, 107.—20, 115. 5. 8.—21,
 17. 22.—22, 52.—40, 33.—41, 37.
 —46, 3.—48, 32.—50, 16.—50, 13.
 —63, 54.—64, 18.—77, 101.—100,
 1².—119, 35.—146, 45.
Moygne, 50, 13.—51, 38.—58, 4.—
 67, 6².—76, 95.—91, 272.—133,
 24.
Moyſes, 5. 9.
Muirhead, 148, 24.
Multra, 58, 6¹.
Multerer, 43, 14.—77, 104.
Muunterſcafduff, 57, 29.
Mur, (perhaps for *Mure* or *More*), 151, 4.
Murdiſone, 19, 87.—95, 299.
Murray, 7, 73.—11, 30.—14, 109.—
 22, 49.—23, 12.—27, 2.—28, 3.
 11².—29, l. 17. l. 24.—31, 30.—33,
 29.—34, 14.—36, 21.—37, 10. 13.
 14. 15. 16.—38, 16. 20. 40.—39, 41.
 —40, 20.—42, 17.—43, 23.—45, 17.
 34.—47, 2. 3. 4.—52, 5. 1. 55.—54, 3.
 4. 7².—56, 1. 11. 19.—60, 14.—61,
 11.—62, 24. 38.—65, 1.—65, 3.—
 69, l. 28.—72, 29.—75, 86. 87.—76,
 90.—79, 129.—87, 228.—96, 305.—
 106, 14.—108, 23. 25.—117, 74.—
 118, 11.—122, 111.—124, 12.—126,
 14.—142, 40.—147, 1.—151, 6. 8.—
 152, 17.—156, 27.
Murray, the Biſhop of, 100, 1³.—101,
 7.—156, l. 19.
Murray, the Earl of, 4, 33.—9, l. 3.
 5.—11, 42.—12, 65.—15, 5.—20,
 15.—25, 21.—26, 22.—28, 9². 10³.
 39, 45.—42, 17.—45, 33.—54, 12².
 —57, 30.—67, 1.—71, 7.—72, 23.
 25.—73, 52. 53, 56.—74, 63.—76,
 91.—79, 125. 134. 135.—80, 150.—
 81, 152.—82, 169.—85, 194.—88,
 235.—90, 255.—101, 7.—106, 14.
 —108, 30.—116, 60.—121, 72.—
 122, 92. 107.—124, 2.—126, 14.—
 127, 26.—133, 14. 15.—136, 19.—
 142, 88.—156, l. 20.
De Muſchamis, 156, l. 10.
Muſchet, (*Monte-fixo*), 19, 96.—59, 1.
 —61, 3.
Muſco-campo, 11, 38.

INDEX TO THE RELIGIOUS HOUSES, PERSONS, &c. 177

N.

Napier, 47, 27.—56, 2.—61, 3.—119, 43.—137, 9.—151, 5.—161, 32.
Neilfon, 5, 18.—14, 119.—25, 3. 10.—40, 26.
Nevil, 107, 19.
Newbattle Abb. 1, 9.—3, 16. 17. 18.—5, 25.—7, 70.—21, 28.—31, 32. 38.—33, l. 39.—36, 23. 39.—55, 5.—68, 3¹.—81. 156.—8³, 173. 179. 182.—4, 184.—85, 193.
Newbigging, 55, 6.—80, 147.—83, 1⁴.
Newtoun, 120, 44.
Niddric, 43, 32.—70, l. 7.—73, 47.—143, 2.—148, 33.
Nifbet, 22, 1.—42, 17.—46, 54.—62, 2.—76, 91.—72, 108.—79, 135.—84, 184.—85, 193.—136, 19.—141, 49. 59.—156, l. 13.
Norie, 31, 17.—86, 205.
Norman, the Sheriff, tempore Davidis regis 1ⁱ, 125, 14.
Northinghame, 17, 35.
Northingtoun, 18, 71.
Northumberland, Henry Earl of, 22, 2.
Nortoun, 93, 281.
Norwich, Bifhop of, 101, 9.—103, 11².

O.

Ochterlowny, 137, 8.—150, 2.
Oge, 26, 27.
Oggu Leifing, 126, 14.
Ogilvie, 1, 5.—132, 7.—141, 54. 62.—142, 68. 82.—143, 91. 92. 94.—149, 41, 42.—150, 61. 2.—161, 3.—162, 8. 9.—165, 2.—167, 20.
Ogftoun, 138, 22.—143, 92.
Oliphant, 7, 57.—18, 72.—24, 15.—26, 28.—28, 9².—51, 23.—82, 166.
Ommid's Son, 17, 48.
Orfuird, 4, 31.—11, 43.
Orkney, the Bifhop of, 3. 2.
Orkney, the Earl of, 51, 34.—118, 27.—148, 30. 33.—151, 7.—163, 29. 166, 10. 13.
Ormyftoun, 122, 102.
Ofbert 67, 5¹.
Ovyot, 64, 20.—77, 109.

P.

Pagainfon, 39, 57.
Paganus de Braiofa, 155, l. 35.
Page, 1, 22.—67, 5.—74, 66.
Paifley Abb. 142, 80. 81.
Palmer, 132, 10.
Paneter, 163, 23.
Panillkyner, 44, 6.
Pankaitland, 7, 55. 68.
Papay, 151, 7.
Papedy, 34, 10².—81, 155.—156, l. 10.
Park, 137, 3.
Parker 80, 140.
Paterfon, (Patrick's fon, Peter's fon), 119, 42.—121, 76.

Patricius capitalis medicus, 18, 70.
Patrikius Comes, filius Waldevi Comitis, 155 l. 36.
St Patrick's chapel, 126, 11. 13.
Paxtoun, 11, 37.—22, 54.—119, 20.
Payinftoun, 121, 83.
Peebles, 25, 21.—39, 44.—114, 16.—139, 10.
Peebles burrow. 15, 4.—133, 25.
Penefax, 12, 67.
Penny, 119, 22.
Pennycuick, 120, 67.—129, 35.
Percy, 5, 17.—9. 3.—18, 75.—54, 2.—101, 9.—103, 11².—104, 11¹. 12.—107, 19.—108, 30.—109, 36.—126, 10.—138, 19.
Pertchay, 5, 17.
Perth burrow, 77, 100.
Peter, 18, 70.—91, 155.
Pether, 81, 155.
Pettinweem, 144, 32.
Pigot, 32, 9. 10.—40, 15.
Pilch, 19, 19.
Pitcairn, 35, 22.—86, 205.
Pitfcottie, 43, 38.—70, l. 10.—73, 52.—74, 61.
Pittendreich, 143, 21.
Pittillock, 38, 25.—56, 6. 15.—59, 5.—62, 23.
Plegmann, 50, 9.
Polworth, 76, 91.—119, 38.
Pope Boniface VIII. 100, 3.
Pope Innocent VI. 108, 25¹.
Portecunill, 6, 51.
Porter, 24, 16.—52, 15.—87, 221.—90. 253.—135, 11.—147, 12.
Poft. 163, 32.
Preaching Friars, 80, 149.—85, 194.
De Prebenda, 156, l. 8.
Prendergaift, 21, 19.—39, 56.—156, l. 13.
Prefton, 30, 8.—35, 8.—40, 12.—41, 11.—79, 135.—82, 128.—84, 184.—85, 193.—114, 28.—120, 65.—122, 10².—126, 10.—129, 33.—146, 38.—143, 36.—149, 37.—162, 12.—166, 10.
Pringle, 5, 7.—55, 7.—56, 6.—59, 5.—61, 23.—66, 1.—69, l. 23.
Punkyne, 151, 7.
Purvoyis, 60, 20.
Pyugil, 72, 27.—8, 117.—83, 175.—125, 28.—128, 1.

Q.

Quarentaly, 8, 26.—27, 6.
Queens of Scots 57 20.—72, 28.—76, 99.—98, 328.—100, 4.—122, 97.—132, 5.—158, 56.—
Quhyt, 14, 117.
Quincy, 79, 137.

R.

Ramorgny, 137, 5.—162, 14.
Ramfay, 1, 12.—32, 8. 12.—33, 35.—35, 23.—36, 1. 3.—38, 27. 34. 35. 36.—

42, 6.—44, 1.—45, 22.—54, 5.—56, 17.—58, 12².—59, 8.—65, 11.—69, l. 11.—71, 13.—76, 90. 91.—78, 116. 118, 122.—80, 140.—82, 169.—86, 207.—88, 238.—108, 23.—118, 17.—125, 28.—134, 41.—143, 10.—146, 33.—157, 37.—162, 13.
Randaliltown, 34, 8.—78, 124.
Ranulph, 9, 1, 2, 3, 4, 5, 6, 7, 8, 9.—11, 55.—23, 2.—25, 21.—26, 22.—28, 9².—39, 45.—42, 17.—45, 33.—54, 12².—57, 30.—72, 23.—85, 194.—88, 235.—106, 14.—116, 60.—126, 14.—155, 8.—156, L 20.
Rate, 52, 12.—54, 9.—65, 10.—87, 218.—88, 237.—91, 287. 288.—96, 314.—97, 322.—98, 331.—112. 7.—114, 13.—122, 97.—124, 4.—125, 1.—128, 8.—130, 9. 10.—131, 25. 28.—134, 5
Re.lheuche, 11, 26.—35, 17³.
Regifter, the Clerk of, 61, 31.—67, 3.—68, 1¹.
Reid, 42, 15.—58, 8.—59, l. 18.—71, 21.—85, 1²3.—117, 69.—132, 10.—151, 5.
Reiltriil, 56, 8.
Reidpath, 123, 112.
Reilwall, 50, 22.
Reitenret Abb. 4, 42. 43.—39, 30.—41, 4.—57, 38.—55, 10.—78, 118.
Retire, 121, 75.—124, 5.
Reyntoun, 60, 17.
Richard I. King of England, 104, 13
Richardfon, 8, 78.—7, 94.
Kicklingtoun, 34, 12.—43, 45.—6³, 2.—73, 5⁰.—74, 64.—76, 91.—82, 169.—84, 184.—85, 193.—136, 19.
Rici, 12, 56.
Riddell, 43, 26.—50, 17.—69, l. 29.—72, 12.—79, 137.—133, 22.
Robardftoun, 77, 108.
Robbiflaw, *brdnes de*, 71, 11.
Robert I. King of Scots, 23, 9.—101, 7.—106, 14.
Robert II. King of Scots, 100, 4.
Roberton, 126, 8.
Robertfon, 31, 25.—35, 17¹.—92, 275.
Roche, 19, 108.
Rogerfon, 7, 73.
Roll, 54, 10.
Rollandus Senefcallus, 156, l. 12.
Rollo, 30, 15.—31, 31.—36, 16².—36, 22.—118, 8.—121, 79.—162, 12.
Rolpot, 32, 11.
Ronfoune, Roderickfon, Rorifon, 48, 2. 3.—97, 316.—99, l. 5. l. 6.—100, 1³, 2.—131, 1⁷.
Rofeins, 46, 48.
Rofs, 1, 11.—2, 44. 45. 49. 50. 56. 58. 59. 60.—3, 4.—5, 4³.—26, 33.—28, 3.—35, 21.—39, 4.—42, 20.—51, 44.—52, 50.—56, 19.—58, 12.—60, 18. 26.—69, 6. l. 21.—72, 16.—73, 40.—81, 162.—86, 202, 205.—91,

Y y

INDEX TO THE RELIGIOUS HOUSES, PERSONS, &c.

273.—9[R], 327.—113, 6.—116, 55.—
118, 18.—119, 20. 40. 41.—127, 64.
—122, 99. 111.—124, 20, 21. 22.
25. 26.—125, 27.—126, 8.—128, 7.
12.—129, 31.—133, 31.—143, 99. 3.
—14", 6.
Rofs, the Bifhop of, 98. 327.—100, 1¹.
—101, ".
Rofs, the Earl of, 7, 44.—15, 17.—16,
4. 5. 7.—28, 11².—20, 1³.—45, 27.
—51. 34.—52, 9.—53, 2.—58, 11.
—62, 3".—86, 205. 5.—20, 258.
—91, 2⁷⁴.—98, 327.—10. 1, 5.—
100, 1³.—101, 7.—103, 9.—114, 10.
—120, 64.—124, 2". 21. 25. 26.—
125, 27.—129, 32.—146, 29.—149,
53.—159, 9.—160, 10.
Roffie, 18. 84.—141. 55.
Roffine, 7, 70.
Rothfay, the Duke of, 104, 12².—146,
42.—162, 13.
Roucaftle, 26, 13.
Rouk, 141, 45.
Roull, 51, 39.
Rouloch (fee Rollo), 30, 15.—31, 31.
—15, 16¹.—36, 22.
Rowlin, 39, 55.
Roxburgh, 87, 227.
Ruffell, 5, 26.—44, 3.
Rutherfoord, 11, 52.—122, 107.—12".
23.
Ruthven, 119, 22.—137, 16.—144, 24.
—163, 24.
Rynd, 66, 6.—81, 161.

S.

Salter, 58, 6.
Sanɛlu Michaelε, 78, 119.
Sandilands, 32, 16.—38, 38. 39.—11⁶
37.—132, 9.—139, 40. 7.—144, 21.
Sandocks, 46, 1.
Sanquhar, 164, 34.
Saryn, 42, 1.
Saulfeat Abb. 41, 5.
Scampe, 131, 26.
Scarlat, 19, 100.—122, 111.—125, 28.
Schaklok, 83, 172.
Schiltown, 26, 17.
Scoon Abb. 4, 40. 41.—37, 19. 20.—
98, 326.—15, 43.—144, 26.—152,
17.
Scott, 38, 26.—56, 15.—62, 32.—142,
75.—159, 1.—166, 7.
Scrimgeour, 20, 115.—22, 52.—113, 5
—115, 34.—122, 100.—128, 6.—
133, 19.—151. 14.—152, 17.
Scroupe, Scrop, 97, 325.—101, 9.—
103, 11¹.
Seatoun, ", 56.—10, 19¹. 20¹. 21². 22¹.
23¹.—1, 25, 3⁸.—1, 89.—15, 8.—
16, 2.—11, 41. 42.—22, 43. 44. 4⁸.
60.—27, 1². 2². 3². 4². 5.—57, 3.—
61. 39.—91, 271.—114. 9.—121, 75.
83.—126, 14.—134, 6.—135, 8.—
143, 7.—156, l. 22.—163, 25. 27.
32.
Selkirk, 93, 283.—114, 2.

Sempill, 7, 52. 69.—38, 15.—116, 63.
—145, 5.
Seres, 164, 43.
Shaw, 47, 13.
Sibbald, 76, 90.—127, 24.—139, 6.—
159, 1¹.
de Sigillo, 156, l. 8.
Silver, 33, 40.—67, 7².—87, 224.
Simpfon, 145, 24.
Sinclair, 7, 67.—12. 57.—21, 40.—25.
20. 21.—31, 35.—36, 26.—42, 9.—
43, 40.—58, 10. 11.—62, 25, 3".—
66, 9.—71, 15.—73, 51.—76, 9".—
79, 135.—82, 164.—84, 184.—85,
193. 194.—91, 273. 274.—119, 11.
—129, 17.—131, 36.—138, 2".—
144, 20.—151, 6. 7.—163, 29.—166,
l0. 13.
Sircatho, 51, 30.
Siward, 20, 117.—25, 10⁸.—28, 10³.
—51, 23.
Skirling, Dominus de, 29, l. 25.
Skynnech, 80, 40.
Slingifbie, 55, 8.—83, 176.
Small, 81, 15. 6.
Smerles, 45, 19.—134, 5.
Sodrighay, (perhaps for Fodrighay), 36,
18.
Somer, 67, 8.—74, 70.
Somerlede, Somerledy, 40, 25. 27.—
47, 14. 20.—51, 29.—54, 14.—72,
39.
Somerville, 24, 15.—33, 33.—97, 320.
—118, 8.—131, 21.—15¹, 11.
Souche of Afheby, 101, 9.—103, 11⁸.
104, 11². 12.
Soullis, 3, 5. 21.—5, 28. 29.—6, 33.
—7, 91.—10, 13. 19.—11, 29.—12,
54.—15, 2.—20, 7.—21, 17. 22.—
22, 47.—39, 3.
Spalding, 149. 43.—152, 17.
pens, 54, 7.—57, 36.—58, 9¹.—60,
23.—64, 9.—150, 2.—159, 5.—163,
2".
Spittell, 34, 4.—78, 122.—148, 16.—
159, 6.
Spot, 147, 10.
Spottifwoode, 84, 184.—85, 193.
Spring, 5, 43.—66, 19.—57, 6.—69,
l. 7.—71, 8.—89, 246.
Sprouttoun, 12, 58.
Sirane, 141, 46.
Starheved, 63, 46.
Stewart (Seneſcallus), 1, 8. 10. 19.—4,
l. 38.—6, 32. 39. 41.—7, 54. 63. 64.
66.—9, 10. 11.—10, 13. 14.—
13, 82. 83. 94.—21, 22. 23. 31. 32.
—16, 32.—28, 1.—33, 24.—37, 5¹.
8¹.—40, 2.—42, 17.—44, 23. 27.
—44, 5¹.—45, 33. 35. 39. 41.—46,
49.—47, 11.—48, 19.—49, 2¹. 7. 5².
—51, 17. 27. 1.—55, 17.—58, 5¹.—
59, 15.—60, 30.—61, 11.—68, l. 22.
—69, l. 30.—71, 8.—72, 29. 33.
—73, 42.—4, 58.—75, 86. 87.—
76, 91.—77, 100. 108.—79, 125.
134. 135.—80, 137. 140. 150.—81, 1

152.—82, 165. 167. 168.—93, 177.
178.—84, 184. 185.—88, 235.—90,
255. 268.—91, 264.—92, 276.—93,
277.—94, 286. 207. 294.—95, 303.
304.—99, 310. 311.—98, 327.—107,
19.—108, 27.—113, 7.—114, 8. 20.
—115. 30. 42.—116, 58. 59. 60.—
117, 64.—118, l. 2. 3. 4. 12.—120,
45. 46. 59. 60.—121, 68.—122, 97.
107. 111.—123, 112. 114. 119. 120.
121. 122. 123.—124, 13. 14. 15. 20.
21. 25.—125, 27. 29.—126, 7. 14.—
127, 15. 21. 26.—128, 8.—129, 22.
27. 28.—130, 4. 8. 131, 15. 16.—
132, 3.—133, 22. 23.—134, 6.—
135, 8. 9. 13. 17.—138, 31. 18.—
139, 39. 8.—140, 19. 29. 33. 4.—
141, 5.—142, 71. 75.—143, 9. 14.—
145, 3. 11. 26.—146, 28. 35. 4.—
147, 7.—149, 50. 52. 57.—50, 60.
—151, 3. 5. 8.—154, 25.—156, l. 12.
—157, 33.—158, 41. 42. 45. 51.—
160, 9. 10.—61, 1.—162, 13. 163,
17. 19. 20.—164, 37, 40.—166, 14.
—167, 24. 25. 26. 27. 28.
Stirk, 157, 37.
Stirling. 19. 97.—30, 12.—37, 2.—38,
28.—45, 26.—61, 16.—68, 9.—77,
107.—82, 166.—159, 6.—165, 2.
Stirling Burrow, 62, 34.
Stowpie, 46, 50.
Strabogie, 17, 41.—32, 18.—33, 42.—
118, 11.
Strawbrock, 1, 21.—2, 34.—45, 20.
Straithbocis, 1, 21.
Strang, 117, 68.
Strathachine, 34, 10.—17, 6.—48, 34.
—4, 6. 8.—51, 37.—78, 116.—79,
126.—121. 78.—24, 19.—149, 39.
40.—163, 18.—166, 5.
Strathawrie, 46, 7.
Strathenrie, 25, 4¹.
Stratherne, 19, 103.—60, 21.
Stratherne, the Earl of, 11, 38.—19,
69.—33, 29.—38, 40.—39, 41.—41,
23.—44, 55.—45, 39.—46, 49.—51,
21.—54.—53, 17. 27.—56, l. 11.—
71, 8.—72, 29.—3, 42.—74, 54.—
75, 87.—79, 125. 134. 135.—80, 150.
—81, 152.—82, 167. 168.—84, 184.
185.—90, 255. 258.—91, 264.—92,
276.—93, 277.—94, 286. 293. 294.
—9¹, 303. 304.—96, 310.—98, 328.
—108, 27.—114, 14.—120, 59. 60.—
121, 79.—122, 107. 111.—129, 22.
2". 28.—130, 4.—131, 15. 16.—149,
57.—166, 15.
Strathy, 121, 84.
Stratoun, 35, 18.—78, 116.—80, 138.
130, 48.—145, 13.—149, 54.
Struther, 137, 18.
Suche, Souche, 5, 18.—6, 41. 50.—7,
51. 56. 58.—10, 22¹.—13, 9.—12,
44.—27, 1³.—93, 278.—101, 9.—
1, 3. 11².—104, 11². 12.
Suppyld, 34, 6⁵.

INDEX TO THE RELIGIOUS HOUSES, PERSONS, &c. 179

Sutherland, 43. 30.—69, l. 32.—72. 36.—137, 2.
Sutherland, the Earl of, 32, 5. 13.—33, 49.—39, 42.—43, 36 —49, l. 26.—63, 53.—65, 15.—66, 2—72. 36. —81, 157.—89, 247.—108, 23. 25.
Swyntoun, 120, 44.—121, 92.—129, 19.—131, 38.—151, 12.—156, l. 13.
Symondstown, 121, 83.

T.
Tabert, 27, 5¹.
Tait, 144, 31.
Tarale, 98, 327.
Tay, 119, 34.
Taylor, 7, 71.—58, 8.—87, 226.—144, 25.
Telch, 28, 17.
Tennand, 6c, 25.
Terry, 47, c.
Thorntown, 1, 13.
Tollare, 157, 29.
Torholtoun, 93, 284.
Tore, Torrie, 21, 23, 24.—35, 34, 35.
Torfopy, 81, 151.
Torthurald, 6, 30.—67, 12.—74, 73.
Toulch, 50, 12.
Towers, 27, 2¹.—39, 9.—48, 30. 31.—51, 35.—62, 33.—121, 62.—142, 89. 143, 96.—149, 55.
Trapont, 77, 110.
Traquair, 1, 6.
Trollop, 19, 104.
Troupe, 40, 24.
Trymblay, 76, 90.
Tullach 1 8, 15.—125, 2.—138, 32. —146, 3:.—147, 8.
Tungland Abb. 3. 14.—31, 25.—36, 36.
Turing, 45, 10.
Turnberry, 47, 15.—72, 39.
Turnbull, 5, 22.—33, 48.—57, 40.—57, 32.—65, 21.—82, 167.—127, 23. 147, 2. 3.—155, 1.
Tweedy, 27, 10—29, l. 25.—43, 28. 59 19.—72, 34
Twynefhiels, 141, 49.
Twynham, 166, 14.
Tynnynghame, 101, 4.

U.
Ulmstoun, 54, 10.
Umphraville, 8, 88.—18, 75.—24, 15.
Uiquhart, 35, 20. 21.—45, 27.—36, 204. 205.—110, 1³.
Urrye, 67, 5¹.—68, 9.
Urwell, 41, 9.—42, 17².—50, 19.—

54, 12¹.—68, 11,—69, l. 20.—72, 23.

V.
Valence, Walence, 158, 55.—161, 13.
Vall, 71, 12.
Vallibus, 71, 7.—72, 25.
Valoniis, 79, 125.—120, 58.—129, 26. 135, 16.—151, 8.
Vaus, 80, 142.
Vaux, 42, 19¹.—45, 37.—60, l. 5.—71 7. 12.—72, 25. 3.—80, 142.—108, 23.
de Veteri ponte, 27, 7².—76, 93.—79, 130, 137.
Vienne, 112, 71.
Vikers, 5. 14.

W.
Wain, 144, 18.—161, 2.
Wake, 9, 91—12, 64.
Waldefield, 98, 24.
Walderus, 81, 155.
Wallevus Comes, pater Patricii Comitis, 155, l. 37
Waleranus the chaplain, 126, 14.
de Waletoun, 156, l. 11.
Wallace, 23, 5³. 68.—25, 6².—27, 4¹. 3·, 4.—31, 46.—41, 11.—50, 1. 2.—53, 22. 23. 24. 30.—55, 16.—61, 4.—68, 8.—87, 218.—91, 260. 261. 262. 267.—94, 28¹.—97, 324.—115, 3·, 38.—130, 10.—131, 25.—138, 32.—142, 80—145, 4.—157, 38
de Wallibus, (see Vaux), 42, 19¹.—69, l. 5.—72, 33.
Wallingford, 11, 30.
Walter, a Cardinal, (probably Bishop of St Andrew's) 151 3.
Walter's-fon, Watson, 26, 30.—46, 42.—65, 5.—77, 108.—83, 174.—96, 1.—98, 232.—119, 3¹.—123, 120.—134, 12.—156, l. 14.—157, 31.—183, 28.—164, 48.—166, 9. 11.
Wan, 144, 18.—161, 2.
Wardlaw, 5, 17.—29, l. 19.—44, 48.—69, l. 37.—73, 41.—136, 19.—143, 98—146, 41.—156, l. 28.—158, 40.
Wardrobe, 04, 205.—131, 17.
Warrenne, the Earl of, 56, l. 11.
Warrick, the Earl of, 108, 30.
Watson, see Walter's-fon.
Wattyltoun, 164, 33.
Wauchop, 121, 80—147, 9.
Wawayne, 97, 325—131, 26.
Webster, 44, 10.
Weir, 15, 12.—75, 86.

Welham, 120, 55—121, 75.—129, 24.
Wellis, 127, 23.
Wemyss, 19, 110.—20, 112.—39, 43. 48.—46, 54.—108, 23.—135, 16.—138. 29. 37.—150, 58.—158, 53 54.
Welchell, 54, 15.
Westoun, 5, 15. 16.—39, 9.
Westray, 151, 7.
Wesage, 50, 9.
White, 147, 117.
Whitehorn Priory, 3, 21.—4, 22, 23. 24.—23, 2¹.—24, 8.
White Friars, 51, 31. 32.
Widow, 5¹, 33.
Wighame, 3⁴, 9³.
Wight, Wichtis, Wacht, Wych, 34, 5.—53, 31.—64, 4.—69, 4.—75, 62.—78, 123.—81, 159.—85, 201.—91, 268.
Wigtoun, the Earl of, 30, 10.—34, 3¹.—35, 15¹.—41, 10.—50, 2.—61, 31.—71, 12.—81, 154.—92, 2·5.—115, 39. 50.—117, 65.—134, 5.
William King of Scots, 22, 4.—23, 9.—24, 15.—49, 1¹.—55, l. 18. 9.—104, 13.—126, 14.—156, l. 5.
William, the fon of an Earl tempore Dav. reg. 1¹, 24, 15.
Williamfon, 21, 14.—119, 42.—128, 1.—135, 12—164, 41.
Williemus capellanus, 135, 7.
Wiltoun, 78, 116.
Winchburgh, 113, 2.—122, 95.—128, 148, 17. 18.
Winterwambe, 19, 90.
Wintoun, 8, 74.—27, 3.—124, 23.—148, 17. 18.
Wintoun, the Earl of, 20, 6.
Wifeman, 2, 57.—33, 42.
Wifheart, 27, 8⁸.—50, 16.
Withing, 156, 10.
Wodyfeld, 77, 106.
Wygmer, 84, 188.
Wygun, 61, 9.
Wyllie, 143, 13.
Wynd, 121, 71.
Wyton, 98, 327.

Y.
Yla, Yle, Yles de, 5, 7. 8.—26, 23.—28, 8.—41, 7.—44, 57.—74, 60.—80, 142.—97, 316.—99, l. 2. l. 11.—100, 1⁸. 2. 2¹.—107, 19.—108, 27.—118, 12. 13. 14.—131, 29.—136, 18. 19.
Young, 18, 68.—67, 7.—74, 69.—77, 102.—100, 1³.—116, 7.

INDEX to the Lands, Towns, &c. and to the Matters mentioned in the Charters.

A.

Aberbothry, 120, 55.—121, 75.—129, 24.—161, 6.
Aberbrothock Abbey, 97, 319.—158, 46.
Aberbrothock Burgh, 54, 8¹.
Aberbuthnot, 17, 56.—18, 60.—39, 42.—66, 8.—82, 163.
Abercorn, 11, 31.—42, 13.—67, 12.—74, 74.—129, 16.—133, 35.—145, 6.—150, 60.—159, 7.
Aberdeen, 15, 12. 21. 22.—16, 29.—32, 11.—34, 18.—38, 14. 23.—42, 1. 3.—44, 6.—46, 42. 55.—54, 8. 9¹.—57, 2.—62, 33.—64, 19.—69, 5. l. 7. l. 9.—71, 8. 10.—79, 133.—86, 203.—91, 2²0.—122, 9².—125, 2.—127, 20. 21.—128, 1.—132, 3.—132.—133, 16.—138, 55.—151, 3.—158, 51.
Aberdour, 4, 33.—9, 4.—34, 11².—81, 156.
Aberkerdour, 52, 14.—65, 16.—87, 230.—89, 243.—122, 66.—129, 34.
Aberlachwich, 23, 4¹.
Aberlemno, 18, 77. 80.—23, 11. 4¹.—24, 3¹.—34, 21.—78, 121.
Aberluthnot, 52, 14.—60, 15.—63, 53. 65, 15.—89, 242.—121, 78.—123, 125.
Abernethy, 33, 44.—61, 6.—134, 40. 125, 17.—129, 8.—146, 35.
Aboyne, (Obeyn), 2, 36.—163, 20.
Abtele, fishing of, 119, 2⁰.
Abthain, 46, 48. 50.—51, 71.—90, 259.
Achanyll, (Achavil), 120, 64.—129, 32.
Achenus, 15, 9.
Achibetoun, (Archibetoun), 1, 8.—62, 18.—142, 87.
Achinback, 126, 8.
Achinbert, 140, 37.
Achingowne, 142, 76.
Achlore, 129, 39.
Achmacoy, (Achmacuy), see 1, 21.
Achray 66, 23.—90, 250.
Achtukis, 20, 14.—32, 4.
Achteveny, 98, 328.
Achyclare, 37, 6.
Achykilhicham, 1, 10.
Achynker, 125, 5.
Acounfield, 65, 23.—78, 123.
Accumonyth, 8. 83.—119, 26.
Act of Settlement of the Crown of Scotland, 111, 63.
Adamtoun, 44, 58.—49, 2¹.
Acockitoun, 37, 3.
Airth, 34, 9.—129, 16.—159, 7.
Airth-byfet, 132, 9.
Akencarne, 45, 15.
Akintor, 53, 6.

Akthynfore, 45, 15.
Akynheuid, 114, 23.
Albany, Duke of, declared innocent of the death of David Duke of Rothfay, 104, 12².
Alcathie, 11, 27.
Aldcambus, 154, 4.
Aldeham, 153, 1.
Aldene, 162, 11.
Alderminnyn, 35, 9.
Aldermuny, 61, 4.
Aldmanyn, 30, 9.
Aldmar, 91, 275.
Aldy, 43, 23.—72, 29.
Allantun, 38, 22.
Allardes, 37, 15.
Allirtoun, 94, 190.—131, 12.
Alloway, 14, 118.—31, 25.—145, 17.
Aloeden, 2, 32.—11, 26.—33, 34.—58, 6².
Alrethis, 18, 58.
Alternmony, 129, 18.—133, 37.—142, 73.
Altoun, 60, 15.
Alveth, (Alva), 30, 12.—35, 12².
Alvya (Avon) river, 66, 24.
Alyth, 4, 38.—23, 3¹.—39, 51.—119, 4².—121, 75.—129, 24.—133, 13.—142, 86.
Amerciaments of Court, 139, 9.
St Andrew's, 43, 34.—69. l. 34.—72, 38.—74, 71.—137, 5.—148, 23.
Angus Earld. 139, 8. 9.
Annandale, 9, 93. 7. 9.—10, 18.—12, 74.—21, 29.—30, 45.—115, 46.—126 9.—164, 47.
Annotouris, 97, 324.—131, 25.
Anftruther, 144, 32.
Appletree, 11, 53.
Appletrethwaytes, 9, 92.
Arduche, 1, 21.—3, 3.—16, 12.—32, 3.—45, 18.—60, 16.—68, 14.—78, 119.—164, 47.
Ardacht, 152, 19.
Ardber, 66, 21.
Arde, 129, 27.—167, 21.
Ardegowar, 136, 18.
Ardendrauchts, 16, 16.—17, 38.—21, 18.—58, 4.—91, 272.
Ardeuly, 63, 17.
Ardgowan, 141, 52.—145, 11.
Ardin, 18, 68.
Arckeyy, 57, 33.
Arillere, (Ardblere) 89, 248.—145, 21.
Ardliry, (Ardlory, Ardlowrie), 56, 8.—112, 101.—164, 40.
Ardnamurchin, 2, 51.
Ardormy, 117, 74.
Ardowran, 26, 30.
Ardre, 116, 64.

Ardrofs, 85, 197.—140, 41.
Ardroffan, 6, 51.—129, 29.
Ardfkodnifh, 26, 18.—28, 4.
Ardwell, 2, 43.
Arefaig, 48, 3.—97, 316.—99, l. 6.—100, 2.—131, 29.—136, 18.
Argyll, 14, 122. 123.—128, 3.—126, 15.
Arketys, 167, 21.
Arncoft, 144, 15.
Arnele, 115, 51.
Arnyuche, 122, 103.
Arran. 49, 1¹.—75, 86.—145, 23.
Arroch, 113, 7.—122, 97.—128, 8.
Arveninche, 2, 39.
Arry, ifland in Tay, 60, 20.
Arynfaugh, 25, 1.
Afchome, 30, 11.
Afdury, 81, 151.
Affaying of money, 31, 40.—36, 41.
Affint, 48, 6.—99, l. 12.—100, 2⁴.
Athelftaneford, fee 11, 34.
Atheren, (Aithrey), 67, 3¹.
Atholl, 19, 88. 105.—80, 141.—124, 26.—140, 19. 20.
Athy, (Ethy), 80, 140.
Auchdale, 151, 7.
Auchidovenald, 2, 32.
Auchinbedie, 62, 41.
Auchinbothie, 2, 57.
Auchincarny, 17, 51.
Auchincrofs, 1, 15.
Auchindald, 148, 17.
Auchindonan, 8, 81.
Auchindrain, 14, 100.—21, 24.
Auchinfichlah, 1, 26.
Auchinlefkis, 4, 39.
Auchinfour, 25, 6.
Auchintelketye, 33, 30.
Auchintoly, 124, 19.
Auchlan, 126, 4.
Auchluchty, 58, 4.
Auchmar, 68, 7.—83, 182.
Auchmayre, 115, 47.
Auchmoden, 17, 32.
Auchmore, 68, 6.
Auchmyln, 53, 2.—150, 1.
Auchnacuy, 1, 21.
Auchnahamper, 162, 11.
Auchranys, 84, 187.
Auchterarder, 19, 96.
Auchterhoufe, 1, 12.
Auchterrony, 17, 32.
Auchtertyre, 18, 72.
Auchtidonald, 2, 32.
Auchynmare, 83, 181.
Aughenlo, 13, 81.
Augherthyne, 49, 8.
Aughingowne, 146, 28.
Aughinrofs, 113, 3.—122, 95.—128, 4.
Aughinfluiks, 20, 14.—32, 4.

INDEX TO THE LANDS, TOWNS, MATTERS, &c.

Aughteveny, 125, 5.—141, 67.
Auldlandys, 119, 36.
Auldtoun of Pethwer, 151, 8.
Auldtounayle, 50, 9.
Auldwick, 137, 2.
Aulifay ifland, 14, 121.—142, 69.
Autitigill, 6, 49.
Avyn, (Awyn, Avon), river, 90, 251.—126, 15.
Aweluchis, 14, 112.
Awne, (Enzie), 16, 15.—32, 1.—42, 18¹. 16.—15, 37.—71, 21.—74, 6.
Ayemuthe, (Eyemouth), 51, 40.—82, 167.
Ayntflare, 143, 5.
Ayr, 6, 41, 44.—14, 102.—21, 38. 39.—25, 12. 13.—82, 166.—95, 302.—96, 306.—119, 39.—158, 41.
Ayrickilane, 6, 31.
Aythnakethil, 4, 38.
Aytoun, 154, 4.

B.

Bachber, 142, 22.
Bad, 140, 43.
Badcafs, 42, 21.—72, 27.
Badenach, 94. 266.—96, 309.—118, 1. 3.—23, 119. 120.—124, 21.—130, 3. 8.
Badfod, 144, 40.
Badinbach, 147, 11.
Bagillo, 18, 83.
Baglillie, 35, 16¹.
Bagraw, 161, 7.
Baiky, 43, 24.—44, 51.—72, 30.—167, 21.
Bailliary, office of, 46, 46.—134, 6.—135, 7.
Bairfkimmyng, 117, 69.
Balbartane, (bret), 32, 12.—36, 3.—3², 36.—97, 319.—130, 6.
Balherdy, 36, 1.—38, 36.
Blblaine, 135, 13.
Balbot, 16², 23.
Balbrochie, 1, 15.
Balcaly, 166, 6.
Bacerifften, 116, 59.
Balclowcheris, (-clowcheris), 18, 74.
Balcolme, 2¹⁰, 7.—120, 62.—144, 38.
Balcory, (Balcrny), 20, 14.—54, 13.
Baldavie, 67, 8.—74. 70.—141, 61.
Baldowrie, 66, 21.—89, 248.
Baldwynyfgill, 166, 11.
Balecharum, 8, 85.
Balgallie, 68, 13.
Balgefchache, 14³, 20.
Balgillo, 18, 65. 83.—56, 12.—125, 1.
Balglaly, 80, 145.—85, 191.
Balglaffie, 18, 77.—140, 40.—144, 23.
Balgochry (-thrie, -orthie), 47, 23.—62, 37.
Balgony, 139, 6.—159, 1².
Balgram, 14, 5.
Balguchraignen, 64, 20.
Balguery, (Balgynery), 80, 145.—85, 191.

Balhelvie, (-lmy), 2, 37. 4⁸.—17, 37.—50, 5.—52, 55.—58, 4.—91, 272.—123, 121.—147, 8.
Balhevy, (Balheny), 96, 308.
Balhoutie, 59, 14.
Ballachaye (Ballachachie, Ballachach), 53, 31.—56, 4¹.—78, 123.—81, 159.—91, 268.—125, 29.
Ballachys, 125, 29.
Ballalie, 39, 48.
Ballayachie, 122, 110.
Balledone, 41, 16.
Ballendallache, 44, 54.—63, 2¹.—73, 57.—83, 178.
Ballelenache, 60, 23.
Ballemontyre, 51, 29.
Ballenclonochaus, (Ballichlewnekans), 51, 45.—75, 89.
Ballernach, 119, 22.—144, 24.—163, 24.
Balleichane, 59, 14.
Balleve, 122, 110.
Balleynch, 140, 38.
Ballhawell, 150, 61.
Ballinbreich, 46, 47.—72, 89.—156, 27.
Ballingall, 59, 9.
Balliony, (Ballouny), 18, 71.—122 109.
Balloche, 53, 31.—59, 4.—85, 201.—91, 269.—16, 64.
Ballwood, 36, 39.
Ballygillachy, 15, 6.—18, 63. 70.—65, 10.—88, 237.—145, 21.
Ballyntrayle, 83, 181.
Balmachanmore, 25, 11.
Balmachennachie, 132, 4.
Balmachothlie, 49, 4⁸.
Balmaclewhane, 93, 282.
Balmaculy, 23, 4¹.
Balmady, (Balmedy), 66, 3².—70, l. 6.—73, 45.—150, 1.
Balmadyfide, 157, 37.
Balmakewin, 60, 15.
Balmaledy, 123, 125.—132, 4.
Balmalyn, 2, 47.—17, 35.—61, 5.—89, 246.
Balmany, 34, 3¹⁰.—78, 121.
Balmariot, 68, 6.—83, 181.
Balmaw, (Balmow), 64, 1.—76, 92.
Balmekeran, 27, 4.
Balmethnach, 123, 125.
Balmonth, 50, l. 1.—52, 52.—53, 17.—65, 18.—86.—89, 245.—90, 256.
Balmofchenore, 135, 12.
Balmuto, 25. 5. 6.
Balnabriech, 127, 17.—157, 37.
Balnagown, 120, 64.—129, 32.
Balnerofe, 3, 14.
Balnefcry, 162, 13.
Balnegal 97, 317.—131, 30.
Balnegetht, 162, 13.
Balnerofs, 46, 8.
Balnkel, 57, 18.
Baloyngy, 118, 29.
Balqwy, 77, 109.
Baltrody, 116, 62.—120, 57.—142, 66.

Baluery, 153, 1¹.
Balveny, 38, 22.—140, 40.
Banbreiclie, 43, 23.
Banchory, 121, 87.—149, 56.
Banebory-Davery, 17, 44.—43, 22.—69, l. 24.—72, 28.
Banff burrow, 22, 50.—37, 12¹.—80, 144.—141, 63.
Banff bar, 96, 308.—117, 74.—142, 8.
Bangore, (our), 48, 7.
Bankes, 52, 170.
Bannerbearer, office of, 20, 115.
Bannock, Wefter, 115, 37.
Bar, 140, 34.
Barbe, 48, 34.—51, 28.
Barbethe, 142, 72.
Barcenonade, (Barcenon Adae), 12, 64. 21, 35.
Barchar, 40, 31.
Bardre, 120, 53.—129, 22.
Bardynghathe, 120, 53.—139, 22.
Barleythe, (-leith), 40. 27.
Barnbougal, 21, 17.—50, 13.—64, 10. 18.
Barnburne, 162, 17.
Barnclench, 39, 19.
Barngor, (Bangour), 14, 99.
Barns, 17, 56.—27, 5².—32, 8.—37, 4².—23, 4¹.—96, 208.—137, 4.
Barntoun, 142, 89.—149, 55.
Barra iiland, 48, 3¹.—97, 316.—79, 1 5.—100, 2¹.—131, 29.—136, 18.
Barrecloych, 93, 282.
Barrelach, 93, 282.
Barres, 53, 24.—86, 210.—91, 262.—115, 37.
Barrinne-heurie, (Barnhourie), 47, 18.
Barroweban, 45, 25.
Bartenonale, 12, 68.—21, 35.
Baftard empowered to difpofe of his effects, 133, 18.
Baftardie, grant of, 51, 43.—140, 32.
Bathewou, 141, 73.
Bathkat, (Bathgate), 9, 11.—21, 31.—40, 21.—58, 5¹.—122, 102.—164, 38.
Bauds, 55, 2.
Baulay, 52, 53.
Bavilay, 128, 13.—133, 32.
Bedrule, (Bethocrule), 5, 12.—10, 23.—46, 48.—55, 18.
Beinitown, 42, 21.
Beith, 144, 34.
Beldy Gordon, 162, 32.
Beliachis, 25, 4.
Bellifernc, 6, 31.
Bellitane, 8, 76.—27, 6¹.
Benederdeloe¹, 26, 31.
Benhame, 125, 3.—140, 17.
Bernis, 9, 11.—10, 20².—7, 56.—21, 31. 42.—23, 4¹.—2⁷, 5².—32, 8.—37, 4¹.—119, 30. 38.—143, 7.
Bertoun, 5, 14.
Bervor, 55, 4.
Berwick on Tweed, 9, 6. 7.—1, 28. 31.—5, 9. 14. 25.—10, 25.—11, 41. 43.

INDEX TO THE LANDS, TOWNS, MATTERS, &c.

—5, 17.—104, 13.—116, 58, 59.—151, 15.
Berwick, North, 99, l. 16.—111, 63¹.—114, 16.
Biggar, 24, 24.—140, 26.—143, 97.—156, 34.—147, 6.—146, 26.—159, 2¹. 3¹. 4.
Birkside, 92, 277.—114, 4.
Bishops, empowered to tell, 92, 276.
Biffethad, 46, 4.
Biholg, 49, 4¹.
Blackford, 116, 63.
Blacklaw, 6, 34.—141, 57.—142, 85.—148, 20.
Blackness, 11, 35.—133, 26.
Blackmoor, 150, 2.
Blaicklaiche, 14, 99.—125, 5.
Blairfensche, 65, 16.—49, 243.
Blairtown, 17, 37, 42, 50.
Blancaurig, 62, 26.
Blanne, 59, 15.
Blaregis, 143, 97.
Blarernache, 78, 116.
Blarseuche, 51, 29.—54, 14.
Blary, 134, 39.
Blauntyre, 86, 195.—120, 54.—129, 23.
Blenherne, (Blanerne), 44, 48.—73, 41.
Blenserken, 63, 2².
Bogtoun, 125, 33.
Bolden, 63, 2¹.—127, 26.
Bolgy, 139, 14.
Boltoun, 33, 45.—79, 137.
Bombry, (Bowbey), 31, 41.—36, 42.—40, 32.
Bondingtoun, 5, 9.—6, 46.—9, 11.—18, 64.—21, 31.—32, 23.—45, 36.—57, 37.—58, 7¹.—87, 225—94, 289, 291.—97, 321.—118, 15.—119, 20.—128, 15.—131, 11. 13. 22.—133, 34.—135, 14.—139, 24.—146, 35.—148, 20.
Bondland, 98, 328.
Borjedworth, 10, 17.—21, 27.—59, 5.—139, 7.
Bonkill, 123, 112.—139, 8.
Bord, 116, 64.
Bordland, 19, 110.—22, 52.—33, 40.—137, 11.
Borgis, (-gue), 40, 35.
Borrowfield, 164, 35.—
Borthwick, 166, 7.
Borthwickshiel, 116, 54.
Bothe, 51, 42.
Bothill, 124, 11.
Bothkenner, 37, 6².—53, 25.—87, 222.—118, 10.—132, 32.
Bothmachan, 34, 6.
Bothoynck, 145, 21.
Bothwell, 32, 55.—61, 11.—145, 16.
Bottill, (Buittle), 10, 20.—139, 7.
Bouchtanis, 138, 30.
Bourland, 86, 211.
Bowlands, 138, 29.
Bowne, 164, 45.
Buyne, (Boyen), 16, 15.—45, 37.—55, 19.—80, 144.

Bracman, 98, 328.
Braddal, (Bradvale), 34, 7¹.—76, 90.
Braid, (Brade), 52, 53.—58, 6¹.—68, 4.—83, 182.—128, 13.—133, 32.—145, 12.
Braidburgh, 20, 13.
Braidshaw, 148, 31.
Braidwood, 24, 11.—120, 67.—121, 88.—129, 35.
Brakanwra, 6, 36.
Brakyefield, 24, 13.
Brambaine, (Brenbeyn), 58, 5¹.—87, 223.
Branxholm, 5, 24.—46, 2.
Brathewell, 120, 59.—129, 27.
Bray, 58, 11¹.—91, 274.
Brechin, 18, 66.—19, 103.—26, 34.—51, 42.—52, 6. 10.—96, 212.—87, 216.—149, 41.—167, 20.
Brechin barony, 113, 7.—122, 97.—128, 8.—138, 38.—140, 31.—149, 57.—158, 43.
Bredles, 138, 29. 37.
Brekmoune, 138, 29.
Breky, Eafter, 143, 92.—165, 2.
Brenan, (Birnam), 36, 43.
Brenglefe, 6, 30.
Brerobanks, 55, 2.—82, 170.
Brettalach, 5, 28.
Brewland, 119, 42.
Brichtie, 166, 16.
Bridgend, 13, 93.
Bridgetoun, 149, 40.
Bridgide, St, 49, 1¹.—75, 86.—145, 23.
Brimmerlands, 144, 34.
Brochlach, 98, 328.
Brockloucht, 141, 67.
Bromchean, 30, 11.
Brome, (Broom), 9, 11.
Brothertoun, 1, 16.—68, 11.—83, 181.
Broufterland, 125, 33.
Broxmouth, 12, 55.—15, 5.—153, 1.—162, 8.
Bruchtoun, 34, 11¹.—59, 18.—79, 127.—143, 4.—148, 14.—157, 30.—164, 39.
Bruiflands, 113, 5.—122, 100.—125, 28.—128, 6.
Brulane, 52, 5.
Brydeburgh, 12, 66.—13, 86.—164, 46.
Brykenhead, (Birkin-), 148, 31.
Bruntwood, (Bruntwood), 162, 17.
Buchan, Earldom of, 2, 44.—17, 38.—21, 18.—97, 324.—131, 25.—138, 32.
Buchan, 2, 47.—11, 26.—16, 18.—17, 35.—29, 21.—123.—147, 7.
Buchan in Dumfries-shire, 67, 11.
Buchan in Stirlingshire, 8, 90.—39, 58.—80, 142.
Buchannan, 58, 12¹.—60, 10.—91, 275.—119, 25.
Buchany, 33, 39.
Buchaum, 8, 90.

Buchowys, 133, 13.
Buchrommys, 163, 21.
Bufrak, 123, 121.
Buky, 74, 69.
Bulingard, 142, 74.
Bull by Pope Boniface VIII. afferting the Independency of Scotland, 100, 3
Burclfield, 148, 14.
Burellie, 97, 317.—131, 30.
Burland, 40, 30.
Burliche, (Burlie), 59, 9.
Burrowmuir, 124, 8, 9.—146, 32.
Burtrees, 6, 50.
Buryfield, (Bouryfield), 50, 8.—82, 168.
Bute Ifland, 146, 35.
Butland, (Butcland), 51, 39.—141, 45, 167, 29.
Buttergaik, 167, 21.
Butterland, 30, 16.—36, 27.
Byugane, 114, 15.—120, 58.—129, 26.
Byris, (Byres), 30, 18.—36, 29.—62, 17.—67, 12.—77, 109.—81, 152.—114, 17.—142, 79.—150, 2². 7.
Byrkinhead, (Brykinhead), 148, 31.

C.

Cabrauche, 115, 47.—139, 7.
Cadzou, 27, 4.—35, 15.—40, 19.—84, 190.—94, 289.—119, 36.—131, 11.—135, 14.—138, 26.—139, 3.
Cairney, 64, 3.—76, 94.
Caithnefs Earldom, 29, 24.—79, 132.—120, 59.—122, 111.—124, 26.—129, 27.—137, 2.—149, 57.
Calange, 77, 109.
Calcare, 142, 81.
Calcow, (Kelfo), 127, 26.
Caldcoats, 155, 26.
Calder-cleir, 23, 8.—7, 59.—121, 73.
Caldor, 16, 28.—22, 57.—144, 21.
Calfs of Man, 9, 2.
Calkilkeft, 59, 10.
Callentar, 38, 25.—58, 3.
Cambingftoun, 59, 14.
Cambo, 25, 9³.—120, 62.—129, 30.—132, 11.—144, 38.
Cambufbarun, 81, 153.—120, 61.—129, 16. 29.—143, 97.—147, 6.
Cambufkenneth, 116, 60.
Cambuflang, 121, 90.—134, 5.
Cambufnethan, 8, 79.—33, 24.—151, 11.
Camby, 78, 117.
Cambyfenew, 59, 10.
Cameroun, Nether, 158, 53.
Camloden, 25, 2.
Campfy, 163, 18.
Canet, 64, 6.—76, 97.
Canetgatefend, 64, 6.—76, 97.
Canrenis, 59, 10.
Cantuly, 62, 24.
Caplochy, 121, 89.
Capronneftoun, 81, 160.—140, 34.
Caprounflats, 37, 3.
Capringftoun, 24, 8³. 9.—66, 5².
Captain, office of, 57, 27. 29.—39, 54.

INDEX TO THE LANDS, TOWNS, MATTERS, &c.

Caputh, 143, 95, 9.
Carcary, 165, 2.—167, 20.
Carcathie, 18, 69.
Cardenacho, 33, 34.
Cardenbarclay, 48, 34.
Cardenenie, 47, 25.
Cardeny, 2, 57.—16, 24.—47, 25.— 116, 55.—143, 99.—146, 47.
Cardrofs, 8, 90.—15, 14.—42, 15.—71, 21.—141, 50.
Carewyne, 32, 12.—36, 3.
Cargill, 47, 9.—163, 36.
Carlaverock, 12, 75.—13, 89.—15, 13. —37, 12.—42, 7.—96, 312.—131, 19.
Carlukes, 8, 75.—27, 5¹.—117, 66.— 145, 22.
Carmelite friars, 38, 21.
Carmichel, 55, 18.
Carmole, 35, 14², 15².
Carmulache, 46, 3.
Carmylie, 36, 6¹.—124, 19.—149, 39. 40.
Carnagie, 61, 14.
Carnbic, 144, 38.
Carnbrowys, 162, 11.
Carncorthie, 51, 42.—59, 14.
Carnduff, 125, 33.
Carnefmole, 13, 91.—25, 17.—97, 318.
Carnfewald, 68, 17.
Carnowne, 137, 7.
Carnowfie, 53, 19.—90, 257.
Carntoun, 80, 140.
Carnwath, 8, 74.—27, 3.
Carny, 139, 13.
Carnyfmull, 13, 91.—97, 318.—130, 5.
Carrick Earldom, 3, 10. 11.—6, 45.— 14, 105, 106, 108, 112, 119.—33, 32. 46.—42, 11.—51, 29.—54, 14.—62, 35.—71, 17.—72, 39.—75, 89.—93, 282.—115, 35.—116, 59. 61.—134, 6.—135, 7.—149, 49.—164, 36.— 167, 26.
Carridden, 64, 2.—76, 93.—79, 136. 137.
Carringtoun, (Kerringtoun), 31, 38.— 35, 23.
Carris, 9, 11.—14, 114.
Cars, 9, 11.—14, 114.—30, 12.—74, 58.—76, 97.—118, 10.—119, 29.— 127, 18.—152, 16.
Carfegownie, 18, 82.
Cartland, 128, 15.—133, 34.
Cafdughly, 140, 40.
Caſkiegour, 60, 19.—28, 328.—125, 5.
Caſs, (-is), 66, 6.—81, 161.—142, 72.
Caſligwar, 141, 67.
Caſlillis, (Caſllys), 43, 37.—69, l. 35. —72, 39.—149, 39.
Caſlindole, (ly), 64, 20.—77, 109.
Caſlebeg, 151, 8.
Caſtlecary, 120, 48.
Caſtledrummy, 147, 7.
Caſtlefield, 37, 5¹. 11².
Caſtletown, 1, 12.—135, 13.

Caſtlevallie of Rutherglen, 137, 13.
Cathyr, 91, 275.
Catnea (Kettens), 34, 17.
Caverays, 53, 6.
Cavers, 61, 2. 13.—121, 83.—139, 7. —147, 7.—148, 26.
Cavirtoun, 10, 13.—21, 22.
Ceres, 64, 20.—159, 1¹.—166, 6.
Ceſſeworth, 5, 11.—12, 57.—21, 40.— 119, 31.
Cefsford, 10, 13.
Ceſſion of the Iſland of Man to Alexander III. King of Scots, by Magnus IV. King of Norway, 101, 7.
Chalachbreck, 164, 36.
Chambirlayne-Newtoun, 116, 54.—121, 81.—159, 7.
Chambirlayne, office of, 162, 16.
Channan, 62, 26.
Chapel in the Garioch, 54, 7.
Chapels, 13, 89.—23, 3.—54, 7.—70, 5.—72, 30.—73, 282.
Charles IV. le bel, King of France, Treaty betwixt him and Robert I. King of Scots, 106, 14.
Charles V. le ſage, King of France, Treaty betwixt him and Robert II. King of Scots, 100, 4.—111, 64. 68.
Charles VI. King of France, Treaty betwixt him and Robert II. King of Scots, 112, 69. 70. 71.
Charles VI. King of France, Treaty betwixt him and Robert Duke of Albany, Regent of Scotland, 111, 61
Chawfield, (Shawfield), 24, 16.—30, 21. —36, 32.
Chethynrawache, 123, 117.
Chirnefide, 141, 49.
Chriſſwell, 145, 2.
Chuluhundy, 19, 91.
Clackmannan, 30, 12.—145, 17.—146, 43.
Clan-Clenconnan, 57, 27.
Clan-Kenelman, 57, 28.
Clan-Macgowin, captain of, 39, 54.
Clan-Munterfeafduff, 57, 29.
Clarkfland, 13, 77.
Claſleuchan, 141, 67.
Clathock, 124, 4.
Clayants, 116, 53.
Clayhills, 167, 22.
Claypots, 64, 1.—76, 92.
Cleis, (Cleith), 137, 11.—148, 17.— 159, 6.
Clenacheth, 116, 59.
Clenaghe, 159, 7.
Clenconnan-Clan, 57, 27.
Clerigenache, 47, 26.
Clerkingtown, 31, 58.—36, 39.—48, 2². —65, 3.—87, 230.—140, 22.—150, 59.
Clerk-Regiſter, 119, 28.
Clifloun, 11, 52.
Clintertoun, 35, 12⁴.
Ciochnahule, 117, 72.

Clocharby, 86, 204. 205.
Clogiuſheach, (Clonſkeach), 37, 1.— 116, 63.
Clonech, 115, 47.
Clonyfchenah, 119, 36.
Cloungwarn, 116, 63.
Cloveth, (Clova), 43, 29.—72, 55.— 142, 84. 87.
Cloynts, 25, 9¹.
Clunche, 143, 5.
Clune, 138, 30.—163, 21.
Cluny, 16, 24.—19, 91. 109.—32, 13. —36, 12.—116, 55.—119, 40. 41.— —143, 5.—164, 44.
Cluthry, 123, 119.
Clyde river, 3, 19.
Clydeſdale, 3, 3².—7, 72. 73.—21, 2¹. —22, 45.—24, 14.—27, 1. 2. 4. 9. —58, 1.—62, 26.
Clyntreys, 84, 187.—134, 4.
Clyth, 122, 111.
Cnapadene, 153, 3.
Cnockenculrach, 6, 49.
Cnolle, 153, 1.
Cnudewith, (Knoydart), 48, 3¹.—277, l. 6.—100, 2¹.—136, 18.
Cockburn, 10, 22¹.
Cockpen, 150, 59.
Cocquet, 9, 5.—46, 43.—52, 22.—55, 22.—56, 3.—63, 47.—133, 27.
Coining, office of, 139, 12.—142, 77. 78.
Colbanſtown, (Culbowſton), 11, 26.— 162, 11.
Colbrandſpath, 42, 20.—66, 24.—90, 251.—126, 15.
Colcarny, 93, 28.
Colden, (Coldoun), 7, 62.—57, 36.-- 78, 116.
Coldingham, 44, 48.—51, 40.—73, 41. —81, 167.—154, 4.
Colla Iſland, 48, 1¹.—99, l. 2.—100, 1¹.
Colle, fiſhing of, 119, 20.
Colley, (Cowie), 17, 55.—61, 25.—70, l. 11.—73, 51.—117, 72.—160, 11.
Collieſtown, 16, 16.—17, 38.—21, 18.
Collutbye, 157, 37.
St Colm, Iſland and Abbey of, 57, 319.
Colmanitoun, 52, 53.
Colonlopayache, 51, 29.
Colonſay Iſland, 41, 7.—48, 1.—59, l. 1.—100, 1¹.—118, 12.
Colſtoun, 16. 16.—17, 38.—145, 9.
Commendator of a Shire, 57, 30.
Conerary, 119, 41.
Conheath. ſee 40, 30.
Connyantoun, 13, 84.
Conſtabulary, 19, 103.—26, 12.—32, 2, 21.—42, 19.—46, 49.—60, 8. — 69, l. 5.—71, 7.—74, 25.—94, 255. —142, 70.
Confervator and Liberty, 58, 10².
Conwath, (Conevath), 29, 23.—31, 27.— 34, 1.—6, 18.—78, 115.—123, 123.
Conynghameheid, 60, 18.

Conyrtoun, 54, 5.
Copprofhill, 149, 39.
Corletlny, 117, 73.
Coroner, office of, 30, 4.—35, 4.—39, 50.—41, 42.—44, 50.—50, 4.—51, 37.—54, 8².—61, 8.—70, l. 2.—73, 43.—97, 322.—98, 331.—114, 13. —124, 19.—131, 23.
Corral, 116, 59.
Corrocks, 42, 8.—43, 32.—53, 3.
Corfby, 94, 296.—95, 298.—142, 81.
Corfchogil, 44, 9.—115, 52.
Corfcunnyngfelde, 125, 34.
Corfelflat, 48, 1².
Corfetrechache, 47, 12.
Corfmychell, 116, 56.
Corfoche, (-ock), 45, 33.
Corfturphine, 59, 8.—120, 49.—148, 24.—162, 12.—163, 26. 29.—162, 12.—164, 42.
Cortachy, 24, 7¹.—164, 37.
Corton, 14, 118.
Corty, 120, 64.—129, 32.
Corveny, 36, 3.
Cofligover, (Cafkigower), 60, 19.
Cotis, 6, 34.
Cotraw, 97, 321.—131, 22.
Coudon, 7, 62.
Coull, 38, 27.—51, 36.—145, 26.
Coulperfauch, 117, 73.
Coultan, 51, 29.
Coulter, 48, 3¹.—55, 6.—65, 3.—83, 174.—87, 230.
Coulyr, 65, 9.—67, 11.—74, 73.—83, 236.
Counecis. 2, 55.
Coupar, 45, 22.—99, l. 13.—158, 52.
Coverhill, (Caverhill), 144, 35.
Cowal, 119, 19.—142, 76.—146, 28.
Cowaustoun, 15, 9.—18, 67.—58, 4¹. 52.
Cowie, 17, 55.—18, 61.
Crabifloun, 150, 1.
Craggock, 39, 44.—163, 23.
Cragoc, 81, 151.
Cragynbat, 80. 145.—85, 191.
Craig. 4⁸, 34.—83, 180.
Craigeneneur, 59, 10.
Craighill, 128, 6.
Craigie, 1, 4.—17, 55.—18, 81.—25, 16. 19.—46, 44.—47. 28.—49, l. 3.— 51.44.—56, 5.—60, 18.—64, 1. 16.— 76. 22.—77, 101.—113, 5.—114, 20. —117, 72.—123, 100.—123, 120.— 131, 25.—143, 3.—145, 4.—151, 14. —161, 1.
Craigilloun, 3, 21.
Craiginfernier, 50, 6.
Craigining, 18, 6¹.
Craiglockhart, 52, 16.—46, 1.
Craigleys, 149, 56.
Craigmillar, 114, 28.—120, 65.
Craigorth, 129, 16.—163, 22.
Craigolt, 34, 6³.
Craigs, 56, 13.—64, 18.
Craigtoun, 167, 21.

Craigueir, 77, 109.
Crail, 20, 114. 118.—25, 3¹. 8¹.—32, 8.—17, 4².—53, 18.—57, 24.—19, 13.—90, 256.—94, 295.—117, 68. 70. —127, 24. 25.—137, 4.—138, 37.— 139, 6.—143, 12. - 167, 23.
Crailing, 22, 1. 3.—97, 325.—131, 26.
Crakneftown, 38, 35.
Crambeth, 34, 8².—78, 115.—115, 40. —157, 28.—158, 55.—159, 1¹. 5. 6.
Crammefmouth, 154, 4.
Craustoun, 43, 26.—45, 34.—69, l. 29. 72, 32.—124, 12.—163, 28.—166, 9.
Crawfurd, 61, 16.—64, 3.—133, 13.— 141, 64.
Crawfurd-Lyndefay, 87, 226.—122, 107.—128, 15.—133, 34.
Crawmont, 30, 16.—36, 27.—60, 25.— 121, 77.—141, 96. 2.—148, 33. —149, 55.—151, 5.
Crechyjofy, 83, 181.
Cree river, 61, 8.—88, 283.
Creholloch, 45, 15.
Cremond, 147, 7.
Crefwall, 8, 74.—27, 3.
Crichen, Adm, 17, 40.
Crichen, Lady, 17, 40.
Crichen, Walter, 17, 40.
Crichmelade, 72, 40.
Crichtoun, 146, 48.
Crifloun, 115, 33.
Crocks, 12, 71.—21, 36.
Crofmartyn, 98, 328.—125, 5.—141, 67.
Crogiltoun, 34, 11¹.
Cromar, (Cramar), 43, 33.—64, 4.— 72, 37.
Cromarty, 2, 50.—35, 21.—45, 27.
Cromby, 148, 17.
Cronantoun, 47, 16.—51, 33.
Crookftoun, 32, 17.
Crofbie, 11, 39.—24, l. 4.—94, 296.— 95, 298.—142, 81.—146, 46.
Crofgate, (Corfgate), 44, 48.—69, l. 37. —73, 41.
Croffard, 26, 26.
Croffewell, 37, 8².
Croffragwell, 116, 59. 60. 63.—142, 69.
Crown of Scotland, Act of Settlement of, 111, 63.
Croy, 116, 64.
Croyxtoun, (Crukyftoun), 32, 17.— 103, 17.
Cruden, 167, 21.
Crutertloun, 61, 2.
Cruvy, 138, 29.
Cuinzie-houfe, 31, 24.—43, 33.
Cukiftoun, 127, 24.
Culafe, 167, 21.
Culbakie, 63, 2¹.
Culbarnic, 66, 14.
Culbyne, 141, 40.—147, 1.—152, 17.
Culcarny, 53, 2⁴.—91, 265.—98, 328. 125, 5.—139, 11.—145, 19.
Culcuchone, 66, 209.
Culenchopagache, 54, 14.

Culhornloche, 40, 26.
Culken, 31, 41.
Cullen, 32, 2.—129, 17.—141, 65.
Cullindach, 36, 19.
Culmalonis. }
Culmalows, } 16, 30.
Culmellie, 114, 26.
Culnaltoun, 52, 2.
Culuhethe, (Conheath), 14, 105.—40, 30.
Culpedauchis, 2, 31.
Culpreffauch, 1, 18.
Culquhork, 167, 21.
Culfhogil, 12, 73.
Cult, 21, 11.—46, 53.—49, 4⁸.—80, 147.—123, 113.—164, 48.
Cultbuy, 60, 23.—78, 328.—125, 5.
Cultcarny, 141, 67.
Cultnachy, 59, 9.
Cultvoy, 141, 67.
Culuhach, 14, 105.—40, 30.
Culuthy, 162, 13.
Culven, 13, 40.—31, 28.—36, 42.— 47, 1.—55, 20.
Culyn, 13, 85.
Cumerpolfloun, 52, 48.
Cunnock, 47, 25.—57, 25.—85, 195. —120, 54.—129, 23.
Cunyngham, 6, 42. 50.—7, 53. 54.— 9. 10.—14, 109.—23, 12.—49, 1¹. —95, 302.—96, 306.—138, 2.— 142, 34.—141, 81.—143, 5.—146, 31.—148, 31.—152, 18. 19.—167, 24, 25.
Cuperm cultis, 2, 55.
Curenokeculrach, 6, 49.
Curdabow, 161, 3.
Curmyre, 78, 116.
Curr, 6, 49.—123, 19.
Curry, 85, 197.—140, 40.—145, 9.— 148, 18.—158, 40.
Curwen, 77, 110.
Cuffeny, (Cufhny), 114, 26.—127, 17.
Cuthayldrayne, 79, 125.
Cuthilduran, 151, 8.
Cuthilmyre, 6², 2¹.—75, 81.
Cutting, 167, 22.
Cuvnathifrigie, 32, 22.

D.

Dahewacht, 75, 89.
Dalacharmy, 141, 47.
Daiguborne, (-gworne), 42, 15.—71, 21.
Dalhoufie, 65, 11.—150, 59.
Dalkeith, 12. 62.—44, 7¹.—40, 11.— 44, 49.—52, 8.—54, 1.—65, 32.— 69, l. 4.—86, 214.—88, 239.—122, 102.—123, 113.—131, 31.—135, 15. —136, 19.—140, 27.—144, 29.— 151, 9.—153, 23.—166, 11. 12.
Dalkernefkan, 27, 5¹.
Dalmany, 11, 29.
Dalmarnock, 124, 13.
Dalmellingtoun, 115, 38.
Dalmorton, 69, l. 35.—72, 35.

INDEX TO THE LANDS, TOWNS, MATTERS, &c.

Dalnotar, 116, 64.
Dalrenache, (Dalrevache), 43, 23.—47, 14.—72, 29.—129, 18.—133, 37
Dalrimpill, 94, 285.—122, 105.—130, 7.—149, 50.
Dalruscan, 41, 41.
Dalry, 28, 10¹.—44, 8.—51, 35.—140, 37.
Dalserf, 162, 17.
Daldunghy, 134, 39.
Dalfupin, 60, 27.
Dalfwintoun, 13, 77. 86. 94.—45, 33
Dalthoran, 116, 59.
Dalwelache, 57, 20.
Dalziel, (Dalzel), 43, 27.—54, 11¹.—69, 1. 36.—72, 33.—115, 37.—132, 9.—139, 40
Danyelltoun, 59, 8.—158, 50.
Dargarlat, 141, 67.
Darlache, 143, 5.
Darnway, 35, 14.—84, 189.
Darnly, 37, 8¹.—151, 11.
Davach, 31, 28.—141, 47.
David, son of King Robert I. conditions of his marriage with Joanna, fister of Edward III. King of England, 101, 9.— 02, 11².
David II. King of Scots, treaties, and proceedings about his liberation from his English captivity, 107, 19. 22. 23.—108, 25. 26. 28. 29.—109, 31. 32. 33. 34. 39. 40. 42.—110, 43. 44. 47.
David Duke of Rothfay, his death, 104, 12².
Dean, 7, 6.—86, 208.—129, 16.—133, 35.
Decliment, 40, 15.
Dee, Loch of, 167, 22.
Dee river, 16, 17.—41, 34. 41.—52, 54.—141, 30.
Deer, 1, 22.—142, 90.
Dekarwand, 141, 47.
Dempster, office of, 132, 8.
Denburn, 16, 17.—128, 1.—167, 22.
Denhouse, 124, 4.
Denoon, 121, 83.
Deutrone, 18, 71.
Dereagis, 26, 30.
Dermore, 41, 15.
Desforde, (Deskford), 16, 11. 12.—45, 18.—124, 26.—151, 6.
Devellie, 84, 189.
Dewre island, (Jura), 41, 7.
Din, 25, 15.
Dingwal, 15, 17.—16, 4.—99, l. 3.—124, 29.
Dirletoun, 148, 21.—149, 43.—163, 24. 27.—166, 13.
Ditchener, (Difcher), 52, 47.
Dolphingltoun, 119, 37.
Donfandalltoun, 61, 2.
Donypais, 8, 88.—20, 15.—39, 41.
Durifdeer, 6, 32.—33, 82.—97, 324.—115, 30.—131, 25.
Dornock, 16, 3. 6.

Dorfhan, 32, 15.
Dorfquhen, 5, 26.
Douglafdale, 8, 77.—10, 15.—55, 18.—142, 71.
Douglas, Earl of, his creation, 31, 42.
Douglas, Earl of, declared innocent of the death of David Duke of Rothfay. 104, 12².
Douglas of Douglas, fymbol of his feifin, 10, 26.
Dounbouk, 139, 7.
Doune, 16, 13.—66, 3.—67, 7.—69, 6.—81, 158.—86, 202.—113, 6.—122, 99.—124, 22.—128, 7.
Douny, 39, 52.—53, 6.—63, 53.—96, 307.—121, 79.—142, 87.—161, 4.
Douuycane, 161, 4.
Dovan, river of, 145, 10.
Dovellie, 35, 14¹.
Dregerum, 6, 41.
Dreghorne, 115, 31.—146, 46.
Drem, 33, 44.—36, 45.—117, 75.—159, 7.
Drippis, 163, 19.
Drochdreg, 37, 8².
Dromedyn, 28, 11².
Dromdynan, (Dromdyvan), 20, 113.
Drome, 47, 17.—54, 12².
Dromecarn, 30, 11.
Dronan, 37, 17.
Droudraylleo, 26, 27.
Droullied, 63, 2².
Drum, 17, 53. 54.—25, 5.—42, 17.—54, 12².—69, l. 20.—72, 23.—133, 24.—137, 6.—166. 18.
Drumadicht, 149, 39.
Drumbeth, 32, 2.
Drumblate, 167, 21.
Drumbordach, 2, 34. humcauchie, 141, 50.
Drumcarne, 30, 11.—35, 11.
Drumcondland, 58, 7².
Drumcrofs, 122, 102.
Drumdow, 179, 92.
Drumelzier, 59, 19.
Drumterne, 41, 11.—53, 22.—91, 250.
Drumgaronade, (Drumgarlet), 37, 7², 98, 328.
Drumgerluch, 125, 5.
Drumgethe, 48, 53.
Drumgran, 47, 27.—50, 7.
Drumliane, 162, 11.
Drumkeith, 32, 2.
Drumlangryg, 44, 9.—115, 52.—139, 7.
Drumlaw, 140, 30.
Drumlorach, 19, 95.
Drumly, 43, 46.
Drummayeth, 37, 6¹.
Drumiinure, 140, 34.
Drumnozirr, 14, 108.
Drumpullen, 13, 81.
Dromraoct, 59, 13.
Drumingard, 29, l. 17.—117, 74.
Drumslied, 63, 2¹.
Dryfield, 64, 6.—76, 97.

Drylaw, 162, 12.
Drymmie, 67, 6².
Duffus, (Duffhous), 39, 47.—43, 31.—70, l. 5.—73, 46.
Duglyn, 144, 23.
Dulgarthe, 13, 86.
Dull, 46, 46.—53, 21.—90, 259.
Dumbarric, 45, 36.
Dumbarton, (fee Dunbartan).
Dumblay, 143, 5.
Dumfries, 13, 89.—64, 15.—66, 7.—77, 106.—134, 5.—137, 12.—149, 48.
Dun, 33, 42.—118, 9.—158, 44.
Dunbar burgh, 65, 12.—89, 244.—136, 19.—158, 39.
Dunbartan, 8, 82.—56, 10.—126, 11.—13.—132, 10.
Duncanlaw, 61, 32.—145, 13.—165, 4.
Duncarum, 11, 31.
Dunchouall, 100, 1.
Duncoll, 13, 77. 86.
Duucrub, 121, 79.
Duuduff, 116, 64.
Dundas, 10, 23².—22, 48.
Dundee, 3, 1².—18, 81.—26, 19.—43, 39.—50, 15.—52, 7.—54, 8¹.—57, 38.—94, 15.—62, 29.—67, L 21.—74, 75.—8, 213.—87, 216.—113, 5.—122, 100.—123, 116.—128, 6. 10.—132, 3.—133, 13. 29.—140, 25. 33.—143, 100.—144, 25.—150, 2.—151, 14.—152, 21.—157, 35.—161, 4. 5. 6. 7.—162, 8.—164, 43.
Dundovau, 43, 23.—72, 29.—162, 17.
Dundrome, 14, 99.
Dunegrelache, 23, 13.—116, 58.
Dunfermling, 38, 16. 20.—126, 14.
Dunfynd, 164, 4.
Dungernock, 41, 34.
Dunipaice, 8, 88.—20, 15.—39, 41.
Dunlop, 167, 25.
Dunlopy, 127, 17.
Dunmanyh, (Dalmeny), 72, 34.
Dunmore, 45, 35.
Dunuchyne, 110, 53.
Dunnot, 20, 27.
Dunnotter, 33, 49.—124, 4.—144, 17. 19.
Dunnure, 26, 27.—93, 282.
Duurod, 125, 33.
Duns, 20, 2.—43, 46.—73, 56.
Dunilaflaage, 141, 124.—15, 15.—26, 13.
Dunfyir, 55, 6.—83, 173.
Duntablay, 149, 49.
Durdoman, 48, 1².—99, l. 3.—100, 1.
Durham, battle of, 62, 27.—67, 11.—74, 73.
Durham, Abbey of, 152, 22.
Durn, 166, 5.
Durris, 18, 59.—60, 14.—65, 2.—68, 81.—87, 229.
Durifclume, (Durfeune, Darfhine), 67, 6¹.—75, 79.
Durydarache, 146, 44.
Dya, (Dyce), 38, 29.
Dyfart, 153, 29.

INDEX TO THE TOWNS, LANDS, MATTERS, &c.

E.

Ealchull, 42, 12. 13.
Easter Breky, 165, 2.
Easter Fordy, 57, 21.
Easter Forfar, 18, 62.
Eccles, 142, 87.
Edderlings, 59, 10.
Eddirsloun, 7. 73.
Edelwood, 21, 21.—35, 15.—84, 190.
Edinbanchory, 149, 56.
Edinburgh, 3, 6.—44, 10.—49, 5².—50, 14.—64, 16.—65, 22.—66, 11.—67, 2.—68, 8¹.—74, 64. 68.—77, 107.—78, 111.—82, 165.—83, 176.—84, 188.—8°, 227.—113, 2.—117, 64.—12 , °0.—122, 95. 107.—123, 126 —124, 16.—125, 31.—127, 15. 19.—128, 3.—132, 3.—134, 5.—138, 34. 36. 38.—139, 10.—140, 27. 39.—144, 26.—145, 8, 11. 25.—146, 36.—147, 10—151, 5. 9.—154, 25.—157, 32. 38.
Edinburgh castle. 104, 13.
Edindovat, 1, 20.
Edindurnache, 54, 7.
Edinghame, 9, 11.—24, 12.
Edirdye, 1, 6.
Edirinche, 3, 17. 18.
Edirsloun, 7, 73.
Ednam, 21, 3¹.—24, 12,
Edrehame, (Edrom), 55, 1.—82, 169.
Edringtoun, 11, 37.—22, 54.—24, 1.—40, 17.—62, 20.—119, 20.
Edward III. King of England, treaty betwixt him and Robert I. King of Scots, 101, 9.—103, 11¹.
Egghee island, (Egg). 4³, 3¹.— 97, 316.—90, l. 6.—10c, 2.—131, 29.—136, 18.
Eglismalesocks, 3, 3¹.—22, 45.
Eiller Balnegal, 131, 30.
Eistertyre, 58, 10¹.
Eitun, (Ayton), 154, 4.
Ekfuird, 21, 22.
Elantirym, 136, 18.
Eldenthe, 69, l. 91.
Elgereth, 69, 38.
Elgin, 42, 19.—133. 15.
Elginshire, farms and duties of, 80, 149.
Elietis, 13, 88.
Ellem, 147, 5.
Ellon, 2, 27.
Elphinstoun, 11, 25.—15. 8.
Elstaneford, (Athelstaneford), 11, 34.—141, 58.
Elvingloun, 7, 64.—44, 49.—69, l. 4.
Elystoun, 14*, 2*.
Enache, 13, 83.—14, 114.—53, 1.—62, 40.—139, 30.
Enachrache, (Enachre), 60, 19.—9°, 318
Enot, 42, 21.
Enzie, (Aune, Awne), 16, 15.—32, 1 —42, 18¹. 16¹.—45, 37.
Erbentoly, (Erventuly, Arutully), 4, 26.
Erchles, 167, 21.
Ernecraig, 148, 33.

Ernock-Sabunsoy, 126, 8.
Eroly, 119, 24.— 120, 65.— 129, 33.
149, 54.
Erroll, 58, 9¹.—61, 1.—143, 9.
Ersch, 82, 152.
Erskine, 49, 5.
Erskinamerchin, 40, 25.
Erskyndy, 118, 9.
Erth, (Airth), 79, 125.
Ertbbeg, 73, 40.
Erth Byset, 115, 37.
Ervyntoly, 124, 13.
Eryngaith, 9, 11.
Escheilis, (Esschlis), 67, 6².—75, 85.
Eschom, 35, 11.
Esk river, 21, 26.—12. 46.—57, 20.
Eskdale, 3, 4².—10, 16, 19¹.—12, 71.—21, 36.—39, 1.—55, 18.
Eskylluh, 60, 14.
Esslmonth, 122, 103.
Essintoly, 114, 17.
Essuly, 1, 15.
Essye, 1, 9.—142, 82.—149, 41. 42.—167, 20.
Esthbernys, (Eastbarns), 86, 208.
Ester cragy, 77, 101.
Ester-rothnem, 72, 77.
Ester-tyry. 91, 273.
Estir-Balnegal, 97, 317.
Est-rifton, 78, 124.
Est-fpot, 76, 91.
Etterschinschap, 144, 33.
Ettrick, 10, 24¹.—59, 3.—142, 71.
Euisdale, 39, 1.
Evchame, (Evinhame), 35, 13².—55, 1.
Exchange of money, 31, 23. 24.—36, 34. 35.
Exemption from vassalage, 68, 1¹.
Extent, old and new, 110, 44.
Eyemouth, 51, 40.

F.

Facfield, 125, 33.
Fail, kirk of, 133, 13.
Faillickyll, 63, 44.
Falkirk, 129, 18.—155, 26.
Farinis, (Fernis, Ferns), 4, 23.—24, 8¹.
Farneroflken, 15, 17.—1 , 4.
Farndun, 154, 4.
Farnydounc, 97, 25.—131, 26.
Fafdauache, 65, 2⁵.
Faulkland, 50, 4.—162, 13.
Faunys, (Fawns), 163, 27. 32.
Faufide, 7. 58.— 1c, 22².— 22, 44.— 2 , 1³.—55, 4.—98, 172.—114, 9.
Fedreffe, 46, 56.
Fentoun, 7, 60.—50, 3.—56, 17.
Ferachy, 117, 72.
FerJill, 37, 5².—44, 47.—70, l. 1.—73, 42.
Feres, 141, 66.
Fermall, 149, 43.
Ferme, near Rutherglen, 9, 12. — 21, 121, 90.
Fernerosker, 15. 17.—16, 4.
Ferne, 122, 108.—134, 5.
Ferny, 49, 10.

Ferryfield, 4, 30. 32.
Ferrytounfield, 46, 313.—131, 20.
Fethane, 123. 113.
Fetherneum, 14, 116.
Fethill, 47, 23.
Fettercairn, 39, 42.—52, 14.—63, 53.—65, 15.—89, 242.
Fife, Earldom, 25, 7¹.—74, 62.
Filorth, (Philorth), 69, l. 21.—72, 24.—86, 204.—91, 273.—160, 11.
Findony, 121, 79.
Finevin, (Fotheneven), 18, 82.—23, 2¹.—52. 9.—86, 215.—120, 63.—129, 31.—132. 12.
Fingask, 167, 20.
Finlargis, 19, 99.
Finlater, (Findlater), 66, 9.—82, 164.—129, 17.—133, 36.—140, 38.—151, 6.
Fintray, 17, 35. 36.
Fintrygask, 2, 47.
Fifewick, 153, 3.
Fisherflat, 7, 66.
Fisshertoun, 141, 57.—142, 85.—148, 20.
Fishings in rivers, 39, 55.—52, 54.
Fithkill, 124, 26.—146, 29.—159, 9.
Five-penny land, 59, 7.
Flask, 144, 40.
Fleminglauche, (Fleminglaw), 61, 2.
Flemyngtoun, 78, 121.—140, 40.
Fogo, 140, 23.—163, 32.
Fohellery, 35, 20.—86, 204.
Fondowie, 62, 36
Fordell, 114, 20.—138, 29.
Fordoun, 4, 35.—20, 3.
Fordy, 57, 21.
Fordyis, (Fordyce), 67, 7¹.—74, 69.
Forfar, 18, 62.—21, 55.—96, 313.—117, 71.—131, 20.—135, 12.—144, 30.
Forgund, (Forgan), 19, 100.
Forgundenny, 124, 26.
Forling, 47, 14.
Formartin, 2, 46.—16, 30.—17, 40.—36, 2.—39, 4².—43, 47.—53, 6.—63, 53.—66, 2¹.—81, 157.—126, 10.—148, 36.—149, 37.
Fornauchty, 149, 43.
Fornwyre, (Furnewyre), 58, 11¹.—9¹, 274.
Forres, 133, 15.
Forrests, 16, 7.—17, 52.—66, 6. —67, 64.—68, 3¹. 8².—81, 152.—114, 19.—117, 72. 73 —119, 21.
Forteviot, 19, 87. 104.—95, 299.—124, 14.
Forth mills, 60, 19.
Forth river, 62, 34.—63, 50.—146, 42.
Fortrie, 33, 47.
Fortyre, 35, 20.—86, 205.
Fossache, (Fosseiche), 19, 106.—53, 81.—90, 259.
Fothergill, 19, 88.—51, 46.—54, 15.—57, 25.—134, 39.
Fothey, Wester, 138, 29.
Fothryl, 50, 4.—73, 122.

INDEX TO THE LANDS, TOWNS, MATTERS, &c. 187

Foulertoun, 18, 78.—38, 17. 29.—40, 30.—95, 297.
Foullerysland, (Fowlersland), 121, 83.—141, 59.
Foullis, 67, 1³.—75, 80.
Foulscheils, 119, 34.
Foultoun, 127, 23.
Fovern, (Foveran), 1, 21. 23.—45, 20.
France, Kings of, treaties betwixt them and the Scots nation, 100, 4.—106, 115. 116.—107, 16.—111, 61. 64. 68.—112, 69. 70. 71.—141, 59.
Freedom, charter granting, 66, 22.
Freirtoun, 155, 26.
French language, charter in the, 27 5¹.
Friendraught, 1, 19.—137, 7.—149, 46.
Freswick, 166, 8.
Red Friars lands, 149, 44.
White Friars lands, 149, 46.
Fruchie, 159, 5.
Fulbakater, 141, 44.
Fuleth, 8, 87.
Fulwood, 115, 50.—128, 15.—133, 34.
Futy, (Foot-Dee), 167, 22.
Fyndoun, 157, 36.—165, 2.
Fynglen, 114, 24.
Fynlawys, 133, 22.
Fynlawystoun, 158, 50.
Fythkill, 124, 26.—146, 29.—159, 9.
Fyvie, 126, 10.—148, 36.

G.

Gage in the burrows, 40, 18.
Gage and meafure, 37, 8¹.
Galachan, 66, 1¹.
Galbrydstoun, 143, 95.
Gallartlauds, 140, 36.
Galloway, 10, 20¹.—13, 80.—20, 4.—25, 6¹. 10¹. 19.—37 8¹.—41. 5, 6.—88, 233.—114, 19.—119, 21.—124, 26.—145, 16.
Galloway, men and liberties of, 13, 80.—33, 26.—134, 5.
Galloway, the indigenous inhabitants of, 134, 5.
Gallowhill, 9, 11.
Gallyitoun, 162, 17.—164, 38.
Galnethe, 142, 72.
Galowfeiyde, 119, 38.
Galvan, 147, 11.
Gannay, 116, 53.
Gardens, the King's, 39, 57.
Garfer, 45, 15.
Garlet, 142, 64.
Garleyis, 45, 33.
Garloucht, 161, 3.
Garmauche, 17 39.
Garmyhoun, 119, 43.
Garmyltoundunyng, 7, 63.—50, 11.—121, 76.
Garmyhoun Noble, 121, 82.
Garnach, 40, 25.
Garquhill, (Gadeholl, Gairbull, Gilchil), 41, 12. 13.—54, 10².—69, l. 16.—71, 18.—91, 263.

Garrow, (Geroib), 48, 3¹.—99, l. 6.—100 2.
Garrow Morwarne, 48, 3¹.—99, l. 6.—102, 2.
Garrowoll, 53, 26.
Garfcadden, 116, 64.
Gart, 123, 21.
Gartgarthe, 14, 103.—22, 56.
Gartheyre, 30, 11.
Garthyes, 120, 46.
Gartindoe, 64, 6.
Gartneker, 43, 35.—70, l. 8.—73, 48.
Garvald, 59, 10.
Garvan, (Girvan), 51, 45.—60, 27.—75, 89.
Garvard, 59, 7.
Garviauche, (Garrioch), 1, 25.—8, 84.—15, 16.—16, 19. 25.—17, 33.—31, 34.—36, 25.—46, 57.—54, 7¹. 7². 11². 15.—59, 16.—61, 2.—139, 7.—141, 53.—147, 7.—166, 14. 18.
Garvock, 1, 14.
Garyncloe, 76, 97.
Galk, 43, 23.—61, 5.—72, 29.— 89, 246.—167, 21.
Galkenes, 16, 28.
Galkin, 66, 19.
Gatyfend, (Gatefend), 76, 97.
Gauinfpot, 7, 71.
Gauylichtoun, (Galftoun), 41, 6.
Gaylis, 95, 297.
Geday, illand of, 48, 1.—99, l. 2.—100. 1.
Gelackbane, 78, 117.
Gelechan, 41, 21.
Geleftan, 72, 27.
Gemily, 8, 76.
Gerloch, 98, 327.—114, 10.
Gerpot, 114, 20.
Gerfmanyftoun, (Gerfmanftoun), 64, 6.—76, 97.
Giblultoun, 56. 15.
Gilberthill, 54, 7.
Gilcolmftoun, (Gilcolmyftoun), 42, 10.—69, l. 22.—72, 4².
St Gile-grange, 146. 4.
St Giles, 119, 27.—138, 34.
Giletre, 149, 44.
Gilgirgyftoun, (Kilgarftoun), 77, 100.
Gilhaine, 139, 5.
Gillinderftoun, 8, 84.—15, 16.—16, 19.—17, 33.—115, 47.
Gillaltoun, 38, 26.
Gilletnachis, 2 46.
Gilmertoun, 11, 29.—21, 17.
Gilmordall, 3, 76.
Gilftoun 69, l. 25.
Girton, (Girthon), 25, 18.
Glaceiter, 115, 34.
Glak, 144, 35.
Glammis, 67, 3².—74, 76.—96, 315.—131, 27.—147, 8.
Glandriftoun, 115, 47.
Glafbany, (Clafbany), 58 ⁵.
Glasfenne, 34, 9.—52, 16.—79, 125.—87, 223.—90, 254.

Glafcullach, Glaftullach), 18, 61.—117, 72.
Glasford 116 63.
Glafgow burgh, 132, 10.—162 12.
Glafgow forell, 38, 32.—59, 46.—68, 19.
Glafochy, 98, 32⁸.—125, 5.
Glafmache, 20, 112.
Glafmonth, 20, 112.—46, 54.
Glenabeukan, 12, 68.
Glenbreeriche, 14, 111.
Glenbervy. 34, 9¹.—78, 116.—141, 46.
Glencairethe, 40, 25.
Glencarne, 13, 95.—53, 29.—60, 28.—91, 266.
Glencavine, 13, 81.
Genearnie, 42, 14.—69, l. 17.—71, 20.
Glenchomure, (Glenchomyre), 4, 1².—99, l. 3.—100, 1.
Glenchungall, 35, 18.—80, 138.
Glencoy, 13, 23.—72, 29.
Glencraig. 65, 21.—77, 110.
Glenere, 116, 53.
Glencrofts, 12, 72.
Glendochyre, 19, 98. 99.—26, 24. 29.—115, 31.—118, 7.—120, 50.
Glendouachy, 2, 45.—124, 18. 26.—141, 53.
Glendovan, 72, 29.
Glenducky, 157, 37.
Gleneche, 30, 3.
Glenegle, Glenelgenie, Glenelg), 48, 4.—99, l. 8.—100, 2¹.
Glenefk 18, 79.—51, 46.—61, 16.—66, 4¹.—74, 7².— 7, 20. 21.—132, 12—142, 87.—150, 2.—166, 15.
Glenefflane, (Glenfkere), 31, 29.—36, 10.—47, 10.
Glenfache. 149. 46.
Glengarg, 65. 21.—77, 110.
Glengary, 37, 8².
Glengleiche, 3. 3.
Glengonvir, (Glengunvour), 114, 24.
Glenhargie, 12, 1.
Glenhifernemore, 11, 53.
Glenkenne, 13, 87.—5, 25.—85, 195
Glenlitherner, 24, 7¹.
Glenluce, 3, 11. 13.
Glenlyon, 51, 27.—80, 141.
Glenmannache, 45. 33.
Glenmope, 40 24.
Glenogweris 2, 54.
Glenopper, 45, 15.
Glenquharae y, 16., 3.
Glenrath, 144, 35.
Glenrufluck, 146, 37.
Glens, 37, 1.
Glenfcanchel, 20, l. 18.
Glenfmantoun, 20, 118.
Gleniumtault, 4 22.
Glentall, 142, 72.
Glenurchy, 44, 7.
Glureth, (Glorat), 30, 3. 5.—35, 3. 5.
Godfraytoun, 48, 23 31.
Gogar, 10, 21².—42, 43.—166, 15.

INDEX TO THE LANDS, TOWNS, MATTERS, &c.

Gordon, 140, 23.—163, 32.
Gorlay, 14, 118.
Gormal, 148, 32.
Gortoun, 40, 12.—41, 1.
Goscroft, 8, 87.
Gosford, 46, 44.
Graggeford, 47, 24.
Graindud, 53, 7.
Giardin, 17, 32.—141, 53. 65.—150, 1.
Grange, 118, 10.—119, 27.
Green, 167, 22.
Greenford, 59, 14.—137, 8.
Greenhead, 31, 33.—36, 24.—39, 4.
Greenhill, 6, 34.—58, 6².—144, 21.
Greneland, 122, 111.
Greshiltoun, 164, 48.
Grey, 143, 5.
Grievefchip of Cullen, 129, 17.
Griobishuide, 39, 4.
Grogary, 64, 6.—76, 97.
Gr-ffmanitoun, 25, 8².
Grugar, 7, 53.
Guynifcaftle, (Greencaftle), 119, 32.
Guli-yn, 91, 2/2.—131, 14.
Gurdnies, 126, 10.
Gurdy, 143, 9.
Guthrie, 42, 87.
Gythy ifland, (Gigha), 41, 7.

H.

Hachethnreach, 116, 57.
Hackmangerum, 37, 6.
Haddingtown, 3, 6.—7, 65.—10, 20¹.
  21¹. 24².—21, 42.—2", 5².—37, 3.
  —43, 25.—45, 36.—53, 32.—6,
  I. 27.—72, 31.—82, 168.—89, 244.
  —63, 263.—114, 2. 12.—121, 91.
  —132, 1.—139, 7.—147, 7.—157, 32.
Haircleuch, 58, 8¹.—87, 216.
Haknak-Iteldun, 27, 7¹.
Hakwrangdrum, 149, 29.
Hale, (Hales), 28, 11.—61, 31.
Half, Well, fishing of, 39, 55.
Halkhead, 147, 6.
Halland, 6, 40.
Hallys, (Hales), 28, 11.—61, 31.
Haltoun, 3, 3.—29, 23.—122, 104.—
  123, 125.—132, 4.—144, 21.—161,
  5.
Halyroodhoufe, 66, 20. 24.—114, 3.
Hamtoun, 125, 3.
Hanerch, Haverch), 91, 275.
Hardiwood, 78, 116.
Harperland, 95, 301.
Hartfchaw, 6, 46, 48.
Haffin dev, (Haffyngtown, Halfyng-
  toun), 5, 12.—11, 3⁸.—12, 61.—
  22, 60.—146, 2⁹.—157, 31.—159,
  8.—161, 2.—162, 28.
Haffingdenebank, 165, 1.
Haftheupland, 125, 33.
Hathingill, 14, 111.
Haueftand, 123, 118.
Hawdene, 164, 39.
Hawick, 5, 24.—27, 7¹.—33, 29.—
  45, 17.—46, 2.—54, 4.

Hawkefhaws, 6, 35.—114, 24.
Hawlafte, 136, 18.
HawthornJean, 54, 5.
Hawthornfyke, 144, 29.
Hebeddees, (Hebeddys), 66, 2¹.—70,
  I. 4.—72, 44.
Henderitoun, I, 6.
Henriland, 124, 11.
Hepop, 144, 33.
Herber, 143, 54.
Herbertfhiels, 33, 40.—141, 57.—142,
  85.
Herbertfhire, 61, 32.
Herdmanfloun, 12, 57.—21, 40.—126,
  7.—124, 23.—148, 18.
Heroud, 115, 36.
Hertfollings, 141, 49.
Herthornehill, 135, 15.
Hertifhuyde, 33, 28.
Hertop, 133, 13.
Hertfhaw, 6, 46, 4⁸.
Heryte, (Hirta, St Kilda), 97, 216.—
  131, 29.—136, 18.
Heffilden, 62, 26.
Hefefcrews, 32, 16.
Hethirwick, 151, 1.
Hethonfields, 143, 8.
Hettoun, 115, 37.
Hevedie, 24, 11.—121, 85.
Hevirterrigis, 1, 17.
Hi'clyf, 125, 32.
Hill, 55, 20.—125, 30.
Hillfield, 20, 114.—22, 52.
Hiltoun, 44, 4⁸.—73, 41.—124, 4.—
  175, 1.
Hochkellou, (Hopkailzie), 32, 6.—43,
  28.—57, 6¹.—72, 34.—75, 85.
Hogefloun, 135, 13.
Holclush, 133, 13.
Holme monaftery, 68, 5.
Holmefide, 6, 34.
Home, 43, 46.
Honemener, 146, 37.
Horfeburgh, 32, 16.—67, 6¹.—75, 85.
Horverdcne, 153, 3.
Hucheonfelde, 125, 34.
Huchtererne, 76, 95.
Humdalwalfchope, (Hundlefchope), 57,
  32.—145, 15.
Hundwater, fifhing of, 119, 20.
Huntington Earldom, 105, 15.
Huntlaw, 138, 23.
Huntly, 163, 32.
Hurderics, 119, 7.
Hwytmyr, (Whitemire), 8, 87.

I.

St James's hofpital, 141, 51.
Jedburgh, (Jedworth), 10, 17.—12, 59.
  —2¹, 27.—22, 1 2. 3.—63, 1¹.—
  127, 23.—130, 7.—143, 14.—147,
  7.—5¹. 6.—152, 25.—157, 33.
Ila ifland, 41, 7.—48, 1¹.—99, I. 2.—
  102, 1.
ncharry, 117, 67.
Inchbrenys, 134, 39.

Inchecalleche, 30, 10.—35, 10.
Inchecret, 117, 67.
Inchetuthyle, 135, 9.
Inchmertein, 19, 100.—29, I. 2.—121,
  86.
Inchore, 50, 20.
Inchftare, 137, 6.
Inchture, 34, 7¹.—78, 114.—120, 69.
  —145, 20.
Inene, 143, 54.
Indigena, indigenous inhabitants of Gal-
  loway, 134, 5.
Inglifmalholks, 58, 1.
Ingliftoun, 1, 12.—97, 324.—131, 25.
  —149, 40.
Inneralmeffie, 54, 11¹.
Innercaritie, 20, 14.—52, 13.—65, 14.
  —143, 91.—148, 29.
Innercarrewchie, 143, 91.
Innerkerratis, 20, 14.—143, 91.
Innerkyn, 47, 17.
Innermaith, 115, 30.—133, 23.
Innerpeffer, 11, 26.—58, 8¹.
Inraloun, (Inverallan), 120, 61.—129,
  29.
Iprouy, 18, 83.
Initrothir, (Anftrothir), 80, 139.
Inveraritie, 87, 219.—89, 241.—142,
  87.—161, 52.
Iuverafren, 2, 59.
Inverbervie, 1, 16.—35, 18.—54, 8¹.
  80, 138.
Invercabock, 2, 30.—120, 45.
Invercnych, 120, 55.—121, 75.—127,
  24.
Inverdovat, 76, 90.—147, I. 2.—152,
  17.
Inverighty, (Invereechtie), 18, 73.—50,
  17.
Inverkeithing, 4, 29.—20, 115.—45,
  24.—47, 24.—89, 248.—133, 19. 23.
  —145, 10.—146, 33.—146, 45.—147,
  51.—149, 52.—157, 29.—162, 15.
Inverkip, 123, 118.—141, 52.
Inverlethan, 37, 4¹.—52, 51.—157,
  31.
Inverlicth, 7, 61.—36, 1.—134, 41.
Inverlunan, 1, 11.—57, 33.—125, 114.
Invermealan, 41, 35.
Invermeth, 151, 8.
Invernate, 125, 29.
Invernauchty, 61, 2.
Invernefs, 9, 5.—26, 22.—60, 26.—
  85, 194.—113, 1.—122, 94.—128,
  2.—134, 19.—148, 34.—151, 6.
Invernorfyn, 134, 39.
Invergny, (Inverugy), 151, 13.
Invcrwyk, 97, 324.—131, 25.
Invelting Dowglas, form of, 10, 26.
Juhanna, filter of Edward III. King of
  England, to be married to David,
  only fon of Robert I. King of Scots,
  101, 9.—103, 11.
John King of France, letters from to
  the Scots nation, 106, 15. 16.—107,
  16.

INDEX TO THE LANDS, TOWNS, MATTERS, &c.

John King of France, his treaty with Edward III. King of England inimical to the Scots, 107, 17.
John of Yle, his submission to King David II. 108, 27.
Irwine, 6, 40.—14, 107.—95, 297. 302.—96, 306.—146, 46.
Iseleborgh, 99, l. 4.—100, 1.
Island of Man ceded to Scotland, 101, 7.
Jara island, 41, 7.—48, 1¹.—99, l. 2.—100, 1.
Jury, decrees by, 119, 23.—157, 37.
Justiciary, 39, 45.—62, 21.—63, 49.—67, 5¹.—74, 65. 67.
Justiciary, mills of, at Aberdeen, 167, 22.
Justice-Clerk, 44, 52.—68, 2¹.—85, 199.—114, 29.

K.

Kargill, (Cargill) 47, 9.—114, 26.
Katerlyne, 124, 4.
Kathnes, 62, 22.
Keith, 162, 11.
Keith-Mareschall, 11, 26.—58, 8².—115, 4³.—162, 11.
Keith-Symon, 11, 26.—58, 8².
Kelg, 91, 275.
Kelluiture, 25, 9¹.
Kellachaffie, 25, 10¹.
Kellie, 10, 14.—20, 117.—21, 23.—25, 10².—18, 10².—51, 23.—55, 17.
Kellis, 4, 24.
Kelor, 18, 76.—124, 10.—143, 94.—167, 20.
Kelso, 39, 5.—41, 14.—63, 2².—127, 26.
Kelsoland, 142, 81.
Keloun, 13, 90.—31, 41.—32, 20.—36, 42.—55, 20.
Kelwood, (Keldewood) 13, 78.—42, 30.—52, 5.—86, 211.
Kelyn, (Killyn), 26, 29.—91, 275.
Kenachan, 123, 211.
Kenelman-Clan, 57, 28.
Kenkynoll, 134, 6.
Kenmore, 10, 79.—46, 5.—56, 9.
Kennedy Clan, chief of, 149, 51.
Kentaill, (Kintaill) 48, 2¹.—99, l. 5.—100, 1².
Kepawenate, 60, 4².
Kepmad, 34, 14.—75, 83.—70, 120.
Keringtoun, (Carringtoun), 51, 38.—35, 32.—86, 207.
Kernock, (Carnock), 58, 12².—162, 13.
Kernorborch, 99, l. 4.—100, 1.
Kerr, Wester, 3, 4¹. 5.
Kers of Stirling, (Carse), 9, 11.—44, 55.—127, 16. 18.—144, 36.—146, 34.—152, 16.—155, 26.
Kerse, 35. 12².—64, 6.
Kerymure, 143, 91.—147, 50.
Kettens, 1, 5.—34, 17.—152, 21.
Keypoll, 26, 27.
*Kilbaberton, 7, 71.—140, 40.

Kilbothok, (Kilbnebo), 54, 1.—121, 73.
Kilbride, 9, 12.—21, 32.—94, 290.—116, 63.—125, 33.—131, 12.—140. 29.—145, 11.—146, 27.—159, 8.
Kildonan, (Kildonwhan), 27, 1¹.—128, 12.—133, 31.
Kildrummy, 76, 95.—149, 56.
Kilkennet, 31, 37.
Killanell, 17, 42.
Killerenache, (Kilrevache), 47, 14.
Killyn, 26, 29.—91, 275.
Kilmahew, 50, 7.—61, 3.—163, 30.
Kilmarnock, 6, 46.—117, 65.
Kilmaronock, 4, 34.—30, 10.—54, 11¹.
Kilmartin, 28, 4.
Kilmawrs, 141, 54.—146, 27.—159, 8.
Kilmechanache, 14, 99.
Kilmoris, 145, 49.
Kilmumkyn, 20, 114.
Kilmychill, (Kilmichael), 26, 27.
Kilpatrick, 21, 33.—58, 2.
Kilfyth, (Kyllynsyth), 47, 5.—69, l. 10.—71, 12
Kilvynet, (Kilwinnet), 36, 38.
Kinaltvy, (Kinaldy), 2, 51.—117, 68.—132, 7.—137, 1.
Kinbaldin, 2, 51.—117, 68.
Kinblackmont, (Kinbrackmont), 18, 66.—48, 2².—65, 4.—88, 241.—123, 115.—125, 3.—139, 5.—140, 40.
Kinbuyscher, 49, 7.
Kinbrede, 143, 92.
Kinbuk, (Kemback), 35, 8.
Kincairny, 2, 43.—45, 24.
Kincaldrum, 158, 53.
KincarJany, 2, 43.—45, 24.
Kincardine, 1, 13.—7, 57.—32, 14.—63, 53.—65, 15.—75, 79.—80, 220.—90, 242.—119, 23.—148, 35.—159, 9.—162, 8.—163, 26.
Kincavil, 7, 59.—23, 8.—25, 1.—121, 73.
Kinclevin, 121, 13.—125, 29.
Kinckrawmont, (King's Crawmont), 148, 33.—151, 5.
Kindeny, (Kindavy), 25, 1.—80, 148.
Kinell, 141, 57.—148, 20. 28.
Kinellour, 45, 25.
Kinfauns, 19, 101.—26, 33.—40, 9.—98, 326.—113, 6.—114, 14. 26.—125, 27.—123, 7. 12.—143, 3.—145, 4.
Kingaldiicrofts, 143, 121.
Kingasplace, (Kingsplace), 26, 35.
Kingedward, (Kinnedwre), 1, 24.—6, 20, 104.—124, 21.—140, 16.—141, 40, 101a.
Kinghorn, 20, 112.—32, 12.—33, 43.—36, 3.—37, 7¹. 11¹.—41, 12. 46, 50.—47, 25.—4, 2¹.—6, 12. 19.—75, 87.—80, 145.—8, 191.—92, 319.—121, 57.—130, 6.
King's chapel, 45, 10.
King's door, keeping of, 47, 26.
King's gardens, 39, 5².
Kingisland, 27, 4¹.—53, 51.

King's isles, 137, 13.
King's lour, 48, 33. 34.
King's meadow, 88, 238.—133, 25.
King's muir at Crail, 57, 24.
King's park, 65, 11.
King's revocation, 52, 49.—62, 23.
Kingstoun, 42, 2.
Kingstour, (King's lour), 48, 33. 34.
Kininmonth, 34, 4¹.—78, 122.—123, 117.—148, 16.—163, 21.
Kinkell, 19, 103.—38, 29.—63, 2¹.—166, 15.
Kinloch, 4, 37.—20, 6.—26, 34.—53, 27.
Kinmonth, 138, 30.—159, 6.
Kinnarde, 17, 45.—50, 20.—141, 56.—165, 3.
Kinnedy, 19, 97.
Kinneff, 164, 41.
Kinneil, 11, 27.—16, 28.—139, 1.
Kinneir, 113, 4.—122, 98.—124, 5.
Kinnell, 142, 68.—159, 2¹.—165, 2.
Kinnettil, 140, 28.—149, 40.
Kinnoul, 22, 57.—34, 5¹.—62, 28.—68, 2¹.—80, 150.
Kinpunt, 9, 11.—21, 71.
Kinrofs, 3, 9.—25, 2¹.—28, 6.—29, 24.—60, 19.—72, 30.—93, 323.—175, 5.—141, 67.
Kinrossie. 167, 21.
Kintail, 48, 2.
Kintillache, (Kintullo), 49, 3.
Kintore, 2, 41.—11, 26.—31, 34.—36, 2.—38, 32.—39, 42.—58, 8².—62, 19.—63, 53.—121, 72.—124, 2.—162, 11.
Kintumer, 138, 25.
Kintyre, 14, 121.—15, 2¹.—76, 15.—32, 41, 7.—60, 30.—118, 14.—125, 15.
Kippo, 50, 259.—140, 30.—143, 94.
Kirk, 12, 79.
Kirk of St Mary in Ettrick forest, 59, 3.
Kirkaldy, 20, 2.—146, 45.
Kirkandris, 5, 2²—6, 33.—9, 91.—42, 40.—27, 1.—25, 7¹.—47, 3¹.
Kirkassily, 65, 11.
Kirkbothewick, 5, 20. 21.
Kirkgunyan, 68, 5.—84, 186.
Kirkhope, 144, 35.
Kirkhuird, 124, 11.
Kirkintullo, 8, 20.—113, 33.—146, 49.
Kirkland, 27, 118.
Kirkmaho, 54, 9.
Kirkmichael, 8, 77. 82.—10, 15.—12, 65.—13, 84.—20, 8.—26, 27.—47, 1².—50, 4.—119, 35.—133, 13.
Kirkornock, 45, 33.
Kirkofwald, 116, 59.
Kirkpatrick, 9, 94.—12, 69.—13, 35.
Kirktown, 16, 5.—162, 17.
Kirkubry, 32, 21.
Kittockside, 125, 33.
Knapdale, 15, 1²—118, 14.
Knocis, (Knocks), 12, 71.—21, 36.

3 B

INDEX TO THE LANDS, TOWNS, MATTERS, &c.

Knockenblane, 17, 48.
Knockgy, (Knocky), 18, 79.
Knockingulran, 14, 111.
Knochebirvan, 35, 15¹.
Knodworth, (Knoydart), 2, 53.—48, 3¹.—9⁹, 316.—131, 29.
Knok, 49, 6.—66, 1¹.—69, l. 23.—72, 27.—78, 117.—137, 14.
Knokhill, 37, 8².
K:okinglas, 54, 11¹.—116, 63.
Knotis, 12, 71.—21, 36.
Kolbak, 114, 20.
Kolbakie, 138, 29.
Kolzilauche, 4, 13.
K adeny, (Kindeny, Kindavic), 19, 87. 95, 299.
Kylcadyow, (Kineadow), 117, 66.
Kyldeleth, 132, 33.
Kyldmithane, 118, 18.
Kyle, 14, 104.—22, 58.—32, 19.—41, 11.—44, 58.—55, 16.—64, 17.—77, 108.—24, 292.—95, 297. 301—117, 69.—131, 14.—140, 36. 37.—149, 50.—162, 17.
Kylllowrie, 145, 21.
Kyllelare, 119, 17.
Eyllofbarne, (Clofeburne), 164, 46.
Kylmald, 136, 18.
Kilzilany, 142, 70.
Kynbeonn, 72, 27.
Kynehubr, (Kychumb'), 69, l. 36.—3, 40.
Kyndeloch, 91, 264.
Kyneff, 83, 172.
Kyneil, 165, 2.
Kynzenny, 8c, 140.
Kyngerok, 166, 6.
Kyraffalde, (Kirkufwald), 77, 110.
Kythreul, 34, 11.

L

Lachis, 95, 3¹.
Lachkerelien, 26, 30.
Lachopes, 52, 55.
Ladcashy, 121, 79.
Ladeglaßhun, 59, 6.
La lytoun, 33, 45.
Lagb, 3, 45.
Lagrelaier, 20, 9.
Lalanis, 14, 9¹.
Lalchmure, 40, 22.
Lainzie (Leinzie, Leny, Leigne), 30, 6.—35, 6.—54, 11¹.—67, 2¹.—113, 52.—11¹, 63.—124, 24.—146, 34.
Lamlingitoun, (Lamingtoun), 36, 18.—22, 19.
Lambertoun, 4, 6.—5, 18.—7, 53.—15 23—3 , 17.—39, 7.—45, 14.—5², 35.
Lambrechtoun, 7, 53.—15, 23.—146, 27.—50, 85.
Lanach, 28, 3.
Lanark, 8, 76.—23, 38.—74, 12.—82, 170.—139, 3.—144, 27.—145, 24.—158, 47.
Langbank, 142, 81.

Langforgund, 9, 6.—11, 42.—26, 19. 20.—29, l. 3.—55, 7.—83, 175.—114, 25.—121, 86.—125, 28.
Langformacus, 9, 6.—11, 42.—144, 80.
Laughall, 144, 35.
Langherdmanfloun, 7, 71.—140, 40.
Langleyis, 48, 34.
Langnewton, 10, 13.—21, 22.—116, 6.
Languuddrie, 7, 69.
Langriggs, 12, 74.—15, 7.
Langlyde, 162, 17.
Langtoun, 22, 1. 2. 3.—79, 137.
Larache, 60. 19.
Largauche, (Largo), 49, 2¹.
Largis, (Largs), 7, 52.—95, 302.—96, 306.
Larglan, 51, 29.—54, 14.
Lafingitoun. 47 9.
Loffintulach, 123, 121.
Laltairig, (Reftalrig), 7⁰, 104.
Lattounshiells, (Liftounshiells), 57, 31.
Lutheirich, 08, 328.
Lathrocht, (Lathrifk), 141. 67.
Lauchaw, (Lochow), 26, 18.
Lauder, 10, 21¹.—(Lawedre), 93, 278. 280.
Lauderdale, 2, 38.—55, 18.—79, 127.—142, 71.
Laurefloun, 60, 25.
Law, 117, 66. 67.
Law, (Fleming-Law), 61, 2.
Leckie, 8, 9.—119, 25.—163, 30.
Ledlewan, (Leydlovane), 50, 10.—59, 6.
Ledrewlewle, 59, 6.
Ledynturk, 166, 5.
Lege Flemingo, 61, 2.
Legge island, (Lewes), 48, 1.
Legevyn, 78, 116.
Leith, 119, 18.—145, 7.
Leky, 163, 30. 31.
Lennox, 8, 81. 83.—30, 11.—35, 3.—118, 2.—119, 26.—122, 96.—128, 4.—134, 3.—158, 45.
St Leonard's near Lanerk, 144, 27.—156, 47.
St Leonard's near Perth, 50, 19.
Lefcraige, 2, 31.
Leftogotoune, 37, 18.
Lefnachatis, 27, 5¹.
L´sma'ago, 24, 15.—27, 5¹.
Lafkdevin, (Luffidden), 5, 19.
Lefynarne, (or Lefyvarne), 47, 15.
Letany, 26, 21.
Lethernard, 61, 31.
Letham, 11, 32, 33.—46, 3.—55, 5.—98, 3².—79, 134, 135.—83, 173. 173.—119, 20.—149, 47.—155, 26.
Lethbert, 8, 89.—11, 27.
Lethbertfhiells, 58, 6².—67, 7¹.—87, 234.—118, 16.
Letteir, 142, 18.
Lettirlochlethe, (Lettir-lochlettre), 134, 39.—136, 18.
Lerache, 30, 11.
Leven river, 3, 19.—59, 4.—145, 10.
Levenax, (Lennox), 8, 81. 83.—30, 11.

35, 3.—118, 2.—119, 26.—128, 4.
Levenax Earldom, 118, 2.—122, 96.—134, 3.—158, 45.
Leviland, 21, 19.
Lewes island, 48, 1¹.—99, l. 3.—100, 1.—124, 26.
Ley, 128, 15.—133, 34.
Leydlovane, 50, 10.—59, 6.
Libbertoun, 4, 25.—37, 9².—38, 34.—49. 1¹.—63, 48.—65, 11.—75, 86.—8², 238.—162, 12.
Liberties of Galloway, 13, 80.—33, 26.
Liberty and confuetude, 3, 11.—4, 40. 41.—13, 80.—15, 4.—58, 10².—62, 35.—64, 1.—66, 20. 24.
Liberty, grant of, 16, 26.—47, 22.—66, 22.—89, 249.
Lickein, 20, 5.
Liddall, 21, 22.—39, 3.—139, 7.
Liddifdale, 12, 54.—15, 2.—121, 91.—122, 92.
Lieutenant, office of, 118, 1.
Linach, 47, 14.
Lindoris, 64, 1.—140, 21.
Linlithgow, 9, 11.—35, 17².—5c, 18. 67, 10.—74, 72.—78, 6.—125, 30.—132, 3.—137, 3.—140, 24.—154, 25.—15², 52.
Lintoun, 166, 11.
Lintoun-Rudericks, 15, 1².—27, 7¹. 8¹.—121, 73.
Lintrethin, 161, 3.—163, 18.
Lifelefe, 11, 40.
Litilbarras, 85, 210.
Litilgrethy, (or Littlegrewie), 65, 21.—77, 110.
Littlegurdie, 32, 10.
Lobri, 14, 68.—21 35.
Loch, (Luchy), 21, 25.—136, 18.
Lochaber, 2, 52.—21, 25.—4³, 1.—96, 304—99, l. 3.—100, 1.—118, l. 3.—130, 3.—136, 18.
Locharkage, 136, 18.
Lochaw, 26, 18.—142, 76.—149, 38.
Lucherward, (Lochquharret), 1, 26.—16, 9. 13.
Lochflats, 34, 7¹.—76, 90.
Loch-houfe, 31, 26.
Lochindurbe caftle, 68, 8².—83, 183.—94, 286.—118, 3.—130, 8.
Lochleboghide, 120, 5.—129, 20.
Lochlettre, 134, 39.—136, 18.
Lochleven, and caftle, 31, 45.—36, 46.—98, 328.—114, 14.—125, 5.—141, 67.
Lochlomond, 30, 10.—35, 10.—91, 275.
Lochmertenah, 14, 120.
Lochorn, 135, 16.
L chtoun, 68, 16.—140, 30.
Lochulhke, 58, 5¹.
Lochyardoche, 36, 18.—79, 119.
Loganhoule, 166, 10.
Logibride, 49, 4.
Logtoun, (Lugtoun), 40, 14.—65, 5.—88, 232.—125, 4.—128, 14.—131, 33.
Logy, 31, 43.—42, 10.—69, l. 15.—

INDEX TO THE LANDS, TOWNS, MATTERS, &c. 191

71, 16.—138, 29.— 139, 11.—145,
19.—163, 23.
Logyachray, 148, 35.
Logyardoch, 56, 5.—123, 123.
Logymigill, 124, 5.
Logymurtache, 36, 30.—150, 58.
Logyumchauche, 30, 19.
Lonyanys, 118, 8.
Lorkane, 116, 59.
Lorne, 15, 19.—30, 2, 3.—35, 2.
Loseragie, 2, 31.—166, 8.
Lothian, 7, 60.—41, 1.—57, 37.
Luthurmure, (Luthermure), 41, 40.
Louchdouc, 115, 8.
Lounan, 124, 15.—135, 13.
Luur, 48, 33.—127, 17.
Levat, 165, 2.
Lowdoun, 6, 38.—163, 17.
LowJounhill, 164, 36.
Lucheris, (Leuchars), 19, 110.—20, 119.—58, 11².—61, 12.—114, 20. —138, 29. 37.—141, 60.—150, 58. —162, 13.
Ludniche, 147, 50.
Lufnes, (Lufno), 41, 3.—146, 52. 53. 38, 1².
Lumger, 124, 4.—125, 1.
Lumlethan, 34, 6².—59, 44.—81, 151.
Lummissaine, 3, 20.—39, 6.—154, 4.
Lumquhat, 33, 35.
Lundie, 51, 21.—139, 16.
Lunrois, 43, 24.—44, 51.
Luthris, 19, 110.—20, 119.—58, 11².
Lyandcors, 115, 44.—144, 34.
Lychnoch, 123, 121.
Lyddall, 39, 3.—85, 197.
Lygeardwod, (Ligertwood), 93, 277.
Lykewyne, 2, 30.
Lynearem, 39, 42.
Lynd miln, 64, 7.—76, 97. 98.

M.

Machan, 7, 72.—24, 14.—27, 1¹. 13¹, 26.—139, 3.
Macherderly, 60, 19.
Mockeritoun, 60, 11.—115, 32.—124, 6—148, 27.
Macoiche, 60, 19.—98, 32⁸.— 2⁰, 5 —141, 6².—(Maucnyth, Maucloyeh, 146, 7.—145, 9.
Maculmstoun, 146, 7.—145, 9.
M lesport, 83, 180.
Maines, Maynes, 38, 27.—51, 36.
Mair, office of, 120, 68.— 121, 71.— 127, 25.
Meirsland, (Marisland, 20, 115—22, 52.—44, 12.
Mertown, 120, 68.—127, 25.
M killandis, 142, 36.
Maldesly, (Maaidesly), 8, 76.—117, 66. —13⁴, 33.
Maler, Easter and Wester, 19, 93.—2⁶, 16.—8, 13.—47, 28.—58, 7¹.—6¹, 12. 141, 3.
M erby, 44, 58.—74, 61.
Mulnanc, 4, 22.
M mylcroft, 86, 207.
Mac fl nd, 9, 2.—16, 22.—39, 45.— 101, 7.—131, 31.

Man island ceded to Scotland, 101, 7.
Manderstoun, 34, 10².—81, 155.
Manner, 24, 3. 4. 5. 6. 7.—28, 5.— 5⁵, 12.—137, 18.—144, 35.
Manuel, 97, 320.—131, 21.—156, 27.
Many, 17, 37.—42, 50.
Marhardlery, 98, 328.—125, 5.—141, 67.
Marbottle, 11, 50.
March, Earldom, 74, 63.—85, 195.— 89, 244.—126, 9.—136, 20.— 147, 5.—161, 2.—163, 27.
Marches, keeping of, 108, 30.— 109 38. 37.—147, 54.
Markinche, 158, 53.
Marr, Earldom of, 76, 95.—147, 7.— 166, 14—16⁷, 21.
Marshall, office of, 11, 26.—58, 8².— 115, 48.—162, 11.
St Mary's isle, 23, 10.
St Mary's kirk in Arran, 75, 86.
St Mary's kirk in Ettrick forest, 59, 3.
St Mary's well, 167, 22.
Mastertoun, 3, 16.—7, 70.—21, 28.— 38, 1².
Mauearier, 98, 328.
Maxtoun, 5. 16.—10, 13.—21, 22.— 115, 37.—143, 11.
Maxwell, 5, 14.—115, 42.
Maybie, 45, 28.
Maybole, 93, 282.—114, 1.
Meadowfat, 15, 9.
Meaduwis, (Parc-Meadows), 64, 6.
Meadowspot, 68, 4.
Mearnes, 1, 11.—4, 35.—7, 57.—20, 3.—119, 23.
Measure and Gage, 3⁷, 8¹.
Meiklegall, 148, 25.
Meikle Wardars, (Wardhous), 54, 11².
Melfort, (Melfirthe), 39. 10.
Melginche 142, 84.—161, 7.
Mellowstanes, 163, 32.
Melrois Abbey, rebuilding of its church, 88. 235.
Meminure, 66, 10.—78, 118.—158, 43
Mendrie, 8, 85.—15, 11.—15⁸, 49
Merchinghoun, 28, 16¹.—31, 35.—36, 26.—83, 171.
Merkill, Nether, (Merkill), 67, 1².— 74, 19.
Merlingtoun, 42, 20¹.
Mertoun, 5, 15. 18.—31, 35.—42, 9 —6², l. 14.—71, 15.—93, 276.—
Mishop, 6, 34.
Old M file, 137, 7.
Methelkiche, (Methblick), 15, 18.—16. 18.—114, 18.—119, 23.
Methven, 10, 14.—12, 63.—21, 23.— 51, 1⁰.—90, 255.—114, 15.—119, 42.—120, 58.—12², 26.—151, 3.
Methyvenayn, 12, 63.
St Michael's kirk, 5, 14.
M ⁱ casil, 6, 34.
Mc arland, 148, 31.
Milnarhort, 92, 317.—131, 30.
Mindat, 124, 41.

Milnhauch, (Mylkhauch), 43, 46.—73, 56.
Milntoun, 64, 1.—76, 92.—151, 14.
The Mint, (Cuinzie house), 31, 24.
Minthow, 5, 21.—32, 48.—127, 23.— 141, 14—157, 33.
Mochrum, 25, 16.—85, 195.
Muderwell, 43, 27.—69, l. 30.—72, 33. —115, 37.—132, 9.
Modworth, (Moydart), 2, 53.—48, 3¹. —97, 316.—99, l. 6.—100, 2.—13¹, 29.—136, 18.
Moffat, 6, 37.—50, 9.
M gil, (Mygbill, 128, 9.—133, 28.— 139, 2.—142, 83.
Mulben, (Mulben), 2, 57.— 63. 6.— 83, 181.
Molenadall, (Molevadall), 14, 119.
Molyn, (Moylin), 27, 5².—28, 7.—47, 16.—51, 33.
St Monance, 86, 208.
Monblary, 166, 14.
Monbudok, (Monbodo), 63, 2².
Moncur, 37, 6¹.—149, 39.
Monegoe, 4, 37.
Moneythin, 35, 22.—36, 206.
Monimusk, 46, 8.
Monorgund, 125, 26.
Monslane, 137, 17.
Montfod, 11, 43.
Month, forest and muir of, 117, 72.— 146, 40.
Montroise, 52, 11.—54, 8¹.—87, 216. 217.—143, 6.—162, 9.
Munycabbock, 48, 34.—148, 25.
Monyseithe, 18, 70. 74.—22, 53.
Monygaip, 31, 34.—51, 33.
Monyhagane, 119, 29.
Monykipper, 47, 16.
Morar, 47, 7.—48, 1¹. 3¹.—77, 316. —99, l. 3. l. 7.—100, l. 2.—131, 29.—136, 18.
Morehouse, 135, 13.
Morsemulun, 143, 10.
Morhanic, 61, 32.
Morintoun, 40, 23.
Morphie, 32, 14. 15.—14, 12.—38, 33. —55, 6.—62, 24.—67, 6.—73, 70. —9, 146.—148, 20.
Morlatoun, 141, 30.
Mortlingtoun, (Mordington), 9, 6.— 11, 41.—13⁵, 19.
Morthyll, 118, 17.
Moritoun, 23, 2. 32.—36, 26.—43, 43. —70, l. 12.—73, 55.
Murwarne, (Morven), 48, 3.—99, l. 6. 101, 2.
Mott, 138, 23.
Mountilory, 4, 33.
M ftoun, 93, 177.
M swuray's lands, 16, 10. 14.
M yden, 15, 14.
M ⁱ s, 15, 14.—16, 4.
Muchilvre, 117, 41.
Muculas, nsuls., 19, 89.—26, 14.
Mudelob, (Mudelub), 58, 8.—87, 280.

INDEX TO THE LANDS, TOWNS, MATTERS, &c.

Muirhouse, 7, 57.—84, 184.—85, 193.
Mukelere, 164, 44.—(Meiklour), 144, 28.
Mukerify, 4, 26.—125, 29.
Mukler, 144, 28.
Muldakatu, (Muldavit), 141, 61.
Mull island, 26, 23.—41, 7.—48, 1°.—100, 1.
Mundole, 162, 13.
Munge, 123, 120.
Munlochy, 28, 11².
Muntercaffenff, clan of, 57, 29.
Murebrakis, 166, 6.
Murecroft, 164, 34.
Murlach, 138, 27.
Murletyre, (Murletter) 53, 30.— 63, 44.—91, 26°.
Murray, Earldom, 9, 1.—84, 189.—96, 309.—118, 1.—130. 3.
Murthelache, (Mortlich), 20, 14.—138, 27.
Musfald, 9, 92.
Muthulane, 43, 46.
Mussleburgh, 20, 2.—146, 45.
Myrihall, (Muirhall), 56, 14.
Mylnetelame, 141, 52.
Mylfilliltoun, 43, 45.—70, l. 15.—73, 55.
Mylyis, 27, 1².
Myadewith, (Moydart), 99, l. 6.
Myreairny, 158, 55.

N.
Nachtane, 162, 8.
Narn, 2, 48.—130, 9.
Nairn Honours, 16, 26.—17, 21.—66, 22.—81, 162.—85, 201.— 89, 241. 240.—91, 255.—96, 307.—134, 4.
Nauhame, 144, 42.
Neith river, (Nith), 51, 25.—88, 233.
Nemphlar, 143, 75.
Netherdall, (Netherdaill), 32, 2.—140, 38.
Nether Gask, 43, 23.—72, 29.
Netherholm, 50, 9.
Nether Liberton, 88, 238.
Nether Merkill, 74, 63.
Nethertoun, 142, 31.
Nether Urd, 145, 18.
Netherwood, 32, 22.
Nevivar, (Navar), 140, 31.
Nevay, (Nevay), 141, 54.—146, 27.—139, 22.
Newbattle, 7, 70.
Newbies, 32, 7.—43, 44.—67, 61.—72, 54.—75, 85.
Newbiggings, 93, 278.
Newbooth, 151, 7.
Newbiskis, 33, 37.—34, 15.—79, 130.—151, 2.—162, 8.
New Forest in Dumfries-shire, 81, 162.
Newhall, 148, 15.
Newtoun, 137, 11.
Newlands, 54, 1.—121, 73.
Newpark of Stirling, 52, 15.—87, 211.—90, 253.

Newtoun, 23, 4¹.—58, 7¹.—76, 90.—87, 225.—120, 44.—140, 36.—144, 40.—147, 1.—148, 29.—152, 17.
New-wark in Aberdeen, 38, 14.
New-water, 119, 20.
St Nicholas chapel in Duncanlaw, 145, 13.
Niddrie, 7, 56.—42, 8.—43, 32.—57, 3.—69, l. 13.—70, l. 7.—71, 14.—73, 47.—91, 271.—147, 9.
Nigg, 63, 1¹.
Nisbet, 7, 55. 68.—10, 13.—21, 22.—22, 1. 2, 3.—55, 1. 6.—82, 169.
Nithfdale, 12, 65.—13, 82.—20, 8.—23, 2¹.—51, 25.—62, 40.—119, 30.—146, 44.—149, 48.
Nodclefdale, 6, 47.
Nodrington, 11, 35.
Northampton, treaty of, 101, 9.—103, 11.
North Argyll, 49, 2¹.
North Berwick, port at, 111, 63.
Northeik river, 87, 217.
North halls, 42, 21.
North-raw, 164, 42.
Nortoun, 57, 37.—93, 279. 281.—97, 321.—114, 6, 8.—131, 22.

O.
Oboyn, (Aboyne), 2, 36.—49, 3¹.—50, 13.—53, 6.—163, 20.
Ochiltree, 49, 2¹.—161, 1.
Ochluchry, 91, 272.
Ochterbannok, 53, 23.—91, 261.—132, 9.
Ochtereny, 53, 2.
Ochterhuyd, 43, 45.—73, 55.
Ochyngill, 106, 8.
Odilltoun, (Udston), 27, 2.
Ogilface, 155, 26.
Ogilvie, 46, 3.
Olivercastle, 146, 37.—150, 3¹.
Oncill, 22, 57.—76, 28.—145, 26.
Onyne, (Unyne, Oyne), 16, 25.—54, 15.
Ordis, 16, 10.—13², 23.
Ordyrheyes, (Ordyquith), 68, 6.—83, 151.
Orcheisy, 68, 6.
Orkney, 101, 7.—151, 7.
Ormonay, 32, 12.
Ormishuch, 6, 42.—167, 24.
Ormuchilane, 37, 4.
Ormystoun, 84, 184.—85, 193.
Olbarnytoun, 145. 16.
Otterburn, 63, 22.—115, 45.
Otterstoun, 14, 8¹.—144, 37.
Ouchterhouse, 118, 17.
Oville, Uill, 97, 3.6.—131, 29.
Oulmesti, (Old Melli), 137, 7.
Oures, 52, 12.—87, 218.—94, 287. 288.—95, 314.—122, 97.—144, 4.—125, 1.—130, 9, 10.—131, 28.—137, 6.
Ovircrayline, 131, 26.
Ovirmerkill, 74, 63.

Oxinhame, 50, 1.—115, 37.—127, 23.—133, 22.—143, 13.— 148, 36.
Oyglethic, 59, 6.
Oywalds, 59, 10.

P.
Paisley, Abbey of, 138, 23.
Panbryde, 1, 7.
Panmure, 48, 34.—50, 14.—61, 14.—137, 8.—149, 39.
Parbroath, 48, 34.
Park, 11, 49.—64, 6.—133, 24.
Parkhill, 126, 10.
Parkmeadow, 76, 97.
Parliaments of Scotland, 8, 84.—90, 258.—108, 26.—109, 39. 40. 42¹. 42².—110, 43. 44. 47.—111, 52. 54. 55. 60. 63.—111, 72. 73.—122, 97.—130, 3.—158, 56.
Parnbogal, (Barnbougal), 77, 101.
Passage-boat on Forth, 132, 5.
Passold, 28, 11.
Paxtoun, (Paxtoun), 84, 184.—85, 193.—143, 99.—153, 2.
Pedenan, 11, 49.—31, 30.—36, 21.
Peebles, 40, 17.—63, 51.—68, 1¹.—85, 198.—133, 25.—137, 9.
Peil of Linlithgow, 50, 18.
Pekerlyngi, 72, 29.
Pelainilat, 42, 15.—69, l. 18.—71, 21.
Pencaitland, 7, 55. 68.—38, 18.
Pendreche, 23, 7.
Penefax, 12, 67.—20, 12.
Pennycouk, 148, 15.
Pensions, 42, 6.—45, 38. 39. 40.—46, 47.—50, 5.—52, 3. 7. 50.—62, 42.—63, 49.—64, 8.—67, 3. 4. 5. 9.—69, 6.11.—71, 6. 10. 13.—72, 31.—73, 51. 52.—74, 65. 66. 67. 71. 72.—75, 82.—78, 120. 123.—81, 156.—97, 323.—114, 21. 29.—115, 49.—117, 65.—118, 5.—119, 33.—121, &c. 85. 91.—122, 93.—123, 116.—124, 3.—129, 19.—131, 24. 132, 2.—133, 21. 38.—137, 3. 5.—138, 19. 20. 35. 38.—140, 24. 27. 28. 33.—141, 62.—148, 22.—150, 2.—151, 3. 4. 10. 12.—154, 25.
Pentland, 7, 67.—149, 30. 33.—166, 10.
Pentland Firth, 118, 1.
Perilloun, 6, 39.—140, 34.
Perknoc, 6, 3.
Periluun, 140, 34.
Perth, 19, 86. 91.—22, 50.—26, 35.—36, 22.—50, 19.—62, 30.—64, 9.—66, 5².—70, l. 10.—73, 50.—74, 78.—77, 100.—115, 43.—117, 67.—118, 8.—122, 52.—124, 7.—129, 21.—133, 27.—137, 15.—14, 35.—38.—143, 91.—146, 19. 40.—149, 45.—164, 32.—166, 13.
Petachruch, 146, 33.
Petardy, 117, 68.
Peterllingia, 43, 23.—72, 29.
Petcoks, 148, 1.

INDEX TO THE LANDS, TOWNS, MATTERS, &c. 193

Petcouran, 59, 14.
Petdunedy, 28, 7.
Peteclache, (Pittilloch), 56, 4.
Petfethick, (Pitfichie), 46, 8.
Petfoulden, 64, 6.—76, 97.
Petfour, 47, 27.—50, 7.—61, 3.—76, 94.—124. 15.
Petgarvy, 121, 78.—166, 5.
Pethver, 151, 8.
Petkenny, 32, 12.—36, 3.—38, 36.
Petlony, (Petlouy), 19, 110.—138, 29.
Pet-M'Duffigyll, 28, 7.
Petmagarterache, 63, 2¹.
Petmalduc, 28, 7.
Petmuckſtoun, 17, 46.—121, 71.
Petquhonardy, 158, 48.
Petrevy, 38, 16.—51, 24.
Pettacherache, 47. 24.
Pettachop, 157, 37.
Petta-rach, 26, 19.—52, 29.
Pettedie, 60, 29.
Petten-Wathyner, 19, 108.
Pettie, 41, 39.—44, 5.
Pettinbruynache, (Pattinbringan), 32, 2.
Pettindreich, 140, 38.—144, 16.
Pettland, 63, 43.
Petvet, 72, 29.
Petye, 143, 99.
Philiphauch, 5, 22. 23.
Philorth, 29, 22.—35, 19.—42, 18.— 58, 10⁴.—69, l. 21.
Philphill, 125, 33.
Philpſtoun, 4, 36.
Pillein, 32, 16.
Pilmoore, 68, 1¹.
Pinkertoun, 20, 116.—143, 12.
Pitcorthie, 20, 117.
Pitedye, 33, 43.
Pitglaſſie, 167, 14.
Pitkery, 50, 16.
Pitmillie, 58, 11¹.—59, 13.—167, 23.
Pitſcottie, 44, 5⁸.
Pittencrieffe, 138, 29. 37.
Pittenweem, 2, 34.
Pitvar, 43, 23.
Place-Muylin, 27, 5².
Plain, 56, 13.—64, 8.—76, 98².
Plat, 164, 42.
Platter foreſt, 4, 43.—38, 30.—52, 9. —66, 6.—81, 161.—86, 215.—120, 63.—129, 31.—132, 12.
Plenderlathe, 27, 8².
Plewland, 119, 20.
Pocknave, (Polnave), 147, 8.
P ibuthy, 10, 18.
Polcairn, (Polcarune), 28, 9.—64, 17. —77, 108.
Polgavit, 61, 32.—166, 4.
Polgownie, 164, 34.
Polgield, 158, 53.
Polkanet, 119, 34.
Polles, 3, 15.
Pollinfiche, 57, 1.—91, 269.
Pollock, 18, 22.—140, 25.—144, 40.
P o...ie, 68, 11.
Polmais Marſhal, 135, 10.

Polnekill, 143, 5.
Polquharne, 146, 27.—159, 8.
Poltoun, 13, 96.—34, 11.—79, 127.
Poltrayl, 133, 13.
Portmelen, 33, 39.
Poſſaw, (Poſſo), 144, 35.
Powis, 56, 13.
Pownchie, 21, 29.
Pratum regis, 133, 25.
Pren, (Pirn), 144, 31.
Preubowgal, (Barnbougal), 21, 17.
Prendergueſt, 3, 10.—154, 4.
Preſcoly, (Preſtoly), 17, 32.—53, 2.— 150, 1.
Preſliſfield, 119, 27.—146, 41.
Preſtoun, 63, 54.—121, 73.—123, 112. —125, 32.
Pronny, 167, 21.
Protection, 79, 128.—89, 247.—98, 32.—114, 11.
Pruſtkis, (Puſkis), 19, 110.—138, 29. —150, 58.
Puddleplace, 15, 11. 22.—16, 20. 21.
Pulterland, 127, 25.
Purgeny, 161, 3.
Putterlane, 138, 28.

Q.

Quarrellpottis, 57, 34.
Queensferry, 4 27.—10, 23¹.—22, 48. —146, 45.
Quithope, 165, 1.
Quhitſum. 5, 8.—30, 20.—36, 31. —70, 91.—141, 59.
Quhuhame, 55, 19.
Quhylta, (Quinilt, Cult), 23, 11.—46 53.—49, 4¹.—80, 147.—123, 113. —164, 48.
Quhytburn, (Whythurn), 64, 11.—67. 5².—75, 84.—77, 102.—148, 24.
Quhytthope, 127, 23.
Quintin, 99, 37.
Quuſquen, 167, 21.
Quorthie, 60, 19.
Quyltoun, 55, 16.

R.

Rachan, 8, 83.—119, 26.
Radynauane, 78, 116.
Rahill, 47, 16.—51, 33.
Railltoun, (4, 11.—77, 105.—139, 39.
Rainfarnly, (Ramfurly), 146, 27.— 159, 8.
Raite, (Rate), 22, 56.—35, 17.—38, 15.—85, 192.—98, 326.—124, 14. —144, 39.—146, 43.—158, 53.
Ramertuk, 55, 18.
Ramorgny, 162, 14.
Randilltoun, 53, 30.—143, 12.
Ranliſhaugh, 13, 91.
Raplach, 22, 2.—69, l. 8.—71, 9.
Raſk (Riſk) 147, 11.
Ratho, 9, 11.—21, 31.—40, 21.—57, 37.—93, 279. 261.—94, 89. 27¹.— 122, 104.—131, 11. 13.—135, 14. —145, 9.—164, 42.

Ratray, 97, 324.—131, 25.—138, 32.
Raviniſouik, 52, 53.
North Raw, 164, 42.
Raw of Weſterker, 12, 72.
Raynaldiſtoun, 127, 22.
Reccor, 83, 172.
Recreiſſ, 23, 3¹. 4¹.
Redcaſtle, 18, 75.—48, 32.—54, 2.— 68, l. 22.—83, 177. 178.—135, 13.
Red Friars, lands of, 149, 44
Redhall, 68, 1³.—115, 31.—118, 7.—138, 31.—146, 27.—159, 8.— 161, 1.
Redhewis, 140, 40.
Redmyre, 1, 17.
Red-Plewland, 119, 20.
Redy, 157, 37.
Clerk-Regiſter, 119, 28. (See under " Names of Perſons."
Regniutun, 154, 4.
Reliefs, Wards, &c. in Roxburgh, 3, 2¹.—4, 23.
Rene, 123, 20.
Renfrew, 96, 311.—97, 324.—115, 44. —120, 51.—123, 118.—126, 8.— 129, 20.—131, 18. 25.—137, 14.— —139, 15.—142, 80.—146 27.— 147, 11.—152, 20.—158, 50.—159, 8.
Rellalrig, 64, 13.
Reſtenuet Abb. 4, 42. 43.
Aeſton, 78, 124.
Rethy, 137, 1.—142, 70.—167, 21.
Reverden, 63, 2¹.—127, 26.
Revocations by the King, 52, 49.—52, 23.
Revuana, 6, 34.
Aeythenan, 26, 27.
Riccarton, 9, 11.—21. 31.—53, 30.— 136, 12.—145, 4.—158, 40.
Richard I. King of England diſcharges all claim of ſuperiority over Scotland, 104, 13.
Richitdraw, 34, 9¹.
Kidren, 116, 63.
Kinns of Galloway, 4, 23.—25, 19.— 27, 1⁵.—37, 8¹.—41, 35.—47, 1¹.
Rires, 39. 42.—15.—58.—150, 53. 54.
Riſtun, (Reſtoun), 154, 4.
Rubbiſlaw, 16, 17.—17, 46.—42, 4.— 71, 11.—124, 1.
Robert I. King of Scots, treaty betwixt him and Haquin V. King of Norway, 101, 7.
Robert I. King of Scots, treaty between him and Edward III. King of England, 101, 5.—103, 11.—104, 12.
Robert I. King of Scots, treaty betwixt him and Charles IV. (le Bell) King of France, 106, 14.
Robert II. King of Scots, treaty between him and Charles V. (le Sage) and Charles VI. Kings of France, 100, 4.—111, 64. 68. 112. 63. 70. 71.
Robert II. King of Scots, coronation of, 111, 58.

INDEX TO THE LANDS, TOWNS, MATTERS, &c.

Robert Duke of Albany, Regent of Scotland, treaty betwixt him and Charles VI. King of France, 111, 61.
Robertoun, 145, 15.—166, 11.
Robertfon, 146, 31.
Robertftoun, 24, 10.—33, 27.—135, 15.
Robucky, 67, 7¹.
Rogertoun, 125, 33.
Rollandltoun, 42, 21¹.
Romannock, 142, 71.
Rofay, 140, 42.
Rofenethe, 134, 3.
Rofline, 148, 30. 33.—151, 7.—166, 10.
Rofs, Earldom, 16, 7.—28, 3.—53, 20.—50, 25ᵃ.—124, 20.—150, 9.
Roffie, 141, 55.—166, 17.—162, 8.
Roffythe, 45, 41.—159, 1².—162, 15.
Rothemay, 16, 8.—20, 16.—26, 34.—32, 18.
Rotherftoun, 52, 54.
Rothes, 2, 57.
Rothneim, 69, l. 33.—72, 37.
Rothuen, 73, 57.
Rothy, Little, 2, 19.
Rothynorman, 42, 41.—72, 27.—127, 17.—140, 43.
Roucan, 13, 76. 85.—65, 9.—74, 73. —88, 236.
Rowallan, 54, 4.—143, 5.—152, 18. 19.
Rowbaiky, (Robebuky), 67, 7.—74. 69.
Roxburgh, 3, 2ᵇ.—5, 14.—11, 51.—12, 60.—5, 8.—74, 59.—126, 12. —131, 10.—139, 7.—147, 8.
Roxburgh caftle, 104, 13.—128, 11.
Rulwod, 121, 83.
Rune, (Roumme, Rum), ifland, 48, 3¹. —97, 316.—99, l. 6.—100, 2.—131, 29.—136, 18.
Rungiftoun, 31, 28.
Ruffel-land, 142, 81.
Ruthirfurd, 5, 16.—127, 23.—166, 12.
Ruthirglen 8, 79.—9, 12.—23, 9.— 55, 18.—121, 90.—132, 6.—133. 17.—137, 13.—157, 34.
Ruthven, 43, 33.—44, 54.—140, 31. —142, 87.—144, 24.
Ryinholme, 142, 81.

S.

Salachethe, 8, 85.
Salary, 114, 29.
Sakehy, 91, 275.
Saline, (Sawline), 25, 5¹.—45, 24.— 147, 13.
Sallochill, 68, 9.
Salmakeren, 14, 114.
Salmelloun, (Sametoun), 46, 51.—143, 98.
Saltcoats, 16, 18.—84, 186.
Sałtoun, 137, 1.
Salveueich, 45, 24.
Sanaigh, 31, 25.—36, 36.
Sandford, 144, 40.
Sandhaugh, (Sandhaulch), 62, 41.— 166, 14.
Sandie-water in Tay, fifhing of, 47, 23.
Sannacks, 13, 90.—32, 20.—36, 42.— 55, 20.
Sanquhar, 5, 27.—12, 70.—21, 34.— 42, 17.—47, 21.—54, 12¹.—69, l. 20.—72, 23.—164, 34.
Safine, fymbol of to Douglas of Douglas, 10, 26.
Safine taken in the fame manner in 1367, as at prefent, 110, 47.
Sauchop, 2, 46.
Scarry, 49, 8.
Scathochy, 138, 37.
Schauen, 69, l. 35.—72, 39.
Scheils, 11, 36.
Schelgreine, 5, 23.
Schelynlaw, 157, 31.—163, 28.—166, 9.
Schenval, 97, 317.—131, 30.
Schephalche, 120, 61.—129, 29.
Schithun, 138, 22.
Schleples ifland in Tay, 26, 13.
Schyrwaghthyne, 26, 25.
Schyvilt, 158, 42.
Senon, 4, 33. 40. 41.—49, 85.—22, 51.—27, 19.—122, 97.—130, 3.— 158, 56.
Scotland, act of fettlement of the Crown of, 111, 63.
Scottifberyn, 1, 10.
Scuttitloun, 29, 23.
Seraling, (Skirling), 24, 10.—43, 28. — 72, 34.
Serelburgh, 12, 74.
Serogiltoun, 79, 127.
Seuchale, 153, 1.
Seafield, 20, 113.—37, 7¹.—97, 319. —130, 6.
Seatoun, 10, 19¹.—21, 41.—27, 2¹. 3¹. 4³.
Second teinds, 51, 25.—62, 31.
Sceflat, 119, 38.
Segey, 59, 6.—148, 21.
Schenvllis, 56, 10.
Selkirk, 21, 30.—34, 16.—60, 12.— 79, 131.—139, 7.—145, 15.
Selkirk foreft, 10, 24.—55, 18.—63, 1.
Semell, 144, 40.
Senefchar, 5, 27.
Seres, (Ceres), 64, 20.—159, 1¹.—166, 6.
Serjeandry, office of, 8, 83.—33, 46.— 63, 46. 48.—64, 12.—67, 5¹.—77, 103.—119, 26.—124, 9.
Seying, (Affaying), of money, 31, 40.
Shanbody, 61, 11.—83, 177. 178.— 114, 20.—135, 13.
Shangwer, 41, 17.
Shawfield, 24, 16.—30, 21.—36, 32.
Sheks, 60, 24.
Sheriff, office of, 39, 49.—42, 19.— 46, 45.—4³, 35.—51, 22. 37 38.— 53, 25.—63, 45.—68, 3¹.—69, 4, 5. —74, 7.—72, 25.—85, 200.—87, 222.—98, 330.—114, 12.—137, 15. 16.—139, 7.—142, 79. 88.—148, 26.—162, 10.—163, 19.
Shetland, 101, 7.—151, 7.
Shualtoun, 95, 297.
Sindegaits, (Suidegaits, Snidegaits), 2, 28.
Skathachy, 138, 29. 37.
Skeagmorchky, (Skeoch Morchy), 41, 5.
Skeen, loch of, 16, 24.
Skeith, 16, 12.—32, 3.—45, 18.—60, 16.—68, 14.
Skeldoun, 14, 120.
Skelmurly, 146, 27.—159, 8.
Skeok, 66, 23. 25.—90, 250. 252.— 129, 16.—145, 18.
Skirling, (Scraling), 24, 10.—121, 88.
Skonie, 59, 14.
Sky, 2, 56. 58.—53, 20.—90, 258.— 124, 26.
Slamannan, 21, 19.—34, 9¹.—79, 125. —115, 37.—132, 9.
Slanes, 1, 35.—55, 4.—83, 172.—120, 47.—123, 17.
Slavery, emancipation from, 89, 249.
Sleplets ifland in Tay, 26, 13.—60, 20. —117, 67.
Slochan, 12, 68.—21, 35.
Smallgyllis, 115, 40.
S.nethieltoun, 116, 64.—132, 4.
Smithfield, 54, 6.
Smithiehill, 123, 125.—132, 4.
Smithieland, 44, 12.
Smyld, (Sivyld, Swild, Sinyld), 14, 110. 113.—53, 22.—91, 260.
Snath, 6, 31.—13, 95.
Snegil, (Suegil), 12, 72.
Softlaw, 115, 42.
Somerftoun, 97, 325.—131, 26.
Sorne, 162, 17.
Sornefawlache, 144, 21.
Soureby, 25, 9¹.
Southaiks, 46, 6.
Southall, 41, 12.—42, 21.
Southbarn, 116, 59.
Southborland, 20, 115.—22, 52.
Southefk river, 86, 212.—87, 216. 217.
Southfield, 8, 87.
Spey river, 42, 16.—69, l. 19.—71, 22.
Spittletoun, 119, 27.
Spott, Eaft, 34, 12.—76, 91.
Sprouftoun, 12, 56. 58. 62.—15, 20.— 45, 17.—54, 3.
Stabilgortoun, 10, 16.—21, 26.—55, 18.
Staluire, (Stair), 14, 115. 117.—119, 29.
Stanchoufe, 56, 19.—62, 26.—73, 40. —138, 25.—139, 4.—148, 14.
Stancleye, 98, 311.—131, 18.—152, 20.
Stenypath, 32, 16.—46, 1.—166, 11.
Stevingftoun, (Steinltoun), 6, 38.—45, 21.—144, 18.
Steward of Scotland, 46, 49.
Stewartoun, 14, 109.—23, 12.—167, 24.

INDEX TO THE LANDS, TOWNS, MATTERS, &c. 195

Stirling, 8, 87.—9, 11.—27, 10.—28, 15.—51, 41.—87, 227.—114, 3.—121, 84.—132, 10.—134, 6.—139, 41.—163, 22.—159, 4.
Stirling, Carſe of, 30, 12.
Stirling caſtle, 53, 25.—87, 222.—104, 13.—132, 32.
Stirling, old and new parks of, 52, 15. —67, 4¹.—75, 83.—87, 221.—90, 253.—93, 284.—135, 11.—147, 12.
Stobbs, 61, 13.
Stockertoun, 37, 2.
Stocket foreſt, 2, 42.
Stockrude, 167, 22.
Stodfauld, 68, 4.—83, 180.—118, 10.
Stormont, 56, 12.
Strachur, 116, 57.
Straglas, (Strathglas), 2, 60.
Straloch, 32, 4.—141, 47.
Stranraer, 25, 4.
Strathachin, 42, 21³.—72, 27.—78, 117.—111, 73.
Strathalvechi, 147, 7.
Strathbarbus, 142, 82.
Strathawn, 2, 30.—118, 4.
Strathbogie, 1, 20.—2, 40.—11, 26.—58, b¹.—118, 11.—147, 55.—162, 11.—163, 32.
Strathbran, 31, 43.
Strathbrock, 11, 2².—34, 17.—79, 132.—141, 45.—151, 13.
Strathconnan, 2, 60.
Strathean, 1, 15.—15, 17.—15, 4.—17, 41.—120, 45.
Stratherbin, 66, 1.
Stratherne, 24, 7¹.—72, 29.—94, 294.—95, 303. 304.—96, 310.—120, 53. 60.—121, 79.—129, 2. 27. 28.—130, 4.—131, 16.—149, 57.—167, 21.
Strathes, 149, 39.
Strathevin, 40, 20.—41, 17.—59, 15.
Strathnarn, 132, 12.—133, 14.
Strathipey, 2, 59.
Strathurd, 31, 43.—36, 43.—49, 4¹. —52, 47.—63, 43.
Strathy, 167, 21.
Stratoun, 142, 72.
Stroglaſh, 159, 9.
Stron, 146, 28.
Strowan, 141, 48.
Struburne, 138, 29.
Strugartuay, 23, 6¹.
Stukroger, 67, 2¹.
Stulecherberth ſhiels, 33, 40.
Suchayche, 25, 8.
Sunderland, 27, 7.—124, 11.
Sundrum, 20, 10.—53, 12.—57, 16.—91, 260.—115, 38.
Suneereech, 141, 67.
Suegill, 21, 37.
Superiority over the kingdom of Scotland, the extorted conceſſion of, charged by King Richard I. of England, 104, 13.
Suthayk, 25, 8.—56, 18.

Suthbarn, 116, 59.
Sutherland, 15, 17.—16, 4.—32, 5.—72, 36.—120, 46.—124, 26.
Swanſtoun, 68, 1¹.
Swinewde, (Swinewood), 154, 4.
Swintoun, 122, 92.
Swynſide, (Swynhede), 127, 22. 23.
Swynwort, (Snoydart), 136, 18.
Syandford, 139, 5.
Sydſerff, 114, 16.
Syllynghowys, 115, 46.
Symonitoun, 8, 78.—27, 9.
Sympleland, 44, 3.
Synellſhope, 166, 10.
Sypeland, 13, 97.

T.

Tah-Unyſtoun, (Thurſton), 97, 324.
Talligartis, 64, 7.
Talling, 64, 20.
Tannadice, 18, 65.—39, 56.—67, 3¹. —74, 76.—89, 249.—164, 33.
Tarbard, 120, 64.—129, 32.
Tarbettis, 17, 56.
Tarnaway, 35, 14.—84, 189.
Tarnedell, 2, 59.—16, 15.
Tarres, 162, 13.
Tarrodall, 2, 59.—16, 5.
Tarvate, 158, 53.
Tay river, 39, 55.—47, 23.—86, 212. —82, 216.—117, 67.
Techyntulchy, 60, 18.—98, 328.—125, 5.—141, 67.
Teinds, ſecond, 5, 25.—29, 10.—62, 31.—167, 19.
Telin, 61, 32.—166, 4.
Teminynane, (Tomenaygne), 59, 9.—98, 328.—125, 5.—141, 67.
Tempar, 123, 121.
Templeland, 119, 38.
Templeſtoun, 11, 56.
Templihall, 84, 184.—85, 193.
Teviotdale, 5, 12.—10, 23¹.—150, 6¹. —17, 37. 46. 47. 55. 56.—18, 59. 60. 61. 70. 77. 80.—23, 4³.—28, 6.—32, 4.—33, 37.—36, 2.—37, 19.—38, 22. 32.—39, 42. 56.—52, 14. 60.—14.—62, 19.—63, 53.—65, 2. 15. 16.—66, 3.—67, 3⁴.—70, l. 11. —73, 51.—4, 76.—78, 121.—79, 130.—80, 144.—81, 157. 158.—80, 220. 229.—89, 212. 243. 249.—96. 307. 315.—117, 72.—121, 72. 75. 78.—124, 2. 13. 18. 25. 25.—129, 24.—131, 27.—133, 13.—164, 33.
Thainitown, 38, 17. 29.—124, 2.
Themalw, 141, 67.
Thirleſtane, 33, 45.
Thuſtcotys, 166, 7.
Tholoche, 162, 17.
Thomaſtoun, 68, 15.
Thomcury, 141, 4⁷.
Tnor, 61, 44.
Thorboll, 43, 30.—69, l. 32.—72, 36.
Thorn, 18, 68.

Thornley, (or Thornyle), 97, 324.—131, 25.—142, 80.
Thorntoun, 1, 13.—125, 33.
Thornwell, 145, 4.
Thornydike, 148, 19.
Thriepwood, 30, 15.—35, 16². —65, 7. —88, 234.
Throſs, 141, 67.
Thurſton, 46, 45.—53, 30.—91, 267. —97, 324.—123, 124.—131, 23. 25. —145, 4.
Tibbers, 41, 5.—43, 43.—70, l. 12. —73, 53.
Tiningeham, 153, 1.
Tirade, (Tirœ), iſland, 48, 1.—99, l. 3. 100, 1.
Todſchaw, 143, 98.
Tolee, 38, 22.
Tolecandalantum, (probably for Toke and Allantun), 38, 22.
Tollie, (Towie), 17, 34.—43, 40.—167, 21.
Tolligdunache, 34, 3.
Jullamache, 60, 23.
Tulygart, 76, 98.
Tolyquonlach, 78, 121.
Tolvry, 97, 317.—131, 30.
Torboltoun, 53, 5.
Torbreakis, 8, 87.
Tornakyders, 94, 295.—131, 17.
Torranys, 116, 63.
Torrinturks, 15, 19.
Torſa iſland, 15, 10.
Torthorald, 5, 29.—13, 76.—15, 1¹. —140, 18.
Torwood, 129, 16.—145, 6.—159, 2¹.
Toſkertoun, 13, 93.
Tothia Darroch, 146, 44.
Touich, 50, 17.—139, 14.—159, 6.
Toulche-Adam, 38, 31.—65, 1.—87, 228.—56, 27.
Toulche-Fraſer, 8, 86.—163, 19.—167, 27.
Toulche-Maler, 38, 31.—65, 1.—87, 228.
Trabeoch, 14, 104.—22, 58.
Trabreiche, 14. 104.—22, 53.—167, 26.
Trabuyage, 167, 26.
Traquair, 10, 24¹.—37, 4¹.—44, 11. —57, 26.—64, 15.—77, 106.—121, 17.—157, 31.—163, 28.—166, 9.
Trauerigliſs, (Terruglis), 64, 5.—76, 96. —149, 57.
Trauernert, (Tranent), 7, 56. 58. 71. —10, 22¹.—15, 8.—22, 44.—27, 1¹.—141, 9.—163, 25.
Treaty betwixt Robert II. King of Scotland and Charles V. King of France, 100, 4.
Treaty by which Magnus IV. King of Norway ceded the iſland of Mann to Alexander III. King of Scots, confirmed by Haquin V. King of Norway and Robert I. King of Scots, 101, 7.

INDEX TO THE LANDS, TOWNS, MATTERS, &c.

Treaty of Northampton, betwixt Robert I. King of Scots and Edward III. King of England, 101, 9.—103, 11.
Tregvere, (Troquier), 116, 56.
Trepren, (Trapren), 41, 12.
Treuchan, 93, 282.
Treuercrageis, 14, 114.
Trona et Tronariis de, an act of parliament, 109, 42.
Trone, 95, 100.
Troupe, 53, 3.—166, 18.—162, 10.
Trouterneis, 2, 58.
Tubcrache, 63, 2¹.
Tulachard, 21, 25.
Tulchgorne, (Tulchgorum), 52, 2.—86, 209.
Tullibeltyn, 124, 12.
Tullachgorme, 123, 119.
Tullachroskie, 123, 121.
Tullenedy, 26, 14.—143, 32.
Tullibody, 71, 21.—138, 37.
Tulliboyl, 17, 5⁰.—42, 16.—71, 22.
Tullicultry, 43, 36.—51, 26.—70, l. 9.
—73, 49.—134, 2.—139, 7.—167, 28.
Tullicurran, 141, 82.
Tulliebardine, 43, 23.—69, l. 26.—72, 29.—151, 8.
Tulliecravan, 37, 17.
Tullimaddis, 48, 34.
Tullimuchache, 61, 10.
Tulliwhenland, 140, 64.
Tulloch, 69, l. 20.—72, 23.
Tulquhurst, 166, 14.
Tulybrek, 158, 53.
Tulyochys, 37, 7².—98, 328.—125, 5.
Tutyngford, fishing of, 119, 20.
Tweeddale, 24, 5.
Tweed river, 3, 17, 18.
Twehener, (Toyer), 52, 47.
Twenethwany, 23, 4¹.
Twecurie, 116, 64.
Twinhame, 30, 13.—32, 20.—51, 36.
Twyndschiels, 141, 49.
Tyne river, 33, 45.
Tynot river, 41, 16.—71, 22.
Tyrebrg, 135, 12.
Tyrie, 37, 7.—91, 273.—97, 319.—130, 6.
Tyringis, 26, 23.

U.

Uchiltrie, 49 2¹.—161, 1.
Uchteardore, 19, 96.
Uchterbanpok, 23, 5². 6¹.
Uchtererne, 64, 4.
Uchterhouse, 1, 12.—149, 42.—150, 2.
Uchterfeatmiln, 143, 98.
Uchtertyre, 18, 72.—163, 26.
Uist island, 48, 3.—99, l. 6.—100, 2. —131, 29.—135, 18.
.lks, 26, 23.

Unrowris, 2, 54.
Unthank, 54, 7².
Unyn, (Oyne), 16, 25.
Ur, 9, 3.—41, 38.
Urde, 24, 2.
Urecis, (Oures), 52, 12.—87, 218.—124, 4.
Urmotstoun, 93, 280.—114, 7.
Urquhard, 49, l. 25.—94, 293.—96, 309.—130, 3.—131, 15.
Urwell, (Orwell), 24, 7¹.—25, 2².—41, 9.—125, 5.—141, 67.
Uster, office of, 119, 24.
Uvinmomunde, 162, 17.
Uvyrereline, 97, 325.

V.

Valiferne, 13, 95.
Vassalage, exemption from, 68, 1.
Velachis, 19, 100.
Veldelle, 98, 328.
Venedududoch, (Benedududoch), 26, 31.
Vogry, 122, 106.
Vynwale, 136, 18.

W.

Wachopdale, 12, 74.—15, 7.
Wachuphead, 147, 3.
Wairistoun, 26, 19.—158, 40.
Wallachan, 60, 19.
Wallecungy, 19, 110.
Walteris, 1, 12.
Walylloun, 62, 38.
Ward, 159, 1².
Wardhoule, (Wardurs) 54, 11².
Wardland, 16, 14.
Wards, Reliefs, &c. in Roxburghshire, &c. 3, 2¹.—4, 23.
Warekewry, 47, 11.
Warwickhill, 6, 39.—140, 34.
Warwicks, 140, 34.
Water port of Berwick, 39, 53.
Watertoun, 35, 12.—84, 187.—134, 4.
Wathyner, 19. 108.
Wattystoun, 164, 33.
Wauchopheid, 147, 3.
Wauchton, 117, 75.—164, 41.
Wectoun, 164, 41.
Welew, 6c, 19.
Wellcroft, 8, 87.
Wellstats, 34, 7².—76, 90.
Welltown, 84, 187.—134, 4.
West-Barns, 119, 38.—137, 4.
West-Binns, 74, 74.
Westbow of Edinburgh, 44, 10.
Wester-Brichtey, 166, 16.
Westercraigs, 22, 48.
Wester Fothey, 138, 29.
Westerkennet, 146, 43.
Westerker, 3, 4¹. 5.—10, 19¹.—12, ¹. 72.—21, 36. 37.—22, 46. 47.
Westerraw, 11, 49.

Westertulachy, 141, 67.
West Ferny, 49, 10.
Westfield, 119, 3d.—151, 14.
Westuird, 56, 7.
Westhall, 57, 37.—94, 289. 291.—97, 324.—131, 14. 13. 22.—135, 14.—164, 42.
West Mater, 47, 28.
Whitburoe, 64, 11.—67, 5¹.—75, 84.
White Friars lands, 146, 46.
Whitehill, 149, 39.
Whitelaw, 145, 9.
Whitemyre, 8, 87.
Whitsum, 5, 7. 8.—30, 20.—56, 6.
Whittingham, 136, 20.
Whytflad, 93, 277.
Wichcrofs, 59, 16.
Wigtoun, Earldom, 35, 14².—81, 154. —97, 318.—130, 5.—134, 5.
Wigtoun, Rinns of, 67, 1².
William King of Scots, discharge to him by King Richard I. of England, of King William's concession of superiority over the kingdom of Scotland, 104 13.
Wiltoun, 9, 17.—39, 2.—143, 98.
Winkystoun, (Winkstoun), 65, 23. 24. —78, 112. 113.—135, 34.—145, 14. —148, 14.
Wintoun, 147, 7.
Wistoun, 38, 38. 39.—132, 9.—141, 21.¹.
Witfield, 59, 14.
Withitoun, 68, 2².—83, 178.
Withnybope, 159, 3.
Wodefield, 97, 319.—130, 6.
Wodgrenyntoun, 65, 23. 24.—78, 112, 113.—145, 14.
Wodland, 148, 25.
Wodolry, 123, 124.
Wolmaniston, 138, 29. 37.
Woodhall, 115, 31.—123, 124.
Wool, custom of, 147, 4.—154. 24.—158, 26.
Wool, an act relative to the weighing of, 109, 42.
Worg, 30, 13.—35, 2.
Worgar, 35, 13¹.
Workachglen, 14, 106.
Wrights Houses, 124, 23.—137, 9.
Wroklache, 60, 19.
Wymachy, 80, 140.

Y.

Yester, 61, 32.—166, 4.
Yhethame, (Zethame, 115, 33.—148, 27.—164, 39.
Ylle island, (Yla), 48, 1.—99, l. 2.—100, 1.
Yuleshiells, 24, 11.
Ywest island, (Uist), 48, 3.—99, l. 6.—100, 2.

APPENDIX.

OBSERVATIONS, by the Editor of the preceding Index, relative to an Act of Settlement of the Crown of Scotland, passed in the First Year of the Reign of King Robert II. 27th of March 1371.

Of which remarkable Instrument a Fac-simile has been engraved, by the direction and at the expence of LORD FREDERICK CAMPBELL, Lord Clerk-Register for Scotland.

THE succession to the Crown of Scotland, anterior to the days of King Malcolm III. appears not to have been directed by any fixed rule. The sceptre, indeed, seems to have been always swayed by the descendants of the same family. But we see brothers succeeding to brothers, and nephews to uncles, much more frequently than sons to fathers (*a*). The succession to the crown of Scotland, anciently irregular,

Even on the supposition that superior merit, and greater ability for government, were, by the usage of that remote period, understood to constitute a preferable title to the throne, still it is obvious that cabal and faction must have had a powerful influence on the elevation of the different Sovereigns to the regal dignity. Hence plots, assassinations, and all the miseries of civil war.

To avoid those calamities, ruinous to the public in general, and productive of perpetual disquiet and alarm to the reigning Prince in particular, it became an object of most anxious desire to the whole nation, that the right of succession to the crown should be ascertained by some clear and certain rule.

Various attempts accordingly appear to have been made to attain an object in every view so desirable: But private ambition for a long while combated the general advantage with too much success.

At length, however, the crown of Scotland seems to have become strictly hereditary in the descendants of King Malcolm III. by his Queen Margaret, of the Saxon royal family of England. Becomes at length strictly hereditary.

The more effectually still to guard the public tranquillity from the effects of private intrigue, a custom became prevalent, during a period of more than two centuries, of making a public declaration, during the life of the reigning sovereign, in favour of the prince who was to succeed him in the throne. Customary for the reign of King to declare his successor.

Thus we learn from Fordoun, that King David I. the third and youngest son of King Malcolm III. immediately after the death of his only son Henry Earl of Northumberland and Hunting- King David I. orders his grandson Malcolm to be proclaimed his successor.

(*a*) Of five and forty kings who are stated to have reigned in Scotland between King Fergus II. and King Malcolm III. only three are said to have been succeeded by their sons.

(A)

APPENDIX.

don in the year 1152, ordered Malcolm, the eldest son of that Henry, to be conducted through the provinces of Scotland, and proclaimed heir of the kingdom (a).

That King Malcolm died prematurely, in the 26th year of his age.

King William has his son Alexander acknowledged his successor.

King William, the brother and successor of King Malcolm IV. followed with peculiar care the example set him by his grandfather King David.

As early as the year 1195, during a tedious illness of King William at Clackmannan, the greater Barons (*Magnates*) having been assembled there, swore fealty to a daughter of King William's named Margaret, as his true heiress, in case he should not have a son by his Queen Ermengarde. Afterwards in the year 1201, the greater Barons in like manner swore fealty, at Musselburgh, to King William's son Alexander, then an infant only three years old: And about four years after, David Earl of Huntington and Garioch, King William's brother, did homage to the same Alexander. Finally, we are told by Fordoun, that when King William was on his death-bed, his son Alexander was, by the Bishops, Earls, and Barons, again recognised as heir of the kingdom (b).

It is likely that King Alexander II. used the same precaution, although our inaccurate historians have overlooked the circumstance.

King Alexander III. gets the right of succession of his grand daughter acknowledged by the barons of Scotland.

Alexander III. actuated by the same motives, rendered still more urgent by an alarming emergency, namely, the death of his eldest son, and, by that event, the probable extinction of the male descendants of Malcolm III. obtained from the Earls and greater Barons a formal obligation to receive as their Queen, and as rightful heir of the kingdom, his grand-daughter Margaret, called the *Maiden of Norway*, and the issue of her body, in the event of his dying without leaving a son *or daughter* begotten of his own body, or of the body of his son (c). This, though overlook-

---

(a) That historian relates the transaction in the following words: " Rex autem David, dissimulato mœrore super " morte unici filii sui Henrici, erat enim sapiens valde, et ex præcedentibus futura cupiens præcavere, attendens idem " Simeis de Moribus, Quicquid a sapiente diligenter providetur, cum ad rem agendam perventum fuerit, facilius superatur atque " decernitur. Melius est enim ante tempus occurrere, quam post vulnus datum remedium quærere: nam serum est cavendi tempus " in medio malorum. Hæc ipse. Timebat enim, propter variabilitatem quæ emerserat in regno suo per patruum suum " Dovenaldum Banum, et fratrem suum Duncanum Nothum, rixantes pro regno, et legitimos hæredes exiliantes, et " paulo post in *Anglia*, in Stephanum regni nepotis sui Henrici filii imperatricis sororis suæ invasorem ; propterea tulit " continuo Malcolmum primogenitum filii sui prædicti, dato eidem rectore Duncano Comite de Fife cum exercitu " copioso, quia ipse senuerat, et fine detrimento corporis regnum peragrare non poterat ; jubens eundem suum nepo-" tulum per provincias Scotiæ circumduci ac hæredem regni proclamari." Book 5. cap. 44. vol. 1. p. 296.

(b) Scotichronicon, vol. 1. p. 509. 516. 519. and 535. where we read as follows, viz " Ubi de die in diem " visibus deficiens, et aliquandiu languens, filio suo Alexandro ab episcopis, comitibus, et baronibus, in regem futu-" rum comitatio et recepto, rebus excessit humanis plenus dierum et senectute bona."

(c) The preferring of any daughter to be begotten of King Alexander's body, to the daughter of his eldest daughter the deceased Queen of Norway, was not only repugnant to the Scots law of representation, by which, in heritable succession, a child comes in place of its deceased parent—the ground on which Baliol's pretensions to the crown were afterwards founded—but was likewise a direct contravention of the marriage-articles between the King of Norway and his Queen; by which it was expressly stipulated, that, failing King Alexander without a son, or without issue of a son, the Queen of Norway and her children should succeed to the throne of Scotland. " Si vero con-

APPENDIX.

ed likewife by our hiftorians, is proved by an original inftrument ftill extant in the Chapter-houfe at Weftminfter (a), expreffed in the following words, viz.

"Omnibus Chrifti fidelibus ad quos præfens fcriptum pervenerit: Alexander de Cumyne Comes de Buchan, conftabularius et jufticiarius Scotiæ; Patricius Comes de Dunbar; Maliſius Comes de Strathern; Malcolmus Comes de Levenax; Robertus de Brus Comes de Carrik; Dovenaldus Comes de Mar; Gilbertus Comes de Anegus; Walterus Comes de Meneteth; Willielmus Comes de Ros; Willielmus Comes Sothirland; Magnus Comes de (Cathania); Duncanus Comes de (Fife); et Johannes Comes Athol; tunc - - - - lleti; Robertus de Brus, Pr. (Pater); Jacobus Senefcal. Scotiæ; Johannes de Balliolo; Johannes Cumyne; Willielmus de Soulys, tunc jufticiarius Laodoniæ; Ingeramus de Gynis; Willielmus de Moravia, filius, Walterus de Moravia, milites; Alexander de (Bal)liolo; Reginaldus le Chen, Pr. (Pater); Willielmus de Sanclo Claro; Ricardus Syward; Willielmus de Brechyn; Nicholaus de Haya; Henricus de Graham; Ingeramus de Baliolo; Alanus filius Comitis; Reginaldus le Chen, filius; J(ohannes) de Lindefey, Patricius de (G)raham; (Herber)tus de Macifwell; Simon Frafer; Alexander de Ergadia; Anegus filius Dovenaldi; et Alang. filius Rotherici; Barones regni Scotiæ; falutem in Domino. Noveritis quod, cum, ficuti placuit Altiſſimo, Dominus nofter Alexander, primogenitus filius———Alexandri, viam fit univerfæ carnis ingreffus, nulla prole legitima immediate de corpore dicti Regis fuperftite, Obligamus nos, et hæredes noftros, artius per præfentes, dicto Domino noftro Regi, et hæredibus fuis de corpore fuo immediate vel mediate (defcen)dentibus, qui de jure ad fucceffionem ipfius debent admitti; et in fide et fidelitate, quibus eis tenemur, firmiter et fideliter promittimus, Quod fi contingat dictum Dominum noftrum Regem, filio aut filia, filiis aut filiabus legitimis de corpore fuo non extantibus, vel de corpore dicti Alexandri filii fui. diem fuum extremum claudere in hac vita: Nos omnes, et quilibet noftrum, inclitam Puellam Margaretam, filiam filiæ dicti Domini Regis Margaretæ bonæ memoriæ, quondam Reginæ Norwagiæ, genitam de Domino Erico Rege Norwagiæ illuftri, recipiemus, et prolem legitimam ex ea defcendentem, in dominam noftram et rectam hæredem dicti Domini noftri Regis Scotiæ, de toto regno,—de infula Manniæ, et de omnibus aliis infulis ad dictum regnum Scotiæ pertinentibus, nec non et de Tyndallia et de Penereth, cum aliis omnibus - - -, juribus et libertatibus ad dictum Dominum Regem Scotiæ fpectantibus vel fpectare debentibus, et - - - - - -fius contra omnes qui vivere aut mori poffunt, manutenebimus, fuftinebimus, et defendemus pro totis viribus noftris et toto poffe noftro (b), &c. &c.——In cujus rei

"tingat, quod Dominus Rex Scotiæ fine filio legitimo in fata decedat, nec aliquis filiorum fuorum prolem legitimam "reliquerit, et dicta Margareta ex dicto rege Norwagiæ liberos habuerit, ipfa et liberi fui fuccedent ditto Regi Sco-"tiæ et liberis fuis, tam in regno quam in aliis bonis."—Rymer's Fœdera, tom. 2. page 1081, article 16.

(a) This inftrument is one of thofe which were carried away from Scotland by the orders of King Edward I. as appears from *Catalogus Munimentorum Scotiæ*, (printed in Sir Jo. Ayloffe's Calendars of Ancient Charters, page 327.) where it is entered thus, viz. " Obligatio Magnatum Scotiæ, facta Regi Alexandro, quod tenebunt Domicellam Nor- " wagiæ pro Domina et Regina Scotiæ." See Introduction, p. 11. l. 10. But it is more fully entered among the *Tractatus Pacis et Trugarum*, p. 288. of the fame book, in the following words, viz. " 1283.—Obligatio Nobilium et " Magnatum regni Scotiæ, per quam obligant fe ad recipiendum Dominam Margaretam, filiam filiæ Domini Alexandri " Regis Scotiæ, genitam de Domino Erico Rege Norwagiæ, in Dominam fuam, et rectam hæredem r gni Scotiæ, " et ad manutenendam prolem legitimam ex ea defcendendam, cafu quo contigerit dictum Dominum Alexandrum Regem " fine filio aut filia de corpore fuo legitime procreat. moriturum.—Sub 3, Iduiis.—Dat. 5 February, 11 Edward I." i. e. 1283-4.

(b) The reft of the inftrument contains an engagement by the barons faithfully to carry into execution the laſt will and teftament of the King. It is therefore immaterial to the prefent queftion.

APPENDIX.

" *teftimorium, plures de nobis apponi fecerunt figilla fua huic fcripto. Dat. apud ········on quinto
" Februarii anno Gratiæ millefimo ducentefimo octuagefimo tertio, et anno regni Domini nostri Regis
" tricefimo quinto (a)*."

But the sudden death of King Alexander III. followed a few years after by that of his infant grand-daughter, rendered those precautions abortive and unavailing; and the nation was involved in all the miseries of a disputed succession to the crown, aggravated by the artful policy of that powerful monarch King Edward I. of England, their ambitious and enterprising neighbour.

We find King Robert I. conducting himself with still greater anxiety in regard to this matter of the succession to the crown: and the peculiarity of his situation demanded extraordinary circumspection. Baliol's pretensions to the crown had been, by King Edward's decision, found preferable to those of Bruce's grandfather; that decision was acquiesced in by the nation; Baliol himself was still alive; a powerful party in Scotland was secretly attached to him; and he had a son, named Edward, whose right could hardly be invalidated by his father's misconduct, or rather, perhaps, by his misfortune.

Besides, Bruce's personal title to the crown could not, at the time when he assumed the government, stand in competition with either that of Baliol or of Baliol's son For the plea of Bruce's grandfather against Baliol, disclaiming the principle of representation, rested entirely on *his being nearer by one degree to the common stock than Baliol was*. But the grandfather, as well as the father, of Bruce being at this time both dead. Baliol was now nearer to the common stock than Bruce was; and Baliol's son, who was in the same degree with Bruce, had the advantage of being descended of the elder branch.

King Robert therefore, aware of all this, after having attained the throne, and vindicated the independency of his country by a persevering intrepidity almost without example, availed himself of the first moments of tranquillity to obtain from the different states of the kingdom a solemn acknowledgment of his own right to the crown, through the medium of the right of his grandfather.

The States of Scotland declare the right of King Robert I's great-grandfather to their crown to have been preferable to that of John Baliol, and admit King Robert himself for their Sovereign.

This measure appears to have been carried into execution in a general council assembled at Dundee in February 1309-10, where the original question about the right of succession to the Crown, as it stood at the time of the competition, having been resumed, an instrument, still preserved in the General Register-House at Edinburgh, was drawn up in the following terms, viz.

" *Omnibus Christi fidelibus ad quorum notitiam præsens scriptum pervenerit: Episcopi, Abbates,*
" *Priores, ac ceteri de clero in regno Scotiæ constituti, falutem in salutis Auctore. Noverit universitas*
" *vestra, quod cum inter Dominum Johannem de Baliolo dudum regem Scotiæ per regem Angliæ de facto*
" *promotum, et recolendæ memoriæ quondam Dominum Robertum de Brus avum Domini Roberti Regis*
" *qui nunc est, orta fuisset materia quæstionis, quis eorum videlicet proximior esset jure sanguinis ad he-*
" *reditandum et regnandum super populum Scoticanum, fidelis populus sine dubitatione semper tenuit,*
" *prout a suis antecessoribus et majoribus intellexerat et crediderat, verum esse quod dictus Dominus Ro-*
" *bertus avus, post mortem Regis Alexandri ejusque neptis filiæ Regis Norwagiæ, verus heres extitit,*
" *et cunctis aliis ad regni regimen præferendus, licet humani generis inimico Zizaniam seminante, diversis*

(*a*) Rymer's Fœdera, tom. 2. page 266.—*N. B.* The syllables here printed within the parentheses are left blank by Mr Rymer.

APPENDIX.

" machinationibus emulorum et cautelis, quas per singula longum esset enarrare, in contrarium res sit
" versa, pro cujus eversione et carentia regie dignitatis dampna gravia regno Scotiæ et ejus incolis ex
" tunc evenerunt, prout facti experientia, rerum magistra, hactenus sepe repetita, manifeste declaravit;
" videntes igitur populus et plebs predicti regni Scotie multarum tribulationum aculeis fatigati dictum
" Dominum Johannem per Regem Angiie pro diversis causis captum, incarceratum, regno et populo pri-
" vatum, ac regnum Scotie per ipsum proditum et in servitutem reductum, ingenti populatione vastatum,
" crebri doloris acerbitate respersum, pro defectu recti regiminis desolatum, omni periculo expositum, et
" occupanti concessum, populumque bonis spoliatum, bellis cruciatum, captivatum, vinculatum, et incar-
" ceratum, stragibus immensis innocentum et continuis incendiis oppressum subjectum et mancipatum, ac
" perpetue ruine proximum, nisi divino concilio circa regni sic deformati ac desolati reparationem, et ejus
" regimen, celerius tractaretur summi Regis providentia, sub cujus imperio Reges regnant et principes
" dominantur ; tot et tanta dampna gravia morte amariora rerum et corporum sepe contingentia pro de-
" fectu capitanei et fidelis ducis, diutius ferre non valentes, in dictum Dominum Robertum regem qui
" nunc est, in quem jura patris avique sui ad predictum regnum judicio populi adhuc resident et vigent
" incorrupta, auctore Domino, convenerunt, ac de conscientia et consensu eorundem assumptus est in
" regem, ut regni deformata reformet, corrigendaque corrigat, et dirigat indirecta, et ipsorum auctori-
" tate regno profectus, Rex Scotorum solemniter est effectus, cum quo fidelis populus regni vivere vult et
" mori, tanquam cum illo qui jure sanguinis et aliis virtutibus cardinalibus preditus, aptus est ad reg-
" nandum, ac dignus regis nomine et honore regni, quod salvatoris gratia injuriam propulsando, regnum
" sic deformatum et proditum gladio reparavit, prout multi retro-principes et Scottorum reges dictum
" regnum, olim sepe proditum, per gladium reparaverant, quesierant, et tenuerant temporibus retroactis,
" ut in antiquis Scottorum gestis magnificis plenius continetur, ac sudores bellici Pictorum contra Britones,
" et Scottorum contra Pictos, de regno fugatos, cum multis aliis antiquitus ense fugatis victis et expulsis,
" manifeste testantur ; Et si aliquis ex adverso jus vendicet in predictum regnum, per literas in prete-
" ritum sigillatas, consensum populi et plebis continentes, sciatis hoc totum de facto processisse per vim et
" violentiam, quibus non poterat tunc resisti, et metus multiplices, cruciatus corporum, ac terrores varios
" qui sensus prefectorum et animos avertere poterant, et cadere inconstantes ; nos igitur episcopi, abbates,
" priores, et ceteri de clero pretaxati, promissa veritati subnixa scientes et corditer approbantes, dicto
" Domino Roberto Regi nostro Scotie illustri fidelitates debitas fecimus, ac sibi et heredibus suis per suc-
" cessores nostros in posterum fore faciendas recognoscimus, et tenore presentium profitemur ; et in signum
" testimonii, et approbationem omnium predictorum, non vi compulsi nec dolo inducti aut errore lapsi, sed
" pura et perpetua ac voluntate spontanea, huic scripto sigilla nostra fecimus apponi. Datum in conci-
" lio generali Scoticano, in ecclesia Fratrum Minorum de Dende, xxIIII die mensis Februarii anno
" domini MCCC nono, celebrato et anno regni ejusdem quarto."

  This instrument was authenticated by twelve seals, appended by labels of parchment. But the seals are now all crumbled away. Even four of the labels are entirely gone, and part of a fifth. On the remaining labels we see written as follows, proceeding from the left hand corner, viz on the first, " St Andr." 2d, " Abirdonens." 3d, " Morauiens " The 4th label is gone; that part of the 5th on which the inscription has been written, is torn off; on the 6th, " Glasguens." the 7th is gone; on the 8th, " Brechenens." on the 9th, " Dunkeldens." on the 10th, " Lismorens." the 11th and 12th are quite gone. Hence the seals seem to have been those of twelve bishops (*a*).

 (*a*) In the British Museum there is a book consisting of three manuscripts, formerly separate, but now bound to-

(B)

APPENDIX.

But, besides this declaration by the whole body of the clergy, the bishops executed a separate instrument by themselves, exactly in the same words, *mutatis solummodo mutandis*, and concluding with the word *apponi*, the date being by that means omitted.

This instrument too still exists in the General Register-House at Edinburgh, though much decayed. Like the former, it was authenticated by twelve seals. Of three of those seals the greater part still remains, namely, those of the Bishops of St Andrew's, Aberdeen, and Murray. But the rest are crumbled away; and three of the parchment labels are likewise gone (*a*).

King Robert next judged it necessary, in imitation of preceding kings, to ascertain the order in which the descendants of his body should succeed to the throne.

With this view, two different acts of parliament were passed; the first in the end of April in the year 1315; the second, in the beginning of December in the year 1318, a few weeks after the death of Edward King of Ireland, King Robert's only brother.

The originals of those two acts are not now among the other records in the General Register-House at Edinburgh. Whether they still exist any where else is uncertain. They are both inserted in the MS. of Fordoun's history, who was cotemporary with the event. Copies of both are likewise in the MS. of Sir James Balfour above mentioned, viz. No. 4694 of the Harleian

---

gether, viz. No. 4693, 4694, and 4697 of the Harleian collection, which appear to have been written by Sir James Balfour of Kinnaird, Lyon King at Arms, about the years 1628 and 1629; and which were attentively perused by the editor in August 1793.

On folio 1. of No. 4694 (which is the second part of the book as now bound) there is a copy of the above instrument; and in a different part of the same manuscript there is another copy of it, to which this singular remark is subjoined by Sir James, viz. "This declaratione is vorde for vorde formerly sett doune in fol. 1. wich I had out of ye castell of E-" dinburghe; and this preciding declaratione is verbatim the same wich I my selve extracted off a double keipt by Sr " Robert Cottone in his thesaury of antiquities at Vestmister; wich I did, to lett posterity see yat ye tuo declarations " ar all one, and differs not, thoughe one be keipte by us and ane uther in England."

The editor wished to see this original instrument among the Cottonian manuscripts; but being informed that it was lost, he made a transcript from Sir James's copy, on the 28th of August 1793. And here justice forces him to observe, that Sir James, though a very industrious, appears to have been a careless transcriber, and that his copies abound with inaccuracies. Between Sir James's copies and the original instrument in the General Register-House a striking and material discrepancy occurs. Both his copies of the declaration are " dat. in parliamento tento apud Sanctum Andream in " Scotia, 17 die Martii anno Gratie MCCCVIII," (i. e. 1308-9.) Sir James adds, " Sex sigilla cere viridis episcoporum " sunt appensa." Whereas, in the original instrument, the date is thus expressed, viz. " dat. in concilio generali Scoti- " canu, in ecclesia Fratrum Minorum de Donde, XXIIII die mensis Februarii anno Domini MCCC nono, celebrato et " anno regni ejusdem quarto," (i. e. 1309-10.) And instead of *six* seals, the number mentioned by Sir James Balfour, *twelve* seals appear to have been appended to this original instrument.

(*a*) The commencement of this instrument, containing the names of the bishops, is expressed thus, viz. " Omnibus " Christi fidelibus ad quorum notitiam presens scriptum pervenerit: Willielmus de Lambertoun ecclesie Sancti Andree, " Robertus Wyscard ecclesie Glasguensis, Willielmus ecclesie Dunkeldensis, Henricus le Chen ecclesie Abirdonensis, " David de Moravia ecclesie Moraviensis, Nicholaus de Balmyle ecclesie Dumblanensis, Thomas de Donde ecclesie Ros- " sensis, Ferchardus Delegannibe ecclesie Cathanensis, Johannes de Kyninmonth ecclesie Brechinensis, Andreas ecclesie " Lismorensis, Thomas ecclesie Candide Case, et Alanus ecclesie Sodorensis, Dei gratia Episcopi, salutem in Domino " sempiternam cum benedictione divina. Noverit universitas," &c. *verbatim et literatim* like the preceding instrument to the word *apponi*, with which word this instrument concludes.

APPENDIX.

collection; and from the words subjoined to Sir James's copies, particularly to his copy of the second, he appears to have made those copies from the original acts themselves, which therefore must have been then existing, and in his custody.

In Sir James's copies there are, as usual, various inaccuracies. But, correcting those inaccuracies by Fordoun, (vol. 2. p. 257. and 290. where the instruments seem to be accurately printed), the tenor of those instruments may be exactly ascertained. The first is expressed in the following terms, viz.

" *Declaratio Parliamenti quod Eduardus de Bruce debet succedere, hæredibus masculis*
" *Roberti Bruce Regis Scotorum deficien.* (a)"

" *In nomine Sanctæ et Individuæ Trinitatis, Patris, Filii, et Spiritus Sancti, Amen. Anno ab*
" *incarnatione Domini millesimo trecentesimo decimo quinto, Dominica proxima ante sestum Apostolorum*
" *Philippi et Jacobi, congregati apud Ayre, in ecclesia parochiali ejusdem loci, episcopi, abbates, pri-*
" *ores, archidiaconi, decani, et ceteri ecclesiarum prælati; comites, barones, milites, et ceteri de com-*
" *munitate regni Scotiæ, tam clerici quam laici, ad tractandum, deliberandum, et ordinandum super*
" *statu, defensione, et perpetua securitate regni Scotiæ, unanimiter concordaverunt et ordinaverunt in*
" *forma quæ sequitur; viz. Quod ipsi omnes et singuli, tam clerici quam laici, magnifico Principi et*
" *Domino suo ligio Domino Roberto Dei gratia Regi Scottorum illustri nunc regnanti, et hæredibus suis*
" *masculis de corpore suo legitime procreandis, tanquam Regi suo et Domino ligio contra omnes mortales*
" *parebunt in omnibus fideliter et assistent. Item ordinaverunt, de consensu dicti Domini Regis, et*
" *Marjoriæ filiæ suæ die præsentis ordinationis hæredis suæ apparentis, quod si contingat, quod absit,*
" *prædictum Dominum Regem sine hærede masculo de corpore suo procreato superstite et permanente diem*
" *claudere extremum, nobilis vir Dominus Eadwardus de Bruce, dicti Domini Regis germanus, tan-*
" *quam vir strenuus, et in actibus bellicis, pro defensione juris et libertatis regni Scotiæ, quam plurimum*
" *expertus, et hæredes sui masculi de corpore suo legitime procreandi, ipsi Domino Regi in regno ipso*
" *succedant; quibus omnes supra dicti, tam clerici quam laici, tanquam Regi suo et Domino successive*
" *parebunt in omnibus, prout superius de persona Domini Regis et hæredum suorum est expressum.*
" *Item ordinaverunt, de consensu dicti Domini Regis, et dicti Domini Eadwardi fratris sui, quod*
" *deficientibus, quod absit, dicto Domino Eadwardo et hæredibus suis masculis de corpore suo legitime*
" *descendentibus, prædicti regni Scotiæ successio ad prædictam Marjoriam, vel, ipsa deficiente, ad pro-*
" *pinquiorem hæredem de eo parte Domini Regis Roberti linealiter descendentem, sine contradictione*
" *cujuscunque, revertatur: dum tamen de consensu Domini Regis, vel, ipso deficiente, quod absit, de*
" *consensu majoris partis communitatis regni, dicta Marjoria matrimonialiter sit copulata. Item*
" *ordinaverunt, quod si prædictus Dominus Rex decedat, relicta hærede masculo minore, vel dictus*
" *Dominus Eadwardus germanus suus, in casu de ipso loquente, simili modo decedat, nobilis vir Do-*

The First Act of Settlement passed by King Robert I. and his Parliament.

(a) This title has probably been composed by Sir James Balfour.

" minus Thomas Ranulphi Comes Moraviæ, ipsius hæredis et regni custodiam habebit, quousque
" communitati regni vel majori parti, visum fuerit ipsum hæredem ad sui regni regimen posse suf-
" ficere. Ordinaverunt insuper, quod si dicta Marjoria in viduitate decedat, hærede relicto mi-
" nore, in casu de ipsa superius expresso, ipsius hæredis et regni custodiam habebit dictus Comes,
" sicut de hæredibus Domini Regis et germani sui in suis casibus est expressum, si idem Comes ad
" hoc suum tunc præbuerit assensum. Si vero dicta Marjoria, nullo hærede relicto de corpore
" suo, aut nullo hærede de corpore Domini Regis Roberti superstite, in fata decedat, quod absit,
" prædictus Comes regni custodiam habebit, quousque prælatos, comites, barones, et alios de
" communitate regni, ad ordinandum et discutiendum super legitima successione et regni guber-
" natione, commode potuerit convocare, si idem comes, ut præmittitur, ad hoc voluerit consentire.
" Quas quidem ordinationes, et earum quamlibet, Dominus Rex, Dominus Eadwardus ger-
" manus suus, Marjoria dicti Domini Regis filia, et Comes Moraviæ, prædicti, in suis casibus,
" ac prælati, comites, barones, et ceteri de communitate, tam clerici quam laici, juramentis
" præstitis corporalibus, fideliter et inconcusse servare promiserunt, et se jurisdictioni episcopo-
" rum et prælatorum regni Scotiæ submiserunt, ut ipsos et eorum successores, per omnimodam
" censuram ecclesiasticam possint compellere ad observationem omnium præmissorum. Et in hujus
" rei testimonium et evidentiam, tam Dominus Rex, Dominus Eadwardus germanus suus, Mar-
" joria filia dicti Domini Regis, et Comes Moraviæ, supradicti, quam prælati, comites, barones,
" et communitatis majores, sigilla sua, una cum sigillis conventualium ecclesiarum et monasteri-
" orum regni Scotiæ, huic ordinationi apposuerunt. Act. et script. anno, die, et loco supra-
" dictis (a)."——Sigilla supra dicta circumcirca sunt appensa, viz. Roberti Regis, Eduardi
de Brus fratris sui, Marjorie filie Regis, Comitis Moravie, Epis. St Andre, Episcop. Glasguensis, Episcop. Dunkeldensis, Episcop. Abirdonensi, Episcop. Candide Case, Episcop. Dumblanensis, Episcop. Catranensis, Epis. Ergadiensis, Abbatis de Dumfermelin, Abbatis de Sancta
Cruce, Abbatis de Aberbrothcock, Abbatis de Kelchou, Abbatis de Londors, Abbatis de Insula
Missarum, Abbatis de Balmuren, Abbatis de Deere, Abbatis de Neubottel, Abbatis de Cupro,
Abbatis de Killoss, Abbatis de Jedwood, Abbatis de Cambuskeneth, Comitis de Fyffe, Patricii
Comitis de Marche, Gilberti de la Hayea militis, Roberti de Keth militis, Alexandri Settone
militis, Alexandri de Rattraie, Ranulpbi de Straqubane, Michaelis de militis, Mi-
chaelis de Balfour Vicecomitis de Fyffe, Johanis de Enderpepher, Johanis de Lacey militis,
Christopheri de Incheyreth militis, Davidis de Annandia militis, Davidis de Balfour de Bulga-
puey, Thomæ de Lochor militis, Alexandri de Ramsey de Dalhousie, Nigelli Campbell militis de
Lochau, Andre de Morauia, Thome Vitchard, cum multis aliis sigillis fractis quorum cir-
cumscriptiones legi non possunt, cum multis etiam prelatorum sigillis absq. ullis inscrip-
tionibus.

The second act of settlement by King Robert I. is expressed thus, viz.

(a) Fordoun stops with the word *supradictis*. From *Sigilla* to the end of this page is taken from Sir James Balfour's manuscript.

APPENDIX.

" *Ordinatio facta de communi consensu totius communitatis regni Scotie, super tuitionem et defensionem jurium et libertatum ipsius regni, et super violationibus dictæ Ordinationis, ac super definitione successionis ad regnum: hoc instrumentum manebat penes Dominum Regem.*" (a)

" In nomine Sanctæ et Individuæ Trinitatis, Patris, et Filii, et Spiritis Sancti, Amen. Anno ab incarnatione Domini millesimo trecentesimo decimo octavo, die Dominica proxima post festum Sancti Andreæ Apostoli, cum continuatione dierum subsequentium ; Serenissimo Principe Domino Roberto, Dei gratia Rege Scotorum illustri, suum plenum parliamentum apud Scouam tenente, cum prælatis, comitibus, baronibus, ac ceteris de communitate regni sui, communi consensu omnium et singulorum prædictorum, inter cetera ipsius regni negotia pro communi utilitate et securitate ipsius regni ibidem tractata et ordinata, ordinatum fuit in forma quæ sequitur, viz. Quod ipsi omnes et singuli, tam clerici quam laici, prædicto Domino Regi, et hæredibus suis, tanquam Regi suo et Domino ligio parebant in omnibus, quilibet secundum statum suum et conditionem, et fideliter pro viribus eidem assistent, pro tuitione et defensione jurium et libertatum regni memorati, contra omnes mortales, cujuscunque potentiæ, quacumque potestate, auctoritate, seu dignitate præmineant. Et quod si quis in posterum, quod absit, istius ordinationis violator extiterit, eo ipso tanquam regni proditor, et criminis læsæ Majestatis reus, in perpetuum habeatur. Item ordinatum fuit, et unanimi consensu omnium et singulorum prædictorum concordatum, quod si contingat, quod absit, prædictum Dominum Regem sine hærede masculo de corpore suo legitime procreato superstite et permanente, diem claudere extremum, Robertus filius Dominæ Marjoriæ bonæ memoriæ, filiæ dicti Domini Regis, ex nobili viro Domino Waltero Senescallo Scotiæ marito suo legitime procreatus, eidem Domino Regi, tanquam hæres suus proximior et legitimus in ipso regno plenarie succedat ; Cui omnes supradicti de regno parebunt in omnibus et fideliter assistent, sicut de persona Domini Regis superius est expressum. Cujusquidem Roberti, vel alterius hæredis de corpore Domini Regis procreati, si tempore decessus dicti Domini Regis minoris ætatis extiterit, tutelam sive curam, ac totius regni et populi custodiam, de consensu unanimi omnium et singulorum de communitate, nobili viro Domino Thomæ Ranulphi, Comiti Moraviæ ac Domino Manniæ, et ipso comite forsan medio tempore deficiente, quod absit, nobili viro Domino Jacobo de Douglas idem Dominus Rex assignavit, quousque communitati regni vel majori ac saniori parti visum fuerit, ipsum Robertum, vel alium hæredem ipsius Domini Regis, ut præmittitur, ad regni et populi regimen posse sufficere. Quam quidem assignationem tutelæ, curæ, et custodiæ, prædicti Dominus Comes, et Dominus Jacobus, tota communitate expresse approbante, in se sponte præstito ad hæc ab eisdem, tactis sacris evangeliis ac sacris rum reliquiis, magno juramento, quod prædictas tutelam, curam, et custodiam, bene, fideliter, et diligenter, ad utilitatem ipsius hæredis et regni, ac totius cleri et populi, gerent, administrabunt, facient, et mandabunt ; jura et consuetudines regni cleri et populi fideliter observabunt, et ab aliis, pro viribus,

The Second Act of Settlement by King Robert I. and the Parliament of Scotland.

(a) This title again, like that prefixed to the first instrument, is probably an addition by Sir James Balfour.

(C)

APPENDIX.

" *obſervari faciendo. Præterea, cum aliquibus prætcritis temporibus, a quibuſdam, licet minus ſuffi-*
" *cienter, in dubium fuiſſet revocatum, quo jure ſucceſſio in regno Scotiæ, ſi clara forſan non extiterit,*
" *decidi deberet ac terminari ; in eodem parliamento per clerum et populum declaratum extitit ac defini-*
" *tum, quod per conſuetudinem in inferioribus feodis ſeu hæreditatibus in regno obſervatam, eum in*
" *ſucceſſione regni aliqua talis conſuetudo hactenus non fuit introducta, minime debuit, ſeu in futurum*
" *debeat, dicta ſucceſſio terminari : ſed quod proximior maſculus tempore mortis Regis ex linea recta*
" *deſcendente, vel maſculo deficiente, proximior femella ex eadem linea recta, vel illa linea penitus de-*
" *ficiente, proximior maſculus ex linea collaterali, attento jure ſanguinis, quo ipſi Regi defuncto jus*
" *regnandi competebat, Regi, de cujus ſucceſſione agi forſan contigerit, ſine contradictione ſeu impedi-*
" *mento quocumque in regno ſuccedere debeat ; quod juri imperiali ſatis conſonum eſſe cenſetur. Ad*
" *præmiſſa vero omnia et ſingula fideliter, ſine dolo, fraude, fictione, ſive malo ingenio, futuris tempori-*
" *bus obſervanda, Epiſcopi, abbates, priores, et ceteri de clero, in forma jurandi eis a jure ſtatuta,*
" *necnon comites, barones, milites, libere tenentes, et ceteri de communitate, tactis ſacroſanctis Evan-*
" *geliis et ſanctorum reliquiis, magnum ſacramentum præſtiterunt, et in teſtimonium præmiſſorum, ſigilla*
" *ſua huic ſcripto appoſuerunt* (*a*)." *Epiſ. St Andreæ, Epiſ Glaſguenſis, Epiſ. Dunkeldenſis, Epiſ.*
Aberdonenſis, Epiſ Morauienſis, Epiſ. Dumblanenſis, Epiſ. Roſſenſis, Epiſ. Cathanenſis, Epiſ. Erga-
dienſis, Epiſ. Brechinenſis, Epiſ. Gallovidienſis, Abbatis de Dumfermelin, Ab. de Aberbrothock,
Ab. de Sancto Andrea, Ab. de Melros, Ab. de Sancta Cruce, Ab. de Calco, Ab. de Londors, Ab.
de Neubotill, Ab. de Cambuſkeneth, Thome Ranulphi Comitis Moraviæ, Jacobi Domini de Douglas,
Comitis de Roſs, Comitis de Mar, Valteri Seneſcalli Scottorum, Villielmi de Soullis, Gilberti de Haya
Millitis Conſtabularii, Roberti de Keth Mareſcalli, Alexandri de Fraſer, Alexandri Settone militis ;
cum multis aliis ſigillis ita temporis injuria fractis, labefactatis, et exæſis, ut dignoſci minime
queant ; cum autographo collationat concordat ; Jacobus Balfourius.

During the reign of King David II. the ſon of King Robert I. It was found unneceſſary to make any declaration concerning his ſucceſſor. The acts of ſettlement by King Robert were judged ſufficient, as is proved by the inſtrument immediately to be mentioned.

But no ſooner had King Robert II. the firſt King of the family of Stewart, mounted the throne, than he thought it proper, following the example ſet him by his grandfather King Robert I. to obtain a ſimilar act of ſettlement. He was crowned at Scoon on the 26th of March 1371. Next day the ſolemn declaration contained in the inſtrument, of which a *fac ſimile* is here preſented to the reader, was paſſed ; the acts by King Robert I. mentioned above having been firſt produced and read in parliament. Of this inſtrument a copy is here given in modern printed characters, for the eaſe of thoſe who may be unacquainted with the ancient characters in which the original is written.

On the back of the Inſtrument the following words are written by way of title, viz. " *Decla-*
" *ratio Parliamenti ubi Johannes primogenitus Roberti habet ſuccedere in regnum* 1371." The Inſtrument itſelf is expreſſed as follows, viz.

The Firſt Act of Settlement by King Robert II. in the Parliament of Scotland.

" *In nomine Sancte et Individuæ Trinitatis Patris et Filii et Spiritus Sancti Amen. Anno ab*
" *incarnatione Domini milleſimo trecenteſimo ſeptuageſimo primo ſecundum morem et computationem eccle-*

(*a*) The inſtrument concludes, in Fordoun, with the word *appoſuerunt*. What follows here, to the end of the paragraph, is taken from the manuſcript of Sir James Balfour.

APPENDIX.

" fie Scotticane menfis Martii die vicefimo feptimo Sereniffimus Princeps Dominus Robertus Dei gra-
" tia Rex Scottorum illuftris apud Sconam tempore fue coronationis exiftens affiftentibus fibi prelatis
" comitibus baronibus ac ceteris de clero et populo regni fui poft facra vnctionis et coronationis fue
" peracta folennia factaque declaratione juris quo idem ferenissimus Princeps fuceffit ac fuccedere debuit
" Domino David Regi Scotie avunculo et predeceffori fuo tam proximitate fanguinis quam ex quadam
" declaratione per quedam inftrumenta confecta tempore inclite memorie Domini Roberti Regis Scotie aui
" et predeefforis ipfius Domini noftri Regis ibidem exhibita atque lecta necnon receptis homagii et fideli-
" tatis folitis juramentis ab ipfis prelatis comitib s baronibus et aliis de clero et populo ibidem exiftentibus
" in coronatione regum Scotie abolim preftari confuetis et debitis volens mere et exemplo celebris memorie
" ciufdem boni Regis Roberti aui fui coram clero et populo fucceflorem et verum h.redem fuum declarare
" ibidem licet de ipfo clare conftitit atque conftet (ex habundanti et vnanimi confenfu et affenfu dictorum
" prelatorum comitum procerum et magnatum indicauit offueruit et recognouit declarauit et voluit quod
" cum ipfum contigerit pro difpofitione diuina ab hac luce migrare) Dominus Johannes filius fuus primo-
" genitus Comes de Carrik et Senefcallus Scotie erit et effe debet verus et legitimus heres fuus ac fibi
" poft mortem fuam in regno Scotie Domino difponente fuccedet et fuccedere debet et poft
" c m fedebit et federe debebit fuper folium regni fui. Qua declaratione fic facta per ipfum Dominum
" noftrum Regem de prefato primogenito et herede fuo ex habundanti ut fupra unufquifque prelatorum
" comitum procerum magnatum et aliorum ibidem exiftentium voce propria fingillatim pro fe heredibus et
" fucceforibus fuis afferuit affirmauit declarauit recognouit et voluit quod idem Dominus Johannes poft
" mortem prefati patris fui fuperftes et viuus fit diuina fauente gratia futurus Rex Scotie tanquam heres
" legitimus ciufdem patris fui promittens quilibet bona fide et manu in fignum fidei dationis leuata quod
" cum pro Rege et herede legitimo ciufdem patris fui habiturus erit ipfumque iuuabit atque defendet
" contra quofcunque mortales necnon figillum fuum fcripto feu inftrumento fuper hoc fiendo apponet in
" fignum fuorum affenfus et promiffionis predictorum cum ipfi fuper hoc fuerint requifiti. Quibus re-
" cognitione premiffo et fidei datione in confilio Domini noftri Regis fic premiffis et actis idem Dominus
" nofter Rex per venerabilem virum magiftrum Johannem de Peblis doctorem decretorum canonicum
" Glafguen. clericum fuum proponi fecit in publicum qualiter ex habundanti indicauit et declarauit
" prefatum Dominum Johannem filium fuum primogenitum verum fuum heredem prout eft et effe debet
" de jure et poft mortem fuam regni Scotie volente Deo Regem futurum. Et qualiter prefati comites
" proceres et alii de confilio affirmarunt recognouerunt confenferunt et fide media ut premittitur promi-
" ferunt. Et qualiter omnem populum cum clero conuocari fecerat ut in eorum prefentia et de eorum
" confenfu vnanimi fieret et publicaretur ne aliquis fuper hoc ignorantiam pretendere poffit aliqualiter
" in futurum. Tota autem multitudo prelatorum comitum et baronum et aliorum tam clari quam populi
" vnanimi voluntate et clamore confono nullo penitus reclamante affirmauerunt recognouerunt et voluerunt
" ipfum Dominum Johannem tanquam primogenitum et verum heredem Domini noftri Regis patris fui
" fuum fore Regem futurum ac manu leuata in fignum fidei dationis promiferunt quod cum pro Rege fuo
" fut ro volente Deo habituri erunt poft mortem patris fui ipfumque iuuabunt atque defendent de toto
" poffe contra quofcunque mortales. Quibus fic actis prefati prelati comites et barones ibidem exiftentes
" figilla fua huic fcripto appofuerunt ad perpetuam et futuram memoriam in teftimonium omnium premiff-
" forum vna cum figno et fubfcriptione publici tabellionis fubfcripti. Acta fuerunt hec apud abbatiam
" de Scona menfe die et anno fupradictis.
" Et ego Johannes Rollo clericus Moraniensis diocefeos publicus apoftolica auctoritate notarius pre-
" dictis indicationi declarationi affirmationi necnon promiffioni manuum leuationi ac predicti Magif-
" tri Johannis de Peblis populo publicationi vna cum venerabilibus in Chrifto patribus Dominis

APPENDIX.

"Willielmo Waltero et Patricio Sancti Andree Glasguenfis et Brechinenfis ecclefiarum epifcopis ac
diferetis viris domino Johanne de Carryc canonico Glasguenfi Waltero de Byger rectore ecclefie de
Eroll Cancellario et Camerario Scotie nobilibus viris et potentibus Dominis Thoma de Marr Willielmo de Douglas et Roberto Senefcallo Comitibus Thoma de Haya Willielmo de Keth conftabulario et marefcallo Scotie Archebaldo de Douglas Jacobo de Douglas Roberto de Erfkyne Alexandro de Lindefay Thoma de Erfkyne et Duncano Walays baronibus ac militibus Magiftro Johanne de Peblys fupradicto et multis aliis teftibus ad premiffa vocatis pariter et rogatis primo in
fecreta camera predicti Domini Regis in fuo fecreto confilio et poft in camera fui parliamenti in
publico ut predicitur coram populi multitudine hoc approbante facl. anno die menfe et locis fupradictis. Indictione nona pontificatus fanctiffimi in Chrifto patris et Domini noftri Domini Gre-
gorii divina providentia Pape vndecimi anno primo prefens interfui eaque omnia et fingula
fuperius expreffa dum fic agerentur fciui vidi et audiui prefens inftrumentum de manu alterius
fcriptum figno meo confueto ad inftantiam predicti Domini ipfius ^Johannis Domini Regis primogeniti
Comitis de Carryk Scotie Senefcalli fignaui hic me(a) propria manu fubferibens vocatus pariter et
rogatus in teftimonium omnium premifforum interlineatione in vltima linea mee fubferiptionis
Johannis approbando."

To this inftrument fifty-fix parchment labels have been appended, evidently for the purpofe of receiving as many feals. But five of thofe labels are now gone; and there are feals on twenty only of the remaining labels *.

Thofe labels are difpofed in three rows; and on the outfide of each label, the penult of the loweft row alone excepted, is written the name of the perfon whofe feal was to be appended to that particular label. Moft of the labels have infide inferiptions likewife. But as all the feals ftill remaining correfpond with the outfide inferiptions; and, excepting the laft of the upper row (which has " *Prior fti Andr.*") both on the outfide and infide) not one of them with that on the infide; it is pretty certain that the infide inferiptions were erroneous and were neither intended nor expected to be feen. They have evidently been occafioned by a conjectural preparatory operation of the perfon who cut the labels. Perceiving, however, in the courfe of the actual appending of the feals, that thofe preparatory inferiptions were inapplicable, he naturally folded the label the oppofite way, and wrote the infeription right.

But the engraver, anxious to exhibit every circumftance connected with the inftrument, has engraved the infide inferiptions, as well as thofe on the outfide. This gives rather a confufed appearance to the reprefentation of the labels in the engraving.

For the cafe, therefore, of thofe who might be puzzled in this matter by the *Fac fimile*, the outfide inferiptions are printed here in the common character, keeping the order and arrangement of the labels †.

---

* Whether feals were originally put on *all* the other labels, is uncertain; but that this was intended, is clear from the words of the inftrument; and on fome of the labels, at which there are now no feals, minute remnants of wax are ftill vifible. It is not improbable, however, that on fome of the labels no feals have ever been put, becaufe (as a learned and ingenious friend of the Editor's obferves) fome of thofe, " perhaps, whofe prefence on that occafion was expected, " did not attend, and others might not have brought their feals with them."

APPENDIX.

In the introductory part of the instrument it is said, that the customary oaths of homage and fealty had, previously to passing the act, been taken by the Prelates, Earls, Barons, and others of the clergy and people who happened to be present.

As illustrative of this fact, and as intimately connected with the whole transaction, the reader will not be displeased to peruse the following passage, extracted from the most ancient book of record relating to Scotland at present known to exist (a).

The passage is as follows, viz.

Epus Sti Andr.	Epus Glasg.	Epus Dunkeldens.	Dunfermelyn.	Abirbrothok.	Melros.	Scon[a]
Comes de Mar.	(Label gone.)	Comes Marchie.	Dns Alexr de Lyndelay.	Dns Walterus de Hailiburtoun.	Dns W de Conyngham.	Dns J de Danielistoun.
Ste Crucis.	Calcou.	Jedworth.	Dns Dav. fil. Walterl.	Dns Patricius de Hebburn.	Dns W de Diffintoun.	(No inscrip.) Arms a Lion rampant †.

† It is probable that the Lion rampant on He was husband of Eleanor Bruce Countess of Cy's docket subjoined to the Instrument, and likewise in the Record to be imp and 38.

" Iours, ...
" Kenedy Ghillaspie Cambel, Willielmus de Fentoun, Johannes de Sancto Claro Johannes de Crauforde
" Alexander de Stratoun Alexander Skyrmicheour, Johannes de Creichtoun Patricius Gray, Johannes
" de Meygners, Robertus de Normeville, Johannes Dominus de Leuyngstoun, Johannes de Crazy,
" Hugo Frasser, Alexander de Strathachyn et Douenaldus Mᶜ Nayir. Qui omnes fecerunt homagium

---

(a) This is the ancient book of record, delivered in November 1793, by his Majesty's command, from his statepaper office at London, to Lord Frederick Campbell, as Lord Clerk-Register for Scotland, and now lodged in the General Register-House at Edinburgh, after having been inspected by the Lords of Council and Session, and judicially declared by them to be an authentic record. See the preceding Index, p. 109, and p. 111, No. 58¹.

APPENDIX.

" *Willielmo Waltero et Patricio Sancti Andree Glasguensis et Brechinensis ecclesiarum episcopis ac*
" *discretis viris domino Johanne de Carryc canonico Glasguensi Waltero de Byger rectore ecclesie de*
" *Eroll Cancellario et Camerario Scotie nobilibus viris et potentibus Dominis Thoma de Marr Wil-*
" *lielmo de Douglas et Roberto Senescallo Comitibus Thoma de Haya Willielmo de Keth constabu-*
" *lario et marescallo Scotie Archebaldo de Douglas Jacobo de Douglas Roberto de Erskyne Alex-*
" *andro de Lindesay Thoma de Erskyne et Duncano Walays baronibus ac militibus Magistro Jo-*

APPENDIX. 13

In the introductory part of the inſtrument it is ſaid, that the cuſtomary oaths of homage and fealty had, previouſly to paſſing the act, been taken by the Prelates, Earls, Barons, and others of the clergy and people who happened to be preſent.

As illuſtrative of this fact, and as intimately connected with the whole tranſaction, the reader will not be diſpleaſed to peruſe the following paſſage, extracted from the moſt ancient book of record relating to Scotland at preſent known to exiſt (*a*).

The paſſage is as follows, viz.

"*Anno ab incarnatione Domini milleſimo trecenteſimo ſeptuageſimo primo, die viceſimo ſexto menſis Martii apud Sconam. Robertus Seneſcallus Scotiæ Comes de Strathorne nepos inclite memoriæ Domini David de Bruys Regis Scotiæ illuſtris nuper defuncti coronatus et inunctus fuit in Regem per reuerendum in Chriſto patrem Dominum Williclmum de Laundelys epiſcopum Sancti Andree Quibus coronationi et inunctioni interfuerunt Domini prelati, comites et barones ac alii nobiles ſubſcripti cum magna multitudine populi ex omni parte regni Scotiæ congregata.*

Celebratis itaque coronatione et inunctione prædictis rite concorditer et ſollemniter in omnibus vt decebat In craſtino Rege ſedente in ſede Regia ſuper montem de Sconæ vt eſt moris conuenerunt et comparauerunt coram ipſo prelati, comites et barones ac nobiles infraſcripti, videlicet Dominus Williclmus de Laundelys Sancti Andree, Dominus Waterus de Wardlau Glaſguenſis, Dominus Alexander de Kynymonth Aberdonenſis, Dominus Alexander Burre Morauienſis, Dominus Patricius de Lochris Brechynenſis, Dominus Walterus de Coucntre Dunblanenſis Epiſcopi, Dominus Stephanus Pay Prior Sancti Andree, de Dunfermelyn, de Aberbroth monaſterii Sanctæ Crucis de Edynburgh, de Landors, et de Sconæ Abbates. Dominus Johannes Seneſcallus Regis primogenitus Comes de Carric et Seneſcallus Scotie, Dominus David Seneſcallus filius Regis iunior Comes de Stratheryn, Dominus Thomas Comes de Morre, Dominus Williclmus Comes de Douglas, Dominus Robertus Seneſcallus filius Regis Comes de Menteth. Dominus Alexander Seneſcallus filius Regis. Barones et nobiles videlicet Dominus de Leuenax. Thomas de la Haye Conſtabularius Scotie, Dominus Williclmus de Keth Mareſcallus Scotiæ. Domini Archebaldus de Douglas, Robertus de Erſkyne Alexander de Lyndeſay Jacobus de Lyndeſay, Dauid de Grame, Walterus de Halyburtoun, milites, Domini Johannes de Carric Cancellarius et Walterus de Bygar Camerarius Scotiæ Necnon Willielmus de Conynhame, Jacobus de Douglas, Jacobus Fraſer Alexander Fraſer Williclmus de Dyſſyntoun, Dauid filius Walteri, Dauid de Anande, Rogerus de Mortemer, Robertus de Rameſay Alanus Seneſcallus Duncanus Walays, Robertus Seneſcallus, Georgius de Abernythy, Dauid Flemyng, Nicholaus de Erſkyne Johannes de Lyle, Symon de Preſtoun, Johannes de Maxwel Johannes de Strathachin, Robertus de Dalyell et Walterus de Ogleby, Johannes de Tours, Dominus Alexander Seneſcallus et Andreas Cambel, milites. Dominus de Setoun Johannes Kenedy Ghillaſpie Cambel, Williclmus de Fentoun, Johannes de Sancto Claro Johannes de Crauforde Alexander de Stratoun Alexander Skyrmichcour, Johannes de Creichtoun Patricius Gray, Johannes de Meygners, Robertus de Normouille, Johannes Dominus de Leueyngstoun, Johannes de Croſy, Hugo Fraſer, Alexander de Strathachyn et Donenaldus M'Nayir. Qui omnes fecerunt homagium"

Coronation of King Robert II.

Names of thoſe who the day after his coronation took the oaths of homage and fealty to King Robert II.

(*a*) This is the ancient book of record, delivered in November 1793, by his Majeſty's command, from his ſtate-paper office at London, to Lord Frederick Campbell, as Lord Clerk-Regiſter for Scotland, and now lodged in the General Regiſter-Houſe at Edinburgh, after having been inſpected by the Lords of Council and Seſſion, and judicially declared by them to be an authentic record. See the preceding Index, p. 109. and p. 111. No. 58*.

(D)

APPENDIX.

"*dicto Domino nostro Regi, et juramenta fidelitatis singillatim. Preter Dominum Episcopum Dunblan. nonsurret Dominum Archebaldum de Douglas, qui prestiterunt juramenta fidelitatis tantum.*"

But the same King Robert II. in order to obviate as far as possible all disputes about the succession to the Crown among the descendants of his five legitimate sons, judged it proper, about two years posterior to the former act, to pass a second act of settlement more special and precise. The original act is among the archives in the General Register-House at Edinburgh. It is indeed deplorably decayed; but by a patient perseverance it may be still read, excepting a few words in different parts of it which are quite worn away. These, however, may be supplied with perfect accuracy by means of the ancient book of record just mentioned, where the act is fairly entered (*a*).

It is expressed in the following terms:

The Second Act of Settlement by King Robert II. and his Parliament.

"*In nomine Domini Amen, Anno ab incarnatione eiusdem millesimo trecentesimo septuagesimo tertio, et regni Regis Roberti secundi anno tertio, mensis Aprilis die quarto. Prefatus Rex Robertus, tenens parliamentum suum apud Sconam, volensque ac cupiens incertitudinem successionis ac mala et dampna que ex successione sumellarum heredum in plerisque regnis et partibus contingunt et contigerunt retroactis temporibus vitare pro posse, et eis pro se et suis maxime futuris temporibus obuiare, ex deliberato consilio, et cum consensu et assensu prelatorum comitum et baronum ceterorumque procerum et nobilium ac omnium aliorum de tribus statibus sive communitatibus totius regni congregatorum ibidem, declarauit, ordinauit et statuit, quod filii ipsius Regis ex sua prima et secunda vxore nunc geniti, et eorum heredes masculi duntaxat successiue succedent ipsi Regi in regnum et in ius regnandi per modum infrascriptum et sub forma et conditionibus infrascriptis, videlicet, Quod Dominus Johannes primogenitus ipsius Regis Comes de Carrik ac Seneschallus Scotie, pro cuius successionis iure in parliamento immediate precedente plene fuerat declaratum, et heredes sui masculi duntaxat post mortem ipsius sibi in regnum et in ius regnandi succedent, ac ipsis Domino Johanne et heredibus suis masculis deficientibus (quod absit) an quod absit, Dominus Robertus Comes de Fif et de Menctcth filius ipsius Domini Regis ex prima vxore secundo genitus, et heredes sui masculi duntaxat, in regnum et in ius regnandi successiue et immediate succedent. Et ipsis Domino Roberto et heredibus suis huiusmodi deficientibus etiam fortasse (quod absit), Dominus Alexander Dominus de Badenach filius ipsius Domini Regis, ex eadem vxore tertio genitus et heredes sui masculi tantum, in regnum et in ius regnandi post mortem ipsorum simili modo successiue et immediate succedent. Ipsis vero Domino Alexandro et heredibus suis presatis, similiter forsitan quod absit deficientibus, Dominus Dauid Comes de Stratherne filius ipsius Domini Regis ex secunda vxore genitus et heredes sui tantummodo masculi, eisdem sic deficientibus ex toto, in regnum et in ius regnandi similiter successiue et immediate succedent. Ipso vero Domino Dauid et heredibus suis predictis similiter forte deficientibus, Walterus filius ipsius Domini Regis, frater germanus ipsius Domini Dauid, et heredes ipsius duntaxat masculi, in regnum et in ius regnandi simili modo succedent. Predictis autem quinque fratribus, et eorum heredibus masculis, ab ipsis descendentibus, deficientibus finaliter ex toto quod absit, veri et legitimi heredes de sanguine et parentela regali, ex tunc inantea (b), in regnum et in ius regnandi succedent. Quibus sic statutis ordinatis declaratis et actis, omnes prelati*

(*a*) Preceding Index, p. 111. No. 63.

(*b*) So, both in the original deed and in the record.

APPENDIX. 15

"comites et barones oc alii de tribus ſtatibus, ſiue communitatibus totius regni, in ipſo parliamento
" ibidem, propter hec et alia congregati, ipſas declarationem ordinationem et ſtatutum ratificauerunt et
" approbauerunt, pro ſe et ſuis heredibus perpetuis futuris temporibus duraturas. Et nihilominus in-
" fraſcripti prelati, videlicet, Dominus Willielmus Sancti Andree, Michael Dunkeldenſis, Alexander
" Aberdonenſis, Patricius Brechinenſis, Alexander Morauienſis, Andreas Dunblanenſis, Alexander
" Roſſenſis, et Malcolmus Catanenſis, eccleſiarum epiſcopi, preſentibus et apertis ſacroſanctis Dei euan-
" geliis, ac infraſcripti comites barones et nobiles, primo videlicet Ipſi filii Regis ſeniores, et proucde
" etatis, Domini ſcilicet Johannes Robertus et Alexander, necnon Domini, Willielmus de Douglas,
" Georgius de Dunbar Marchie, Johannes de Dunbar Morauie, Comites, Thomas de Haya Conſtabu-
" larius Scotie, Domini, Willielmus de Keth Mareſcallus Scotie, Jacobus de Lyndeſay Dominus de
" Craufurd, Archebaldus de Douglas Dominus Galweidie, Jacobus de Douglas Dominus de Dalketh,
" Robertus de Erſkyn, Hugo de Eglintoun, Duncanus Walais, David de Grahame, Walterus de Hali-
" burtoun, Willielmus de Diſchingtoun, Alanus de Erſkyn, Alanus Seneſcalli, Jacobus Fraſer, Alex-
" ander Fraſer, Robertus Seneſcalli de Inuermeth, Rogerus de Mortuo Mari, David filius Walteri,
" Patricius de Grahame, Andreas de Valoniis, Johannes Walays, Johannes de Maxwell, Andreas
" Cambel, Willielmus de Conynghame, filius, et Johannes de Strathachin milites, Johannes Kenedy,
" et Alexander de Cocburn ſcutifer, eiſdem ſacroſanctis Evangeliis per eorum quemlibet manutactis,
" corporaliter iurauerunt quod preſatas declarationes ordinationes et ſtatuta pro ſe et pro eorum here-
" dibus inuiolabiliter obſeruabunt et ab aliis pro uiribus perpetuo facient obſeruari. Conſequenter vero
" et immediate tota multitudine cleri et populi in eccleſia de Scona ante magnum altare propter hoc ſpe-
" cialiter connocata, ac preſatis declaratione, ordinatione, et ſtatuto ſic juratis alta et publica voce cis
" expoſitis, quilibet leuata manu per modum fidei dationis in ſignum vniuerſalis conſenſu totius cleri et
" populi exprimebat et maniſeſtabat publice ſuum conſenſum pariter et aſſenſum. In quorum omnium
" teſtimonium preſatus Dominus Rex preſenti ſcripto ſiue inſtrumento ſuum magnum precepit apponi ſigillum
" et ad maiorem euidentiam et ſecuritatem pleniorem, omnes Epiſcopi Comites et barones et nobiles ſupra-
" dicti, eidem inſtrumento ſua ſigilla fecerunt apponi, gratia teſtimonii, et ad perpetuam memoriam fu-
" turorum. Acta fuerunt hec apud Sconam in pleno parliamento Domini Regis predicti, anno menſe et
" die ſuperius annotatis."

This inſtrument was authenticated by the King's great ſeal, ſuſpended by a hank of unwoven brown ſilken threads; by a ſet of ſeals ſuſpended by ſtrong woven cords of green ſilk; and by another ſet of ſeals, ſuſpended by more ſlender woven cords of red ſilk. The great ſeal is now crumbled to pieces: Of ſix of the other ſeals, ſome conſiderable bits ſtill remain; and five of thoſe that had been attached by the greeniſh cords, being pretty entire, have been cut away, and are kept in the General Regiſter-Houſe, perfectly diſtinguiſhable by the remnants of the greeniſh ſilken cords by which they had been appended (a).

(a) A copy, too, of this laſt inſtrument, is inſerted in Sir James Balfour's manuſcript, No. 4694. of the Harleian collection, before referred to; but it is by no means correct.

www.ingramcontent.com/pod-product-compliance
Lightning Source LLC
Chambersburg PA
CBHW032133230426
43672CB00011B/2316